Sawdust Caesars

Original Mod Voices

Derek Glover 1965

Tony Beesley

ISBN: 978-0-9565727-4-5

First Published 2014 by
Days like Tomorrow books

Cover designed by Dave Spencer

Layout and design by Tony Beesley

Printed on FSC approved paper by
www.printondemand-worldwide.com

The author Tony Beesley shares a life-long passion for music with his writing

As well as being a freelance writer for Vive Le Rock magazine, he is the author of several books including the 'Our Generation' trilogy

Best wishes

Tony Beesley

Dedicated to the loving memory
of Julie Currie
1965-2014

Front cover photograph: Steve Austin, Clacton, 1964

ESSENTIAL MODERNISM

ACROSS THE DECADES

Gill Evans - 1963

Rob Nicholls - 1964

Gary Wryill - the style of 79

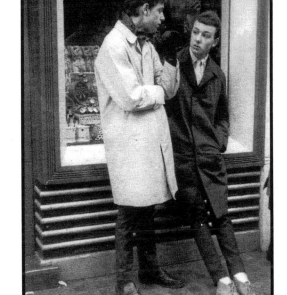

**80's Mods on Carnaby Street
by Paul Hallam**

Acclaim for
'Sawdust Caesars: original Mod Voices'

"Love this book - a great piece of work." - **Paul Weller**

"The Definitive book about Mod Culture." - **Vive Le Rock magazine**

"This book is indeed compulsory for anybody who is the slightest bit interested in Modernism from day one to the present." - **John Hellier**

"A beautiful piece of work. Thumbs up for embracing all aspects of Mod." - **Don Hughes**

"Essential." - **Best of British magazine**

"Exhaustively researched." - **Shindig magazine**

"An awe-inspiring romp through Mod history." - **Street Sounds magazine**

"A major reference to Mod culture." - **My Kind of Town magazine**

"A rich record of Mods from all periods of time and location." - **Classic Scooterist magazine**

"An amazing kaleidoscope of Mod culture in detail. This is the book I will be showing my grandchildren." - **Irish Jack Lyons**

"I dig this book." - **Andy Crofts (The Moons)**

Contents

Scarlett Baylis 2014

Introduction

The Original Modernist appeared out of the post-war period, a black and white world of austerity and conformity, a time when a teenager (a title first coined in the 1940's) had no separate identity and was absorbed into the mundane dull life led by their parents.

In many ways, the early Modernists, the first generation after the war freed from the obligation of National Service, were the antithesis of their surroundings. Mostly from working class families and London centric, they reached beyond their class, with a cosmopolitan interest in music, mobility, clothes and style. Their interest in Modern Jazz, as observed in Colin MacInnes' 1959 novel 'Absolute Beginners', the central (unnamed) character of which is said to be modelled on Terry Taylor - whom many claim was the very first Modernist, was pivotal to their cultural pleasures. Just as important was their obsessive commitment to creating their own style and look in order to allow them to stand out from the greyness of daily life. No twentieth century fashion or cult would rival their dedication to 'Cool'.

Contrary to some studies of the early Modernists, their fashion influences, when coordinated into a cohesive image, were drawn from many sources. The middle class Ivy League look of Brooks Brother's suits, button-down shirts and Bass Weejun loafers of the USA was one profound influence: Ironically, the Ivy League style was originally a partial development of what an English undergraduate would wear (along with the American's addition of button-down collars etc.) and thus was re-imported back to Britain. Cecil Gee in Shaftesbury Avenue supplied this imported Ivy League look along with seersucker jackets, button-down shirts and loafers and - following a visit to Italy in 1956 - the colourful influence of the continental knitwear, jumpers and tops appeared. His Italian season of the same year also helped to create the desired image. John Michael's shop also sold Italian inspired gingham shirts in bright colours and provided Mods an additional outlet for sharp clothing. The Left Bank style and tightly cut Italian mohair suits of the American Blue Note Jazz artists and peacock styles from the Edwardian age, also adopted by rock n' roll addicted Teddy Boys, afforded a further source of inspiration, though the rebellious nature of rock 'n' roll was quickly exchanged for the cool sophistication of Jazz.

Modern Jazz may have been the early Modernists' music of choice, along with its 'Birth of Cool' look, but the next generation of Modernists were in their late teens and early twenties. Soon-to-be Mods, inspired by the originals, started evolving a younger more dynamic movement that developed into what is the popularly recognised image of Mods. These younger Mods (the term now shortened to reflect a less elitist movement) developed and frequently changed their image, which drew on many influences, assimilating many styles and fashion trends. As the 1960's dawned there were significant shifts, which saw Mods adopting the American College Boy look and the Harrington, a zip up jacket favoured by Steve McQueen, coupled with a Fred Perry shirt and Levis.

The smart casual look, along with Mods infatuation with sharp cut made-to-measure Tonic mohair suits and button-down shirts, was one of their many evolving statements of identity. Mod girls, dressed in long pinstripe skirts, bottle green short sleeve jumpers and cropped hair were making an equal impression. Aloof, astute, self-consciously vain and meticulously cool in taste, the Mods regarded themselves far above all other youth movements: the decade would surely be all theirs for the taking.

Mods absorbed black American 'Race music' bought over by Black GI's and played in the clubs in and around Wardour Street. Authentic and electrified rhythm and blues provided Mods with an underground musical identity. The advent of the rhythm and blues nights at the Marquee in 1962 and live sets including Alexis Korner's Blues Incorporated (featuring a young Brian Jones), and a fledgling Rolling Stones performance to an audience of Mods that same year, symbolised the shift from the Modern Jazz of Thelonious Monk, etc. to predominantly black American music. Consequently, the new breed of young Mods had little interest in Modern Jazz and adopted music from the mid-West and Deep South of the States along with Blue beat from Jamaica as their sound track of choice and the most obscure tracks were held in the highest regard.

The popular media conception of Mod probably originated with the widely reported seaside disturbances of 1964. Rumours exist that journalists orchestrated these clashes. Reports of the conflict between teenage Mods and rival rockers were headlined in the Tabloid papers: Gangs, yobs and 'Little Sawdust Caesars' fighting, wrecking and rioting at Clacton and Brighton. Mods had previously gathered on bank holidays at Clacton, Margate and Hastings, with no attendant disturbances. Subsequent Bank Holiday clashes further reinforced a misrepresentative image of Mods which was cemented forever in popular perception, as the phenomenon emerged from a relatively underground subculture into mainstream consciousness.

Many books and essays have been published on the Mod movement, but these have been (mostly) from the position of observers, this book is different from the majority, it is a complete chronicle of Mod from its earliest period to the present and containing many exclusive first person experiences by Modernists and Mods, who were part of the movement's gestation and development, they helped to create the image and psychology that is now call "Mod."

On the following pages, Mods attempt to relive and evoke the experiences of all Mod periods - each as participants in the conception of this great British phenomenon. These Mods have chosen to pass on their recollections in their own words, it may help us to understand, appreciate and empathise with what being a Mod was all about during the cult's formative years and subsequent revivals.

'Sawdust Caesars: Original Mod Voices' supplies essential pieces to the ever expanding Mod jigsaw, a scooter riding, tailored suit-wearing proud passage through the weekends and times of young teenagers who became intoxicated with the scene, embracing the whole ideology of being a Mod. No matter what the background and circumstances or period of involvement, they were driven by a need for self-expression and identity. Casting future anxieties to the wind and the 9 to 5 realities of Monday morning, forever onwards with tomorrow's sharp-suited purveyors of impeccable taste; in music, clothes and razor sharp detail. Leave no detail unattended and let the journeys begin!

BEFORE THE SIXTIES SWUNG

It is hard to visualize now in the 21st century how constrained teenage life must have been prior to the Beatles and the pop-culture explosion of the sixties. In 1960, only fifteen years had passed since the end of WW2 and the consequent rationing and associated hardships were still in effect. In this period of recovery from America came the term the teenager, the frivolities and freedoms of which influenced younger Brits keen to forge a path into a future of self-expression and thrills. Despite the conservatism and apparent lack of independence of the 1950s, British teenagers were soon engaged in a search for identity orchestrated significantly by the primeval and instinctive sounds of American rock 'n' roll. As a consequence this new generation of youth was hungry for a vibrant scene all of their own. Original Mod John Leo Waters explains the Mods' attraction to Black American R&B:

John Leo Waters - "Being brought up in the fifties on a diet of 'Family Favourites' and 'Workers Playtime' this new wave of black music from the USA was a million miles away from the vapid exhortations of Perry Como, Pat Boone and the like we had endured throughout our childhood years. Here was a completely new form of music - edgy, earthy ... almost dangerous!"

Lloyd Johnson - "It's important to remember (despite the myths) that we had little money."

Early Modernist Lloyd Johnson and his family in a classic 1960 period snap

Jeremy Norman - "Before Grammar School in 1961, almost everyone I knew dressed in black, with turned-up jeans and leather jackets."

Adrian Stern - "I had effectively no clothing experiences pre-Mod as I was too young and a schoolboy. In 1958 when I was ten, I had an older brother and I listened to his music: rock 'n' roll, doo-wop, traditional and modern Jazz, and Ray Charles - plus the music on Radio Luxembourg. Soon Wimpy bars and ten-pin bowling became paramount and then we were Mods. No idea how that happened, no one that I knew did anything consciously to be 'Mod.' The name Mod was used after the initial momentum. The press saw youth culture as a way of selling papers even though we did nothing particularly interesting."

Steve Austin - "The movement came through when I was 14 or 15, just as I was getting interested in fashion, so I was always a Mod. But hindsight is a wonderful thing, and I realise now that Modernism wasn't created in a vacuum. What we now call Mod evolved from Lindy Hoppers in the 1940's, via Teddy Boys, Beatniks, and Hipsters. But like every other generation, I hated the one before. For me Teddy boys were like Rockers, their clothes, music, and bikes were so old-fashioned, and we were so new, and so cool!"

Sally Stevens (from West Byfleet, near Woking) - "I started my adolescent life as a rocker, influenced mostly by Eddie Cochran, Elvis, Buddy Holly, Gene Vincent, etc. Before that, at 11 years old, my attire was art school beatnik: Tight black pants, long black sweater. My brother used to call me The Beetle. (This before the advent of the Beatles, who were also rockers until Astrid cut their hair, and Eppy put them in Cardin suits.)"

Alfredo Marcantonio - "People take youth culture as a given, with its many cliques, all with their own dress code, clubs and magazines. When the Modernist movement arrived none of these things existed. There were no decent clothes shops, no music stations and television barely acknowledged young people's existence. Until the sixties swung in, you'd have trouble telling post-war Britain and pre-war Britain apart. Everything was so grey.

   For most of us, the phrase 'fashion victim' had an unintended accuracy; from toddler to teenager, we were kitted out like miniature adults. You were forced to wear scaled-down, short trousered, grey wool worsted suits. If you were lucky! For most of us, going out in your 'best clothes' meant donning the dreaded school blazer. Little wonder we seized the chance to express a bit of individuality."

David Middleton - "It was all new for us back then, we were teenagers and all we heard about was war and more fucking war; my dad did not come out of the navy till I was 13 years old. Elvis went into the army and when he came out, he was singing lots of top ten hits that were just not rock 'n' roll anymore and were mostly ballads. For me, Jerry Lee Lewis was the king of rock 'n' roll. By the late-50s Teddy Boys had really had their day anyway."

Rob Nicholls - "When I met Pat Smitherman at the local fairground in 1959 I was fifteen and already working full-time. My brylcreemed hair was swept back at the sides with a rollover quiff at the front. I wore a Teddy Boy drape jacket and a homemade bootlace tie. Pat had a bouffant and she wore a short white plastic mac worn with matching high heels. My change of attitude began in autumn 1961 when I went to lunchtime dances at the Lyceum with day-release classmates Alan Cowell and Terry Bunyan. The birds there were chic, and for me, Pat compared unfavourably.

   Richard Barnes reminds us that 'in the fifties, girls were still corseted and strapped up in suspender belts, pantie girdles and all that corrective brassiere stuff.' With her suspender belt, stockings and lace petticoat, Pat seemed to belong to an earlier generation. I felt that there must be more to life than this. I felt confined by going steady and my future seemed to be closing in. This wasn't helped by Pat hinting that she wanted to buy some knives and forks 'for the bottom drawer,' which signified a seemingly inevitable and dismal fate. I'd read a 19th century biography 'The Houses in Between' by Howard Spring and I felt a yen for witty conversations across drawing rooms with piano nocturnes tinkling in the background and for new styles based on foppish Regency fashions. I envisioned a light grey double-breasted suit with the royal-blue lining that I would have made as a badge of my new identity. My break-up with Pat in August 1962 precipitated my virtual immediate transition to Mod and I began to develop a new sense of style. I wanted my life to be exciting and I planned to make it so!"

Above: Rob Nicholls before and after (from Teddy Boy to Mod). Photo at left, with girlfriend Pat at the Kursaal in Southend and in an identifiably Teddy Boy style

Photo at right: With un-named friend at Royal Dance Palace, Tottenham in late 1962. He is wearing a grey double-breasted suit, white shirt with a high-winged tip collar with a tiny knot in the tie. Rob states - "The first hair style I had when I was undergoing my transition into Mod was this soft brush-over fringe."

Below: The pre-Mod Ted look, the Tony Curtis cut and early 60's style of suit that was common amongst youths across the country and a pre-Mod David Middleton scootering into the sixties on his friend's LD scooter (1960)

MODERN JAZZ ███████▶

"In London, as an art student, it really was like 'Absolute Beginners' in that you really did either like Modern Jazz, in which case you defined yourself as forward-thinking in art, design, clothes etc. and called yourself a 'Modern', or you were a trad and blues (Leadbelly, etc.) loving Beatnik and hence a 'trad'." **(James Bowden: late 50's original Modernist)**

 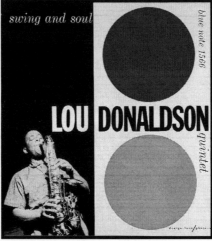 

The original Modernists of the late 50's immersed themselves in the sounds of Modern Jazz as their soundtrack. Rejecting the sounds of the trad-Jazz devotees and goatee beard wearing CND beatniks, and the various other styles of Jazz available, the Jazz music that the Modernists bought into was characterized by asymmetrical phrasing, intricate melodies and erratic up-tempo rhythms that essentially defied the Jazz standards of the day. In theory it was a development of left-field Bebop and a reaction to the familiar accepted trad-Jazz of New Orleans. Artists such as Miles Davies, John Coltrane and Charlie Parker were the pioneers of such styles and the record labels, most famously Blue Note with its expansive recording stable, along with Prestige and Riverside and others, supplied the many styles that were Modern Jazz.

These first Modernists were not initially part of a movement as such, more a collective of like-minded forward-thinking Modern Jazz enthusiasts. They recognised their mutual choices in the music and accompanying tastes in cool clothes, most notably the Italian styled mohair suit and Bass Weejun loafers they so keenly wore. Evolving during the summer of 1958, from around two hundred originals, in the clubs of Soho, early Modernists embraced the exotic stylish sound and visuals of the Modern Jazz musicians, though perhaps not so avidly the associated narcotics. Though massively outnumbered by the rigid followers of trad-Jazz, the Modernists, confident in their exclusivity, soon recognised their importance as the vanguards of a new cultural force. These Modernists aspired to break away from the low expectations of their generation and the monotones of the post-war life of their parents. If any manifesto existed, it would be to eschew the old world of subjugation and tradition for one of cosmopolitan subversion and the shock of the new.

Musically, perhaps two of the most identifiable Mod Jazz greats were Jimmy Witherspoon and Mose Allison, with their Blues-enthused Jazz sounds, although many Modernists swear by the Modern Jazz Quartet and Thelonious Monk as the key Mod Jazz icons. Undoubtedly, the roster of Jazz artists is varied, eclectic and extensive. However, tastes were moving on!

John Leo Waters - "MOD JAZZ? Let me start by saying that I could not be considered a fan of Jazz music! Growing up in the fifties and early sixties the term 'Jazz' immediately conjured up pictures of a bunch of white musicians clad in striped waistcoats and straw boaters playing something called 'trad' – which always seemed to include group members employing banjos, tubas and trumpets! Then there was the 'other' type of Jazz, which was labelled 'modern'. This usually seemed to be represented by a trio of very miserable looking black musicians playing some form of music that seemed to comprise of a number of random notes played in any sequence that came to mind! As for 'scat' – the mere mention of the word caused my teeth to grate and a cold sweat to break out on my brow (still does)!

As a youngster, Jazz was completely beyond my comprehension. I was listening to Elvis, Little Richard, Chuck Berry and Buddy Holly. Nevertheless, as the 50's became the 60's subtle changes in the music coming out of the USA became apparent – R&B/Soul music became the listening choice of the emerging Mod population and compounded within this music was a fair proportion of Jazz. Jazz clubs had existed in Soho for many years. The 100 Club first opened its doors in 1942. Firstly, as a restaurant featuring Jazz it changed its name to the London Jazz Club before settling on the 100 Club some years later. The Nut House Club (lovely name!) on Regent St featured Jazz and made the papers in 1941 when it was raided by the police and several people were taken to court for 'drunkenness' and the landlord fined! The Fullado Club in Old Compton Street opened its doors in the late 40's. Bebop was very popular in the club and US servicemen would often drop in sometimes bringing records unavailable in this country.

Another club that opened its doors in 1948 was Club 11 at 41 Gt. Windmill St. where Johnny Dankworth and Ronnie Scott were the resident bandleaders. The 41 was considered the leading Jazz club in the UK and became so popular they had to move premises to Carnaby Street where the first recorded 'drugs raid' by police in 1950 saw several arrests for drug possession and the club closed soon after!! (Does all this sound familiar?) Cy Laurie opened a Jazz club in Ham Yard (which later became The Scene) which proved very popular although the music tended to lean towards 'trad' rather than Modern Jazz. Just around the corner in Archer St was the Harmony Inn, an all-night greasy spoon where Modern Jazz musicians would gather (along with some of London's most notorious gangsters!) Studio 51, The Marquee Club, Ronnie Scott's and The Flamingo also opened their doors in the early fifties. The Flamingo was owned by Jeffrey Kruger and was originally sited in Coventry Street. It was an 'up-market' nighterie featuring many visiting US Jazz luminaries. One of the first clubs to feature all-nighters, Kruger soon moved the club to new premises in Wardour Street.

It wasn't just the capital that Jazz had infiltrated. Up in Liverpool both The Mardi Gras Club and the Cavern had opened as Jazz clubs (the cavern was actually named after a Paris Jazz club) and in Newcastle, the Downbeat and Club A GoGo were thriving Jazz clubs.

The Modern Jazz fan was seen as having a 'cool' look. Cecil Gee had helped introduce the 'Italian' and 'Ivy League' look to London and the 'studied' image sported by their heroes such as Miles Davis, Theolonius Monk and John Coltrane became the aspiration for many. The stereotypical Jazz look of tight black trousers, roll neck jumpers, beret and shades (not forgetting the French or Russian cigarettes) was the image portrayed by the media. The coolest guy on TV was *Johnny Staccato* played by John Cassavetes. He was a private detective who doubled as a musician. His 'office' was Waldo's basement Jazz club where Staccato sat in the band (amongst them Barney

Kessel and Shelly Manne). Dark and moody the series was essential viewing for fledgling Mods.

But times were changing. Rock and Roll (Rhythm and Blues) had reared its ugly head. Teenagers were flocking to dancehalls all over the country. Modern Jazz was music for the head rather than the feet! Many US Jazz musicians had already dipped their feet in the waters of this emerging sound through sessions and touring bands. Club owners were nothing if not sharp and they soon realized there was a potential new market on offer and began devoting odd nights catering to this new phenomenon. Teenagers began flocking to these 'new' clubs and in no time at all the one time bastions of Jazz were now almost exclusively playing R&B and Soul music.

But the Jazz legacy had not been completely decimated. A new form of Jazz was very popular with this emerging teenage culture. Best described as 'Soul-Jazz' it featured Jazz artists playing in a 'Soul' style. Whether this was a way of expressing their love of all types of music or simply compromising their talents to attain monetary gain is open to debate. Whatever the reason the results were very popular. Our heroes included Jazz virtuosos such as Ramsey Lewis, Hank Jacobs, King Curtis and the 'Holy Trinity' – Jack McDuff, Jimmy McGriff and Jimmy Smith. The mighty Hammond was king. UK musicians such as Alan Price, Graham Bond, Zoot Money, Brian Auger, Stevie Winwood and of course Georgie Fame satisfied our longing for Hammond grooves. Clubs like the Flamingo where Georgie Fame had a residency would feature Jazz alongside R&B, Soul and Ska. Through artists like Georgie Fame, we came to know and love tracks by artists such as Mongo Santamaria, Oscar Brown Jnr and Mose Allison. Indeed early hit tracks by Georgie Fame such as 'In The Meantime', 'Something' and 'Yeh Yeh' were very much in the Jazz mould. Jazz (albeit in a style acceptable to sixties teenagers) had made its mark and will always hold an equal place in my memory bank alongside the sounds of Motown, Stax, Blue Beat and Chess."

The fusion of Soul and Jazz firmly established by the mid-60's was popular with Mods in the clubs of the period. The Hammond organ Soul-Jazz styling's of Jimmy Smith, Jimmy McGriff, Horace Silver and the Godfather of Soul, Ray Charles, released on the 7" single provided popular dance sounds in The Flamingo and other clubs. Modern Jazz and its associated fusion of styles, previously the sole domain of long playing albums (their cover art often as notably cool as the music) was now a crucial ingredient on the playlist of most self-respecting Mods of the new decade, truly the birth of cool!

Lloyd Johnson - "For me personally, I didn't see it (Modernism) as an extension of Modern Jazz, though I knew of some who were bringing Miles Davis albums to music lessons at school. Jazz would arrive later for me, say '63.

Around 1959, we were already calling ourselves Modernists, Stylists, individualists; so much around us was modern, yet take a look around and our friends were still stuck in the past, copying the rock 'n roll idols of the day. From 59-62 the Modernists were a bunch of very smart kids wearing tailor made suits, it was all very much underground."

Significantly, a tectonic shift in the balance of pop culture was about to begin:

Paul Clay (Nottinghamshire Mod) - "It's a well-worn cliché - the quote from Terence Stamp, but when he said that during the 50's everything was black and white and when the 60's came it was all colour, well it's true, it really was!"

CHAPTER 1

LET THOSE COOL CATS BOOGIE WOOGIE

Rob Nicholls from London (like Lloyd Johnson and John Leo Waters), was immersed in the beginnings of Mod, certainly in its early transitional period. He reached his Mod epiphany during the very period that saw the original Modern Jazz-loving stylist's choice of music succumb to a more American-influenced pop culture; taking on board the new and mostly then underground rhythm and blues, later to merge with Gospel and be christened Soul. A genre that was swiftly finding its way into the Mod's clubs and record collections via US servicemen who frequented clubs such as La Discotheque and Flamingo in Wardour Street and the likes of musical enigmas such as DJ Guy Stevens of the Scene Club. Whilst the day of the original Modern Jazz enthusiast/Modernist of the late 50's was over, the dawn of the 60's Mod had arrived.

Typically, Rob received his musical awakening through the emergence of rock 'n roll during the 1950's which, for his generation, provided an important gateway, the wind of change heralding a new decade and the subsequent birth of Mod as we know it.

Rob's story exemplifies a perfectly timed journey of Mod's formative stages. Much of a whole generation's Mod experiences are mirrored in his story. Painting an authentic picture of a period of new possibilities and ideologies when the world was growing up - seemingly intent on losing its innocence - Rob Nicholls' accounts serve to illustrate how the Mod phenomenon straddled the doorstep of the 1960's.

As a whole new cultural revolution took shape, for a few years, Mod was to be the crucial influence in helping to shape and inspire a generation of youth able to exploit a new-found limited affluence and independence. Though it may be true that 'There was no such thing as an overweight Mod' and times were still relatively hard for working class families, the Mod's newly acquired spending power resulted in a sense of subversive pride, by being dressed better than the boss. Clearly, teenage Mods wished to create their very own identity and permanently distance themselves from the shadow and old world influences of the past. By late 1962 the age of the Mod was here: there was simply no retreat. The war was finally over - the weekend starts here!

Rob Nicholls - "From rather vague beginnings in London around 1961 when they were referred to simply as 'Modernists,' by 1963, Mods comprised a full-blown youth movement of scooter-riding, fashion-conscious teenagers who were discovering and buying Black American rhythm and blues records. The year 1963 was pivotal for Mods; The Scene Club, 'Mod central,' opened in Soho in March and by August the TV show 'Ready, Steady, Go!' that featured Mod styles (within its music, fashion and participating audience) was being aired. I was involved in the popular street culture of North London from the age of fifteen, when I left secondary modern school and became a wage earner, until I jumpstarted my academic career at the age of twenty-two. Those years document my experience of being a 'Face,' a fashion setter, and provide descriptions of home-grown dances such as the Bang, the Block, and the Face Twist; and of getting 'blocked' on purple hearts to stay awake during all-nighters. My experiences conclude with a discussion of the coastal fracases of 1964 and how these contributed to the eventual decline of the original Mod movement.

Before the 1950s, teenagers didn't exist as a separate consumer group. Author, Paolo Hewitt argues that after the birth of 'This brand new creation called the teenager,' the youth 'would not settle for lives that were replicas of their parents. They would not think like them nor dress like them.... [Even so] British pop culture was toothless, weak. The music of the time reflected its bankruptcy. There was no glamour, no sex, and no rebels.' As a result of this disenchantment 'Modernism' was born. Patrick Uden argues 'Modernism was a uniquely English idea because it was born from the frustration of having nothing... Britain was ancient, it was falling to pieces.' Mods embraced the new and the modern. Hewitt states 'The working classes discovered their voice, their talents ... [and] the seeds of a new optimism were sown. The sixties would be harvest time.'

Like others Londoners of my generation my road to R&B seemed predestined, starting in 1956 when I saw Little Richard in Bill Haley's movie 'Don't Knock the Rock' at the Rialto Cinema in Enfield. Little Richard's rasped chanting and falsetto in 'Long Tall Sally' uplifted my soul and cemented my identity as a rock 'n' roller. Guy Stevens had a similar epiphany when he attended a Jerry Lee Lewis concert in 1958. It was the same for others of our generation. The Mods' endowment wasn't simply the Mod flair, the clothes or the dancing, but it was their discerning aesthetic taste."

Robs' total absorption of the Mod life style was mirrored by most early Mods: the obsessive interaction with clothes and music - particularly Black American R&B. Mod's birth was driven partly from an automatic reaction to the stale conservatism of the 1950's and the adult-focused crooning's of the popular music of the day, yet was not an immediate metamorphosis.

Rob Nicholls explains his initial exploration of styles in total contrast to the perceived Mod look before providing us with his zestful search for authentic R&B within an uncompromising pre-Beatlemania Britain. Numerous important social and cultural changes are documented within Rob's and other accounts of the period.

Rob Nicholls - "I wore Teddy Boy fashions at fifteen, but as time passed I moved onto dark Italian suits with bum-freezer jackets and winkle-pickers.

At the beginning of the 1960s not much American R&B was played on British radio. In fact Aunty BBC didn't play any at all. Radio Luxembourg played some during the evenings although the reception wasn't very good. In addition to the Fair's periodic visits, we heard the latest sounds on juke boxes in coffee bars, at dances, and in record shops that played music over loudspeakers.

Some singles I purchased at the beginning of the sixties, include Chuck Berry's 1956 track 'Roll Over Beethoven' which was re-released in the UK around 1960; the Coasters 'I'm a Hog For You Baby' (1959); Ray Charles 'What'd I Say' (1960) which was hip clean and cool, and way ahead of its time; the novelty 'Hide and Go Seek' by Bunker Hill (1962); and 'Zip a Dee Doo Dah' by Bobby Socks and the Blue Jeans (1962) a vanguard for the Phil Spector sound.

In order to dance to good R&B, Pat and I started going to the 'Under Twenty-one Night' held at the Royal dance palace in Tottenham on Tuesdays. I complied with their dress code wearing an Italian suit with a tie, but my hair remained Brylcreemed and swept back at the sides. In 1961 the Twist became the rage when Chubby Checker released his cover of Hank Ballard's 'The Twist' and followed it up with 'Let's Twist Again.' Later that year the (movie-featured) 'Peppermint Twist' by Joey Dee and the Starliters was popular. I twisted with Pat at the Royal. It was an energetic dance but the Royal teenagers gave it their all. In due course Little Eva released 'Do the Locomotion' (1962) which included conga lines of dancers snaking like a train, but by then I had become weary with going steady."

Steve Austin (Tottenham Mod) - "[As a Mod] I twisted in 1961-2, it was corny but Joey Dee was cool; it doesn't get cooler than the Peppermint Lounge in New York."

John Leo Waters experienced a typical post-war year working class upbringing of few amenities and a basic cultural environment. John's formative years were driven by a distinctly rebellious streak and also - like many of his generation - fueled by the advent of rock 'n' roll and its essence of danger and anti-establishment attitude. His path to Modernism followed!

John Leo Waters - "I was born in late 1948 in Archway, North London, the eldest of three boys. My parents were Irish, working class and we lived in rented rooms above a shop. Money was tight and both my parents worked. We were not poor in that we never went hungry but had little in the way of spare money and times were pretty tough. Like so many others in post-war years we had the usual luxuries - outside toilet, no hot water, tin bath – Oh the joys of twenty first century living!

The area I grew up in was rough. We lived off the Holloway Road, which was a lively place on a Saturday night. Countless Irish pubs would disgorge their contents of big drunken Irishmen onto the street where 'the fight' would break out. Lots of 'rolling up of sleeves', 'throwing down of caps' and 'squaring up' before huge roundhouse punches would be delivered. They took so long to land that there was almost time to pop for a pint and get back before they arrived!

I attended a local Catholic junior school run by nuns which was a fairly happy environment (I still have the imprint of headmistress Sister Aggie's hand on the cheek of my backside!) and then went on to St. Aloysius College in Hornsey. This was a prestigious school run by a religious teaching order.

This was around the turn of the decade and the world was changing. Post-war teenagers were starting to find their feet and question a life style that involved 'making do' and the dreaded 'national service' had been resigned to the history books. Rock 'n' roll had arrived and the High Street shops were starting to cater to a whole new teenage market.

It was against this background that I suddenly found myself plunged into a world of draconian discipline. The brothers ruled with a rod (or should I say cane!) of iron. Religion was thrust down our throats and while most teenagers were running around in winklepickers, we were parading down the Holloway Road in vivid red blazers with pale green piping! (To say nothing of the red and green cap!).

I was not enamoured with Latin, the finer points of Shakespeare and classical music left me cold. Inevitably, perhaps the lure of the streets became much more attractive than a stuffy classroom. I seemed to spend most of the time I was in school standing outside the headmasters' office awaiting his wrath to descend upon me (in the form of a particularly long thin bamboo cane!). Eventually common sense dictated that it might suit my situation a little better if I withdrew from school and went out to work - in other words leave or be expelled! So at fifteen, I found myself free of the shackles of a stifling education system. The world was my oyster. Not quite!"

In a world of teenage gangs, centered around juke box-equipped café meeting places (a resurgence in the taste for coffee in the early 50's saw a rise of coffee bars in and around Soho, also spreading further around London) territorial street rules and accompanying violence, John was steeled in self-preservation representing a certain breed of tough teenager that would soon establish their identity within the cult of Modernism rapidly evolving around them. Whilst elements of Mods would avoid dirtying their hands and clothes by getting involved in gang skirmishes and the like, John was certainly not of that ilk, a hard Mod.

John Leo Waters - "London in the early 60's could be a pretty intimidating place. The Notting Hill riots were still fresh in the minds of many people. Large areas of North, East and South London were under the control of ruthless criminal gangs such as the Krays and Richardsons. Many areas were policed by teenage gangs and the Archway was no different. The Archway 'Mob' was a loose group of perhaps 80 young tearaways. We guarded the borders of our 'manor' tenaciously. We were surrounded by bigger gangs such as the Highbury mob, the Mars and the Somers Town gang who were all sworn enemies. Skirmishes were frequent and occasionally full-scale incursions would take place. Weapons of choice were hammers, knives and razors. To be caught on another 'manor' meant a beating at the very least. Evenings would be spent hanging around the tube station or in one of our local cafés. These cafes were always Cypriot-owned and a prerequisite were a jukebox, a pinball machine and football table.

The Mod movement had taken hold by this time. A gradual process at first with its origins in the Jazz clubs of the early 60's it had slowly built up momentum as the burgeoning 'baby boomer' generation came of age. Countless thousands of young teenagers nurtured on a diet of inane 'popular' music were becoming aware of a new type of music originating in the black ghettoes of Chicago, Memphis, Detroit and New Orleans in the USA. It is difficult to determine the exact point of entry chosen by this new music. Certainly, there is some credence to the theory that black US servicemen introduced many to this phenomenon in the more enlightened clubs of the capital and the same can be said of visiting seamen in cities such as Liverpool. In the folk and Jazz clubs of London early pioneers such as Chris Barber, Cyril Davies and Alexis Korner were initiating young would be R&B musicians into their magic circle. At the same time, Radio Luxembourg began transmitting specifically to this new teenage audience often featuring R&B tracks.

By 1963, this revolution in popular music had really taken hold. London was home to countless 'R&B' groups and many had started to make some headway into the British charts. The Rolling Stones, Animals, Kinks and the Beatles were all making news and relied heavily on R&B and the infant 'Soul' music for most of their repertoire.

The Archway mob embraced this new form of music totally. Raised on a diet of 50's music this new musical form was like manna from heaven. Listening to the Stones and Animals versions of American R&B was fine but it did not take long before we were hunting out the original versions of their covers. Our eyes were opened to a whole new world of exciting music – Muddy Waters, Chuck Berry, Bo Diddley, John Lee Hooker, exotic names playing raw Blues. We pestered staff in the local Broadmeads or Co-op to order in this new music.

The emphasis began to shift slowly from the earthier R&B to the new sound that was coming out of Memphis and Detroit – Soul music. This was music we could relate to. Brought up in a poor working class environment, we were constantly reminded that we were 'second class citizens'. The signs in lodging houses 'No Blacks, No Irish, No Pets' were prevalent. Holloway Road may not have been Watts or Harlem but there were parallels. I believe it was Bob Geldof who said the Irish in the 50's and 60's were the 'blacks of Europe'. At the same time, the powers that be running the clubs in Soho realized that here was a new market waiting to be tapped into. Almost overnight the West End of London was awash with clubs catering to this new audience."

The appetite for the new Black American sounds soon replaced establishment radio playlists of the early 60's.

Maurice, early 1960's and his band Salty Dogs

Maurice Moore (Nottingham Mod) - "In the early 60s, as a young boy growing up, I started listening to music. The choice on the radio was very limited: chart hits or middle of the road stuff. At night-time, I would snuggle under the bedclothes to listen to Radio Luxembourg. Then a myriad of groups sprang up, like the Beatles, Rolling Stones, Animals, Spencer Davis Group who were predominately covering the songs of Black America - apart from the rock & roll we had been hearing for a few years, there was rhythm and blues, Soul, Motown, Jazz, blues. We had little chance of hearing the original versions of these songs and it was not possible to buy them in the record shops."

Maurice Moore - "Two television programmes had a big impact on me: one was the American Folk-Blues Festival, which introduced me to the blues of Muddy Waters, Howlin' Wolf, Sonny Terry and Brownie McGhee and more; the other was 'Ready Steady Go!', which became compulsive viewing on a Friday night. On the latter, I heard new music and saw the audience wearing the latest trendy clothes and dancing enthusiastically - it was time for me to change my appearance and get out there to join this new scene. At some point, I got my girlfriend to cut my hair into a new more-Mod style, however, this was a mistake as it created patches of near-baldness, it was more like a skinhead cut and I did not feel like going out again until it had grown back!

At this time, as I played the guitar, I joined a band with some friends and the Salty Dogs were born. We learnt many songs by the bands mentioned above and soon the first gig arrived. It went down very well. Two girls there liked what we were doing and suggested we went to a new club in town called the Dungeon, as we would enjoy the music."

JACK THOSE CATS WERE CLEAN!

These early days of Mod's impressionable influence upon young people, also brought the sexes together - occasionally establishing lifetime relationships.

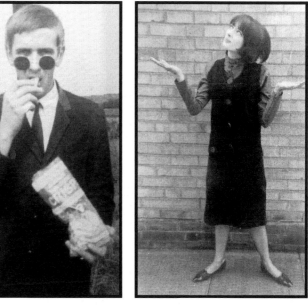

Original 1962 Mods Del and Gill Evans

Gill Evans - "I was at art school in Birmingham, doing Dress Design and Pattern Cutting and I used to go to a coffee bar off the High Street called the Stage Door and meet other art school friends and also a pub, the Old Stone Cross, this would be around 1961. The pub used to have trad Jazz bands playing at that time and that is where I was introduced to Del. He said I gave him the brush off to start with, but I was probably a little tipsy. Anyway, we got on from then and had such happy times together. We found we liked the same styles and music. I can recall, the year after, as myself and Del walked past a poster of the Beatles, who I had not heard of until that point, and Del says to me 'They are really good, they have a single out called 'Love Me Do' which you would like, especially the harmonica sound. Oddly as Mods, we both really liked the Beatles.

Even before this period, I was already interested in the continental style, a distinct French and Italian influence on clothes, simplistic styling. I was into designing my own clothes, something I had always done right from my childhood, and so did Del. I would draw his designs and then he would head off to the tailors to have them made to measure. He never bought any off the peg clothes.

My angle between the Modernists and the '62' period Mods was that I didn't think of us as following on from their late 50's style: they wore a shorter cut of suit and as a dress designer, I noticed this. Del's elder brother liked Mod Jazz but he wasn't particular stylish. It was all about style for me and there was a noticeable division between the styles of the Modernists and us Mods. Being an art student, as had been people such as Charlie Watts and Ray Davies, we had a bit of a different look and slant on things, much more individual. It was certainly more of a personal development for me - the same with Del."

These cool cats of the fledgling Mod era succumbed to little outside influence from the accepted fashions of the day, designing and creating their own individual Mod style via their own tastes and self-expressive nature. With Gill's art school sensibilities and gift for design, along with Del's confident poise and flair for exclusive visuals, together they exemplified the authentic style of early Mod.

Gill Evans - "Even as Mod arrived, there was little in the way of clothes for the Mod girls on the High Street. You could maybe go to to C&A and buy an Italian style Mac, but there wasn't a great selection available, otherwise.

In 1963, Knee Hi socks (left) were the in-thing in the world of Mod, but, as with many things, they soon went out of style. Personally, I thought they looked pretty cute. Mine were black rib with buttons up the side."

Gill's striking looks and style attracted the attention of a model agency, but indicative of the strong parental influence still exerted then, she was refused permission by her father to pursue such a career.

Above: the impeccable style of Del Evans

Gill Evans - "I made a lot of suits. I liked dresses and would never wear casual clothes. Aside from the continental influences, we could also identify with how the Mod groups appeared, in particular the Small Faces when they arrived on the scene and 'Ready Steady Go!' and also the very early style of The Who, who looked great, just like the Mod boys of the time.

I also loved the Jackie Kennedy look (and still do). Her style was popular for us Mod girls and my hairstyle was often Jackie Kennedy inspired. Although the title 'celebrity' was not in use back then, it wasn't uncommon to see members of groups and actors and actresses' just shopping and mingling with us in the boutiques in London and Birmingham, when they began to appear. Coco Chanel has also always been one of my inspirations, working very well with the Mod look. Everything was so exciting and there was always a buzz in the air."

Ever the arbitrators of style, absorbing all resplendent influences at their disposal, these pre-64 period continental influenced Mods, male and female alike, stood at the highest pillar of taste - unquestionably, these 'cool' cats were clean!

Another Mod of the early period was Top Face and Scene Club member, Alfredo Marcantonio, who exemplified the natural poise, style and confidence Mods exhibited during those formative days.

ALFREDO MARCANTONIO

Alfredo Marcantonio was also there at Mod's inception, absorbing the world of Mod style that could be uncovered if you searched in the right places. Alfredo grew up - like many of the early cast of this story - amidst a realization that there really were very few places to go and thus frequented the limited number of venues sought by Mods. For Alfredo much of this early activity was centred on the Lyceum, describing the Sunday afternoon dance at the Lyceum in the Strand as 'a big Mod club'. In such venues the DJ's who selected the records were major architects of teenagers' musical tastes. Accordingly, Ian 'Sammy' Samwell and Jeff Dexter are owed a debt of gratitude for this. Jeff Dexter was involved with much of the activity revolving around the fledgling scene, first entering the Lyceum in August 1961 at the age of fourteen. Alfredo describes his Mod club-life at this point.

Alfredo Marcantonio - "Monday nights we used to go to the Lyceum in Streatham and the Orchid in Purley…. Wednesdays was The Wimbledon Palais, Thursday it was the Locarno in Streatham. At the weekend: The all-nighters at the Scene were the big draw, also La discotheque and the Flamingo. You wanted to be the one who wore things first not the ones who wore it three weeks later. I was in a little 'posse' that included Denzil, who appeared on the front cover of that famous 1964 Sunday Times Magazine article, Pete Sanders who became a DJ and is now a photographer and Mickey Finn who got very pally with the Scene DJ Guy Stevens and went on to team up with Marc Bolan in T Rex."

Adrian Stern a Mod from Hackney Downs fondly remembers the early 1960s period.

Adrian Stern - "We had 45's and record players, transistors and pirate radio, 'Ready Steady Go!' on TV, and discothèques, scooters, and cars. I was only 15, pretending to be 18 of course. We visited most of the coffee bars in Soho and the clubs with afternoon dancing which is how we came to Les Enfants Terribles in Dean St. The interesting thing about Les Enfants was that it became a kind of second family - a core of Londoners with French and Italian visitors staying weeks and months at a time - some coming back year after year."

On leaving school, Adrian worked as an articled clerk earning £3.10s a week, and then switched to a sales position with Century 21 Toys in the Coliseum building in St. Martins Lane. He would walk to Les Enfants for lunch where he would meet up with friends. Working in the West End, he was no longer constrained to the afternoons and his horizons widened. Adrian and his contemporaries, Howard, Theo de Rosé, and Ted Murphy, added French clubs Le Kilt and the Bataclan to the list of regular venues, as well as the Scotch of St. James. Adrian laments, "You could go out for a night for ten shillings in those days! I think a pint was 11½d and a large scotch 2s." Adrian and his mates mostly rotated around the West End—the Whisky à Go Go and Flamingo on Wardour Street, Tiles, and the Golden Egg at Marble Arch, occasionally taking in Klooks Kleek and Eel Pie Island. Adrian remembers, "We went to the 007 bar on the top of the Hilton 'cos my friend Howard's dad's band played there." Regarding music Adrian states, "Alexis Korner, etc., were our music idols and we found the Stones more appealing than the Beatles. But really, rock bottom, our music was black— Jamaican or American, Ska or Soul! But if I'm honest," Adrian admits, "My interest was far stronger for girls than music and this influenced where I spent my time."

As with all Mods, clothes were important to Adrian but money was scarce. "I think I earned around £20 per week at Century 21. My father paid for my tailor-made suits otherwise there would never have been any." "Fashion was invention," proclaims Adrian, and he remembers how he was inspired by the Op-Art movement to decorate his black oilskin coat by putting chequered "go faster" tape round the edges. This and chrome tape was popular decoration for cars and even scooters at that time."

Significantly, the world of Rob Nicholls, and other similar aged youths, was about to take an important and life-defining change of course as the influence of Mod came into full force.

Rob Nicholls - "I was now an apprentice dental technician and my change of style began in autumn 1961 when for one day a week I attended classes in Kingsway, London. At midday a couple of classmates and I would go to lunchtime dances held at the Lyceum in Aldwych where secretarial workers in Holborn socialized with the Covent Garden boys from the Fruit Market. The young labourers' had adopted soft hairstyles and continental clothes and they were setting trends. I remember neat sleeveless V neck sweaters worn over shirts, with tweed trousers, baggy but not belled; and also that mustards and pastel colours held sway. The Lyceum youth were the first Mods I saw, though they were not yet known by that name.

Richard Barnes states, 'Modernists... looked to the Continent for fashion inspiration. They'd see French students and tourists who were much better dressed than themselves. 'Through eyes conditioned by British and American fashions we strived for a look that was overtly, even stereotypically French; for example, when I first rode my scooter I dressed in a striped matelot shirt with a French beret on the front of my forehead.

Recently, I discovered that Kenney Jones of the Small Faces also wore a French beret when he rode his scooter. At the Royal, young Modernist men were appearing in neat clothes, college-boy hairstyles, and with a clean, well-groomed look. By the end of 1962, I had made friends with Jerry Tucker and Malcolm Harvey who had been wearing Modernist styles for a year or more. Both Jerry and Malc wore flared trousers and Pierre Cardin style collarless jackets (later known as Beatle jackets). Malc's was dark blue and short and was cut away and rounded at the front. The collar of his white shirt was high in Eton style and although his tie was quite broad it had a tiny knot that almost disappeared under the collar.

In the company of Jerry and Malc my stamping ground expanded to include cellars in Earls Court, Kensington, and Bayswater as well as clubs in the West End such as the 100 Club on Oxford Street and the Marquee which featured live music; formerly Jazz bands but R&B groups by this time. When, early in 1963, we discovered the Rolling Stones playing on Sunday afternoons at Ken Colyer's Studio 51, we became regular attendees. At that time they weren't considered a pop group, but an R&B group which had the intellectual status of a Jazz band. It's odd to think of it now, but Studio 51 was not very big and audiences were often sparse, sometimes consisting of only a couple of dozen individuals. As history shows, the Stones records sold well and attracted a wider 'pop' audience. Their last gig at Studio 51 was in September 1963 and following the release of Buddy Holly's 'Not Fade Away' they had a large show at Edmonton's, Regal Theatre on 2nd October. I didn't enjoy it, it was too crowded, and in any case by that time I was fully Mod and had different musical predilections.

The term 'Mod' (as opposed to 'Modernist') began to be generally used at about the time Rod Stewart adopted the designation 'Rod the Mod.' I remember a Jazznik guy in Studio 51 waylaying me in the men's room, probably in August 1963 or shortly before, and bemoaning how these young blokes with their hair parted in the middle (describing Mods without using the term), were showing up in significant numbers and spoiling the blues clubs. Although I withheld my council, I was secretly miffed because he didn't identify me as one of those blokes, but it underscores that by that time a distinct Mod identity was being established. That there were Mods (Modernists) a year earlier is unquestioned. That's when I first saw squads of scooter boys wearing parkas and bell bottoms at the Imperial Club in Waltham Cross, and in August 1962, I joined a fashion that was already underway. The musicians that played at the Imperial were pretty much Rockers: Gene Vincent, Screaming Lord Sutch, Johnny Kidd and the Pirates but to the extent that they were good entertainers we enjoyed their music, after all there weren't any performers that looked like Mods at that time, remembering that the Beatles didn't release their first single 'Love Me Do' until 5 October, 1962. Nor at that time was there much of a rift in North London between Teddy Boys and Mods, for example my move from one to the other was a smooth evolution. Teddy Boys were dying out in London anyway.

In various essays Mod life comes across as being rather superficial and effete. It is true that Mods of the early 1960s had a certain arrogance, after all the whole ethic of Mod, based on style in clothes, hairstyles, and dancing, were inherently narcissistic. In his Mods documentation Richard

Barnes states, 'The Mod way of life consisted of total devotion to looking and being 'cool',' while elsewhere it is stated, 'Mod was pure unadulterated style.' But this does not mean that Mods were all show and no substance, instead, the Mods' birthright was an intensity of feeling and a heightened musical sensibility. Some London Mods rose to national prominence as pop musicians, namely Rod 'the Mod' Stewart, members of The Who, and The Small Faces. The Who played regularly at Wolsey Hall, Cheshunt, in late 1964 and early 1965, and my mates and I attended nearly all of their shows. It was a large hall and was not very crowded, so we were able to get close to the stage.

Above: Rob (centre) between friends Mel (left) and Duke (right)
Margarita cafe, Swiss Cottage, London, early 1965

British pop groups took their cue from typical street Mods and not vice versa. Irish Jack, an early Mod, reports that when The Who were starting out at the Goldhawk Club, guitarist Pete Townshend would join the dancers on the dance floor during the intervals and copy their dance moves, then: 'when the band go back onstage he tries out some of the steps he's just pinched from us. Then he perfects the fucking thing.' Pop musicians copied Mods not only in their musical tastes and dance steps but in their fashion sense also, and during the early-mid 1960s the audiences were usually more stylish than the entertainers on the stage. When the Beatles of Liverpool came to wear collarless Pierre Cardin jackets early in their career and Cuban heel boots from Anello and Davide; they were considered passé by London Mods who had worn them almost a year earlier."

David Middleton - "In 1963 I went up to the West end to the 100 Club and Cyril Davis and his all-stars were on: the R&B was all new to me but I was hooked. After buying records by people that was near your own age, you was buying records by old black guys that really had more to give, the labels to go for was Pye international and Sue records.

I was going to clubs on the council estate that shut dead on 11pm, and most of the time the group would turn up in drainpipes trousers and winkle pickers shoes and all they wanted to do was play Liverpool shit to a Mod club. I saw the Moody Blues in an Irish club in Balham and they were good but we all knew that Bessie Banks version of 'Go Now' was far much better. I also went to see one of my favourites The Downliners Sect when they did a ten minutes version of Bo Diddley's, 'Mona' and if you were not dancing to that one, well you must have been dead.

We were buying lots of new R&B records by this time, and some older ones, along with some Blue Beat records if we could pick 'em up, but Motown to me was just Doo Wop for kids. The West End clubs were great and we had some great nights all the way through to the mornings up on Wardour Street. Then that fucking lot from Brixton started getting up West and you got mugging and so on and that mucked it up for all of us."

Irish Jack Lyons - "We were Modernists. Mod fashion started with the rocker/teddy boy Italian box jacket. A reliable account says that the sons of Jewish tailors, primarily in the East End of London and talented like their fathers with a pair of scissors, redesigned the box jacket and added other accoutrements, like bell-bottomed herringbone trousers and bouffant hair. These guys listened to the Modern Jazz of artists like the Dave Brubeck Quartet, John Coltrane, and Miles Davis. They told people they were 'Modernists' because they listened to Modern Jazz. Then, as this wave of style found its way across London, someone came up with the name tag 'Mod.' Brubeck's 'Take Five' is actually the core achievement of the Mod sound.

A Mod was essentially a young boy or girl from the age of seventeen up who dressed in neat-cut French/Italian clothes and this fashion was at its peak, particularly in London, from 1963 to '65. Mods wore handmade Italian cycling shoes and Sta-Prest jeans, usually in high-toned colours like pink, orange, and red. We wore Fred Perry sweaters with a special insignia to denote the fact that the garment was authentically expensive and not a cheap reproduction. Mods wore full-length coats made of suede and leather-buttoned. The great sin for a Mod was to wear leather zipped. Sacrilege! They also wore blue nylon plastic macs to the knee with belts knotted, like an Italian film director, never belted through the clasp. Uncool! That would be more sacrilege."

Tony Foley (South London Mod) - "Mod initiation? There was none. It wasn't some sort of secret society, it was a natural progression. For me, it was the year, 1962 on leaving school. To say we were 'galvanised' is completely wrong, there was no 'grown-ups' resistance."

The paradox that affected many Mods was the conflict, that although they wished to be recognised as individuals, it is also the eternal wish of youth to belong to a gang. Although many hard Mods belonged to gangs, the Mod movement was not strictly a gang driven cult, but how does one stand out in a gang?

Although not the first Mod of the period, Mark Feld was a classic example of the early Mod's obsessive affliction for clothes and the elitism of the individual trendsetter. The famous Town magazine feature of 1962 'Faces without Shadows' - which pre-dated the release of The Beatles 'Love Me Do' by a month - was undoubtedly a prototype media excursion into the world of the Mod. Some dismissed its conservatism and naïve references to right wing ethics and an element of the Mod elite even (somewhat prematurely) declared it as the beginning of the end for the Mod.

20TH CENTURY BOY: MARC BOLAN – MOD FACE

Mark Feld was born on 30 September 1947, the son of a Jewish couple Simeon and Phyllis Feld. He attended William Wordsworth Secondary Modern School in Shacklewell Lane where he was respected amongst his peers for his personality and panache. Music and clothes were obsessions from an early age.

Ian Kleinberg - "When I was at school with Mark, he could be casual but he had the look. He was someone you wanted to be with, and he wasn't even famous then. There were other guys at school, maybe four or five of us, but Mark was the visionary. You know he could put an ordinary shirt and pair of slacks on and look great. We were great friends, but most of it was protecting each other – he more protected me more than I protected him because he was a bit older than me. He came from a more affluent family than I did, so I used to get hand-me-downs. He used to give me his jackets, his shirts – and I was proud to have them." (Town article)

Helen Shapiro - "We were up at the club one evening playing 'You Don't Know' when Mark Feld came in with a load of his pals from a rival club up the road at Stamford Hill. They were 'Modernists' dressed up to the nines in Italian suits, with short bum-freezer jackets and smart trousers. He walked in like he owned the place which didn't go down too well." (Town article)

Mark Feld - "You got to be different from the other kids. I mean you got to be two steps ahead. The stuff that half the haddocks you see around are wearing I was wearing years ago. A kid in my class came up to me in his new suit, an Italian box it was and he says to me 'You're not with it.' 'I was wearing that style two years ago,' I said. I got into the clothes thing when I was about 13. I used to have a black velvet jacket with a white satin collar and a gold walking stick with a white elephant handle and I'd go walking around Stoke Newington. You had to be the heaviest cat in the gang and that meant you had to have the coolest clothes." (Town article)

The famous Town magazine article written by Peter Barnsley and photographed by Don McCullin, later a renowned war photographer was published in September 1962. The article established the use of the word 'Face' to describe a clothes conscious, club going, trend-setting young Londoner. It also brought Stamford Hill and Hackney into the limelight as a place where 'Faces' were to be seen. Although the words Modernist or Mod were not used in the article, it helped to spread the Mod movement. Even at the age of 15 Mark Feld had the qualities of a rock star in the making - immaculate style, arrogance and a desire to be rich and famous. But he was unimpressed by the article.

Marc Feld - "It came out about seven months after they'd come down to see me and taken the picture. During that time a Face's wardrobe would have been completely transformed seven times over." (Town article)

Peter Sugar, Miki Simmonds and Mark Feld. Mark's leather waistcoat, extremely expensive at the time and almost impossible to find in his size, was custom made by his neighbour Mrs Perrone.

Pete Sugar - "Just a bit ago me and Michael were at this dance hall in Hackney. We twist a lot. We were twisting ... and it used to cause a lot of trouble that we were told to stop it. Nowadays everyone twists so we have a different twist. I mean there's the straight twist and the rock twist and the sophisticated twist, you have to be different." (Town article)

In time the specialized twist that the three invented became known as the Face Twist.

In 1964 Mark Feld ditched his Mod look and became, first Toby Tyler, and then aspiring pop star Marc Bolan, releasing his first single 'The Wizard' on Decca records in November 1965. A stint in legendary cult Mods John's Children followed, spawning the release of the Bolan penned 'Desdemona' - earning a BBC ban due to its "lift up your skirt and fly" Lyrics.

STAMFORD HILL MODS

Miki Simmonds - "This was our meeting place, our turf. We were the Stamford Hill Boys. We were hip, we were cool." (Town article)

Benny Hall - "We'd go to the Regent on Sunday evenings. One or two of us would pay and the rest of us bunked in the door at the back. We'd flick Smarties at people in the front." (Town article)

Steve Austin - "Around 1962 we used to go to a coffee bar in Stamford Hill, there was one little Jewish guy who was supercool, he wore his very expensive leather coat over his shoulders, his name was Markie Feld, who resurfaced years later as Marc Bolan. Another face was Peter Sugar, another rich Jewish kid." (Town article)

Stamford Hill was not only Mark Feld/Bolans' Mod stomping ground. The area was a hotbed of teenage fashion activity during the early sixties where young Mods tasted their formative pop cultural experiences: often a springboard onto the burgeoning clubs that provided the young hipsters their weekend highs.

Miki Simmonds - "It was a good place to be a teenager. You could meet up with friends at the Wimpy bar, Montegino's the Italian café, the Casbah café, Carmel's, the E & A salt beef bar where you could get a salt beef sandwich on rye bread with hot mustard. You could go to the Victoria Boys Club or the teahouse in Springfield Park. You could hang out and play pinball at the Amusement Arcade, known as the Schtip. You could go to the Regent Cinema on Sunday evenings, play snooker at the Grange Club or go dancing at the Lyceum Ballroom or the Tottenham Royal. In 1960, the first ten-pin bowling alley in Europe opened in a converted ABC cinema in Stamford Hill. That's where you met the girls.

On Friday and Saturdays nights, you went to clubs such as Loyola Hall in Tottenham or to the West End to Last Chance Saloon, Whisky a Go Go, The Scene Club or The Flamingo. Sometimes at weekends, you'd go on your scooter to Southend or Brighton and get involved in skirmishes with the Rockers. And of course, you showed off your clothes. What you wore was vital. You might spend two weeks wages on a tailored suit or handmade shoes.

In 1959, Helen Shapiro and Markie Feld were both members of Stamford Hill Boys and Girls Club in Montefiore House. Two years later, she had two number one hits and he went on to become the pop idol Marc Bolan of T Rex fame. Some say that Stamford Hill was the birthplace of the Modernist movement, a forerunner of the early Mods.

The schtip was a pinball arcade with a kiosk at the front selling sweets, chocolate and cigarettes run by two-old timers Bill and Phil, Bill was the owner and Phil was the manager who had big bags under his eyes and would carry a huge bunch of keys around his neck, he looked like Bela Lugosi. Some days we'd get barred for pushing (schtiping) the machines, some of the boys had become pinball wizards.

It's the year 1960 and I'd just turned eighteen. We were all full of energy, youth was eternal and life was yet to be, we thought we were going to live forever. With the introduction of the hire purchase scheme, twenty pounds down would get you a Vespa or a Lambretta. With our plastic macs and French berets we were the business, we were mobile. Scooters were to become our first class ticket to independence, I can go anywhere I want, I'd never been south of the Mile End Road before, this is a great time. We were Mods, ace faces, a new culture that had evolved on its own. It's the 1960s an explosive time. Being a Mod is a way of life, it's our generation." (Town article)

Mod friends in 1962 From left to right Stuart Mason, Brian Fenton, Alan Hall, Peter Sugar, Michael (Miki) Simmonds, Garry Skone, Dave Cleaveley, Teddy Davis

Kenny Silver - "There were the great dance halls that us Mods would visit regularly, probably the best of all was The Royal Tottenham, then The Lyceum W1, The 100 Club, The Whiskey A-Go- Go and the very special one in the narrow way in Hackney called Barry's. One night in Barry's the first time that Roy Orbison's song was heard 'Only The Lonely' it was the only record that was played all night.

There was certain places that we would meet on a Saturday evening one of the most popular was on Stamford Hill where there would be at least 200 Mods gathered, showing off the latest in jackets, shirts and shoes, trying to find out where the Saturday party was located. Saturday afternoon was usually reserved for going to Bethnal Green to get a pair of trousers made by the famous Bilgorri tailors shop, then onto Kingsland Road market to get a Mod shirt made to match." (Town article)

After little success with his early recording career (and exiting John's Children), Marc Bolan went on to cult status in 1967 with Tyrannosaurus Rex and in turn achieved 70's Glam Rock stardom as T.Rex. Marc tragically died after crashing his Mini into a tree on September 16th 1977 - a mere fourteen days before his 30th birthday.

Marc Feld centre in photo

Photo: Don McCullin. Thanks to Sue McAlpine, curator, and the Hackney Museum for providing permission to use the photos and materials from the Stamford Hill Mod Exhibition and Town extracts within the previous pages.

Other young Mods shared the same stomping grounds as Marc and the Stamford Hill Mods.

Adrian Stern (right) - "We were Mods at school, some of us. Not many and not friends either but we recognised each other. One character, Phillip Glazer was interesting – well only interesting really, because it was his father who opened the bowling alley on Stamford Hill. That was where we would try and steal bowling shoes! The arrival of a Wimpy Bar cemented the Hill as a meeting place – a place to hang out as no one had any money to spend. I really don't remember there ever being any clubs around Stamford Hill unless they mean the Victoria Club (Jewish) - I only remember the Royal in Tottenham as a place to dance, but mostly we were in Soho."

Rob Nicholls - "The Tottenham Royal is a common Mod thread. We all went there at some time between 1962 and 1964: Mark Feld, Helen Shapiro, Johnny Moke, Steve Austin, Rod Stewart, Twiggy, and me. At the Royal, we could strut like lords in meticulously tailored outfits. Our mate, Roger Danbry, was notably dapper and when we went to the Royal, he wore old-fashioned spats over his shoes and carried a brolly. 'I fancy the blonde with flick ups, what'd'ya think of your one?' I asked my mate Mike. The Royal's dance floor was the birds' preserve and they mostly danced in pairs. We geezers would circle the perimeter surveying the prospects. To approach them you had to have a mate in tow. Asking for a dance was daunting and risked public humiliation. It involved striding into the shiny amber arena with the possibility of striding right back out again if rejected. Often there was an element of doing a mate a favour, which would be returned at another time, but it might require some persuasive patter to reassure a doubtful friend. In order to dance with the bird of your choice, you'd have to apply a sales pitch regarding the finer points of her friend."

ROY ALLEN – BLUE BEAT ENTHUSIAST

Roy Allen in 'Classic Blue Beat style'

Roy Allen is another real deal. When he moved to London in 1961 he adopted the Mod lifestyle immediately. First he lived in fashionable Belsize Park famed for bistros and trendy pubs, and then he moved to centrally located Baker Street in the West End. With his finger on the pulse of the youthful scene he frequented the Tottenham Royal, Ilford Palais, and the Crawdaddy in Richmond where the Rolling Stones, Yardbirds and Zoot Money regularly played. In the West End he went to The Scene Club and the Flamingo, parking his Vespa GS scooter outside Lyons Coffee House near Trafalgar Square.

Roy was an R&B fan, spending his time listening to "Soul music and dancing, and living the life I love." He includes Major Lance, Mary Wells, and various Tamla artists among his favourites. With the advent of Blue-beat he grooved to Prince Buster's hits such as "Madness," and "Al Capone." At that time he had a short razor-cut hairstyle and bought a Blue-beat hat. He regularly attended 'Ready, Steady Go!', where he wore blue mohair trousers and a Fred Perry shirt with slip-on loafers, or alternatively shirts with wide collars, a blue leather tie, and a zip-up-jacket. He wistfully recalls how his scooter was stolen when he was buying records at a store in Balham. He says, "I left the scooter padlocked to a lamp post and when I came back after about thirty minutes, it was gone!" Roy maintains an upbeat Mod outlook to this day and still utilizes the jargon, closing his correspondence with the counsel to "Stay Kool!"

The new Mods fully intended to stay cool - Maurice Moore from Nottingham (where a scene all of its own was fast developing) took trips south for clothes to further enrich the image.

Maurice Moore - "This was the Swinging Sixties: changes were taking place. The music became 'cool'; therefore, clothes had to be 'cool', hence the arrival of the Mods. The look was immaculate, Mods took a lot of pride in their appearance and always wore up to the minute fashion, otherwise girls would say things like 'not very Mod are they'. The boys, with a typical Mod haircut, wore a parka if they rode a scooter, checked or brightly coloured hipster trousers, jeans or a mohair suit, generally Italian and tailor-made. Under the suit would be a shirt with a button-down or pin collar and tie or a casual shirt, sometimes a polo neck. I remember seeing guys with different coloured suits – bottle green, burgundy. On their feet, they would wear Chelsea boots with Cuban heels, Desert Boots, moccasins or bowling shoes.

We regularly travelled down to the 'smoke' - London - to look for clothes, Carnaby Street and the Kings Road beckoned. Jeans were worn, usually Levi's or Wrangler's as there was not the choice we have nowadays; some people, especially the girls, on buying a new pair of jeans would take them home, put them on and get in a cold bath to make them shrink! Both girls and boys liked to wear leather coats, very often long, down to the ground."

Dennis Munday (Southeast London Mod) - I grew up in Southeast London in Barnfield Gardens, a council estate in Plumstead that had a notorious reputation. 1964 and '65 were defining years as I got into the Mod scene. I didn't need drugs to stay up all night, music was my 'speed', which I listened, and danced to all night long.

My mates and I would visit the local pubs and clubs in the area, many had live bands on at the weekend, and some in the week. I remember the Crown & Cushion just by Bell Water Gate [on the Thames], and The Shakespeare, both in Woolwich. I caught The Spencer Davis Group and Zoot Money's Big Roll Band at this pub; it was Stevie Winwood's birthday. I saw Graham Bond at The Black Cat club in Woolwich and during the interval; we popped around to The Bull in Vincent Road. Sat at a table was Graham Bond, Ginger Baker, and Jack Bruce. We nodded to them and spoke a few words before leaving the pub."

Steve Austin (pictured right with Brenda on Clacton Pier, Easter 1964) is a Mod original from Tottenham in North London. He lived in Durban Road near White Hart Lane station, not far from the Spurs football ground. As a Mod he frequented the Royal and other local venues and was a cohort of Willie Deasey, Mickey Mack, Dodger, and other Royal Faces – members of the Mod elite

Steve Austin - "The Royal has been very underrated in the growth of Mods because of the Jewish influence from Stamford Hill. Around 1962 we used to go to a coffee bar in Stamford Hill, there was one little Jewish guy who was supercool, he wore his very expensive leather coat over his shoulders, his name was Markie Feld, who resurfaced years later as Marc Bolan. Another face was Peter Sugar, another rich Jewish kid."

Steve Austin and his mates began to frequent clubs such as the Chez Don in Dalston where The Downliners Sect played and the Blues room above Manor House pub in Seven Sisters Road opposite Finsbury Park. There they saw John Mayall with Eric Clapton, and the Steam Packet with Rod 'the Mod' Stewart. Around 1963, Steve started to go 'up west,' to the Flamingo and La Discotheque in Wardour Street and The Scene Club in Ham Yard. But when The Corner House Cinema on the corner of Seven Sisters Road and Tottenham High Road was converted into Club Noreik in 1964, Steve and his mates became regular patrons. Various groups played there, including local groups such as the Four Plus One, emerging supergroups such as the Rolling Stones and The Who, and visiting R&B legends such as Howlin' Wolf. A Howlin' Wolf gig when Wolf was backed by Bluesology sticks in Steve's memory:

Steve Austin - "They had a funny little fat guy playing the organ. He was right next to me as I was leaning on the stage. I had taken a few Doobs and the way his feet twitched started to annoy me, so I grabbed his leg right in the middle of a song and started pulling it. The organist started kicking me with the other foot, whilst still trying to play the song, then my friends started pulling the leg he was kicking me with and the bouncers appeared and we disappeared. The little fat organist later changed his name to Elton John!

The main places in the Tottenham area for seeing live bands were the Blues room above the Manor House pub on Seven Sisters road, Club Noreik in West Green road, and the Cooks Ferry on the North Circular road. One of the many bands I saw at the Manor House was John Mayall's Bluesbreakers with Eric Clapton on guitar. I remember that Eric was so shy when he played his guitar solos he would disappear behind the bank of speakers so he couldn't be seen by the audience. I spoke to him and many others then, because they weren't stars, they didn't feel like stars (yet) and they didn't act like stars.

Also at the Manor house, I saw The Steam Packet with Rod Stewart. When Rod started singing everyone in the audience started taking the piss out of him, we just weren't ready for that asthmatic voice back in 64/65."

Left: Mods outside The Royal
Right: friends of Steve Austin – including Bronwen
Davies, bottom row at left – in Clacton, mid-sixties

Steve Austin - "The only music a true Modernist was [truly] interested in was black American music. If, as was the case all the time, a British band recorded an American song, we would search everywhere to buy the American original, if nobody stocked it we would have it imported from America. The British copy was always inferior with no feel to it, and of course, the singer singing with a pseudo American accent. We saw the British bands because they were available, but our true musical love was black and American."

Photos, 1964:
Cambridge Mods

Left: Sid Cousins and Pip Carter (R.I.P)

Right: Mod Colin and John Bradbeer

Inter-racial dancing to Ska

Wherever possible during these developing times Mods promoted the acceptance of inter-racial socialising, and whilst there were considerably few black Mods as such, the West Indian rude boy look was a profound influence on Mods who also interacted with American and UK born blacks largely affected by prejudice. From Rick Gunnell's Flamingo club to the US airbases still in place from the days of WW2 to the few record shops that sold Jamaican R&B commonly known as Ska or Blue beat and later referred to as Rocksteady, racial equality was, with few exceptions, the norm.

Many of the black American R&B artists that Mod's respected were little known in their homeland, yet were given legendary status by the Mods. Alongside the widely recognised talents of James Brown, The Impressions, Otis Redding and The Miracles etc., they danced to Bobby Bland, Arthur Alexander, Don Covay, Solomon Burke, Gene Chandler, Betty Everett, Fontella Bass, Etta James and many others. In particular, the Sue, Chess, Stax, Volt, King, Federal and Pye International labels supplied a constant flow of new sounds. Live sets were provided by popular artistes such as Jimmy James and the Vagabonds and Herbie Goins and the Night Timers. Yet not all records picked up by Mods were quite of the expected style. Rock 'n' Roll 45's from Little Richard and Jerry Lee Lewis were often played side by side with the sounds of Jimmy Reed, Ike and Tina Turner and The Upsetters, especially at The Scene Club, where DJ Guy Stevens regularly spun his first love in music - rock 'n' roll.

Guy Stevens (born 13/4/43 in East Dulwich), regularly mentioned within this work, was an highly respected aficionado of Black American music, be it his rock 'n' roll roots or the plethora of R&B and emerging Soul sounds he regularly spun at the Scene Club, starting out his regular residencies on Monday nights - a relatively quiet night of the week at The Scene club - the reasoning being, that it would quickly attract the Mods. It achieved this.

Original West London Mod, Randy Cozens, also, had a keen taste for Black American music. Randy was well known for his love of 60's Soul and, being friends with Dave Godin, also provided crucial input into promoting Northern Soul at the end of the decade. His Top 100 Mod 45's was printed in Sounds magazine in 1979 and provided an inspirational template of Soul and R&B classics for the new generation of Mods as favoured by the originals. That same year, Randy joined forces with fellow Soul enthusiast, Ady Croasdell to set up their club '6ts Rhythm and Soul club'. The love and appreciation of Soul was to be a lifelong passion and involvement for Randy.

A Mod's tastes in music were established in their attention to the original sources and required almost as much consideration to detail as the clothes that they wore. After all, one of this youth phenomenon's primal concerns was to adapt, improve, impress and stay ahead - in style.

CHAPTER 2

MAXIMUM STYLE

Mods defined style, always paying the utmost care and attention to the most precise of details with a view to impress: even when dressed casually, Mods found sources of inspiration - the 1961 film 'West Side Story', for example, influenced elements of Mod's casual attire. Refined details were important, be it the crisp button-down Carlyle shirt or newly tailored mohair suit (with a readily available comb in the inside left pocket), the Italian knitted polo shirt, often sourced from Cecil Gee's, or the spacing between the suit's cloth buttons and the length of side vents on the jacket. The mere suggestion of how something was worn - the demand for perfection and the ever-evolving focus on style for the Mod was all-consuming.

Of course, their dedication to the art of 'looking good' did not come easily and could not be simply purchased 'off the peg' or influenced by some out of touch magazine article's recommendations. It was and still remains an instinctive and personal development of taste, much more than what could be craftily noted and absorbed from within their surrounding social circle; or what the latest Mod fashions were declared to be. Michael Caine's masterful and impressively cool interpretation of a working class man with confidence in his personal style and appearance as Harry Palmer in 'The Ipcress File' may have been a measure of what some generally considered to be the epitome of 60's style. But, as impressive as that may have been, the character's original source of inspiration - the authentic Mod - aspired to be more inclusive.

In addition, the influences did not stop at the visual nuances of film and the twin loves of clothes and music but also the taste in cigarettes, art and transport. Contrary to popular conception, not all Mods adopted the scooter: the bicycle (along with the associated cycle shirt) was also utilised and accepted very briefly as a means of transport for a select few. In context, however, mobility, for these gum-chewing Johnny Staccatos' was merely one essential need, and the methods of acquirement were not always by honest means.

John Leo Waters - "Of course keeping abreast of the changing styles was a problem. A decent suit would cost around 25 guineas and most young lads would be lucky if they were earning a fiver a week! Almost inevitably, the only alternative to young street Arabs like us was to turn to more nefarious means to accrue monies. The cost of keeping up with this newfound life style was beyond most of us. Clothes, clubs and records - all cost money, so we turned to crime."

Don Hughes - "Without a doubt James Bond was the Mod icon. The epitome of cool. 007 had it all. Well he had all that I wanted, that's for sure…. The girls, the chat, the clothes, that car and the cash."

LOOKING GOOD – MOD FASHIONS

Rob Nicholls - "We were striving for what we thought the French look to be."

Jeremy Norman (Midlands born, moved to Northfolk in 1960) - "Until I started work my sole Mod outfit was a cord jacket in green and a pair of Tattershall check trousers (wool) with a pair of suede desert style boots. I remember my mum saying she could knit me a black tie and she did…bless her. After I had worn it twice it had stretched to almost three foot long!"

Rob Nicholls - "I was buying collarless shirts from John Michael's Sportique shop on Old Compton Street in the spring of 1962. By 1963, the Mods' matelot shirts, bell bottoms, Levi jeans and brogues were yielding to 'parallel' trousers, often light coloured, which were straight-legged, neither pegged nor flared and which fell three inches short of the shoes, which were chunky Italian creepers, bowling sneakers, suede hush puppies or Desert Boots. Nehru shirts, button-down tab collars, and high-collared shirts were worn, while Fred Perry shirts were ubiquitous.

Made-to-measure mohair suits were considered stylish though expensive, otherwise Ivy League jackets in linen or madras cotton with vertical stripes, or fitted tweed sports jackets with long vents were worn. Hair styles were layered and shortish with a high crown and parted in the middle or with a high parting. In a critique of Quadrophenia, what existed in reality but not in the movie has to do with the Mod's stance. Mods were never daunted by style but reveled in it and would fall into poses. During the tweed/linen jacket era, which were waisted and usually worn buttoned up with a high collared shirt or a polo neck, a Mod might lean forward a little with hands behind the back, one hand holding the wrist of the other, resembling the Duke of Edinburgh's bearing. Wearing a light grey double-breasted box jacket with my thumbs hooked in the pockets of my Levi jeans and my head cocked slightly to one side, I adopted a Mod pose in the photo of my wrecked GS.

I have been asked whether the cost of staying abreast of fashion required certain affluence, specifically 'did it start with the middle class and filter down to the mainstream youth'? I can state categorically that like many of my peers, I was not affluent. Although the following amounts sound ridiculous by today's standards, remember that in 1966 a secretary might earn as much as £20 per week. A Mod in a 1964 *Sunday Times* article states, 'You need £15 a week to be a leader – most Mods make between £8 and £10 a week and spend about £4 on clothes.' As an apprentice Dental Technician in July 1963, I earned £4. 17s. per week, while by 1965 I earned £8. When my apprenticeship at Upper Wimpole Street finished in October 1965, I transferred to Islington where I earned £13.10s per week; and then I switched to a sales position with Century 21 Toys, in the Coliseum building in St. Martin's Lane in March 1966 where I earned £15. By then the Mod movement was waning, but believe me I was not well off, until 1966 I lived at home but contributed to my upkeep. What little spare cash I had left over went on clothes, mobility, club entrance and occasionally a treat on payday in the form of a 45-rpm record. No, you did not have to be affluent to be a Mod."

Tony Foley (left of photo) - "The whistle [suit] was paramount and conservative. The only real breakthrough was cloth (waisted jackets, number and positioning of pockets, vents, lapels etc. a matter of personal choice). If there is a statement, it is the number of buttons on your jacket and how you did them up. Shirts were a secondary (classic but tailored) item until the Carnaby Mod period burst upon the scene, then it went berserk for about a year... no longer! The single point I can add is the importance of accessories which were fundamental."

Lloyd Johnson - "I suppose, really, the classic Mod shirt was the Tab collar style in 1964 along with the Fred Perry sports shirt and the Button Down collar shirt. Ben Sherman's appeared around '65, they were a copy of an American shirt like Manhattan, Arrow, Career Club and Lion of Troy which were sold at places like Austin's in Shaftsbury Ave. and John Simon's shop The Ivy Shop in Richmond, Surrey. I heard rumours that the people from Ben Sherman actually bought shirts from The Ivy Shop before they started the company in Brighton. I was a seaside boy; I came from Hastings so my take was probably quiet different to that of 'The London Boys'.

Very early on in 1960/61 when I was 15-16 years old there was an old Menswear shop called Cobleys where I would buy stiff detachable round Van Heusen collars which I wore with a blue striped collarless shirt my Granddad gave me: that shirt must have dated to the 1930s and looked amazing when worn with the detachable round collar, black knitted tie, Brown Italian bumfreezer jacket with a half belt at the back worn with grey slimline trousers with 1 inch slits at the bottom of the outside leg seam and a pair of sidelaced Denson Winkle picker shoes bought from Winters Shoe Shop in George St. in Hastings Old Town. I already had the college boy hairstyle from around 1958/59 with a raised side parting.

The look wasn't as defined and strict as it became later and is nowadays, if fact there weren't too many of us with college boy hairstyles then. Some people have taken it to very stylish levels now. Daniel Savare has done just that, he looks great! and has a style of his own. It wasn't always the typical 3-button mohair suit, button down shirt short hair Mod look back in the day. I think of that as the 'Jack the Lad' London Boy Look and I liked it but it wasn't for me - too many people were looking the same in that look.

Lloyd Johnson's proto-Mod style of 1959

In May 62 I did have a 3-button pinstriped suit I wore with - once again - a stiff white detachable collar and the black knitted tie but this time it was a Van Heusen spread collar and the footwear was Annello & Davide Ba-Ba Boots, the boots that The Stones and Beatles would wear later; people like Adam Faith had been wearing them for years before The Stones and Beatles. I thought Adam Faith look great in the early 60s and so did Tony Meehan and Brian Bennett - both drummers for The Shadows.

By '64 it is true that someone could be wearing say a Paisley shirt and some guy across the road would shout 'What are you wearing, didn't you know, Paisley went out at 3 o'clock yesterday afternoon or 'Polka Dot's in Paisleys out' but this was done with humour, just taking the micky out of each other. After all, we were just a bunch of kids having a laugh.

When I read the well-known quotes relating to Stevie Marriott being the first to wear white jeans it makes me smile as I was wearing them in 1959 and have the photo to prove it, not that it's any big deal, it's just these things get written and it's taken as gospel.

There was the Art school side to the Mod Movement too. You had some Art school people who were essentially Beatnik types, yet would mix their style with a Mod Look, wearing things like a black Leather 3-Button blazers bought from places like Gaylords on Shaftsbury Ave. or Lewis Leathers on Great Portland St. Most people these days think of Lewis Leathers as a biker/Rocker brand. But back in the early 60s, they made one of the first leather blazer and lapelless leather jackets, which was outrageous at the time; this was at a time when if you wore suede shoes you were considered a Poof.

I always loved dark muted striped bleeding madras shirts, which were quite rare. You only seemed to be able to get them from The Sportique on Old Compton Street or 'Just Men' in Tryon St. just off the Kings road. For me The Sportique was the best shop in London in the early/mid 60's, but sadly I could never afford to buy anything there, it was below Dougie Millings the tailor who made all the pop stars suits."

Alfredo Marcantonio, describes his continuing quest to be an original, exploiting his imaginative improvisational skills, always an essential bonus to Mods, both to save much-needed hard-earned money and also to promote individuality.

Alfredo Marcantonio - "My late sister was a very early Modernist and was a big influence on my taste in music and clothes. She was a real 'soul sister' and a close pal of Dave Godin. In fact Dave bought my Austin's Madras jacket off me, after it had run its course. I used to come up to London to buy clothes but an awful lot of your stuff you had made, made yourself or found in bizarre places like Woolworths. My mother had been a dressmaker for Schiaparelli and Hartnell and used to make stuff for my sister and I. At that time when we used to go to The Scene we'd try to wear something new each week. I would get my mother to make tartan shirts, polka dot shirts from dress fabric. If a guy down The Scene would have something on and we'd think that's nice, we'd get it made for the following week. Once I saw something on TV about American college kids, who had initials on their shirts. At the time the most sought after thing were these Italian lambswool polo style shirts. I got my mother to make some felt letters and she embroidered my initial onto my one and a 'C' for Cliff onto my mate's. We wore them down the Scene Club and the next week everybody had them."

John Leo Waters - "The music revolution was not the only major upheaval taking place. It was not enough to be 'in the know' as far as musical trends were concerned; we had to look the part also. The new 'Mods' felt the need to make a statement with regard to the way they looked. This new movement took its inspiration from the sharp dressing stars of Modern Jazz and the Ivy League colleges of the USA. Hipster jeans, tab collar shirts, Fred Perry tops, hush puppies, Desert Boots, loafers and perhaps the most iconic of Mod accoutrements - the mohair suit. Sourcing clothing was difficult initially. Good tailors were few and far between (all suits had to be handmade!).

We were lucky in that Aubrey Morris had a shop at Highbury Corner. A small shop that was almost unnoticeable on a small parade, but to those in the know - this was the place to go! A tiny shop piled high with wonderful colourful bales of cloth. A selection of mohair that could not be surpassed and in Aubrey Morris a true artist worthy of such a classic material.

A suit would take at least a month from initial measurement through two fittings to completion. Every garment was a labour of love. I never knew anybody to have a complaint about an item of clothing made by Aubrey Morris. Not that Aubrey was shy about singing his own praises! He was forever telling us of his esteemed clientele and would regale us with tales about several pop singers including Chris Farlowe along with several members of the Kray firm using his services. Of course, we took all his tales with a pinch of salt. However, a couple of years ago I was talking to Chris Farlowe and I asked if he had ever heard of Aubrey Morris. Chris immediately went into a soliloquy about a silver grey Tonik suit he had made there!

Of course, it was not always practical to wear a 'whistle' so other more casual outfits were popular. Wrangler or Levi jeans with a Fred Perry top and a pair of hush Puppies or Desert Boots were my favourites for 'knocking about'. I had a beautiful Prince of Wales check jacket made by Aubrey Morris, which really looked the business with jeans. Fashions came and went. At one stage, overcoats were very popular. The Crombie by Dormeuil was the real deal but due to the cost, most young Mods purchased readily available copies. A trilby with a narrow brim often completed the 'look'. I bought an extremely expensive sky blue denim jacket 'up west'. Three buttons with a 14-inch centre vent - it was the bee's knees. I wore it to a club that night and by morning, it was ruined! Cigarette burns, ingrained dirt and God knows what else consigned it to the bin!!

Another style faux pas that I remember was the fashion for wearing a roll neck jumper under a plaid 'work style' shirt. As wearing a jumper under a shirt was both expensive and uncomfortable Marks and Spencer had the brilliant idea of stocking a small roll neck that finished at the chest. It simply pulled over one's head - no sleeves - a bit like a breastplate. Excellent idea until I had to go to hospital one night and had to remove my shirt revealing this small piece of 'roll neck' jumper sitting on my shoulders! The two young nurses thought it was hilarious! (in the photo on p.58 Rob Nicholls is wearing such a partial roll neck). True Mods created their own look and took pleasure in obtaining elements from many sources, not just entering a shop and walking out as a 'Mod'"

Roger Ames (Muswell Hill Mod) - "London Mods bought clothes from back street tailors recommended through the North London grapevine, made to measure to their own specification, or combed jumble sales for collarless shirts, to team with high cardboard collars. The West Green Road and Kingsland Road provided numerous Greek or Jewish tailors who were happy to indulge the sometimes extravagant instructions."

Gary Maxton (Long Eaton Mod) - "Every Saturday we would go into Nott's to a shop called Birdcage to buy clothes, Ben Sherman shirts etc. and the assistant in the shop was Paul Smith who is now Sir Paul Smith the design guru. We would also go to Burton's tailors for made to measure mohair suits which cost about £30 in 1965. I think a man's wage was about £10 a week back then. We used to buy them on the tick and go in every week to pay 5 or 10 shillings Off (Taking 4-6 weeks to make including the usual 3 fittings). We would choose the cloth from rolls and ask for 16-inch centre vents and specify every detail of how many pockets, buttons etc. Sometimes we would even take in our own length of two tone tonic mohair purchased on one of our trips to Petticoat Lane market in London, which was also great for buying full length leather coats in any colour you wanted, even multi coloured."

Following excursions into the world of Beatniks and Jazz, the influence of Mod inspired Italian born Giovanni Napolitano, now living in Islington, to immerse himself into the scene with an unknown beatnik named Rod. A mutual passion for Mod fashion soon came strongly to the fore.

Giovanni Napolitano (Islington Mod) - "We started off as Beatniks as the teddy boy and rocker scene was more of an outer London thing. This was the whole coffee bar period where all teenagers spent their time in them, it was the very early 60's and from the ardent Jazz scene (places such as trumpet player Ken Collier's club, also known as Studio 51 where most bohemians and students went) we progressed to the Folk clubs, which is where I met Rod Stewart. Rod and myself followed a singer called Rambling Jack Elliott and he was exactly as his name sounds.

Then we all got into the clothes. Myself, my brother Tony and Rod started to go to The Flamingo club which was a Modern Jazz club [now moving into Rhythm and Blues] and had Georgie Fame and the Blue Flames as the resident band. This is where we started to wear Italian styled suits and Pork Pie hats and broke away from the Beatnik scene; although we continued to attend Jazz nights, but to go 'where the action is' we would go where the smart people were going. Above the Flamingo was the Whiskey a Go Go as well. Bang in the middle of all of this there was another Jazz club and that was Cy Laurie's, right across the road from the Windmill in Newport Street. The whole Cy Laurie's crowd had their own style and this is where the Mod style really came in. The guys in immaculate 3-button mohair suits and Anello and Davide Cuban Heels and the girls with Mary Quant dresses and Vidal Sassoon hair styles - before they became known on the High Street. The crowd in there also had their own exclusive dances that were all done very cool.

We would wear the Cuban Heeled shoes, later to be known as Beatle boots, but to stop the Levi's wrinkling up at the bottom, someone came up with the idea to insert a triangle into the side of the shoes so it performed a flair. I am almost certain that this is where the first flared trousers came into being, shirts were often the blue denim button-down style or similar and hair began to be wore longer and smarter but cut into a style rather than just letting it hang long. This is where Rod Stewart found his position and style and the look that he pursued throughout his career.

Ken Collier's club, although being an ardent Jazz club and run by two old showbiz women, Pat and Violet, started a Sunday afternoon Rhythm and Blues experiment with Alexis Korner's all stars performing. Everyone was horrified when they first heard the sounds but to us, it was all still rock 'n' roll. This music being played was something unknown on the Jazz scene. This is where the Stones made their debut and others. The daddy of them all was Long John Baldry who, having been through Jazz, Folk and now Rhythm and Blues, had a vast knowledge of music and was more advanced than us all.

At the clubs we went to, we would be listening to tracks like 'I Got My Mojo Workin'' by Jimmy Smith and all of the classics of the time. We also went to the Marquee too where lots of the Blues and Rhythm and Blues groups played. Rod was still doing his thing and I can remember saying to him, though I often said he was much more interested in the girls than his music and being a singing artist, 'Rod ... You have a bloody awful voice, you are never gonna make it, come and join me in Hairdressing, there's plenty of girls around here.' Rod replied 'You wait and see, I am gonna make it!'"

Giovanni's nephew was Johnny Powell, also from Islington, North London. Johnny, born in 1949, often spent childhood holidays in Sheffield, home of The Mojo club and, thanks to his elder brother Stephen and Uncle Giovanni, along with a certain 'Rod the Mod' Stewart, felt the definitive influence of Mod upon his life in 1963.

Johnny Powell - "I was a teenager from 1963 onwards, my older brother was two years older and he was a Mod, but not as keen as me! My Uncle Giovanni, who was a Beatnik, was Rod Stewart's friend. Rod hung around with his Beatnik friends, but was really always a Mod and the odd one out. I got to know Rod too; this was many years before he was famous. They were real rebels and when Rod went to France busking my Uncle went along too.

My father (who was a professional boxer beginning before the war) had all of his suits made in Oxford Street at a tailors called Barry-

Above: Giovanni Napolitano (between the girls) and a young pre-fame Rod Stewart (right)
Below: a young Johnny Powell in 1963

Chalkham's and it was there that I had my very first suit made – I still have the hanger for it. I was 15 years old and saved all of my wages up to pay for it made to measure. I paid 40 guineas for the Beige Brown suit, the tailors' always charged you in guineas back then. I had a few more suits made from there over the years."

Photos: Johnny Powell wearing his first suit at Butlins aged sixteen

Right: with friends Billy Cobb and George Byrne

Johnny Powell - "I bought my Ben Sherman button-down shirts from a local shop in Islington or Cecil Gee's and would also wear Levi's and Lee jeans, though I would most often wear a suit. I also had the classic American Forces parka with the big fur trim collar, which I bought from the army surplus store where lots of us Mods went. Shoes were bought from a great shoe shop on Shaftsbury Avenue, I can't remember its name, but it was a very Mod place to go."

From Cecil Gee's and Soho tailor Ben Harris - who reputedly made the finest quality American styled suits in London - to the influence of Brioni of Milan, the leading Italian label, founded in 1946 who in turn influenced Cecil Gee, the style of the Mod could be found. Yet it was not only in the capital that the continental style was cited as an influence.

DEL EVANS – THE STYLE OF 1963

Del Evans, referred to in chapter 1, was one of the earliest of Birmingham Mods. When his wife-to-be, Gill (a keen exponent of the Continental style and influence), first met him in 1962, he was already a conscientious Modernist. Del personified Mod perfection and class throughout the whole of the era, enjoying a talent for creativity and improvisation so redolent of the whole ideal and ethics of Modernism.

1) Del wearing his 3 piece navy chalk stripe suit. It's a 4-button jacket with flap pockets and ticket pocket with 8-inch side vents, waistcoat with matching flap pockets. Beneath he is wearing a pale grey shirt with white stiff collar fixed on with studs back and front, a Navy silk tie and pocket handkerchief. Shoes are Black Italian lace-ups. In Gill's very own words "Del always had an incredible sense of style and always looked immaculate."

2) Del designed this suit and had it made to measure at Hepworth's New Street Birmingham. Black & white tweed four-button flap pockets, ticket pocket, 8-inch double vents. Gill adds "A walking stick was a popular accessory for a time and at the West End Ballroom Birmingham, the Mods would dance in a circle with them. We were both fans of 'The Avengers' TV programme and influenced by it, Del liked the style of John Steed"

3) Del wearing his self-designed navy chalk stripe 3-button suit, black and white gingham giraffe tab collar shirt and black knitted square end tie.

Left: Del Evans 1964 in Trafalgar Square. Del is wearing a Chalk Stripe Ghillie Collar Suit designed by Del and made to measure at Hepworth's, New Street, Birmingham. Black & White Gingham Giraffe Tab collar shirt from Cecil Gee, a pale Grey Lamb's wool Sweater Black Leather Coat designed by Del Evans and made by Gill Evans. Boots by Anello & Davide

Right: in Wales wearing what Del described as a dark brown, fine tweed suit with a black silk handkerchief, beige button-down shirt 1964. He always favoured eight-inch side vents and ticket pockets

Del, 1963 black and white tweed trousers with 16-inch bottoms

Far right: 1965, plain navy self-designed 'never off the peg' suit

Alfredo Marcantonio - "As Carnaby Street got going, there were a lot of sharp lads around. But there were some of us who had this all-consuming drive to be 'original'. I don't remember buying anything in John Stephen's shops. To me it was Austin's for USA made button-downs and places like John Michael for Italian and French stuff. But they were so expensive, instead we'd buy cheap cotton cricket whites from C&A and dye them ourselves - bright yellow, orange - because you couldn't buy brightly coloured clothes. We would have them shortened by two inches so you could show off your equally bright socks. That way we ended up doing a bit of DIY - Dye it yourself."

Jeremy Norman - "Clothing could be a nightmare if your parents would not help out. Pocket money was minimal. Summer jobs like fruit picking filled the coffers and a bus trip into Norwich brought a visit to Harry Fenton's. My sympathetic grandparents funded my first pair of Tattersall Check trousers and a cord jacket. I thought I was the dogs.

Levis I think were about £4.19s 6d (£4.97p in new money) and being in the county of several American airbases, Parkas were easy to come by. My first suit, after starting work at Jewson's, was made at a Tailors called Chadd's, still going too. It was a three piece, blue Mohair and cost £34 made to measure. I earned just under a fiver a week so good old Mum loaned me the money."

David Middleton - "Mods came up first with what we called Italian suits, I had a Prince of Wales check, with a half belt at the back and cloth buttons, from a shop on Battersea Rise called Henry London. Then I had bits sewn into jeans to make them bell-bottoms. I also walked into the tailors asking for brown and white Harris tweed 15-inch knees and 18-inch bottoms; I did get some funny looks but I was getting there.

Then there was roll neck jumpers, paisley shirts, crew neck tops, pop pie tops and Blue beat hats. I got another of my suits from a little Jewish boy, Alexander's in Newington Butts, gold, bottle green, and black mohair. I had a grey suit, a pinstriped one and full leather and suede coats from a shop in Tower Bridge road called Lewins. I had a blue suede jacket with leather collar, which did go down well. My tops cost me in-between £4 to £8 and I bought them from all over but not Fred Perry as I thought that they were crap.

I was working over the water in Victoria, in some homeless place and one day eight tops come in, Andy Amoss, Harrod's and some from Italy: they were well way out of my price range and the homeless would be dressed better than me, really class tops, so when no one was about I put the lot on and walked out, going over Vauxhall bridge.

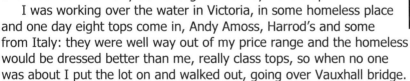

It was a red-hot day and I was glad when I got to Oval, and said to my Mum 'Wash me that lot Mum'.

The shoes came from Ravels as they were nice, a bit on the dear side but you got something that was stylish. In 1965, I bought an overcoat for £22 from Austin Reeds, and I felt good in it. I did really look after my clothes.

Going to Brighton on scooters, we did not have suits. The suits we had were always the one 12 inch vent and not two as we called them fart flaps."

Steuart Kingsley-Inness - "Most Mod kids I knew wore their Levi's without turn-ups; in fact we wore turn unders to give a clean almost tube-like look in order to enhance the style of 'parallels'. The early Levi's had button flys, and the chosen look featured 'worn in' thighs and flys - often helped with Vim and a scrubbing brush!"

David Middleton (right)

Mods were largely working class with little cash to squander - the importance of how they appeared was a desire for admiration and approval and for some a level of respect ... and for others, a desire to alienate.

Don Hughes (left) - "Hush puppies worn with bright-red socks were declared 'in'. Striped butcher's jackets were highly prized. Camel jackets, Suede jackets in blue or brown with a leather collar worn with a white polo neck jumper. And, if you could afford them, Lewis Brothers' casual jackets and waistcoats. The Fred Perry shirt, Clark's Desert boots, Levi jeans with one-inch turn-up – and the ubiquitous maroon, blue or green leather coat, gradually came in. A code of clean smart dressing evolved that was strictly adhered to for fear of being labelled a state. It was the only way to be."

Reggie Webster - "Jumpers and button-down shirts were cheap enough at Petticoat Lane or Shepherd's Bush Market. It was all about the Spartan look, not a fashion statement, just an indication of what you were, a non-participant in an era of exhibitionists and people making serious money out of its pretence. I remember lads who went to Carnaby Street for the walleting, not the silly clothes or the people that sold them. We always thought the peacocks were looking for approval from people, I still do. We looked for disapproval. Being the same as every other trendy was easy, you just needed money."

They were a new breed, with acute self-projection, a cool demeanour and an obsessive aspiration to be the first to add the all-important exclusive detailing to their look.

Wayne Kirven - "I've got friends who put a handkerchief on their shoulder when they were kissing a girl in case they got powder on their jacket. The clothes transported you into a world out of your reach. They cost you an arm and a leg but you had to have them." (Town article)

Mods aspired to be the best. To be known as a 'Face' or top Mod fashion leader, you needed to be preened and perfect and keep up with the ever-changing styles. By 1963, it was penny round collars and short-layered college boy haircuts and close fitting three-buttoned, single-breasted two and a quarter inch wide lapel suits (usually tailored by Jewish tailors of the East End) with hipster trousers and frogmouth pockets.

John Stephen (right), The self-styled Mod king of Carnaby Street

Sometimes derided and classed as effeminate, the original Mods' personal grooming and what was previously considered gay (pink and pastel shirts and white trousers etc.) was in effect ahead of its time. Significantly, the majority of Mods were heterosexual and mostly from tough working class backgrounds - merely pushing the boundaries of male appearance.

Frank Cooper - "We were into clothes big time, Sonny Bilgorri and his offsider Jack, bespoke tailoring no less. Our shoes were handmade by Greek shoemakers from Islington and Battersea. Ronnie Flash was a half Asian cockney shirt maker who had a market stall on the Kingsland Waste in Dalston on Saturdays, pin collars, button down, great fabrics and colours, he could make whatever you wanted, you'd go on Saturday get measured-up come back the next week and its ready, three quid for a stylish tailor made shirt. We were the Beau Brummell's of the day." (Town article)

Rick Brockhume - "I'd get two and a half yards of fabric, cut make and trim, mohair, Prince of Wales check, and get a three piece Gold Tonic Suit made by Bilgorri in Commercial Street. It cost me £12 and with an extra £2 I could get another pair of trousers." (Town article)

Johnny Moke - "We went to the bowling alley wearing old plimsolls. We hired a brand new pair of bowling shoes and afterwards I walked out with mine. That weekend I was the only guy walking round Clacton with bowling shoes on. When I went to Brighton six weeks later, half the kids had bowling shoes on." (Town article)

The name of Glasgow entrepreneur John Stephen is one that is synonymous with the fashion of the 60's, along with his early period Carnaby Street shop where some Mods patronised his pioneering clothes of fine detail and previously little seen use of bold colours and pattern.

Though John Stephen and others were partially responsible for the commercial 'Carnaby Street' explosion and over-exposure, resulting in the broad assumption that Mod equalled merely being young and fashionable, a vast proportion of Mods shunned the easily acquired 'off the peg' attire that was being mass-marketed. Perhaps one of the most respected and least flamboyant of menswear designers was John Michael located on the King's Road. Regardless, some working class Mods dismissed what they saw as 'too many fashionable types' on the scene who merely talked the talk but ... not the walk.

Reggie Webster - "There weren't too many types around in those days, guys with similar hair and suits; ticket pockets and centre vents were not exclusive to Mods, they were quite traditional really: a change from those old fashioned box type short jackets and tapered trousers the older guys used to wear. The smart suited guys with suede shoes we [generally] saw as 'Weekenders', blokes looking for a good time with their mates, not unlike us, really. At times, they looked like Mods yet other times they looked like Joe Normal; no scooters and some looked like the CID or rent collectors. There were plenty of Dandy kids like that, fashionable to the excess, and certainly more middle class and wealthier. Some of that clobber cost a mint. Plus they classed it as old hat within six months. I still see all of that as a futile attempt in trying to buy some credibility, just following to fit in.

There were those that took music seriously, Soul and Motown was something to dance to, not a secret to the meaning of life and something that represented anything, just music. It was pretence, much like the hairies that thought that they could end all wars with a flower and a tambourine. If the music was fast it was either good to dance to or not, or slow enough, whether you could pull a bird to it. As for a DJ?... only a bloke that talked too much between records, something he could be warned about on occasion.

Generally we stood together and away from the the trendies, looking for a dim corner was always a bit of a joke really but a great place to let people know who we were and that we weren't there to socialize, we were there for the birds and a dance. There would be times you were seen as a threat, but, usually, the locals' stayed clear. Arriving outside a place was always a buzz, you could hear the scooters from a distance and you made sure the people outside knew you were there: it was like a show at times, lining up, packing your gear, buttoning your top suit button, loosening your tie and walking in the style, feet at 10 to 2 with your hands in your pockets. It was all about the flash, there were other suited kids around but we never considered them as being like us, they maybe never had scooters or they mixed with the wrong people. It's difficult to explain now, but just looking the part was simply a case of talking the talk, being level and straight up meant little if you couldn't back it."

The compulsion for clothes, looking the part and walking the walk were not the only requirement.

John Leo Waters - "Purple Hearts, Bombers, Dexys - all were freely available - at a cost! Initially we, like so many others, would purchase our supplies from various spots around town but as time went on we realized there was money to be made.

One of our acquaintances had a contact in the trade as they say. He managed to acquire 7,000 Dexys but got word that the 'old bill' were going to 'turn over' his flat. A local villain of some notoriety, he could not afford to get busted so asked if we would be interested in taking his stash off his hands. What a silly question. We agreed to shift the material on a 50/50 basis and so we entered into the drug trade. Our supplier was able to accommodate our needs for some time and the arrangement proved very beneficial to all concerned.

We normally hid our supply on a building site at the bottom of Wardour St keeping enough on our persons to supply initial demands. It did not pay to carry too much at one time. We would make the rounds to La Disc, the Scene and the Flamingo and every so often pop back to the site for fresh supplies. We had usually been cleared out within a couple of hours apart from a little something kept back for personal use! Soft drugs were considered to be something of a nuisance at that time and the police initially treated suchlike as a minor irritant. But pressure began to build especially from the press and soon the police were carrying out raids on the West End clubs. The paddy wagon would arrive outside, police would seal the exits (usually only one!) and the punters would be searched and questioned. They would usually find a few under age kids and sometimes a few drugs (the floors were usually awash with tablets!) and they would be carted off to spend the night in a cell at West End central. Their parents would be informed and they would be charged and bailed in the morning or just given a ticking off."

Rob Nicholls - "I remember one occasion when my bird and I visited her friends. While they sat and nattered incessantly, all I wanted to do was dance by the record player and chew gum - I couldn't stop dancing and chewing. I felt embarrassed, my pupils were dilated but nobody seemed bothered. I'll confess I didn't always feel comfortable on speed. After the initial euphoria, I would often become anxious, and the comedown is notorious. As they wore off some Mods would swallow handfuls of pills in an attempt to forestall the inevitable."

Although pills, namely purple hearts (Drynamil) and black bombers (Durophet) were fairly commonplace, the effects of which promoted self-confidence and awareness for the user, Alfredo Marcantonio argues that the Mod movement wasn't necessarily speed oriented all of the time, even though some Mods did indeed take it to the limit.

Alfredo Marcantonio - "Mostly people only really took speed at the weekend and they did so to keep awake... (but some) stepped up the dosage until they got right out of their boxes."

Inevitably, the constant ingestion of Purple Hearts ultimately took its toll, especially in later years, for two prized members of the early Mod scene.

Rob Nicholls - "Peter Meaden indicates that the suppression of the sex drive that resulted from getting 'blocked' on Purple Hearts (Drynamil) to stay awake during all-nighters, impacted gender relations adversely. In 1942, the British Army provided amphetamines to soldiers to allay fatigue and *reduce their sex drive.* Purple hearts had the same effect on Mods and the purple heart high may be what Meaden is referring to when he argues that 'people were not emotionally involved.'

Unlike regular Mods who scored purple hearts on the street, Meaden had them prescribed for depression. As a result of habitual speed use, Peter Meaden and Guy Stevens, both corner stones for the emerging Mod movement, lived hard and died young, neither reaching the age of forty. Meaden died in 1978 at the age of 37, while Stevens died in 1981 at the age of 38."

Steve Austin - "Purple Hearts, later French blues [amphetamine], were readily available. They were anti-depressants, and I remember reading at the time that they had been prescribed to Churchill, Eden, and Kennedy. There were always local lads willing to break into a chemist to steal a thousand; I heard later that they were breaking into the SKN factory in Welwyn Garden City."

Though there are many aspects important to being labelled a Mod - attention to detail and visual perfection and wherever possible, retaining exclusivity - in addition, there was the crowning glory of a Mod - the important cut and style of the hair.

MOD HAIRSTYLES

Clothes aside, there is no other visible detail that required closer attention than a Mod's hair - commonly described as the barnet. Like the attire that they proudly wore with style and flare, changing with each passing week and day - the many fast-evolving and varied-looking hairstyles also reigned supreme. From the short back and sides of the Ivy League cut (also known as the College Boy style), the straight and severely short fringe of the Caesar cut to the later and longer bouffant style favoured by Steve Marriot, the young David Bowie and Rod Stewart and the short cropped crew cut style - one thing is certain, the style and cut had to be perfectly coiffured, precise and neat- the completion of the Mod's appearance.

Above: The Caesar cut.   **Rob Nicholls**

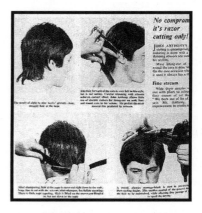

Johnny Powell (left) with his friends sporting the Mod crew cut style

Johnny Powell - "Right from being a kid, I always had short cropped hair. During my Mod years, I kept the cropped style but the barber - a lovely Greek fella called Lou - would do me a half an inch crop and then, with his hairdryer and a steel comb, would style a parting in it. It was so short yet had this great parting - I loved that style, we weren't skinheads, it was far more influenced by the American crew cut and was very Mod."

Jeremy Norman - "Hair cuts? Being at a Grammar School was good for our Mod hairstyles. The hard bit was finding a local barber who was 'Avant garde' enough to give you a razor cut and do some shaping. Mostly you ended up looking like an inmate of Dartmoor! But neat was Mod as far as we were concerned. Once I could drive and started work I could visit an Italian barber in Norwich called Enzo. This guy was brilliant. He had looked at pictures of the hairstyles going around and made the effort to copy them. Charges for a wash and cut and shape was 7/6d."

Rob Nicholls - "Modernists' hairstyles were basically a college boy hairstyle though many included a brush-over-fringe now known as the Beatle cut. This hairstyle was standard among British Invasion groups and was worn, for example, by the Dave Clark Five. Later Mod hairstyles were layered and short with a high crown (bouffant) and parted in the middle or with a high parting. Then there was 'The French Crew' which was like a crew cut but around two inches all over and 'The French Crop' which was the College Boy grown out but with a higher parting, a great example being Rod Stewart's rooster's pompadour, a Mod hairstyle *par excellence*."

Gordon Rath (Sheffield Mod) - "I always wore my hair short. Some of the lads went for the bouffant style, but that was not for me, I would get too sweaty from dancing to have that style."

David Middleton - "After the Beatle look in came the middle parting: you tried to make it look Mod so as to stand out and so people would look at you and know that you were a Mod, I cut my hair myself for years."

Straight-talking South London Mod David Middleton lived the Mod life to the hilt. Epitomising the fast-talking, gum-chewing, pure working class grit of many of his fellow Mods, David lays down some non-negotiable rules and requirements of life as a Mod in the early sixties.

David Middleton - "The Mod culture had come from nowhere in late 1961 and the cult was at its peak by 1964. London was full of Mods as it was a London and English born cult to be a Mod to begin with. The Mod cult did take it's time getting out of London and into the sticks.

Mods for one thing did not have anything to do with America that most cults did in one way or another. Apart from, that is, the best Mod R&B records coming over from America and then there was also the best scooters coming from Italy. The English scooters was just so bad and crap to look at and none of the Mods would buy them anyway and wouldn't be seen dead on any of them. Besides, you couldn't buy any nice looking accessories for the English scooters to make them look good anyway.

Mod culture consisted of scooters, records, nightclubs, clothes, coffee bars, rhythm and blues and the ultimate kick for many of the Mods was popping lots of pills in a club somewhere and dancing the nights away every weekend. The Mod 'hates' were people at work who still thought that they are something big in the Army as well as upper class Bohemian Twits, Beatniks, and most of the records from Liverpool apart from 'Some Other Guy' by The Big Three'. Maybe, most of all, the hates went on the 'out of date' Rockers with their 'oil pissing out all looking the same boring motor bikes' that went with the Rockers cult.

The Mods turned their backs on religion because when they was seven or eight years of age they were made to go to Sunday school. It was the most boring way to spend a Sunday afternoon singing silly songs, kneeling down getting up then kneeling back down again. Besides, playing at war over on the bombsites was much better fun.

Most Mods never bought a newspaper as most of the time it was about things that went on half way around the world in some overseas piss holes where you were never going to go in your lifetime - so why the fuck do we have to read about it all the time? Why should we give a fuck anyway?"

The clothes, the records and the pills. But where did these essential commodities come together. Apart from the popular Ballrooms, which were often colonised with small pockets of Mod contingents, there was The Flamingo (which opened as a Jazz club in the 50's and the most cross-cultural of these clubs). Also popular were the French-influenced clubs La Discotheque on Wardour Street, La Poubelle (Poland Street), Le Kilt (Green Street) and 93 Dean Street's Les Enfants Terribles. The latter, though not strictly a Mod club, was home to whom many consider the very first female DJ, Georgina, who sequenced her records in order of danceability. Then there was the hottest little club in London.

THE SCENE CLUB

The Scene Club on Ham Yard off Great Windmill Street, Soho, opened in 1963 and was formerly The Piccadilly Jazz club, Cy Laurie's Jazz Club. It had begun as Ronnie Scott's Club 11 in 1948, originally a barrow store for the Rupert Street traders. It was part-owned by Irish entrepreneur Ronan O' Rahilly who started Radio Caroline. With its resident hip DJ Guy Stevens it was a natural haven for the Mods to enjoy the sounds and social presence of their own exclusive culture.

Rob Nicholls - "Pete Townshend of The Who was a true believer and remembers The Scene Club, 'The Scene was really where it was at.... It was a focal point for the Mod movement. I don't think that anyone who was a Mod outside Soho realised the fashions and dances all began there.' The fact that such musical luminaries as the Animals, Georgie Fame, Chris Farlowe, the Rolling Stones, and The Who all played at the Scene, was not what secured its status as Mod central; it was Guy Stevens' record sessions, and everyone else was playing catch-up. Richard Barnes describes Stevens as, 'The man with the best R&B collection in the country.' Some of his vast record collection like Howlin' Wolf's 'Smokestack Lightening' and Bo Diddley's 'Who Do You Love? were not the 'latest' both being recorded in 1956, but they were new to the U.K. For me, becoming a Mod was synonymous with discovering great R&B, and later West Indian Blue-beat. We knew what we liked when we heard it, whether it being James Brown's shuffling instrumental 'Night Train' (1961), Wilbert Harrison's throbbing 'Let's Stick Together' (1962), Don Gardner's and Dee Dee Ford's gospel tinged 'I Need Your Loving Everyday' (1962), or Inez and Charlie Foxx's ethereal 'Mocking Bird' (1963)."

Steuart Kingsley-Innes (Hull Mod, relocated to Fulham 1963) - "The hot summer of 64 and Mod was coming to a peak. It was one of those magic moments in time that can never be repeated - you just had to be there!

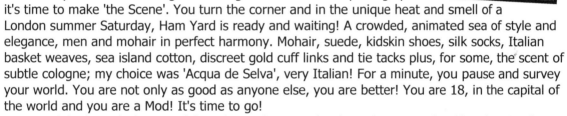

Off the tube (stand up; watch your creases!) and on into Soho; a scotch and coke in the 'French Pub' then a stroll on down to Gt Windmill St, nodding approval and acknowledgement to guys whose style stood out, making mental notes for future reference. Onto Wardour St and the Kontact sandwich bar, a coke to wash down a couple of bombers and a little Rufus Thomas on the jukebox, yeah, jump back baby!

You feel the chills starting to rise and pop in some gum as your mouth seeks a rhythm to chew along to. The night's momentum is picking up and it's time to make 'the Scene'. You turn the corner and in the unique heat and smell of a London summer Saturday, Ham Yard is ready and waiting! A crowded, animated sea of style and elegance, men and mohair in perfect harmony. Mohair, suede, kidskin shoes, silk socks, Italian basket weaves, sea island cotton, discreet gold cuff links and tie tacks plus, for some, the scent of subtle cologne; my choice was 'Acqua de Selva', very Italian! For a minute, you pause and survey your world. You are not only as good as anyone else, you are better! You are 18, in the capital of the world and you are a Mod! It's time to go!

You glide through the crowd, 'weighing in' Una at the door, down into the dilapidated cellar that is the Scene! Guy Stevens is the most famous 'jock' there, the king of R&B but also a massive Jerry Lee and Little Richard fan, always sitting on his box of precious records and looking mischievous, who knows what he's likely to play? But it's Saturday and Sandra's behind the decks and she's already on a roll! 'Where are you going later?' your mate asks. Who knows? The ''Mingo'? 'The Disc'? Maybe even the 20s! We'll see! That's for later, a night time away. Right now the record you've been waiting for roars out 'Got love if you want it' - Slim Harpo's classic 'anthem.' Oh, yes! It's time to dance!

Nearly midnight! Time to get some air; check out who's about and what's new. Plus top up your buzz! You lean on the wall again, survey the still crowded yard but your mind is on the dance floor. Some heavy competition tonight, if you fancy yourself as a dancer that is; looks like all the real 'steppers' are in there and doing their thing. Hey, no surprise, the music is the best. Band? What band? Couldn't tell you who's on! I'm there for the records, the real sound! That new label Tamla has some good stuff out that they're playing, The Miracles and 'Mickeys Monkey', Gino Parks 'Fire' and Martha Reeves 'In My Lonely Room' to name a couple, mind you I prefer her 'Heatwave' for me that's got the better beat, I'm thinking if they keep that standard up they could be a big label one day. Coming back Monday for R&B night? You ask yourself, 'Why not' you decide, some of those old discs are great Jimmy Reed 'Big Boss Man', Elmore James' 'I'm Worried', Wilbert Harrison 'Let's Stick Together'; the easy beat of Sonny Boy's 'Nine Below Zero' and 'Help Me' all still sound fresh yet some have been around for years. Another guy I'm getting to like is James Brown - his 'Night Train' always gets a floor moving. Where they find the records beats me; no wonder Guy sits on his box. He's got everything by Slim Harpo and all the old blues stars plus strange stuff like Jay Hawkins 'Put a Spell on You'. But he still likes to hit you with 'Great Balls Of Fire' and 'Tutti Frutti'! You should see some of those kids jive. You pop another gum in and light up one of your occasional cigarettes, a Players Weight Tipped, as the smoke hits you're already racing - nervous system you muse on for a bit longer. Thinking of R&B, John Lee Hookers' stuff is outstanding and different 'Boogie Chillun' hard to dance to but a great guitar. Talking of hard to dance to - Charlie Fox's' 'Mockingbird' can sort them out. With Major Lance, Jackie Ross, Freddy King, Isley Brothers, Mary Wells, Gene Chandler, The Impressions, Chris Kenner, Solomon Burke and many other top black artists to check out every night, who needs the top twenty? The sound of Phil Upchurch cuts through your thoughts 'You Can't Sit Down'. He's right there! Time to head back, flash your hand stamp, and on into the heat and steam. You slide back into the dancing throng and pick up the Rhythm. It's Saturday night at the Scene!"

Geoff Green - "I first went in 1963 with a group of my friends. I was a Mod (of sorts, I was an apprentice and didn't have a lot of money), but the main reason we went was that the advert in the Record Mirror spoke of records played by artistes including Chuck Berry, Bo Diddley, Jimmy Reed, Howling Wolf, Jerry Lee Lewis and others. I can't remember if they used the term 'Maximum R&B' first, or if this was originated by the Who later. At this time, the Merseybeat boom was getting under way, beat groups were beginning to feature cover versions of rhythm and blues songs, and we wanted to hear the originals. Chuck Berry's records had been issued in this country, but when Chess moved from London to the Pye group, his singles had been deleted. So though there was terrific interest in his material nothing was available.

I remember my first visit, the music seemed incredible. All the great rhythm and blues records, and good rock 'n' roll stuff, plus the current Phil Spector hits like 'Da Doo Ron Ron' and 'Zippadee Doo Dah' I had never been to a club before, only to local dance halls, like the Tottenham Royal, where there was not the same atmosphere. And there were all these guys wearing the clothes I wanted and was having difficulty affording. You went down a staircase, paid your money, had your hand stamped and went into a rectangular room. As I recall the DJ was in a little box to the right of the entrance, but it was flush to the wall. In the right hand corner opposite to the DJ was a bar that only sold soft drinks (I remember cola that was made from powder and water, really horrible).

A bit further to the left of the entrance was a passage to the cloakroom. Along the far wall to to the left were booths. I think the first few times I went there you couldn't see what was going on, but later they were opened up, I think this happened after a raid for drugs. And I think there were benches on the right hand wall between the bar and DJ booth. The rest was a dance floor with a pillar or two. People stood around or danced. A lot of the time, it was a case of being seen at the right place. I went a few more times, but became a regular in 1964.

This was in the later part of the summer, I'd met a girl, and we were always going out to places to hear music and dance. So we went to the Scene, and the music was less rhythm and bluesy, more what we'd call Soul, but it was still called rhythm and blues by us.

Also popular that summer were old rock 'n' roll records by people like Bill Haley and Carl Perkins. Remember this was the year of the Mods and Rockers riots, grossly exaggerated by the papers. But those records had the right beat for the dances of the time, the Block, and later the Bang. Also at that time, I remember the Miracles' 'I Like It Like That' and the Supremes' 'When The Love light Shines in His Eyes' being played. I wore an off-white jacket with patch pockets (very fashionable then) and thought I was really cool. I also had a sort of crew cut; it was the summer of the American look, Levi's with little turn-ups and Desert Boots.

Shortly after that, I joined (instead of using vouchers from the Record Mirror), as did my mates and girlfriend. It was a guinea (£1 5p). That seemed a lot of money in those pre-inflation days to an apprentice. Monday nights were free to members, and Tuesday (the best weekday night) was one shilling (5p). The all-nighter on Saturday was 5 shillings (25p), but I couldn't go to them with my girlfriend, her parents would have gone mad. We regularly went on Tuesdays and often on Mondays.

When the Who started appearing at the Marquee in Wardour Street we would often go to the Scene in the break between their appearances, for about 3/4 of an hour. The music by then was what I would describe as classic Soul, Motown, Chess, Major Lance, Impressions, Gene Chandler, plus tracks like 'Boom Boom' and 'Dimples' by John Lee Hooker, and Jimmy Reed classics. Also Ska (or Blue beat as it was known) was played, but not great amounts, records like 'Madness' by Prince Buster and 'Carolina' by the Folks Brothers. Also, a track 'Jamaican Ska' was a minor hit on the Atlantic label, I can't remember the artist. Incidentally, when I danced with my girlfriend we often jived, this was quite common then.

I remember 'Night Train' by James Brown was regularly played, it had just been re-issued on the Sue label, and people formed a chain and weaved in and out of the dancers. It was led by an attractive blonde who looked like Dusty Springfield; one of my mates fancied her. Organ instrumentals were highly popular, people like Jimmy Smith and Jimmy McGriff. Quite a lot of Jazzy sounding stuff was played as well as almost anything issued by the British Sue label. One Tuesday night an American TV crew were filming, I'd love to see that now.

In February 1965, my girlfriend packed me in for one of my mates, and this broke up our crowd. A couple of the others had girlfriends and were drifting away anyway. At that point, I was pretty down and started to go to all-nighters there with one of my mates. I would meet him at about a quarter to midnight in Piccadilly Circus underground station, outside the Gent's toilets believe it or not. We'd then go straight to the Scene, pay our money and go in to hear the music. It was exciting and the music was brilliant. It was the time that all of the classics were coming out, 'Respect', 'In The Midnight Hour,' 'Nothing Can Stop Me,' 'I

Can't Help Myself,' etc. To a certain extent, they seem a bit hackneyed now; we've all heard them so many times. But they were new then and so exciting. Just like when you hear a Northern Soul or R&B track you have never heard before. I'd hear one of my faves and be out on the floor straight away.

As well as Soul and R&B tracks, some pop stuff was played. GTO by Ronnie and The Daytonas (a sort of surfing sound, but I think actually made in somewhere like South Carolina); 'Yeh Yeh', Georgie Fame; Jewel Atkins' Birds and The Bees; Righteous Brothers 'Hung On You' (a great track and better than 'Loving Feeling'); the Vogues 'You're The One', quite a good pop record, but written by Petula Clark; the DJ (by now an attractive blonde lady [Sandra]) must have liked it; and just before the end 'Lightning Strikes' (Lou Christie) and 'Barbara Ann' (Beach Boys). Also, she liked to play Tallahassee Lassie (Freddie Cannon); 'Summertime Blues' (Eddie Cochran) and 'Lewis Boogie' (Jerry Lee Lewis). At the same time bluesy stuff was still played; as was an EP made by the Animals as a demo tape for Decca featuring 'Boom Boom' and 'Dimples' (Not the versions they did for Parlophone). There was a version of 'Mohair Sam' by someone other than Charlie Rich; it had different and more amusing lyrics; and also Jimmy Hanna's version of 'Leaving Here'. Some things just stick in your mind.

During the all-nighters, we would go out for a walk to get some air and go to the milk machine in Berwick Street. I remember we were once accosted by a lady of the night who offered her services for 30 shillings (£1.50). Needless to say, we turned her kind offer down, music was more important, plus I think she made us a bit nervous. Many of the records played were imports, so we heard many good records long before they were issued in the UK. I started going out with a girl (who eventually became my wife) in January 1966 and I took her there a few times, but there was another drugs raid, and when it re-opened, it wasn't the same. We stopped going around March or April 1966. It later became the King Creole Club but I know nothing of that.

The Scene had a major effect on my musical taste, and I still look for some tracks I remember and have never found. When you're young you are inclined to take everything for granted, and that's how we were. It was good and I am glad I went there; I wouldn't be the person I am today if I hadn't gone there."

Alfredo Marcantonio cites William Bell's 'Monkeying Around', 'Got You on My mind' by Cookie and his cupcakes along with 'It's love Baby - 24 Hours' by Hank Ballard and the Midnighters as "Three Scene favourites... I never, ever heard anywhere else". Other Mod faves of Alfredos' include 'The Clock' by Johnny Ace and Jimmy Reed's 'Big Boss Man'. Fellow Scene club attendee, Rob Nicholls recalls other particular favourite platters of his that were regularly spun at his favourite club.

Rob Nicholls - "The Whisky-a-GoGo and La Discotheque on Wardour Street, were small, a bit gaudy, and were often too crowded for my tastes. I preferred The Scene Club, which although a bit seedy and usually rather sparsely attended, was more my style. On Saturday nights, the West End was just too much of a melee for me, and my mates and I preferred to go to parties.

There were a couple of records that Mods at The Scene used to associate with taking Purple Hearts (Drynamil; an amphetamine/barbiturate stimulant). One was Bo Diddley's 'Pills' (1961) which was played on a regular basis. A worthy local version by Mickey Finn and the Blue Men is performed on stage in Blue-beat style in BBC's Panorama Mod interviews in 1964. Another popular track on the same topic was Willie Mabon's 'Got To Have Some' (1962), a moody R&B record in which Mabon's baritone voice intones 'I must get some, I gotta have some, I really need some.' The record was so successful that Mabon then issued, 'I Just Got Some,' which was covered by Rod Stewart in 1966 as the B-side of his much sought after 45 'Shake' on Columbia. Purple hearts would provide a lift but there was the inescapable 'comedown.'"

'DO THE DOG AT THE SCENE CLUB'

Rob Nicholls - "In 1963, many of the dances at the Scene were adaptations of American dances like the Dog or the Monkey that had caught on, although some were individual expressions. Nineteen year old London Mod, David Holburne talks of attending 'clubs in the West End' in 1964 and reports, 'We do the Shake and Hitchhiker to fast numbers'). Good dancing was appreciated and virtuoso dance steps might be imitated and become the vogue for weeks at a time. Whether it was The Scene's doing or simply the work of individuals, for a while, French chalk was dusted on the dance floor to make it more slippery and better for dancing because it gave less resistance to dancing feet.

Later, coinciding with the R&B acts that toured England, there was a more conscious adoption of Black American dances. During visits to Norwich clubs in 1965, my mates and I learned the Jerk and the Swim from Black GI's who were stationed on nearby American bases and came to town for weekend amusement. However, the Block, the Bang, and the Face Twist were homegrown dances developed by the Mods at The Scene. The Bang had a sideways swaying movement with legs kicking out side-to-side. The bang' part was when one leg shot straight out to the side while the other foot stamped on the floor providing a loud percussive emphasis. It was performed by both males and females, but seemed to be favoured by girls, possibly because their 'granny shoes' had a solid heel which served this purpose well. The Block refers to the Mods' use of Purple Hearts, getting 'blocked,' and the parody was performed primarily by males. The dance had a basically upright posture and consisted of a rhythmical but somewhat spasmodic movement of the legs and arms, crossing of the legs, twisting the torso and spinning around occasionally, with lurches off to the side as if about to topple over, legs buckling but never collapsing.

Within the Mod hierarchy, individuals might be designated as a 'Face' who set fashions or a 'Ticket' who followed them. I was a Face and initiated trends, for example, I bought a pair of black Italian shoes in soft leather with thick crepe soles at Raoul's on Carnaby Street, but because dark shoes were invisible in the dimly lit Scene Club, I accentuated them by using white laces, and in so doing drew attention to my dance steps. Before long, I found other Mods were wearing white laces and furthermore, the Hush Puppy shoe brand who were marketing suede shoes to Mods at the time, started to sell them not only with laces in white, but in pink, green and other colours also.

The Face Twist was popular at the Scene and was performed by both males and females. It was extremely stylish and demanded a lot of self-confidence. It is mentioned in *Time Magazine* (10 April, 1964): 'Mods change dances even faster than they change trouser-widths. The 'Shake' and the 'Bird' are both passé, and only the Rockers would be caught doing the Twist. The current dance craze is something called the 'Face Twist,' which has a tricky hand and heel movement that resembles a cross between a hula dance and a High Noon gun draw.' The Face Twist was done much slower than the regular Twist, leaning forward and with one arm extended with the hand in a thumbs up position (or in a 'High Noon gun draw'), and swaying the rump from side to side ('hula') with the heels pushed back. Although it was slow it could be done to fast or medium tempo music creating an interesting dichotomy."

Alfredo Marcantonio - "We ditched the rotating nature of the Twist and began to move forward and back, with a lot of 'heel' action'."

Marc Feld referred to a sophisticated twist in the 'Town' magazine article previously mentioned, a dance, it appears, that was the exclusive domain of the Faces themselves?

Rob Nicholls (on being a Face) - "Nobody tells you that you have become a Face, you're not elected or appointed or anything. You start out by looking stylish and perpetuating the Mod look, but adding innovations - initial letters on shirts in the case of Freddy Marcantonio and his friend Cliff; pilfered bowling shoes in the case of Johnny Moke. In my case, it was [the afore-mentioned] white shoelaces on dark shoes. All of these trends were copied by key Mods. Thus, you became aware that you had arrived as a Face when your idiosyncratic additions were copied by your peers. At that stage, you might be confident enough to perform the Face Twist. I never saw anybody dancing it who wasn't a Face. By the time a fashion became accepted among the general teen culture the Faces had moved on to new styles. However, staying one-step ahead of the Tickets became more difficult by 1964 when Mod clothes were manufactured and sold off the peg at numerous boutiques, and any Tom, Dick or Harry could buy a Mod outfit. This forced the original Faces to look further afield for inventive ways to project the Mod persona yet still stand out from the Tickets.

During the summer of 1964, old rock 'n' roll records by Bill Haley, Carl Perkins, and Eddie Cochran, were danced to again at The Scene Club and the Last Chance Saloon, and the American look was revisited, for example, by wearing Levi's with little turn-ups and Desert Boots. Some Faces like Mike Tenner and Ted Murphy completed the look by wearing colourful cycling shirts and bomber jackets while others, like me and Geoff Green, wore long sack-style single-breasted jackets, referred to as zoot suit jackets. While Geoff's was off-white, my two-buttoned and long-lapelled jacket was in a light tawny brown synthetic-type material. It had patch side-pockets but no top pocket. I wore it with a white silk-scarf and looked the biz. This is an often neglected era of Mod history and was my last overtly Mod look before my style petered off into Art College bohemianism in the Summer of Love and the ensuing sex and drugs and rock 'n' roll."

THE WEST END CINEMA AND DANCE HALL

As much as Mod evolved most strongly in the London clubs and ballrooms, contingents of Mods soon appeared sporadically around the country, their social meeting places often being the established dance halls of their nearby towns.

Gill Evans - "The West End [in Birmingham] had been open for years. I started to go there just after leaving art school. Del had also been a few times before we were together. Then, later on, we would go together and see groups like Steampacket with Rod Stewart, before we knew who he was, and Long John Baldry, the Spencer Davis Group who we loved and was obviously from Birmingham. It became a meeting place for Mods around late 1962 and into 63.

After the Merseybeat thing, the guy spinning discs would start playing Tamla and other Soul, it was not licenced so, for us, it was a tea or a coffee, but then again, we didn't really drink as we needed to stay at our best and pristine.

Birmingham Mods outside the West End Cinema and Dance Hall, 1965

Left: Del Evans in his Italian Navy nylon Trench Mac, 1963

There was some division on the dance floor. The Mods tended to stay at the top end of the dance floor; while in the middle was the mid-types, neither here or there …. Mockers I suppose. A few rocker types stayed around the stage area. There were dances on Saturday afternoons but the big meeting time there was Sunday nights. All the local Mods met there, they all got on well. There was also another ballroom at the other end of the city called The Ritz and of course there was also the 'Whiskey a GoGo' [obviously not the London club of the same name] where we also would go along to. The two guys who owned the Whiskey also went to the West End. The Mod nights at the West End continued through until around at least 1968."

Back in London, a plethora of inviting options to sample the vibrant scene were at hand.

Johnny Powell - "We used to go the Marquee to see all of the groups. Also a coffee bar called Bungies, we went to all the best coffee bars at the time, and around the corner on Great Newport St, under some shops there was the '51 Club' where I met Rod Stewart for the first time. It was an old Jazz club but on Sundays it was converted for the modern sounds. I can remember the Stones played there before they were known around '63 and also for a surprise gig after they were famous. The other place was the Tottenham Royal where I started going from '65 onwards, that was the Mod place to go. I was always out with my older brother. My Dad used to say 'Stick with your brother and make sure you are back on time. It was a great time being a teenager – all the way through the 60's."

David Birchall - "We would go to dances at the Wooden Bridge Pub in Guildford (the Stones played there), the Ricky Tick Club, the Crawdaddy Club, Eel Pie Island on occasion and the Harvest Moon Club in Guildford. It was across the road from the Ricky Tick and was the cause of its closing. We would see Georgie Fame, Chris Farlowe, Long John Baldry, Spencer Davies and of course, John Mayall. We (my buddy Alan Taylor and I) would also go to the 'Disc' on Wardour Street or rarely, 'The Scene'. The Scene could be intimidating since you never knew if you were going to get rolled! I remember picking up a girl there and dancing for a long time with her until somebody I didn't know whispered in my ear 'She is the girlfriend of the leader of the Mile End Boys!' Exit one wannabe boyfriend ..."

ROGER AMES - MUSWELL HILL HIPSTER

Roger Ames lived initially in East Barnet, but when his parents moved to Royston, Roger moved in with his grandmother in Muswell Hill, to be nearer to Hornsey College of Art. That was late 1962. He found that the worst thing about Royston was dealing with the Royston Rockers. Roger says, "They had never seen anyone with backcombed hair, hipster ankle-swinger trousers in white, and Blue Anello and Davide stack-heeled boots.

Above right: Roger (2nd from right) with North London Mods, Clacton 1963

Right: Roger (at the front wearing shades) with Mod friends at High Beech in Epping

Roger states, "My home dance hall was the Royal [Tottenham], but me and my scooter boy friends visited all the Mecca haunts from Purley to Stevenage." Other dance halls included the Lyceum, Manor House, Cooks Ferry, Club

Noriek and the Athenaeum in Muswell Hill where Rod Stewart used to perform. The London clubs Roger frequented included The Scene, Discotheque, Flamingo, Last Chance, Purple Pussycat, Cromwellian, Scotch of St. James, Poubelle, and Chez Don in Dalston. On Sundays, Roger and his mates would hang out at High Beach, an area of open heath in Epping Forest near Walthamstow where Mods would gather. The photo [previous page] shows Roger and his mates from around Wood Green and Southgate seated on Tex's, ex U. S. Jeep. Roger is in front wearing the sunglasses while Tex is at the left in the driver's seat. Many of Roger's friends were noted dancers, for example, Cyril, at the centre back of the photo, was a well-known dancer from the Royal. In addition to R&B standards such as Rufus Thomas's 'Do the Dog,' Roger was keen on Blue-beat such as Prince Buster's 'Madness' and The Skatalites 'Guns of Navarone. He was also a dance enthusiast and often appeared on Ready Steady Go! (RSG). Roger shared his love of dancing with RSG dancer Sandy Sarjeant, who has gained the status of Mod icon and who Roger dated in the early sixties. He recalls:

"I went out with Sandy for some time, having met at an RSG audition. We used to hang out at quite a few dance halls, the State, Kilburn, Top Rank, Kings Road and many others, we originally got turned down at the [RSG] audition and Sandy kept up the pressure and got the feature dance slot. I had my RSG passport and had to perform a couple of dances on the show. We used to drive around in my BMW Isetta ([Bubble Car) having sold my GS. The Isetta was bright red with two racing stripes that went over the roof."

Roger attended Hornsey College of Art and took many photos of Sandy when she was trying to get into modelling. We can lament the loss of these photos of Sandy, and we can further regret another lost treasure, Roger's thesis at Hornsey on Modernism, titled 'Transient, Mobile, Disposable Generation,' from when he visited all the clubs building up a photo library and a film record. "Unfortunately, it's all gone," admits Roger, "My Liberal Studies tutor took my original document and it was never returned!" In due course Sandy married Ian McLagan of the Small Faces.

These Faces, along with the other ranks of the Mod hierarchy - the tickets and the seven and sixers - those that struggled to keep up with the trendsetters - not forgetting the streetwise scooter boy gangs, all had one thing in common; they aspired to strike out via their own identity and individual vision of Mod. Embracing the new consumerism - yet defying its outcome when their own exclusive choice of style became universal - Mods often elevated themselves to be their own personal tailors and barbers and craved constant change and improvement.

The look of the individual was all encompassing and so was the additional projection of classiness and aura of cool. Be it smoking French Gitanes cigarettes for effect or sketching the style of French 'new wave' star Jean Paul Belmondo in the Jean Luc Godard film 'A Bout de Soufflé' (1960) the look of Alain Delon in 'Plein Soleil' or being the first to hear a record and create the all-important first exclusive dance for it - Mods were consistently the social and cultural embodiment of style!

That recognition of style was also often a less flamboyant yet no less relevant primal reaction to the safe family-friendly pop music of the period and possibly the establishment itself. For some younger Mod-afflicted teenagers, the abrasive raw energy of the new influx of Beat groups - the angry young men of the R&B music scene - was also crucial to the appeal and an incentive to belong to an exclusive gang of like-minded youths.

Reggie Webster - "The formative years of being what the media called 'Mods' had to be 1963-64; style wise and socially, the 1950's didn't seem to end until 1963, pop music was still dominated by showbiz-driven artists like Cliff and the Shadows, Susan Maughan and Johnny Leyton, who's exposure was the BBC, Radio Luxembourg and ITV variety shows. The girls screamed at quiffed blokes in short jackets and film stars, just like they had since the 1940's. 1963 brought something different, Beat music and a wave of (very) rocker-styled Beat groups like the Beatles and The Searchers. It doesn't seem unreasonable that kids with a certain type of attitude, not unlike the teds of the 50's - and well established Greasers - reacted when the next wave of what appeared to be angry young men started singing 'My Generation.' The Who, The Kinks, The Animals, Pretty Things and The Yardbirds brought a very British aggressive take on R&B - a soundtrack the wilder kids could relate too. The music wasn't a motivation but there was an appeal. These guys didn't look like something your Mum would approve of, four guys dressed all the same in winkle pickers and matching waistcoats, a respectable niche in the market for the new teenager who just had to be 'with it' and bought 45's!"

To be 'with it', for most Mods, this also meant the added accessory of a particular method of transport.

Del Ansell (Clacton Mod, with his late brother Bert in white t-shirt) - "Scooters were all that we had, we couldn't use the phone so we had to go and see our mates. They were our life, we had hardly any money, but just enough for 99 shillings HP on a scooter, petrol and of course COFFEE! Best days of our lives!"

Irish Jack Lyons - "The only acceptable mode of transport for a Mod was a Vespa GS or a Lambretta Li 150 scooter. The most beautiful sound in the world is the two-stroke piston pop of a scooter. *Pop, pop, pop.* The fairing on the scooter was held to be sexy, curvy, delicate like Brigitte Bardot. *La dolce vita.* Ooh-la-la. Rockers referred to our tiny two-stroke scooters as 'hair dryers.'"

MODS AND SCOOTERS

Above: Alfredo Marcantonio on his Vespa GS, 1963

Rob Nicholls (pictured above right, with what was left of his Vespa GS after it was recovered.) "I wanted a historical record before I discarded it. Although the photo was taken in February 1965, for the photo, I am wearing the clothes I wore when I bought the scooter in April 1963: a short box-shaped, double-breasted jacket worn over a matelot t-shirt with horizontal stripes and Levi jeans."

Alfredo Marcantonio - "Mods were never interested in live groups. We were into records. So you sought out 'record nights' which is why you needed a scooter as a form of transport."

Rob Nicholls - "I kept my nose clean and while I was a Mod I didn't have much trouble with the law, unlike my hippy years when various infractions tripped me up. Yet I was pulled over by the Old Bill on my scooter for the 'excessive noise' of my twin chrome pipes. In court, the Beak told me to remedy the situation and fined me. This happened more than once. The second time I stopped up the top pipe by stuffing a potato in it. And no, my exhaust did not smell of chips, but it was great fun watching the cop poking in the exhaust with his little probe and saying to his colleague, 'This one seems to be blocked.' 'You're right there, cunt 'stable,' I muttered.

The Imperial attracted a lot of teenagers with Vespa's and Lambrettas and these were an impressive sight when parked in rows outside the club. I bought my Vespa GS Scooter second-hand in 1963. It was silver grey and I kept it plain without the multiple mirrors and decals that some scooter boys added. It had bars at the front and I added a big mud flap at the back, which reached the road. My pièce de résistance was the exhaust system, which consisted of twin chrome pipes, 1 1/2 inches in diameter which gave it a throaty burble, it droned like a Second World War bomber.

Unlike later eras, in the mid-sixties there were no laws requiring crash helmets. Although rockers generally wore them, Mods preferred other headwear or none at all. With the option of the Parka hood if it rained, most went hatless or wore Blue-beat hats. Borrowed from the West Indian rude boy look, a Blue-beat hat is a small porkpie trilby with a tiny brim. In my case, I wore a beret and instead of the standard Parka, I wore a short oilskin coat.

In a friendly critique of 'Quadrophenia' what I admired in real life but found lacking in the film is the way scooters were ridden. Whether ornate or sleek, Vespa or Lambretta, the scooters usually looked serviceable and some were showcases. But the most important part of the ensemble was the Mod's demeanour. A Mod did not just sit on his scooter—he rode it—a charioteer with his chariot, a knight with his steed. With no windscreen or merely a tiny one, when riding, Mods adopted a jaunty upright posture, leaning backwards slightly, knees splayed, and although the heels were behind the fender the toes were pointed out at 45 degrees.

In the depth of winter, I regretted not having a snug Parka. On icy days, I wore mittens and put on extra trousers and jerseys under my oilskin and scarves around my face. Style went out the window and I was wrapped in globular fashion like the Michelin man. Riding home late at night along the tediously straight Cambridge Road I would take my hands off the handlebars and flap my arms across my chest trying to keep warm. In November 1964 my scooter was stolen from its parking place at Turnpike Lane and although it was later recovered it had been repainted and stripped and was a right-off."

Roger Ames was riding his Vespa GS as early as May 1962. His scooter was largely undecorated, although he had a Rolls Royce hubcap on his spare wheel. Like Rob Nicholls, who got his GS almost a year later, Roger sported a huge mud flap at the rear and had to be careful not to trap it when pulling the scooter onto its stand. Both modified the exhaust, Rob, with twin 1 ½-inch diameter chrome pipes, and Roger using "a long copper tube to deepen the note - flattened to increase backpressure and a hole to enable me to pour in small quantities of Castrol R to give that unmistakable aroma." Both Roger and Rob wore oilskin coats rather than the more conventional Mod anorak/parka.

Roger Ames - "At fifteen, I was able to buy my father's friend's Vespa GS for £40 and once I'd removed the massive windscreen, my fate was sealed. At fourteen, my mother had sent me to the N20 School of Dancing and I soon realised that it had advantages. I could dance with girls! Throw off the mohair jumper and 14 inch bottoms and put on my bleached Levis and Fred Perry shirt - feel the music and make the right moves and you're on your way.

I sometimes wore a deerstalker as scooter headgear. When moving out on your scooter, one had to have the feet at the front of the floor with the toes pointing down, the right foot scraping the road until you changed into second and then perched right at the front of the seat. The elbows also should be extended outwards to ensure the correct exaggerated riding position."

Steve Austin - "There was only one scooter to have and that was the Vespa 160. It was more stylish than the Lambretta, and a little bit faster, because it had a slightly bigger engine. Rockers used to laugh at us because they could do the ton and we could only squeeze 50-60 mph out of our little machines. But that didn't matter, we had the style and as much chrome as we could afford. Everyone and I mean everyone came off their scooters at some time, and remember there was no crash helmet law then. You would often see someone limping on to the bus who had just written off their beloved scooter, and also injured themselves at the same time."

Derek Glover and his girlfriend, Dianne in 1966

Derek Glover - "I purchased my Lambretta 150 series 3 'on the knock'. My Mom signed as guarantor and I was given a little card to make my monthly payments. The scooter was a beige colour but after two weeks and some spray cans it changed to blue and red. My girlfriend (now my wife) bought me a spare wheel rack and I purchased a fly screen. I went down the scrapyard and picked up a spare wheel, stopped off at green Austin Mini parked in a quiet side road and 'borrowed' a hubcap, which fitted perfectly into the centre of the spare wheel. Then came a tin of white wall tyre paint and some RAF transfers from the model shop. With a hammer and a six-inch nail, I banged some holes into the exhaust box to get the sound of a powerful roar when I revved up the engine. The transformation was complete. The next step was to get down to the Army and Navy store for an American parka. I had not got a helmet so I got myself a nice little Beret, which seemed trendy at the time.

I remember the day of my scooter-riding test. I removed my fly screen and spare wheel rack. I put on a suit and tie, my highly polished loafer shoes and wore a peaked helmet. I thought the smart, sensible look would give me the edge and create a good impression to the examiner. It did the trick, even though I done some things wrong and answered a couple of questions wrong, I PASSED"

Alfredo Marcantonio - "Scooters were popular in Britain way before the Mod movement got going, but a glance at archive films and photos shows you it was a mode of transport favoured by a very sad looking bunch. It was Soho's Italian waiters, in their bright jumpers and tight suits that helped to give them a 'cool' image. There were a number of Italian makes around, including Isettas and Rumis, but no self-respecting Modernist would get his leg over anything but a Vespa or Lambretta. The big decision was which one? My best pal Cliff loved Lambrettas and moved from a Li 150 to a TV175. But I only had eyes for the Vespa. I was obsessed with getting 'the original' when it came to music or button-down shirts, scooters were no different. It was the brainchild of helicopter designer Corradino D'Asciano and with a patent application dating back to April 1946; it leads the 'Lambo' by a couple of years."

Johnny Powell (left) - "I Bought a scooter in '66 - then I was a real Mod. It was a Vespa SS with a square head lamp, it was bought as a 180 and I had it converted to a 200."

Whilst scooters were the domain of the Mod male and Mod culture was primarily a masculine-dominated environment, Mod girls were just as dedicated to the cause and attention to detail as the Mod guys. As with all youth cults, a certain degree of improvisation was required and the female input into the early Mod look should not be underestimated.

David Middleton - "The first time I saw Mod girls was in a dance hall in Streatham South London. There were groups of Mod girls, to me I wanted one, and it really went from there. I think the girls got into it quicker then the boys did in some places."

David Middleton and his Lambretta series 1 and riding pillion in Brighton

Maurice Moore - "Amongst the first [Mod girls] I saw were girls with closely-cropped, shaped hair, dresses with flower, geometric or op-art designs, very colourful or just black and white. In addition, they wore matching plastic daisy earrings and hair slides. All was covered with a see-through pac-a-mac, a very thin raincoat which could be folded down to purse-size so that it would fit into your pocket or handbag, which, being almost transparent, showed the clothes you were wearing underneath; the dresses of course were getting shorter with the introduction of the mini-skirt; competitions were held to find the girl wearing the shortest mini-skirt. Shoes or boots were made of patent leather, generally quite flat or with low heels."

HIGH ROLLNECK SWEATERS

NOW THEY'RE MOTIFISED!

White heavy bulk cotton sweaters for gals or guys with your own name or that of your favourite group, hand embossed in Black, Red or blue washable dye (up to 10 letters). State size & name reqd.

JUST 20/- Post Paid!

MICHAEL MARTIN LTD

Authentic Mod girls of the era and a mid-60's cash-in advert

CAROL McFEE

FROM LLANDUDNO TO THE WHEEL

The euphoria of being young and caught up in the mid-60's Mod period led girls such as Carol McFee to the legendary Manchester club, The Twisted Wheel. The experiences of sharing her youthful excitement with like-minded souls and the equally thrilling anticipation of creating the right look inspired memories of a lifetime.

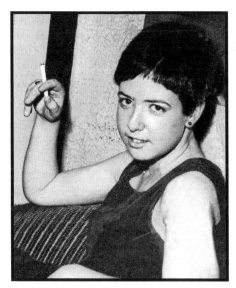

Carol McFee - "I was born in 1950 in the small seaside town of Llandudno, North Wales. When I was about 13 or 14, I watched ITV's 'Ready Steady Go!' the people, the clothes; the music ... It was all so exciting, I was hooked.

The early days of trying to get the look was exciting, hunting in the old ladies' clothes shops for lamb's wool twin sets, pinching my dad's collarless shirt, old men's ribbed vests and dyeing them on the stove, plastic mac from M & S and Clark's for original granny shoes; the rest I made myself, scouring 'Honey' magazine and copying the clothing.

Locally, apart from the Friday night dance 'Teen Beat', we had The Venetia (The Ven) coffee bar, where Mods gathered every evening. Weekends drew people from all over North Wales, Liverpool and Manchester - with the scooters lined up outside, always a fabulous sight.

Further afield over in Rhyl were The Lido on a Saturday night and The Palace on a Sunday and these would be heaving with people from all over. Then when I was sixteen, I discovered The Twisted Wheel in Manchester and from then on, my whole life was geared around getting to Manchester on a Saturday.

As soon as I finished work, my friend and I would thumb it to Manchester, our vanity case held everything we needed, change of clothes, make up, etc. As soon as we arrived, it was straight to Piccadilly Gardens to the underground cloakroom to get washed and changed. Once we were ready, it was over to the Wimpy for a coffee and to meet up with others, ready for midnight when the doors to the Wheel would open.

There has never been anything to compare to the atmosphere in The Wheel, it was the best. After dancing the night away, at 7am we would make our way to the Salvation Army stall set up nearby, for a cup of tea or orange juice, then it was off to Stax for a couple of hours of more music, and sometimes onto Rowntree's for the lunchtime session, phew!

Thumbing back to North Wales on a Sunday afternoon was not much fun and took hours, but it was all worth it, and we couldn't wait to do it all again the next week."

Carol on her 16th birthday with Louis Noble from Shrewsbury on the promenade at Llandudno, North Wales, Sunday 24th April 1966

PAT BECKETT: A MOD GIRL'S STORY BY ROB NICHOLLS

Peter Meaden's description of The Scene Club reflects the sexual insularity that he believed existed. In reality, people *were* emotionally involved, but often less overtly than in an amphetamine-free situation, though even this is hard to maintain in the face of Barnes' photos inside The Scene in 1963, which show hug-up dancers, couples kissing, and romantic clinches in the alcoves. Despite Meaden's assertion, we went there to review the latest fashions and dance styles, promenade and pose, and hopefully to *meet girls.* I had a number of good dates at The Scene at various times; with East End Cockneys such as Elaine Bostock, who lived with her parents in a high rise in Poplar E14 that swayed in the wind; middle-class young ladies who'd adopted Mod styles and came into town, for example from Epping such as Bunty Ward; miscellaneous office workers in bedsits from Knightsbridge, or with Pat Beckett from Tufnell Park who I met at the club in November 1963 when I was nineteen.

Pat (left) with her friend Pauline at Butlin's

Pat was about eighteen when we met and had a round elfin face and black hair styled into a Mod bouffant. Her upper eyelids were completely shaded in mascara, which made her look a bit like a little owl. She was buxom, not very tall and her shapeliness was scarcely concealed by her loose dark roll-neck sweater and the light slacks she wore. Ike and Tina Turner's 'It's Gonna Work Out Fine' evokes that auspicious occasion. Because the music was loud, we went outside to Ham Yard and talked. I learned she lived with her mother in a flat in Nag's Head, Holloway. I got her phone number but did not call her, instead hoping to bump into her serendipitously when next I went to The Scene. But this was not to be. My mate, Alan Baldock, and I were planning to go there on Friday 22 November and I was cutting Alan's hair in my bedroom in preparation for the night out when my mum broke the news that President Kennedy had been shot. Jumping on my scooter we went anyway, but The Scene was closed, as was most of the West End.

The next week I called Pat up and thus began our yearlong relationship. I had purchased my Vespa GS second-hand in April 1963, some six months before I met Pat. However, in December 1964, a month after our relationship ended, it was stolen and trashed. The scooter was our main means of transport throughout our time together. Pat would ride the pillion wearing a nylon mac in dull blue with a large headscarf covering her hair. Nylon macs from C&A's were popular for a while, but whereas the majority of Mod girls were slim and the macs just hung limply, with Pat it emphasized her Shapeliness - wrap a buxom girl in plastic and that's bound to be the result. I became enamoured with Pat, she was pert, she was neat, she liked nightlife and danced well, and she was desirable. Furthermore, we looked good together and despite her cool demeanour, she seemed my Mod ideal.

Like some other Mod girls, Pat demonstrated a superior taste in music and I found out early on that her musical sophistication exceeded that of most of my mates. A penchant for good music carried a lot of kudos with me. It was Pat who introduced me to the *Ray Charles in Person* album. I'd bought Ray Charles's 'What'd I Say' as a 45 rpm single when it came out in 1960, hip, clean and cool, and way ahead of its time. He performs it live on the LP along with the heart wrenching 'Drown in my Own Tears' featuring Margie Hendricks.

Pat lived in a flat with her mum on St. George's Avenue, Tufnell Park, now gentrified and a desirable location for urban professionals, but in 1963 an anonymous and pretty much working-class street. I remember sitting in the kitchen of her mum's flat on the third floor of the four story Georgian row house, while Pat played the album to me. It opens with the honking sax of David 'Fathead' Newman as he launches into the opening bars of the classic 'The Night Time is The Right Time.' The experience of that live performance even though heard through the speaker of a little portable record player made the hairs on my neck stand on end.

On Boxing Day 1963 I picked Pat up on my scooter and brought her to my parent's house in Enfield, where we commandeered the sitting room and listened to my new records on my little red Dansette, including the Drifters' 'Sweets for my Sweet,' Gene Chandler's 'Duke of Earl,' Richie Barrett's 'Some Other Guy' and 'Sea Cruise' by Frankie Ford. This was the only time Pat visited the family home, and sensing some discomfort between Pat and my mum, after a while, I took her back to her place. I think Pat's unabashed manner and extensive mascara made her a 'painted woman' in mum's eyes. Incidentally, I never met her mum, even though I visited her flat on a regular basis, mostly during the evenings, parking the scooter in the front garden. While we sat in the kitchen chatting and playing records, her mum remained ensconced within the inner sanctum beyond the kitchen door.

Sometimes, when we had an evening out, instead of her usual slacks and sweater Pat would dress up in a form-fitting sleeveless dress in a large black and white dogtooth pattern worn over a black crew neck and with black stockings. This emphasized her curves and she looked tasty.

We dated in a rather irregular fashion going to the cinema or visiting coffee bars and when Pat was reluctant to venture out, we'd simply sit in her kitchen. Sometimes we would meet at The Scene not necessarily by pre-arrangement, but were grateful for each other's company nevertheless. Often we would just sit together, listen to the music, and watch the dancers, and merge mindlessly into the evening's unfolding. Although reserved with strangers, among her friends or when we were alone together, Pat had a confident style with cutesy ways, chatty with a wry sense of humour, giggling at her own jokes. During 'duh' moments, she would curl her upper lip and sneer in a Presleyesque manner. This expression suited her and she knew it, although it normally ended in a chuckle. I believe she practised in front of a mirror. I adopted a passive stance with Pat and as her admirer, I was prepared to accommodate her vanities and often let her take the lead. I was captivated by Pat and deferential to her because I admired her self-sufficiency and musical sophistication, and I was dependent on her ability to bestow favours, so despite the fact that my admiration of Pat wasn't fully reciprocated I found that pandering to her vanities secured her attention. However, the Mod milieu didn't encourage steady relationships and our courtship was complicated by the demands of London nightlife, which included Doobs (Drynamil).

Some of the pressure of formally dating was eased by extending the friendship to include Pat's friend, Pauline, and seeing that Pauline was easy to get along with, it worked quite well, and we would do the town together as a threesome in a sort of genderless friendship. This was made easier by the fact that we often took purple hearts and my libido was suppressed. This was facilitated by Pauline who seemed to have ready access to them.

It wasn't until later, maybe 1966, that birth control pills started to be widely used by teenagers. Before then there was more caution regarding sex, though there were always scrubbers ready to screw if that was uppermost on your mind. But Pat wasn't easy - and that was probably part of her allure. Although public shows of affection were taboo, when it came to the good night kissing at the end of the evening she was usually accommodating. We'd say our farewells in the hallway some distance within the front door of her building. Starting off tentatively not to alarm her, the darkness and the privacy of the hallway served to break down her reserve and we'd engage in some serious snogging. She may have allowed herself this secret indulgence against her better judgement.

Both Pat and I earned relatively meagre wages and lived with our respective parents, and I didn't have a car so consummating our relationship wasn't easy. Male-female relationships in the Mod era were rather precarious, and there's no denying that. Sometime around November 1964, I stopped seeing Pat and though she called me a couple of times I didn't renew our relationship. I don't really remember why. It wasn't because I'd found somebody else, although I occasionally had one nightstands with other girls during our time together. I probably found the constraints of our relationship rather wearisome, or maybe the words of The Miracles, 'Shop Around,' had taken root. This was neither the first nor the last time I pre-emptively withdrew from a relationship in which I was over-invested emotionally. Sometimes I wonder if Pat saw me on TV in 1965 when I regularly danced on *Ready, Steady, Go!*"

Rob dispels the myth that there was little interaction between the sexes during Mod's formative years. Indeed, as can also be recognised in many studies of the classic era of Mod, the female presence is one of often-equal importance. Apart from the fashion input, their knowledge of the sounds at hand often matched the most articulate of male Mods of the period.

MOD FASHION BY JACKIE BAIN

Jackie Bain - "As a teenager, I lived in Mill Hill, London, NW7, and visited various dance halls in the North West London area. In 1962, I had backcombed hair like Helen Shapiro and wore white, pointed stiletto heeled shoes and sling backs. I saved 10s a week for six months for a transistor radio. They were expensive then, relative to wages, so I ended up with a pocket-sized radio.

In the evening, I listened to pop songs on Radio Luxembourg (the only station that played pop songs then). I didn't have much money to go out, but I went to see Cliff Richard in the film 'The Young Ones.' I didn't know what kind of dances teenagers did so I went to dancing classes where they taught the waltz and boss nova. Occasionally I went uptown to C&A's to buy clothes. Shift dresses, frilly blouses, Rd. Kildare blouses and low-waist, twist dresses were fashionable that year.

Sam Cooke's 'Twisting the Night Away' reached number Six in the charts around that time and Tommy Roe sang 'Sheila.' I particularly liked Bryan Hyland 'Ginny Come Lately' and Carole King, 'It Might As Well Rain until September.' Other favourites were 'Bobby's Girl' by

In this photo taken late 1964 early 65, Jackie is wearing a pink, floral, flared trouser, cat suit

Susan Maughan, which reached No. 3, in the charts and 'Let's Dance' by Chris Montez, which reached No. 2.

I changed jobs in 1963 and started going around with lots of girls from work. I still had the Helen Shapiro hairstyle. I grew my hair a bit longer and had a backcombed, longer hair, Mod hairstyle that some Mods favoured back then. Some girls had a similar hairstyle to Cathy McGowan. Others favoured a short Mod hairstyle with a side parting. For a while, Mods used those gold and silver, small, puffer bottles to spray a single grey or gold, streak in their hair and girls' eyebrows were plucked to about 2.5 cms. Later Mods wore black chiffon scarfs tied round their hair. At work, I started hanging around with girls from Borehamwood and went to the Lynx Club (a Mod hangout) and Studio Cinema with them. The Beatles were my favourite group. I saw them at Finsbury Park Astoria with the girls from work and also at a 'Ready Steady Go!' rehearsal where I got George Harrison's autograph on my 'Twist and Shout' EP.

Around 1963 there were lots of Mods around Burnt Oak and Edgware. Mod girls wore hush puppies and classic jumper/cardigan twin-sets. Colours like grey or maroon with a few stripes were popular. Skirts were straight, calf length with a small slit at the back. Thicker stretchy, bri-nylon and thinner polyester ski-pants with a stirrup that went under the foot in plain dark colours like navy or maroon were popular. Lots of girls (including me) wore those round-toed, shiny, red, plastic-patent shoes with a strap round the ankle. Navy and brown nylon macs and black and white tweed coats with black leather collars and pocket flaps were everywhere. Later on, Mod girls and boys wore ice blue, shiny, straight leg trousers known as floaters. Other fashions like white pleated skirts and tartan kilts, ankle length skirts and knee high, socks with three buttons came into fashion briefly. Raoul shoes became more popular when a shop opened in Edgware. Suede or leather coats and brown suede jackets with leather collars were very popular. I had a brown, suede jacket and a petrol blue, suede coat (bought at Petticoat Lane shortly before Christmas 1964). Our clothes changed constantly so you had to make most of your clothes to be in fashion. Clothes were out of date once the majority of Mods started wearing them. Likewise, our dance steps were always changing.

I started going to the Ritz in Kingsbury on a Saturday night in 1963. The Ritz was very popular with North London Mods. We used to get off the 140 bus (red double decker London routemaster) at Roe Green, Kingsbury, and walk down to The Ritz most Saturday nights. It was usually packed on Saturdays when I went with my friend Brenda Jackson. We had our regulars who always asked us for a dance. The main band at The Ritz sang a mixture of slow sixties songs and other faster songs like 'Let's Go' and 'Roll over Beethoven.' After the Ritz closed around 1964 many Mods went to Guy Haywards' dance hall (above Burtons) in Harrow. Later, when I worked in an Oxford Street shop with my friend Sue, we used to go to Tiles once a week after work. We also went to The El Partido.

I only saw myself as a Mod around 63/64 when masses of Mods wore similar clothes. I thought Mod fashions were quite slavish. I believe later sixties styles were much nicer than earlier Mod styles which I wore when I went dancing at the Ritz Kingsbury. For me Mod was just a brief, couple of years when I was a teenager."

By 1965, Jackie no longer considered herself a Mod.

SALLY STEVENS and the influence of MOD!

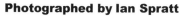

Photographed by Ian Spratt

Sally Stevens personified the generic impact that the growing Mod scene had upon a generation of youth coming of age as the sixties progressed.

Intergrating a mix of Beatnik and art school influences into her photogenic look of glamour and style, Sally welcomed the profound influence of Mod.

Above: Sally with David Phillips and Sue Howard, 1966

Sally Stevens - "To me, the essential difference between the Mods and the rockers was the music they favoured and the clothes they wore. When Paul McCartney introduced the British record buying public to Motown via his recommendation of The Miracles, the break was complete.

Unlike rockers, Mods were great dancers, especially the guys. Locally, at the Ricky Tick in Guildford, it was an honour to be picked to dance with the likes of Rob Kendall, or Brian Brough at the Friday night dances in Woking - sharp dressers and great dance stylists. Like the character played by John Travolta in Saturday Night Fever, these dancing guys ruled.

The music and the clothes took over for the Mods, while the rockers seemed content to remain in the leather and drape jacket world, attacking Mods for being different and progressive, though the Brighton riots were more likely fuelled by the gutter press throwing ten shillings around and asking idiots to start something, while the cameras rolled.

I loved the style changes that came with the advent of Mod. In 1964-65, women's hair went from stiff busbies full of hair spray to the geometric styles of Vidal. Hair rollers were replaced by blow dryers, long soft hair became de rigueur, every young woman wanted to become a fashion model and date a rock star, and even though that wasn't on the cards for many, it didn't prevent young British women from at least trying for the look pioneered by Patti Boyd, Jane Asher, Jean and Chrissie Shrimpton, Verushka, Twiggy, etc. The men abandoned Brylcreem - well, the Mod men did anyway! No more quiffs or D.A.'s. Saturday afternoons were usually spent at the local tailors, watching yet another suit being designed!

The English music scene was bereft of rocker bands. Elvis had gone to Hollywood, Eddie Cochran and Buddy Holly were dead; rockers simply lacked musical and fashion leadership and couldn't adjust to American blues and R&B and Motown, let alone the swiftly-changing fashions. They were left in the dust when it came to style whilst Mods' adjusted: they wished to remain 'Modern.'"

GILL EVANS – NOT LIKE EVERYONE ELSE

Gill Evans from Birmingham epitomised the early to mid-60's female Mod. Continuing her flair for self-created design, her homemade clothes augmented her natural good looks and model styled self-confidence.

Gill Evans – "1964 - I love this suit which I designed and made, I wore it many times as I always felt good in it. It is light navy pure wool with a cream and navy silk collar and buttons. The skirt is a slight A-line hipster with curved back pockets. I loved the scallops on the jacket and collar and took my inspiration design wise from the Chanel Gardenia. In the Original Modernist days it wasn't down to how many clothes you had it was all about being individual and unique and looking perfect always."

Gill Evans - "I designed and made this leather jacket (pictured above right), waistcoat and skirt in early 1963, it is dark brown and I still have it. It was influenced by my interest in French fashion, the jacket has a high round neck and flap pockets with buttons. I am wearing a black polo neck jumper. I love this look and still often wear a black leather knee length skirt and a black polo neck jumper. Simplicity is my favourite look; this photo was taken at the Thames Embankment."

Gill Evans - "My Mum hated my Mod look and style of continental influenced clothes, she would say 'when are you going to get your hair permed and change your clothes.'

I never actually followed any set outline on what anyone else was wearing around me at the time. I had my own individual take, having a vision in my head of how I wanted to look. I wanted to style myself and to be quite unique and was able to do this, being a designer, so was never ruled by what was available in the shops or dictated to by fashion. When I went out, I wanted to be wearing something I had designed myself and was totally exclusive to me.

I remember having this photo taken (right) but I never thought that fifty years on anyone else would want to look at our photo's, at the time we were just enjoying ourselves wearing the clothes we loved and going out to clubs and dance halls in Birmingham. I am wearing a black crepe blouse with a black and white tweed hipster skirt, a grey leather round neck jacket and low heel lace up shoes. The top photo is of me wearing my French-influenced leather jacket and skirt"

The style of the Mod girl would influence and inform fashion consistently as the 60's progressed. Its imagery appeared throughout the glossy pages of Rave, Mods Monthly and the numerous pop magazines that continuously absorbed, referenced and diluted the Mod look, a style that pop stars and celebrities also copied. The Mod girl next door and her keen sense of personal style stamped an identity on the period. The earlier Mod girls, in particular, helped to pioneer and create a very modern and liberated look that would resonate throughout the decade.

Mod's origins and influence in the capital and its surrounding new towns was strongly identifiable - as were the scenes in Sheffield Birmingham and other towns, cities and suburbs - but Mod awareness was about to explode nationwide as the 1964 beach fights propelled the earlier co-existing Mods and Rockers into public recognition. The early days of the Modernist era was fast approaching its closing chapter, it would soon lose its

elitism as the original focus suffered and many stylists scorned the tribal overkill of what was once their own self-contained club of limited membership. However, despite this dilution, the heyday of the original Mod had not yet passed completely.

CHAPTER 3

LET THE GOOD TIMES ROLL

"Y'know, with me, I literally lived for the Mod way of life. It was the biggest thing that ever happened to me. I was nobody until I became a Mod." - **Irish Jack Lyons**

David Middleton and friend, Ace Face Mike Tenner dances with the girls including Sandy Serjeant, (2nd from left) at the Scene Club and Gill Evans – female Face of 60's Mod

It was a true mark of youths' identity, of working class respect and social accomplishment – to be a Mod! Whilst most of early sixties' youth were being swept along with MerseyBeat and the Beatles - as pop culture took a firm grip of the prime interests of the teenager, for some, being a Mod was the epitome of cool: even if the vast proportion of the outside world was not yet aware of their existence.

It would be a Friday evening TV show that would, to some degree, help to push the fashion and style of these weekend ravers into the public's consciousness. Almost eight months before the headlines of 'Mods v Rockers' beach skirmishes, the opening credit music of 'Wipe Out' by The Surfari's proclaimed it was time to say goodbye to the grind and trepidation of the working week and celebrate the weekend's offering of freedom and excitement - of being young and hip!

Above: Stevie Wonder. Left: Rob Nicholls in the light-coloured sweater at the front-centre of the audience watching The Supremes on their 1965 'Ready Steady Go!' special.

Mods had their own TV program, *Ready, Steady Go!* (RSG) which was broadcast live from Studio 9 in Kingsway (later Wembley Studios) and went out nationally on ITV on Friday's between 6:00 and 7:00 p.m. Proclaiming 'The Weekend Starts Here', RSG ran from August 1963 until December 1966, concurrent with the rise and decline of the London Mod movement, which it emulated, yet, initially at least, did not promote or recognise. However once Mod arrived in the studios in 1964, Mods outside of London could stay abreast of music, dances and fashions. Groups performed in front of a live audience of dancers. The roster was impressive and included the popular British groups of the time and visiting American R&B artists. With their love of American Soul music, some Mods, including Rob Nicholls, became members of Dave Godin's Tamla Motown Appreciation Society (TMAS), which was influential in bringing the Tamla Motown Review tour to Britain in 1965. In time, Mods had their own radio station too. The pirate station Radio Caroline started broadcasts in Easter 1964. The station was based in an old Irish ferry moored outside British territorial waters and became essential listening for the R&B/Soul underground.

'Ready Steady Go!' symbolises the mid-sixties heyday for many. With its varied (but significantly not all Mod-related) acts and informal atmosphere, it quickly became the cultural signpost for youth. Once established, the show was regularly graced with the company of authentic Mods and their musical heroes and for a while, the weekend really did start with 'Ready, Steady Go!'

Another authentic early Mod original, and one that will be very familiar with anyone who has viewed Redifusion's 'Ready Steady Go!' over the years, was Mike 'Mickey' Tenner. Recognised for his dance routines at the Scene Club - and consequently on the TV show, Mickey had been a regular Scene Club goer from as far back as 1961 when the club was still known as Cy Laurie's Jazz club, catching such seminal acts as Cyril Davis there and befriending Mod entrepreneur and High Numbers manager, Pete Meaden, who Mike refers to as the 'Modfather'.

Mike was also present and assisted with the 1964 recording of the legendary first Who release (then still under the guise of the High Numbers) 'I'm the Face'. He also confirms that Meaden was present at the famous Mods v Rockers clashes that very same year. Mike's fellow 'Ready Steady Go!' dancers were Sandy Sarjeant and Ted Murphy, and he can be spotted on the footage of the programme, on occasion providing the backdrop for famed groups such as the Beatles. Mike and Ted wore silk cycling shirts during this period with Harrington-style bomber jackets.

Left: The legendary Mickey Tenner between Paul McCartney and John Lennon

Despite the presence of genuine Mods in the studio - displaying many of the latest fashions and dances - some debated the actual authenticity of the show. In balance, Mod fashions were changing so rapidly it would have been almost impossible for any mainstream produced TV programme to have remained consistently in touch with every aspect of Mod's evolution.

RSG dancer Sandy Sarjeant

Adrian Stern - "What always greatly amused me about 'Ready, Steady Go!', was how out of touch it was with what was actually happening, at least where we were in Soho and Belsize Park. I always assumed that the researchers hung out in South Kensington and missed the trends, or they were paid by the chain stores to promote off-the-rack clothing and music for the masses."

However, Ready Steady Go! did successfully reach out into the homes of the nation's youth, providing numerous important influences and fashion hints to aspiring out-of London Mods.

Away from the capital, Jeremy Norman's rural location did not stop him checking out the touring Mod acts, including The Who.

Jeremy Norman - "I saw The Who at The Links in Cromer; I have no idea of the date. The only thing I remember is that I thought 'what a waste' when they smashed their instruments.

The band I followed the most was Geno Washington and the Ram Jam Band. Geno to some extent we took to as almost a 'local'. He had been in the USAF at Bentwater's base in Suffolk. Therefore, he did a lot of gigs in East Anglia. I can remember seeing him at the Wellington Club East Dereham, The Links at Cromer and The Orford Cellar in Norwich. The Orford was a real 'dive', it used to get so packed that you could not lift your glass to drink; when people started to jump to the music you had to join in whether you wanted to or not. No way would it be allowed now. If ever there had been a fire none of us would have got out. Another venue in Norwich was The Gala Ballroom, but by the time I was mobile enough to get to Norwich regularly, it had become a 'Rocker Joint'...so a no go for me."

Mods found their lyrical and cultural spokesmen with The Who, along with a taste for the rapidly evolving blue-eyed Soul of bands such as Zoot Money's Big Roll Band, Georgie Fame and the Blue Flames, Cliff Bennett and the Rebel Rousers and veteran singer Chris Farlowe. They came to empathise and relate to The Who and their live performances. Yet it was the heartfelt vocals and rhythm and blues of Soul that remained closest to the Mod's musical heart

Soul in 1963 was still - relatively speaking - within its formative stages. Artists such as James Brown, The Impressions and Sam Cooke were creatively pushing the style ever forward, musically and politically. Significantly, the Mods promoted Soul's development and appreciation in the UK just as profoundly as their own non-racial stance - unlike their teddy boy predecessors' who often found no irony in being overtly racist alongside celebrating black American-derived music. As the Beatles celebrated the influence of the Tamla acts on their second long player 'With the Beatles', the DJ's avidly embraced a music that in the UK - so far - belonged, almost exclusively within the Mod's protective domain, yet was soon to be celebrated with hit records, high profile tours and unfathomed success. The golden age of Soul was on the horizon.

THE SOUL OF MOD BY ROB NICHOLLS

"The word *Soul* to describe Black musical expression was used as early as 1852 by Charles Day in Barbados to describe dance rather than music: 'Black nymphs sleek as moles ... [their] dark feet writhed like eels'.... This was dancing with the *soul* in it."

Rob Nicholls - "The depiction of Mods as self-absorbed and narcissistic is patently false. Despite arguments to the contrary Mods were not all show and no substance. Our birthright was a heightened sense of fashion, emotional sensitivity, and a discerning musical ear—we knew what we liked when we heard it. In 1956, when I was twelve, nobody had to sell me on Leadbelly's good points. When I first heard 'Ol' Riley' it spoke directly to my soul and gave me goose bumps. It was the same when I first saw Little Richard's 'Long Tall Sally' in the film *Don't Knock the Rock*. My road to rhythm and blues was predestined and in my early teens I was listening to whatever Blues I was able to get hold of, such as 'Drop Down Mama' by Sleepy John Estes with Hammie Nixon on harmonica, which I bought on a 78 rpm when I was fifteen. In my later teens, like other Mods, my appreciation of Black American music extended to up-tempo R&B. We were less interested in pop or British beat music but had an insatiable appetite for hot Black American music; the music that became the heartbeat of the early Mod movement.

The role of 'Skiffle' in the birth of British beat music cannot be underestimated. By 1957 it had seemed as if every street corner from London to Liverpool, had their own Skiffle group with primitive homemade instruments, such as a tea-chest bass and washboard, and were singing about breaking rocks on a chain gang or labouring 'in dem old cotton fields back home!' British beat bands that had Skiffle origins included, the Searchers, Freddie and the Dreamers, David Bowie, Charlie Watts and Bill Wyman of the Rolling Stones, Jimmy Page and Jeff Beck of the Yardbirds, Ray and Dave Davies of the Kinks, Gerry and the Pacemakers, even Van Morrison and Them from Belfast. George Harrison is quoted as saying, 'No skiffle, no Beatles' referring to the Quarrymen Skiffle Group. The Swinging Blue Jeans started out as a Skiffle group called the 'Bluegenes' and British R&B vocalist Chris Farlowe even won the All-England Skiffle Contest! Cyril Davies, the 'father of the British Blues Harmonica,' first discovered the Blues through his enthusiasm for Skiffle, as did many of us early Mods.

The influence of the working class on the music of a people is unmistakable. Most of the significant popular musical movements of recent times originated with the lower classes: Jazz, Flamenco, Country and Western, Blues, and Gospel. Rock 'n' Roll was advanced by 'poor whites' and their black counterparts. R&B flourished in juke joints and honkytonks. Ska, which also found favour with Mods, was born in the Shebeens of Jamaica's Trenchtown.

As stated, Mod lives were centred on two basic essentials: clothes and music. American R&B was largely ignored by the UK's mainland radio stations, yet that was the music we Mods craved. The only station to pay much attention to it was Radio Luxembourg, which played some decent tracks during the evenings, although the 208 MHz reception was erratic at best. Usually, we learned of great records by word of mouth. Pirate Radio wouldn't emerge until 1964, so the sharing of records among friends played an important role in our musical education. Guy Stevens, the DJ at The Scene Club, paved the way. He featured American imports on Monday evenings and is renowned for playing the best, tightest, most soulful, and most danceable music available; a mother lode of music as yet unappreciated outside of the communities that produced it. Many British musicians who covered or copied Black American songs got their material from him. In July, 1964 Fontana released, 'I'm the Face' by the High Numbers who Pete Meaden was promoting as the first authentic Mod band (The Who). Meaden simply put new words to Slim Harpo's 'Got Love If You Want It.'

Originally described as 'race music,' those R&B records of the 50-60's which became popular with Mods in America were purchased almost exclusively by Blacks within what is known as the 'chitlin' circuit' (chitlins i.e. tripe). The Billboard's R&B charts of the early 1960's contained a number of recognizable Mod tracks, which demonstrates the extent that British Mod's tastes paralleled those of Black Americans. Billboard's list of 'R&B singles chart number one hits of 1963' shows that the majority of the twenty singles are Mod favourites; including artists like The Miracles, Bobby Bland, Jackie Wilson, Sam Cooke, Garnet Mimms, and Little Johnny Taylor. Significant Mod hits are included such as 'Two Lovers' by Mary Wells, 'He's So Fine' The Chiffons, 'Workout' Jackie Wilson, 'Hello Stranger' Barbara Lewis, and 'It's All Right' by the Impressions.

SHAKE A TAIL FEATHER – THE MOD GIRLS

Mod was not exclusively about male style - as has often been suggested. With considered dedication, the Mod girl consistently strove to belong and identify with Mod. Early Mod girls wore straight knee-length skirts, high-heeled winkle pickers and backcombed beehive hairstyles. By 1963 nylon macs and three quarter length suede coats were also popular. In direct response and admiration to their male Mod counterparts, the girls styled their hair in a similar style to the boys but accompanied by heavy mascara, which was influenced by the late-50's Bohemian girls of the Soho Jazz scene. In essence, the Mod girl was often deliberately boyish yet attractive - retaining her femininity. Female Mod fashions soon developed and adopted a more swinging 60's influence of extra make-up, the classic 5-point bob by Vidal Sassoon and Mary Quant hairstyles, but the Mod girl's enthusiasm and sense of style remained consistent throughout the decade and beyond.

Rob Nicholls - "Mod girls wore boxy-shaped jackets and straight skirts that reached just below the knee or mid-calf. For a while, lightweight plastic macs were popular, normally in a dull blue. Other Mod girls wore slim three-quarter length suede coats usually worn with slacks (parallels). Old style 'granny' shoes or hush puppies were appropriate footwear. Early hairstyles of Mod girls evolved from the beehive and flick-ups of the previous era and transmuted into a small backcombed bouffant but with shorter fringed edges and a parting in the middle or just to the side. Later Mod girls increasingly styled their hair like the boys. Hardly any jewellery was worn, but heavy mascara adorned the eyes."

Top: left to right, John Water's girlfriend and future wife Pauline (also pictured right), unknown Lincoln Mod girl and Gill Evans

Mods appreciated the rhythm *and* the blues in all their poignancy and this is where the Soul of Mod is aroused. Muddy Water's 'I Just Want to Make Love to You,' for example, is embroidered by Little Walter's gushing harmonica. The haunting harp melody reverberated in our heads at 6:00 a.m. when we emerged from the clubs and wandered, pale and squinting, into the Soho dawn. The harmonica refrain followed us along the gray city streets echoing from the buildings as daylight filtered into our consciousness. The pathos emanating from the bleak brass riffs in 'If You Don't Come Back' by the Drifters is similarly compelling. The Mod milieu did not encourage 'going steady,' but the Soul songs of the era, and there were many of them, were witheringly bittersweet. Listen,

for example, to 'Go Now,' by Bessie Banks, 'That's How Heartaches are Made' by Baby Washington, 'Oh No, Not My Baby' by Maxine Brown, and 'Ain't it Funny How Time Slips Away' by Joe Hinton. These plaintive airs about lost loves and broken promises, gives the lie to the idea that romance wasn't in the air. No, not self-absorbed, instead Mod life was diffused with an emotional intensity—Soul. The ambience of Mod nightclubs is conveyed by Nick Coventon in his novel, *Move On Up.* The Mod, Johnny, is at The Scene Club:

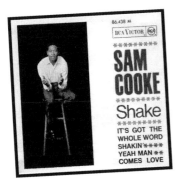

"The DJ put on 'What's easy for two is so hard for one' by Mary Wells, and a giant unseen hand dragged Johnny away from his companions and onto the dance floor. Some records just had to be danced to. It couldn't be explained…. But when the opening bars of particular 45's filled the room, it was like a religious experience. A calling. No it wasn't a hand that dragged him and made him dance. It was the angel of Soul, gently lifting him onto the dance floor. Johnny didn't believe in God but when for instance 'Hello Stranger' by Barbara Lewis was put on he knew there was a heaven."

That was our endowment; it wasn't just the Mod flair, the clothes or the dancing, or even our discerning musical taste, it was Mod Soul!"

MODS MEET THE TAMLA MOTOWN STARS

There can have been fewer memorable occasions for the members of The Tamla Motown Appreciation Society (TMAS) than this monumental and very special event when the roster of Tamla Motown label stars met and performed for their fans. In these rare and exclusive photos the joy and sense of love for the artists can clearly be recognized and almost tasted.

A host of Motown Stars including Smokey Robinson, Marvin Gaye, Martha and the Vandellas, the Supremes, and the Miracles mingled with Mods, John and Barbara McNally, Mick Paige, and others on this historic occasion. Barbara McNally (nee Wetherell) is seen with Smokey Robinson in the photo on the left.

A number of Mods within reach of London became members of The Tamla Motown Appreciation Society (TMAS), which Dave Godin set up in 1963. By 1965 TMAS could boast three hundred members, including Mods, John McNally, Barbara Wetherell, Mick Paige, Don Hughes and Rob Nicholls. Described as an "Apostle of Soul" and now a legend in Mod circles, David Godin (born London 1936; died. Rotherham, Yorkshire, 2004), was soft spoken and a rather unlikely looking R&B fan. Although not a Mod, he was neat and slim with a beard and spectacles and a rather mournful looking face. The son of a milkman, Godin had attended Dartford Grammar School along with Mick Jagger and he had introduced Jagger to black music, playing a minor role in the early jam sessions from which the Rolling Stones emerged. Godin later regretted this because he felt the Rolling Stones exploited black music.

Godin set up Soul City records in Deptford in late 1966 and then became partners with John Abbey and moved Soul City to Covent Garden, WC2. He began writing for *Blues & Soul* magazine and it was in a June 1970 column that Godin coined the term "Northern Soul" for the new Soul scene emerging in clubs in Blackpool, Stoke and Manchester.

Members of the society received regular reports of TMAS activities and updates on the Motor City through the mail. Sometimes members would attend social events at Dave Godin's house in Bexleyheath, to meet, for example, Catherine Anderson and Gladys Horton of the Marvelettes, Claudette Robinson of the Miracles, wife to Smokey, and others. More informally some members enjoyed Sunday afternoons in Dave's black-walled bedroom listening to some rare records from Dave's collection.

Dave Godin interacted with the Motown headquarters in Detroit, specifically with Margaret Phelps who was President of the Hitsville International Fan Club. Impressed by Dave Godin's enthusiasm, Motown President, Berry Gordy Jr. invited him to the USA in 1964 to meet the performers. This was reported with photographs in the TMAS newsletter. During his visit a 45 rpm record was made for TMAS. On this "Hitsville U.S.A. - Greetings To Tamla Motown Appreciation Society" disc, Motown music provides a background to greetings from Smokey Robinson, Stevie Wonder, Marvin Gaye, Marvelettes, Temptations, Martha and the Vandellas, Contours, Eddie Holland, Kim Weston, Diana Ross and the Supremes; as well as Berry Gordy himself.

Dave Godin with Martha Reeves

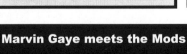

Marvin Gaye meets the Mods   **Harvey Fuqua (above)**
Martha Reeves (right)

A NIGHT OF HITSVILLE USA – UK 65

The highlight of Dave Godin's tenure as president of TMAS was the 1965 UK tour of the Tamla Motown Review. Featuring headline acts, Mods were able to meet Motown stars, acquire autographs, and see performances. A concert was held at the Finsbury Park Astoria that featured the Miracles, Temptations, Supremes, Martha and the Vandellas, and (Little) Stevie Wonder, accompanied by the Earl Van Dyke Sextet.

During that period The Temptations were promoting "Girl, Why You Wanna Make Me Blue?" with Eddie Kendricks singing lead. With her kind heart Martha Reeves oozed Soul and made a big impression on the Mods. She and the Vandellas performed "Heat Wave" and were publicizing "Nowhere to Run." Diana Ross was stunning looking but friendly and described as 'not at all aloof'. The Supremes were promoting "Stop in the Name of Love" with its legendary dance routine. Stevie Wonder was just fourteen and was still known as Little Stevie Wonder, his latest release was "Kiss Me Baby." John McNally and Barbara Wetherell had the foresight to take a camera to some of the TMAS gatherings as can be seen in the accompanying photos.

TAMLA STARS SIGN UP

The story of how Martha & the Vandellas made their first
abounds; like the long mysterious disappearance of Slim
with The Drifters. The lead singer of the group, Marth
Corporation. She landed this job after she spent muc
are in Detroit, doing odd jobs voluntarily and with the eag

**Rob Nicholls' stars of Tamla
Motown signed collection**

Don Hughes – "I'd never met, or indeed spoken to,
any member of TMAS before. I had high expectations.
Stylish Mods, older Mods perhaps? I wore my
favourite outfit, a pair of Levis, Hush Puppies and a
white roll neck sweater. Not exactly ahead of the
curve but tonight with Marvin Gaye on stage I felt it
didn't matter too much.

Dave Godin walked on stage. He introduced
himself. I took a long look at him and discovered he
was no Mod. Looking over twenty five, Dave was
bearded and wore black horn-rimmed glasses and a
sports jacket.

Marvin Gaye finally appeared in the flesh! Blue
suit, white shirt and a slim black bow tie. A living
dream had strolled casually on stage. Marvin burst
into song and we were treat to powerful yet different
renditions of his recent singles; 'Can I Get a Witness',
'Wonderful One' and 'Try it Baby' and his best yet, an
uptempo gospel-inspired number called 'Baby Don't
You Do It.'

John McNally with Martha Reeves and Claudette Robinson

In 1967, Barbara married John and became Barbara McNally, and Dave Godin and Mick Paige attended their wedding in Loughton ("Still together 47 years in June [2014]," says Barbara, "must be our good taste in music and partners"). When recalling the TMAS years, John and Barbara have a few tales to tell, "Do you remember the get together at - I think Kennington at the house of the guy who ran the Irma Thomas fan club," asks Barbara, "John was designated to pick up Irma Thomas and Doris Troy (d. 2004) from their hotel in his beat up old Ford Consul (which he paid £25 for). He picked up Irma ok, but Doris Troy refused to travel with her ('I'm not getting in that car with that bitch'). Irma was not impressed with the car; I think she expected a limo. However, it was a memorable night but then there were so many."

Tamla Motown – now such a household name – was historically a Mod's choice for Soul, along with the numerous other popular Soul labels - many only available exclusively as US import singles. Showcased by Mod club DJ's such as Guy Stevens at the Scene Club, these new black American sounds shaped the tastes of Mods as did the Jamaican version of R&B newly christened Ska – extensively released on the Blue Beat label and sparking off a new musical term ('Blue Beat) in homage to the label itself.

The Mods' obsession with Black American R&B was now the accepted badge of Mod taste. Therefore, of course - in the true Modernist ever-changing chameleon-like sense of cool – an additional musical genre was required to complement their existing soundtrack.

RUDIE'S CAN'T FAIL – THE OTHER COLOUR OF MODS

Rob Nicholls - "To stay ahead of the mainstream, Mods moved on to Jamaican Ska and began to assimilate West Indian 'rude boy' fashions. Some wore the trilbies with tiny brims favoured by West Indians. Mods referred to Ska as Blue-beat, because of the name of the record label that much of it was on. The Blue Beat label was owned by Melodisc records and started up around 1962. Many of the biggest artists recorded for them including Prince Buster, Derrick Morgan and The Folks Brothers. An article titled 'It's the Blue-beat Craze,' appeared in *The Record Mirror* on February 15, 1964. It defined Blue-beat as 'a strictly Jamaican sound with a pulsating on-beat played on stop chords throbbing mercilessly through the disc. Most of the songs are down-to-earth items that don't usually deal with love, and the tunes are strictly secondary to the beat.' The article further explained, 'The craze has been 'in' with the Mods since last summer [i.e. 1963] because of the marvellous dance beat.' We liked our Blue-beat raw and hard-edged. Prince Buster's 'Madness' was a big seller, as was his 'Fire in the Wire.' The Skatalites' instrumentals featuring Don Drummond on trombone were Mod hits and their 'Guns of Navarone' was heard all over town. Some early Maytal's 45s such as 'Matthew, Mark, Luke, and John' were popular, as was The Flames 'Broadway Jungle' (1964) usually referred to as 'Dog War.' Blue-beat got a boost in late 1963 when 'My Boy Lollipop' was a hit for Millie (Smalls) on Fontana, and she appeared on Ready Steady Go! singing this song. Later in 1964, Prince Buster also appeared on RSG. I don't remember Guy Stevens playing much Blue-beat at The Scene Club, but he probably played 'Oh Carolina' by the Folks Brothers, which was a favourite and epitomizes those Mod days for me. Instead, we danced to Blue-beat at other clubs including La Discotheque on Wardour Street or at 'blues parties' hosted by West Indians.

There were Blue-beat nights at both the Marquee and Flamingo where the Duke Vin Sound System played records. In 1964, nineteen year London Mod, Paul Walsh, admitted 'We all took purple hearts, marijuana and hemp.... We meet at someone's house, draw the curtains and shut the doors and windows, and play Blue Beat records and smoke drugged cigarettes.... Girls are there too'. During all-nighter Blue-beat sessions, the relentless vamping on the offbeat was hypnotic and really drew you in. It was a high energy music that put you in a trance—good Doob music and a vigorous work out!"

In 1959 a Jewish couple called Rita and Benny King opened the R & B Record Shop at 282 Stamford Hill and then a few years later moved up to number 260 on the same road. By 1963, they were releasing records on their own label, first the parent label R & B and then others such as Giant, King, Ska Beat, Hillcrest, Caltone, Jolly and Port-O-Jam. They were the first to release a record by the Blue Flames with Georgie Fame. Without question, owners, Rita and Benny were among the very first to release Jamaican music in Britain. They stocked hundreds of Ska, Rocksteady and Blue Beat records - artists such as Laurel Aitken, Dandy Livingstone, Junior Smith, Jackie Opel, The Wrigglers and numerous others - musical genres extremely difficult to track down, resulting in young black people and fledgling Modernists keenly paying the shop a visit. Rita and Benny's shop lasted for 25 years, finally closing in 1984.

Ian Kleinberg remembers the first record he bought there for his Mum's birthday - "Rita's always had it. Vinyl's in those days were like gold dust. If you wanted something, you'd heard on Luxembourg or whatever programme you were listening to, you'd go to Rita and say have you got this, she'd trundle off upstairs and come back with a pile of 'em."

Ska originating from Jamaica during the early sixties combined the style and influences of Calypso, Jazz, Caribbean mento and most importantly American rhythm and blues. The very first Ska recordings were made at Kingston, Jamaica's Studio One recording facilities and later recordings inherited the strident optimism of the country's 1962 independence from the UK. It was inevitable that the music would soon gain the attention of the Mods and the sounds of Prince Buster (and his world-famous and hugely respected Blue Beat label recordings), The Skatalites, Derrick Morgan, Jimmy Cliff and a huge influx of Ska artists would be given their-very own spot on the Mod clubs' dance floors. Again the Stamford Hill area of London would prove to be pivotal and the small but indispensable R & B Records Shop was a true pioneer in exposing Mods and young people to the new sound of Jamaican Ska. Yet, how were the black people who imported and championed these pioneering sounds, themselves, received?

John Walters - "As the fifties moved into the sixties many teenagers were frequenting dance halls around the capital. Live bands and/or records supplied the music for jiving or showing their prowess at the 'twist' rage that was sweeping the world. But black teenagers were not welcome in the dancehalls. How ironic that whilst thousands of white teenagers were dancing to a 'black' recording the UK's black teenagers were 'shown the door'."

Despite this retrogressive intolerance, undeterred, the rising population of black citizens in the UK of the late 50's and early 60's - West Indians in particular, primarily in the areas of Brixton and Lambeth - chose to create their own means of musical entertainment via their afore-mentioned 'blues parties'. The downside to this was that, unlike the rock 'n' roll gatherings of their white counterparts, these social occasions of joyous dancing to the Jamaican rhythm and blues now being termed Ska and Blue Beat were shared with their family including their parents. Much like teenagers the world over, young coloureds spread their wings elsewhere.

Rob Nicholls - "Regarding the question 'Were there any black Mods?' Well, Peter Kester was one in 1964-65. He was a member of a well-established black family in the Oval in Lambeth and had a Lambretta and wore a parka. Sandy Sarjeant was half-caste. But, in all truth, in London in the early sixties, there were not many black teenagers because the initial migration from the West Indies occurred in the 1950's, and the immigrants did not bring tots with them, such that, they would have been teenagers by 1963-64.

Nevertheless, the young blacks we did meet were mostly smartly dressed with interests in nightlife and dancing similar to our own. For North London Mods, interaction was most noticeable at the club above the Manor House pub in Harringay where a handful of young black men would dance with their white girlfriends. While some white blokes may have felt resentment they didn't voice it and there was no overt friction; rather there was a grudging admiration at the way the West Indians handled their girls during their stylish 'hug-up' dances. Some Mods took this admiration to extremes. In 1964, nineteen year-old London Mod, David Holburne stated, 'At the moment we're hero worshipping the Spades (blacks) …. The more sophisticated teenagers can go to Spade clubs in the West End… We're going back to dancing close - because the Spades do it.' Although some Mods' parents, even older brothers and sisters, might have been bigoted; as a group I didn't find London Mods to be particularly prejudiced and racial issues were rarely discussed. Ian Hebditch states, 'Mods were open-minded. Not narrow. There was a great degree of respect between the Mods and the West Indian community.' I personally found that. Within the Mod movement I don't recollect any element of racism at all, and by racism I mean anti-black feeling.'"

John Leo Waters - "The one place that did cater for this burgeoning black population was the Flamingo in Wardour St. The Flamingo had started out as an upmarket Jazz niterie and had gradually changed its clientele becoming a magnet for black GI's and West Indians alike. The club eventually became 'off limits' to US servicemen but by the early sixties the club was known as a 'black club'. The club's unique mix of R&B, Soul, Ska and Jazz coupled with the best in visiting live acts from the USA and West Indies was a magnet for black clubgoers. There were other clubs in the West End of course but the Flamingo was the place for black teenagers to be seen. The young black clubgoers always 'dressed up'. Mohair suits were very much the order of the day. They often sported a 'Blue beat hat' (trilby with a narrow brim) and the hat became almost synonymous with the club. The Mod movement had really moved into full gear by 1963 and the commercial world had moved in. [When] 'Ready Steady Go' came onto our TV sets and the pirate radio stations were in full swing, the target of all the commercial enterprises was the young 'white' teenage population.

The black teenagers were left ostracised. There were very few shops stocking Ska music outside the areas they lived in. Integration was not an option and it was very much a case of 'them and us'. But by 1966 the climate had changed somewhat. The Flamingo had become more of a melting pot. Count Suckle had opened The Roaring Twenties, which catered specifically for black teenagers. The Gunnell's opened The Ram Jam in Brixton, which pulled in a lot of black customers due its location. Across London other clubs such The Club Four Aces and The New All Star were aimed at the black population. Integrated groups had sprung up. Georgie Fame had fronted an integrated group in The Blue Flames for some time and groups such as The Ram Jam Band and The Nightimers were white bands fronted by black singers from the US. Jimmy James and the Vagabonds, The Ramony Sound (later the Foundations) and The Equals were all multi-racial in membership. Things were definitely looking up.

But to the question 'were there any black Mods'. The answer has to be yes there were but only as far as they were Mods in style and musical tastes. They were never part of the mainstream Mod movement simply because the door had not yet opened to racial integration.

I only knew of one black family in the area I grew up in and the gang I ran with after school was again white only. We knew little about London's black population and many of the members of our group were extremely racist! I can remember black people that occasionally passed through being subjected to abuse and derision. I always felt that it was somewhat ironic that many of these sons of immigrants were subjecting black people to abuse when their own parents had themselves often been discriminated against. In the same vein it was quite acceptable to champion the music of black America and Jamaica but completely unacceptable to mix with black people! I feel it was much the same with other youth gangs. I can only remember two other black youths associated with gangs, one from Highbury and one from the Elephant and Castle. The only reason they were 'accepted' is that they had a reputation as 'hard guys'. As I grew a little older (and wiser) I began to question the racist opinions of many of my mates. I went to a few blues parties (much to the disgust of some!) and found that I was made welcome. The Flamingo was the club for live music and although I felt a little bit of an atmosphere at times this was probably due to our manner as much as anything else and indeed, I got to know one or two black guys who frequented the club. Thankfully, times and attitudes have changed and these days we can accept people for who they are rather than what they are."

Unquestionably, the most profound social crime was the prevalence of racially motivated prejudice directed towards the blacks of this country and even throughout elements of the media. Perhaps, the greatest irony though, was - as noted by John Leo Waters and others of the time - the unfathomable contradiction that numbers of young whites could so easily embrace and enjoy the music created by black Americans, yet be so equally resolute in their intolerance to those that perform that very music and their race. In context, however, as briefly mentioned earlier, one of the greatest attributes to the 60's Mod legacy is the progressive re-evaluation generally implemented by Mods towards black people. This was a scene that - despite its relative transgressions, that, as John considers, were indicative of the social climate - openly welcomed, not only the Blues and Soul performed by blacks, but also their presence and equality within their midst. It could be said that this was a blueprint for a multi-racial scene. One that celebrated the premise that all Mods are equal with regards to colour: the only prejudice likely to be administered would be with regards to the projection of taste in clothes, music and personal style.

Mod was the province of the young, but for young blacks the freedom for self-expression required a stronger desire to break out of not only wider society's prejudices but also the strong family control exerted by the parents of young Afro Caribbeans. Young white Mods however revelled in the casting of the constraints inflicted on them and were determined to seize the moment. One of the youngest of the fledgling Mods was Jeff Dexter of Newington Butts. Jeff recognised the appeal of R&B as early as 1958 and by 1961 was perfecting The Twist at the Lyceum. His commitment, knowledge and unrelenting passion for the scene and its soundtrack would lead him to be resident DJ at London's Tiles Club and recognised as one of the key authorities on Mod.

The Twist craze swept through the UK ballrooms in early 1962, the first of many new dance fads, a number of which were adopted by Mods. In 1963 The Beatles released their E.P. 'Twist and Shout,' its title track, being a rousing rendition of The Isley Brothers original. Although The Beatles left many early Mods unimpressed, their cover versions of R&B originals helped to inform and encourage considerable portions of affected youth - in turn leading to their obsessive searches for the originals in place of the accessible substitute versions.

John Hellier - "Around 1963. I was 14 and still at school. Most schoolmates of mine, both male and female, were starting to dig both the Beatles and Stones. Their first albums were full of great songs but they were, in the main, covers of obscure American records. I'd go out of my way to seek out the originals and when I did, I was amazed at the quality of the unknown versions. While everybody in the school seemed to be digging the Fab Fours versions of 'Twist and Shout' and 'Money' I'd be playing the Isley Brothers and Barrett Strong! My first musical heroes were Bo Diddley and Chuck Berry. By the time I'd picked up on them they already had very strong back catalogues.

In '63 I never consciously said to myself 'I wanna be a Mod'. It was something that I just drifted into without much thought. We had a few really fab clothes shops in Romford, my local town, such as Brent and Collins (who were later bought out by Take Six) and they would stock pretty much everything that Carnaby Street catered for anyway. The mainstream Mods and Rockers rivalry thing started with the tabloids and the fighting on the beaches stories of '64. Myself and my local mates were very proud to be called Mods but we would disassociate ourselves with the street level guys on scooters that were just out for a punch up. We saw ourselves as a bit above that - pure snobbery.

In '63/'64 I was wearing white Levis, Desert Boots (only tan ones), hooped crew necks, tailor made tonic mohair trousers from Leslie Andrews in Romford, you'd go in there every week and pay half a crown (2s. 6d) off of the bill, and for a very short period even a French beret! I had my trousers made bespoke and would wear contrasting jackets with them. I did have suits but they'd be off the peg. Suits were, for me, always tonic mohair. I loved that material and still do. Personalised only with the likes of the essential silk hankie overflowing from the top pocket. That was just me, many others would personalise much more so.

The clothes scene changed rapidly. Early on winkle pickers, then chisel toes, which were a pointed toe with the end abruptly cut off. After that toes became very rounded off. I remember patent shoes being very popular, they were highly glossy shoes previously worn by dancers also lots of basket weave (still THE ultimate Mod shoe) and two-tone brogues and slip-ons. Clothes wise, early on it was all about being suited and booted, tonic mohair being preferable but by '66 it was largely smart casual with Fred Perry (type) shirts being very popular. It wasn't all about names though as it is nowadays. You'd be pretty happy to buy a Fred Perry type shirt from your local High

Street it wasn't necessary to have the label. As Steve Marriott famously told Nicky Horne in an '85 interview when asked 'How did success change you?' He replied 'Well, I stopped going to Woolworths and went to British Home Stores instead!'

I loved the Wardour Street Marquee. A very intimate atmosphere where the only drink on sale was Coca Cola (well it was back in 65/66). I saw many bands there that went on to superstardom including the Who, Small Faces, Cream and Jimi Hendrix Experience. I also saw the first gigs from Humble Pie and the Faces there. I loved the Scene club in Soho as well.

That was pretty elitist and very snobby and owned by the guy that ran Radio Caroline. You'd only ever hear original American artists in there, with the possible exception of Georgie Fame, Chris Farlowe or Zoot Money. That was where I first met Pete Meaden, a fast talking, over the top sort of guy who managed The Who in the early days as well as working with Andrew Loog Oldham and the Rolling Stones. Pete was a mate, perhaps more of an acquaintance really. He was a bit of a pain and the type of guy you went out of your way to avoid if you could. He died young and has now achieved legendary status amongst Mods. Dying before your time is certainly the way to achieve that! Other groovy clubs of that era include Tiles in Oxford Street, Billy Walkers Uppercut Club (he was a famous boxer) in the East End and the fantastic Lotus Club in Forest Gate. There were also some great venues near to my home in Romford such as the Wykeham Hall and Willow Rooms, tiny places but very atmospheric."

John Hellier would continue his love of the Small Faces far beyond their original short-lived career. A life-long passion for the band has earned John the continuous respect of fans and quite possibly, he is the man who knows the most about the Small Faces.

Dennis Munday - "Another great venue to see live music was at The Black Prince Hotel, Bexley. It was a barn of place, but they did have some great groups appear there on Sunday nights. The Steam Packet, featuring 'Long' John Baldry, Julie Driscoll, Brian Auger, and Rod Stewart. Chris Farlowe and the Thunderbird's, featuring Albert Lee [who grew up in Blackheath], a guitarist every bit as good as Clapton. Cliff Bennett & The Rebel Rousers was a regular at the Prince."

The soundtrack being so consistently favoured by Mods further impressed yet more white Blues and Beat acts into presenting their own take on the diverse American black music on offer. The roster of talent from 1964-66 is virtually endless - from the outstanding soulful vocals of Mike Patto in Timebox, Steve Marriott in The Small Faces and Reggie King in The Action alongside The Creation, Spencer Davis Group, The Who, The Birds, Alan Bown Set and Richard Kent Style to lesser knowns' such as The Poets and Riot Squad, The Eyes, The Attack, Soul Agents and a certain David Bowie in The Manish Boys - some of these latter groups never to achieve true recognition and Mod respect for decades, others making positive impressions from the start.

Chris Farlowe - one of the most formidable and credible of blue-eyed Soul singers, who released 'Buzz with the Fuzz' under the pseudonym of Little Joe Cook, a release rated highly by the Mods, is right up there amongst the higher echelons of the great white singers that have loved and sung Blues and Soul – demonstrating, in his case at least - that those white boys really can sing the Blues.

Above: Guildford Mods, friends of Sally Stevens (who took the photo) in 1966

CAN THOSE WHITE BOYS PLAY THE BLUES?

'Talkin' about the white Blues explosion'

John Leo Waters (left) - "It was Muddy Waters who was quoted as saying (after a UK visit) - *'White boys can sure play Blues guitar but they still can't sing!'.* The subject of 'Blue Eyed Soul Singers' always raises a few hackles and is a contentious subject but even more so when relating to UK singers! The term was the prerogative of The Righteous Brothers, the American Duo famous for ' You've lost that loving feeling'.

The sixties saw a proliferation of R&B/Soul bands springing up all over the UK. Many bands and featured singers went on to achieve fame (and in some cases, fortune!) – Manfred Mann, The Rolling Stones, Spencer Davis Group, Animals, Georgie Fame, Rod Stewart, Small Faces, Kinks, Yardbirds - all started off as R&B/Soul bands gigging around the UK club scene. Others achieved a modicum of success – Chris Farlowe, Cliff Bennett, Pretty Things, The Downliner's Sect, John Mayall, Zoot Money, Alex Harvey, Long John Baldry, Them. Some bands became minor one-hit wonders like The Undertakers, and The Dennison's. The vast majority never achieved success even though they included some excellent musicians. Bands/singers such as Graham Bond Organization, The Action, Mike Cotton Sound, Gary Farr and T Bones, The Artwoods and the Bo Street Runners all proved popular on the club circuit but were never able to achieve real success chart wise.

The sixties R&B/Blues scene in this country owed a great deal to insightful jazz musicians such as Chris Barber and Ken Colyer who promoted the Blues within their Jazz bands often featuring a certain Tony Donegan (re-christened himself Lonnie after Lonnie Johnson) along with blues chanteuse Ottilie Patterson. Two other musicians within the band were Alexis Korner and Cyril Davies and in the mid-fifties they broke away and started the Blues and Barrelhouse Club at the Roundhouse pub in Soho. In 1962 they formed Blues Incorporated and opened a blues club in Ealing. The club and band was seminal in the story of UK R&B. Regular visitors included Mick Jagger, Rod Stewart and Paul Jones. The band was very fluid in membership and over the years included such luminaries as Jack Bruce, Charlie Watts, Long John Baldry, Graham Bond, Duffy Power and Ronnie Jones. A musical difference led to Cyril Davies leaving to set up his own Cyril Davies R&B All Stars taking Long John Baldry with him. When Davies sadly passed away in 1964 Baldry renamed the band The Hoochie Coochie Men and brought Rod Stewart in on shared vocals.

By 1962 the R&B revolution was in full swing. Former Jazz clubs up and down the country were booking R&B acts. In Newcastle the Downbeat and Club a GoGo featured the Alan Price Combo with the raucous vocals of Eric Burdon. In Liverpool the Iron Door and Cavern clubs had dropped their Jazz policies in favour of R&B and in the capital clubs like the Flamingo and Marquee embraced the musical form booking top US R&B, Blues and Soul stars. These visiting stars needed backing groups and the demand for good R&B bands was high. By 1964 a plethora of clubs had sprung up throughout the UK. The Twisted Wheel in Manchester, The King Mojo in Sheffield, The Dungeon Nottingham, The Whisky A GoGo in Birmingham as well as a dozen or more in London. A huge circuit now existed for bands and good residencies were at a premium.

The new teenage Mod population's craving for R&B/Soul music could not be sated by the trickle of US stars that visited our shores so they looked to home grown talent to appease their appetites. Only Jimmy James, Geno Washington, Ronnie Jones and Herbie Goins were black singers 'in residence' so the 'Blue Eyed R&B/Soul Singers' were highly sought after.

Most of the popular bands could be divided into two camps - the R&B/Blues based bands and the Soul/Jazz orientated groups. The more popular R&B/Blues bands included the likes of The Rolling Stones, The Yardbirds, [mentioned previously] along with the Hoochie Coochie Men, John Mayall's Bluesbreakers, Downliner's Sect, Gary Farr and T Bones and Jimmy Powell & Dimensions. Although the bands featured some excellent musicians only a few had vocalists of note. Eric Burdon of the Animals and Long John Baldry from the Hoochie Coochie Men both possessed powerful voices. Their guttural vocals were probably the nearest thing to authentic R&B the UK was capable of producing. They came from vastly different backgrounds - Baldry was from a middle class Middlesex background whilst Burdon was raised in working class Wallsend but both possessed rich blues infused voices, which had more in common with Chicago than London and Newcastle! Both Paul Jones of Manfred Mann and Mick Jagger were singers of note but not quite in the same league as Burdon or Baldry. In Jagger's case it was often felt that his styling owed a little too much to Don Covay!

Some of the Soul/Jazz aggregations popular in the clubs around the country included Georgie Fame and the Blue Flames, Spencer Davis Group, Cliff Bennett and the Rebel Rousers, Zoot Money, Graham Bond Organization, The Undertakers and The Alex Harvey Soul Band. Georgie Fame's Jazz inflected vocals were right on the money but the 'Blue Eyed Soul' of Cliff Bennett, Alex Harvey and the young Stevie Winwood from Spencer Davis Group were hard to beat. Whilst we could never truly replicate the gospel drenched vocalizing of Otis Redding, Wilson Pickett or James Brown some of our homegrown vocalists were more than capable of holding their own. The first Spencer Davis Group LP released in 1965 highlighted Stevie Winwood's Soulful tenor and on tracks such as '*Every Little Bit Hurts*' the vocal similarities to Winwood's hero Ray Charles are obvious.

Alex Harvey had been a stalwart of the Glasgow scene since the late fifties and with his 'Soul Band' he was a popular live attraction. His mix of R&B and Soul was exactly what the doctor ordered and whilst his vocals may have lacked the depth of Stevie Winwood he was still considered to be one of the best interpreters of black music on this side of the pond. Cliff Bennett had started his apprenticeship as a Rock and Roller with Joe Meek in 1957 but gradually made the switch to R&B, a genre that perfectly suited his rich soulful tones. One of the most under rated UK R&B singers his voice has definite comparisons with another famous blue-eyed soulster – Bill Medley. The one singer I have only briefly mentioned is perhaps the daddy of them all – Chris Farlowe. Hugely popular on the club circuit Chris Farlowe and the Thunderbirds crossed between R&B/Blues

and Soul like no other band. Farlowe's booming powerhouse vocals were suited to up-tempo Soul covers and down home Blues alike. There cannot be many who are not familiar with his recording of 'Stormy Monday Blues' under the pseudonym of *Little Joe Cook* for Chris Blackwell's Island Records, which led many to believe that this was a genuine US Blues singer. It has been listed by many as one of the best Blues recordings of all time. It was no coincidence that Otis Redding requested he join him on the RSG special after witnessing his act at the Flamingo Club. He had started his career in London as a skiffle singer before making the transition to R&B in the late fifties. Often referred to as 'The Voice' he is still belting out Blues and Soul classics in small clubs and concert venues throughout Europe.

We should not forget the distaff side of the 60'S R&B movement. Whilst female singers were spread thinly on the ground mention should be given to the likes of Beryl Marsden, Kiki Dee, Barry St John, Julie Driscoll, Dusty Springfield and even Lulu (her first LP with the Luvvers contained several R&B/Soul numbers). Julie Driscoll possessed a great voice and her 'Mod' look made her a real favourite. However, it was Dusty Springfield who voice came closest to emulating the perception of a 'Soul' singer. Her sultry vocals held just the right amount of angst to elevate her to the rank of the finest 'female white Soul singer' of the sixties. The fact that there were so few UK female R&B singers may have something to do with the rather dodgy club circuit of the sixties. Many clubs were pretty seedy, there was a widespread amphetamine problem and many clubs had links to the criminal world. Only Beryl Marsden and Julie Driscoll really toured to any great extent.

Alan Bown Set

The Mod phenomenon had reached its peak by 1965. Many more clubs had opened their doors to cater for the ever-expanding younger Mod population. The Animals, Spencer Davis, Georgie Fame, Them, The Rolling Stones and The Pretty Things were all enjoying chart success. Several new bands began to make their mark in the clubs The Action, The Alan Bown Set; The Birds all appeared in 1965. Excellent bands all, and they put out some great music but only The Action featured a vocalist of any great note in Reggie King. Reggie King had formed the band in Kentish Town, North London an area prolific in producing/nurturing R&B talent during the sixties within a three mile radius were domiciled Chris Farlowe, Rod Stewart, Elton John, The Kinks, The Equals, The Tea Set (Pink Floyd) and The Gaylords (Marmalade).

Down in an East London above Stratford pub The Two Puddings a band of young Mods had been rehearsing. Their vocalist was called Steve Marriot and when the Small Faces first graced the charts in 1965 with 'What'cha Gonna Do About It' it was obvious that the UK had found another 'Blue Eyed Soul' singer of note. Like their West London counterparts – The Who – they were soon portrayed by the media as the face of Mod. Both bands had R&B backgrounds but whereas Roger Daltrey's raucous voice was more suited to the Rock idiom that The Who later pursued, Marriott was blessed with a set of pipes that had real depth. Unfortunately their early promise did not last (just listen to *You Need Lovin'* on their first LP – eat your heart out Robert Plant!) and they soon forsook their R&B roots (as did the Who) in search of the mighty dollar. In all honesty neither bands really hit the spot with established Mods – The Who were considered to have jumped on the bandwagon and the Small Faces were too young for a generation that had come of age some two or three years earlier.

The sixties Soul/R&B revolution had peaked and the street orientated Mod movement had now been taken over by commercial forces who guided the record buying public into psychedelia, flower power and heavy rock. R&B/Soul vocalists were no longer in vogue and although one or two singers of some note did pop up in the later sixties (Steve Ellis and Andy Fairweather Lowe to name two) the moment had passed. Over the years the term 'Blue Eyed Soul singer' has been bandied about willy nilly in the UK but one only has to listen to Messrs Farlowe, Winwood, Marriot, Baldry, Harvey or Bennett to appreciate the true meaning of the term."

It is almost inconceivable to consider, during these re-evaluated times, that such a vast array of talent amongst the UK Beat and pop fraternity of the sixties should have been virtually ignored and under-appreciated. Whilst, scores of acts did manage to experience considerable success, countless others remained to be enjoyed almost exclusively by the young Mods of the day – who in effect, were just as influenced by the same musicians as the artists themselves.

Dennis Munday - "At the time, there were many groups and artists around that never quite made it. The Action had one of the best drummers in Roger Powell, and Reg King had a voice and a half. There was The Alan Bown Set and Jimmy James & The Vagabonds, who were big favourites with the Marquee crowd. Herbie Goins an American R 'n' B singer and The Mark Leeman 5 were both good. Another good band was The Creation, as well as Fleur De Lys, The Downliners Sect, Winston's Fumbs, A Thin Red Line, and the Shakey Vick Blues Band. There were many local bands on the southeast London circuit, including Edwick Rumbold, who I recall, because my mates were in this band.

The first time I saw Georgie Fame & The Blue Flames was at the Prince, with drummer Red Reece, bassist Tex Makins, guitarist Colin Green and Mick Eve on tenor.

You wouldn't miss Geno Washington when he appeared at the Prince, or anywhere else, and he was well liked by the Mods. He had a great live act, which for some reason he couldn't re-produce on record. Nevertheless, who can forget him singing 'Michael'. John Mayall appeared there, this time with Peter Green on guitar and the crowd heckled him, as Eric Clapton has just left the band, which was a shame, as he was an excellent guitarist. When we got on the bus to go to the Prince, Hughie Flint, Mayall's drummer was sitting on the backseat.

We also hit Soho and did the clubs in Wardour Street, The Flamingo, The Whisky-A-Go-Go, and the Marquee club. Strange as it may seem, none of these were my favourite London club. That honour belonged to Tiles, situated in a basement, at 79 – 89 Oxford Street. Most of the bands that played there were not famous. Jeff Dexter was the resident DJ. Sam the Sham and his Pharaohs appeared here, as well as Amen Corner, when they were a quasi-blues band."

By 1964, and certainly the following year, the same youthful enthusiasm felt by London Mods for these blue-eyed soul artists had spread out into the provinces as the taste for the music and the associated Mod lifestyle proved to be just as infectious as was being experienced in the capital.

Derek Glover - "The Kings Head pub on Hagley Road, Bearwood had a cellar called The Morgue and was a great venue for R&B bands. Regular bands there were The Spencer Davis Group and Jimmy Powell and The Five Dimensions. The Spencer Davis Group were the all-time favourites of all the Smethwick Mods. They could do nothing wrong. We would also go and see them at Thimblemill Baths, or go into 'Town' to The Golden Eagle, The Whiskey, and at the all-nighters at The Birmingham Town Hall. I remember Stevie Winwood once asking me to get him a pint, he was only seventeen and not yet old enough to go up to the bar.

Thimblemill Baths in Smethwick was a just a normal swimming baths during the summer. Then during the autumn, the pool would be covered up with floorboards and open back up as a ballroom for the season. Top names would visit 'The Baths' such as The Beatles, The Who, The Pretty Things... unbelievable times."

PAUL CLAY '64' MOD

Paul Clay, also from Nottingham, came of age as Mod was gaining its public profile. Quickly sussing the essential codes of Mod ethics, he was soon addicted to the essence of being a Mod.

Paul Clay - "I never decided I was going to be a Mod, I just just kind of became one by noticing what was going on. I suppose to have been there right from the off, you had to have been born in the 40's, I just scraped in. It all started in the 50's really, noticing the rock 'n' rollers and the Ted's styles of dress, but by '62' there were noticeable changes going on, certainly, for me, by 1964. I started work that year and I really wanted to look smart, it was all about looking good!

It went two ways for us all, the Teds went scruffy and became rockers and we went smarter and were Mods. I drifted away from the interest I had previously had in bikes and bought a scooter. But, let me say this, scooters were only a small part of it. A means to get from one place to the other, whilst looking cool.

I suppose I was very lucky in that I had four really good quality suits, up to 55 guineas a throw. That's the other myth when you hear guys go on bragging off that they had ten mohair suits, are they kidding or what? Who could afford that amount of suits, no that's a lie? There's lots of bullshit about the time I suppose and there's the 'looking through rose-tinted glasses' too but we have to remember the truth – how it really was!

Paul, left with Trevor Westbrook

I went to the Dungeon Club and the Boat Club but most of the time, we stood around in our little group on street corners, just like most other working class youths of the time did. We [as Mods] did want to belong to the same gang, but we didn't want to look the same, we were always after some item of clothing that would help us to stand out, sometimes it may be a change of what you wore with what you already had as the fashions changed that much, but as long as you looked different to your mates that was cool. The worse thing was trying to get hold of some decent shoes. Until Ravel, we used to wear grey or brown Hush Puppies. We wouldn't wear our trousers tight (that was for the Teddy Boys) but wore Parallels, suits came with twelve inch vents. One mate had to go even further and try for fourteen inch side vents. I can remember the tailor arguing with him, saying 'You can't do that; it will totally ruin the suit'.

My fave bands were some of the obvious ones, The Who, Spencer Davis Group, the Small Faces etc. and there was a lot of Soul in there too, Tamla, Booker T and the MG's. I also loved the Stones, to which some of my mates said were not a Mod band, but I differ, they were liked and enjoyed by Mods. But then I also loved the Blues, which is where the Stones came from.

It was a time of just a little affluence, but we were not greedy. Our parents had come back from the war with an aim to make things better. I suppose in our own way, that's what we were doing, trying to make our world better. We all thought that we were a part of the revolution, a sexual revolution too, which we were."

Gary Maxton (right) - "When I was 15 my best mate in Solihull was a lad called David Rice Davies (you may remember his infamous sister Mandy Rice Davies). He had his dad's old Lambretta and a Parka with a fur trimmed collar, so I decided to sell my motor bike and join him. I'm not sure if I initially called myself a Mod, but I soon bought a reefer jacket, some Hush Puppies and a Fred Perry shirt.

We went to see the Stones at Birmingham town hall and at our local youth club we saw Denny Laine and the Diplomats. My favourite gig in Brum was the Spencer Davis Group (I think Steve Winwood was about 16 then). I then went to Australia with my parents for a year clutching my Stones, Animals and Pretty Things albums, but I was soon back in England living in Long Eaton Nottingham where I originally came from.

This is when my Mod days really took off, and I started clubbing in Nott's at the Dungeon, Beachcomber and Boat Clubs. Within a year I had seen The Who, Small Faces, the Yardbirds, Otis Redding, Ike and Tina Turner, Georgie Fame, Ben E King, Mary Wells, The Drifters and most of the Stax artists. During this time I was at a Geno Washington gig where I took my first couple of Purple Hearts."

REGGIE WEBSTER SIXTIES SCOOTER BOY

No realistic investigation of the mid-sixties Mod era would be complete without an accurate balance of it's contrasting influence upon the various youths of the day. Despite Mod's often flamboyant aspects and elevation of self-image as a prime requirement, not all Mods were as fastidious and over-concerned with what they regarded as the 'Peacock' tendencies of some elements of the Mod elite.

Separate from the fashionable clubs and light years away from the commercialisation of Mod, there existed an underbelly of significantly more street-wise, working class, scooter-riding Mods. Belonging to pockets of gangs, fiercely loyal to their friends, spartan in their love of clothes, they were as equally inspired by the post-Beat boom of British R&B bands as the swinging Chelsea set and more fashion-conscious Mods were. These harder edged young Mod urchins held their honour and Mod prestige highly (though not always recognising the term 'Mod' as a description). They would soon emerge as the first skinheads of the decade.

Reggie Webster - "There were always scooters around when I was a kid; ridden by the conformist guys in white 'pisspot' helmets who were in clubs and spent weekends away with their chums from the office singing folk songs around the camp fire. Those very people became a great point of supply for used scooters. I say 'used' because the majority of kids like me came from the working classes, no cars in our streets and extra money was something you scraped for.

I was 14 in 1965 and was always destined to be like the kids that had shown some spirit at Margate and Brighton. I'd already worked weekends in service stations, some of my mates had even left school early to work. I dealt a moped, a T100 scooter and a Triumph 500 Speed twin to raise enough cash to get my first Lambretta on the road: 25 quid from a respectable Nigel who wasn't that pleased to sell it to me and another few quid customising it with anything I could find at the scrappers or swap with the other odd guy with the same intention.

I passed my test at 1pm on my 16th birthday, after spending over a year on the road underage on L-plates, something that didn't seem that important to anybody back then and certainly not uncommon. I'd even done my first Brighton Bank Holiday on a '64' Sportique with chrome panels - 35 quid from Reading, paid for by the profit on the Lambretta after I'd finished with it. I'd enjoyed something we'd all dreamed of, the V formation drive in on the Prom and then the line-up waiting for the next crew.

If you planned on staying the night, you just packed up an army bedroll or a parka and kip (or try to) under the pier. I don't remember it ever being above freezing at night, despite being the middle of Summer. Some of the guys stayed awake all night because they'd taken a few blockers, not hard to get hold of in those days: you could walk into Boots and buy amphetamine slimming tablets for a quid. Three or four was enough to keep you awake, eight would make your guts ache and eyes bleed - never saw the point myself, rather have a 'yella fella' after a dance (Valium, usually at least one kid's Mum was on 'Mothers little helpers') coming down was better than going up anyday.

By 1966, (I'll use the word 'Mod' now, but back then we never did - it was derogatory but amusing, the scooters and the army surplus clothing of the crew spoke for itself), local celebrity Mods (the bad lads that most girls mums wanted them to stay away from) had generally established a uniformed image, compared to '64'. I'd like to mention that being a 'Mod' now meant you were bordering on juvenile delinquency more or less, the very same connotation as being a greaser: I always assumed it meant we were just a modern version of their attitude. Now I look back, I feel we had more in common with the greaser as far as attitude was concerned. There were certainly no rules as far as violence was concerned, but, like most things, it was blown out of proportion and resorted in banter and rowdiness, something frowned upon by society in those very conformist days where you were expected to dress like your Dad and get your name on the council list for your future wife. Plus, in all honesty, most of us knew at least one greaser at school or locally and had helped or been helped by one for mechanical stuff. Nothing was ever as black and white as history says. A 'stand up bloke' was OK whatever he was.

To us there was us and Rockers, nobody else. By 66-67, there were plenty of Paisley-clad Dandy-looking blokes and it wouldn't be unreasonable to say that they were just replicating the 'pop group' look of the era. They wanted to look like the kid called Brad in Jackie magazine that everyone loved and the birds all wanted to look like Mary Quant or July Driscoll. The Mods had maintained their Spartan look, a decent suit to go out in, very plain sportswear - something nobody wore if they weren't doing sports at the time - and, of course, decent jeans, two quid Desert Boots and some weatherproof gear from the army surplus. My first suit came from a second hand shop on the Portobello Road. Mates were the same really, we never had a made to measure suit. Logic says when you took £4 17/6d a week home and three quid of that was for digs or rent, running a scooter took the priority, not rushing down to your personal tailor for yet another attempt at making you look like a top kiddy: you earned that title not bought it.

Popularity amongst some of the girls was a great motivation. There was always the image of the teenage gangsters, the Jack The Lads that knew their way round. Some girls would do anything for a ride on the back of your scooter and young kids would pay you two bob to take them round the town so their mates could see them. Three trips got you a gallon of 2-stroke. I fondly remember Saturday afternoon at The Continental in Woking (a cafe come scooter shop), it was a guaranteed earner, a posing afternoon where we'd sit and drink Pepsi with all the scooters lined up. Quite often, a gang of birds would stand ten yards away plucking up enough courage to speak to us dangerous kids because of what their parents had told them about Britain's teenage public enemy number one.

There were no hard and fast rules, certainly a pecking order because we were fairly outgoing but no 'shrinking violets' and most could handle themselves. But importantly we had a sense of humour, confident rather than arrogant. One kid, after riding his scooter into the front of a fruit a veg shop one Saturday, had Fyffe's Banana stickers stuck on his side panels, carrots tied to his backrest on string etc. Another time, my back wheel was loosened and fell off while going down a hill. Or [maybe] a fight where the guy against three was left on his own for a couple of minutes before we joined in to help; it was a strong sort of camaraderie - these blokes were your family, we shared everything but our girlfriends."

DAVID BIRCHALL

David Birchall was another classic example of a younger, yet equally clued-in, element finding their way into the early scene, his affiliation coinciding with the 64 to 66 high tide of Mod.

David Birchall (Godalming Mod) - "I was born in Paddington but we moved south of London when I was still a small lad. I was involved in the Mod scene around Guildford starting in the summer of 1964. Since I lived alongside the A3 (the main road south out of London) that's where I first saw what subsequently became known as Mods in 1962 and 63. They were on very smart scooters - not the 'mum and dad' type with a windshield, but very smart - with accessories but not overdone. The riders wore parkas and trilby hats. I was gob-smacked and knew that was what I wanted to look like - problem was I was fourteen and making ten bob a week on a paper route...

I bought my scooter - a Lambretta Li150 - in the spring of 1964, just after leaving school. I painted it in two-tone red and white but ran it in 'skeleton' form, minus front mudguard and side panels, quite a bit. It made it easier to nick chrome side panels when the opportunity arose. I fitted a two tone red and black striped seat (from Pride and Clarke's?) plus lights, mirrors, carriers and a fly screen. I fitted one of those silencers with the megaphone on the end that sounded wonderful until the whole thing plugged up! I took it off and soaked it in acid but couldn't clean it out so I took a big hammer and a chisel to it and punched a hole in the front - best thing I ever did! It restored the performance but made the Lambretta sound like a Vespa GS! Instead of the putt, putt, putt of the Lambretta there was this turbine like howl of a Vespa - very cool!

I didn't have much money - I only made four pound ten a week initially, so buying clothes was a creative affair. We had a small 'boutique' tailors in Guildford at the time - I forget the name but they were next to the Ricky Tick Club (as the main ballroom was named). I had my first suit made there and they took a lot of trouble over it. When I subsequently worked at Austin Reads, the tailors there were very impressed with the cut and hang of this suit. Otherwise we wore what was 'the latest thing' for the London guys - striped jackets, button down collars, Levis (of course - although getting the Levis was a major operation), Desert Boots and parkas. The parkas were a fashion thing but they were bloody useless for stopping the cold and rain - especially the rain! I think that must be the reason we all fitted 'fly screens' to the scooters - to give us some protection, in addition to looking cool. I started out with a skinny white fur roll on the hood of my parka but when I acquired a really good brown roll I used the white fur on the epaulettes - I never saw anyone else do that and it looked really good, even if I do say so myself. There had been a fashion for the 'Barrow Boy' look in about 1963 and I still had the flat hat but I found that by undoing the clasp between the peak and the body of the hat it would stay on and also looked good - I saw others do this but I can honestly say that I arrived at this idea on my own. We stole the mirrors off Honda 50s so that we could 'accessorize' our scooters in addition to front and rear carriers, fly screens, lights and crash bars. Nobody considered the weight all this accumulated stuff was having on performance. I was one of the few people who knew how to work on an engine and

I managed to make my scooter go quite well.

I became involved with the local band of Mods - all were older than me and made more money (I made four pounds, ten shillings and eleven pence a week as an apprentice compositor). I want to make a point of the age thing. The Baby Boom Generation is generally considered as those born between 1946 and 1964 (US Census info) - I was born in 1948. My mates were all generally born four or five years before me. I contend, M'Lud, that this gave them a distinct advantage - with jobs, opportunities (birds) and with 'creating' styles. There were also far fewer of them, thanks to Adolf. Think of the ages of the Beatles, Stones, The Who and I suggest, M'Lud, the early Mods. (please don't bring up Mark Feld/Bolan he was a freak of nature!). Those of us in the Baby Boom generation had to follow them - we had no bleedin' choice!"

John Hellier - "Well up until the Who we never listened or liked anything that was wasn't American. From late '64, we realised how good a lot of the homegrown talent was. Artistes such as Georgie Fame, Zoot Money, Chris Farlowe, Rod the Mod Stewart and Chris Farlowe were not only great live acts, they were making great records as well, albeit mostly cover versions."

John went on to form his own band – The Music Box (pictured below in 1966)

John Hellier - "I was in several bands in the 60s but the one that I was with the longest was MUSIC BOX previously known as THE CIRCLES. Formed in 1966 in the Romford/Ilford area to the East of London, we were a 6-piece group that used to specialise in American West Coast material. We were signed to Galaxy Entertainments in London, which was one of Don Arden's off shoot companies and had big ambition at the time. We honestly thought it was just a matter of time before we hit big...alas we were wrong. The line-up of the band was Lead Vocals Rob Etherington and Mick Brown, Lead Guitar Brian Meeks, Rhythm Guitar Terry Moore, Bass Guitar Steve Eastman and yours truly on Drums. There were personnel changes but the afore mentioned line up was the most consistent. We toured up and down the length of the UK and played some prestigious venues none more so than the Lyceum Ballroom in London. After the band split I went on to play with a similar band called PINK GIN.

One day in 1966, I answered a Drummer required ad in Melody Maker. It was for an established band called JOHNS CHILDREN (pre Marc Bolan). I rehearsed with them for about a month in a church hall in a place called Ickenham (Middlesex I think). I even got as far as having a promo photo shoot done with them although I never got to see let alone own any of them. It was great until their previous drummer Chris Townson wanted to return and they opted to take him back. Chris had stepped in for Keith Moon on a European Who tour. That tells you his pedigree I had no chance. I remained mates with them and a re-formed version of Johns Children played for me at my sold out Steve Marriott Memorial Show in 2001."

Lloyd Johnson - "I was out of the country when The Small Faces and The Who hit. I came back early '66 and everything was over commercialised: for me I didn't like that whole fighting yobo thing that started in 64, the idiots had joined in, so I just did my own thing, I got more obsessed with clothes ..."

IRISH JACK LYONS FROM SHEPHERD'S BUSH

One loyal and keen fan of The Who would attain Mod legend status in a twist of fate meeting that would- in due course - have a profound impact on his self-identity.

"I focused on this guy playing guitar and afterwards introduced myself 'Hello I'm Jack from Shepherd's Bush.' Townshend replied in his cockney twang 'Hello Jack from Shepherd's Bush, I'm Pete from Ealing.'" - **Irish Jack Lyons**

He is the man from Cork: a Mod legend, close friend of Pete Townshend and The Who and significantly the man that Townshend is rumoured to have based his 1973 Mod epic 'Quadrophenia' and its central character, Jimmy upon. Irish Jack Lyons - who was 19 at the time he very first set eyes on Townsend in his pre-Who act The Detours in 1962 - has become somewhat of a fully deserved Mod celebrity over the years, his enigma and affable Irish charm drawing admiration from the whole of Mod's wide-reaching fraternity. Earthy, clean and cool and loyal to his friends, Jack's Mod experiences are truly worthy of a book of his own: here Jack recounts, in his straight-talking endearing manner, just a few of his Mod memories down at The Goldhawk Club - bringing back to life the edgy and electric atmosphere of being a Mod in West London' Shepherd's Bush.

Irish Jack Lyons - "There was one thing about the Goldhawk Social Club in Shepherd's Bush where Mods went every Friday and Saturday night in '64, and that was if you weren't from West London it soon got around. And that was when the trouble might start - if you were looking for it. Like the night, someone said there was a bit of a ruck going on upstairs in the bar. I was one of the crowd dancing on the floor who heard about it and went up to have a look.

**Irish Jack Lyons
Early Shepherd's
Bush Mod**

It turned out that some geezer called Big Jim from Mile End had walked into the Goldhawk Club with a couple of his mates intent on causing trouble. By the time I got upstairs this bloke, Big Jim, was lying on the flat of his back in the middle of the bar with his mates standing around him looking like a whiter shade of pale. The manager of the support band was doing everything he could -short of the kiss of life- to revive Big Jim. While over at the other side of the Goldhawk bar some skinny-looking guy called Martin Gaish - from Hammersmith, had a small crowd of friends and well-wishers gather round him advising him to cool down. But the way I picked up on this guy's nervous energy, he looked more like he was getting ready to take on the whole Goldhawk Club. I'd seen this particular guy around Hammersmith before but had never taken too much notice of him. Now I found I couldn't take my eyes off him as I studied him from where I stood at the bar counter.

Irish Jack watching the dancer

Gaish was five-foot nine, maybe even five-ten. He was loose and skinny, gangling almost, like when he moved it looked like every joint in his body had been well oiled. His dark hair had been cropped in the French-cut style with a neat parting in the middle. And though their natural colour was sharp blue, the pupils of his eyes contained a certain brilliance obtained only through that well-known artificial energy known as 'leapers'. In other words, he was pilled to the eyeballs, and spots of blood trickled down from a cut above the right eyebrow on to his freshly pressed Fred Perry. And what really struck me about this guy Gaish was the fact he already had a smart handkerchief puckering from the top pocket of his jacket - which he wouldn't dream of ruining - some girl had actually stepped forward and given him a tissue to swab the bloodstains from his jacket collar. As I stood there and watched, I knew then that I had just witnessed one of the reasons why people looked up to this guy Gaish. But he was more than just a well-dressed Mod, this fella Martin Gaish. He was a face in every sense of the word without lifting a bloody finger.

The guy on the deck, Big Jim, was no chicken. Built like a tank the shoulder pads of his Burton suit looked like they'd had half a fucking mattress stuffed into them. On the other hand, Martin Gaish was one of those real wiry, bony; characters you'd expect to see get pushed around in a crowd. About the only thing he had going for him was the speed of his hands and a left hook like a piston rod. A human piston rod. He wasn't the sort who went looking for trouble - but when it came knocking he was the last person in the world you'd expect to see fight his way out of it. He went missing from the Goldhawk Club for a couple of weeks, and just when I thought he'd been barred for life he turned up one Friday night dressed in a Henley jacket and wearing inch-roll Levi's looking like he'd stepped off the front cover of Town magazine.

Irish Jack Lyons at the Marquee 1965

I have to admit that I admired this guy because I considered him the all-time clothes wearer and stylist - which was something that I, Irish Jack, a filing clerk with the London Electricity Board on Shepherd's Bush Green, five-foot six in stocking vamps - could never be. And instead of the envy, I usually felt in the presence of better-dressed Mods, with Gaish I felt as though I was falling thousands of feet through the air into a warm sea of admiration. Everything about him looked so right, see. He was taller than me for a start. And subconsciously I had always felt that I was too much on the short side to really carry my clothes right. Once I had studied Gaish, it didn't take me too long to realise that the reason why my clothes didn't appear to 'hang' like his was simply because-

I wasn't tall enough. Soon I was scouring the small ads in the back of music magazines for the 'Gain 2-Inches' tablets. But who the fuck was I kidding?

Philip Grants in the King Street or John Stephen's in Carnaby Street - it was all the same to me. I could wear exactly the same gear as Martin Gaish but he'd still look a million times sharper. And then there was his face. Moody's not the word for it. It had a kind of built-in sullenness about it that could accommodate a thousand more expressions of defiance than I could ever conjure up. Sometimes he'd do something in a certain way that you'd swear he must have known how good he looked doing it. Ten minutes later he'd do something equally as good as if looking flash was the furthermost thing from his mind. Being flash was a kind of secret with Gaish. An unwritten code of behaviour you could never get in on. And I reckoned that about the nearest anyone could get to that natural cool of his was to be constantly in his company. Something I planned on doing.

Later that first evening, I instinctively followed the little knot of friends who coaxed him out of the Goldhawk bar back downstairs to the dance floor. I watched him as he laughingly explained to friends how the fight had started. Meanwhile on stage the support band The Clique entertained the Goldhawk crowd; and when The Who came on practically everyone clambered to the front of the stage for a look - but not Gaish. He remained at the back of the hall dancing with a handful of others. I'm not kidding; his legs must've been made of rubber the way he kept going when others had flaked out on the sofas... 'Road Runner', 'Parchment Farm' and Benny Spellman's 'Fortune Teller'... this guy Gaish could out-dance anyone. And he had this dance move where the open palm of his hand came across his face... like it was the dance of the seven fucking veils.

It turned out that Martin Gaish lived with his parents Fred and Joan Gaish in Riverside Gardens off the King Street in Hammersmith. His younger brother Lee was also a Mod and walked around with a harmonica belonging to Roger Daltrey in his back pocket and permanently a pair of drumsticks in his side pocket which knowing Lee and his connections he would have 'borrowed' from Keith Moon. Martin worked as a tile layer for a small building firm. The first time I ever had reason to use the toilet in his parent's council flat, I went in and discovered to my surprise that Gaish must've been doing a handy bit of nicking on the side from his firm - cos the entire bathroom was covered top to bottom with tiles of every description, shape and colour. Talk about a fucking kaleidoscope. And while I sat there on the seat as nature took its course I realised that what Gaish was obviously doing was coming home from work every night with whatever tiles he could lay his thieving hands on and he just stuck them on as he went along.

I got on well with his mum Joan. Martin told me his old man Fred worked as a night sorter in the Hammersmith post office so maybe that's why I never saw too much of him. There was one thing I could never understand about Gaish the more I got to know him - and that was how he never owned a scooter. One day we happened to be talking about scooters so I just came out and asked him why he never bothered. Gaish just shrugged it off, 'Scooters? They're okay, I suppose. But you can't knock-off a bird on the back of one, can yer?' I gave it some thought and had to agree. Then he added, 'Anyway I'm gonna start saving up for a mini-van...' 'A mini-van?' I replied, not sure of what he was getting at. 'Yeah, sure. That's what you want,' he assured me. 'What'd' you want a mini-van for?' 'To put a fucking mattress in the back, dick.' I looked back at Gaish still unsure of what he'd meant. He looked at me: 'Jesus! Haven't you ever heard of sex, Jack?'

I don't have to say what an idiot I felt. I didn't pursue the matter any further. I still reckoned Gaish would've looked a thousand times sharper riding around on a Vespa or Lambretta than sitting behind the wheel of a silly looking mini-van. I might've been wrong but I always reckoned there was something very un-Mod about driving around on four wheels. You weren't really a Mod or seen to be a Mod until you stepped out of the car. Unless of course it was a Jaguar Mark 11.

'Don't mention nuthin' about pills....' Gaish warned me as we climbed the stairs to his parent's council flat in Riverside Gardens. It was my first time ever going round there. It was just meant to be a quick pop-in while he changed his shoes for the 'Off The Record' night at the Hammersmith Palais. The shoes he had on were kind of soft, sponge-soled and they stuck to the floor for the special dance steps to John Lee Hooker's 'Dimples'. He'd just remembered the shoes as we were about to go into the Palais so I had agreed to walk back with him. His mum Joan was in the kitchen as we entered. She popped her head around the door and cheerfully asked if I'd like a cup of tea. I was just about to say 'no thanks' when she arrived with a cup and saucer in her hand. By the time I had managed to gulp half of it down Gaish was standing by the door in his change of shoes and ready to leave. I heard him sigh a breath of impatience as I answered his mother and told her I was living over in Shepherd's Bush in Kelmscott Gardens just off Askew Road. Joan nagged Gaish for being so impatient and impolite. Much against his will he sat in the settee. Mrs. Gaish wanted to know where I worked so I told her. Then she asked me if I lived near St. Stephens Roman Catholic Church on Ashchurch Grove, I told her that I could see the church from my back window. She asked me did I worship there. I told her that I went to Mass there about once a fortnight - which was a lie. I could sense Martin snarling at me from out of the corner of my eye.

I said good-night to Joan Gaish and followed Martin down the stairs out into the courtyard. I sensed he had something to say. Then he said it: 'I don't believe in nuthin like that no more.' He sounded as if he had made his mind up about it some time ago. 'Why not?' I heard myself ask. I wasn't sticking up for religion or anything like that. I was just curious as to why he thought that way. 'Why not?' he replied, 'I dunno. I just refuse to believe any more that there's any such place as heaven or hell. That's all.' I was a bit taken aback. It had come out of him as if he was discussing the weather. 'Yeah, but look...' I said, 'If you don't believe in heaven and you don't believe in hell, then what's the point of believing in God?' Gaish looked back at me hard, 'Who said anything about believing in a God? You don't mean to tell me that you actually believe there's a big God up there in the sky keeping an account of all your stupid little sins?' I looked back a bit sheepish at him. I knew there was no way I was gonna win this argument. 'Well, do you?' 'Do I what?' I replied. 'Do you believe that there's a big God up there keeping an account of all your sins?' I waited for a moment. I was really pissed off with myself for falling into the stupid trap of arguing about religion. 'Yeah, I suppose I do believe there's a God there. Yeah.' 'Oh don't be a prat Jack,' Gaish snarled with a half a smile on his face like he had every intention of passing this on to someone else...'Look, it's like A-B-C,' we stopped by the Broadway as he vented his spleen, 'If I refuse to believe that there's a heaven there, and I refuse to believe that there's a hell there, right? Then what's the bloody point of believing that there's a God there? It stands to reason.' 'Alright,' I said, 'You've made your point. But if you don't believe in heaven or hell and you don't believe that there's a God there... where do you think we go when we die then?' Gaish was looking back at me with an incredulous expression on his face. 'Where do we go? We don't go anywhere. You just go. Y'know, you go. You rot. Or you get cremated. That's where you go.' His words made a kind of terrifying sense. Where in fact you *went* after you died was a subject, which had always occupied my mind from school to work. And even lately on a score of Black Bombers when the 3-D horrors had set in, I couldn't stop thinking about places like heaven and hell. After the bombers had worn off and the come down arrived, first you'd feel every muscle in your body tighten up. Then you'd get an attack of cold shakes and your brain - or what was left of it after leapers- would pound ahead of you and all the bleeding art galleries of your mind would flicker open and shut, open and shut, open and shut, like somebody mucking around with the cord of a venetian blind. I have to admit that even as a little kid at school I was never too pushed about heaven but I could never stop thinking about hell.

The simplicity of what Gaish had said seemed a thousand times more honest, more practical, than all the hours and hours I'd spent sweating in my bed and wondering would there be a bright blue heaven waiting for me when I died. As we headed into the Hammersmith Palais it occurred to me that I had gone through life living in a kind of fear-world. And then, someone like Gaish comes along and blows away everything with three little words...*you just go!* But that was the thing about Martin Gaish, see. The way he'd just barely let you in on what was going on in his head. He never went in for detail. With him a thing was either good or bad. Right or wrong. Black or white. He never bothered with gray areas and never went in for big words either. Sometimes it was practically impossible to have a discussion with him. I mean a real discussion. Y'know, you'd get so far with him and then he'd suddenly clam up. Like if he was talking about a particular subject, say, for longer than ten minutes he'd suddenly start looking at you as if he suspected you were trying to pick his brain. I mean, when he was on pills he'd talk all bloody night, really rabbit on and on. But it was always about girls and parties and records - never about himself. Almost as if he had a time limit on everything.

I was nobody until I became a Mod. And yet Gaish could be so cool about the whole thing. So cool that in a way he appeared bigger than it. He was in control of it whereas with me it swallowed me up without trace. I must have suffered a thousand agonies privately trying to attain the face look and yet I still clung to the idea of being a Mod cos Mod was the only way I could express myself. Mod was the only way I could channel my deepest fears and frustrations. Mod was the only way I could get a girl into bed... if I ever got that lucky. I'd swear that if someone came up and told Gaish that Modernism had just died or went out of fashion at ten minutes past five; he'd have shrugged his shoulders and been in the queue for the Odeon in a sloppy pullover by eight o' clock. I mean if that had been *me*; I would probably have been picked up by the police standing on the edge of Hammersmith Bridge contemplating suicide.

I not only lived, ate, slept and dreamed Mod - I romanticized about it as well. Every week I'd be the trend setter with my ham roll and half a Watney's Brown staring at the Sunday colour supplements with front page Terence Donovan close-ups of leading atheists, anyone with something intellectual and provocative to say. I always had a hankering-after, a secret admiration for people like Shelagh Delaney's 'Taste Of Honey', Brigid Brophy and Malcolm Muggeridge the way in which they were able to express themselves and some of them so cool about disbelieving in God. It seemed so anti-establishment, so rebellious. I used to live for every minute of it.

We fell out over Brighton, Martin Gaish and I. Practically everyone in the Goldhawk Club was talking about going down there for the Whit weekend in '64. But ever since the trouble in Clacton over the Easter, I got the feeling that something was going to go wrong. In Clacton the shops put up their shutters and Mods were just shunted along the pavements like a herd of cattle - and it pissed out of the heavens. There had been a lot of people fined over the minor rioting at Clacton and newspaper columnists were urging the Government that if anyone got nicked at Brighton they should be gaoled. One old geezer in the House of Lords woke from his snooze, had to be helped to his feet before declaring that Mods should be publicly flogged. On the Friday night of the Whit weekend the whole Goldhawk Club was buzzing with Brighton. They were even discussing it in the toilets where French Blues and Drynamil were being sold in large quantities for the long weekend. The bar was packed with geezers making plans. Gaish bragged to his friends in a corner about the prospect about doing three months if he got nicked. I listened to the wisecracks and watched him hold court. The crowd in the corner was growing as each person after another verbally committed themselves to travelling to Brighton – 'for a giggle'. Some jester mentioned Holloway if any of the girls got nicked and Chris Covill was in like a shot: Holloway? Blimey, fancy doing three months there with all those women? Fuck the remission.' Even the club secretary Ted Woolgar who usually went about his business like someone with a bad gas pain couldn't resist smiling.

The Goldhawk Club

I must've told Gaish and anyone else who enquired that there was no way I was going down to Brighton. Of course Gaish had to be told over and over again. But he kept on about it and kept on telling me what I'd be missing out on. From what I'd heard about Clacton I didn't really fancy being herded along the pavements like cattle by the police. It seemed to me that half the Mods in the whole of London

were heading that way and I had no intention of being part of a shunted herd. When I mentioned this to Gaish he responded with 'Don't be daft, Jack. There'll be plenty of pills, there's the Aquarium and there'll be hundreds of birds all sleeping on the beach, some so cold they won't mind sharing a sleeping bag.' He might've been right but I had my mind made up and I had made plans for something else which I hadn't told him about yet.

By ten o' clock eighty per cent of the Goldhawk Club were committed to Brighton. Apart from the real bloody lunatics that wanted to set out for the coast at twelve midnight, most of those with scooters had promised lifts and others had planned to travel down by train the next day, Saturday. Gaish told everyone in the corner that he had arranged to go early Saturday morning with a friend who owned a mini-van. There was a hush as those in the group realised that nobody else had thought of such a practical way of travelling. Little Joey Bitton from the White City estate shook his head in genuine wonderment, saying 'A mini-van? Jesus, Martin, you don't half come up with them.' Terry Roche made everyone's feelings known as one of the girls jabbed him playfully in the ribs, 'You won't have much trouble pullin' someone tomorrow night then?' Suddenly Ian Moodie gave vent to a brain wave, 'Ere Martin, wanna hire out a fucking mattress?' Everybody laughed as Gaish soaked up the attention. 'It's been thought of already.'

Gaish looked down along the bar towards me. Our eyes met and he raised his eyebrows wondering if I had changed my mind. I looked straight back at him and carried on drinking. Gaish ignored me and turned to one of the McCarthy twins and appeared to whisper something humorous. I half expected what followed next as the McCarthy twin looked down towards me and said, ''Ere Jack, you coming along with us tomorrow?' Up until then I hadn't minded some of Gaish's jibes about me not going but what came next was like a knife in the back as he shouted along the counter for everyone to hear... 'Don't worry Jack - they've got a church down there.' The group in the corner sniggered as they pretended they didn't have a clue as to what Gaish was talking about. I finished my drink and walked out of the Goldhawk Club hoping that the stupid lot of them would get their silly fucking brains kicked in. Gaish especially.

Some girl I had gotten to know in the Goldhawk Club called Carol had invited me over to her house in Penge for the Sunday of the Whit weekend while her parents were away. Although it seemed like a pretty long way to travel from Penge to Shepherd's Bush for the Goldhawk Club, Carol would usually go Up West like a lot of others after the Goldhawk and return home by train Sunday morning. I knew I couldn't go wrong with this invitation. I packed a few half pint bottles of Watney's Brown and half a dozen Blues LP's under me arm. I was so horny about the whole thing

I just couldn't believe my luck. I arrived sometime in the afternoon. She was definitely up for it and so was I. We opened some of the bottles and everything seemed to be moving the way it was expected to. Then the phone rang in the hall and I said 'You don't have to answer that.' She giggled and said she had to ... just in case. I heard her talking in a surprised tone on the phone and stood by the room door trying to catch what was being said. 'Oh no, mum. That's terrible. Are you and dad alright?' My jaw dropped when she came back into the room and told me that her parent's caravan had been kicked to shit down in Hastings. And they were on the way home. The funny thing about it is that it would have taken bloody hours for her parents to get home what with the Bank Holiday traffic jams and -Jesus- she could've had bloody triplets in the time. But as soon as she heard about the caravan it put a damper on everything and I couldn't get her back into the mood. She mooched about between the kitchen and the sitting room as I watched a cowboy film on TV. I was sitting there wondering what to do next and the next thing I heard on the telly all the trouble down at Brighton. I leaned across and turned the telly up loud just to hear it. She came in from the kitchen and turned the sound down. I said, 'What the fuck are you doing? All my mates are down there.' And as I watched the newsreel showing TV cameramen running after Mods along the beach I felt a complete parasite sitting in a nice terraced house in Penge while all my friends from the Goldhawk Club were probably having the time of their lives. I knew I was in the wrong place. I turned to her and told her I was sorry I shouted. Told her I really had to go. She just ignored me and shifted the cushion behind her and stared straight ahead at the TV. I gathered up my LP's, let myself out and headed for the station.

I was so disgusted with myself. It wasn't until I reached the ticket barrier at Hammersmith that I realised I never bought a ticket at Penge, which had been British Rail. The old ticket collector looked really pissed off having to work on a long weekend. He put his arm out and asked me where I'd travelled from. I hesitated for a moment and then said the nearest station that came into my head... 'West Brompton.' I knew the fare wouldn't be much from there it was only a couple of stops. The old geezer looked back at me a bit wary and said, 'You'll have to think again cock, that stations closed on Sundays.' I mumbled something and looked around me in embarrassment to see who else was having a good smirk. There was nobody behind me so I decided to make a run for it and bolted towards the street exit. 'Oi!' The ticket collector called after me. When I reached the exit I shouted back in at him... 'Brighton, mate. That's where I got on. Fucking Brighton!' The old boy put a distress whistle in his mouth and started to blow. And that was the end of my Whit weekend - tear-arsing down the Shepherd's Bush Road like a lunatic with a half-dozen LP's under my arm. A romantic. A helpless dancer, that was me, always.

I didn't see a sign of Martin Gaish for a few weeks. Never saw him at the Goldhawk Club; never saw him Up West or the Hammersmith Palais. Someone told me he got a bit of a doing over. I didn't bother going round to his mum and dad's at Riverside Gardens; anyway I was still pretty well disgusted with what he had said to me about a church. Sometime later I spotted him along the King Street. He saw me and stopped. I got up close and saw the after-effects of a pretty bruised face. He looked a little embarrassed. 'Well, how did you get on at Brighton then?' I enquired with sarcasm. 'Well, you might as well know cos someone's gonna tell yer... I walked into a few fucking lamp posts dressed as rockers.' He was smiling. 'What about you? How did your bunk-up in Penge go? I heard.' 'Disaster. She was never really up for it ...' I replied, unconvincingly. 'Fancy a drink?' Gaish asked. 'Yeah, why not.' We walked along King Street towards the Builders Arms. Gaish turned to me and said, ''Ere Jack, you're not gonna go on rabbiting' about God, are yer? So there you are. I was at Brighton. And then again I really wasn't."

In true screen-to-life relativity Jack had been a clerk just like Jimmy's character in 'Quadrophenia'. Yet working for the London Electricity Board - a means to an end so typical of any aspiring Mod's day job utilisation - was a chore compared to Jack's Mod epiphany once he became transfixed and dedicated to The Who and the Mod lifestyle.

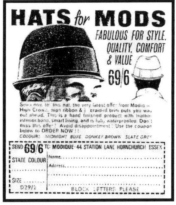

Soon becoming something of a regular mascot for the band, Jack travelled around with The Who for early outings, contributing in helping them set up, and avoiding becoming a roadie as in his own words 'I'm a bit of a snob like that'. Christened by Who manager Kit Lambert, Lyons was - remarkably - unaware of his nickname for a good while. However. the legions of Who fans and Mods alike are certainly aware of the enigma and legend that is Irish Jack Lyons.

By 1964 Mod was big commercial news as illustrated by these adverts of the period

Music, clothes and scooters - not forgetting the recreational medicinal fuels needed to enjoy these - all were paramount to a Mods lifestyle. The Mod was a true enigmatic individual that strove to be the best, yet often felt the timeless inner sexual and personal frustration of youth. If any group of the period came to symbolise the lifestyle of the Mods and reflected those frustrations and stuttering teenage angst - most potently with their debut Brunswick release 'I Can't Explain'- then that band must surely have been those volatile young friends of Irish Jacks - The Who.

THE WHO BY ROB NICHOLLS

For many The Who epitomised both the heyday and commercial height of 1960's Mod. With their musical and visual aggression, Tamla and R&B covers, mischievous boyish looks and a penchant for utilising (often belatedly) what their Mod audience was wearing - and a guiding light in their mentor Pete Meaden; they came to be recognised as the first identifiably and marketable Mod group. Whilst their early period was in parallel with what many would consider the demise of the underground Mod scene as it became increasingly over-commercialized - thus diluting its exclusivity and focus - nevertheless from mid-64 until the end of 65, The Who came to lyrically empathise with and dynamically represent their Mod fan base. Like a speeding aural and visual whirlwind, The Who captured the peak and stuttering cultural climax of the Mod generation! London Mod, Rob Nicholls was one of many at the time who succumbed to their enigmatic spell!

Rob Nicholls - "Some London Mods rose to national prominence as pop musicians, namely Rod Stewart, Davy Jones/David Bowie, Mark Feld/Marc Bolan, The Who, and the Small Faces. With a nod in direction of Georgie Fame, the Kinks, and Long John Baldry, no other British bands were truly Mods back in the day. The Who preceded the Small Faces and were the only real Mod band around for a while. In the spring of 1964, under the management of Peter Meaden they changed their name to The High Numbers and a few weeks before cutting their first record Meaden went to Guy Stevens' flat in Regent's Park and picked out a couple of suitable songs. Meaden chose Slim Harpo's 'Got Love If You Want It' and 'Misery' by the Dynamics. He prepared some new lyrics and changed the former to 'I'm The Face' and the latter to 'Zoot Suit.' These were released in July 1964. I dutifully bought the single but didn't enjoy 'I'm The Face' much, preferring Slim Harpo's version. The lyrics of Zoot Suit contained sartorial advice:

> 'And to get you wise I'll explain it to you,
> A few of the things that a Face is supposed to do.
> I wear zoot suit jacket with side vents five inches long,
> I have two-tone brogues yeah you know this is wrong.'

Mods never wore Zoot Suits, but this is a reference to the long sack-style jackets that came into vogue for a while at The Scene Club. I had a two-buttoned, long-lapelled, lining-less sack jacket in a light tawny-brown synthetic material. I also had two tone brogues in maroon and black. Concurrent with the release of 'I'm the Face,' in July 1964 the music journal *Disc* wrote -

> 'Hailed as 'the first authentic Mod record,' four hip young men called The High Numbers are out right now with 'I'm The Face,' backed with 'Zoot Suit' –a Fontana disc. Two numbers penned by co-manager Peter Meaden. How Mod are this Mod-mad mob? VERY Mod. Their clothes are the hallmark of the much-criticised typical Mod. Cycling jackets, T-shirts, turned-up Levi jeans, long white jackets, boxing boots, black and white brogues and so on.'

The High Numbers performed at Wolsey Hall in Cheshunt on 19 October 1964, but Meaden was soon bought out by a new management team of Kit Lambert and Chris Stamp and the group reacquired the name of The Who. During the latter half of the year, they were performing about four times a week with a series of Wednesday night gigs at The Scene. They played at the Marquee and the 100 Club in the West End and other London venues including the Goldhawk in Shepherd's Bush, St. Joseph's Church Hall in Archway, the Railway Club in Wealdstone, and Club Noreik in Tottenham. I saw them mostly at The Scene Club and Wolsey Hall. Their early shows consisted of R&B standards such as 'Daddy Rollin Stone' by Derek Martin, 'Ooh Poo Pah Doo' by Jessie Hill, 'Fortune Teller' by Benny Spellman, and 'Shout and Shimmy' by James Brown. They also included Tamla Motown material like 'Heatwave' by Martha and the Vandella's, 'I Gotta Dance to Keep from Crying' by The Miracles, and Eddie Holland's dynamic 'Leaving Here.' The Who rose to fame with a series of top ten hit singles, boosted in part by pirate radio station Radio Caroline and by appearances on Ready, Steady, Go! In January 1965, their self-composed 'I Can't Explain' was released and was followed in October by 'My Generation.' The lyrics reflected the Mod attitude ('Why Don't You All, F, F, Fade Away'). The Who continued to perpetuate the Mod ethos and is evident later, for e.g., in Townshend's existential 'Teenage Wasteland' ('Baba O'Riley' 1971).

For me, The Who were the seminal Mod Group, and Pete Townshend with his long face, big nose and cool hair was the most Mod looking and as a result he tended to be featured on posters more. Keith Moon with his round face and fringe also had the Mod look and was chirpy like the proverbial Cockney sparrow, while Roger Daltrey and John Entwistle were also Mods. Pete Townshend was a showman from the start. Early in his career he was creating feedback from his guitar, unconventional at the time and using his signature 'windmill' action of swinging his arm in a circular motion as a windup to striking a power chord on his guitar- the guitar smashing came later. Townshend's tempestuous guitar style first appeared in their version of Bo Diddley's 'Road Runner,' whereby the established guitar riff soon dissolved into an electronic cacophony. This noise was unfamiliar to us Mods and, conditioned as we were by Clapton's guitar solos, we weren't used to such unbridled improvisation; we preferred tight rhythmic numbers. But The Who looked the part and performed with such conviction that they won us over. There were some precedents. Some people point to rock 'n' roll guitarist, Link Wray as a formative influence and certainly, his instrumental, 'Rumble,' was popular among Mods. He is credited with inventing power chord guitar playing and is said to have inspired Neil Young and John Lennon as well as Pete Townshend. Accompanied by the metronome clicking of the bottle tops on the soles of his shoes, some of John Lee Hooker's early instrumental tracks pushed the electric Blues guitar to extremes and explored the outer-reaches of Blues tonality/atonality. Accompanied by Keith Moon's relentless drumming, Townshend's guitar solos also possessed this quality. In Pete Townshend's autobiography 'Who I Am', although not mentioning Link Wray, he does say John Lee Hooker's 'Devil's Jump' was among a few records he was 'listening to ... over and over again.'

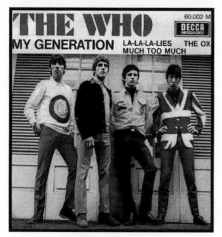

After they had established themselves with some hit records, The Who's performances became even more forceful and, urged on by their promoters, their act sometimes included Pete Townshend smashing his guitar into the speakers and Keith Moon knocking over his drums. In the aftermath of the skirmishes on the coast, the pundits argued that the Who's violence on stage embodied the aggression inherent in the Mod subculture, which sounds like nonsense to me. Personally, I didn't appreciate the guitar-smashing much. I felt it slighted many audience-members who would have loved to own a quality guitar, but couldn't afford it, and disrespectful of the craftsmanship that went into it. However, it was novel at the time and, followed by Jimi Hendrix's guitar burning, the visual spectacle of pop performances became increasingly epic in scope. The Who's fame grew internationally with memorable appearances at the Monterey Pop Festival in 1967 and Woodstock and Isle of Wight festivals in 1969. Pete Townshend had discovered performance art when he originally attended Ealing Art College, hence the Rock Operas Tommy (Pinball Wizard) and 'Quadrophenia'. The Who were early innovators in both the visual and audial dimensions. When released in 1979 the movie 'Quadrophenia' played a large part in the subsequent Mod Revival.

I had continued to attend The Who's shows until they became too popular to perform in small clubs. The last time I saw them live was late-1965 at the Marquee and it was too crowded for my tastes, but Peter Townshend and Roger Daltery recognized Mel and I as Faces from the small club days and had the good grace to come into the audience during the interval and chat with us for a little while and, although I didn't realize it at the time, this was in essence a form of goodbye."

That small but poignant farewell would prove to be profoundly significant. As early as their second single of May 1965, 'Anyway, Anyhow, Anywhere', The Who had been keen to move away from strictly Mod sensibilities, proclaiming Pop Art's influence as the way forward. Their December '65 debut long player 'My Generation' could be considered their Swansong to Mod, certainly by that stage the original Mod era was closing in. By their 1966 second album, 'A Quick One While He's Away's' closing mini-opera title track, the journey from Shepherds Bush Mod figureheads to the world stage of 'Tommy' and 'Woodstock' had begun! Meanwhile as The Who were recording their departure from Mod, another young group were releasing their own first records.

WHAT IS MOD? BY THREE SMALL FACES

For many, few other UK bands of the sixties captured the spirit of Mod as purely as the Small Faces. All, with the exception of Ian McLagan, were already ardent Mods prior to forming the band in 1965, their taste for Mod clobber being enhanced by the guiding hand of Jeff Dexter. Their lead singer was charismatic former 'Oliver' child actor, Steve Marriott - a pint-sized ball of energy and mischief with a voice that came to personify blue-eyed Soul. Ironically, the Small Faces were sadly rarely taken that seriously by a good proportion of original Mods due to their pop appeal, a stigma that they collectively despised. Releasing a diverse catalogue of, ultimately influential music - three studio albums and a collection of singles - the band imploded in 1968, their legacy and stature growing within the ensuing decades.

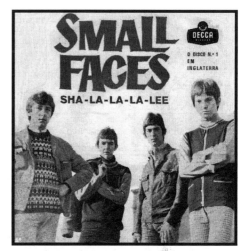

Steve Marriott - "I was a Mod; I had my anorak (a parka). I think to establish yourself, in the very early stages, clothes can really set an image for you, really work for you or it can make you a laughing stock. It was a cool thing while it lasted."

Kenney Jones - "We were all Mods before we formed the band, when we met up we were already Mods. We had all identified individually with what we wanted to be before we had actually met. It was absolutely amazing that when we all bumped into each other we all looked the same. Same taste in clothes, same taste in music and the same outlook generally. We were the first young generation to be born after the war and I remember growing up as a kid in black and white. Everyone wore black, white or sometimes grey. Our generation were the first to wear bright colours. We always wore bright things and it was acceptable to dye your hair as well. A lot of Mods actually dyed their hair blonde. It wasn't called dyed, it was called bleaching your hair back then. We actually used bleach, no hair dye from the chemist."

Ian McLagan - "By then Roger [Daltrey of The Who] was a real Mod. Pete [Townshend] had only just got out of art school so couldn't afford the clothes and John, of course, wasn't. Yeah, Daltrey was a Mod; he was quite a heavy little tough bastard! I wasn't a Mod until I joined the Small Faces. I was at art school, like Pete, and didn't have any money for clothes. It was like a brown corduroy jacket and jeans for me. There was a couple of guys at art school who had the parkas and scooters. I liked the clothes, well apart from the parkas. I thought they were stupid."

Steve Marriott - "I was one from around 1963. There weren't a lot of Mods to begin with, only a few around where I was living. I used to save up all my dough and go down to Carnaby Street. The funny thing about the street was that it was only a handful of dingy little shops early on and they used to import all their stuff from France. An actor mate of mine, who I used to hang around with at the Square Ring coffee bar in Manor Park, first turned me on to the place. He'd always turn up wearing all the latest gear but it was expensive. I had to save up for it. But really, we used to get laughed at. Me and Ronnie and Jimmy, Kenney wasn't really a Mod, used to get wolf whistles from geezers on building sites and my ol' man didn't like that. I mean it did take a lot of courage in those days. It was nice to be different, well that's the way I felt about it anyway. It's all to do with mates as well. I mean you look around and there's always one geezer that looks different. You clock him, ask him where he got the gear, he tells you, and you become a Mod without really thinking about it. That's the way it went."

Early Small Faces line-up with original member Jimmy Winston who was replaced by Ian McLagan

Kenney Jones - "I had my Mini then. I'd get home, park outside and all I did was clean it, polish it and put clocks and stuff on it. It was my extension of a scooter really."

Ian McLagan - "We could go down Carnaby Street and fill a taxi with shirts and jackets and hats and stuff. I just wish I had kept some of the gear. I remember a beautiful suede jacket with a leather collar. Actually, Kenney wore it on an album sleeve picture and then he gave it to me and I wore it for years. And some of the shoes and suits...Yeah!"

Steve Marriott - "We never tried to impress an image; it was just the way we were. I think the difference between us and groups like The Who was that they actually had managers that saw Mod and deliberately dressed them like that. We were just of the street. The Small Faces were what they were before anyone discovered them. We were just a little Moddy band whereas The Who actually got things bought for them. I thought The Who were great, it's only in retrospect that you can look back and see that Pete Meaden, a great mate of mine, and Kit Lambert kitted them out. But then you had the legitimate Mod bands like The Action they were of the same age as us and they were just off the streets as well, they were not groomed. There were a lot of bands that were groomed though, bands like Grapefruit and Johns Children, they were sent to go and get all these clothes from a particular shop. There was a lot of rotten, horrible bands that had a lot of money spent on them and they amounted to fuck all really. Out of that quagmire of bands the Small Faces came to the top because they were legitimate and I think it showed."

Steve Marriott - "Mod meant money. A way of life gone wrong. It went up its own arse. As soon as too much money gets involved, the people who are in it can't get into anymore, as soon as it starts to cost money if you see what I mean. Mod never really did cost money at first. You'd buy the cheapest things but in the style you wanted and then they'd start producing it because they realised there's a demand for it and then up the price. The whole original idea was to be individual and as soon as they started mass marketing the stuff and up pricing the hell out of it then the thing of being an individualist is lost. Mod was individual at the time, it's like saying that you want to be an individual but within a group. That's a contradiction but it's a good one. You want to be an individual but just a little bit, not too much just a little niche. It is down to the individual what they want to wear within some set rules. There were some set rules, no doubt about it, like the length of trousers, colour of socks, length and style of hair, that kind of thing. That was the code that said you were a Mod. The rest of what you covered your body with was up to you. But then it all got out of hand and, like anything, as soon as it got out of hand all was lost. The media gave us the name and called us Mods. We didn't know what the fuck it was, y'know, we just liked button downs and when I look back on it now it was fucking great!"

STEVE MARRIOTT interviewed by JOHN HELLIER in March 1985. IAN McLAGAN AND KENNEY JONES interviewed by JOHN HELLIER in February 2001

129

The Small Faces, like many other acts of the time, were understandably subjected to increasing media attention and seemingly endless magazine interviews and photo shoots. In some ways, the high profile given to 'pop stars' (a label that many artists despised, especially The Small Faces) would also prove to hinder their status and credibility with the Mods. This was a time of colour, glamour and pop music overkill; London was swinging by 1966 and many of young Mod's favourite bands would be swept up within the euphoria of the times. Britain led the way for the world in pop culture in 1966 - the high tide of commercialised Mod. Yet, away from the world of pop, most of the pop-afflicted acts could be caught performing the music they loved to the audiences that knew and appreciated them the most.

Derek Glover - "The place to be on a Friday night was the Whisky a GoGo in Birmingham. It later changed its name to The Pink Elephant but everyone called it 'The Whiskey'. Georgie Fame, Spencer Davis Group, the Moody Blues, The Steam Packet were almost regulars there. I also saw Ike and Tina Turner and Sony Boy Williamson play there too.

I remember one evening during 1965 arriving early at the club with my friend. The Small Faces were appearing and were unloading their equipment out of a van. We asked if we could help. They accepted our invitation and we helped to carry speakers, guitars and an organ up the stairs. The Faces were dead chuffed and thankful for our help. What a night, not only were we The Small Faces roadie mates, we also got in for nothing which was a fantastic extra bonus.

The first thing that struck me was that they were really small as their name suggested. Ronnie Lane was polite and grateful for our help. He asked if R&B would go down well with the local crowd, unaware that the Mod crowd would only require that of them. The organist was Jimmy Winstone and he set up a weird rotating box on top of his organ, which gave it a whirling sound, which can be heard on 'Whatcha Gonna Do About It'. He couldn't go wrong with the crowd when he played 'Green Onions'. Steve Marriot hammered out all the R&B standards of the time and kept everyone dancing. That's what most of The Whiskey Mods were there for - dancing their dance steps to their music.

Plonk wore tweed dogtooth hipster trousers with a wide belt that was red, white and blue striped. I had never seen a belt like that before - it was definitely Pop Art. I really wanted a belt like that, so I bought three rolls of electric tape, red, white and blue and stuck the tape along my existing leather belt and there I had one Pop Art belt. The Who were doing Pop Art and now I'd seen The Small Faces doing it, I loved it and even painted targets on the record labels of my 45s as they spun round on my Dansette, but only on records that were worthy."

Dennis Munday (left) - "The Bromel Club at the Bromley Court Hotel was another favourite with the southeast London Mods. The Who played there in '65, as well as the likes of Zoot Money's Big Roll Band, Kinks, Spencer Davis, Gary Farr & the T-Bones and Graham Bond. When The Small Faces made an appearance, they were in the charts with 'Whatcha Gonna Do About It', and only did the gig because it had been booked, well before the hit record. Girl's lined the front of the stage, with several screaming 'Stevie' and making a right soddin' nuisance of themselves, before the bouncers chucked them out. This kind of behaviour was OK when you're watching the Beatles, but not down The Bromel.

One summer's night we were in the club watching a band, suited and booted. I have no idea what the temperature was, but it was soddin' hot. We were wearing ties and the top two buttons of our jackets were firmly done up. I could feel the perspiration seeping through my shirt and jacket, but would I undo my tie? No way. On arriving home, there were large sweat stains under the armpits of the jacket, and the next day I took it to cleaners, as it needed to look pristine for next week's show.

There's one person who had a huge influence on me, and that's Georgie Fame; he was the 'Guv'nor' as far as I was concerned When a mate played me the 'Fame At Last' album, it knocked me out and I went to see him whenever he was playing. I saw him three times in seven days, once at that Black Prince and twice at The Ram-Jam club in Brixton. On the second night, a Sunday, the show was being filmed for French TV and it was free to get in. We had to wait a long time for the band to come on and we nearly missed the last train home, but it was a great gig.

On stage, Fame wore the pink and blue check button down shirt that he wore on the front cover of 'Sweet Things'. The line-up consisted of Pete Coe (ten), Glen Hughes (Bari), Edward 'Tan-Tan' Thornton, Nii Moi 'Speedy' Acquaye and Glen Barton (bass). The drummer was Mitch Mitchell, who would later join up with Jimi Hendrix. Incidentally, Barton was a top bass player at the time and died tragically young from drugs, as did Glen Hughes.

I was so into Fame that I bought a Hammond L100 organ, and started to take weekly lessons. After two years, I gave up and sold it. I could read music, and my teacher wanted me to take the exams and go to a music school. However, by then I'd discovered girls, and I didn't think I was going to make it. Mates have said, I should have carried on and joined a band, but it wouldn't have made any difference. Do I regret this decision? No, although, if I hadn't ended up in the record business, I might have. For me, Fame has never really received the accolades he's due. He was one of the first musicians to play the Hammond Organ in the UK. He fused Jazz with rhythm and blues into a unique sound of his own ... and he played Blue-Beat [Ska], before the 'Two-Tone' crowd were swinging in their Dad's trousers."

By the time bands such as The Who and The Small Faces and the vastly under-rated at the time The Action were being listened to and enjoyed on Dansette record players by Mods and pop fans alike, the original UK Mod scene had reached its peak. Exploding across the country into an uncontrollable money-orientated marketing tool, its original exclusive appeal and individualism now appeared diluted and compromised almost beyond repair.

Rob Nicholls - "The idiosyncratic creativity in dress of the original Mods was gone and it had become that Mod clothes could simply be bought off the rack at menswear shops in Carnaby Street and elsewhere."

Left: Early period Mod, Rob Nicholls with friends Jerry Tucker and Ann At Rockley Sands Caravan Park, 1963

Sid Poulton (photo across right) - "By 65 and into 66 Mod was becoming over commercialised. Guys were simply buying old scooters putting a parka on and calling themselves Mods. We referred to them as scooter boys. Also around this time a lot of the lads had cropped hair and certain newspapers started calling the younger Mods Skinheads, the first time I heard this phrase was in The London Evening News around 67 when it referred to trouble at the coast between rival skinhead gangs who were actually Mods."

Steuart Kingsley-Inness was another original period Mod. Steuart relocated his passion for the scene, moving to Bristol in 1966 and working as the resident DJ at the Bristol Locarno (left).

In defiance of Mod's mid-60's popularisation, Steuart held firm to his original commitment to the cause, the affirmation of self-belief remaining untainted.

Steuart Kingsley-Inness - "[Mod was] knowing who I was; what I wanted to say, and not giving a damn!"

Despite Mod's new-found status of popularity, its underground beginnings had created an undying code of style - one that had also been embraced by sections of the scene with a certain air of danger around them. Elements of original Mods, some of whom had fit the bill as Mods before they had even heard the term, still held their Mod ethics very closely to their heart. Stylists with an undying love and respect for mohair and their working class origins and territory.

CHAPTER 4

THE MAGIC OF MOHAIR

'Fast talking, slow walking, good looking' - **Mohair Sam**

John Leo Waters - "So goes the chorus of a Charlie Rich sixties song 'Mohair Sam' which is, in essence, a paean to the mohair suit. What is it about wearing a mohair suit that evokes a feeling of absolute sartorial elegance? Mohair the very word has an exotic ring to it! To anybody who came of age in the sixties it conjures up a picture of the ultimate in male chic. Of nights in clubs and Dancehalls absorbing the latest sounds attired in the iconic symbol of a generation - the mohair suit. What is mohair? Why did it come to represent the ultimate in sixties chic?"

Early Birmingham Mod Del Evans wearing self-designed mohair suit, 1964

Steuart Kingsley-Inness - "Back in the 50s, any man with a well-tailored suit was respected, he was going places. No wonder Modernists and later Mods based their look around them. Mohair had an 'exotic' edge to it: A touch of Italy, France, the US, even a touch of 'Showbiz'. It stood out, it shone in the light and it came in amazing colours - although midnight blue, sand and silver grey were early favourites. It looked great with good simple accessories. It held a sharp crease (except kid mohair). Whilst understated, it was in your face as well and above all it said 'Here I Am, Check me out!'"

The real thing: Gary Wood and John Reading (Mod friends of John Leo Waters) Nottingham Mod, Gary Maxton (1965) and bottom right, Del Evans, 1963

John Leo Waters lived the Mod lifestyle to his very core. Whilst being an acutely observant and meticulous purveyor of the Mod aesthetic, John also had a hard and uncompromising nature - embodying Mod's distinct street level edge of tough stature and lifestyle. His journey encompasses much of the scene's cultural growth, integrating its development from exclusive beginnings to the wide appeal of 1964 and beyond. Continuing his authoritative exposure of his experiences, John talks us through the importance, history and relevance of a Mod's most cherished fabric- mohair!

John Leo Waters - "Mohair is made from the hair of the Angora goat. Angora goats evolved originally from Tibet but came to Turkey in the 16th century. The goats were later introduced into USA in the mid nineteenth century. The USA is now the one of the world's main producer of mohair along with South Africa and Turkey. As material mohair has been in demand for much longer and there is evidence that the pharaohs of ancient Egypt wore clothing made of mohair. So King Tut was a Mod?

Mohair was introduced to Britain in the 8th century and during the industrial revolution, the mills of northern England became the world's leading exporters of mohair. The material itself has a wonderful sheen, which contributed to its popularity as suit material. Being lightweight, wrinkle and moisture resistant meant that mohair suits were the ideal fashion accoutrement for sixties teenagers who often spent his evenings in sweaty clubs dancing the night away.

It is difficult to determine exactly where and how the mohair suit became *de rigueur* for a generation of British teenagers. Undoubtedly, the wave of 'cool' Jazz musicians that emerged in the formative years of what became 'sixties pop culture' had an influence. Artists such as Charlie Parker, The Modern Jazz Quartet (left) and the ubiquitous Miles Davis were all to be seen sporting mohair suits. Italian style was an influential factor in the development of the sixties look. Innovative clothing outlets such as Cecil Gee had been championing Italian styled suits since the late fifties. Short 'bum freezer' three buttoned jackets and tight trousers often in mohair were a staple of their shop windows. Many influential US sixties musical heroes such as the Drifters, Otis Redding, The Temptations and Four Tops all appeared in publicity shots clad in mohair. Indeed, almost all the artists emerging from the flourishing Motown record label were clad in mohair. Whilst by no means an influence on the sixties teenage generation musical tastes it had to be said that even 'The Rat Pack' looked pretty 'cool' clad in shimmering mohair!

The influence of television should not be underestimated. By the turn of the sixties, the 'box in the corner' had become a welcome addition to many households. Early American TV series such as *'Route 66', '77 Sunset Strip', 'The Naked City'* and *'Johnny Staccato'* all featured the heroes decked out in sharp clothes. *'The Naked City'* and *'Johnny Staccato'* in particular were relevant to the emerging teenage penchant for the mohair suit. *The Naked City* starred Paul Burke as detective Adam Flint. Impeccably dressed with a button down shirt and tie and always wearing a suit, often made of mohair complemented with a narrow brimmed trilby, he cut a fine figure. It is easy to see how fashion conscious young teenagers could relate to the 'cool looking' characters. *Johnny Staccato* starred John Cassavetes as a Jazz pianist come private detective using *Waldo's* basement Jazz club as his office. The epitome of 'cool' Staccato was impeccably turned out and the smoky club with its resident band (featuring such Jazz luminaries as Barney Kessel and Shelly Manne) added enormously to the overall 'feel'. Set in Greenwich Village the club could just as easily have been transposed to Soho in the early sixties. The short-lived series was written in part by Stirling Siliphant (now that is a name!) who went on to do such sterling work in films such as *'In the Heat of The Night.'*

Back in the clubs of London's West End the burgeoning Mod movement wasted no time in noting the advantages of this wonderful new material and soon small-bespoke tailors all over the capital were being besieged by young Mods wanting to acquire their own unique suit made from mohair.

**John Leo Waters (far right photo) and main photo his, friends –
The Archway Boys, Terry Parker, Dougie Robinson, Gary Wood, Terry
Malone and John McCarthy in the Lord Nelson pub on Holloway Road**

Although the '*mohair suit*' came to be viewed as an item of Mod '*uniform*', in reality nothing could be further from the truth. Far from being uniform, every suit was tailored to the individual in so many different ways. Every mohair suit was made to precise requirements with regard to styling. The only common 'thread' was the material itself (I cannot believe I just used that phrase!). The style of the jacket was normally fairly uniform in length but in every other respect, no two were the same. The number of buttons on the cuff was normally three or four but some individuals opted for five as a mark of individuality. Two, three or four inside pockets were fitted according to taste. Jacket vents were almost obligatory. The single vent was very popular and lengths varied from six inches up to fourteen inches. The number and type of pockets was very important and normally consisted of two standard pockets and one ticket pocket (two ticket pockets were not uncommon). Pockets were usually slanting and the angle was again a matter of personal choice. The width of lapels had to be determined. Was a buttonhole required? Even the type of buttons was important. Buttons came in different colours and materials or maybe cloth covered? And let us not forget the lining! Silk linings were very popular and colours were many and varied. Often in a darker or lighter shade of the material colour but often, a complete contrast was used to great effect.

Trouser widths were fairly slim and usually between twelve and fourteen inches and never more than sixteen! Two waist pleats were fairly common but again very much left to personal taste. Side adjusters were often fitted. A small waist fob pocket was normal sometimes often with a buttoned flap. Rear pockets were usually a standard requirement and again a buttoned flap was quite popular. The length of the trousers was very important. When standing upright the trousers should just touch the throat of the shoe – just the right length to show enough sock without 'flapping in the wind' At various periods' small refinements were added to trousers. Stepped bottoms were an option at one point – where the rear sections of the trouser legs were 'stepped' down between a half and a full inch. Another variation was small 'vents' up to an inch long at the bottom of the seams.

Finally there was the material itself. Mohair came in a variety different mixtures and colours. Mohair suits were normally available in two or three ply signifying the number of yarns or cloths used to manufacture the material. Mohair was mixed with worsted or polyester to produce a different finish. Sometimes different coloured yarns were combined to great effect resulting in the 'two tone' effect. Tonik mohair was the *piece de resistance.*

Tonik was Dormeuil's trade name for tonic, they were a fine cloth manufacturers founded in Paris in 1842, and they specialized in supplying finely woven fabrics sourced globally. In 1926 they centred their operations at Dormeuil House, off Regent St and in 1957 they introduced Tonik to the world. Basically a three-ply mixture of mohair, the secret lay in the purity of the raw materials they sourced. With a reputation for producing '*the world's best clothes*' Dormeuil Tonik mohair was the Holy Grail for any discerning young Mod.

The material itself was only half the equation, of course. Just as important was the tailor. All over the country small corner shop tailors (usually Jewish) were the preferred choice of young Mods in search of perfection. Although it was possible to have a suit 'made to measure' at High Street chain stores such as John Collier and Burtons at a cheaper cost than bespoke, the thought of faceless factory cutters and machinists 'knocking up' suits on piecework was no substitute for the loving care afforded by the smaller tailor.

Being born and brought up in Islington, North London we had a plethora of good quality tailors within a stone's throw. By far the best was Aubrey Morris. Aubrey Morris had a little shop on a small parade at the bottom of Holloway Road next to Highbury Corner. The slightly tired looking shop façade belied the treasures that were held within! A large cutting table in the centre of the shop was surrounded by bolts of cloth piled to the ceiling. Every hue and type of material was to be found although only Aubrey himself knew exactly where!

A small bespectacled man, Aubrey Morris was the archetypal '*east end*' tailor, if such a thing existed. Assisted by his son, he worked at breakneck speed with a dexterity and eye for detail that was hard to match. He was not shy in telling the world what a good tailor he was and would regale clients with stories of how well known local singers such as Chris Farlowe and The Equals had all been in to get measured for suits. We tended to take his tales with a pinch of salt but I had the opportunity a couple of years ago to ask Chris Farlowe if he remembered Aubrey and he went off at a tangent describing a 'wonderful silver grey Tonik suit' that Aubrey Morris had made for him!

Every item made was a labour of love. All his garments were hand finished with beautiful stitching that was perfection in itself. Suits always required at least two fittings and could take up to a month to completion after initial 'measuring up'. Prices were not cheap and a standard two-ply suit would set you back around twenty five guineas! Small potatoes in comparison to today's marketplace but when one considers that the average wage would be around £15 a week and young teenagers would be getting far less than that, then one can appreciate the cost in real terms.

There was no way of rushing Aubrey. Endless trip to phone boxes in attempts to hurry things along were always in vain. Then finally the words we had waited to hear – 'The suit is ready'. The trepidation as we made our way down to Highbury Corner, the approving looks on the faces of friends as the garment was brought down from the rail, and finally the feeling of absolute contentment as the jacket was slipped over your shoulders – a perfect fit! Who could forget the first time they stepped out wearing their new Tonik suit. The envious looks from our contemporaries and the admiring glances of the young ladies!

'Fast walking, slow talking, good looking' – You had better believe it!

The expensive mohair suit did not come cheap. Although Mods by and large worked in full-time jobs, the lucrative side-line of dealing in pills provided an extra income and occasionally led to more dangerous means of supporting that option.

John Leo Waters - "We had many ways of making money – some turned to burglary, others to robbery and others to less dangerous occupations. At one stage I was employed to keep 'doggo' for street vendors selling Pop art jewellery on Oxford St. This was a nice easy 'earner'. I simply kept an eye out for 'Old Bill' whilst my mate sold the goods out of a suitcase. We met up with our Guv'nor every morning in a café in Soho. He would dole out the material – mainly cuff links, ear rings etc. – from the back of his van and off we would go. We were on commission and if caught the worst the seller could expect was a small fine. The only problem was that the material might be confiscated and in that case the debt had to be repaid and the gentleman we were working for was not the type to accept excuses! Another little scam we had going was working as casual labour for a well-known removal company. We had a friend working in the office who would inform us when there might be a lucrative job due. We would queue up outside in the morning and make sure we were picked for the right trip. The pay was 50 bob a day (£2.50 in modern money) but the pay was of little consequence.

One of the better jobs was moving a small workshop to West London. They specialized in silver plating ladies dressing table sets (all quality stuff). We made a nice killing on that particular job! We were never too greedy though as one had to be careful or we might get no more work!

We had all kinds of schemes going - another one was Record Vouchers. A young lady I knew worked in the record department of a well-known electrical shop and she would supply us with large books of vouchers. We travelled all over London exchanging vouchers for LP's which we had on order from customers at half price. That lasted for a couple of months until the unfortunate young lady got the sack! Of course a lot of the shenanigans we got up to were much more serious such as smash and grabs (the London smog had its advantages!) and shop breaking."

....

Dennis Munday - "In early '65, I acquired my first tailor made two-piece suit, from Alexandre's in Powis Street, Woolwich. It was on the 'never-never' and after putting thirty-bob down, I paid a five bob a week until it was paid up. It was a blue Mohair/wool mix, the jacket had three buttons, and ten-inch side vents. The pockets were slanted and on the right hand side, a ticket pocket. The trousers were self-supporting, with one pleat, a French bearer, and 16-inch bottoms. I used to buy my shirts from a little shop in Powis Street, although American button down shirts were out of my price-range, and I had to settle for copies, or Ben Sherman's. One thing that is true, if the Labour government hadn't amended the Hire Purchase Act in 1964, the Mods couldn't have afforded their clothes, scooters etc. We bought everything on hire purchase.

By the spring of 1966, there were two more mohair's in the wardrobe, one in green, and a nice maroon number. For some reason my Father objected to this colour and told me to return it to the tailors. I pointed out to him that it was tailor-made and the shop wouldn't take it back, which pissed him off no-end."

How about the Rockers?

John Leo Waters - "Rockers, Greasers call them what you will, they were the sworn enemies of all things Mod. Greasy long hair, leather jackets, motorbikes, rock 'n' roll – all these things represented the very antithesis of all things Mod. The Rocker has, thankfully, almost ceased to exist as a sub culture. The bikers of today bear little resemblance to the leather jacketed greasers of the sixties!

There were no Rockers around the Archway, or if there were they kept themselves well hidden! In fact it was extremely rare to even see a Rocker on our turf! The Rockers tended to keep to their own encampments. The Ace Café was the most famous of these and although only a few miles from our manor it was considered to be strictly 'out of bounds'. Another venue was the Busy Bee up by Watford. Both these cafes were close to the M1 which made them ideal for Rockers wishing to 'do the ton' up the motorway!

Another enclave was the 59 Club, which, if memory serves me right, was run by a vicar down in Hackney! That a vicar should be running a youth club for tearaway bikers always seemed rather strange to me! The club moved over to Paddington at one time before going back to Hackney. There were even photos in the press of the vicar blessing Rockers and their bikes in church! God must have been a bit of a Rocker! There were various other smaller divisions of greaser gangs around the capital usually based around greasy spoon cafes and usually on the outskirts where they were able to use their bikes with comparative freedom.

We had occasional run-ins with Rockers but these tended to be 'off the manor'. One such incident came when we were asked to back up another gang at Ally Pally. Alexandra Palace was a venue that tended to be used by Rockers. There was a fairground and roller skating rink there. Fairgrounds always seemed to attract Rockers. I am not sure why but there were always a fair few in attendance be it at Hampstead Heath Fair on Bank Holidays or the Kursaal at Southend – there were always Rockers! It was a strange situation, in that surrounding gangs such as the Highbury mob were our sworn enemies but it was an unwritten agreement that certain destinations were deemed to be neutral ground – a no man's land almost. Soho was one of these and another was St Pancras Boxing Club. Several of our number trained at the club as did members of the Highbury mob and it was an unwritten law that any 'bovver' was restricted to the ring!

Major battles between Mods and Rockers were few and far between. There were odd confrontations such as the '*Battle of Upper St*' but these were blown out of all proportion by the press and were usually no more than minor skirmishes. We tended to keep to our own 'patch' as did the rockers but on occasions the two cultures would clash. One such altercation was at the Gatehouse pub in Highgate. The pub had a large back room and it was decided to put it to use by holding a dance. Of course, being on our manor we attended. So to, did a small group of Rockers. Needless to say a fight broke out and the Rockers were put to flight. The occasion only sticks in my mind because as the Rockers were being chased I picked up a lump of concrete from some road workings and aimed it at the head of one of the fleeing Rockers. It missed him completely (I was rubbish at cricket also!) and promptly hit my best mate full in the face! What a mess – there was claret everywhere. Luckily no lasting damage was done but several years passed before I broke the news that it was I that had caused his 'war trophies'!

The Bank Holiday fair at Hampstead Heath was another choice of destination for gangs of Mods and Rockers. Fairgrounds have traditionally attracted gangs of teenagers and still do for that matter but Rockers seemed especially keen. I am not sure if it is the adrenalin rushes of the rides or the music pumping out or a combination of both but fairgrounds and violence seem to go hand in hand.

A few of us 'worked the fair' on Bank Holidays. I worked on the *Pirate Ship*. This was an early forerunner of today's rides. The ship held about twenty or so and there were no harnesses or safety belts. The rope mesh around the upper sides were all there was to hang on to! It was my job to collect the fares. This had to be done whilst the ride was in motion and involved leaning into the direction of the boat as it swung up and down! We had to learn how to jump from the boat onto the wooden platform as it swung past on its downward motion – no health and safety in those days! Of course there was an ulterior motive! When we returned change to screaming punters they would inevitable shout 'put it in my bag' or 'put it in my pocket' as they were hanging on for dear life. So we were able to pocket a little extra but then that is expected at fairgrounds?

Gangs from all over North London would attend the fair over the holiday period and fights were common. Of course, the one gang nobody picked a fight with were the fairground workers! They were a tough bunch and if there was a confrontation with one then it was with them all. Rockers would make their presence felt at the Heath. They would arrive in sufficient numbers to be a major threat. Several times over the weekends there would be outbreaks of sporadic violence usually in the surrounding fields where police presence was limited. Although major clashes were avoided the local ambulance crews were kept busy!

One occasion when we came face to face with our *deadly enemies* was on a trip to High Wycombe. A girl I was seeing at the time told us of a party in High Wycombe. Now High Wycombe was way out in the sticks as far as we were concerned (in fact most of us had no idea where it was!). In those days 40 miles was a looong way! Four of us decided to take a trip up there with a couple of the girls in tow. We had no invitation of course but ... hey, who was going to stop us?!! We duly arrived at the house and barged in only to find the whole building was full of greasers! Talk about 'doing a wrong 'un!' We thought we were in for a good kicking but to our surprise the guy running the party came over and made us welcome. We were absolutely gobsmacked to put it mildly. We had a great evening and even managed to shift a lot of gear (who said Rockers didn't do drugs!). As a mark of our respect we didn't even steal anything!

At one time I was seeing a girl that lived on a housing estate in Hornsey Rise. I would spend quite a bit of time on the estate where the two local 'hard boys' were a couple of die hard Rockers. Through the girl I got to meet the two guys in question and over a relatively short period we became good mates! They loved their music as we did albeit a different type. They were rebels and chose to show their rebelliousness in the way they dressed and behaved. The comparisons with our own Mod culture were there to see for all. The only difference was that they had chosen one path and we had chosen another. Both paths were different but the goal was the same! But enough philosophy – they were Greasers and we were Mods and never the 'twain shall meet!"

Away from the presence of Rockers, John continues his Mod escapades: venturing into far darker and potentially dangerous areas and clientele – right at the centre of the raw unforgiving fast lane of sixties Soho at its height.

John Leo Waters - "We had started frequenting the clubs in the West End - The Flamingo, La Discotheque, the Marquee and The Scene. Soho in the sixties was very place different from the trendy 'village' it is today. Where nowadays the area is full of bijou restaurants back in the sixties it was full of sleazy clip joints and clubs. The streets were thronged with prostitutes and their punters, pimps, tourists, gangsters and of course Mods. What is now a relatively safe corner of the capital was then a very different proposition. Stabbings and 'stripings' were commonplace. Muggings and beatings were rife whether for cash or drugs or more often where strip joint customers had 'made a complaint' about being ripped off!

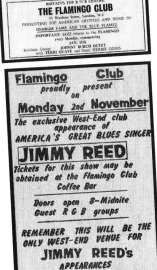

In addition we made forays into the East End. Pubs such as The Green Gate, The Two Puddings, The Ship, The Salisbury all featured live bands. Occasionally we might go for something a little different like The Duragon (live comedians) or the Top House in Tottenham for drag artists. Inevitably we began to mix with what I can only term as real villains.

We looked up to these people. They seemed the epitome of cool. Always 'booted and suited' and as often as not sporting Crombie overcoats, handmade shoes and shirts, they seemed to have money to burn and above all they commanded respect (albeit through fear!). It wasn't long before we began to visit drinking dens (or nightclubs as they were called!) such as The Regency Club, City Club and ill-fated Tempo Club.

We combined the 'gangster look' with our own Mod fashions. Velvet collared overcoats were popular although we fell well short of being able to afford true Crombie's. I took to wearing a pork pie trilby. A nice white silk cravat with matching silkie set off the effect nicely. We may not have been able to afford Anello and Davide but we could afford to do the next best thing and shop at Ravel!

Looking good cost money and we became increasingly involved in criminal enterprise to support our lifestyle. By now I moved into a small flat in Highgate and had embarked on several small scams locally, which brought in enough money to pay the rent and living expenses.

London fogs were still quite prevalent and would give an excellent opportunity to carry out 'smash and grabs' when the covering fog would make the risk of being spotted much less and help deaden the noise. We even tried our hand at safe breaking! A little team broke into an office in Highgate and attempted to blow the safe. They were disturbed and were forced to abandon the attempt. The local paper quoted a police inspector as saying that there was enough explosive packed around the safe to 'blow half of Highgate off the map!!'

There were times, of course, when we let our 'hair down' so to speak. On Bank Holidays we would dress in something a little less formal like levis and Fred Perry's. We would catch a train down to Brighton or maybe head up to Hampstead Heath fair. In Brighton we would indulge in mindless violence fuelled by drink and drugs. Mindless rioting was the norm at the expense of any poor unfortunate who happened to get in the way. Hampstead Fair was similar in that we were simply looking for trouble. As often as not it would be with rival gangs but occasionally a gang of Rockers might put in an appearance and we would all join forces to fight the common enemy. Most fights were no more than a lot of 'posturing' and we would be put to flight by the local constabulary before any real violence occurred but there were odd skirmishes when blood would be spilled!

Inevitably perhaps, my criminal career came to abrupt end when I was arrested on several counts and ended up at the Old Bailey where I was sent down for Borstal training. I have read several theories that the 'hard Mod' originated in Detention Centres and Borstals. That is a misguided conception. These institutes were full of Mods and Rockers and everything else in between! The inmates arrived fully equipped with their share of attitude rather than obtaining it whilst inside! I was ensconced in a maximum establishment where we were initially subjected to a harsh regime, which was meant to break the spirit of any so called 'hard nuts'. It was very hard, of course. Getting up a six o'clock and running around the snow laden parade ground in vests, shorts and army boots was not my idea of fun!

Of course the Mod population tended to group together. Their similar tastes in music, clothes and lifestyle were a great bonding tool. Obviously it was difficult to maintain an 'appearance' inside but a little tobacco here and a 'bob or two' there ensured that there were decent creases in our trousers and haircuts were neat and tidy rather than 'basin' style. Old habits die hard and I was soon involved in several little schemes to make life a little more comfortable!"

HERE COMES THE WEEKEND!

One thing is for sure, despite the almost-mythical and much-celebrated focus on the Mods' passion for the weekend - the often-clichéd ideal - this time, it is perfectly true. Counting down the days from the dreaded gloom of Monday morning's drastic come-down, Mods existed amidst numerous types of weekday jobs, earning and surviving throughout the humdrum of the 9 to 5 - with only the possibility of a mid-week excursion to some favoured club or dance hall. For those graced with extra energy and enthusiasm, a swift indulgence in lunch-time music sessions was an option: in any case, the Mod with few exceptions fully embraced the forthcoming weekend.

Steuart Kingsley-Inness - "There was plenty of work around but much of it was blue collar and hard. Barrow boys, tradesmen, physical labour of all kinds; the hours were also long for most. There were many who went up West during the week or local clubs, but most of us looked forward to 'The Weekend' the most. Cash in pocket, suited and booted, London was our playground and we were going to make the most of it as, by Monday, it was time to 'Come Down' and back to the graft. Ah well, only five more days."

John Leo Waters - "Saturday night was what we all lived for. All week we would look forward to the weekend. Friday evening would always start with 'Ready Steady Go!'. Often cited as a Mod institution, in our eyes nothing was further from the truth! We considered the programme to be pants! Staffed by presenters we considered to be totally at odds with everything truly Mod. Keith Fordyce looked like someone's grandfather, Cathy McGowan (self-proclaimed Queen of the Mods) was some 'posh bird' who had no street cred and according to all the Mod girls we knew had no influence whatsoever.

Then there was Patrick Kerr - showing everybody how to dance! Please! Go into any West End club on a Saturday night and one could see the real dancers! It's a bit like Lionel Blair giving instructions to Northern Soul fans on how to dance at Wigan Casino! No, the only reason we watched 'Ready Steady Go!' was the music. The programme featured many of the artists we had come to revere. I can remember James Brown, Otis, Prince Buster, Sonny Boy Williamson, Marvin Gaye, Supremes, Martha and the Vandella's, Solomon Burke plus all the UK R&B bands like the Stones, Animals, Kinks etc.."

John Water's girlfriend Pauline (centre) with friends, Linda Cook (left) and Mary Nicholson (right) in the mood for Newcastle's Club A 'GoGo in 1965

Away from the popular appeal of 'Ready Steady Go!' and the clubs of the capital were venues such as Newcastle's Club A 'GoGo which opened up in 1962 on the top floor of a Percy Street building. Like most of its southern counterparts the club was originally a Jazz club (A pre-Animals Eric Burdon performed in the Jazz Lounge there), but by the following year the club's Jazz policy was dropped once American Blues artists Sonny Boy Williamson and John Lee Hooker performed on stage, soon to be followed by touring acts of the time including Mod favourites The Graham Bond Organisation, Spencer Davis Group, The Who, Georgie Fame, Rolling Stones, John Mayall's Bluesbreakers and Soul stars Wilson Pickett and Ike and Tina Turner. The resident group were the Alan Price Combo soon to be The Animals and later on, in 1964, Newcastle's other home grown group, The Junco Partners (Below). The club was the authentic port of call for a generation of Mod and Beat group fans. The 'Marcus Price' shop (only a few doors down from the club) sold clothes to the Mods. Sadly as the 60's came to a close, like the decade itself, the venue had lost its magic vibe.

Newcastle Mods The Junco Partners

John Leo Waters - "Friday night would sometimes be spent visiting pubs – many of which featured live bands. The Green Man in Bethnal Green or The Two Puddings in Stratford or perhaps the Angel, Edmonton or the Somers Arms in Kings Cross or even further afield like the Apples and Pears at the Elephant and Castle. We had to be careful as we were on foreign 'turfs'. Occasionally we might venture into dancehalls such as the Tottenham Royal or the Downbeat in Finsbury Park or even out in the sticks to Watford Top Rank or the Stevenage Locarno.

Occasionally we might get an invite to a Blues party. One of our number worked as a butcher in Hornsey Road. The shop had a large West Indian clientele and he developed a good relationship with the ladies. This led to invites to Blues parties. These parties were held at the house or flat of the lady in question. There was a small entrance fee and once inside we were able to buy curried goat and rice and Red Stripe lager (all at a cost of course!). The organizer made a little money and these were great nights featuring some fabulous music. Blue beat (early Ska) was the order of the day and it was at these parties we were introduced to the music of Derek and Patsy, Higgs and Wilson, Derrick Morgan, Laurel Aitken, The Folks Bros and the mighty Prince Buster.

But it was Saturday that was the highlight of the weekend. We would meet up in the pub early in the evening and draw up our battle plans. As far as I was concerned there was only one final destination - Wardour St. Wardour St on a Saturday night - the pavements were alive with prostitutes and their minders, nervous looking punters, doormen, touts, villains, a few tourists and hundreds of Mods all looking for excitement.

The quest for the 'buzz' meant different things to the many characters that thronged Wardour St but to the Mods it meant the clubs! The Flamingo, La Discotheque, The Scene, the Last Chance, The Marquee, Ad Lib, London Cavern – all within a few hundred yards of each other. There were the coffee bars - The Coffee An, Le Macabre, Freight Train, 2 I's - pubs such as the Intrepid Fox and the Eagle - all full of Mods with one thing on their mind - to have a good time!

The excitement of entering a club for the first time – walking up the stairs to La Discotheque, handing over my cash then the door was opened. Stepping into the darkness, dozens of sweating bodies dancing in a frenzy, the heat was oppressive and then there was the music! The opening bars of 'In the Midnight Hour' earthy, edgy almost dangerous – I was hooked for life. This was where I belonged!

Mods of the period and Solomon Burke

My first experience of a Soul giant live - Solomon Burke at the Flamingo. Struggling to get near the front, pushing through the crowd. The band taking the stage resplendent in their mohair suits. Suddenly there he is dressed in all his finery. The ermine robe and the crown – the King of Rock and Soul! I can remember little of the next hour until finally the band break into opening bars of 'Everybody Needs Somebody to Love'. The crowd goes wild. Solomon beckons a young lady to join him. It's Dusty Springfield! They bring the crowd to a new high.

Then all too soon it's all over. King Sol has gone and Dusty is back at her table with Madeline Bell. A night that will live in my memory for ever! It seemed that this was all we ever wanted in life. The music, the clothes – it could not get any better, could it?"

HARD MODS DID THEY REALLY EXIST?

The term 'Hard Mod' is undoubtedly one that has been used belatedly as a reference to the mid-60's period onwards Mod that influenced and merged into the style of the early skinhead. These Mods were committed to the sharper, shorter-hair style and 'spartan' basics of Mod's origins, eschewing the Dandy-leaning extravagances of elements of the London core of Mod Faces for a smart, more casual but no less visually dynamic look. Predominantly working class purveyors of taste and style they perhaps perfectly exemplify the over-used Pete Meaden declaration of - 'Clean Living under Difficult Circumstances'.

In some aspects this return to street wise Mod sensibilities was a direct response to the over-commercialisation of Mod post-1964. In relation to this revival of Mod's profile, it is also a fact that a fair proportion of 60's Mods could be classed as hard of nature, thus re-enforcing the popular description of the Mod transition to skinhead as being of a harder Mod persuasion.

John Leo Waters - "So, was there such a thing as a 'Hard Mod'? Well, certainly there were plenty of Mods who could be considered to be 'Hard'. It very much depends on what your conception of the term is. If, as is generally accepted, it means somebody who is able to look after themselves physically then yes, the term certainly has validity. However, if the term is to be applied to a sub – culture then I would have to disagree. I do not believe there was a specific genre that could be termed thus. The fact is that there have always been gangs of delinquent teenagers. They may have been Teddy boys or Punks in the past or Hoodies today but they do not constitute a culture in their own right. They are simply one small part of a whole rather than a body in their own right."

The term 'Hard Mod' has been bandied around for quite some time now and has almost been given credence a sub culture in its own right. I have been labelled (*by others I hasten to add*) a 'hard Mod' so I felt I had a 'duty' to try to ascertain just what the label actually represents. So what is a hard Mod? Did they really exist or was it simply a convenient label for a hard core hooligan element?

The term 'hard' has many different meanings but various dictionaries refer to the term in this context as '*someone who shows no fear and can look after themselves in a situation*' another definition is '*naturally tough, strong minded*'

In the world I grew up in 'hard men' were usually violent criminals who refused to conform or submit to authority, men who would stand their ground no matter what. In fact, the kind of person you would like 'watching your back' in a fight. Stories of legendary fighters abounded in our circle. Local villains would go up West to '*pick fights*' with bouncers just for the sheer hell of it.

Of course the term 'Mod' needs no explanation but one interesting definition describes Mods as *'sixties group noted for their clothes consciousness often as a symbol of their alienation for conventional society'* Descriptions such as this merely give credence to the theory that Mods were a gang of delinquents. Of course nothing could be further from the truth. The vast majority of sixties Mods were just normal everyday teenagers who enjoyed dressing up in the latest fashions, dancing to the latest sounds and having a good time generally. Exactly the same behaviour you would expect from teenagers the world over in any era.

The media had a field day building up the myth of the wars between Mods and Rockers. The Bank Holiday invasions were seized upon by the press and given massive coverage depicting Mods as nothing better than a drug crazed mob bent on violence and creating mayhem. Of course, there was a grain of truth in the garbage spewed out by the press. There were a hard core of Mods whose sole purpose in visiting Brighton, Margate and the rest was to create anarchy. I must admit I was a part of that core. So what constitutes a 'Hard Mod' if such a thing really existed and what made them so different from the majority. Well, I can only draw on my own experiences to attempt to answer that question.

I was fifteen years old and the 'sixties' were coming into their own. There were jobs a plenty for those who wanted them. I had fifteen jobs in that first year although to be fair some only lasted a day or two! The shortest, in fact, only lasted two hours! I was now a fully-fledged member of the Archway and we ruled our 'manor' ruthlessly. There were strict borders between the various gangs in North London. Our closest rivals were the Highbury and the Somers Town gangs. The Highbury in particular were our sworn enemies and fights and incursions were commonplace.

By now the Mod revolution had taken off and we were quick to embrace this new revolution. We had been brought up in the austere post war years where 'make do and mend' was the ethos our parents lived by. Suddenly there was a life for teenagers! Music, Clothes, Clubs were all accessible – all that was needed was money! Most worked for their rewards but I had decided that work was for losers!

Reputation was everything. I had taken to carrying a weapon (an axe) and had shown willingness to use it when required. A reported fracas in a local burger bar ended with a guy being injured with an axe. The assailants fled and the injured party was taken to hospital. Some friends of his returned later that evening looking for the offenders. I was ensconced in a local pub when a member of our little fraternity ran into the pub telling us of the incursion. We were not interested but he wanted to go down with a few others to 'sort them out'. He borrowed some tools including mine and went off to getting himself arrested in the process. This guy was a member of a well-known South London family but as soon as he was given a slap in the cells he blamed everybody else and claimed the weapon was mine! I was put on an identity parade where a waiter picked me out (after being *advised* by the local constabulary!). I found myself on a charge of attempted murder! Of course, by the time the case came to court matters had sorted themselves out. The waiter decided to tell the truth and that he was mistaken and our other 'friend' told the court he had simply implicated me in a panic. The case was quite rightly thrown out.

This gained great kudos from my contemporaries but reputations have to be maintained and there were many moments when I came very close to being caught by our adversaries but only on one occasion did I come out on the wrong side of a good hiding when I was ambushed by four members of the 'Tolly Park' (a small local gang aligned to the Highbury mob). I received a few lumps and a badly scored face where one guy had given me a 'wash and brush up' with a wire brush!!

Having a reputation could as often as not serve as a deterrent to others and if you could enhance that by waving an axe around whilst screaming and shouting threats then that was often enough to put adversaries to flight! Of course, it was not enough to 'talk the talk' - one had to look the part also. The 'look' became all important. The mohair suit was almost obligatory preferably Tonik and lovingly tailored by the right artisan."

Of course the spectre of violence was not always as prevalent or participated in by all members of the Mod community.

Rob Nicholls - "Regarding violence, or in my experience, lack of it. In the London Mod clubs that I went to I didn't witness much. Apart from an enclave at 'Alley Palley,' there were hardly any Rockers in London. Alexandra Palace was a roller-skating rink housed in a monumental building on top of a hill in North London that also served as a broadcast tower, and some Mod firms would harass the Rockers from time to time. I heard about a bunch of Rockers from the provinces that came into town for a night out and somehow wound up at The Scene where they proceeded to poke fun at the 'prissy' Mods. The Mods rose up en masse and I was told 'pushed them through the walls.'

I've heard reports about punch-ups in Ham Yard and Mods being mugged in Soho for their leather coats, but I couldn't afford a leather coat and remained unaffected. John Leo Waters lived in Upper Holloway and was a member of the Archway mob in the early-mid sixties. He differentiates between scooter boys and 'Hard Mods' and identifies himself with the latter. Hard Mods, according to John Leo Waters, 'would not be seen dead on a scooter, their preferred mode of transport being a car.' They belonged to Mod 'firms' or street gangs each with their own manor, e.g. the Highbury mob, the Archway, Somers Town, Elephant and Castle, Mile End, etc.' Apart from Mod/Rocker enmity, Mod on Mod violence sometimes occurred, as Mod, David Birchall, remembers. 'The Harvest Moon Club was the main centre for Mod action in Guildford, thirty miles SW of London, and played a good selection of Blue-beat.' David recalls one night when some guys came down from Mile End in East London in a Ford V8 Pilot: 'They got into an argument with some locals and the next thing they are pulling claw-headed hammers out of their inside pockets. They beat the shit out of several friends of mine. We had not experienced this degree of violence before and it was a wakeup call. We waited for them to come back but they never did.'"

Paul Clay - "In my experiences, it was often more a case of more chasing than actually fighting. There was one real bad exception to this when I was set about by around thirty rockers in the town square. In fairness I was a cocky little shit. Me and my mate were heading that way, I thought 'they are not stopping me passing to where I wanna go' and as I passed one hit me in the cheek and some of the others joined in. Mind, I gave as good as I got, they started it and I just wanted to pass by. I was carrying a stone-coloured Mac of mine and as I got up, and people dragged people off, I was more concerned by that as it was ruined in the scrap. But considering the amount of time we spent out and about the real violence was quite rare. The violence thing was all because of the papers and their headlines of Mods and Rockers scraps on the beaches. If that is all Mod is remembered for, well, I have to say, it's a sad and sorry state to remember it by."

Steuart Kingsley-Inness - "Sadly history has defined our early days by the seaside violence and the 'Mods v Rockers' spectacle, but history has it wrong. It's all a part of growing up for young males to be aggressive, ask the army! Also once given a choice of 'causes' and sides will be taken. Sure fights took place, not just on the beaches, but also in the clubs and on the streets. But for many, myself included, Mod was more than that; it was a release from the old ways, it was a way forward. With girls, clothes, music and good times to be had ... well why waste your time 'rolling in the dirt' for no sensible reason? In the end, the scrapping caused many to leave the scene altogether."

So did Hard Mods exist, was the question? As John Water's honest and constructive insights, and others of the time illustrate, there was certainly a considerable element of the 60's Mod generation, brought up amongst rough working class surroundings and post-war hardship that were assuredly of a tough and 'Hard' nature - and were undoubtedly Mods. Youths of a genuine Modernist persuasion who had no qualms whatsoever of asserting their will via the use of their fists, boot or weapon(s) at hand if so needed. The climate of the period and within their social circles was one of survival and self-preservation. Some of these London Mods also had close connections and were on first-name terms with certain elements of the criminal underground of the time, often being just as influenced by the gangsters' own affinity with violence as they were with their mohair suits and ice-cold poise. Their stripped down vision of Mod was, in some way, a reaction to the Dandy-like foppery of elements of their fellow Mod crowd. Yet did such a Mod-spawned youth cult as the Hard Mod exist in isolation? Probably not? The true answer surely lies in the minds and experiences of those of the time that were identifiably Mod, but adopted a more street-wise interpretation of Mod - in some ways not altogether dissimilar to some elements of the pre-63 Mods attitude- and who were not afraid to assert their allegiance to the culture by all means appropriate.

CHAPTER 5

NORTHERN MOJO

"If you went up north there were no Mods up there at all to begin with but eventually they took it up and Manchester and Sheffield did become very Mod indeed." - **Steve Marriott**

Left to right: Wiggy with Rick Spencer (Spanner) outside the Viking coffee bar, Lincoln, 1966, Mik Sykes (Doncaster) with catalogue model Audrey Chambers and Lincoln Mods, including Glenn Field (far right)

Although there is little question as to where the Mod cult originated, and as a serious underground scene, its heart rests predominantly in the capital. Yet, once the movement was recognised, Mod attitude spawned formidable self-contained scenes further afield. From the suburbs of London and the south, upwards to Lincolnshire, Nottingham, Yorkshire, Lancashire, Newcastle and the North-East and onto Scotland, Mod spread its intoxicating influence. Clubs sprang up such as the legendary Twisted Wheel in Manchester, Sheffield's Esquire and Mojo clubs, Hull's Kon Tiki, 51 club and Gondola clubs, The Birdcage in Portsmouth, Dewsbury's Bin Lid club, the variously located Ricky Tick Clubs and the Club a 'GoGo in Newcastle. The exposure to the very latest Mod sounds may not have been - initially at least - as rapid as those heard within its spiritual birthplace - and fashions would undoubtedly have been far more difficult to keep up with, yet regional Mods swiftly became just as impeccably attired and clued-in to the whole Mod ethos and lifestyle as their pioneering southern counterparts.

Sheffield teenager Keith How was perhaps a classic example of the later Mod period's devotees: a younger generation of Mod born just that slight few years too late to taste the very earliest of Mod's offerings. Nevertheless, these young and impressionable youths quickly absorbed and assimilated the mid-60's Mod period sounds, styles and subsequent weekends of club action. Despite the suburban out-of-town location of Mods such as Keith and many others, the enthusiasm and dedication was just as ardent and all-encompassing. In addition, the creation of their own local scenes would supply enough action.

Keith How (Sheffield Mod) - "It was always the music: or as long as I can remember. Before television came into our house the radio was never off. My mother was in love with music. She liked the modern stuff much to my Dad's disgust. He worked on Saturday mornings so I heard 'Saturday Club' with her old mate Brian Matthews. But who were these mysterious artists who sang about heartbreak and girls? The folks next door were the first people to have a television around 1965 and one summers evening I was passing the window and there on the screen in glorious black and white was Cathy McGowan. She introduced The Rolling Stones and my young life turned on its axis. From that moment on, even though at 15, I wouldn't realize the effect, my life would be influenced by music and clothes.

My parents' biggest mistake was buying me a tiny transistor radio with an earplug. They forbade listening at night which was a little foolish. Radio Luxembourg - Station of the Stars on 208 I listened every night falling asleep and waking with the whistling in my ear. But I knew about Otis

Redding and Sam Cooke, Dave Brubeck and Alexis Korner, John Lee Hooker and 'Live from the Marquee Club', The Beatles, The Yardbirds and The Pretty Things. Eventually I could pick up pirate radio stations. What an amazing time to be alive.

I suspect my first real encounter with Mods was on holiday with a couple of mates in Great Yarmouth around 1966. We were in a hotel and hooked up with some guys who, as I recall, were suited and booted and had great haircuts. They were cool and (being) older they also picked up the waitresses that we were trying to impress. I recall thinking that I needed a look like that.

Back home the 72 bus dropped you at the Sheffield Moorhead before Pond Street. You could buy Levi's 501 shrink to fit jeans and get your inside leg measured for a pair of Sta-Prest Chinos from a shop, 'Harry Fenton', I think, at Furnival Gate [also Chappel Walk]. They sold Harrington Jackets and Ben Sherman button down shirts. I walked down to the Castle Market for my Clarks Desert Boots and Hush Puppies. Some weeks the clothes gave way to buying a couple of singles say Junior Walker and the All Stars maybe Otis or even a long playing record from Cann's record dept. on Chappel Walk. Parkas were always available at the Wakefield Army and Navy Stores along with "Tuff Boots". It was a good time. Even though you were no-one you felt 'someone'.

Living 16 miles away from any action was difficult so we made our own scene in local pubs and at the 'Marquis'. Weekends were amazing when the scooters came up the valley. I couldn't wait to have my own. When I could have 'Hire Purchase' my first scooter was a Vespa which I promptly wrote off. But at least I could move further afield from the legendary 'Marquis'. Somehow I was able to own a lovely Lambretta LI 150. I spent a week's wages on accessories. Mirrors, backrest, aerial and 'tigers tail'. I came out of the club one night to find them all stolen. I pared things down after that. Gigs were difficult to get to although I remember Arthur Conley (at Down Broadway), Geno Washington, and The Small Faces."

One club was pivotal in keeping the flame of Soul alive. Manchester's Twisted Wheel club was the king of all of the R&B and Soul clubs so favoured by the Mods in the north. The Wheel's status amongst Soul fans is legendary and some cite it as the birthplace of what would soon develop into the Northern Soul scene.

Roy Allen outside The Twisted Wheel

The Wheel's first location was on Brazennose Street off Albert Square. Opening in 1963 and owned by the Adabi Brothers, the club rapidly became the leading Blues and rhythm and blues club in the city, soon attracting members from all over the north and beyond, its only realistic competition being the close by Oasis club. The DJ was local R&B and Soul connoisseur, Roger Eagle - perhaps the north's equivalent of The Scene Club's Guy Stevens. Roger went on to open the Stax Club prior to his 'Summer of Love' initiation. Meanwhile the clubs near complete immersion into Soul arrived when it switched dwellings to Whitworth Street and the Mods and Soul Boys made it their own. As well as the club's highly reputable and greatly enjoyed Soul sets, the venue also played host to a regular flow of Soul and R&B stars, from Stevie Wonder and Edwin Starr to the Soul Sisters, Joe Tex, Bob and Earl and Junior Walker. Many touring Mod acts such as St Louis Union, The Action, Mike Cotton Sound and The Artwoods also regularly appeared.

THE TWISTED WHEEL STORY BY DAVE FAWCETT (also known as Harry from Sale)

THE GREATER MANCHESTER/SALE CROWD AND THE TWISTED WHEEL:

"It all kicked off for us in the autumn of 1965. I started to spend my nights hanging around the centre of Sale with three mates. We weren't alone, there were up to a score or so similar groups of Mod lads and lasses, and it didn't take too long before we integrated and 50 or 60 of us were rendezvousing by the benches in the middle of the shopping centre every night. 'Mod' in those early days was all very individualistic. Although I'd considered myself a Mod since '64, I was guilty of more than a few fashion fax-pas. Soon we'd all smartened our act up and by spring of '66 there were well in excess of a hundred or so of us, and what was to become the 'Sale Crowd' was formed.

I was just 17 at the time, and had left grammar school in the summer of '65. Although some of my mates had already briefly experienced a couple of the clubs in Manchester (six miles down the road), financial restrictions and an enforced curfew had meant that I'd had no chance of contributing to the Mod scene before I left school. To gain financial independence and freedom of movement I'd bucked my father's wish for me to go into the sixth form in favour of being a Mod.

Soon we were all going to Sale Locarno on a Thursday night, which was teenagers' night- local group and a disco! They had chart-topping groups on there - Wayne Fontana, Freddie and the Dreamers and Georgie Fame to name but a few. When we started going to the Locarno, the mix of kids was probably 30% Mod, 20% greaser and 50% ordinary kids. Within 12 months it was 80% Mod, 20% ordinary kids and no greasers.

The Locarno, like many other venues back then, also had a strict policy that only dancing in pairs (girl/girl or girl/lad) was allowed on the dance floor. The fast rise of the Mods altered all of that: we danced in a group, a circle or individually, and nobody was going to alter that. Remember, we were the very first teenage generation. There was no way we were going to act, dress or even dance like our parents. As opposed to today's teenagers, there were no well-trodden paths to follow - we made our own rules. But having got the taste for it, there was no way we were going to stay local. Soon we'd started going up town four nights a week to clubs like the Oasis, Jungfrau, Jigsaw and the Twisted Wheel. We met Mods from other parts of town and got loads of new ideas fashion-wise and music-wise.

By the summer of '66, we had a bit of a routine. Thursdays and Sundays were either local clubs or up town, Mondays and Wednesdays we hung around the centre of Sale and Tuesdays and Fridays were definite clubbing nights in Manchester. Saturdays were either partying or clubbing in town. There was also a couple of hundred of us now, with Mods drifting in and out of the Sale crowd. We were also intertwined with the 'Alty Crowd'. Altrincham being the town that bordered Sale, and having an even larger older established Mod crowd than Sale.

Gradually though, the Twisted Wheel was becoming the biggest influence in our lives. Fashion-wise, we were in the middle of a massive change. Those of us who went up town clubbing had discovered mohair suits. All the top Mods were starting to wear them. This was a godsend for me in particular, as my co-ordination of Mod gear had been somewhat woeful on occasions. But so long as I picked a decent cloth and copied the latest style, my fashion faux-pas days were over. Add our new suede haircuts to our suits and we well looked the part. This was important as to go to Manchester's premier club you needed to look the part, but the Soul-Mod look wasn't just for the wheel, it elevated our standing at other clubs as well.

Although the Sale crowd was a loose confederation of a couple of hundred or so, by the summer of '66, we'd realised that you couldn't afford to be a clubber, and a scooter lad, and be in a relationship with a lass. Money was limited, you couldn't afford everything, and you had to choose the direction that best suited you. Those in relationships weren't clubbing as much as the rest of us, and the scooter lads, who were usually paying for their bikes on the drip, couldn't afford the clubs. I was definitely a clubber, I could always get a pillion ride if there were any scooter runs but clubs was where all the excitement was.

The change in fashions worked wonders for my love life as well. There were only half a dozen or so lasses whom I fancied in the Sale crowd, and all of those were unavailable to me for one reason or another. There was never any problem trapping off at parties, but I was competitive back then and didn't like any of my mates to have a better-looking girlfriend than me. Mod girls looked great, with smarter haircuts, straight, long, bobbed or pageboy; no beehives like the greasettes, or perms like your mother. I loved the era of the mini-skirt and the long leather coat. I picked my first couple of girlfriends on looks alone, but once the Mod scene really kicked off, girls for me had to be good-looking AND Mod, as I now had appearances to keep up and standards to adhere towards.

Although the Sale and Alty crowds loosely numbered a few hundred, a lot of Mods still went to venues with their original mates, majority rule! Not so me, I realised that I could go to whichever club in the Manchester area that I fancied... and see people I knew, and widen my circle even more. Clubbing for us lads was a mix of socialising, drinking, dancing and meeting lasses. There was something of a sexual revolution in the mid-sixties, so we lived life to the full. Funny enough though, the Wheel was never a 'trapping' club. There were available Mod lasses by the score in the Oasis, 'Frau and most of the local clubs, but Wheel lasses were that little bit more sophisticated. They were there for the music and the ambience rather than to pull. The Wheel was one of those clubs you took a lass to, rather than trap off with one there.

The parties, though, were something else. Us core crowd members had learned never ever to be the one to hold a party.... fatal! However every Saturday night there was a choice of parties. Kids on the fringe of the crowd and those who wanted to be part of the crowd fell over themselves to throw parties, thinking that was the best way to gain acceptance. Parties were great; music, fraternisation, drunkenness and uninhibited girls made it so. The main drawback to holding a party were the gatecrashers. Yes, we all gatecrashed loads of parties, most of us with fun in mind but there were always unscrupulous individuals who just created mayhem with wrecking and robbing. In the film 'Quadrophenia', there's a party scene that illustrates sixties parties brilliantly. Mind you, the scenes where Mods arrived at clubs on their scooters wearing parkas over their mohair suits is far-fetched: most of us knew to keep mohair well away from oily scooters. On the scooter front in Manchester, it was 95% Lambrettas. Vespa's were not thought to be cool even though they seemed to be the preferred choice down south.

Every Saturday afternoon, we congregated on 'the benches' to find out where the parties were and decide which one(s) would be graced by our presence. But the best time of all was had in the clubs, and the Twisted Wheel was outstanding.

Two things struck me on my first visit to the wheel. Firstly was the fact that this was where all the top Mods hung out and everyone looked the part. Secondly, the music was different; it was nearly all Motown, Stax, Atlantic and Blue Beat, as opposed to the mainly chart and pop music played at the other clubs. The Wheel fast became our preferred destination Tuesdays and Fridays.

The cherry on the bun however were the Saturday night All-Nighters featuring top live acts and playing great dancing music. Even in the early days of the all-nighters, Mods were attending from 60/70 miles away, and remember there was little social media in those days, news only really spread by word of mouth. A lot of records in the charts were songs originally recorded by black American artists, and re-recorded over here by white British artists. However at the Wheel, the opposite was the policy, we were treated to the original recordings at the Wheel. Black artists were badly discriminated against in the States, and even when their songs charted they were re-recorded in the U.K. by white artists, and it was those versions that were plugged. Easy to see how delighted and astounded they were at the adulation and appreciation they received at the Wheel. At the Wheel we were one united crowd of Wheelers. We came from all over town, but there were never any petty rivalries or unpleasantness whatsoever. In three and a half years I never saw one fight at the Wheel.

Best dressers there were the Jewish lads, they were always immaculately suited, and more than happy to point you in the right direction. Coolest were the lads of West Indian parentage from Moss Side. We got dance moves off them, plus a taste for pork pie hats, and some great wordage. They also introduced me to the shebeens of the Moss, and the infamous Nile Club, where I honed my love for blue-beat and ska. A famous incident occurred early in the Rolling Stones career, having done a concert in Manchester based on their new LP, they visited the Wheel after, where the D.J. played all the numbers from their earlier concert, but by the original artistes.

By the time I started going to the Wheel in 1966, it had moved from its original location in Brazenose Street to an excellent cellar club in Whitworth Street. As Wheelers, we looked, lived and acted the part. We were the elite of Manchester's Mods, but we never gloated about it, we just acted cool and nonchalant. Those of us who went to the all-nighters became known by our name or nickname and the place we lived; although I was a 'Dave', I'd been nicknamed Harry in my school years, and that's what stuck. I was henceforth always known as 'Harry from Sale'.

Getting the look right was paramount. mohair suits were the top item. Mohair was essential as it was lightweight and easy to dance in. But you had to get the suit right as 'the look' was always changing. First it was side vents, then centre vents, and vents invariably got longer. You had to pay attention to the pockets and ticket pockets as well, not to mention lapels, cuffs and buttons. Whether you had two buttons or three, you always had the bottom one unfastened. Each new suit had to be bob-on- the latest style. Smart plain shirts with military or old school ties complemented the suit, as did a silk hanky in the top pocket. Shirt-wise, Ben Shermans were especially popular. Shoes were Italian leather slip-on or brogues (all with leather soles for dancing). A crombie overcoat topped the ensemble, but it had to have a top pocket and handkerchief. Last part of the wardrobe for all-nighters was an airline bag (usually containing change of clothes for the morning, brush, comb and chewing gum! Away from the clubs, messrs Levi ,Wrangler and Lee were the main influence on our wardrobe, worn with casual shirts.

Some Friday nights back then in '66 and '67, we could get on the Altrincham to Manchester train at Sale, and when it pulled into Oxford Road station, there might be as many as 60 of us walking down Whitworth Street to the Wheel. Saturday night though, was all based around the All-nighters. We'd either go direct from another club in town, or more usually catch the last train or the all-night bus from a party in Sale or Alty.

Most of us agreed that taking amphetamines enhanced the All-Nighters, but how did we obtain these banned substances? Originally general practitioners everywhere were prescribing pep pills or 'mothers little helpers' to women up and down the country, so there was a steady supply. However by 1967, what with the bad publicity, supplies halted. Throughout the land, chemists (who in the main had woefully little security) found themselves the victims of break-ins. More enterprising individuals were able to gain access to supplies from warehouses. A member of the Sale crowd who worked in the local pharmaceutical warehouse, supplied the Sale and Alty crowd with ample supplies, which meant we didn't have the hassle of trying to score gear in Manchester on a Saturday night when the drug squad was out in force. Needless to say, the perpetrator was eventually brought to justice, but only when most of us were coming to the end of our Wheel experiences and moving on to new adventures.

The All-nighters were the best club experience I've ever had. Near on eight hours of with a live act such as Edwin Starr, Junior Walker, Ike and Tina Turner, the Drifters or Geno Washington. They had the club heaving, sweat running down the walls. When the act finished we were still high on it, dancing, socialising and having a great time.

When we poured out of the back doors of the club afterwards, we made our way to Piccadilly Station where we'd stored our airline bags in the luggage lockers. Wash and brush-up first on the agenda, together with a change of clothes if necessary. Next stop was the salvation army stall outside Victoria Station. They provided us with drinks for no charge whatsoever. Ever since then I've always bought their 'Warcry' magazine in pubs. After hanging around Victoria for a while, it was across town to Stax on Fountain Street for a couple of hours, and then at mid-day back across town to Rowntree's Sounds for the 12 till 2 session, after which we dispersed our separate ways.

The Mod movement (we were a part of) started coming to an end in 68/69. A lot of the scooter lads found they were restricted as they were still paying for their scooters on the drip. Plus a lot of them were now well over 18, and becoming interested in four wheels rather than two. Selling the scooters wasn't really an option as there was often more owed on the bikes than they could get for them. A perfect solution presented itself to lads in this predicament. A lad wanting to get rid of his bike would park it up at night only to find that it had disappeared by the morning. Of course he knew it was going to 'disappear' but didn't report it till the next day by which time the culprits had already started to dismantle it for spares. After a few insurance payouts, the police started taking scooter theft seriously, and a few of us, including the owners of the missing bikes, found ourselves in court.

By mid '69 there were fewer and fewer of us 'Soul Mods' still going to the Wheel. The crowd there was getting younger, and the youngsters did not have the same fashion sense as us veterans. Gradually most of us stopped going to the Wheel and the new arrivals became the original Northern Soulers. Lots of people have asked me since 'why if the Wheel was so good, did you stop going?' You need to remember things were much different back then. Nowadays all the youth sub-cultures are established, but back then we were still creating them. It was like a helter-skelter out of control.

But by '69 we'd exhausted all the Soul-Mod options. We'd used every reasonable conceivable variation on mohair suits, and the new young Wheelers weren't interested in the look. Most of us were now entering our twenties, and were more into the over-18 clubs such as Rowntree's, Sounds, Takis and Top of the Town. And in fact we were moving on from that even, growing our hair and experimenting with hallucinatory drugs which were more suited to the hippy scene than the Mod scene, and so we just moved on to different lifestyles.

The Wheel kept on going till early 1971, when it changed style and became a disco (Placemates). The good news though was that ex-Wheeler Peter Roberts re-opened it in 2000, and with a lot of us old Wheelers going back, and new Mods being converted, it's still as strong as ever in 2014. Albeit in new premises, the twice a month Sunday sessions are attended by hundreds, and we still have the same great time.

The Sale crowd basically drifted apart as the Mod population shrunk. We broke up into smaller groups, depending on which pub we preferred. The Alty crowd survived a little longer, but by 1970 Mod was no longer the biggest teenage cult out there, although it has had a few reincarnations since and no doubt will go through a few more, because quite frankly, it's the coolest look around."

A YOUNG MOD'S UNFORGOTTEN STORY – GROWING UP IN THE SIXTIES BY KATH CHAMBERS

A relatively short journey away from Sheffield and Manchester, the city of Lincoln had also developed its own fledgling Mod scene: comprised of young and energetic teenagers, eager to mark their own identity as hip young scene-goers. As with most of those inspired by the cultural signpost of Mod, the journey to their music and clothes-obsessed destination would be born of an earlier age of popular culture.

Kath Chambers - "Born in the Fifties, growing up in the Sixties, perhaps I didn't realise until much later how lucky I was. The radio was on most of the time and I was five when music started to sound different to me – I can remember my oldest cousin singing 'All Shook Up'. Out of the miasma of Perry Como, Al Martino and Rosemary Clooney came the sounds of Elvis, Lonnie Donegan and Jerry Lee Lewis. My sister and I were given a second hand record player and a box of 78's dating from the 30's and 40's to which we soon added Mum's Fats Domino LP and my auntie's Elvis 78's. It was a few years before we could afford to add to our collection but Radio Luxembourg filled the gaps. A very youthful youth club allowed us to dance to Cliff and The Shadows, the Everley Brothers and the various products of the Joe Meek stable. We soon stopped listening to Children's Favourites on the BBC – introduced by 'Uncle Mac' who clearly hated children! - and moved on to Saturday Club with Brian Matthew. At the time, it was the only programme on the BBC that played pop music. It was a curious mix of British and US pop, skiffle and Jazz, where you would hear Marty Wilde, Bert Weedon and Chris Barber and, eventually, visiting US stars such as Gene Vincent and even Bo Diddley.

It seems strange now, when we are presented with an almost unlimited range of music and countless ways to hear it, but there was a small number of artists and only two radio stations to listen to - BBC Light Programme or Radio Luxembourg. There were a number of TV shows but they usually featured British artists who performed US hits as, for a long time, it was difficult for foreign musicians to get permission to play in the UK. Of course, everything changed in 1962-63.

I lived in London until 1962; we moved to Lincoln when I was 10. I used to go back quite often so got the chance to see 'Swinging London' first hand and go to shops like Biba or Bus Stop and go down the King's Road or to Kensington on a Saturday. (Although I was only 12 or 13, I was used to travelling around in London on trains or buses from the age of six.) Like most teenagers then, my main interests were music and clothes. I couldn't afford to buy a lot of clothes so I started designing and making my own or borrowing from my Mum. She had a couple of 1940's grey two-piece suits and I found an old 1930's black crepe dress belonging to my grandmother. We used to get send parcels of clothes, from relatives in America, which could be worn, remade or customised, plus there were vintage finds from Oxfam. I even wore a Fair Isle cardigan that had been a 10th birthday present. I met up with an old school friend a few years ago and she asked me if I was still making dresses out of my Mum's curtains! I also remember finishing off a dress in the back of class one day and getting my friend John to help sew the sleeves as I was going to wear it to see Stevie Wonder at the Gliderdrome the next night.

Kath's friends, Susan Hanley and Gina Gregory on the Duke steps, September 1967 with Sugar from Leicester and Bob Garrard. Left: Adverts for Boston's Starlight Room.

A former pre-war open-air skating rink, that was burnt down in 1959 and re-opened the following year, Boston's Starlight Room Gliderdrome played host to many of the Mod attractions of the day, including Otis Redding, Solomon Burke, The Who, Yardbirds, Lee Dorsey and more. The venue was one of many that northern Mods, including sections of the Lincoln contingent, regularly visited.

Boston Gliderdrome was another great venue to see American soul stars that came over – such as Ike and Tina Turner, Otis Redding or the Temptations. A rickety bus left Union Square in Lincoln at 6.10 on a Saturday night, just within sprinting distance from my Saturday job at Woolies, get changed and made up on the bus, ready for a big night out.

The trick [for Mod fashions] was to have some key fashion items. Various 'must have' items came and went, such as fur coats or gangster trilbies. The most important items of clothing were a pair of Levi's, shrunk to fit and scrubbed on the draining board, and shoes you could dance in. I always wanted a pair of Courreges style white short boots – but could never afford them! I did have a white PVC mac – which might have come from C&A. Buying clothes from catalogues was great because you could pay weekly. Quite a few of us bought knee high leather boots from my Mum's Freeman's catalogue because they were only £5, or 5 shillings a week, affordable out of babysitting money. The High street shops were Chelsea Girl or Dorothy Perkins but local boutiques were very better to find something different. Of course, all the clothes were wasted unless you had somewhere to go to show them off. This started with youth club or school dances and on Saturday we would go into Lincoln and go to the Viking Café. Everyone went there and you would always meet someone you knew and it was a good way to find out what was happening.

There were certain clubs that were popular and that people aspired to go to, such as the Mojo and the Twisted Wheel, but local clubs were also quite influential in building up the scene. In October 1966, the Duke of Wellington Soul Club opened over a pub in Lincoln. It was started by people who went to the Mojo and Twisted Wheel – they would bring back the latest records and dances so we would be aware of these within a day or two. Some of the founder members had appeared on the 'Ready Steady Go!' Otis Redding Special in September 1966, recruited from the Mojo. It was originally on a Sunday night to keep the all-nighter vibe going. Later it was open on Wednesdays and Fridays as well, so this fitted round going to a Saturday night out or all-nighter at Nottingham, Sheffield, Manchester or Retford. The first time I went to the Duke was New Year's Eve 1966. I walked five miles into Lincoln with my friends, Susan Hanley and Pauline Smith, as there were no buses. When we got there, we found it was all ticket so despite pleading with the legendary doorman, Dick Barnsdale, we had to sit on the stairs until Susan's Dad rescued us. Of course, we were back next week to get our memberships! We would go two or three times a week; when my friend Gina moved to Manchester she used to phone me at the Duke, as we had no phone at home.

At first, it was quite scruffy, full of old furniture from the pub downstairs, the chairs were prone to collapsing if you sat down too hard. Of course, the ladies' toilets smelled of Youth Dew and the men's of Brut! I remember being quite shocked coming back from a trip to London to find it with a Mojo-style makeover with black walls and psychedelic swirls. A bit hippy – but I got used to it. The Duke was also popular with people from other towns such as Newark and Leicester.

You would travel all over to go to a good night. If you were living at home, you never told your parents you were going to an all-nighter, so you had to say you were staying with a friend and maybe just going to a local dance. There were dances at the Raven Club at Waddington RAF camp, which were usually good soul nights, so it was a good excuse to say you were going there.

It was unusual for people to go with their girlfriend or boyfriend to an all-nighter. It was definitely something you did with your mates. One of the issues would be transport as not many people (and almost no girls) had cars – of course some of us were not old enough to drive anyway. So you had to rely on lifts or public transport, which would affect where you could go. For me Nottingham was the easiest to get to by train. The main clubs were the Dungeon, the Beachcomber, the Boat Club and the Britannia. I knew a crowd from Leicester so quite often would meet them there. I even used to go on my own sometimes as there would always be someone you knew. I used to joke that my overnight bag went to the Twisted Wheel more than I did, as friends used to borrow it. I occasionally took amphetamines but I went off them when I saw someone take a huge handful and it made me feel sick. I probably would only take a couple – they were cheap eight for £1.

In the morning, you would go somewhere like the bus or train station and get washed and changed as your clothes would be sweaty and damp! Then maybe find somewhere to have a coffee or a pint of milk from a milk van. Sometimes go to the bowling alley – I knew someone who once went to the ice rink in Nottingham. Eventually you would make your way home and try to conceal the fact that you had been up all night from your parents. Probably have to sit through Sunday lunch (although you wouldn't be hungry if you had been taking amphetamines); go out again Sunday night. The crunch usually came on Tuesday morning when you would realise how knackered you were. You probably had to fit homework in at some point if you were still at school!

Above: Lincoln Art School Dance

Below: one of the Duke club's three founder DJ's Steve Carter with Lyndsey Preedy

For me, the most important thing was the music. I started off with the usual pop groups, the Beatles and the Stones but I didn't really spend money on their records. You could hear this music on the radio all the time. However, these bands brought Motown and R&B to our attention and that sounded more interesting to me. I also had a friend who had a great collection of Blues like Howling Wolf or Sonny Boy Williamson. I bought records out of my babysitting money and Saturday wages and I always asked for an LP for Christmas or birthday presents. A prized possession was my portable tape player. It cost about £13 from a second hand shop and I used to copy my records onto tape so I could listen anywhere. Better than having them chewed up by a Discotron. In the 1960's it was unheard of for girls to DJ. You were not even really expected to have a record collection.

On my trips to London, I would go to record shops or second hand stalls and pick up some bargains. Susan and I did occasionally help a mobile DJ but I think he just wanted a couple of go-go dancers so we didn't do that for long! I did at least get to play for junior discos at school. I would have loved to play at the Duke but couldn't compete with Steve Carter and Neil Blanchard, the resident DJs. Steve had an amazing collection, which he sold in about 1972; the £2000 price tag was way beyond my reach. Of course, he later regretted selling his records and spend a lot of time and money replacing them. I did eventually get my chance to play at the Duke when Steve and I shared the decks at a reunion. [Thankfully] I still have all the records I bought back then.

We certainly felt as if we were the 'In Crowd'. There was a certain self-confidence that came from feeling you were ahead of the mainstream. When pirate radio finished and Radio 1 started, 'our' music started to move away from the pop scene, which preserved the 'different-ness'. I suppose the Wheel closing coincided with a lot of people moving on, going to college or settling down and having families. We certainly stopped travelling so far to go out. More local clubs were opening up but these were smart disco's not old cellars. It was a new generation of kids who (now) went to the Casino, The Torch, Blackpool Mecca or the Catacombs."

MOD 'DUKES' OF LINCOLN

From the left:
Paul, Lance and Glenn Field

Life-long Mod connoisseur Glenn Field and his brother Lance embodied both the obsession to detail of Mod, but also its carefree approach to substances.

The Duke Mod nights were set up by landlord Tom Blanchard's son, Neil on October 15th 1965. The original DJ, along with Neil, was Steve Carter: Bill 'Wiggy' Hildred joining in on the decks in 1967.

Glenn Field - "The Lincoln Mod scene owes an awful lot to the guys who started 'The Duke' Soul nights at the Duke of Wellington pub in 1965. These guys brought the tunes back from the all-nighter scenes in Manchester, London, Sheffield and Nottingham. We also had a meeting place between pub opening times at The Viking coffee house where we would swap information about where the best night to go was. No mobiles in those days. All word-of-mouth.

Word of advice-don't get carried away with a bespoke suit when pilled up with mates. I had to have the lot, but be different. Woolen brown and white pin-striped, double-breasted, three covered buttons, hand stitching on the lapels, working cuffs, turn-ups and then to top it all two, fourteen inch vents! To accommodate the vents the tailor made the jacket longer looking like a cross between Beau Brummell and a Teddy boy. The girls loved it though! Another word of advice - don't ever throw up on a woolen suit. I did a month later and that was the end of that suit.

Always aware of amphetamines in our family. Our father was a pilot in the war and they were given Wakey-Wakey pills whilst flying. Bombers, Blueys, Bennies were the order of the day. Black and whites (also known as dominoes and Jesters), green and clears, brown and clears left you with a horrible taste in the mouth and hours of Doobie dust floating out of your mouth every time you spoke. Not to mention the 'horrors' (imagining little devils trying to grab your ankles from the skirting boards. You knew they couldn't be real but you still moved out of their way.)

Living in Lincoln the nearby RAF Waddington Raven Club put some brilliant bands and groups on. Rod Stewart and the Steampacket, Brian Auger Trinity, Walker Brothers. All great Mod stuff.

Saturday nights we would meet in our best clothes at the Falstaff pub (it was one of the few pubs with a Juke box with records on we would actually pay to hear) The only guys not dressed up would be in jeans and plimsolls so we knew a chemist was going to be cracked that night. If we couldn't get a lift to an all-nighter from the pub (usually to Nottingham's Dungeon or Beachcomber) the gear wasn't wasted as I shared a flat and a few of us would spend our blocked up night discussing the Vietnam war and listening to Bob Dylan, Blind Lemon Jefferson, Leadbelly and other Blues men.

Sometimes we did have transport. A friend had a Mini so we took two girls to a club in Birmingham to see the Drifters. Motorways were new to us and the roads all looked the same. We seemed to be driving for hours on the way home to Lincoln. It was only when we saw a sign saying Bristol 20 miles that we realised we were heading in the wrong direction! It didn't matter. We were young. We were Mod!!!"

Duke 60s Soul club regulars, including Glenn Field second on the right at the back with the blond girl on his lap (top photo) and (below) second on the right with the dark suit on. Bottom right photo is Duke and Mojo regular, Mick Gregory

THE MOD WORLD OF ELLA DONNOR

**Ella Donnor (right)
with Helen Murray**

Lincoln born-and-bred Ella Donnor could well represent the classic example of the 60's teenage girl with a fascination of Mod and its mid-sixties culture: both wisely astute in her choice of scooters and Mods, alongside her love of the music and fashion of the scene, Ella undeniably also epitomises the photogenic innocence and appeal of the period.

Ella Donnor - "I was born in December 1948 and brought up on the St Giles Estate in Lincoln. I attended the St Giles Infants and junior schools and then after passing my Eleven Plus went on to South Park Grammar School for girls. I met Helen at the junior school, she lived round the corner from me and we became best friends.

On reaching 15 I worked at Woolworths on Saturdays earning 15 shillings and a penny and at 16 started work at the Lincoln Telephone Exchange as an operator which is when I started going out to with Helen and other friends, we went to the Viking coffee bar where we met others and as we preferred the guys with scooters rather than motorbikes and liked to dress smart we became Mods.

From there we all met in the Viking café and frequented places such as Ruston's club on a Sunday night, the RAF camps at Retford, Scampton and Waddington and to clubs in Boston, Nottingham, Sheffield, Doncaster, Scunthorpe and Leicester at weekends. During this time, a disco opened at the Duke of Wellington pub and we went there regularly. Helen and I hitch-hiked to lots of places often late at night and once went to London where we arrived really early in the morning and walked the streets for miles seeing lots of sites before hitching back to Lincoln tired out, it was all for something to do.

There were parties and get together's at Lincoln, Skegness and Cleethorpes when all the Mods went on their scooters, a good time was had by all as the parties were all-nighters and a lot of the people were high on 'mild' drugs at those times. In the mornings after dancing almost all night a lot of us caught buses to the bowling alley where we stayed chatting for a good part of the day with coffee, tea or soft drinks and even breakfast to rest our weary feet before going back to the

Viking at Lincoln, sometimes we would go home for food and get changed ready to return to the Viking and on to the Duke disco in the evening. I remember one time when we were lucky enough to get a lift back to Lincoln we (five or six in the car) all nearly ended up in a ditch as the driver was high on drugs and was hallucinating, he thought he saw an animal in the road which he tried to avoid by swerving.

Ella and friends, Skegness 1965

During these years I also had a Mod boyfriend, at the beginning we often ended up together at the clubs then later we went places together with other couples, unfortunately we broke up after 4 years and I had to 'drop out' of the scene and start afresh, Helen by then had moved away and got married and a lot of other friends were now 'couples' so I began to do bar work at the Pye-Wipe as an extra job and concentrated on my career, most people by now were 'pubbing' rather than 'clubbing' so I still had a good social life going with workmates."

Nigel Brandt-Bellamy - "Lincoln for all its remoteness of a Shire town was often at the centre of the Mod revolution. Skegness, too, for the occasional battle with the Biker boys. We would meet at the Viking café to plan the weekends ahead and where we would be heading. It could be an all-nighter or just a local do where we would all turn up in force, Parkas and all. Dress was so important and to look good with the right suit and tie. Just about everyone had a nickname of some sort like, Spanner, Tonk, Big Fred, Wiggy to name just a few.

Everyone had scooters and there was internal rivalry between those who had Lambrettas and those who had Vespa's. There was always somewhere to go to have fun and listen to Tamla and Soul. The Summer hols came round at the end of July beginning of August when we would head off to Newquay."

Lincoln's Mod social mecca, The Duke, attracted Mods from further afield, whilst it was also the regular place to congregate (along with the city's Viking coffee bar) prior to an out of town journey to other venues. Mod clubs such as Tinned Chicken in Castleford, The Broken Wheel in Retford (surely a play on the popularity of Manchester's Twisted Wheel?), Sheffield's Mojo and numerous others were within reach and proved popular with the Lincoln Mod crowd.

Bill 'Wiggy' Hildred - "I was a regular at the Duke. Our weekends were made up of a night at The Duke on Fridays followed by whichever all-nighter we were to attend on the Saturday, either The Mojo, Twisted Wheel, The Tinned Chicken in Castleford and sometimes The Dungeon in Nottingham and then Sunday for another night at The Duke to finish the weekend off, back home at my parent's house at the stroke of midnight; fantastic times."

Left: Wiggy with girlfriend of the time, Angela
Above: with friends Greg and Rob and some of his membership cards

Right: Lincoln and Leicester Mod crowd outside Retford's The Broken Wheel club

Glenn Field - "'The Duke' was the local gateway to what was happening on the wider scene. Its reputation as a great place to go meant visits from the serious club goers. The Leicester lads were regular clubbers. In fact, the first time I had seen dance moves like it when they all lined up and did their moves. Cool guys. They even rolled up in an American motor one night. It was always a thrill to walk up the stairs to the clubroom with the music banging out. Pay to get in and have your hand stamped with the Duke name. We felt part of something special that only a few like-minded souls would understand. We were under the radar. The lighting in the room illuminated everything that was white. Girls with white dresses ended up see-through. Guys with dandruff on the collars of their dark jackets. You really had to be careful with what you wore and how well groomed you were. The music transcended everything. Some of our favourites were - Marvin Gaye 'Ain't That Peculiar', Bobby Sheen 'Dr Love', O'Jays 'I Dig Your Act', Bob Kuban and the in-men 'The Cheater' and tracks from The Olympics, Flamingos, Little Hank and 'I Spy for the FBI' by Jamo Thomas."

Glenn's brother, Lance was also an ardent Mod and a regular on the Lincoln Mod scene. Here he recounts events not unlike scenes from the film 'Quadrophenia' to be released over a decade later.

Lance Field - "I remember we used to flatter the girls who worked in the local chemist shops. This 'grooming' resulted in what we were really after. Nicked jar full's of 'Doobies'. The police had a notion of the 'usual suspects' if a chemist was done on the Friday night. The Viking Coffee Shop was Lincoln's Mod hangout so the police knew where to go. One of the guys who was wearing a borrowed suit jacket was pulled Sunday lunchtime outside the Viking. He was cocky, as he hadn't any gear on him. However they searched him and found a solitary bomber in the borrowed suit jacket. He had no idea that it was there was there. For that, he got sent down to North Sea Camp borstal!"

Lance Field – with Janet Nissler and friends - upstairs in The Duke Soul club (at the Duke of Wellington pub, Broadgate, Lincoln.)

Below: The Rolling Stones at Lincoln ABC 1964

Lance Field - "Venturing from Lincoln, we went to the Flamingo. During the day, we would visit an East Ham Jewish shoe shop. Then to the Prospect of Whitby pub. We would use toilets to change into our all-nighter gear. Herringbone hipsters were in with us. Outside the Flamingo, very young 'rude' boys tried to con pass-outs from you as if they were part of the club. Obviously, they were sold on or used by their selves! A great club: Long John Baldry coming in at 4am and getting on stage with Chris Farlowe and Georgie Fame."

Glenn Field - "I remember going to Boston Gliderdrome in a van with a group of Lincoln mates about 1966 to see the Small Faces. The support act was announced as a group's first visit to the UK. Out came Edwin Starr with a full band, backing singers the lot. About 15 of them on this huge stage. Their sound, their songs, their personalities. Awesome. We knew we were witnessing something special. If this was the support act what were our 'gods' the Small Faces going to do for us? Sadly, they bombed. Big time! The stage was too big. They looked, well, so small. They couldn't reproduce the studio sounds of their records. Booing started, followed by some bottles being thrown. One actually drew blood on Kenny Jones' head. Steve Marriott and Plonk Lane, to give them their due, stood at the front of the stage giving the worst of the crowd verbal's. The chant began from the crowd. Edwin, Edwin, Edwin. Back he came and the crowd went mad. No band on this night would ever be able to compete with a guy who would soon become a true legend to the Mod/Soul scene."

THE LINCOLN IN CROWD

Top photographs - Nigel Brandt-Bellamy and (insert) Duke club regulars. Bottom Left: Mick Osborne, Wiggy, Malc Butcher and Mick Wilson in Skegness, 1967

Bottom right photo taken on the stairs at the bottom of the 'Duke' Soul club at the Duke of Wellington pub, Lincoln. From the left Bob Moore, Neil Blanchard, Nigel Brandt-Bellamy, Jimmy Jarman

Duke Club regulars

From the left: Mel Barnard, girl in white (unknown) Jimmy Jarman, unknown and then Lynda Beevers, Neil Blanchard wearing the suit. The tall guy at left is Jodie Bustin and 'Mocker' Cawdron (arms folded). The guy with his hand on Mocker's arm is Bob Moore.

Eddy Grundy (left) with Wiggy in The Duke 1967

Andy de Soosa on the left and Nigel Brandt-Bellamy with Grantham Mod girls

Left: Wiggy wearing his much-loved leather Levi's jacket in 1967

Above: Malc Butcher, Gwyneth and Rob Hughes

Above: the landlord of the Dukes' son Neil Blanchard who was one of the three guys who started (and DJ'd at)The Duke Soul club in 1966.

Left Lincoln Mod regulars at the Duke

Below Mick Gregory and Carol Gregory with Mod friends

The Lincoln scene, though not reaching first gear until 1966, was one of the healthiest and most close-knit in the north, preferring the common bonds of music, clothes and friendship over Mod's southern elitist tendencies. Its' nucleus, The Duke Club - like the scene itself - holds many fond memories for those who were a part of the action.

Over in Sheffield, another club was also having a strong impact on Mods in the north, including many hailing from Lincoln.

SHEFFIELD'S MOJO WORKIN'

Sheffield's Mojo club (renamed King Mojo shortly after opening) was a Mod mecca for northern-based Mods. An enterprise of the Stringfellow brothers - Peter and Geoff - the club was the latest venture in Sheffield, following on from Club 60 (which held brief, though unsuccessful, forays into Modern Jazz on opening in 1960),The Black Cat club and The Blue Moon - where the Kinks performed whilst breaking through with their 'You Really Got Me' debut single.

Situated at the junction of Burngreave Road and Barnsley Road in the Pittsmoor area of the city, the Mojo - former Dey's ballroom and rented out for £30 a week from local businessman, Ruben Wallis - opened in February 1964 (its closest Mod themed rival, The Esquire opened October 1962) and swiftly attracted big names and a loyal Mod crowd. The club soon became one of the prime Mod clubs of the north.

Amongst the many quality acts to perform at the Mojo were the Eric Clapton period Yardbirds, Ike and Tina Turner, Spencer Davis Group, Geno Washington, Isley Brothers, The Animals, Wilson Pickett, Rod Stewart, Julie Driscoll, six visits from John Mayall's Bluesbreakers and numerous outings from Mod icons Small Faces and The Who along with a Stevie Wonder daytime set.

Top photo: The Yardbirds (with a young Eric Clapton) at the Mojo

Right: Mods crowd The Mojo's dance floor

Mojo regulars Carol and Mick

Carol Gregory (Sheffield Mod) - "I went to Sheffield's Mojo club when I was just 15 years old seeing such Mod fave acts as Amen Corner, Stevie Wonder, Chris Farlowe, Them, Georgie Fame and The Temptations. We would meet up with Sheffield's 'In-Crowd' at the La-Fav Café and (as well as The Mojo) also go to The Esquire Club amongst others."

Mick Gregory - "I would go to Nottingham's Boat Club on Friday nights, where I saw The Foundations, otherwise it may have been Leicester's Night owl, The Twisted Wheel in Manchester and The Mojo.

Carol and I met one Sunday munch time at the Cavendish Club and yes, it was love at first sight. We both went to The Twisted Wheel seeing Ben E King and others. It was a brilliant Soul night there and some of us would dance on the stage. We would meet up with people from all over the country – the lads in their smart mohair suits and the lasses looking fab in their mini-skirts and dresses - for the Saturday all-nighters and also Stringfeller's all-day Sunday events. No wonder we were so knackered by Monday morning."

Sonny Boy Williamson with the Stringfellow brothers at the cancelled Mojo gig

Dave Manvell (Sheffield Mod) - "With the advent of Mod groups like The Who and the Small Faces, hair styles changed yet again becoming slightly shorter and lots of back combing going on. This was when the Mojo's own fashion styles started to take off. One of the fashions at the time was pin stripe suits, brown brogues and the need to carry a blue nylon mac - a derivative of the black pac-a-mac. The length of vents in your suit would be changing daily. Many of the coats were double-breasted and even the number of buttons became important with hand-stitched lapels and button holes."

171

Ella Donnor - "My friend Helen and I hitchhiked to the Mojo, an 'all night' club at Sheffield every Saturday and danced the night away, some people were lucky enough to get seats in the café area but others sat or stood on the floor when they weren't dancing. A lot of Soul groups came to the club so the music was mainly Tamla Motown, which was and still is my favourite music today.

As everyone came out of the Mojo it was rather funny to see people looking so strange in the daylight, one time I had been with a good looking man (or so I thought) but when I saw him in the daylight he was covered in spots, I made a quick exit from his side. The strobe lighting seemed to change everything even the colours of our clothes.

Even though the club served no alcohol, the use of uppers (usually obtained in the city's cafes beforehand) was inevitable, but they were not always the genuine article.

Lance Field - "One of the Lincoln 'faces' King Pill was ripping off young 'tickets' at Sheffield's Mojo by soaking aspirins in Quick ink and selling them as 'blueys'. The police arrested him for pushing illegal drugs. He said they couldn't as they were only aspirins so they tried to do him for selling pharmaceuticals without a licence!"

Nottinghamshire Mod Gary Maxton was a regular at many of the northern Mod clubs, including the Mojo.

Gary Maxton - "When I started going to the Mojo Club all-nighters in Sheffield, I really discovered the Highs and lows of French Blues and Black Bombers, and had soon graduated to selling them. For a couple of years I thought I was a gangster and formed a lot of friendships with people who went to the Mojo. They came from all over the country Nottingham, Derby, Ipswich, Peterborough, London, and Lincoln. We really did think we were something special and of course, as teenagers, we thought that anyone who wasn't a Mod knew nothing and must live a boring life. I remember going into Pete Stringfellow's poky little office to ask him for 10 bob to get home because I had lost all my money.

One Bank Holiday we all went straight from the Mojo on a Sunday morning to Skegness for Mods v Rockers madness, it seemed great at the time, but not so good back at work on the big comedown with no sleep for 48 hours."

Gary Maxton with friends in 1965

Rivalry with the city's other Mod club, the Esquire never really escalated much further than a line of scooters outside the Mojo being kicked over (though that was never proven) and the occasional invasion of an older group from the Esquire.

Dave Manvell - "They used to send gangs of youths up from the Esquire to do raids on the Mojo. Brian the doorman would say 'right, I want everyone inside. I've had word that they're coming up from the Esquire. Whether any of these gangs appeared or not I don't know because we were all inside."

When Mod faves, The Spencer Davis Group played the club, the coffee bar collapsed. Later Issues with an application for an alcohol licence, complaints of noise pollution and a local drug dealer's bragging's about selling pills in there spelt trouble.

In May, 1966, a group of Mods, including Lincoln Duke club and Mojo regulars Gordon Rath and Rob Taylor, ventured to the studios of 'Ready Steady Go!' after winning a Mojo dancing competition: perfect timing indeed, as it turned out to be the legendary Soul singer Otis Redding's special.

Rob Taylor (on the left in the suit, Gordon Rath in the white shirt) on the set of the 'Ready, Steady Go! Otis Redding Special'. Gordon won tickets through a dance competition at the Mojo.

Gordon Rath - "It was fabulous! You have to remember how much of a major event or us at the time, it was unreal, definitely a major event for us.

How did it come about? Well, Stringfellow used to DJ warming up the audience for 'Ready Steady Go!' and every so often (three times I was aware of) he would put on a competition for the best dancers at the Mojo and the winning prize was to go and be part of the audience on the show. When we won, it was eight of us, a mix of lads and lasses. We went down by car, a lad we knew from Lincoln, Gregg Organ who now lives in Canada, took us. We met Neil Blanchard and others from up north down there too. When we got there, we were all sheparded into a certain spot. There was no animosity from anyone there, we did keep ourselves to ourselves in our little group, but it was a great atmosphere, everyone there for the same reason, just like back up at the Mojo. There was Chris Farlowe and Eric Burdon there, who both performed up on stage with Otis Redding and also mingled with us all in the audience. I remember trying to get on the camera as much as I could, while dancing. He came back the same night; we couldn't afford hotels back in those days, we were all always skint!

I lived in Lincoln and would meet guys from all over the country to go to all-nighters – Leicester, Peterborough, Nottingham and other places. We would all meet and soon we would be going to the Mojo. Though, I didn't make a great start going there. I got done (along with my mate, Pete) for selling aspirins' for uppers and Stringfellow went mad, he had been getting hassle, already, from the police, so was none too pleased at this. It went to court and I got a fine of 1'n' 6 for something along the lines of 'obtaining money under false pretences and defrauding the public'! It was desperate days; we would do allsorts to get to and get in these clubs and live the Mod lifestyle. I wasn't the only one dealing pills in there either.

Another money scam was asking people to contribute for a mate who we said had been nicked and everyone would chip in with half a crown (a lot of money in those days); everyone was such a friendly bunch at the Mojo and we would all help if anyone was in trouble, we used to do the same, help others out.

I first saw Little Stevie Wonder - as he was called at that time - at the Mojo. Stevie (obviously being blind) kept banging his head on the low roof joists of the building (it was an old church so they were low, and Stevie was quite tall). It was mostly Soul and the Tamla acts I saw there, Four Tops, The Supremes, Jimmy James and the Vagabonds etc. One thing that Stringfellow used to sometimes do was advertise a name act, say The Supremes, and we would all buy tickets and then on the day, he would say they wouldn't be turning up so he would give us a discount for the next time. But... it didn't matter, it was such a fantastic atmosphere, we would be there anyway. It was the comradeship with like-minded Mods and all coming together under one roof and a chance to get away from the humdrum of life outside that was the most important thing. I never saw or heard of any violence in there when I was there, there was nothing to prove in that way. There were some real characters, Toots was one and Margate Tony another, everyone knew of them, but we were all there for the same reasons, to enjoy the music and meet mates in, along with The Twisted Wheel in Manchester, was one of the best Mod clubs in the whole country."

By 1967, the Mojo - now fondly known as 'The Beautiful Mojo' - had indulged in the dominant influence of psychedelia resulting in a period-defining performance by the Jimi Hendrix Experience and an all-day event with Pink Floyd amongst other 'hip' happenings. The mood of the times had changed at The Mojo just as significantly as it had nationwide. The writing was on the psychedelic mural-adorned walls that the end was nigh for what had been Sheffield's favourite club amongst Mods.

Over in Rotherham, a few miles from Sheffield's Mojo club - a town that boasted its own quota of Mod clubs such as The Pendulum and Mod 21 clubs, Up and Up Club amongst others - local Mod girl Katrine Greenwood was frequenting similar club nights as the Mods over in Lincoln.

Left: Dave Growns and friends at the Mod 21 club

Above: Sue Watts at the Pendulum club, 1966

Rotherham's Pendulum club, 1966

Katrine Greenwood (Rotherham Mod, left with young family member) - "I never intended to become a Mod but the alternative was being a Rocker and not liking the clothes, music or motor bikes I didn't have much option. So progressing from Sunday night dancing at a venue which was above the Odeon on Corporation street, I started going to the Baths Hall on Sheffield Road, there I was fortunate to see many bands including 'Them' singing 'Here Comes the Night' and The Gaylords later to become Marmalade (not so great!).

Clifton Hall was always good, in my memory it was huge and took ages to walk round to see who was there, I went just before it was demolished and it seemed tiny! I frequented the LBJ club, which was somewhere near Masborough and this was always a popular event. The Assembly Rooms was also good. My favourite place though was the Pendulum, which was at the top of Moorgate. This was always a good night and the music I loved At this time. I was working as a Saturday girl in Saxon shoes in Rotherham (THE place to get your shoes) so every Saturday morning I got there early to choose the shoes I would be purchasing for that night! All my Saturday money went on this. All our coats were worn long (I still like this style now!) with often something very short underneath, famous words 'you will catch your death in that'! I don't remember ever getting a taxi; you caught the last bus or walked. If you were lucky, some nice person with a scooter would take you home!"

Gary Maxton (right: a morning after a Mojo trip, 1965) - "I lived in Long Eaton, Nottingham, and used to hang about with the Ilkeston lads and also a few from Nott's. Our regular Haunts in Nottingham were The Dungeon Club, The Beachcomber and the Boat clubs. On Saturdays we usually went to an all-nighter at either The Twisted Wheel in Manchester or the Mojo in Sheffield. I saw some great bands in small venues back then; The Who, Small Faces, Yardbirds, Ike and Tina Turner, Ben E King, Sam Cooke and The Drifters. I even saw Otis Redding twice in one night at the Starlight Rooms in Boston first, then a late show at the Beachcomber in Nottingham."

If Found please return to the address overleaf, or to the:-

Dungeon Club
6 Stamford Street, Nottingham
Telephone : 54749

THE DUNGEON CLUB

The Dungeon club in Nottingham was an essential venue for Mods of the region. Like the Twisted Wheel, The Duke and the Mojo, the club quickly tuned into the favoured Soul soundtrack. Maurice Moore experienced first-hand the intimacy, live acts and the sounds played at the Dungeon and other clubs.

Maurice Moore - "The first visit to the Dungeon was to change my life. It was a dark, cold, sometimes damp place and, although the main room was just below street level, you felt like you were some way underground in some subterranean underworld. From the road, you walked up some stairs to enter the club; past the doormen, the cloakroom and the ultra-violet light, which was used to see the pass-out stamped onto the back of your hand. To the right on this level was the first room, which had a small dance floor, some alcove seats round the sides, a jukebox and in the corner a bar where a guy would serve you with an ice-cold coke from a big red coke machine or coffee in glass cups. No alcohol was served on the premises, but we would walk up to a local pub for a drink, usually the Royal Children, Salutation or Trip to Jerusalem. Next to the pubs was a graveyard where couples would go for a 'cuddle'.

Leaving the first room, you would go down the stairs, where posters were attached to the walls (I remember one advertising John Mayall's Bluesbreakers featuring Eric 'Slow hand' Clapton, another for the Farinas, a band from Leicester who, I believe, dressed as 1920s American gangsters and later changed their name to Family). At the bottom of the stairs, round the corner, you would enter a dark room, painted predominantly black, with very loud music throbbing from large speakers and a throng of people dancing. To one side was a stage and the DJ's desk, there was no seating. I had not heard music played like this, volume–wise or the content and it was life changing. The place was not big like the arenas of today but more like a large pub and we were within touching distance of the artists. On one occasion, I remember standing next to this small guy on the dance floor, before realising it was Keith Moon.

Songs I remember dancing to from those early days include 'Night Train' by James Brown, 'Open the Door to Your Heart' by Darrell Banks, 'The Entertainer' by Tony Clarke, 'Tell It Like It Is' by Aaron Neville, 'Boogaloo Party' by the Flamingos. Two records played regularly on the jukebox upstairs were 'Soulful Dress' by Sugar Pie Desanto and 'Walk on the Wild side' by Jimmy Smith. Amongst the Artists I remember seeing on the stage are Soul singers like 'Little' Stevie Wonder, Inez and Charlie Foxx, Patti LaBelle and the Blue Belles, the Drifters, Geno Washington and the Ram Jam Band, bands like the Who, Small Faces, the Steampacket, Mark Four, Dave Dee, Dozy, Beaky, Mick and Tich, Family, more bluesy artists like Screaming Jay Hawkins and Jesse Fuller.

With the love of dancing, all-night sessions developed. These were held at the Dungeon, but the Mods also attended sessions at other clubs, in particular the Twisted Wheel in Manchester and the King Mojo in Sheffield. I think I saw Ike and Tina Turner at the Mojo. Pete Stringfellow was the DJ there and he used to come over to the Dungeon to play a set. After hearing all the soulful sounds played, the Salty Dogs incorporated many of these songs into their set, songs by Otis Redding, Wilson Pickett, Sam and Dave."

Previous page: Ann and Tiggs by the Dungeon jukebox

Above: Maurice Moore

Left photos: Nottinghamshire Mods outside Nottingham Castle and town hall

Maurice Moore - "I went to the Dancing Slipper on one occasion to see the Spencer Davis Group with the amazing Stevie Winwood. On the same night Wilson Pickett was appearing somewhere in town. I remember going up to the DJ at the Slipper to request him to play a record that we were dancing to at the Dungeon, 'In the Midnight Hour'; not only did he not have it in his collection, but he had not even heard of it!

Mods liked to congregate in the Old Market Square in Nottingham meet by the Lions in front of the Council House or just sit and chat in the square or one of the nearby popular coffee bars such as Lyons Tea Shop, the Kardomah, the Four Seasons Restaurant and the L-Shaped Room. They all liked to show off their scooters and would park them in front of the Council House; all sorts of Vespa's and Lambrettas were there and my bright orange DKR Defiant, as I was always different. Suddenly everyone would leave, sometimes moved on by the police, to go nowhere in particular and a large snake of scooters would wend its way through Nottingham. One group who were always around were known as the mini-boys, as they drove around in Mini cars as well as scooters; they were held in awe by many of the group. At the weekends, either instead of or after a trip to the Dungeon, there were always parties to gate-crash. Although the Dungeon was probably the most popular of the Nottingham clubs at the time, there were others like the Beachcomber and the Boat Clubs – the Brit, the Boat and the Union.

The electrical system in the Dungeon was not great and I remember the fuses being blown more than once – certainly during the Mark Four's set and when Screaming Jay Hawkins sang 'I Put a Spell on You', he stepped forward, there was a flash and … all you could hear was the horn section. After his performance, Jesse Fuller was outside giving out very small slips of paper containing his autograph.

In March 1967, the Dungeon, which by then had lost some of its popularity, had an all-nighter featuring the Drifters. People came from all over the country and the club was packed. At some point during the early hours, I went outside to get a breath of fresh air, to be greeted by the arrival of a double-decker bus and an orderly line of marching policemen arriving at the club. It was a raid. They made everyone stay inside the club, with no music and the bright house lights switched on, while they searched every person, then either threw them out onto the streets or, in the case of those who were underage, rang their parents to go down to collect them. I believe the bus was used to search the girls. My friend sat on the floor at one stage, only to disturb a jumper under which was hidden a very large pile of pills. We decided to inform the police, who proceeded to search us and throw us out. Luckily, for us, there was another all-nighter in town that night at the Beachcomber, so we went over there, where Lee Dorsey was performing. Eventually word got back to us that the police had finished and the Dungeon was reopening. The place was quite empty by now, as most people had gone home, however I seem to remember that the Drifters appeared sometime around 6 or 7 in the morning. The next day we were 'celebrities' as the raid appeared in the national newspapers, however I doubt it was very successful for the police, as I don't think many arrests were made.

The Dungeon had Sunday afternoon sessions, sometimes with a live band, often just a DJ playing records. We would go down, and when it finished go to Lyons tea shop in the square for a drink and then drive up to the Hand and Heart near Canning Circus for a pint and to watch 'Batman' on the television, before sometimes going back to the Dungeon for the evening session or going to the 'funnies', a cinema where they played cartoons, but had double seats where you could get close to your girlfriend. The 'Bung', as the Dungeon was known by many regulars, had shaped my life and had been a great place giving me a wonderful experience. I had been introduced to a wide range of fabulous music, met some great people, some of whom are still friends, had a lot of laughs and fun, given me a certain style. We lived, for a short while, in our own unique and exclusive Mod world.

Sheffield's Mojo Club closed its doors in December 1967 - the final song played was the appropriately titled 'I'm Gonna Miss You' by The Artistics; whilst The Duke's original Mod nights had run their course as the 'in' place to be by 1969 and became less of an underground 'elitist' event. The Dungeon lost its impetus following the March 1967 raid, changing its focus and Mod appeal, whilst venues such as The Assembly Rooms and Clifton Hall in Rotherham would become just as popular for a new generation of Mods a decade later. Manchester's Twisted Wheel would move into more northern Soul waters as the Mod scene faded towards the end of the decade.

Northern Mods, who largely by-passed psychedelia in comparison to their southern counterparts, continued their love of Soul and Black American music throughout the remaining years of the decade and beyond. They were fiercely loyal to their clubs and many of those clubs have seen special tribute events in recent years, and, on occasion, updated versions, where original Mods and new generation Mods alike share their undying love of rhythm and blues and Soul.

CHAPTER 6

FIGHT THEM ON THE BEACHES

"It is not likely that the air of this town has ever been polluted by the hordes of hooligans, male and female, such as we have seen this weekend. These long haired, mentally unstable, petty little hoodlums. These Sawdust Caesars, who can only find courage like rats hunting in packs, came to Margate with the avowed intent on interfering with the life and properties of its inhabitants."
Margate Magistrate Dr. George Simpson's sentencing speech, 1964

"There was no way that a Face would scuff their shoes by kicking somebody or something!" –
John Hellier

The unfolding decade saw hordes of families set their sights on the good old British seaside for some respite from their typical daily grind of hard labour. Leaving the suffocating London smog and its suburbs, for the sand, sea and jellied eels of Brighton, Clacton and Margate, amongst others hot on their heels came the young and newly independent teenagers. They came spilling out from the coffee bars, clubs and workaday grind, groups of rock 'n' roll leftovers, motorbike-riding leather-clad wild ones and greasers (often known as ton-up boys), university Dropout beatniks and the most culturally striking, cleanest and confident of them all - the Mods!

This was no pre-planned or premeditated confrontation. The first known clashes took place at the British seaside resort of Clacton during the Easter Bank Holiday 1964. This confrontation between Mods and their apparent adversaries the Rockers was more likely a mere random clash of youth cultures, a relatively inconsequential spark, that once the media learnt of its occurrence, remarkably and literally overnight, it metamorphosed into a sizzling stick of dynamite.

Of course, there was genuine violence, some upheaval and disturbances. Photographic evidence displays numerous skirmishes and scenes of crowds of Mods being chased across the beach by mounted policemen as deck chair-hugging holidaymakers looked on in disbelief. This was a new generation of youth who had shed their post-war past and embraced the freedom and autonomy that their war weary parents had never tasted. One of the first generations to have been denied the obligation to fight in foreign lands to preserve their country and way of life. Once the fuse had been lit and the electricity of youth was switched on, the press and the establishment had their desired field day and the historical perceptions of the Mod v Rocker beach fights was thus created, yet so placed out of context and exaggerated.

Nottinghamshire Mods, Skegness beach

Alfredo Marcantonio - "The end of it was Brighton in 1964 and the riots. These guys weren't real Mods. It was all watered down. They'd bought a scooter and a parka but that was it. What broke your heart was that it got so big, plus it didn't help when the paper blew up the stories about the pills…. For me it was all over. I pulled out"

John Leo Waters - "Of course, the big Mod and Rocker confrontations were at Bank Holidays. The coastal towns were the favourite destinations and there was much posturing and 'drive pasts'. There was relatively little confrontational violence however in spite of what the press would have us believe! Rockers very rarely left the comparative safety of their bikes, which enabled them to pass along the front as leisure but with the advantage of being able to escape at speed if desired. They were more of a threat outside the towns where they could harass and confront smaller groups of Mods on scooters."

John Hellier - "The media were influenced by what they read in the newspapers and Mods and Rockers fighting on the beaches was all that they were interested in. That type of headline sold papers. There were two types of Mods really. The first (and the one I would associate with) were Faces. Faces were very vain and would never even contemplate a fight for fear of damage more to their clothes than themselves. Blimey! I wouldn't even sit down in an empty railway carriage for fear of losing the crease in my trouser! The second type of Mod were more into being Scooter boys than Faces. This was more street level and these guys were always happy to cause a riot! Real Faces disassociated themselves with the second type but it was the second type that the public would ultimately associate Modernism with."

Jeremy Norman - "When you only had one set of decent threads no way were we going to Yarmouth for a 'bundle' with Rockers and get them destroyed. We would sit on the beach when the tide was coming in and let our Levi's soak while we rubbed the legs with sand and beach shingle to help fade them."

Maurice Moore - "Bank Holidays were spent in 'Skeggie' (Skegness) or Mablethorpe to have fights with the Rockers or 'Greasers' or just cause general mayhem. I never took part in any fighting but went along for the buzz. The towns would be flooded with scooters."

Mods and Mini at Margate 1966

Inset: Sid Poulton, Great Yarmouth beach

Sid Poulton (Enfield Mod) - "We Mods used to frequent Gt Yarmouth quite a lot. A few of the lads had jobs in the Birds eye factory in Lowestoft and stayed the summer. The Mods v Rockers thing had almost died out, but there were skirmishes between rival towns. Also, trouble at The Tower Ballroom between northern Mods and us Mods from the London area"

David Middleton - "You simply did not go fighting in a suit, no sod went to Brighton in a suit, mind you what we had on was near the price of a suit."

Rob Nicholls - "Given the opportunity, Londoners would head for the coast during the summer for daytrips or weekends away. Prior to my break up with Pat, we would go on coach trips to Southend or Clacton organized by her factory. Later, my Mod mates and I would occasionally grab a battery-operated record player and set off for the coast in a convoy of cars for a beach party. In the summer of 1963, Jerry Tucker and I and some other friends rented a caravan at Rockley Sands Caravan Park just outside Poole in Dorset. In these out-of-way areas, the Mod panache worked well for picking up birds. Sometimes we would hitchhike to Brighton or another coastal resort, but I did not like hitching-I'm not rough or tough enough to endure it. Motorists would jeer at us as they sped by or worse still, spit at us.

I never took the early morning milk train from Charing Cross to Brighton after an all-nighter in the West End, but many Mods did. They were following a tradition established by their Jazz Boho

(Bohemian) predecessors. Two trains per day were required for the milk trade of London. They Brought milk to London and in the early hours returned with empty urns and tanks providing a cheap and convenient transportation for sleepless club-goers. Always eager to experience the Mod lifestyle, Pete Townshend took the milk train, as Peter Meaden recalls, 'Pete and Nick's ex-girlfriend [Nick Goderson] spend a weekend traveling around Brighton in late summer 1964; sleep together 'platonically,' did speed, shared a compartment on the milk train back to London.'"

Gordon Rath - "We had a few runs to Skeggy on the Bank Holidays and there were a couple of fights with rockers who came on their bikes. To be honest I don't think anyone won, we all had big fat lips to prove it."

Adrian Stern - "We went to Southend one of those weekends in 1964, my sister, cousin Roberta, and others. My sister had a suede coat, which was very 'in' at the time. But seeing no confrontations we went to the Kursaal amusement park. I had to wear my blue nylon 'Pac-a-mac' all day to hide my embarrassment when my new tight white trousers split from seat to crotch.

Remember, that in the early 60's T-shirts were still considered underwear and were only just starting to be worn exposed. My brother brought me back one from St. Tropez with an embroidered anchor badge on the front, but for RSG I persuaded my mum to modify a plain white T-shirt with a big felt letter 'A' (for Adrian) attached to the front. This was worn with straight cotton trousers, parallels, and black Hush Puppies and finally, a steel comb in the back pocket for the 'Barnet' - never without one!"

Recalling the beach disturbances of '64, Mod, John Bentley professes a little dismay at the way they have been portrayed by some sources.

John Bentley (South Wales Mod) - "This was my first scooter in 1962, it's the only photo I have of me on it then - during those days we never took photos. I went to Brighton in 1964 from Newport South Wales on the A40; there were no motorways back then, on a Vespa GS 150. By the time we got to Brighton, there were about seventy Scooters plus all the others that got there before us. It was a great sight to see so many of us there."

Derek Glover - "We had been to the Welsh coast for a Bank Holiday weekend and were travelling back to Smethwick on the Lambretta. Riding through Shrewsbury the engine started to stutter and died. I ended up pushing my Lammy through Shrewsbury and Dianne was walking at the side carrying our luggage. Along came a helpful Bobby. Who asked 'Are you in trouble?' He walked with us to his house, gave us a cup tea and told me I could leave the scooter in his backyard. He then arranged for a panda car to take us to the A5 and we were dropped off at the best place to thumb a lift, which was easily done in those days. Later in the week the policeman sent me a letter (most homes were phoneless) to tell me that he had repaired the scooter and was now up and running. I travelled to Shrewsbury on the train and rode back home on top of the world. Looking back now, I don't think I showed that caring Bobby enough gratitude, he never asked to see my licence, insurance, etc. His only concern that night was for us to get home."

MOD DAYS ON THE SOUTH COAST BY LLOYD JOHNSON

Lloyd Johnson personifies the cool and inspired suss of the period. Quickly tuning into the early Mod sounds and style, Lloyd, from his Hastings setting, experienced a classic south coast Mod journey.

Lloyd Johnson - "Hastings like many other seaside resorts in the early 1960s was a London boys/Scooter Boys destination. The hangouts were The Pamdor, best coffee bar in my opinion and home to both Mods and Rockers. The local rockers/bikers were known as The Stonefield Mob as a lot of them lived on Stonefield Road. There was never any trouble between us because we all went to the same schools. The worst that would happen is that we would nudge the jukebox so their records would reject, for some reason they were always playing Jim Reeves. We preferred Stax or Tamla and some regular hit parade stuff. Other coffee bars were The Fiesta, The Sombrero (more of a beat hangout), The Continental (short lived), and The Scene (short lived). The pubs in The Old Town were very popular with Mods, Beats, Art Students, and Foreign Students. The main three were The Anchor, The Pump House and The Nelson which was the only place in town to have The Cyril Davies E.P. on the jukebox, four records for the price of two!

During the summer months there were dances at St. Clements Caves which consisted of Trad Jazz with local pop and R&B bands in the interval. The Caves were very reminiscent of The Beat Girl movie that featured Adam Faith that came out some years earlier.

In our crowd there was: Micky Piesley, he of the pink ankle swingers; Sue Piesley his sister; Helens Evans who the best at the French jive in town; Liz Hayer; Timmy Hayter; Carry Hayer; Lance Tilbury; Lexley Thewenetti; Steve and Barry Davis; Ronnie Bradshaw; Pete Smith and his mate Eric and many more. At weekends our ranks would be swollen by a group from Tunbridge Wells including Bruce Gearing and Johnny Penfold. We'd also get the London Mods coming down and crowds from all towns in between. The Pamdor would be so packed that they'd be people sitting on the tables which didn't go down well with Eric who ran the coffee bar.

The Pamdor was above Hepworth's the Tailors and above the main Coffee Bar there was a small club which Les Martin, who ran it called 'The Take Five Club,' but we just called it The Pamdor Club. It had a small dance floor where we'd workout new dance moves with the help of the girls, Helena, Lexley, Sue, Liz, and others, after watching RSG on telly.

In 1964 The Stones played the Pier on Bank holiday weekend. The Police were flown in and marched us all over the town. I got bored with it and went back to The Pamdor. I read in the newspaper a few days later that a kid had fallen off the East Hill Cliffs. With so many people herded together something like that was bound to happen. What was going on? Can't kids have a bit of fun? There seemed to be an influx of sheep (followers) around this time. I got disillusioned and left England for Sweden. But it was a great period and I'm really pleased I was born at the right time to live it to the full."

183

THE FACE FROM HASTINGS

Lloyd Johnson - "The girls often stayed up in London with various boyfriends and went to The Scene Club so they were well up on the dances. Style-wise apart from what was going on in England we'd pick up a lot from the French kids from Paris and the Swedish girls from Stockholm who would be wearing things like Ski Pants and clogs in the early 1960s. One French guy use to come to the Pamdor with his hair in rollers, his name was Xavier; he had just finished his time in the French Army fighting in Algiers and could handle himself. He was a real laugh. He didn't care what anyone thought of him, a real character and always immaculately dressed in dark mohair suits, with great wavy hair two inch off-centre parting and a curtain fringe, sideburns and back-combed on top.

We would often go to Brighton and hangout in The Starlight Rooms, The Scan (a Scandinavian Coffee Bar), the Mecca Ballroom by The Clock Tower or The Aquarium. My big memory of Brighton is the scooters at 45% in front of The Electricity Board Offices/showrooms where loads of Mods would wait for the birds that worked there to finish work and whisk them away on their scooters, peeling off one at a time like a Squadron of Spitfires going in for the kill. At this particular time crew necks, Paisley or polka dot tab collar shirts, Levis red socks and hush puppies were popular.

At other times such as Sunday afternoons we'd go to Finch's in Eastbourne, a dive club in a basement but very hip, a great little place. That was around the time of 'Let's Dance,' by Chris Montez and 'The Locomotion' by Little Eva. The best Coffee Bar in Eastbourne was The Continental, the namesake of the smaller one in Hastings. The Continental in Eastbourne had a dance floor in the middle of the coffee bar, and it somehow felt special to have it all going on in one big space.

The best night in Hastings was Saturday when the big name bands played The Pier Ballroom. The Witchdoctor club opened around 1964 and stole The Pier's glory. For a short while both would battle it out with top name bands, neither won the battle. Some people preferred to go to The Pier while the 'Mods' went to The Witchdoctor. The first place I'd ever seen with under floor lighting and fabulous Voodoo Witchdoctor décor, think Screaming Jay Hawkins. The Nashville Teens played the opening night and the list of bands that played there reflects the times: Steve Marriot's Moments, Georgie Fame and the Blue Flames, the Moody Blues with Denny Laine, The Who, and hundreds more."

THE WITCHDOCTOR CLUB - HASTINGS

Lloyd Johnson - "The Witchdoctor was amazingly ground breaking for a club back then as you can see by comparing it with places like The Scene and The Starlights Rooms. They put a lot of work into the décor and it was in a fabulous building being in Marine Court St. Leonards Hastings - it was on the first floor where the vertical windows are at the front of the building."

The popular Witchdoctor club of St. Leonard's on Sea was reputedly the first club with underfloor lighting and complete with voodoo wall images. It was managed by Tony Powell who booked many of the best upcoming bands of the period. Tony went on to become an MD for MCA records and is now retired living in Battle.

The Confederates photo is at St. Clements Caves

Roger Ames - "One Easter in 1964, I went down to Hastings in My Triumph Roadster, the weather was pretty cold with flurries of snow. Anyway one night we went to see The Stones performing in the Pier dance hall, only about forty odd people had bothered to show up, but most were Mods, who had heard the jungle telegraph going round the Mecca dance halls, that Hastings was the place. Not much was going on, so me and my mate Kevin left and mooched around the sea front looking for some talent. We drew a blank, so later on we were looking for somewhere to sleep.

We walked down to the east of the sea front, climbed up the cliffs, and found an unoccupied cave, laid down our sleeping bags and nodded off. Woke up a couple of hours later, the cave was crowded with both Mods and Rockers looking for somewhere to doss down. It was all amicable and we all made the best of it.

My Roadster ran a wheel bearing on the seafront, so jacked it up and removed a wheel, quite a crowd of Tottenham Mods gathered round to discuss last evening events, as a number of Rockers drove by on their assorted BSAs, Triumphs and Matchless's. As they drove past a cheer went up from us, as one of the Rockers Bus conductor hats flew off. They kept on driving up the road and Cyril, one of the notable dancers from the Tottenham Royal, stepped into the road, picked up the hat, promptly pissed in it, and put it back in the road. The rocker soon returned, picked up and donned his cap to further shouts of derision; I don't think it did much for his Brylcreem and possibly Mod and Rocker relations.

Sunday night, Kevin and me managed to pull a couple of girls from Hackney, so we drove up on the fields by the Hastings castle, there were quite a few other Mods around sitting round improvised camp site with small fires. We took out our folding camp bed and sleeping bags from the car and settled down with our female company. About an hour later the field was raided by many police, who chased away everybody, except us four tucked up by my car. I never under stood why we were left disturbed, but unmoved."

David Birchall - "I would say that from the summer of '64 until summer '65 me and my mates put in 40,000 miles on our scooters. Which speaks volumes for the quality of those abused machines. We would go to Brighton or Bognor (bugger Bognor!) frequently. The scene in 'Quadrophenia' where they are sleeping under the bandstand I can recall well since I did it too. My favourite memory of time at Brighton is in 1964, the police rounded all the Mods up and told us to head out of town. I was about fifty yards back from the lead scooter as we left Brighton - two abreast and probably a thousand scooters when the lead scooter simply turned around and headed back into Brighton - we all followed and the police were completely unprepared - we took over!

I recall one trip to Brighton, we had left it a bit late and it was very dark crossing the 'Sarf Dans' so we started looking for somewhere to stop overnight. Somebody spotted a hay barn so we pulled down a bit of fencing and rode the scooters over the field to this barn. We all had sleeping bags of course and we just kipped down in the hay. Just as we were dropping asleep there is a commotion and it transpires that we are sharing the barn with about two dozen pigs (The four-legged variety)! Not much sleep was had that night - bloody pigs didn't like us being there and let us know it.

Another trip we were going through a pea soup fog somewhere on the main Brighton road. You couldn't see more than ten feet and we were almost certainly going too fast when I see two pairs of legs standing beside the road - the bodies were lost in the mist. As I ride by I hear 'DAVE!' yelled in desperation. I managed to turn around and it was two friends whose scooter had broken down and were hitching - this was about midnight! They had recognised the unique sound of my scooter - if it had been somebody else they might have got their heads kicked in.

The Battling Mods Invade A Hamlet

MORE than 60 Mods on their scooters, together with minicar loads of their girl friends, descended on the hamlet of Puttenham, near Guildford, last night, to do battle with village teenagers.

Jostling youths filled the street and local people ran to their homes and locked their doors.

Police from Guildford, Godalming and Farnham were sent. They rounded up the Mods and restored order. They spent nearly an hour taking names and addresses.

A youth was taken to hospital with facial injuries.

David Birchall - "This photo is of three of our group - Tony Whiteman, Roy 'Fingers' Proll and Stewart Poustie in 1964 - they have just returned from a trip to Bristol to meet some girls but it was so wet they had to ship the scooters home on the train!"

Violence was a major part of the Mod scene, no getting away from it. The group that I hung out with were all in the building trade and were a pretty tough bunch, but it was usually a matter of six or more on one. One night at the Wooden Bridge Club there was a confrontation between us and the Guildford Mods. After this they were all gathered in a group discussing tactics and didn't notice me standing on the edge of the group listening in - I would have got my head kicked in if they had seen me. Anyway, they planned to invade our area and 'sort us out' at 7.30 the following Tuesday - as they inadvertently told me! I went back to my group, told them what I had heard and by Tuesday we had reinforcements in and were lining both sides of the street as the Guildford boys rode into town. They saw the situation and didn't stop but we exchanged some insults except for me - being the youngest, and possibly the mouthiest - I stepped forward as one of them rode by - he swung his leg, I swung mine and we both had badly bruised shins for our troubles. That was the only time I ever exchanged a blow with another Mod. I was mouthy but I was no fighter.

We made up with the Guildford boys after that. A few weeks later, we went to a dance at a local village and it turned out to be a Rocker hangout. We were way outnumbered and some of our guys got roughed up quite badly. This would not do so a call was put in to the Guildford boys – would they come and help us out? They were delighted! The ensuing melee' made the front page of the Evening Standard or News, I forget which. The headline read - 'More than sixty Mods on their scooters, together with Minicar loads of their girlfriends (actually the Guildford boys) invade village!' General disgust all round. If any of you computer geniuses can find that from late 64 I would love to have a copy. We saw very few Rockers generally and they stopped going to the resort towns after 1964 - they were outnumbered."

Roger Ames - "We were in Brighton in the summer of 1964 and saw the Who at the Aquarium by the pier. All I remember was that they were absolute crap and not a Mod band. The place stunk of fish, so we soon went outside to see if we could pull a bit of talent to while away the night, but no luck. On the back cover of 'Quadrophenia', Townshend dedicates the album to the Mods they played too in 1965 at The Aquarium and other venues, but I'm sure it was 1964; I suppose 1965 may have been a return gig!"

BRIGHTON ON MY MIND BY DON HUGHES

During the mid-1960's, Brighton was a beacon for Mods such as Hounslow, West London youth, Don Hughes and others intent on casting caution to the wind and living it up at the great British seaside resort. This was a time when a certain untarnished pride still held supreme for our coast and its array of splendour and old Englishness, remnants from a fast-disappearing Empire of old. The Victorian seaside resort of Brighton, though in the midst of its final flurry of popularity, still attracted a sizeable proportion of southern holidaymakers, Bank Holiday revellers, families and scooter-riding 'Sawdust Caesars' - the latter with a media-spread reputation for creating havoc, destruction and disorder in their wake.

Mods such as Don Hughes and his scooterist friends simply wanted to have a good time and grab a taste of the action and experience the thrills on offer. If that involved a bit of a ruckus along the way, then so be it, it was all a part of the excitement and euphoria of being young - after all, nothing lasts forever.

Don's Mod days had grown out of an early addiction to the girl group sounds of the Orlons, Dee Dee Sharpe and the catalogue of the Cameo Parkway label, moving onto early R&B and Tamla Motown (including a memorable meeting with Marvin Gaye). In April 1964, by then a committed Mod, Don absorbed the newspaper headlines and TV reportage of 'Wild Ones Invade Seaside' and 'Scooter gangs beat up Clacton' wishing he had been there. As the nation digested the subsequent 'Mods v Rockers' riots media reports in Don's own words 'the phrase Mods and Rockers was now on the tip of everybody's tongue. Aunts and uncles, neighbours the lot.' By August 1965, Brighton beckoned!

One of Don's first purchased import singles, Marvin Gaye 'Baby Don't Do It'

Don Hughes and his friend Dave Brown, 1965

Don Hughes - "My friend John and I were chatting non-stop about the events along the south coast over the last year. How it all kicked off just before we left school. How my school pal Les found out about it, long before the papers had gotten hold of it. Alan Taylor's story and how he somehow managed to get his ugly boat race into Brighton's Evening Argus last Whitsun and how the silly prat tore it out to show everyone.

Then there was poor old Mickey Robinson getting nicked down there for threatening behaviour. Stories such as girls sleeping out rough down on the beach of a night - up for almost anything. The clubs and ballrooms in the town such as the Barn, the Florida and the Regent. As good as any found in the west end I was informed. Fantastic groups such as The T-Bones, The Abandoned, The Motion and The System. Apart from Gary Farr's mob, I'd never heard of any of 'em but at least they sounded like Mod groups. Doobs? Not a problem-get yourself along to a Beats coffee bar called the Cottage over in Middle Street. It seemed too good to be true. Like some sort of paradise! And here was I raring to go! From nobody to somebody I kept thinking-on my brand new SS180.

That evening Setch approached John and I from out of nowhere by the cloakroom in the Zambezi Club. 'We've been looking for you in here mate, I said to him, where ya been?' 'Down the alley with Mandy' Setch informed us with a cocky smile on his face. The three of us gave each other a knowing grin for we all knew Mandy could knock out a blinding hand shandy. Talk soon turned to Brighton and Setch was puzzled as to why John wasn't going. We decided to go for a coffee before The Chessmen came on.

Behind the latticework in the coffee bar we somehow managed to squeeze in and park our arses. The club was thick with smoke and heaving. Not that Tony Knight and his Chessmen were considered to be some big draw. The subject of Brighton was the 'big draw' here tonight pulling in nigh on all of Hounslow's scooter boys desperate for information about the weekend. A rumour kept going round that the 'theatre of war' maybe moving inland and closer to home. Box Hill or to Richmond Park maybe. The $64,000 question was why? Well the consensus was that the boys in blue had finally got it sussed at Brighton this summer. All kind of stories were floating about what'd been going on down there. Men and women armed with clipboards had been approaching Mods asking all sorts of dumb questions (and getting some dumb answers too, I've no doubt). Plain clothed coppers some had suggested. Then there were the dodgy looking foreign geezers strolling about day and night with cameras slung over their shoulders. Some bright spark came up with the idea that they were coppers too or possibly working for them. But I'd also learnt these so called coppers were shelling out a few bob here and there bribing boys to leg it up the beach! I didn't like the sound of all this. It made me feel uneasy. I mean I was only going there for a giggle. But to be handed up to half a sheet to run up the beach? Why? What for? Did they intend to hand the photos over to old bill? Well I couldn't figure out any of it. So it'd crossed my mind more than once whether it was simply worth going. It all boiled down to one thing really. And that one thing was getting me collar felt. To be honest it niggled me especially after John gave me a blow by blow account of what he saw inside. I'd left me thinking ever since that I couldn't stomach the idea of three days bird let alone three bleeding months!

We sat in the Zambezi's coffee bar most of the evening. Chin wagging non-stop with all our mates had somehow taken our minds off dancing and a bit of pulling. Brighton was on. My anxieties melted away. A meeting place was somehow thrashed out. 8 o'clock tomorrow morning outside the Bell pub or the same time and place on the following day if one chose not to stay overnight. Some kind of scooter pecking order was agreed upon. A contingent of GS/SS and GT's would head off followed by the rest on a motley assortment of Sportiques, LI's and TV's. The idea was to create an impression. To show Brighton, the Hounslow boys owned the best scooters money could buy. Then a real surprise as Setch bent under the table to produce some Doobs from inside one of his socks. He gulped a few down, whispering that he had another two dozen tucked away, a tanner each if we wanted any? He didn't have a care in the world. I declined. Anyway I had my eye on the Jacky Nelson over the other side.

The next morning there wasn't a cloud in the sky and here was I heading for a weekend in Brighton. 'Wow', I said to myself pulling up onto the Bell pub forecourt. Before my very eyes at least fifty or sixty scooters stood on their stands glistening under the morning sun. Small groups of boys had gathered to chat. One or two of them here and there under-taking a few final spot checks on their machines. I knew 'em all-well give or take a couple. And not a bird in sight, thank God. There in the thick of it was Setch. A small crowd had congregated to admire his SS so I gently manoeuvred my way through the crowd to pull up alongside.

Setch was posing. At first he pretended not to notice me. Dressed to the nines, shades on and sitting upright against the spare wheel with his legs stretched out. He busied himself answering questions. I'd dressed up too and not for some beach fight either. A neat all white outfit of white cotton trousers and a T-Shirt. The same gear I wore to the Jazz Festival. Now the crowd really had something to talk about. Two identical SS180's alongside each other. I continued to gaze about me well above the crowd. An explosion of chrome and colour as far as the eye could see.

I introduced Setch to Chris and Nick. Scooter boys...nothing more and nothing less but top of the range scooter boys and that's what mattered. We managed to park our four Vespa's together. Two white and two red models lined up. The perfect match we thought. All that was missing was a camera but no one ever carried one of those around. And then another thought. Had anyone brought a tranny (transistor radio) with them? One was fished out of a tool box. It was Bob's and as he waved the radio high in the air he turned it onto high volume. I could hear a Caroline jingle emanating from it. Brilliant I thought... at least we'll have some decent sounds on down there.

By now the crowd appeared restless. The sudden presence of two coppers on Noddy bikes didn't help matters. It was time to move on. Everyone agreed that the three top models would lead the pack. The cream of the crop if you like - the GT followed by the SS and coming up at rear the Mk2 GS. Slowly but surely we began to kick start our machines into life. And with the noise already deafening I nodded approvingly to George astride his gleaming GS. Ten minutes or so went by as we slowly inched our way forward into Bell Road, allowing the rest to form a convoy behind us.

Heading out towards Kingston we meandered along doing around thirty in order to keep together. I kept glancing over my shoulder to keep an eye on things. One could almost hear buildings shake as we snaked our way through Twickenham. The roads were empty and ours for the taking. However those at the vanguard were becoming impatient. Stuck forever in a lower gear and revving hard I realized it would be impossible to reach the coast together. Word soon passed through the line that beyond Kingston lay the open road and therefore an urge to open up. Exiting the Toby Jug roundabout, those heading the convoy suddenly dropped a gear to accelerate with the Vespa's in hot pursuit. Our patience had finally snapped.

The race was on! Before we knew it we'd reached Burgh Heath. Passing through Reigate we ignored all the birds thumbing lifts. I clocked a road sign for Gatwick. Half way already! Approaching the airport on the A23 dual carriageway we caught sight of still more scooters. Dozens of 'em there were, caning it too. Sixty seventy mph! Approaching Crawley at a set of lights we finally caught up with them and for a split second it was eyeball to eyeball.

As the lights turned to green, the roar was palpable. South and West London riding out together. Dozens of us plus a few birds they'd dragged along riding pillion. Scooter boys and not a hard case or Stylist in sight. And with the Sportique and Li riders trailing somewhere behind maybe a hundred or so scooters in all. Enough for an invasion. And that's what it felt like-an invasion! Next stop-a roadside transport café at Hickstead.

As we rolled into the forecourt, a lorry parked up indicated the café was open. We all drew to a halt placing our scooters onto their stands. Chatting for a while all seemed quiet and peaceful as we made our way towards the entrance. Suddenly the door flew open and there stood this massive geezer. He was wearing an apron. It had to be the guvnor of the café and about to make his presence felt...loud and clear. He told us to clear off, the lot of us. We stood our ground. A few deep inside in the crowd mumbled. Others made discreet gestures. A few V signs here and there, a casual Nazi salute. And with no hard cases along for the ride - what now I thought? Who on earth is gonna take him on? Seconds ticked by. A somewhat bold South London boy suddenly piped up telling him that we had only dropped by for a jimmy and a cup of tea. The guvnor blanked him as we stood there face to face. You could have heard a bloody pin drop as the forecourt fell into a pall of silence. Suddenly the lorry driver leapt from his cab bawling out 'These louts causing trouble Bert?' as he marched over to his side. 'Another stroppy bastard,' I whispered to Setch, 'that's all we fuckin' need.' Setch ignored me. Wearing his brand new Madras check jacket, I sensed he was in no mood for a stand-off. And neither was I. And it appeared, the South London boys. Common sense prevailed. Enough was enough but as we melted away the old boys rolled up their sleeves and limbered up. The guv'nor gestured again telling us to Bugger off with his pal joining in with 'Sling yer hook, before we call the law'

Trouble before we even enter Brighton? No one had bargained for that. One by one we kicked over our scooters. However Bob who'd by chance managed to keep up with us, had to open his big mouth. 'Up yours!" he shouted indiscriminately, pointing two fingers into the sky whereby the café owner and his mate stormed straight over. Smack! And with no if's or butts, Bob cops a fat lip from 'Bert' knocking him clean off his scooter.

'That's the trouble with you boys today, he argued rubbing his knuckles, you've all got too much what the cat licks its arse with!' 'Now I'm warning you lot, the lorry driver chimed in pushing his sleeves up still further by way of making a point, clear off before someone else gets hurt!'

With blood flowing copiously from Bob's mouth, two of the Croydon birds rushed over to help. Tissues and hankies pulled from handbags. Meanwhile George went to pull Bob's battered TV175 off the ground and onto its stand. He kick starts it in readiness. As the two men sauntered back to the café one could see their eyes raking over us. Round one to them and time for a hastily lit fag.

'Come on, one of the South London boys suggested, let's get out of here or we'll have the law to deal with next.' And with Bob hastily patched up we all rolled back onto the A23...

10 minutes later zooming passed Brighton's roadside 'Welcome' towers, a huge cheer rang out with a few fists thrown in the air. 'Brighton... we'd made it!'

Don and pals on Sussex Downs above Brighton town

And so began our prearranged split into smaller groups. Some of us headed for a campsite outside of town while others kept riding towards the seafront. Meanwhile our group followed the map readers and headed for the hills to the small hamlet of Hollingbury. It was blowing a right old gale up there so the map readers and rest of their gang made a decision to ride on further down into the valley. We stayed put. Surveying the scene a dozen or so small tents, their canvas straining against the wind stood pitched across the brow. A few scooters stood alongside swaying and creaking. An old car, a convertible with its hood up sat nearby. Rockers, maybe? But with the sun high in the sky, not a soul could be seen or heard. 'What a view!' I said taking in the fresh sea air. 'Bollocks to the view, Setch groaned, come and help me fix this tent.'

Alongside us were Bob, George and the owners of the other two SS180's...Chris and Nick. We'd agreed to stick together over the weekend, the six of us, two to each tent. Bob flashed the ash so we all lit up. Setch said he didn't like the look of the place. I made a comment about the other tents. Just who was in them? Mods yeah, but there maybe a few hard cases ready to pick on us?

After having to explain which part of London we were from, we ended up introducing ourselves to some lads called Colin, Wattsy and Kevin (who informed us that it was bigger than last year - the law had penned in the Rockers at the West Pier while Mods had been herded like cattle onto the beach by the Palace). The hard cases are bored stiff they told us, plenty of in fighting. Mod vs. Mod... town vs. town, birds stripped and thrown in the sea. Cops galloping around on horseback, truncheons swaying. Meat-wagons there at the ready. TV crews filming. Journos' snapping shots. Men and women with clipboards asking all sorts he informs us. And Stylists sitting around posing-letting the world by, they joked. Amazingly we also ended up with a supply of pills from them. Dexamphetamine Sulphates - the real McCoy. We'd never seen so many pills in our lives. And for once Bob kept his trap shut. Transfixed but not fully understanding Wattsy's pharmaceutical spiel we asked no questions and got straight down to business. A decision was made in a flash. We were buying. Five bob each gave us £1-10-0d in all so we clubbed together all the lolly we had going spare giving us enough to get our hands on sixty of 'em. Ten each! Wattsy kept his word on the price - a tanner a throw. The deal was done and dusted in minutes. After stuffing the envelopes into crevices of our scooters we relaxed and got chatting.

While we stood there listening to advice, we learned of the whereabouts of the cafes. Where to go such as the Cottage, which we'd heard so much about, the Zodiac in St James Street, the Continental, the Whiskey a Go Go and the Mallacca in Duke Street. Where not to go, the Little Chef in Marlborough Place, the Rockers hang out Wattsy warned us. And don't venture into the boozers either he added, or The Skylark on the seafront, who would call the law at one look at us.

Excitement filled our senses as we strolled back to our tents. Wattsy and Co seemed ok. Promised to keep an eye on our tents too! I knew they were drug peddlers and I'd always taken it that peddlers were kinda gangsters. But after our meeting, I felt I'd got it all wrong. I didn't give a fuck to be honest. We'd laid our hands on a load of Doobs for the weekend, and that's what mattered.

The midday sun was unrepentant. Astride our scooters we snaked our way down the steep hill onto the A23 towards the town centre. All appeared quiet. Too bloody quiet. Then trouble. Passing Preston Park to our left, a small group of Rockers had gathered by a small roadside café. First came the jeering, followed by a shower of pebbles they'd snitched from the beach. Wallop! Poor old George, his new GS landed a direct hit creating a nasty dent on a side panel. Shaken up a bit we rode on towards the seafront.

Minutes later at a standstill in heavy traffic we finally caught sight of the sea. Like a lake it was. Could see ya face in it! And as the hot sun beat down, I could hardly contain my excitement. We had to remain cool though as folks began to stare. We sat there on our chrome horses aloof. I gave Setch a nod and a wink for he knew how I felt. Like a fucking King!

As we turned a corner we caught sight of the Palace Pier. The clock tower read 3.30. We headed slowly out from the Grand Junction along King's Road out towards Hove. The seafront was jam packed with row after row of scooters. Moments later girls began waiving. We smiled over at them. Small groups of Mods began to jeer- friendly like but we took no notice. Young school boys stopped in their tracks and began pointing. We ignored them too. I could hear my beloved Radio Caroline blaring from transistors. The 'Sound Of The Nation' was on everyone's dial. And that's when it hit me. There wasn't a motor bike or a Rocker in sight.

A hundred yards from the West Pier we encountered our first run in with the law. A lone traffic cop suddenly jumped into the road, gloved hand outstretched. 'Stop! Your kind are not allowed beyond this point' he told us in no uncertain terms. The cop ordered us to do a u- turn. We duly obeyed. It was just as well as ahead we saw a few spaces up for grabs outside the Astoria café, where we went and ordered six teas and a plate of chips from its hand-written menu crudely cello-taped to the window; we were bloody starving. Food and drink at last. Our faces said it all as the gang fell silent. Within a flash, our chips were wolfed down, swiftly followed by mugs of piping hot tea. The Astoria got our approval rating despite its appearance and the sullen waitress who had made it clear she didn't trust us saying 'No trouble do you hear or you'll have the police to deal with!' As we said our goodbyes a tramp who we had seen smiling over from us flew out of his chair. It turned out he had lost his right hand at Anzio in the war and was after a spare shilling or two. We ended up giving the tramp nigh on a shilling between us. As we argued the tramp grabbed the money off the table and flew out the door. We all followed suit.

Returning to our scooters I mentioned the hidden drugs. Setch was adamant. He'd made his mind up. We'd take them when the sun went goes down. It made sense so we all agreed. Heading towards the Palace Pier tension rose upon each and every step. Mingling with the crowds we were distracted by rows of saucy postcards and various nick-nacks that caught our eye. Chris went wild at the sight of the 'Kiss Me Quick' cowboy hats on sale. He suggested we all buy one to attract girls. He was told to grow up and act his age. Then Bob insisted on buying a stick of candy floss. It was the last straw for me and Setch so we walked on ahead. To be seen shoulder to shoulder with the rest suddenly seemed like a bad idea. Off the scooters it didn't work. Meanwhile Bob scoffed his candy floss. He looked a right state and the others didn't look much better. Setch agreed with me looking over his shoulder sneering. I had to remind him they were all scooter boys. Cut from the same cloth maybe - but scooter boys. We wondered how long it would be before we came across any of the Hounslow and Richmond boys?

George and Bob fell silent while the other two fell way behind talking between themselves. Step by step we become ever more anxious as we approached the theatre of war... the Palace pier beach. The clock tower came into sight. It now read ten past five. Were we too late for a beach? fight? I hadn't a clue. Whatever the case, I wasn't dressed for one. And where were the Rockers? I still hadn't seen any on the seafront. It didn't make sense.

We walked on through the crowd. It seemed like a fashion parade on the seafront. Mods were everywhere. I looked good though and didn't feel intimidated - in fact I felt like a million dollars. It was a chance to check one another out. You know...North London, East and so on. Who's who and who is dressed the best. But all wasn't what it seemed to be. Amongst the Mods were groups of hard cases, tough nuts looking for a ruck. To the untrained eye all would pass as Mod but nigh on all the hard lads had shorter hair with a neat parting. Fred Perry, Levi jeans and Clark's Dessert boots completed the look. They had their own uniform. Clothes I'd never owned.

We were now close by. A nervous silence fell upon us. My heart was beating like a drum. Two coppers on horseback stood side by side on a plinth by the sea surveying the scene. Their eyes peeled looking for any sign of trouble. We marched on under the pier reaching a point of no return. It was then as we emerged, I noticed a gang of Hounslow boys grouped up. Hard cases, the lot of 'em but we'd already been clocked so reluctantly we had to approach them. All appeared primed and ready for action. Edgy, fidgety, eyes flickering all over the show. We acquainted ourselves with a simple nod here and there. Mickey Robinson broke the silence. He told us he'd nicked a scooter out Kingston way, after getting blocked at the Cellar Club all-nighter.

'Fuck knows how I got down here on it, he said bragging, I just dumped it in some bushes outside Hove.' Mickey wasn't giving any old flannel. It was common knowledge around Hounslow that he nicked scooters to get home on. Flanking him was another hard - case I was on nodding terms with, Tommy Roach who together with his band of miscreants had arrived by train.

I glanced over to Setch and the others. They all had a kind of uneasiness about them, for the unspoken deal with any hard - cases was to leave well alone. But here on the beach those rules of engagement were soon forgotten. You stood together and fought together. So I approached Tommy asking, like I had known him for years, what was to happen now?

He gave me the run down on what had been happening since they arrived. Setch and the others meanwhile managed to slip away leaving me on the beach alone chatting with Tommy and his mates. It put me in a bad space. The problem was I couldn't just walk off. I grinned and looked on nervously as Tommy continued when suddenly about a dozen or so boys ran through the crowd causing mayhem and panic. 'Zigga Zagga! Zigga Zagger! Oi !Oi !Oi !' they yelled.

The Mods war cry wrung out. The next thing I know I'm running with Tommy and the rest. Police were running too. Two mounted cops gallop into the crowds swinging their truncheons. I heard girls screaming. Shouting. Scuffles broke out. Dog's barking. A panic welled up inside me as I heard the sound of pebbles crunching under my feet. Up along the pier Joe Public were cheering and waiving as a boy was frog marched off the beach by two coppers. A right old commotion but ten minutes or so later an uneasy calm was restored. Gangs regrouped. Cigarettes lit. Journalists milled around with cameras at the ready. And do you know what? I never even saw a fucking Rocker!

I melted into the crowd and was gone. The beach was fast becoming a battlefield. Mod vs Mod.

Town vs Town. Our very own Anzio! After taking a leek, I walked onto the steps up from the beach. I gazed into the crowds for Setch and the others. As I suspected they'd slipped away too so I headed back to the scooters. The stash of pills came to mind. Huh- they'll perk me up I thought. There was a problem though. It was still broad daylight. Plain clothed coppers came to mind. Those camera swinging journos' and the oddballs armed with clipboards. Other Mods! It was just as well as I was walking along a few yards away I noticed a plod standing over my scooter taking notes. I enquired what was wrong and was asked if I owned the scooter and if so I was parked over the stud of the zebra crossing, he issued me a ticket, despite my protests. 'You should study the Highway Code, instead of wasting my time down here' he snapped at me before storming off. I grabbed the ticket and stormed off. 'Now where do I go?' I thought to myself.

And so I headed off in search of the Cottage. Confused I ended up in Duke Street where I come across the Mallacca Coffee Bar. Heads immediately turned as I walked through the door. A deadly silence hit me as a folkie deep in a corner strummed away at a guitar singing a bloody protest song. Dark, spooky and brim full of Beatniks. I felt uncomfortable as some continued to stare. So I said to myself, oh, no way - walking straight out to resume my search for the Cottage. It took me a while but after asking a few passers-by I finally caught sight of the place situated at the end of a narrow alley.

Once again I found the place full of Beats. However my first impression of the Cottage struck me as more relaxed so I walked inside to pick up a dog eared menu. Pretending to browse through I discreetly glanced around from table to table. A few Stylists were enjoying a coffee together but otherwise like I said, full of pipe smoking bearded Beats chatting with girlfriends. Traditional Jazz boomed out of a juke box. Jazz I thought? Chris Barber? Humphrey Littleton? In this day and age! About to walk out, a pretty girl wearing a matelot shirt and a red beret caught my eye. Glancing down at her fishnet stockings I stopped to gaze. She smiled at me as she crossed her legs and it did cross my mind to... well you know. As I stood there pondering she pointed over to a narrow stairwell. I took the hint. Mods go upstairs. On my way up I heard familiar laughter. It was Bob.

'Blimey look whose here!' he gasped in disbelief. Setch was surprised how I had found them. I told them about the riot and hundreds of us legging it up the beach. 'Wow! gasped Chris, I told ya we should have stayed down there Setch.' He ignored him as I filled them in on the latest letting him know about Tommy being walloped with a truncheon by a copper on horseback and the claret everywhere. 'And some of those South London boys we met got a right old' pasting too,' I added.

I kept banging on and on until something dawned on me. They were all fucking blocked. 'You've all taken the gear ain't ya? I enquired...you been back to the scooters.' They turned to each other and grinned. The rest of the gang laughed as they waited for my next move. But I couldn't help noticing George with his head slumped back facing the ceiling. He looked ill. He had taken the lot. Once again they all broke out into laughter at George's misfortune. 'Of course we have!' Chris confessed to me. 'And don't worry about him, Bob cut in, he'll liven up in good time.'

I soon forgot about George's plight. A feverish excitement came over me. The shakes, a dry throat- you name it. Nerves I guess. I gazed for a while at the dozens of scooters parked up. Row after row with their fly screens reading... Wembley, Acton, Tottenham, Streatham and many more. Half of London in fact. After a quick shufti I got to work removing both side panels and the plug from my scooter. So far, so good. I knelt down further to pull out the package I'd tucked behind the spare wheel. It'd gone! I fished around. In a panic I forgot the world around me as I groped clumsily for my stash. And there they were. Phew! Thank God for that! And like a kid with a tube of Smarties, I gulped 'em down there and then sat by the road side. Feeling euphoric I screwed back the plug and slung the panels back on. It was just as Setch said it would be...easy peasy.

Back at the Cottage I walked in feeling like I owned the bloody place. It wasn't the pills kicking in just a familiarization I guess. The Beat chick smiled once more. Should I or shouldn't I. Nah I thought as I took to the stairwell, there's too much going on. Reaching the top I glanced over at the gang. They looked comfortable, too comfortable. I suggested we go and see Graham Bond at The Florida club. Nobody was keen to move on. George sat there in a heap out of his brain. Nick complained of the heat while Chris and Bob continued to grumble of the cost. Desperately I turned to Setch suggesting instead that we try The Barn with Gary Farr on stage (I had seen it on a poster) – it was only five bob to get in. Setch thought it over but I could see he wasn't impressed.

Nick told me the reason Setch wasn't so keen was because he had his eye on a Beat chick wearing a red beret downstairs. Apparently, she was after going for a ride on his scooter. A fucking beat on a scooter? I was in no mood to listen to all of this. No club, no beach and as yet no bird for the night. I knew I was cornered. I stared across at George who was about to keel over. Huh! What a night this is turning out to be. So I made [another] suggestion. 'We should get him out of here, I demanded...take him to casualty or something.' 'Don't be so bloody stupid, argued Bob, they'll start asking questions.' 'But what if...? 'Blimey Drugsy, he exclaimed, ya sounding like Margery Proops!'

The three of them sat there rolling up. It appeared no one gave a fuck about George. I became anxious. I kept thinking he may have overdosed or had some sort of nervous reaction my Mum warned me about. Despite my unease I never found the courage to say or do more. As we all looked on the lads hollow laughter ground gradually petered out. Maybe they too were having second thoughts. A chilly silence permeated until Setch returned with our chip rolls and Pepsi's. 'Ice cold these drinks, he enthused as he carefully put down the full tray, I saw the old girl take 'em out of a fridge!' We all tucked in. Suddenly ears pricked up as a Zombies single began to play on the downstairs juke box. Bob leapt from his chair and threw himself over the bannister making a plea for it turning up. Thinking we were about to be slung out, the room shuddered to the sound of 'Tell Her No.' The Cottage café had agreed to Bob's demands. I couldn't believe it! We were now staying put. The Cottage had lived up to expectation. And as the night rolled on we soon forgot about The Barn, The Florida, the beach and poor old George. Ok it wasn't the Zambezi Club but a few home grown Soul groups had now made the grade and the Cottage juke box stacked them all. Why even a local group was on the rack, none other than Gary Farr and the T-Bones..

Throughout the evening we mingled peacefully amongst the Beats and the Stylists. It gave me an opportunity to check out their current soundtrack. I fed the juke box to listen to some genuine Blues men. For the first time ever I heard Memphis Slim, Jesse Fuller and Big Bill Broonzy. I became more and more interested as the evening rolled on listening and chatting away with the Beats down on the ground floor. They were helpful and courteous informing me of a new Blues show on the pirate station Radio 390 hosted by Mike Raven. 'You'll hear everything on there', I was told. I hung on their every word. It gave me a feeling I was moving onto new vistas maybe. Totally engrossed I suddenly heard a panic struck voice hollering at the entrance. 'Quick! - quick!- there's a bundle going on down the seafront, quick- hurry up- hurry!'

The Beats completely misunderstood. Thinking it was a raid, the cafe descended into chaos and confusion. As the seconds ticked by, small bags of Mandies dropped to the floor. Dozens of 'em! 'Anyone from Croydon in 'ere, a lone voice pleaded, South London?' 'Why? I shrug, it's gone bloody midnight!' 'Come on, he demands pointing to the end of the street, gotta get down the seafront- now! Some lads in a motor have been nicked, there's a right ol' ding dong going on down there!'

A crowd of us from inside the Cottage soon gathered asking questions. Another bunch of Mods had already congregated at the end of the alley. I did a quick head count. There had to be around twenty of us. Enough for now I thought. Finally Bob, Chris and Nick appeared from upon the stairwell. 'Where the hell is Setch?' I yelled out to Bob demanding to know. 'Take one guess,' he shouts suggests grinning from ear to ear. 'And George?' I ask impatiently. 'He's in the bog throwing up,' Bob shouts above the din, we'll have to leave him.' 'Well come on then, I yelled again, let's get down the seafront with the rest.'

Within seconds we arrived at the bottom of Middle Street looking out onto the seafront. All of us primed and ready for action. Once again there wasn't a Rocker in sight. Instead a screaming crowd had gathered around a number of meat wagons and a car. The car was identical to Wattsy's. A number of fights were breaking out. Heads were butting. Fists were flying. Coppers steaming into the fray with dogs on leashes and truncheons pulled. The boot was going in good and proper. It was time to wade in.

As on the beach earlier, the excitement was palpable. I pushed my way through along with the rest, screaming, shouting, pushing and punching. I felt nothing until I slipped and fell to the ground. I couldn't get up. I was on my own. My ankle was throbbing and all I could see was legs kicking. I panicked but managed to crawl away to a nearby shrubbery. The dogs began taking chunks out of us all. Hoping for the best I curled up into a ball. My luck soon ran out as an Alsatian suddenly tore into my left foot ripping my shoe! In the mayhem the copper mistakenly pulled the dog off me. Lucky I guess so I continued crawling to the side of a seafront bench where I played dead. Well almost. My ploy appeared to work as the fighting continued all around me. I looked in desperation for Bob and the others. I saw no sign of them. My adrenaline was pumping fast and furious. I had to get up. I just had to! And as I was about to I heard... 'You're nicked sunshine!'

I froze. However I soon realized it wasn't my collar being felt. It was none other than Wattsy, who'd struggled free but caught and thrown to the ground. Then it hit me- it was their motor! I hid my face away from him. I didn't wanna be roped into Wattsy's kinda shit, all that drug peddling kinda shit. It made me think for a second. He had to be looking at a few years bird. Hiding my face still, I looked on as his last moments of freedom ebbed away. Sat there huddled up on me jack I watched as Wattsy was bundled into the back of the van. I was scared shitless. I had to scarper. Get away. Back to the Cottage, the scooter even. Anywhere but here!

We clomped over the pebbles to the seashore and I was more concerned about the state of my suede shoes. They were ruined. We watched on from relative safety as sirens rang out. Three meat-wagons were pulling away heading back to the nick. Conscious that we'd slipped the net we drew breath to consider our next move. It was almost daybreak and as the sun slowly peeked above the horizon we sat there watching the rippling of the waves discussing the plight of Wattsy 's gang and the rest of the passing day. The brawl and how it started. Setch and the Beatnik bird. Tommy's gang. The Croydon boys and not forgetting George. We had a great deal to catch up on.

Another hour had passed and before we knew it daybreak was upon us. We'd been up nigh on 24 hours. The Dexy's appeared to have worked we concluded! It was time to go. Making our way back to the scooters we stopped to take a gander at local fishermen pulling their haul from huge nets. Some of the fish were still twitching we noted. Up and away from the beach, the main road was all but deserted. A few scooters parked up here and there suggested a few of us had slept along the seafront. All was quiet as gangs of Council workers busied themselves sweeping the length and breadth of the promenade in readiness for the next big day - Bank holiday Monday. For us though the pills were finally wearing off. The come down was upon us. We were gasping for a drink and began to feel tired. We were concerned about one thing and that was George. He was left on his jack upstairs at the Cottage but hours later here outside the Astoria Café, his scooter remained parked up. We all began to worry but felt it was down to Bob to find George so we persuaded him to return to the Cottage. Ten minutes later he returned alone. The Cottage was shut. George had gone missing. So now what? Call the police? Or run a full scale search party? No way - not at this hour of the day. He's big enough to handle himself we concluded - so we headed back to the tents to find Setch there. Setch had the pretty Beat girl from earlier tucked up under his parka. She was fast asleep so with the prospect of naked flesh on view I took a closer look inside. And with not so much as an ankle in sight, I grabbed my belongings, closed the flaps of the tent and sauntered over to Bob's for some kip. It'd been a long day.

'Come on its almost lunch time - I'm bloody starving!' Bob was shaking me to come to, the following day. 'Did George turn up?' I said to him rubbing my eyes barely awake. 'No' 'I wonder where he's got to then.' 'Fuck knows, Bob snapped, Setch has gone too so let's get down the seafront and find out eh.' I got the message. Bob was clearly worried about his mate. He crawled out of the small tent so sensing his anxiety I quickly followed suit. Chris and Nick were outstretched on the hillside enjoying the sunshine and their first cigarette of the day. Taking in the view some might say. I looked around me. Saw no sign of Setch, the Beat chick or his scooter. In fact there was no sign of any other scooter, tents or lads either. The four of us were left alone so Bob and I moseyed on down the hill to join the other two. With Setch disappearing again and George missing we needed to discuss our next move. However their minds were already made up as Chris and Nick planned to head back home. They'd had enough. I pleaded why, trying to sound persuasive, proclaiming that it was going to be massive that afternoon; a right laugh, even though the afternoon was already here and it was clear that Chris and Nick had already made up their minds. Bob and I looked at each other unsure. We were staying put. We simply couldn't or wouldn't abandon our mates.

And so we all began the task of dismantling our tents and packing up the rest of our belongings. Despite our differences there were no hard feelings between us. If the truth was known I wasn't 100% about returning to the beach myself. We'd been up all night and had our fun. But the fun was far from over as we hadn't met any crumpet and that I guess was the tipping point for Bob and I. The four of us said our goodbyes and split. Next stop the Astoria.

George's scooter was still in the same place which gave us cause for concern, but he must have been around somewhere? We took off our parkas and strolled across the main road to the seafront. 'Hey look over there, Bob suddenly exclaimed, that row of scooters- do you recognize them?' It looked as if the rest of Hounslow were here. Bob and I became excited. The rest of Hounslow 'had' arrived. The Monday contingent. We grabbed some bacon sandwiches and cups of tea out of the Sunray and went back outside. Everywhere you looked there were Mods with hoards of pretty girls following behind all giggling. One or two smiled at us as they passed while others walked on ignoring us. Fed and watered we headed off towards the Palace Pier.

I felt good about myself. I'd only been here a day but it felt like a week. My fear had gone. I felt invincible! Trouble was though I looked like the fucking tramp. My clothes were filthy and then there was my shoe. Ripped and torn so much it made me walk with a slight limp. Bob kept taking the piss claiming I'd never pull a bird in a million years. I began to believe him. My thoughts turned to Tommy and his mates. They'd got it so right with their regulation uniform of Fred Perry, Levis and Dessert boots. A white outfit was strictly for Stylists. A few minutes later I noticed the toilets. It was time to take a quick jimmy. Then through the crowds we saw some sort of commotion going on by a hot dog stand. Tables and deck-chairs in the air flying about, men looking on and cheering, girls laughing and small boys darting in and out trying to obtain a better view. A couple of Old Bill stood there just looking on, arms folded and chatting, no doubt waiting for a meat wagon to arrive before they steam in. Asking a nearby Mod what the knockabout was all about, I was told that the Tottenham and Edmonton Mods were tearing limbs out of each other as they hated each other's guts. Bob and I walked on. Nearing the Palace Pier I felt my heart pounding again. I glanced at Bob. He looked distinctly nervous.

We were now under the pier entering the theatre of war. Just as it was yesterday only better! The beach was jam packed with Mods from all over town. Peppered amongst them were the hard cases. Some were huddled in groups smoking. Others were simply looking on waiting pensively. A few Stylists dressed up to the nines stood near a stairwell - just in case. Across the breakwater I saw another world. Mums and Dads relaxing in deck chairs while kids busied themselves making sandcastles A few pensioners huddled around a wind break were enjoying ices together. A small dog wandered about pestering folks for tit-bits. All were blissfully unaware of what lay ahead. I stood there in awe. And then somewhere in the distance I could hear the sound of Radio Caroline... the soundtrack of a generation. Our generation. Better still - my generation. We eventually found the rest of our mates who'd turned up for the day and there in the thick of it was Tommy and the rest of his team. As bold as brass I approached him and tapped him on the shoulder. 'Alright mate...' 'Fucking hell-what you been up to, he said to me in astonishment, just look at the fucking state of ya!' 'It's a long story Tommy,' I said all nonchalant glancing at his ear. 'Well come on let's hear it then, he responded eagerly, spill the beans-tell us what happened?'

So I told Tommy the story and he was all ears [well one and a half I'd say] as I gave him a blow by blow account. He flashed the ash as I spoke. The rest of 'em stood hanging on every word. Even big mouthed Bob kept schtum. And for the first time in my life the eyes and ears of those that mattered were upon me. As I continued to explain the events of last night, I gradually felt this feeling come over me. A euphoric feeling that I'd finally arrived. It occurred to me that here on the beach I'd become a seasoned player overnight. To some I looked evil incarnate. I took a look around me. Way above me along the promenade Joe Public had turned out in droves waiting for the show to begin. Behind me a heavy mist had settled upon the sea like a backstage curtain. The stage was set.

Overnight I'd become a programmed weapon of destruction. Volcanically unstable, a bloody savage. Christ, I'd become Tommy! And for one brief minute I seized the moment. I found myself lifting my arm to shout the beach war cry, Ziggy zaggy ziggy zaggy oi oi oi! The beach erupted. Hundreds of us ran amok. Police gave chase. All along the promenade Joe Public cheered them on. I caught a glimpse of more police streaming onto the beach backed up with dogs while two on horse-back gave chase with truncheons drawn. Girls screamed as boys began to shout. Moments later all around us, the dogs were baying like wolves, scuffles broke out, a candy floss stand turned over. Deck chairs went flying, picnic tables, pots of tea, crockery went the same way. I saw children under my feet, crying. I panicked and so I ran, ran and ran till I could run know more. Exhausted I collapsed spread-eagled behind a breakwater way up the beach. It was deserted.

Laying there all I could hear were the barking dogs and the distant cries of the children or maybe the injured. I looked around. I was alone but for some reason, a crippling guilt had come over me. I had to get out of town - quick.

A few miles out I saw a bird thumbing a lift. Young and pretty, she wasn't one of those dirty Beatnik types you generally saw hitch-hiking. I pulled up. With her blond hair cut into a fashionable bob, she wore a green suede jacket and a cream skirt above the knee. Nice legs, very nice. She was real cute, there was no denying it. I gave her a lift home to her Littlehampton which turned out to be a small run-down council estate. You know the sort of place, door numbers painted on the front with car engines sitting in the garden.

Back home I watched the evening news on the telly. To my amazement the Brighton beach scenes had been filmed. I saw Tommy being dragged along the beach by three coppers. I couldn't believe it! 'You haven't been down there have you?' Mum asked me. 'Oh no way Mum, I've been to see a girl I know in Littlehampton. She's gonna write to me soon.' 'But you told me you were going camping?' Mum then asked me as sharp as a needle. 'And what happened to ya shoe, she added, and why you so filthy rotten dirty?' 'Blimey Mum, I snapped, it's all questions questions with you!' 'Huh, she replied desperate for the last word, you wanna watch it with these girls you keep seeing, I don't want you bringing no trouble home - do you hear me?' 'Don't be daft Mum, I'm a big boy now and I know what I'm doing. Anyway, I added gathering up my belongings, we're just good friends...' She ignored me and got up to turn the telly over. I said no more and went upstairs to bed. It'd been a long weekend."

EPILOGUE

John: Spent the weekend quietly with the rest of his family. He never did explain to me why he never came to Brighton that weekend. At the time I simply ruled it down to parental pressure.

Setch: After spending the rest of the day with the Beatnik girl he headed back home dropping the girl off in Wimbledon. He never saw her again.

Bob: Having run amok along the beach with the rest of us, we lost contact. He later slipped away with the rest of Hounslow's scooter boys attending the Florida later that evening.

George: Wound up in the early hours of Monday morning at the casualty department in Brighton General Hospital. Suspected of taking drugs he was ticked off and finally released around midnight with a clean bill of health whereby he rode home alone.

Chris and Nick: Having left the camp site they arrived in Hounslow by early Monday evening where they spent the rest of night in the Zambezi Club.

Tommy: Was later charged with possession an offensive weapon [a length of rubber tubing] and remanded in custody pending reports. Two of his mates were remanded on bail accused of using threatening behaviour.

Wattsy: After an argument over drugs and cash, the fight on the seafront broke out initially between Wattsy and Co and a gang of Mods. When the police arrived both gangs attacked them. As a result the car was impounded and over a dozen boys were bundled off in the back of three meat-wagons. They all appeared at a special court in Brighton early on Monday morning. Wattsy along with his two sidekicks Colin and Kevin were remanded in custody for three weeks for medical and probation reports. All three were all facing stiff jail sentences.

Don Hughes third instalment to his 'Friday on My Mind' trilogy is called 'Get the Picture' – and is an illustrated view of his experiences, with new exclusive stories included.

BRIGHTON BANK HOLIDAY 1965

John Leo Waters - "Brighton... Where to begin? I went to Brighton twice in the sixties. I cannot remember the exact dates but I know for certain that one was on Bank Holiday Monday in June 1965. The reason I know is because that weekend was one of the most memorable in my life!

It started at La Discotheque on Wardour St. This was our favoured club (we being a little firm from Archway in North London). Following the previous Bank Holiday 'events' at various seaside destinations this weekend was being discussed in some length by many club goers. Not that there was any chance of discussing anything in the club over the sounds of Stax and Motown blasting out of the speakers! No, we had met up earlier in the 'Coffee A' cellar coffee bar down Whitcomb St and had arranged with some girls from Borehamwood to meet up on the Monday morning at Victoria station. There was going to be around 20 or so of us in total, which was a nice number (safety in numbers!)

The Saturday night was like most other nights in Soho – lots of great music, dancing and a few of 'mothers little helpers' to keep pace! Sunday was normally a 'day of rest' but this being a bank holiday was different. The sun was shining as I remember and we spent most of the morning just mooching around our local coffee bar – De Marco's at Archway. I got some kip Sunday afternoon in the local Odeon (this was par for the course!).

Sunday evening was a big event - The Who were playing at St Joseph's Hall on Highgate Hill. The hall had started putting on concerts a short while ago and this was the big one. The band had a following within the Mod community featuring regularly at some of the West End clubs. They had hit the big time with 'I Can't Explain' and were currently riding high with 'Anyway, Anyhow, Anywhere'. Although both songs were very popular with Mods we found the 'B' side of their first single more interesting being a version of the Kinks 'Bald Headed Woman'.

Early evening found us ensconced in the lounge bar of 'The Cat' on Highgate Hill. Not one of our regular drinking spots it was however, next to the venue and was soon full of punters. Most of the talk was of the following day and our 'trip to the seaside'. We were building up in preparation for the event. We had a few 'sherbets' and had been joined by a couple of the top local 'faces' – 'Haggis' and 'Birdy'. Obviously, Haggis was of Scottish origin and Birdy? – no idea! All of a sudden, we found that we had been joined by Keith Moon and Pete Townshend who knew Birdy and the trip down to Brighton was mentioned several times. Moon said he was going down but we took that with a pinch of salt! By now, the place was heaving and it was time to make a move. The hall was sold out and the band was – well, as you would pretty much expect. Loud, brash and full of energy! Lots of young girls squealing and shouting seemed to be the order of the day.

We were mob handed as the event was on our manor and there were probably fifty or sixty of us in the hall. We danced, looned about and tried showing out to a few birds as we normally did. Then someone spotted a small contingent of faces from another local firm! The sheer effrontery of them! On our turf as well! Of course words were exchanged and before long there was a fight. I was across the other side of the dancehall and seeing the melee dashed across with all guns blazing, so to speak only to be met by a right hook smack on my jaw which sent me flying down the highly polished dance floor to end up in a heap under a table full of girls by the front of the stage! Talk about embarrassed – I was livid! The fight was broken up by the bouncers (all good local chaps) and the invaders were put to flight very quickly.

The night continued and the skirmish had whetted our appetite for the Bank Holiday. The Who were giving it large with the guitar-smashing bit, which livened up the crowd (although it seemed a bit pointless to me). My mate 'Mac' and I had scored with a young lady who had come in with the other firm but decided to stay on after they 'left'. My family had moved from the area recently but I still had the keys to the old place and there were a couple of old beds left behind so along with another lad, John (who had his girlfriend with him) we decided to camp for the night. I won't go into detail but suffice to say that we didn't get a lot of sleep and John in the next room got even less! The reason for which became apparent the next morning when he discovered countless bites inflicted by bed bugs!!!

The following morning found us meeting up at Victoria station. There were around a dozen of us in all (not sure where the remainder were!). A few paid for tickets, some even bought returns! I didn't believe in paying for anything if I could avoid it so I just bundled my way through with the crowd (no turnstiles in those days!). The train was packed with Mods heading off to the seaside (minus buckets and spades!). We settled into a compartment to ourselves – not difficult as the few other members of the public around were not really partial to sharing the journey with a bunch of herberts!

All the talk was of what we were or weren't going to do when we got to the coast (most of it just waffle). Word came that Keith Moon was on the train but I am not sure if that was true? At one stage a ticket collector tried to make his way down the corridor checking tickets. I hid in the overhead luggage rack (just a basket like arrangement in those days) covered with coats etc. I am sure he was perfectly well aware of what was going on but did not fancy getting involved!

We hit Brighton like a plague!! Dozens of erstwhile hooligans disgorging onto Queens Road and heading down to the beach. The sight of a beach full of Mods numbering in the hundreds was a sight to behold! All along the promenade were police shepherding and cajoling Mods onto the beach where they could be kept under some kind of control I suppose – at least that was the theory!

It was like Soho on a Saturday night. Groups from various clubs and different manors in London mixed side by side oblivious to the fact that under normal circumstances they might have been at each other's throats! All around the beach many girls had transistor radios, which were tuned into pirate stations, which were blasting out a heady mix of Motown, Soul and chart hits. There were familiar faces everywhere and most of the day was spent wandering up and down the beach/front catching up with others or trying to chat up the ladies. Rockers were few and far between to be honest. Every now and again a convoy of bikes would make its way along the front but going fast enough to avoid direct confrontation and keeping within sight of the accumulated police forces. The pebble beach made for some very handy missiles, ideal for pelting at the passing enemy!

The previous year (1964) had seen a much larger Rocker representation and there had been more skirmishes but they were massively outnumbered in 1965. The Rockers tended to keep to the outskirts of town where they could ambush Mods as they came in on scooters. Whenever boredom set in some bright spark (Birdy a couple of times!)would stand up and shout 'Grease' or some such war cry! Immediately a large mob would rise as one and head off at speed chasing the 'invisible' enemy. To be fair there were a few instances when Rockers were really being chased but on most occasions it was simply an excuse to rampage through the town creating havoc!

The damage caused was mainly superficial and consisted of knocking over signs, litterbins etc. with the odd shop window being put through. There were a few minor cases of theft from shops but again this was minimal. Most of the fighting consisted of scuffles with the police. I was grabbed on a couple of occasions but managed to get away without having my collar felt (leaving one member of the constabulary with a sore shin!). I saw at least one of our number dragged into the back of a paddywagon though.

There were several coffee bars around the town some which were equipped with jukeboxes and a few with pinball machines. These were popular spots but tended to be packed out. My abiding memory of walking about the town is Sonny and Cher's 'I Got You Babe', which seemed to be playing on every jukebox or radio. The song still evokes memories of Brighton today. We had decided to stay overnight and make our way back to London by train the following day.

The year before we had spent up and attempted to hitch a lift back to town. There were four of us and we walked for a full day and into the evening eating 'scrumped' apples for sustenance without one lift. Eventually we had to hide behind a hedge and let one of our number hitch a ride. A Mini eventually stopped and we all jumped out and piled in! To be fair the driver was a real diamond – he was a French student of some kind and not only dropped us in Sloane Square but bought us all tea and toast on the way. No, this year it was going to be the train!

We were hanging around the town centre trying to 'get lucky' with some local girls with the view to finding somewhere to crash out for the night but without much success. There were very few venues in Brighton in those days and to be honest I think a lot of places just shut up shop in case of trouble. The area around the Aquarium was very busy and the Florida was open if I remember but packed out so no chance of getting in there. We decided to find somewhere to 'kip' once the pubs had closed. Of course, there were plenty of others with the same idea! We eventually picked a spot in the grounds of the Pavilion and made ourselves as comfortable as possible. I drifted off to sleep only to be awoken by a copper's size 10's in my ribs. We were told in no uncertain terms to 'move on' although the terminology was a little more blue in content.

After a while wandering around we settled under the pier with a dozen or so other sorry looking Mods and spent a sleepless night to put it mildly what with the breeze off the sea and the sound of the waves. I remember I was wearing a pair of bottle green Desert Boots. We had taken to dyeing Desert Boots in various colours (seemed a good idea) and at one stage I removed my shoes to find that my feet were a lovely shade of deep green where my boots had got wet whilst messing about on the beach!

By morning we were damp and miserable. Whatever cash we had brought was just about gone and we decided to head back to London. There were three of us by this time and my two mates both had return tickets. Not to worry, I thought – a quick check revealed enough cash to get a ticket to Redhill, which was just outside Brighton – once on the train I would be away. We duly made our way up to the station where I purchased my ticket and we headed toward the platform where the London train was waiting. We showed our tickets and walked past the ticket inspector toward the train when I felt two hands grab me by the shoulders! I spun round to be confronted by two coppers (of some considerable size!). 'Going to Redhill, are we?' 'There's a special train just for you.' They dragged me across to the other side of the platform where a sorry looking bunch of similar Mods were waiting 'under guard' to be put on a slow local train that was only going a few stops!

Now I was sweating! I watched my mates get on the train and then the whistle sounded and she began to pull away. My mates were at the door and I made a decision and as the train began to build up a little speed I broke away and made a dash along the platform. The lads had the door hanging open (no locks in those days) and I ran alongside until I made a grab and jumped aboard. James Bond would have been proud of me. The journey back was uneventful as almost everybody was asleep and we exited Victoria without any trouble.

That was the last trip to the coast as Mods. The following year was the World Cup so our minds were on other things and by 1967 things had begun to change. We were a little older and wiser perhaps or simply a little less energetic!"

TORQUAY '66' – AWAY FROM THE BEACH FIGHTS

There was also a much less vibrant side to visiting the great British seaside for some Mods.

By the mid-60's, the package holiday experience was now in its stride, but not for most working class people, it was still largely the perogative of the middle class and above. For the masses, Mods being no exception, the British seaside still reigned supreme.

In contrast to the high profile beach fights elsewhere, Gill and Del Evan's trips to Torquay were tranquil and sociable.

Gill, Del and Pam holidaying in Torquay

Del Evans (smoking cigarette) with friends, Mike and Pam, Torquay 1966

Gill Evans - "Torquay? We wanted to go away with our friends Mike and Pam and Mike said he had heard that other Mods saying that they were going there. It would be the last week in July and first week in August, what we called the industrial weeks, and we set off with all of our best gear – or togs as were often called them. We went down in our MGB and Mike and Pam in their Volkswagen Beetle.

It was very tranquil, nothing like what had been going on a year or two previously in Brighton and those other seasides. There were a couple of nice pubs down by the harbour and we would go in there and meet up with some of the other Mods we knew that had gone down there.

In these photos, Del is wearing the right clothes, is lighting up the right French cigarettes and looking the part. It was all about these certain things, not only the clothes and the look, but drinking the right drinks, the right colours of clothes, the right shoes, the right shades, the right attitude. Del had all of that, he was meticulous."

By 1966, the infamous beach fights would gradually subside as the youth driven Mod generation adopted less confrontational methods of self-expression - change was in the air.

Still, the exuberance of that time would leave a lasting impression upon many of those who participated.

Reggie Webster - "Brighton was a regular hop for us really. The Guildford-Woking area was an hour and a half away from Brighton so as soon as the good weather came it was off to the coast en-mass. Crew meeting crew on the way down, South and West London kids, Redhill, Kingston, Croydon, Middlesex and so on. Just a quick wave and a nod and the group would get bigger. Later in the 60's it was important to stay remote. Local coppers were OK, but they would draft in the Met for Bank Holidays. There was always a three-way split, a few up the A23, rest to Hove or left to Lewes. Always road blocks checking documents and scooters, any excuse to turn you back or give you a nick. It was easier to go by car in 69-70 as nobody took any notice.

The Top Rank was OK, probably more Mods in there than anywhere else in the UK on Bank Holidays, but in the low hundreds not 1000's as imagined now. There were a couple of clubs near the car park but they just seemed to be the usual 'swinging sixties' type places, trendy Paisley shirts and bouffant haircuts. Nine times out of ten they wouldn't let you in, just like the landlady's 'No Mods or Rockers' signs posted in the windows. The same with some of the cafes. It seems ironic that nowadays they look forward to a version of them arriving because it's a pay day."

John Leo Waters - "Brighton 1964 and 1965 will always hold a special place in my memories. It was all a part of coming of age I believe. The camaraderie, the sense of belonging, the excitement, the sheer bloody mindedness and being part of that wonderful revolution will stay with me forever. I still visit Brighton and I love the place. Outside of Soho there is no better place for a sixties Mod to relive those heady moments."

John Bentley - "They were great times but a lot of guys have got it so wrong about what happened that day, [Brighton] we were just young kids having fun."

John Bentley's friends in 1965: left to right Vicki, Snowy, Jack, Angie and John at the bottom. Vicki is now a matron at a hospital in Newport South Wales. Snowy, Jack and Angie have all sadly passed away.

Like punk, a decade later, Mod in the mid-60's was in effect partially ruined by negatively focused media overkill. The famous 'beach fights', though symbolic of the period, were largely exaggerated and in some instances premeditated set-ups by the headline-hungry press. Whilst at best a release of youth's energy and pent-up aggression, they would be forever associated with Mod's image. Scorned and misunderstood by adults and the establishment, these 'Sawdust Caesars', who supposedly came to fight their foes on the very beaches Churchill had vowed to defend from the Nazis twenty four years earlier, had now reached their cultural precipice.

CHAPTER 7

CHANGE IN THE HAIR!

Sally Stevens 1967

Lynn Betts and Pam Cliffe 1968
Rob Nicholls pictured in 1968

While die-hard post-64 era Mods engaged in the occasional final seaside confrontations and as the core of the original stylists seemingly disassociated themselves from popular Mod fashion, change was clearly in the air. Male hair grew significantly longer, clothes became more outlandishly extravagant and rock music grew up. London club UFO (Underground Freak Out) had heralded UK psychedelia and with the arrival of a new drug on the scene - LSD - the once pill-popping generation were now experiencing a new high. The musicians associated with the new tide of adult-themed rock that followed in the wake of The Beatles 'Revolver' and 'Sgt Pepper' long players, embraced the times of transition. The Small Faces released their ode to LSD with 'Here Comes the Nice' (and unbelievably cheekily dodged the censors), Townshend penned The Who's 1967 gift to psychedelia in 'I Can See For Miles and The Creation, already sonically well in front of the game with their soundtrack of 'Music that is red with purple flashes', offered 'How Does it Feel to Feel'.

Meanwhile a young guitarist arrived in London by the name of Jimi Hendrix and Rock music reached new heights of showmanship. Kaftans, military jackets - as worn by Jagger and Keith Moon on 'Ready Steady Go!'- Paisley and polkadot shirts and the influence of the Regency period replaced the mohair suit. It would be easy to be fooled that the phenomenon that was Mod had truly ended, yet even as the winds of change swept throughout the UK - greatly enhanced by the sounds of USA psychedelia - the spectre of Mod was still evident in places, perhaps most noticeably at the coast.

Though few would doubt that it is Brighton that appears to symbolise the Mod's association with the coast, a fair proportion of other UK seaside resorts also shared Bank Holiday visits from the Mods. Clacton, Hastings and Margate in the south - places where much of the media furore had actually begun - Great Yarmouth and in the north, Scarborough and Skegness; all of these seaside towns still continued to be popular for Mods.

Don Hughes' earlier mid-sixties encounters could well mirror the colourful jaunts of numerous other youths who experienced these trips of unadulterated coastal thrills of fun, pills and rhythm and blues. Consequently, for a while these excursions continued to occur unaffected by the sweeping changes in the Capital.

Whilst the famous Mods v Rockers seaside riots remained most prominent at the southern resorts mentioned, with additional skirmishes elsewhere, if one digs further into Mod history of the 60's, a different location of beach fight unravels.

Mods at Skegness Easter 1966 (John Wood)

As early as 1964, the same year that the police and authorities were trying to keep the swarms of Mods and their foes in check at the traditional locations, a Welsh version of the riots was also taking shape. The seaside town of Penarth in Wales was first introduced to the sights of shorthaired youths in smart casual clothes, taking on the obligatory local Rockers later in the year, on the event of Bonfire Night the 5th November 1964.

The first Welsh Mods v Rockers stand-off was reported as taking place in an atmosphere of friendly rivalry with youths in generally good spirits throwing humorous jibes and good-natured insults at each other's respective gang. Little more than two to three hundred turned up and, apart from a light police presence and a few sporadic warnings handed out, all went without incident. By the following year's Bonfire night, the situation had changed to represent a much closer image to the widely reported south coast riots of recent years. As a result, a heavier police presence was out in force - helmets and riot shields included.

Shops, restaurants, public houses and residents' homes along the sea front boarded their windows up, whilst the fire brigade stood ready for action. Scooter gangs and a surge of biker gangs began arriving from the mid-afternoon, many travelling from further afield. As night time drew in the gangs goaded each other and fighting kicked off, resulting in police charges, general rioting and mayhem across the beach and esplanade. Fireworks were thrown; Bangers, Roman candles and rockets being used as grenades against the opposing force. Dozens of Mods and Rockers were hurt with numerous arrests as, yet again; the TV and media reporters arrived to cover the story. By 10.30pm, the trouble had subsided leaving behind a scene similar to the earlier Brighton riots.

Consequently, the Penarth Mods v Rockers fights became an annual event continuing throughout 1966, peaking in 1967 and reaching a conclusion in 1968 when bad weather, poor attendance and changing fashion influences, sealed the end of the Welsh beach fights. The police were not required to leave their coaches to hand out any arrests or warnings on this occasion and November the fifth could return to its more traditional annual event and leave fireworks to be lit for less violent purposes. Elsewhere, the aggressive confrontations appeared to move further inland.

Don Hughes - "Fleet Street soon grew tired of the 'riots' but the confrontations still carried on regardless. By 1965, the police and the local authority at Brighton were back in control. Assisted by Brighton council, an army of social workers and various observers has been sent out to report on the issue. As a result plans were drawn up in readiness for more conflict.

However the increasing police activity during the years of 1964/1965 eventually lead to the theatre of war moving inland to Box Hill in Surrey. This caught the local police napping as hundreds of Mods riding scooters or arriving by train suddenly descended upon the beauty spot during the first Sunday of March 1966. Once again the Mods and Rockers hit the headlines."

An unlikely Swedish invasion of a different kind also occurred in the clubs of the south coast.

Ted Reynell (Torquay Mod) - "The 'riots' of 64' had captured the imagination of every school kid in the country. The burning question in every school lunch break was no longer 'Who is your favourite Beatle' but 'Are you a 'Mod', a 'Rocker' or a 'Waste of space'. Thousands of kids across the country became 'new Mods'. It was no different in Torquay only I can't remember any 'rockers'. Too 'posh' I suppose. Instead of 'Rockers' in 65/66, we got invaded by the 'Swedish birds' who blew the local 'Modettes' right off the dance floor. Over here on 'student exchange', they were like an army from Venus. They were so beautiful. So game on lads. Blue blazer with vents, 'Fred Perry' shirt, white 'Levi Sta-Prest' and loafers - all from 'Costello's' in Union Street. So a little conversational skills in the 'Union' bar with the girls just to welcome them to the country and offer your 'tourist guide' credentials. 'Thank you Ted, that is so nice!' Off to 'The Hot Spot' with Marie and Marina to see The Fascinations' 'Baby Make Your Own Sweet Music'. Sorted!"

Away from the disturbances, Mods recognized the changes that were manifesting in various ways.

Bill 'Wiggy' Hildred - "Around '66' we Mods started to trade in our scooters for cars. At the Mojo, in Sheffield, there were fewer scooters and when everything went all Flower Power, Peter Stringfellow turned the Mojo that way too. We started going over to the Twisted Wheel instead."

Gill Evans - "I knew it was changing, but I still wanted it to last forever. Clothes were changing, for the men it was becoming more casual and for the girls the skirts were getting shorter: for instance the classic Mod look for girls in 1962/63 was knee length or just below the knee, by '65' it was about four inches above the knee and into 1966-67 it was much shorter.

In 1966, we were still into the Mod thing, but people were drifting away from it. One of the things I noticed was that people spent less time in record shops. This was where we met, shared our tastes in records, checked out what we were all buying and listening to in those record booths (there was even telephones you could pick up and listen to records too in the Co-op). Up to that point, it was the day of the 7 inch single, Georgie Fame, Righteous Brothers, Chris Farlowe, all the Tamla records and the Stax and Atlantic ones. Record shops were an exciting meeting place; they were a real social occasion. As albums came in more popular, a lot of that was lost as people would take them home and listen to them alone.

Gill pictured in 1965 (left) and 1966

I did like and listen to some psychedelia but it wasn't really mine and Del's thing. We still preferred our R&B and Tamla singles. As for the clothes, they were just not smart enough for us. Another thing is that by this time - I was eighteen in 1962 and twenty-three in 1967 when we got married - but unlike us, who had our first child in 1973, many other Mods were getting married, having their first child and settling down, being Mods was just not an option for them anymore"

Left: a classic image of 1966, Dennis Munday (far left) and friends recreating an iconic Graham Bond Organisation 'Sound of 65' shot

Roger Ames - "By 1966, I was growing out of the obsession of belonging to the Mod generation, growing older, I looked down on what us older Modernists called 'Mini Mods', a rather scathing moniker for kids probably only a couple of years younger than ourselves, who we felt just aped our image and life style in a very diluted version.

I became more involved in the creative and visual world during my time at art school, although always distinguishing myself and my college associates who embraced the Modernist ideas, from the sloppy jumper and sandal image of the typical art school students. I still used to go clubbing, justifying my nights out to lecturers at college by explaining, that as I was going to work in the world of communication, it was imperative to stay in touch with street society, as these were the people, in the future, you would be expected to influence. My interests were now directed to graphic images, film, and photography.

The period as a fully integrated Mod was over, but that formative period of my life, gave me the direction I wished to travel. The visual aspect and creative force that drove mods to create their own identities, stayed with me, but that experience allowed me to expand my horizon into new and experimental arenas. Modernism, for me, was about moving on, so as the decade progressed, it was necessary to adopt new styles and interests, leaving the skinheads behind, as antiquated as the rockers that we so derided for their stagnation and entrenchment in a single idea."

David Birchall - "I sold my scooter in late 1965 - the whole Mod scene just seemed to be finished. Between the press and the TV they had made being Mod seem passé' - if that is the right term. I would love to find my old scooter (it was either RPA215 or 215RPA - I had one number on the front and the other on the back). When I decided to sell it I only had to let it be known and it was sold - I suppose it had a bit of a reputation by then. With the money I financed a trade in 'mothers little helpers' that we got by the thousand from a club called 'The Ace of Spades' up near Charing Cross tube station and a friend and I sold them at the Harvest Moon Club. (Sorry to those who got nineteen in a packet intended to hold twenty...). I worked the door at the Harvest Moon on Sunday nights and one night I actually bounced somebody! Since I weighed nine stone dripping wet that was as surprising to me as it was to him!

My parents emigrated to Toronto in 1966 and I announced, the week before the ship was due to sail, that I was perfectly happy to stay in England with my mates. It was seven years before I saw my parents again. In 1968, I finally decided that it was time to see the world and went up to the P&O Shipping offices right at the entrance to Petticoat Lane in the East End and signed up to work on liners for a few years. After seeing the world I realised that I preferred the look of Vancouver so moved here in 1973 - no regrets. My wife's closest friend (who immigrated to Vancouver with her) used to go on holiday with the Kray family! They had caravans together in Burnham on Sea and would spend weeks together. Charlie, the oldest Kray brother went to school with her father."

Sally Stevens - "Drug culture continued to influence fashion, notably the fashions of 1966 onward, showing a distinct psychedelic influence, mingling with Courreges, and Mary Quant, followed by Barbara Hulanicki and Biba Fashions. 'Mods' moved with the times, and ultimately so did I, leaving the UK for good in 1969, to move to Los Angeles, where I lived in blue jeans, t-shirts and bare feet, and didn't wear make-up any longer, but that's a story for another time!"

Sally Stevens with John McManus, London, 1967. John is the brother of Ronnie Money, Zoot Money's wife

THE IMPACT – TAMLA MOTOWN APPRECIATION

Whilst music, fashion and attitudes changed, the music of the Mods was being further absorbed into mainstream popular culture, the Tamla Motown label and affiliated releases growing rapidly in popularity. Notably, by 65/66 the Tamla soundtrack was of a much more pop orientated style.

Tamla covers by genuine Motown fans The Impact being performed in 1966 to a crowd of locals, including numerous Mods, in Stratford, East London.

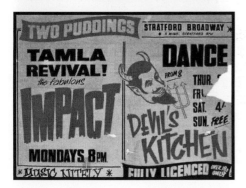

By '66, the popularisation of one of Mod's greatest and most-loved musical genres - Soul, in particular via the Tamla Motown label, saw aspiring beat acts across the country include the label's hits into their live sets. This acceptance of Black American music was surely a positive result of the Mods continuing promotion of the genre?

1966 AND ALL OF THAT!

1966 - the year that Great Britain ruled the world! Swinging London, led by Carnaby Street and its Boutiques, saturated with Union Jack adorned commercialisation was the cultural capital. A world of flamboyant and colourful hip young gear appropriated in part from the Mods who had pioneered the fashions, styles and colours of a generation. Here it was in its entire tourist attracting glory. When England triumphantly won the World Cup that year, it seemed that the Empire had been restored: pride, respect and success were once more firmly back in place.

Maurice Moore pictured in 1966

Yet, for the first generation Mod, time was almost up. In a world of 'one High Street uniform fits all' - with even a unisex Mod range on sale that year - there was simply too little creative space for the self-respecting Mod to move in. Despite this compromise of its identity, American journalist Tom Wolfe came to London, considering that these 'swinging London Mods' still deserved study.

Ironically, the music of the Mods showed little sign of losing favour. That year was a huge success for Soul, its profile further raised the following year by the Stax/Volt revue tour: likewise the key proponents of Mod were releasing quality long players. However, the rising media and fashion exploitation and the dilution of what Mod represented for the individual appeared conclusive: To paraphrase the Kinks 1966 album, the Mods were 'Face to Face' with the challenges of either adapting and accepting significant changes or perhaps rejecting the commercialisation and simply retreating to their underground roots. Decisively, many former Mods succumbed to the mind-expanding creativity of psychedelia, taking Mod's rich influence along and in turn pre-empting the imminent 'Summer of Love')

Maurice Moore - "Much happened in 1966. Harold Wilson's Labour government were endorsed by winning the General Election, Times Magazine coined the phrase 'Swinging London', and everyone in the country was happy and in good spirits, especially after England beat Germany to win the World Cup, where everyone jovially crowded round a small black and white television to watch the match. There was a general mood of optimism; Britain was the place to be.

Black American music, in particular Soul and Motown, was now very popular in the mainstream and readily available in record shops. There was a 'Ready Steady Go!' Special shown featuring Otis Redding and in a later Melody Maker poll, he was voted the Best Male Singer, replacing Elvis Presley. Soul Music had arrived. I was starting to travel more, playing many gigs with the band, seeing a wide selection of live musical acts and generally having a fun time."

Derek Glover - "In 1966 we stayed in London during the same time as England won the World Cup. We rode into Trafalgar Square on the night of the final. It was one big party. People from all over the world just dancing, singing, passing drinks around even the Germans."

Derek Glover's girlfriend and wife to-be, Dianne on Carnaby Street in 1966. Note the poster for The Move.

The tide of Great Britain's prestige continued: along with the hugely influential sounds that emanated from it. Architecture, design and cinema were experiencing a surge of optimism and creativity. British directors such as Lindsay Anderson ('This Sporting Life' and 'If') Ken Loach and artist Peter Blake amongst others epitomised the period. Yet a sense of betrayal was still prevalent amongst many Mods.

Derek Glover - "Up until 1966, the Mod army had evolved naturally. They had chosen their own heroes, their own styles and their own music. No outside commercial influence only influence from within their own circle of peers. Most of the classic Mod club tracks were never UK top twenty hits yet you could travel from London to Birmingham to Manchester and hear the same 45s being played in Mod clubs. Songs like 'Night Train', 'Needle in a Haystack', 'Ride Your Pony' were never hits. 'Green Onions' never charted here till 1979. Suddenly in 1966, our American Soul singers were not only charting but were recording Beatles songs. The British Mod groups, who we considered to be our very own, had now gone mainstream. Chris Farlowe, Georgie Fame, Spencer Davis, Cliff Bennett, even the Yardbirds were now top ten artists. Instead of playing down our club, they were doing Top of The Pops and NME Awards. They weren't ours any more.

With Carnaby Street now gaining worldwide attention, commercial business soon started moving in, dictating the styles, attempting to create fashion trends that suited their stock, trying to turn everyone into trendy Dandy's under the pretence of being Mod. Everyone wanted to jump on the Mod bandwagon after it had been almost underground for the three to four previous years and 1966 probably was the start of the end."

Maurice Moore - "The Mods had encapsulated a neat, immaculate look and an energetic lifestyle based on shaking their bodies to vibrant dance music. The new hippie culture saw a wilder look of abandonment, perhaps more colourful, and the music was more complex and cerebral: more spiritual, mind-bending and thought provoking and maybe more political. Instead of dancing the night away, people would sit on the floor and listen earnestly to all that was being said."

Rob Nicholls - "By late 1966 the London Mod scene had run its course. Its demise was heralded on 15 October, when the Roundhouse in Chalk Farm hosted the launching of the IT (*International Times,* an underground newspaper). The Who, Geno Washington, the Cream, and Pink Floyd played and Marianne Faithful, Jane Asher, Paul McCartney (disguised as an Arab), and yours truly attended. This served as a precursor to 1967, the release of *Sergeant Pepper's Lonely Hearts Club Band* and the ensuing 'Summer of Love' and 'Flower Power. The original Mod movement petered out when, overtaken by emerging psychedelia and Victorian kitsch fashions, it splintered into different factions. 'Art school Mods,' and I was one, accepted the transition to Hippies who were essentially middle class, while 'Hard Mods' did not and instead rediscovered their working-class roots and became Skinheads. Eventually in September 1967, BBC reacted to the popular appeal of the Pirate Radios by initiating a new pop-oriented station, Radio One, and by March 1968 Radio Caroline had been forced off the air.

The music, drugs, and clothes were changing. As Hebdige points out, 'Dress was no longer innovative - anybody 'discovered' items like Levi jeans or hush puppies. Style was manufactured from above instead of being spontaneously created from within.' But here was a chance to be original and inventive again. The uniforms the Beatles wear on the cover of *Sergeant Pepper* gives a clue as to which direction clothes were heading at that time. In 1967, I purchased sailors' bell-bottoms in white from an Army and Navy store. I went to a school outfitter and purchased a large boy's red flannel blazer to wear with them—hardly a Mod outfit, but by that time I sported a freaked-out and back-combed hairdo, and was working towards a degree in Art."

The unisex Mod look of '66' and a mid-60's Levi's advert

Despite the sense of anti-climax and compromise, the resplendent fashion and style of mid-60's London was being immortalised in songs crafted by the dedicated leaders of 60's pop. For some, it was possible to recognise and appreciate the new mood that followed the classic Mod period.

John Hellier (right) - "As for songs about the London Mod scene well you've got the fairly obvious Kinks 'Dedicated Follower Of Fashion' and the Small Faces 'Here Come The Nice' but much more importantly check out the REAL Mod anthem which has to be 'London Boys' by David Bowie from 1966. An autobiographical account of pill-popping Soho in the mid-sixties."

Above: Stuart 'Dinky' Dawson and Dave Growns, 1967

THE TIMES A CHANGING – LLOYD JOHNSON

Lloyd Johnson - "After leaving Hastings late summer '65, I returned from Sweden the following summer. All through '66, there were no beach fights or anything like it in Hastings. The Witchdoctor club was still going - I think it may have disappeared around late '67 - but in the summer of '66, there was a new club that had opened that we went to beneath the Queen's Hotel called The Flying Machine (probably an indication of where things were going at the time). It was opened by people with connections to the visiting Foreign students, we helped decorated the walls with Foreign newspapers and painted French and Swedish swear words in red on them... very Punk Rock, many years ahead of its time! My Swedish girlfriend, Sara, worked there behind the bar so I was there all of the time.

The local R&B band called The Talismen played the usual stuff of the time there and were very popular, 'High Heel Sneakers', 'Walking the Dog' and Coaster's numbers. There was also a band from London, which fluctuated its membership to meet the finances of the club's budge: if the Club could only afford so much they would turn up as a four-piece, or if the club's takings were flushed they could expand to a ten-piece. Whichever version it was, they would play the same set. That was the Club that summer along with a few others we went to.

During the summer of '66, I was wearing Ivy League clothing with a bit of French influence thrown in, Shetland sweaters - which you would wear tied around your shoulders or waist if it got too hot. Then, I managed to get a job at Cecil Gee's in London. On the first day of that job, we drove to London early and dropped Sara my girlfriend off at the station. She was going back home to Sweden. I still recall 'Ticket to Ride' playing on the car radio during the journey, quite poignantly.

My first day working at Cecil Gee, Johnny Walker of The Walker Brothers walked in. I was awestruck. I was a guy from the sticks brought up in a 3 up-2 down working class environment, I suppose I was naïve too, I wasn't used to being in the company of such highly successful people from the music scene... But, it was something I was to get used to. This was the place where the

Rat Pack and visiting American Jazz musicians would buy the amazing clothes that were on sale.

Following a prank by the other lads who worked in the shop I ended up standing in the lift as lift boy. Little did I know it only went up the one floor to Cecil Gee's office. Cecil Gee (who was a really nice guy, a very well dressed Jewish businessman) arrived at work, entered the lift and said 'what are you doing in the lift son?' I told him what had happened and he said I was in the wrong shop and that I should report to the Charing Cross Road shop the following Monday. My first day working there Mick Jagger walked in. When he asked what new stock we had in, the window dresser Mike McVeigh said 'We've got these', how about a Dr Kildare shirt' to which Jagger answered 'How about a punch on the nose?'

Kavan Cooper, who also worked there told me that, Mike - who had first choice of the sun-damaged window dressed stock - bought a brown suede jean jacket and his mother made him return it because it cost £4/10/- half his week's wages. John Lennon then bought the jacket and wore it on the front cover of the 'Rubber Soul' album. Cecil Gee in Charing Cross road was a great experience for me.

During my lunchtime round this time, Autumn '66 and yes, the L.P. was played in the shop. I occasionally went to a coffee bar in Denmark Street called The Giaconda where many musicians would frequent. I would sit in the corner with my coffee just people watching and listening to the great times they were having. After work one day, I walked over to Wardour Street and hung out in The Ship: I overheard a group's members tell their stories of mayhem at a concert in Germany. The auditorium had been destroyed and I realise now that I was overhearing tales of John's Children.

Back then (even by '66), it was all still mohair suits, classic Mod attire and college boy haircuts plus the classic 2-inch parting with backcombed top hairstyles with a lot of Beatles and Rolling Stones influenced haircuts. At the time, I had my hair in the kind of curtains style, which was basically the next step to growing my hair much longer than before – this was my transitional period. I hung out with a guy I met at The Ship and spent some time around Soho but became tired of running around behind him when he had got himself (and us) into one scrape after another.

Groups of the time such as St Louis Union and The Small Faces would shop in the Charing Cross road branch of Cecil Gee's. They had a Coffee Bar in the basement where the more conventional bands could buy matching band uniforms, the likes of Acker Bilk, Kenny Ball and the remaining bigger bands from another time. It was a constant flow of bands, Soho gangsters, bouncers and Mods buying in that shop. When I left Cecil Gee, I got a job in the 'CUE' department at Austin Reed on Regent street and during my lunchtime would walk through Carnaby Street. I remember thinking everyone is looking the same, Hair backcombed bouffants and the clothes were all commercialised many of these guys seemed like they just

LONDON'S CECIL GEE AND HIS INCREDIBLE NEW FASHIONS

OPPOSITE PAGE: THE DISPOSABLE JACKET AND SHIRT; THE DISCOTHEQUE JACKET AND RED DISPOSABLE OVERSHIRT. ABOVE LEFT: DISPOSABLE BLUE AND GOLD MAHARAJAH SHIRT. LEFT: FUR TRIMMED WINTER COAT; THE INFLUENCE OF ZHIVAGO IS MARKED. ABOVE LEFT: "PLUS TWOS" WITH MATCHING HAT AND WIDE LAPEL JACKET RIGHT: "ZIP JACKET WITH SHORTS. -51 didn't belong, very low hipsters and cropped tops showing the midrifts … all a bit too camp for my liking at the time.

During those lunchtimes I started to go down to 'Tiles' and this is where I first met Jeff Dexter who was DJ'ing at the lunchtime sessions in the club. My friend Patrick Cockell managed a shop on Tiles street and we'd meet up with Sebastian Keep there, we were all [originally] from Hastings.

During the Summer of '67, one day in the 'CUE' department, two boys came; in one was wearing a guardsman's jacket and the other was wearing what reminded me of a priest's outfit. It turned out this was Pete Sutch and Paul Reeves and we became friends. Whilst working at 'CUE' a fellow salesman named Wayne came in during his lunch break with a record and asked us to put it on full blast, which we did. It was the first album by The Doors. Music was changing!

Left: Paul Reeves and Pete Such

Hastings in The Old Town High St - Sid, Chris who lived in Hastings: and Sebastian Keep and me, we'd moved to London by then and were visiting for the weekend.

Pete Sutch and Paul Reeves were selling Budgerigar bells on leather thongs and Kaftans made from Indian tablecloths, they had come to show them to Colin Woodhead who ran the 'CUE' department. Clothes really were changing too and my hair was growing but not yet quite long enough – I was aiming to grow it like a French bob and started to dress more that way, wearing 'Just Men' trousers and bought my first shirt from 'Granny Takes a Trip' - it cost around 4 and a half guineas, a near fortune. Walking down Wardour Street I would hear the sounds of 'Summer in the City' by The Lovin' Spoonful and all the typical sounds of the period.

A girl called Katcha came in to 'CUE' Dept. selling floral ties and I thought 'I bet she's making a fortune, I could do that?' so along with my friend Patrick Cockell we started making ties in the evening from our bedsit in Clapham. We sold them to 'Granny Takes a Trip', 'Hung on You', 'Just Men', 'CUE', 'Blades', 'Washington and Tremlett', 'Irvine Sellers' and many more shops. Some of these shops were on the King's Road. We thought 'Bloody hell, it's great over here, look at all these birds! So we moved West and got a flat together.

We then ended up opening a stall on Kensington Market, which we had to build ourselves. I painted it silver like a submarine and we bought some old Victorian styled Gothic looking chairs and a Victorian chest of drawers as a stock fixture, and followed this up with a trip to Paris after our French Mod/Minet friend, Marcel Laussance, suggested we sold Newman's jeans, which were big in Paris at the time. We went to Paris in our Mini clubman with six hundred quid and bought as many of the Newman stovepipe jeans that we could afford, there were loads of colours in cord and velvet which were an incredible cut knocking spots off the traditional Levi's jeans that they were based upon. The colours were phenomenal. We went back to Paris frequently and visited the Renoma shop where Jacques Dutronc bought his suits - great clothes. I bought myself a two-button navy blue velvet jacket with concaved shoulders and the back of the jacket had blade seams which finished at a horizontal waist seam. There was an inverted pleat up to the waist seam which double as a buttoned up ven – a very cool jacket. I also bought a pair of French Loafers with bulbous toes (extra high on the big toe) with a large brass buckle, lilac Burlington gold cup socks, a navy blue shirt (one-inch high at the back), 1930s spear point shape collar and some light sage green trousers. The front of the shirt had self-coloured embroidery down both sides of the Plaquet. I thought I was the bee's knees!

Shops were springing up all over, the most notable and some of the best were 'Granny Takes a Trip', 'Universal Witness' (by Paul Reeves), 'Just Men' in Tryon St. off the Kings Road plus various stalls in Kensington Market: Deborah and Claire on Beauchamp Place did fantastic shirts. Elsewhere people were buying crappy and cheap looking loon pants, 3-button vests, and the like. There was Sweeny's a great hairdressers in a basement on Beauchamp Place, when you walked down their stairs you would be completely stoned by the time you got to the bottom. They did the hair for Hendrix and Clapton's afro. Eventually, it all got very 'hippy trippy' and silly and people were beginning to fall by the wayside, overdoses were becoming more frequent, people were doing Mandrax for the buzz and a lot of smack was doing the rounds. Patrick and I thought that this was really not the way to go and decided to take a different path to this. We just didn't get involved in all the drugs. Also, the thing to remember, is that I was maybe around two years or more older than most of these guys, especially the ones who were doing the Mod thing in '66 in 'Tiles' club and afterwards up north. I remember thinking 'This was all over in '64 as far as I was concerned the business in Brighton and Hastings etc. had killed it for me?'

Groups would drop off records to our stall to play and promote, so we would get the records as freebies. It wasn't all obscure Soul like it was up north, though I still played my musical preferences such as Jimmy Reed and Sonny Boy Williamson, Howlin' Wolf, Booker T and the MG's, Otis Redding, Wilson Picket, Mose Alison and all the Brill building stuff such as The Coasters etc. which are, basically, my favourite styles of music. And later on we played Buffalo Springfield, Country Joe and the Fish, Commander Cody and The Lost Planets Airmen, Captain Beefheart, Doctor John ... that was late 60s.

At that time I was wearing Gohill boots in William Morris printed velvet, a full length bottle green narrow shouldered coat with six-inch black velvet cuffs and collar with a waist height back vent worn with a black roll neck, black crushed velvet trousers, hands adorned with loads of Art Nouveau silver rings and an Art Nouveau silver enamel pendant on a silver chain over the roll neck. By now, my hair was shoulder length, cut straight across the bottom and worn with an off centre parting: I had become a Dandy and it was great fun! I didn't realise I was living in a fantasy world being in Kensington Market and only meeting people of my own age or younger. I Loved that period apart from the drug casualties it spurned, the Clubs we went to - The Cromwellian, Blaises, Cafe Des Artist, The Speakesay. J.Arthurs opened up way down the Kings road - that was laugh. I remember Malcolm 'Percy' Raines party there, he went as a nun and Johnny Moke went as Noddy in a small open top Italian yellow car, they looked really funny sitting side by side. Two of the coolest guys around in fancy dress without a care in the world. Great Times!"

Gill Evans - "When Radio One began, the very first record that they played was 'Flowers in the Rain' by The Move, and that is when myself and Del both recognised, and always remembered, as being the turning point."

Psychedelia did not arrive overnight, yet its impact on pop culture was considerable. Whilst elements of this particular generation realised that here was an ideal opportunity to continue one's journey, others gave up the ghost of Mod for social concerns and the onset of adulthood. Regardless, the era of mysticism and mind expanding acid trips, alongside musical experimentation, was in full swing.

Gill Evans picking up some Flowers in the Rain

Tony Foley - "The cut-off point, in my case was 1967. For various reasons - bureaucratic as well as social - but generally, in 'working-class' South London it was no reason other than getting serious; getting serious with yer bird, getting serious with yer life, getting serious with your family responsibilities etc. all very banal stuff... but true."

In January 1967 the future cult film classic 'Blow Up' by Michelangelo Antonioni was released. Including a memorable Yardbirds performance and a tasty Jazz score, the film, sadly, did little to promote Mod's real face, moreover, it added further to the swinging London art-house depiction of Mod; an assumption that middle to upper class boutique-dependent hip young things were as relevant to mid-60's Mod as Italian suits and the black American music of its origins. Perhaps the closest on-screen interpretation of Mod's profile and ethos of self-improvement was Dennis Waterman's portrayal of a frustrated class conscious Mod in Peter Collinson's 1967 kitchen sink drama 'Up the Junction', previously broadcast on BBC as a Wednesday Play in 1965.

Some original Scene Club regulars and notable Mod Faces such as Mickey Tenner (left) found much to enjoy in the UK psychedelic scene. Persuaded by the flamboyant creativity of psyche-influenced fashion, perhaps ignoring the middle-class aspects of the genre, in essence reflecting the original Mod ethics of moving forward and celebrating the new.

Look closely and you can even spot Mickey Tenner in a London club at the height of the swinging sixties period in the Boris Karlof and Ian Ogilvey starring Tigon Horror Thriller 'The Sorcerers' (1967).

Psychedelia swept along the twin commodities of music and fashion and in balance helped to create a vacuum for new and challenging exploratory music and lyrical progression to fill. When LSD replaced Purple Hearts, the music scene (in the south at least) changed colours almost immediately. The UK psychedelic vision was realised most notably in December 1966 with the UFO club in Tottenham Court and Pink Floyd's acid-soaked happenings. Pockets of Mods decided to check out this new 'Turn on, Drop out' scene for themselves and were mostly won over with the permissive, free-spirited alternative scene: when Townshend, himself, began attending, the transition to psychedelia was complete for certain sections of the Mod community. Elements of stylists, until recently, sporting bouffant Marriott style Mod haircuts and the latest sharp Mod look of the time were now wearing kaftans, beads, Paisley shirts and matching long hair in reflection of their now-found enlightenment.

In contrast, the remaining Mods were no longer seen as hip and culturally relevant by an ever-swiftly progressing pop culture: its fashion now almost completely swallowed up into the swinging sixties mainstream. Devoted Mod, Don Hughes's descriptions of this period - interspersed with a blunt dose of personal honesty - vividly evoke the post-66 fall-out.

Don Hughes - "Sadly the Ricky Tick (club) had jumped on the Flower Power bandwagon. Soul music had been foolishly relegated to just two evenings a week by mid-summer placing Wednesdays and Sundays over to a mundane 'discotheque Soul session'. A paltry half a crown entrance fee attracted an ever-growing hoard of 'shaved to the head 14 and 15 year olds. Peanuts, all in their uniform of Levi jeans, Harrington's and Clark's brown Desert Boots. The so-called 'new take on '64' which the Ivy shop owner over in Richmond was mainly responsible for.

By Autumn Flower Power had been dismissed as a mid-summer craze. A short-lived fad. Wandering about in a Kaftan complete with Jesus sandals and jingly cow bells draped around my neck was already passé. The Small Faces who'd taken to wearing the whole Hippy kit and caboodle just a few months back were now back in Carnaby Street threads. Ok, with the odd satin shirt, a silk scarf and longer hair thrown in, but I could live with that.

But this short-lived Flower Power fad would leave a long-lasting legacy. The urgency of Mod replaced by a laid-back cool. The music had fragmented beyond belief. 'Sgt Pepper' together with our own blossoming Hippy movement had changed the face of the business forever. To put it bluntly, you were either into pop groups or rock bands. It was as simple as that. But for me, I seemed to have somehow 'slipped through the cracks'. I didn't fit in anywhere. Still smarting from the abuse I received wearing a Kaftan, I found myself rudderless as I attempted to navigate my way through the new worlds of Rock and Pop. Drifting, searching, observing, evaluating one scene after another.

Then more bad news. A newsflash on (Radio) Caroline informed us that Otis Redding had died in a plane crash. As with Kennedy, I would recall the moment forever. I looked out my window towards London thinking ... what now? He was the key player in many ways. The main man. The Soul man! Destined for even greater fame after his successful appearance at the Monterey Pop Festival a few months earlier. His death left a vacuum that the Suits found impossible to fill and frankly if I had to pin a date on the day London Mod really drew its last breath, it would have to be December 10th 1967.

Up in the West End, that old Mod Mecca, the Flamingo Club once the coolest place in town had suffered the indignation of being renamed the Pink Flamingo. Still a Soul Club, its biggest draws were now discothèque nights featuring the first mobile disco acts like the Toni Rockett Disc Tet with Cleo the go-go girl. A sad reflection of the times.

One new thing London had to offer me was the Roundhouse in Chalk Farm which had such delights as The Majestic Heads or The Philosophers Stone playing regularly. Freak out bands as I called them.... Geranium Pond, Magic Mixture, Katch 22, Doctor Marigold's Prescription. These were at the eye of the Hippy storm and to me a right old bunch of mystic miscreants. One act that did catch my eye was none other than Zoot Money, an old raver from the Mod days. Renaming his band Dantalion's Chariot he issued a sensational acid-laced single called 'The Madman Running Through the Fields'. I did consider checking them out live too but never made it. Once again, because of my Mod indoctrination, I'd confined myself to Soul and Ska so convinced was I that the final answer still somehow lay there.

I really enthused about The Love Affair pinning high hopes on the group [Love Affair singer Steve Ellis had previously fronted The Soul Survivors]. Just like The Small Faces who'd more or less returned to their Mod look, Love Affair appeared to follow suit. I felt they could rekindle interest in Mod someway - after all, lead singer Steve Ellis had made claim to once being a Finchley Mod! Ok, maybe they were not the calibre of The Who or Small Faces but Ellis dressed the part and sounded every bit as good as Daltrey or Marriott. This brief optimism brought about by Love Affair - that they might spark a possible Mod revival - persuaded me, albeit incredously, to buy another decent scooter. Since the sale of my SS180, I'd owned a Lambretta Series One L1150."

Keith How - "Not all Mods seemed willing to embrace change even though their heroes were moving on. Hair grew, the Summer of Love offered new delights. My two good friends the Healy brothers lived and worked in Sheffield and kept us abreast of the latest gear and also as Michael was a hairdresser my longer hair was kept tidy. 1968 brought the opportunity to be more flamboyant. Every day wear was always 501's, Ben Sherman shirts or a crew neck sweater but the 'dandy' look became more popular with us. Velvet Corduroy double-breasted jackets, hipsters, silk shirts, cravats and brogues."

Don Hughes - "There were seismic shifts to the pattern of events during 66-67. Hailed as the 'Summer of Love' the rise of the Hippy gave the press another photo opportunity... 'Love in's' at Woburn Abbey. The following year however, saw the rise of the Skinhead and the Greaser and once again Britain's beaches became a battleground. According to the Daily Mirror front page headlines of September 3rd 1968, Brighton saw 'over 200 boys in seaside fight' over the Bank Holiday weekend. The tag 'Mods and Rockers' had now been dropped in favour of 'hotheads' and 'Death's Angels'. I was in Brighton with my girlfriend in Sept 1968. A huge fight kicked off so we fled. It made the headlines the next day but neither Mods nor rockers were mentioned... only a fleeting reference to leather jacketed Deaths Angels."

John Leo Waters - "I was released in 1967 to find that things had changed drastically! Gone were the clubs - many had been closed by the police and others had morphed into psychedelic palaces belting out weird electronic noises and screeching guitar solos! Many 'Mods' had turned their back on their lifestyles and joined the 'flower power' movement. Even the bands I had regarded as heroes had eschewed their roots and taken the road to 'peace and love'!

The street gangs had almost ceased to exist and to my horror, I found that many of my compatriots were out drinking with lads from the Highbury Mob! I was mortified. So many former gang members had moved on to other things. A few had settled down with girlfriends, some had moved literally and quite a few more were banged up! The Krays and Richardson's had long gone and most villains seemed to be taking a short hiatus for the moment. In short, most of my former running partners had 'grown up'. Not me though! I made a decision to move up to Newcastle where the nightclubs were still in full swing and I could enjoy a few more years of *walking the walk and talking the talk*!'

CHANGING FACES – CHANGING DECADE

Sally Stevens by Ian Spratt

John Hellier pictured in 1969 and outside the famous Lord John shop, early 1967 with what he describes as his "Bouffant hair in tribute to 'Rod the Mod' Steam Packet era."

It was a period of experimentation for virtually all of the genres that Mods had held close to their musical hearts during the previous few years. The Brit-invasion sound which influenced a new generation of US garage bands and Folk/Rock, most successfully personified by The Byrds, had inspired a flowering of talent, successfully merging into the sounds of psychedelia. The UK artists further honed their skills into developing a more serious and progressive interpretation of their talents: introspection and spirituality replaced the vibrant rhythm and blues of recent years. The previously regimented legions of Berry Gordy's empire also fell in love with the drug-influenced vibes of the time when Tamla Motown tasted the Acid tests of psychedelia, generated largely by the talents of Norman Whitfield. Yet, would the Mod generation themselves manage to remain as optimistic and at ease with the cross-generic dilution of their cherished and purist sounds?

John Hellier - "By 1967 Mod turned into psychedelic Mod. The bands were no longer playing the R&B classics and the style was now very firmly influenced by what was going on in San Francisco. Incidentally one of the very best live acts on the London scene at this time was Winston's Fumbs led by ex-Small Face Jimmy Winston. Don't let anybody fool you that he couldn't play, this band really cooked!

What a lot of people don't realize is that many of the 70's superstars had roots in 60's Mod. Rod the Mod we all know about but David Bowie, Marc Bolan, David Essex (yeah, David Essex was the drummer in a very cool Mod outfit called Mood Indigo) and even Status Quo were strutting the stages in their peacock suits! Check out pictures of Quo from 1968 with Rossi sporting a Marriott haircut!"

Gill and Del Evans adapting to the times. Centre: Gill wearing: "Hot Pant outfit with my favourite type of blouse, this one is white and I had it in a lot of different colours."

Rob Nicholls - "Acoustic folk and blues guitar styles had come full-circle and political messages were contained in protest songs. Bob Dylan's 'Masters of War' was released in May 1963, while 'The Times They are a Changing' was released in January 1964, and Dylan's records appeared on the jukebox alongside the customary R&B records and pop records at Mod haunts like the Oakwood Station Café near the northern end of the Piccadilly Line. 1966 saw the flourishing of guitarist singer/songwriters. The folk and blues club, Les Cousins, a former skiffle cellar in Greek Street, Soho, had a new lease of life. It was known as the spawning ground for the best finger-style guitarists around including Alexis Korner, Bert Jansch, Roy Harper, Davey Graham, and Cat Stevens. Even Joni Mitchell, Bind Gary Davis, and Paul Simon played there. A poignant memory illustrates the intersection between the Folk and Mod scene at that time. The sad spectacle of a white junky squatting on the floor just inside the entrance to the Flamingo Club, flailing away on small bongo drums which couldn't be heard above the sound of the music. I recognized him as one-time guitarist virtuoso, Davey Graham, composer among others of the influential instrumental 'Angie,' which was recorded by Bert Jansch on his debut album in 1965 and later appeared as 'Anji' on Simon and Garfunkel's 1966 album 'Sound of Silence'. Davey Graham got so zonked during the Mod era when folk blues went out of fashion that he wasn't ready for it when it came back round again, and he missed the boat."

Keith How - "Musically I loved Stax, Atlantic and Motown but I became a sonic explorer. I guess The Beatles were mostly to blame but who could resist The Byrds and Jefferson Airplane from across the water? Even The Temptations and The Supremes started to experiment as did The Isley Brothers and Muddy Waters. 'Ogden's Nut Flake Gone' was amazing and even our beloved Who bent the mind with 'I Can See for Miles'. One Friday evening at the Healy Brothers house they turned up with 'Axis Bold As Love' by Hendrix which we played and sat transfixed and realized that the era of the single seemed to be passing. I often wonder if Mod passed away in 1967 even though the influence lives on. I cut my hair short again in early '69 but something had changed.

There was a much stronger Skinhead presence around with what seemed to have an aggressive stance which did not sit well with me.

I was one of those who embraced change. I have never wanted to be categorized or labelled. Modernism has always been about personal class, taste and responsibility for me. Later Jimmy, in the Who's 'Quadrophenia', seemed to mirror my often restless spirit and I identified with his disillusionment portrayed in the album and later the film. As the 1960's faded I remember discovering The Faces and being blown away by the song 'Flying'. The '70s were looming but that is another story."

For one ex-Mod, the late-60's period meant indulging in the influence of psychedelia with equal nods to the recent progressive boom, yet still keeping a love of Soul close to his heart.

Maurice Moore (right) - "The Mod subculture did not last very long, perhaps a couple of years. Some people continued to wear the clothes, listen to the music and Northern Soul was born, others became 'skinheads'. Many evolved into the hippie subculture, which had developed in the States.

My hair grew longer; I listened to and saw more rocky and psychedelic bands – Pink Floyd, Jimi Hendrix, Cream, Captain Beefheart and the Magic Band. People I had seen at the Dungeon in backing bands became bigger names, for example Rod Stewart, Elton John, Peter Green, and Mick Fleetwood. My band, The Salty Dogs added a keyboard player, changed their name to the Velvet Explosion and added more psychedelia to their set."

Dennis Munday (left) - "Things started to change, psychedelia had arrived, and I started to grow my hair longer. I swapped my 16-inch bottomed trousers for flares, which I had first seen at school in late 1963, though they were called 'bell-bottoms'. It was also time to grow up and face up to the daunting prospect that although, 'Life is a drink, and you get drunk when you're young'; it was ending."

Don Hughes - "Occasionally I'd hear this voice in my head saying that I must attune with the times... but I just couldn't become a bloody Hippy, still less a Peanut. The Suit thing had fizzled out, replaced by yet another moniker, the Smoothie. They were simply younger versions of the Suits who found the now familiar '64 stripped down Peanut 'Mod look' somewhat beyond the pale.

Hippies, Suits, Peanuts, Greasers, Smoothies, Freaks. These were the new tribes beyond the Summer of Love but I didn't feel motivated by any of them. The magic wasn't there. I felt stranded amongst these new barren cultures. I was in danger of joining what appeared to be the lunatic fringes. The Hippy revolution had moved through the music and clothing industry like an unstoppable juggernaut. It was as if Mod had been wiped out of history. Swept aside the cult was soon forgotten about. In the end, I got bored defending Mod. The Hippy and Skinhead cults had ruined everything as far as I was concerned. In time, I would come to despise Hippies since they were, mostly, a bunch of middle class tossers. I despised the cult of skinhead too. The Skins had inherited all I valued about Mod but promptly went about brutalising it."

SKINHEADS ON THE WAY!

They could just as easily have been termed Peanuts, but the name skinhead - obviously referring to their close-cropped hairstyle - was far more descriptive of their sparse, casual but smart, tough nature and appearance.

The original skinheads -themselves a direct descendent of Mod's '64 period style further absorbing the influence of the smart look of West Indian rude Boys - were first noticed on the football grounds of Tottenham, West Ham and Chelsea around 1968.

Their tough working class background, passion for football and its often-accompanying violence on the terraces reinforced a reputation that often preceded them, yet the original skinhead was meticulous in their taste in fashion as the Mods had been. Equally studious in their love of Black American music, the skinhead exchanged the Mod's love of Soul for Jamaican Ska and later reggae.

Fashion, for the skinheads, changed quickly and between 1968 and the early 1970's, there were numerous varying styles and accoutrements adopted along the way: from sheepskin coats, the classic Crombie, braces, Harrington's, Sta-Prest trousers, button-down check shirts, corduroy and suede jackets, donkey jackets, bowlers and brollies, red socks, brogues and DM's all of which merely scratch the surface: the attention to detail and self-identity was second to none.

As with most youth cults, a negative angle often aligns itself to the progression of its ethics and ideals – sadly the skinhead became often unjustifiably associated with racist tendencies and an unwillingness to accept social and cultural progress. Without exploring, or giving any credence whatsoever to the subject of Racism, suffice to say, there can be few collectives of youth movements throughout the post-war years and recent times that has not been hindered by its less-acceptable downside elements. Most importantly, the skinhead style, like that of the Mods, evolved despite their continual bad press and uncompromising image.

Photos: Ex-Mods adopt the incoming skinhead look in photos from Nigel Brandt Bellamy's collection.

As skinheads arrived on the scene, many Mods, themselves, were still approaching the closing chapters of their Mod journeys.

Gordon Rath - "By 1969, it was all over for me. I married quite young and it was family first. There simply was not enough money available to do the Mod lifestyle as well. In the following decade, I did security work which included doing a Rod Stewart gig (who by now was not the young Mod we saw play in Leicester in 1965 and had become a bigheaded little shit). Another Rod gig I had words with him about his attitude to his fans and his missus of the time came and had a go at me and Keith Moon, who - after drinking from a huge hamper of drinks he had brought along and then moving onto the Rod tent we shouldn't have been in - pulled down the middle pole of the tent, which came crashing down on us all."

The whole of UK Pop culture was swiftly changing yet again as the onset of the late sixties Blues boom and fledgling prog-rock made its first forays into an ever-changing Rock scene. Ahead was the advent of adult Rock and the post-psychedelic fall out and its associated Hippie dream - a dream that was brought to a crushing end with Altamont and Woodstock. Consequently, Rock music became studious, proficient and seriously intellectual as the Rock generation came of age.

Johnny Powell (top) and friends pictured late Sixties - a photo perfectly illustrating the contrast in hair lengths during this period

The closing chapters of the decade could not have been any further removed from the dawn of the 60's, so much had occurred. The innocence of the first half had been superseded by the spectre of vast political and social changes. Youth had experienced autonomy and the cultural revolution had been explored, enjoyed and tasted. The 60's had been a decade of protest and questioning of establishment values resulting in an explosion of artistic self-expression. Undoubtedly, Mod had been a huge and crucial part of this development of change. When Townshend and The Who created their 1967 released 'The Who Sell Out' album (long players were no longer an extension of the hit single, but a progressive concept all of their own) the combination of Mod, Pop Art, swinging London, psychedelia and pirate radio - perhaps the most single important promotional commodity for pop music of the decade - culminated in one of the period's most vital representations of Mod's wide-reaching influence: perhaps the flagship of British pop of the 60's?

By 1968, however, with the Paris Student Riots, Vietnam in full flow, political assassinations and the many aspects of social and political changes, nothing could ever be the same on the world scale. The sixties ideal was dying, its generation of youth had grown up. Cynicism and the drugs fall-out had replaced youthful optimism. Fashions changed reflecting this new mood and as a consequence, Britain no longer ruled the world as a cultural force.

Despite the recent influence of psychedelia and the changing fashions in the Capital, the Hippie revolution and its promises of Free Love and spiritual enlightenment, the 'Granny Takes a Trip', 'Lord Kitchener's Valet' endorsed Regency style had not been the way forward for all. For many, despite being no longer under the spotlight of late 60's fashion, the fundamental appeal of Mod had not dissipated and the origins of Mod's street level leanings would re-emerge across the suburbs and council estates of the country.

Far from the Carnaby Street fashions and longhaired extravagances of the late 60's period, Mod-inspired youths such as Reggie Webster were embracing the harder-styled smart but casual Mod look favoured by the growing skinhead cult.

Reggie Webster - "As the 60's progressed, certainly by 67-68, the whole Psychedelic Progressive Hippy thing was happening. I think that [for some] was the motivation for the next small step towards what the media called skinheads.

Our hair was fairly short anyway and we all owned a pair of work boots Doc Martens meant little then; I had hobs and wore them when I worked at the garage so it was normal. Going from a college boy cut to a Number 4 crop in Summer was quite usual for some. Certainly the crop was a representation of your working class roots, not a statement, but enough to let people know you were up for it: Grammar school and posh kids probably only ever saw a crew cut on a kid that had head lice at some time, not uncommon back then.

I remember all the Brutus's tapered check shirts hitting the shops, 1/4 inch Gingham being the first and most common, not expensive and, in my mind, it seems the most colourful period of our decade. Perma-pressed strides had been around for years, in some form or other. Levis took a large part of the market, of course, but after a year or so were too commercial. Brutus v Levi battled it out for a new generation of kids, younger and with not as many scooters. By '71' it was all nearly new GS's and two year old SX's in their simplest form with a bit of a rally look and even murals: they seemed to be much wealthier than we were in our formative years. A few of the guys stuck with it but it wasn't a great look if you were 19-20 years old whilst some of the new kids were only around thirteen year old.

The seudehead look wasn't that much different in essence, the emphasis being more on the Spartan style again - plain shirts etc. Brutus did a great Panda collar, rounded, but a short and blocky shape on a trim fit base and white or black with a half sleeve detail resorting back to that colourless thing I always remember. Grey trousers in lieu of the cheap two tone imitation tonic shiny ones or the extravagant Rupert checks. Penny round heavy print shirts and loud tank tops. I guess it was just the end of our time really, certainly clothes wise we'd moved on drastically from the skinhead norm.

It was basically a circle really, the Mod to Skinhead thing. Following that, it was the longer hair and the more popular the skinhead thing got, then the more we grew our hair and got a little bit flasher. We began separating ourselves because we were all late teen to early 20's and the skin scene had gone onto the football crowds and there were hundreds of 'em everywhere aged between 11 and 18, mostly with no Mod background either. I suppose it was the last throw of the old Mods really: the best part too really, as we all had money by then."

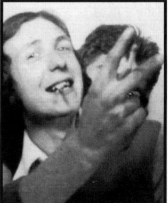

BOOTS AND STA-PREST – THE STYLE OF THE ORIGINAL SKINHEAD

Skinhead hair styles were basically short and neat, with varying lengths and detail across different areas; side-partings, sideboards and mutton chops optional. Brutus button-down shirts with their authentic check often won over Ben Shermans, though many individuals refused to conform to wearing either. As with suits, there was a certain way of wearing and carrying the clothes that were clearly a statement of style and class; the original skinhead consistently cared and, like their Mod cousins, their identity and sense of style was paramount.

Female skinheads generally wore their hair either short (some favouring the style of Julie Driscoll) but with the later Suedehead interpretation, hair was kept longer with a back-combed bouffant, layered both sides and back - perhaps the most recognisable female skinhead image when complimented with the obligatary Crombie. The obsessive nature towards clothes, detail and staying ahead of the crowd, or 'the Mob' as Lester Owers states, also reflected their Mod ancestors.

Lester Owers (Basildon Skinhead) "You always had your own take rather than a uniform style, no use being a clone of somebody else. You have to try to have an edge over the mob.

I used to shop in my local town Basildon, but I grew tired of shops like Harry Fenton etc. I had already moved on from Burtons to Bespoke tailoring at Barringtons in Basildon where you could be more precise in the cut of your suit. You had the fitting with pins and chalk etc. That suit cost £29. My next one, in late 1969, cost £46 and more than two weeks wages; it was Blue/green 3-ply Mohair with a Herringbone stripe in the material, it changed colour in the light. The usual refinements hand-stitched lapels, ticket pocket, cash pocket, flaps on both back pockets.

Lester Owers with his cousin Wayne in 1968 and right in 1969

On the shirt scene I had grown out of Ben Shermans, and I never bought Brutus. I started to buy clothes from the Squire shop in Brewer st Soho and Austins Shaftesbury avenue. I bought career club shirts from the squire shop, Barracuta Jacket for £12, Royals for £7 guineas. I bought trousers, shirts and Arrow golf Alpaca and golf cardigans from Austins. Meanwhile, I was buying record imports from Contempo, Musicland and HMV Bond street. I never thought of myself as a hardcore skinhead. Rather than the stereotype version, which I tried to steer away from, I veered towards an almost Ivy League version"

Skinhead fashion changed regularly, yet consistently retained the basic sharp look throughout the heyday of 1968 to around 1971. Continuing Mod's constant requirement for detail, the skinheads created their own exclusive style, utilising a smart casual look for everyday wear (Ben Shermans, Fred Perrys, Harringtons and Levis in London and – from 1970 – Wranglers in the Midlands and the north) and a flashier tailored two-tone suit for evening wear. Dr Marten boots shared preference with Oxblood Brogues. Importantly, preferences of style varied with each individual.

SKINHEAD BY STEVE BUSH

Original skinhead Steve Bush also utilised the smart Spartan-style of Mod's mid-sixties period.

Despite, the shaven-head fascist-leaning cliché of the late 70's, the skinhead must be one of youth cultures most misconstrued and harshly interpreted. Far from being of a thuggish nature – though be assured, like many of their earlier Mod relatives, the skinhead was of a strictly working class grass roots background - the early skinheads, a proportion of whom had been too young to have truly embraced Mod, were clean, clothes-obsessed, smart and not necessarily of a right-wing political persuasion.

Steve Bush (Sheffield skinhead) - "1969, the migration to Skinhead had been a natural move for me and my friends. Born in the mid-50s, we were a bit too young to be fully fledged Mods, and had lived in the shadows of our elder siblings, especially when it came to questions of fashion and music, but at the age of thirteen and fourteen we were starting to make a fresh mark.

There was a new development in teenage fashion sweeping across the country, so when we had the chance to be at the birth of our very own movement, we jumped at it. Off we toddled to 'Alfredos' on Southey Green to exchange our flowing locks for a Number 2 head-shave. I, being the mouse who put the bell round the cat's neck, went first. Alfredo shaved half my head and then said, in his Italian-accented broken-English 'Gimme five pounds or I leave it like this!' My mates, sitting queuing, laughed and relaxed a bit, and within half an hour, all five of us were done. Walking back down Adlington Rd, we felt the sensation of a fresh wind on our scalps for the first time ever, and the feeling of being leaders rather than followers slowly fell upon us.

That evening when I met my girlfriend on the way to Mansell youth club, she turned and ran off in the opposite direction. It would be a few days before she got used to the strange new me, although it wasn't long before most of the young ladies had also joined in, adopting the popular 'cropped top and longer sides' haircuts favoured by the skinhead girls, and later, Chris Waddle.

On the music front we were building up new interests in the strange rhythms coming from the Caribbean - Blue beat, Ska and Rocksteady. On Saturday mornings, we would congregate in Violet May's listening to Prince Buster, The Skatalites and other early stars of the genre. We flicked through the 45s carefully examining any Trojan or Island label vinyls, then we would head back to mine to practice the new range of dance movements. We worked hard at getting the poses right, thumbs through the belt loops, heads slowly shaking, and exaggerated stomping steps, reminiscent of walking on the moon. Many of the vocals utilised a strange Jamaican patois, which we tried hard to imitate without sounding like a prat, which we no doubt did.

Even more radical than the music though was the fashion. To be a proper skinhead required a complete change of wardrobe. Gone were the pointed shoes, tight trousers and paisley shirts of last week. Now it was a case of saving up your Paper-Round money and heading to the city centre, to shops like Harrington's and Bunney's, for the radical modes. Some of it was interchangeable with Mod gear, but much of it was totally new.

Steve and girlfriend, 1969   **Late period Mod wear advert**

There were two types of popular jacket, the Harrington and the Wrangler cord (corduroy). Both had to be worn in a certain way, with the Harrington being zipped about one third of the way up. The Wrangler was fastened with one button only at the point between the breast pockets, and would have the cuffs turned back. Colour was also important. The most popular colour for Harrington's was black and for Wranglers it was beige or petrol blue. It was also okay to wear a standard Levi's denim jacket, but this would now be worn in a different style, similar to that of the Wrangler. Shirts were either a Fred Perry or a Ben Sherman style shirt. Here the choice of colours was wide and varied, my own favourites being a white Fred Perry with navy blue trims and a black-and-white gingham short-sleeved Ben Sherman.

The jeans that we wore with the same makes as worn previously but we now had them in a completely different style. Levi's and Wranglers were the most popular choice, but instead of a leather belt they would now be held up with very thin elasticated braces, and the bottoms were turned up to 3 inches above the ankle to accommodate the most interesting of the new fashions, the footwear.

These Dr Martens boots were the one thing that really separated skinheads from everyone else. Originally worn used as industrial footwear, and displaying their trademark air-cushioned soles, they now became the symbol of this rapidly expanding movement. They came in a variety of styles and colours, but the ultimate was a pair of cherry red 18-hole boots. These we would bring to a high shine, using Kiwi (never Cherry Blossom!) Oxblood polish. The spit-shine technique, used by soldiers worldwide, had to be developed, but once learned was never forgotten. The first time you wore a pair of 'Docs', you knew you were moving into new territory. They were quite unlike any other footwear, and you really could feel the cushion of air beneath your feet. It was a shame that these boots, along with other aspects of the skinhead movement, became associated with violence and vandalism, as most skinheads just wanted to dance and have a good time, much like the Teddy Boys and Mods before them.

A number of clubs sprung up in and around the city, catering for this new movement. 'The Ark' at Crookesmoor and 'On Broadway' beneath a shoe shop in the high Street, were two of the most popular. Many youth clubs, especially across the north side of the city, also became assembly points, and the normal diet of pop records changed quite radically to incorporate the new fad. Dancing was easier than before, as boys could now dance in a group, or even alone, and a female partner, although still desirable, was no longer necessary. For the first time we began mixing with kids from different parts of the city, sharing a common desire for 'Shantytown' and other floor fillers.

That first stage of the skinhead movement lasted only about a year, and we very quickly moved into the next phase, letting our hair grow a little bit longer, swapping the denims for Sta-Prest trousers, and exchanging the beloved Dr Martens for leather soled shoes, (although many of us still wore 'Docs' to the factories where we worked). This was a smarter, more formal look, and came just as we were making the adolescent step up into pubs and nightclubs, so it suited us perfectly. Even the musical tastes changed, and we now sought the dancing rhythms of what would become Northern Soul, but that's another story for another day."

Don Hughes - "The turn of the decade witnessed Skinheads having their bootlaces confiscated by police at Southend. Meanwhile over in Brighton, large groups of older ex-Mods had arrived in hired Ford Transit mini buses. The sea front boozers now took precedent over the coffee bar scene of the early 60's. Suitably tanked up at the newly opened Volk's bar, the ex- Mods were raring to go only this time it was town against town. By the early 1970's they had no natural enemies so the theatre of war shifted once again - to the football ground. And that's another story."

Richard Arlen's controversial paperback novel

Far left: younger skinheads of the era

Right: Lester Owers in 1970

Below: Wiggy and friend late 60's

In a twist of cultural fate, some elements of these original skinheads would return to a love of Mod's Soul beginnings. By the late 60's, Soul had adopted even further exploratory musical influences including psychedelia and a steadily increasing injection of Funk. Sadly, the eventual dilution of Soul and its commercial overkill was just around the corner, but then there was Northern Soul.

THE JOURNEY TO NORTHERN SOUL

It should be recognised that the twin influences of Manchester's Twisted Wheel club (including the hugely influential DJ Roger Eagle) and the professor of Soul, Dave Godin were crucial in the growth of Northern Soul. With their stamp of approval (not forgetting Godin's terming of the genre in 1970), great knowledge and promotion of Soul there followed a surge of interest in recordings that continued the heritage of Mod. Northern Soul's origins of Motown pastiche indie-released obscurities sought by DJ's eager to hold the crown of one-upmanship by playing these undiscovered Soul gem 45's spread across the north almost in parallel with Mod's demise in the south. Yet, contrary to its accepted biographical profile, its influence reached the ears of southern Mods too. Ted Reynell's journey to Northern Soul begins with late-period Mod experiences reflecting the changes of the times.

Ted Reynell - "Nice place to grow up Torquay. Of course, at school you were a 'Mod' or a 'Rocker' or a 'Nobody', there was simply no choice. The 'Mod' birds were better. 'Julie Driscoll' haircuts, 'Mary Quant' make-up, skinny-rib sweaters, little black mini-skirts and shoes from Ravel.

At the time there were only the English based 'Mod' groups playing live at the clubs like 'The Scotch' in Torquay. 'Geno Washington and the Ram Jam band'. 'Jimmy James and the Vagabonds, 'The Foundations, 'Zoot Money' and 'Freddie Mack'. Then the 'Mods' from the Midlands and the 'North' brought their 'Mod' music down for their holidays because of course travelling to Benidorm hadn't been invented by then.

It was a completely different music. London was drifting further and further into 'funk' but the rest of the country stayed solid digging deeper and deeper past the influences of the major labels in your record shop, Motown and Atlantic. Rare sounds like Brooks and Jerry's' 'I got what it takes' and Cliff Nobles 'The Horse' were changing the 'face' of 'Mod' music.

When I moved to Redditch in the Midlands' I hit the 'Mod' hardcore. You had to look the part. Made to measure suit from Burtons, 16-inch centre vent, two and a half inch ticket pocket flaps, trousers 21inch at the knee and 23 at the bottom. Ben Sherman shirt, cardboard handkerchief, Ox blood loafers. It gave you a pride being a 'Mod'. Dead smart. Everybody looked at you when you walked down the street. I suppose in a way we personified a very 'right-wing' English look. Almost flying the flag against those dirty rockers and their greasy birds that hung around the hot-dog stand. I remember once when our local 'ace face' parked his Lambretta (and what a work of art they were) and walked straight up to the 'dog' stand full of rockers to order one with no onions. He ended up in hospital but what a hero.

Saturdays and a few drinks in the Unicorn pub and a brief check and we are sorted for the 'Blues'... then off mob-handed to the greatest 'Mod' club in the world, 'The Twisted Wheel' in Manchester'. It was an altar of style. A mate of mine once was chased out by the Manchester mob 'cause his hair was too long. No alcohol but who needed it. We were buzzing, chewing gum like maniacs, talking rubbish, just don't look at the other crews from all over the country in the eyes.

Having said that never saw a fight in my life as opposed to your local pub. Mutual respect for the clothes and the music.

The dancing had now turned into another art form. Jackie Wilson back 'flops and multiple spins. And of course, the heroes of our vinyl that 'The Wheel' had booked from the States to perform in front an adoring crowd. Inez and Charlie Foxx. Ben.E.King. Edwin Starr, Sugar Pie Desanto et all. Then (followed) the frenzy in the morning to buy fave rare records imported from the States from the dealers. I once spent a week's wages paying a fiver for 'Heaven Must Have Sent You' by The Elgins. With the help of a top-up, still buzzing on Sunday for the legendary 'Chateau Impney 4-7 Club' in Droitwich just outside Birmingham.

Set in the cellar of a beautiful French Chateau it was the last weekend spot for all the 'Mods' from the Midlands. The Derby lot, The Stafford lot and the mob from Walsall. There was a sort of 'peer' thing with the 'Mods'. All the 'modettes' in Redditch thought the Walsall lads were the 'ace faces' and wouldn't touch us preferring to spend their time at 'The George' in Walsall. They did have a point though. They were a majorly cool bunch.

Of course from the first days back in Torquay the rare records that were played like 'Six by Six' (Earl van Dyke) and 'The Fife Piper' (Dynatones) were 'Northern Soul' but it was only years later that Dave Godin of Blues n' Soul dubbed it 'Northern Soul' to differentiate to customers in his shop the soul music that was being played in London as opposed to the rest of the country. The scene changed of course. 'Northern Soul' records got faster at Wigan Casino and the fashion evolved into the 'loons' and vests."

The political connotations associated with the struggle for civil rights of Black Americans had a significant influence on South Yorkshire Irish-bred youth Sean Hampsey's initiation to Soul.

Sean Hampsey (from Sheffield) - "It's well documented that the 1960's was a time of struggle, revolution and liberation, chronicled and supplemented by a wealth of incredible and inspirational music. It seemed to me, for one reason or another, that all had played a significant part in my life, while growing up. Certainly, it was a very 'noisy' decade. Peaceful protest and parlour music were a thing of the past. My parents were Irish. We'd attended the first Civil Rights March, in 1968, before the 'troubles' broke out over there, echoing Martin Luther King and singing 'We Shall Overcome'. At home, they played loud music; rousing jigs, reels and rebel songs, on a Sunday afternoon. My mother had the kitchen windows wide open, she said to let the steam out while she cooked the Sunday dinner, but I always suspected it might be to make a point to the neighbours. My dad was a Union man. An immigrant. A Sheffield Steel worker and then a Yorkshire Coal Miner. A hard man who had felt embittered by social disadvantage and prejudice, but who knew the value of work. So I guess an unconventional upbringing and outlook came with the package. But despite the rebellious nature, 'decency' was always imperative. I remember, when very young, being told to beware of growing up like the Beatniks and Teddy Boys that hung around town. In retrospect it was pretty good advice!

Back then, most kids picked up a guitar and tried to imitate the Beatles and Stones, but, at eight years of age, I took to learning the Trumpet, purely because it was 'different'. And after a few years, I was a serious horn player. A few years later though, in 1968, came the initiation into Soul Music; when I first heard a Black American record on the Stax label, featuring the Memphis horn of Wayne Jackson. The music was born out of Gospel. Cries of freedom and passion, forged in injustice and inequality; it was inevitable that this would be the backing track to my formative years and beyond.

We lived in a small South Yorkshire pit village. A shanty town of concrete dwellings, knocked up in the early 1950's for the settling mining population, who came, in the main, from Eastern Europe. My mates were all of interesting origin. Poles, Ukrainians, Latvians, Lithuanians and Italians. And a few like me, second generation Paddy's. Looking back, I guess we had a lot in common with folk in Brooklyn or the Bronx, but it didn't always feel like that at the time. These were difficult days in a tough neighbourhood and a bit of glamour or escapism would never have gone amiss, so I was very ready for what was on the horizon.

The guy that introduced me to Soul music, was the son of a Polish father and an Irish Mother. A switched on older guy by the name of Ervin. A well-respected Mod in the village. My older sister had been a Mod for a few years and she and her friends knew he was the business. On Erv's leather school bag were the strange felt-tip inscriptions, Stax, Atlantic, Carla, Otis and Aretha. On one occasion, curiosity got the best of me and I was bold enough to ask him what these peculiar and unfamiliar words actually meant. That afternoon he introduced me to Sam and Dave's brilliant stupefyingly 'Hold On I'm Coming'. It had an intro from Horn Heaven and drew me in like a moth to the light. After a few hours induction, he sent me packing with a couple of albums; 'This Is Soul' and 'Memphis Gold' – his generosity was part of his cool! This black Soul sound was raw and emotional and I was soon completely hooked, playing them over and over. I started to seek out more of the same, spending my spare time and weekends in second hand shops, scouring for old 45's on Blue Stax, Black Atlantic, Stateside, Sue and Tamla Motown. Trawling through the Russ Conway, Val Doonican, Animals and Searchers discs to find the 'black' stuff.

This would have been early '69, it wasn't long before my older Sister, and her friends began to take an interest. I might have been the kid brother, but I had the records they all danced to. They'd gone to the Twisted Wheel in Manchester and the Mojo in Sheffield. They'd hear and buy new records and bring them back to the village. Clubs like the '1812' in Dinnington and 'Up & Up' in Rotherham were where Mods assembled to dance to Soul. And most nights of the week, there'd be a line of scooters at the front of the house and I'd be in the corner of the room, playing the sounds. Style wise, they set the trend and I naturally followed. Sharp Jackets and Hipsters soon were unavoidable. It never occurred to me to dress any other way.

The major venues in the Midlands and the north, such as the Golden Torch in Stoke and the Highland Room in Blackpool, were essentially Mod Clubs which carried on the tradition of the King Mojo in Sheffield and Manchester's Twisted Wheel, attracting those who had 'kept the faith' into the new decade. For many of us, Soul music was still a 'cool' thing to be into. At the time when southern mods started to embrace other music styles, northern Mods had stuck to the original soundtrack of Soul. These days the North / South divide is more blurred, if it still exists at all, but back then, it was certainly more pronounced.

By the Summer of '69, I was learning more new words. Sta-Prest, Doc Martens, Loafers, Harrington... aggro and bovver. The young Mod felt he needed a tougher image and Skinhead fashion started to influence the style. Sheepskin Coat, turned-up Levis and Ox Blood 'dockers' gave the right impression. It was important to get it right. There was no substitute for Ben Sherman (I had a wardrobe of 16 shirts, which everyone thought was obsessive at the time) or Levis Sta-Prest in a pale green we called 'pewter'. I even wore white Ben Sherman's and grey Sta-Prest for school. Just wouldn't be seen in anything else.

Thankfully, the harder 'boot boy' apparel was 'fashion' for only a couple of years, and evolved into a 'smoother' more 'Mod-like' look once again. As the hair grew back, Suedehead became the norm. The dress code got back to being 'smart' again and more socially acceptable, on the face of it at least. Although the irony had escaped me at the time; we believed we were seeking nonconformity, but trailed each other instinctively, as a pack, with a 'uniform' and a new set of rules to follow.

Some of the lads I hung around with were a few years older, and the vocabulary was ever expanding. I wanted to grow up fast and dressing 'right' was a great way to fit in. But clothing was only part of the culture for me. Once you understood the specific requirements, that bit was easy. Music was still my first love and demanded most of my time and energy. My passion for Soul had very quickly led me to Sam Cooke: the classic 'Another Saturday Night' became the benchmark. But even then, nothing summed up, what we were all about, better than Dobie Gray's 'The In Crowd'. Composed by Billy Page, we were five thousand miles from Hollywood but it always felt as though he'd written it about us.

Aged 15 I now had a significant collection of albums and Soul 45's. The Spellbinders, Bobby Sheen, Tommy Neal and Bobby Wells were far enough away from the pop charts for comfort. School and studying, by then, had taken a back seat. Being Mod, collecting the sounds, was all that mattered. I left school and started work. The teachers were disappointed and tried to talk me into staying on, destined for a College of Music, but I needed money for clothes, records and the nightlife."

Mod's late sixties influence - via the skinhead cult's extension of Mod's style and tastes - had left a profound impression upon many young teenagers, especially those too young to have embraced Mod's heyday yet keen to sample its ongoing legacy and influence. Sheffield skinhead Steve Bush felt the strong musical influence of Northern Soul's recent development on the dance floors of the northern clubs. Through this continuation and undying love of Soul and the later Mod's love of obscure up-tempo pastiches of Tamla Motown records, the Northern Soul scene thrived into the next decade.

Steve Bush - "As the 60's drew to a close; we teenagers were drifting between two trends. We had been skinheads for about a year, but that was getting left behind as we grew our hair slightly longer, exchanged turned up jeans for smartly pressed trousers, and confined our precious Doc Martens to the work wear cabinet, choosing instead to socialise in leather soled shoes, brogues or two-tones.

As well as changes in clothing styles, we were also moving in a new direction musically. Throughout the sixties, we had all been fans of Motown and other American Soul labels, Atlantic, Stax and Vee Jay among others, and had enjoyed the chart success of many of the associated artists. What we hadn't realised, but were now discovering, was the seemingly endless supply of great songs on these and many other smaller, but no less cherished labels. Many of them had an addictive beat and raced along at a tempo, which screamed 'Get up and Dance' - and dance we did. Clubs were suddenly springing up around the city, which catered for these new dance disciples. Meynell Rd Youth Club in Parson Cross and 'The Ark', held in a church hall at Crookesmoor, were among the first to truly exploit this cult. Dancing became a very athletic pastime, and required hours of practise. Lightly stepping round in short quick circles with lots of arm movement, occasional quick spins and even the odd gymnastic leap, we took the discipline to a whole new level. Dancing hierarchies were established, with the more accomplished practitioners forming an exclusive semi-circle around the DJ, where talc was spread liberally across the floor and frenetic motions even included an infrequent back flip. It was mostly guys dancing on their own, but a few girls joined in, and there was still room for couples when the slow burning ballads drew the evening to a close.

One of the most exciting aspects of this trend was searching out and discovering new records, previously unheard of tracks that fitted the genre, and persuading the DJ to give them an airing. The main supply in Sheffield was Violet Mays, a small independent record shop, hands-on managed by Violet herself. Situated just off The Moor, it had grown up as a Jazz specialist store, but had now expanded to include a prime selection of second hand music, and a wide range of imports, which fell under the 'Soul' umbrella. On Saturday mornings, the shop was full of teens combing through albums by the likes of Martha and The Vandella's and The Four Tops, and asking to listen to tracks, which might meet the required standard.

As the momentum increased, we became ever more adventurous in our search for suitable sounds. Whenever United or Wednesday were playing in London, me and my best mate would don the appropriate scarf and catch the SUT coach from Pond Street, but instead of going to a game, we caught the Tube to the fashionable arcades in the likes of Carnaby St and Covent Garden, where there were lots of specialist music stores, and would spend the afternoon pouring through the low profile American Soul labels, hoping to discover a new gem. We noticed that we were part of a crowd of likeminded guys from other northern cities, Bolton, Blackburn and Manchester to name but a few, all in the guise of footy fans, but like us, trying to root out dance diamonds. The store assistants caught on quickly and would have lots of the appropriate vinyl on display and ready. They even made recommendations, presumably having listened to them during the week, and were responsible for unearthing many of the classics for us. Dave Godin, the manager of one such shop, identified this trend and, in order to separate us from local customers in search of the latest releases, gave it the title 'Northern Soul'. The name stuck and we loved it for many reasons, not least of which was that it excluded Londoners. I can well remember the first time I walked into a shop and saw a large selection of 45s grouped under the heading 'Northern Soul', getting the same buzz I still feel whenever I hear that unique tempo.

The night club scene in Sheffield was still stuck firmly in the 'cabaret' mould, but there was a slow switch over to evenings dedicated to soul dancing at places like Samantha's and The Heartbeat. Perhaps the best was 'Turn-Ups' at The Nether Edge Hall, where on Friday and Saturday evenings, the floor was packed with swirling windmills measuring the beat to songs like 'At the Discotheque' by Chubby Checker, Dobie Gray's 'Out On The Floor' and the classic Gloria Jones floor filler 'Tainted Love'. Around this time, '72/'73, emblems began to appear, Sew on badges, proudly displaying the names of all-nighters in other cities such as The Torch in Stoke and Cleethorpes Pier. There was also a universal emblem, based on the clenched fist of the Black Power movement and accompanied by the motto 'Keep The Faith', which we wore on backpacks (we needed *somewhere* to store bottles of water) and bowling shirts, sported for their loose fit. There was also a new trouser style, the high-waist baggy 'Oxfords', favoured for their freedom of athletic movement.

Disc Jockeys tended to use these evenings to buy and sell records, and there was always stories of discs changing hands for increasingly ludicrous sums. My particular favourite, 'The

Playground' by English MOR singer and TV actress, Anita Harris, was much in demand, but I wasn't ever going to part with my treasured copy. There was also a few guys selling tablets with various properties, but we steered clear of those.

By the mid-70s, many of those who were originally involved had moved on to other areas, American garage bands such as The New York Dolls, and our own punk bands, were becoming headline trends. But there was a handful of us who stuck with it, and it's great to see a resurgence of Northern Soul themed events all around the city today. The bottomless pit of up-tempo, addictive beats is still there, waiting to be excavated by a new generation of Soul fans. The gift that keeps on giving helps us all to 'Keep The Faith'."

Do old Mods never die, or fade away? By the late 60's and early 70's, the recognisable version of Mod had certainly faded, though only temporarily, whilst the continuation of its lineage and influence had become merged into various interpretations.

SMOOTHIES BY REGGIE WEBSTER

For Mod, Reggie Webster, the journey from 1964 had taken him through the progression of the skinhead, Suedehead and now the logical next step – the smoothies.

Reggie Webster - "The Smoothies, were just old Mods that had served their time, Prince Of Wales or Dogtooth suits, 3-piece, plain shirts and a return to the pastel plain or striped Oxford as well as panda's. Shoes were important, double soled Royals of a traditional type, like Loakes, heavy waffled tassel loafers with a rear kicker and a split seam toe, top of the tree were what we called 'Americans', a plain Gibson,(771's now I believe),so hard to get hold of, but brown ones polished with oxblood to get a chestnut colour and plain coloured socks to emphasize the bottom heavy aggressive look of a thick leather sole full of Segs, it was a move towards a gangster look, a parody of the city gent, the last-last act of defiance, good for nothing aggressive kids dressing as the establishment.

I could go into miles of clothing details and their motivations, the silk hanky draped gaily into the top pocket of the top end military blazer, your initials embroidered in gold on the pocket, the old Etonian school tie that I still wear today, this was and had always been about kids from working class backgrounds showing a finger. Even the cars that had now become our mode of transport, the 'Old Lumps Of Flash' we called them, Austin Westminster's, Ford Zodiac Flying Pigs and old MkII Jags, certainly a better way to go down to the coast on the weekend, always plenty of room to sleep in those plus there was nothing wrong with looking like a gangster, because by This time we all knew at least one.

Summarizing, for me, 1969-71 and probably most of the old boys that still hadn't got hitched or done stir, was the real time - the sorts were great, they'd got their own identity for the first time really, suits from Etam or Chelsea Girl or the like, a hairstyle akin to the earlier sportswoman look of the 60's, white tights and heavy shoes, smart, clean cut and very feminine, almost like a business woman, quite a step from the now standard skin girl who was a few tears younger in her monkey boot and shiny tonic. Two years previous the sorts might have been impressed by a scooter, but a car with a walnut dash and leather seats that went well just made them feel special compared to the trendy popsters little Mini with a flower stuck on the door and a stuffed rabbit.

The working class kids who had very little when they were alone, had everything when they were together, fond memories with the moral 'defiance and deception', we weren't the no hoper's the older generation thought we would always be and every now and then I spot another old boy, he's got the walk, the confident swagger and pays you the respect of just a confident inexpressive nod as he gets into his BMW 7 or S Class Merc. Nobody knew or liked us, that was the appeal, it was never a popularity contest

The Smoothie look was different, half vent Ben Sherman's with loose half sleeves, a vent on the front of the trousers, a much more sophisticated look to the standard skin Suedie set up. The self-monogrammed blazers, loose silk pocket hanky, old public school military tie, heavy soled shoes. Crew neck or skinny fir polo neck sweaters, even the trousers has a slight flair or French inverted pleats, 3 button jackets had been around for years, it was nice to be able wear 2 button tailored fit for a change. Suits in bottle green, mid-blue or beige when we weren't wearing traditional checks. A much more mature look in comparison to the now normal look of the next teenage generation of skinheads, a sign of our affluence at the time in, I suppose, young gangsters.

Smoothies of the era

There was a mutual respect for the skin kids, they came from similar backgrounds and we'd share venues at times, but because we were older we tended to continue with our aloofness, most of us had grown up together and if we hadn't, we still all felt a part of the same crew and seemed to understand each other. New things were happening, reggae was popular for the younger guys, but the 'prog wallies' were in big numbers, even the nucleus of Quo types, lots of denim, same with the Northern Soul type blokes, baggy strides and stripy tank tops were a long way away from our attire and mentality, we were a defiant parody of upper class gents that represented the old ways, to be honest, we had more in common with gangsters, they were realistic as far as we were concerned, maybe not well educated, but street smart and alert, common sense, some flash, humour and confidence, just like it always had been from the start."

GLAM ROCK AND POST-HIPPIE FALL-OUT

Ex-Mods from left, Dave Fawcett, David Middleton with friend and Rob Nicholls – in his Glam Rock phase and wearing a self-designed zipper sweater

Dave Fawcett - "A year [or two] later and a lot of us had followed the hippy trail which was a great experience and an integral part of our rites of passage, but looking back, the best years of all had been the Mod years."

David Middleton - "I wasn't really buying that many records by this time but was a fan of Rare Earth, Iron Butterfly and Stray. Then I got married in 1973 so most of the music went out of the window. I had had some great times over the years as a Mod. Despite never seeing The Who and The Small Faces as they came along around 1965. I had been a Mod since 1961, long before those bands were around."

Original Mod, Del Evans moves Into the 70's (pictured in 1972)

Rob Nicholls - "Although at the time I didn't call it anything, in retrospect I call it my Afro-glam rock era—the sweater was an African textile—I was teaching in Nigeria by that time, but returning to UK during the summer holidays. Funk and Soul was flourishing by then and the club scene was racially well-integrated. After that, young blacks and whites diverged again as the music scene splintered into diverse genres. Disco often gets a bad rap, but in a way, the Disco era was a sensationalized version of the Mod lifestyle. In fact, Pete Meaden boasted that John Travolta's character in *Saturday Night Fever* was based on him."

Like Disco, Glam Rock was a dominant musical force as the 70's progressed, its appeal could even be considered as a gateway between the aspirations of two separate generations - the 60's Mod and the 70's punk? Perhaps it is not altogether surprising, though, that some original Mods took keenly to Glam Rock considering the connection via the likes of Bowie and Bolan. 'Bowie's 'Jean Genie', single, had it been released a few years previously, would surely have been applauded by Mods of the time.

Meanwhile, the ongoing legacy of Northern Soul was also continuing its momentum.

Sean Hampsey - "If the 60's was considered a decade of revolution, the 70's and early 80's must be characterised as a time of diversity, division and disruption on the Northern scene. During only a very few years we witnessed a great deal of change, both in the style of music played and in the way the Soul fan was outfitted. A large proportion of those of us on the early scene had come from within grassroots Mod culture and there was a strong allegiance to that style of dress, general approach and lifestyle. Consequently change wasn't always seen as a good thing.

Our early 'Northern' Soul fashion included strong elements of the classic Mod style, such as barathea blazers, Ben Sherman and Fred Perry shirts, Windsor knotted ties, tassel loafers and leather soled brogues. But, because of an obvious and innate interest in clothes and trends, in 1973 when Oxford Bags made a huge resurgence many started to wear these and other light and loose-fitting clothing (sports vests or bowling shirts) more for reasons of practicality and comfort (particularly when dancing) than style. To me it was never a particularly attractive look, but I must admit to having fallen victim to a few pairs of high-waisters at the time.

Musically, by the mid-70's, the safe and recognised conventionality of 60's Soul had been broken by more adventurous DJ's who'd taken to playing newer releases, alongside the more traditional 'Northern Stomper'. The repercussions were significant and divisive. I was certainly one of those in favour of the 'mix'. I suppose at the time believing that being 'Mod' was more about 'being modern' and progressive than necessarily 'retro'. And, after all, I was a Soul Music fan. Whatever Black America had in mind, I would aim to get behind it. Just so long as it was soulful! However, this new diversity led to what could only be seen as a 'split' with different factions entrenching and quarrelling while offering the crowd an alternative approach.

The main protagonists were the famous Blackpool Mecca, a trendy 'clubby' environment providing a smooth mix of Motownesque finger-snappers and new soul releases (...by 1976 embracing New York Disco) and the Wigan Casino; a drug fuelled sweat box, full of acrobatic, wide-eyed, youngsters and heavy sixties beats. I favoured the former, but was still hugely attracted by the latter. There was simply nothing like the excitement, feverish atmosphere and 'edginess' of Station Road. Blues & Soul magazine introduced us to even more records and brought me to meet other like-minded souls from further afield. Clubs that played our music were sought with serious intent and travelled to, as often as possible... and as far as money would allow. Blackpool Mecca, in November '72, where I first heard the Sapphires 'Gotta Have Your Love' and was convinced that it must be the Supremes under another name! (today the naivety makes me smile). The Charade, in Rotherham, a legendary South Yorkshire Soul Club (where a few years later I got to ply my trade) played the big 'Torch' discoveries of the time such as Dean Parrish 'I'm On My Way', Bobby Hebb 'Love, Love, Love', Dusty Springfield 'What's It Gonna Be' and the Cooperettes 'Shing A Ling' all programmed superbly alongside club classics from Willie Tee and Jamo Thomas and the new releases from Millie Jackson, Syl Johnson and the O'Jays.

The following year, 1973, with a burgeoning room filled with boxes of vinyl, I was asked to do my first professional gig. It was the start of a DJ career which lead me to work every weekend through the 70's (during the dynamic Samantha's and Wigan Casino era). I enjoyed several Club residencies, including the legendary Charade where I played rare Soul and new release imports. Northern Soul was at its height and the sounds were turning over thick and fast. I ran the Record Stall on Rotherham Market for 4-5 years, which kept me up to speed and provided access to the latest releases. These were exciting times for someone so heavily into the music."

Northern Soul, despite its lean years and dissenters, would continue to prosper and grow within its active underground scene of clubs and record collecting obsessives: in truth, it's ethos was not so far removed from the origins of the Mod clubs that preceded it, perhaps, only the discarding of Mod's focus on visual style and fashion being the main distancing aspect?

By the time of these closing excursions in post-Mod year's fashions, a much younger breed of 60's child was nurturing a love of the previous decade. Virtually ignoring the prevalent mid-70's music scene, their individual experiences would soon collide with an almost preordained revival of Mod style and ethics. A fresh explosion of Mod culture re-designed for the 1970's.

IN SEARCH OF MOD BY A YOUNG TERRY RAWLINGS

THE GREAT | paul revere
AIRPLANE | and
STRIKE | the raiders

Whilst the early to mid-1970's are forever associated with Glam Rock, Prog-Rock, Disco and for those who continued the Mod heritage - Ska, Reggae and Northern Soul - ultimately a welcome return to rock 'n roll basics in the R&B soaked pub rock scene would emerge. Meanwhile young kids such as Paul Weller and a certain Terry Rawlings found solace in the previous decade's Mod recipe.

Terry Rawlings (South London Mod) - "The only similarity I shared with the sixties Mods regarding my personal Mod origins was my fascination and love of American music. However, it wasn't the ultra-cool Blues and rhythm and blues dudes that turned on the original Mods for me. No, it came by way of all things lightweight, pithy and poppy. It was super-shallow bubble-gum turns like *Paul Revere and the Raiders*, *The Turtles Lovin' Spoonful* and even *The Archies*. These acts were whiter-than-white; all the bands looked healthy and tanned, dressed in bright candy-striped trousers and tops. They were always pictured on beaches without pebbles or windbreakers, and surrounded by beautiful long, blonde-haired girls. Their songs were all breezy, jolly and sunny; it was the American Way, and it looked fun, fantastic and (frankly) out of this world - especially to a young council kid from the back street of Bermondsey.

And it wasn't just the music; it was pretty much anything American. I was totally obsessed by the US way of life, spurred on by our first colour television and sitting square-eyed, glued to every American TV show that was ever beamed into my drab, grey South London world. The first time shows like 'Land of the Giants', 'I Dream of Jeanie', 'Bewitched' and (most important of all) 'Batman' burst out of that bulky, fake-pine box, was like that scene from 'The Wizard of Oz' when everything turns from black and white to glorious Technicolor. I was a stay-at-home kid.

I was a sickly child; asthmatic and prone to bouts of bronchitis, so when I say I was a stay-at-home kid, I mean it quite literally. There was no daytime TV back then, apart from a couple of shows at lunchtime called 'Watch with Mother' which were meant for toddlers, that I watched anyway. I spent my time drawing and watching the clock counting down the hours until I could once again lose myself in 'The Time Tunnel' or 'Voyage to the Bottom of the Sea'. Then, I would check out how close my sketches of the submarine Seaview; the Flying Sub, or the 'Lost in Space' flying saucer, Jupiter Two, were to my fictional favourites.

It was due to my TV addiction that I can pin-point exactly when IT happened! The two days when two seminal televised events occurred for me! Two momentous musical moments that without a shadow of a doubt makes sense of how my life panned out. The first was a Friday night in June 1972 when my weekend started with me watching my first ever episode of *The Monkees*. I was ten years old and after twenty-five glorious minutes of *Monkee*-mayhem, I was instantly a life-long *Monkee*-mad fan.

The second epiphany happened on Boxing Day, 1973 with the BBC screening of *The Beatles'* 'A Hard Day's Night'. To say I was blown away cheapens that worn-out cliché and - yes! I know it's shocking that it means I'd seen *The Monkees* on TV before I'd seen the *Fabs* but, hey! That's how it went down.

My brother is three years older than me and in 1973 a teenager he had thrown his lot into Glam Rock! Our bedroom was full-on *Bowie, Bolan* and *Roxy Music* - complete with a string of coloured light bulbs and a record player housed in a home-made fake speaker cabinet covered in glitter. Alongside glow-in-the-dark plastic model kits of Frankenstein, Dracula and Wolf Man, stolen workmen's battery-powered neon flashing road markers completed the picture. Needless to say, Ziggy Stardust haircuts, platform shoes and feather boas just weren't for me; I wanted Beatle-boots, hooped sweat-shirts and white jeans. I immersed my imagination in all things 1960s, and my fascination for that most magical musical era was ignited; it's a fascination that still fuels me to this very day. However, back in 1973 I soon realised I had a problem; I was eleven-year-old kid with no money, and little access to acquiring any! Therefore, my tentative steps into building a sound-track to my life and thus embracing the sun-kissed, swinging idyll of a lifestyle choice I'd now became aware of, meant starting at a lowly level.

The Church Jumble Sale! Our Local Church at Dockhead, Bermondsey was (seemingly) forever holding some sort of fund raising, cake-baking, tea-drinking all Saturday long bore-fest and I remember I went to every one of them. It was at these events that I first became aware of the fickle nature of teenage girls and their callous ability to cast aside from a mere few years ago dreamy crushes on Davy Jones and Peter Noone and replace them with *The Sweet's* Brian Connelly and *Cockney Rebels'* Steve Harley! So what did this mean? Well, it meant... I coerced a friend from school who had more pocket money than me to go along. In short I made him come with me to the record stall in the church hall where a couple of sixth form goddesses were off-loading their older sisters' entire *Monkees, Partridge Family* and *Beach Boys* unloved album collections, plus...wait for it: a whole box of *Beatles* vinyl. Guess the price? Twenty pence an album! Yes twenty bleedin' pence an album! I didn't have a penny on me, and my mate from school had his eye on a Captain Scarlet car but I managed to convince him to buy virtually the whole lot. We scarpered back to his home on the Neckinger housing estate (a red brick council dock-workers' pile of flats just south of Tower Bridge) and played every album back to back whilst ogling the covers and absorbing every single word written on the sleeves. Within weeks we prided ourselves on being able to recite who played what, on every track – well, maybe not in *The Monkees'* case! This was far more life-affirming information memorised in a single sitting than the pair of us had learnt in our entire combined school internments!

We were instant 'just add water' Record Heads. Now we needed more! There was a local record shop in Southwark Park Road called 'Track and Groove' that we started to basically loiter around in pouring over the record sleeves and blagging the out-of-date promotion posters and cardboard displays. We also found out that most record companies at that time did budget album releases like Decca's 'World Of' series, plus cheap 'Best Of' compilations by labels like 'Marble Arch', 'Embassy' and even 'Bell'. These were normally quite a disappointment; a simple single 12-inch wallet with an out-of-sync picture of the artist on the cover and next to no information on the reverse!

Still, they were within my (recently allotted) pocket money purchase capacity so we snapped them up greedily. This pattern continued for years augmented by my liberal pilfering of my brother's now largely ignored record collection; he'd discovered girls!

By the time I left school (actually expelled, but that's a whole different story, folks) I considered myself a very knowledgeable and well-versed academic in all things rock and pop related. So what if I didn't have an 'O' level or a 'CSE' to my name - I could tell anybody who the bass player was in *Chicory Tip*.

I came to *The Who* by way of the album 'Meaty, Beaty, Big and Bouncy' - a cobbled together collection of random hits and misses which intrigued me enough to research the band in great detail. Magazines like *Zig-Zag* loved them and the weekly *Melody Maker* featured them regularly - albeit the hairy, beardy boiler suit incarnation. Nonetheless I became an avid follower, especially once I'd discovered the band's early pop-art leanings. Now, at this point I must reveal my nerd-omiter was on full-tilt mode and my *Marvel* comic collection (alongside my record fixation) had grown so huge it was housed in its very own pram-shed.

That early *Who* sound and image seemed to fit right in with my comic book fascination; it was all Biff Bang Pow, arrows, chevron motifs and bullseye targets. It was as perfect an accompaniment imaginable. Lucky for me my Mum had always bought me clothes from Marks and Spencer's because they were a safe bet. By that, I mean their high-street style hadn't exactly kept abreast of the times that were a changing. For example, they still sold traditional straight-legged trousers as opposed to flares or loons; their sensible tops were cotton and (for the most part) hooped; they always stocked polo shirts and they did a pretty decent range of blue and white deck shoes and Hush-Puppies. Get the picture?

I may have looked totally unhip in the eyes of most of my peers but I knew I had a good look going on. I convinced myself it was close enough to the look that stared out at me from the covers of most of my favourite records – well, almost. Not that it wasn't without its drawbacks, these mostly arose when it came to attracting girls. The problem was that girls in mid-seventies London weren't hot for the Brady Bunch look at all; they wanted cheese-cloth and denim. I remember getting into a bewildered fight with some girl's fella who took offence to the one-inch turn-up on my jeans.

I became quite inventive in accessorising my M&S basics; my old Nanny Ivy who (some years earlier) had knitted me a Mike Nesmith green wool bobble hat (complete with eight pearl buttons) was put to work knitting me a jumper with pop-art symbols. She also did me an identical black and white cardigan to the one Starsky wore in 'Starsky and Hutch' but we won't go into that...

Now, I'll be the first to admit that back then I never cared for what I regarded as 'older brother' music. Bands like *Genesis*, *Pink Floyd* or *Led Zeppelin*; that stuff sounded far too long-winded to me. I didn't like Soul either, it felt like you really needed patience to listen to that stuff, and I for one had no patience whatsoever. I needed instant gratification when it came to all my tastes whist growing up in the 1970s.

It was a three minute pop song - not a dragged out noodle-fest; a comic book, instead of a worthy weighty novel; an episode of the 'Persuaders' or 'The Man From Uncle' rather than the predictable snore that I consider (still do) even the most lively of James Bond films to be.

I also hated (once again, still do) what I perceived as any sort of pretentiousness and loftiness, and I don't care who knows it but when I first heard the album 'Quadrophenia' I considered it four sides of hoity-toity, excruciatingly self-indulgent clap-trap. I thought it just stunk up the place, it was so up itself! Nowadays, however, it's one of my favourite albums! I still think it's a tad too long but hey, I'm still impatient!

My first impression of Pete Townshend's Mod odyssey may have been well and truly wide of the mark, but it didn't extend to the record's packaging and most certainly NOT to the booklet! No sir, no way! Boy oh boy, that little black and white insert to me was like discovering my own personal Dead Sea Scrolls. This was it! This was where my many obsessions had been leading me all these years. That's what I needed to be! That coat, those white jeans, that badge and... that scooter!

I tracked down my first original US army regulation Parka from an army surplus stall on the corner of Club Row and Brick Lane in East London. They also had the American air force insignia and sergeant stripes. It was a one-stop shop, as right next door to it was a stall that was selling pull-on pigskin boots with elasticated sides. Once home and, with badges sewn on, I assembled my outfit. This, I thought to myself, was what years of listening to and learning about all those great 60s groups had led me to. That, and the hours spent reading the hundreds of comic books, now housed in their very own council shed annex. It felt like I had a new identity and a personal sound-track to boot. The year was 1978, I was sixteen, and I thought I looked (and felt) a million dollars!

I didn't become a Mod by any cool means whatsoever; it wasn't through leaning about obscure Jazz or Blues players. It wasn't in order to smoke French cigarettes, take pills and dance, and it certainly wasn't due to watching French art films, or wanting to run with the pack. No, it was a single-minded personal pilgrimage born out of a childhood and teenage fixation with all things 1960s. Cool TV shows; fantastic Beat and Pop groups; classic clothes, cars and scooters; pop-art and comic books. All these things and many, many more were what inspired me from such a very early age. They all fed my mind and fired-up my imagination, and that old green army parka was simply a second-hand coat that I could wrap them all up in. I wonder what ever happened to it?"

Above: Terry (right) with fellow Mod Gary Crowley

Bottom: Terry circa 1980 by Graham Cooper

The future of Northern Soul - the genre that had significantly been influenced by the original Mod soundtrack and much of its code of ethics – was, by the mid-70's reaching an unclear crossroad.

Sean Hampsey - "Inevitably there was some crossover with the 'sounds' as each club endeavoured to be ahead of the game they also readily picked the very best from one another. However, the politics and bickering began to undermine the true good nature of the scene and the camaraderie that went with it and by the end of the decade, both had met their unhappy demise. The thousands that had rushed to get involved during the 'popular' years seemed to drift away just as quickly, taking their bags, badges, vests and beer towels with them. The crowd had reached maturity, gone off and started families and assumed a new bunch of priorities."

Meanwhile, an upcoming generation, who would soon come to converge with the enigma of Mod, were discovering, for the first time, the classic Mod sounds of the previous decade.

Robert John Manton (Purple Hearts) - "Simon, Jeff and myself were all in the same class at school from 1972 -1977. By about '76 we had all started to get into 60's music via Bowie's 'Pin ups' album and Little Nicky Horne's Friday night 60's oldies show on Capital Radio. At the same time we were looking at the Who's 'Quadrophenia' LP in Downtown Records in Romford. Speaking for myself I think it was The Kinks/Animals/Stones/Yardbirds who I really connected with as a teenager. I felt much more attuned to the doom and gloom of songs like 'Evil Hearted You' and 'We've Gotta get out of this place' than 'Smoke On The Water'."

Ray Margetson (Stoke Newington, London Mod) - "1975, whilst other people at my school in East London (Clapton) seemed to listening to Pink Floyd/Yes/Led Zep etc., I found that so boring and tedious and started looking for something fresher, something more creative, imaginative and exciting especially when I had been into Bowie and Roxy Music - all these other bands just paled into comparison. I came across the sounds of James Brown, a real funky get-up-and-go sound and then 'Al Capone' by Prince Buster, WOW! That really set the tone for delving further into good music. I came across that record at a club in Dalston (East London) called Cubies. This was a predominantly black club unearthing some great contemporary sounds as well as some old stuff, which I latched onto.

In 1976 I was wearing stuff like 'carpenters' jeans, jellied plastic sandals and mohair jumpers as most of the sussed black and white kids were into. I was always searching for something different and a year later, during the early summer of 1977 (when I was still 15), went to study Spanish at Holborn after my exams, for the sheer hell of it and came across two girls who really got me into Punk after they had seen the Sex Pistols."

By late 1977 and into 1978, Terry Rawlings, Robert John Manton, Ray Margetson (who would soon earn the middle name moniker of 'Patriotic' after his Mod fanzine) and others of such Mod persuasion would be in like-minded company. Almost two years previously, a new youth cult had arrived, itself ultimately spawning a second coming of Mods. This new generation of Mods - though influenced by the originals - would assume quite a different outlook to their cultural ancestors: a decidedly more aggressive stance and politicised environment would create an altogether different interpretation of Modernism!

CHAPTER 8

A 1970'S REBIRTH

Lloyd Johnson outside his shop

The Mods of the 60's were seemingly an irrelevant force by the early 70's. The Bank Holiday Mods v Rockers clashes - good feeding ground for a desperate story-seeking press only a few years earlier - were now folklore - a near-forgotten part of British cultural history. The 1970's soon descended into a decade of long-hair, width-defying jeans and prog-rock excess's, glam rock and disco abounded. It was a period of varied influences, which ultimately lacked soul, a circus of commercial excess and adult-orientated rock that stretched all the way through the decade until a young bunch of 'Foul mouthed yobs' - themselves a bastard off-spring of The Who and the Small Faces - declared 'We hate Pink Floyd' on their torn t-shirts. A group to revolutionise the very core of pop culture and its shallow establishment: that was the Sex Pistols!

The original Mods had been absorbed into the fabric of society: their lasting image a yellowing newspaper feature of the famous beach fights or a creased membership card of The Scene Club or Flamingo. Ironically, it would be almost as a direct result of those punks, their anarchic vision and re-exploration of rock's most basic structures that would help to ignite the next Mod explosion! The 1979 Mod revival.

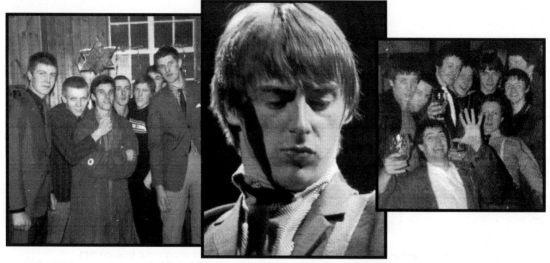

In hindsight, it could be said that all branches of Mod intertwine. The family tree of the original Mods had spread far and wide. From psychedelic Mod Rock, the Northern Soul scene, the original skinhead movement and spin-off cults the Suedeheads and Smoothies, the grit and sweat of the R&B driven pub rock scene to the early garage rock of Punk, it all links together, in one way or the other.

The scooter clubs of the 70's, too, had continued with the legacy of the original Mods. Often complimented with veteran Mod members as the driving force, they had kept the ideals largely intact, keeping the faith alive with their roots in distinct Mod beginnings acknowledged and respected. Now, as the 70's neared their conclusion, some fresh inspiration, whilst adopting the spirit of Modernism, was required to provide a way forward for Mod, if the genre was to survive.

In 1976, one of the UK's most dedicated Mod-obsessed teenagers - Paul Weller - saw a new hope for youth music in the previously mentioned Sex Pistols and also The Clash. Never shirking his love of all things Mod, his Who, Small Faces, Dr Feelgood, Soul and rhythm and blues fixations, Weller - with his band The Jam - was keen to be a part of this new youth explosion... but - most crucially - without any defined allegiance to the party line of punk.

Soon antagonising and distancing himself from much of punk's elite, Weller's growing disenchantment with the new order was something that resonated profoundly with a certain clutch of fellow punk generation new wavers, as The Jam seemed to cultivate their audience of like-minded fans. Weller – the personification of punk attitude within a Mod context and style –soon discarded his regulation off stage punk gear fully realising the actual ideals of punk were far more important than its fashions. Significantly, early Jam gigs around the country saw elements of the audiences wearing a punked up 70's version of the classic Mod attire, skinny tight blazers and ties, winkle picker shoes, feather cut hair styles and an obligatory 'Jam' badge... the look soon spread throughout the new wave scene and beyond.

In essence, Punk was born of the 1960's and shared the same drugs as the Mods - many of its protagonists, such as Clash manager Bernie Rhodes, were teenage Mods in the 60's, whilst a considerable influence on early UK punk were The Hammersmith Gorillas led by R&B stalwart Jesse Hector who released their proto-punk rendition of 'You Really Got Me' in 1974. In context, glam rock and pub rock aside, it appeared as if the punk-inspired generation had almost completely erased the whole of the 70's so far, dismissing its excess's and outlandish grandeur in favour of a

return to the rudimentary basics of rock ... a celebration of the danger, impulsive nature and youth involvement of rock 'n' roll, effectively a continuation of where mid-60's Mod had left off.

Punk's much-celebrated year zero rejection of rock's past has also since been exposed as virtually non-existent. Despite pinning their allegiances to the youth explosion of the present, the main players of punk secretly held great regard for the established music order. Later punk luminaries such as UK Subs leader, Charlie Harper had once been a regular Scene club attendee - enjoying sets from The Who and Pretty Things amongst others, for example. Mick Jones of The Clash had referenced the Kinks, Stones, Yardbirds and the US Garage punk of the late 60's as his greatest influences in 1977, while his fellow clash city rocker, Joe Strummer had been motivated by the Stones and the mid-60's R&B explosion. The Clash, initially referenced for their Mod style in early reviews, also embraced an updated interpretation of Pop Art via their paint-splattered Jackson Pollok influenced clothes alongside their recycled Kinks and Who riffs. Scene Club legend, Guy Stevens also produced early Clash Demos and later went on to work with the band on their 1979 double album departure to punk, 'London Calling' in which they incorporated a plethora of styles and musical genres. The fledgling Sex Pistols themselves also covered Who and Small Faces songs. Punk's birth was littered with connections to the heyday of Mod.

Punk arrived with many intentions, spawning various interpretations, class issues and political agendas and just as many contradictions. Yet it remains the most vital youth cultural explosion since the Mods of the 60's and has rarely seen a truly competitive rival since.

Punk was an ideal, a sense of possibilities that could be grasped and achieved. Its fashion was merely a statement - proclaiming self-identity, not a premeditated uniformed look. In many ways, punk failed - eventually subsiding into a cartoon parody decorating tourist postcards, inspiring nostalgic gatherings and greatest hits compilations, to name just a few of its obvious failings - yet in numerous other aspects, punk succeeded. Its life-defining inspiration for following generations is immeasurable as are its wide-ranging influences in music and the arts. From film to journalist, writer to poet, musician to politicised spokesman, its ideals and links are everywhere. Mod too achieved elements of that, only much less politically. Some may dispute Mod's connection to early punk but its post-punk offerings of Power Pop and the subsequent early Mod revival period bands owe numerous direct roots to punk, surely significant signposts of the affiliation.

In 1978-79, Punk Rock had begun its descent into depths of parody, nihilism and often sheer moronic and predictable play by numbers rock, easily recognisable by its 1-2-3 intro and (by the next decade), accompanying studs and leather. The forward-thinking post-punk digging Weller and like minded members of his generation took influences from Mod's past with a determined dedication to create something new and of a Modernist persuasion for pop culture's future. In truth, Weller had recognised and shared a love of 60's Mod influences with his band The Jam since before punk, anyway. By the end of 1978, for many, the Mod sounds of the 60's appeared far more relevant and inspirational than the recent stirrings of throwaway pop and punk's creatively stifled cul-de-sac: consequently a new generation of Mods slowly, at first, then quickly, began to emerge.

A further connection was its nods to a musical heritage (linking punk's new rebels to the aggression and Mod sensibilities) of the Who, The Creation (whose 'Makin' Time' and 'Painter Man' singles were re-issued on punk label Raw records in 1977) and the 60's garage bands.

Whilst The Jam, musically at least, would pin their direct allegiance and style to punk most obviously across their first two albums (Weller's punk-spawned ideals always remaining to the very end) – integrating their raw R&B and 60's Mod influences into the aggression and energy of punk, they would undoubtedly help raise the profile of the fledgling Mod bands that were also making their first outings as punk acts. The Jolt, New Hearts (soon to be Secret Affair), The Sockets (Purple Hearts), The Chords, The Killer Meters all kick-started their careers as punk and new wave influenced bands. Numerous others too.

The Skunks (seen left) were another Mod influenced London punk band. They were spotted by Pete Townshend and Keith Moon, whilst supporting Generation X at The Vortex in 1977, and subsequently signed to Townshend's Eel Pie label. The similarities with The early Who were evident in their first single, written by lead guitarist Frank Cornelli, 'The Good From The Bad', recorded at Eel Pie studios and produced by Townshend. The Skunks were good friends with The Merton Parkas until a falling out when Merton's' drummer, Simon Smith started rehearsing with The Skunks, at their Brixton studios culminating in a blazing row with Mick Talbot.

Singer and rhythm guitarist, Gerry Lambe will go down in history as being the only known person to smash one of Pete Townshend's guitars, his favourite original 1952 Fender Telecaster no less, at St Marys College Twickenham. Like the Who, The Skunks were high energy and built up a loyal following, and similar to The Jam, a good mixture of punks and Mods attended their explosive and usually raucous gigs. The band's songs expressed their frustrations of being teenagers growing up in late 70's Britain and of their often depressing South London surroundings.

By early 1979, an ever-expanding collective of Mod inspired bands were playing in and around London, often paired on the same bill at venues such as the Bridge House, The Wellington and others. Punk, though a polar opposite in many aspects, yet sharing various fundamental ethics, had essentially laid the bridge for a new Mod absorbed scene to evolve.

In some ways, it is one of rock 'n' roll's shortcomings that this new Mod scene rapidly became known and celebrated as a revival - significantly adding to its eventual fashion status demise. The flood of media focus also brought with it elements of bandwagon jumpers and tribes of scruffy un-

Mod-like sheep, along with constant accusations of a retrogressive attitude. Superficially, it could be argued that this new interpretation of punk-generation Mod would have been categorically dismissed as irrelevant by the originals - as defying its original ideals of forward-focussed Modernism. While some of this has validity, it must also be considered that this fresh celebration of Mod was not simply a regurgitation of its 1964 period style. Contradictions aside, the negative elements of this 'Modern World' (the rise of unemployment, social conditions and further class division to name a few) were being dismissed and channelled into creating a new youth movement of positive focus and progression. During punk's formative days, Weller spoke of punk-inspired art, poetry, writers and of course music, focusing on optimism and creativity as opposed to punk's doctrines of anarchy, destruction and 'no future'! This set of ideals continued to influence the growth of the new movement and spread its enthusiasm into the early Mod crowd.

Despite Mod's image of Peter Blake-influenced RAF roundels and the tribal sea of parkas rapidly appearing at Jam gigs, there was plenty of contemporary influences to be recognised and utilised within this new scene. Much like punk before it, one needs to appreciate the positive creativity that can be found beneath the public profile and outer edges of its popularisation. Most importantly, from both punk and the so-called Mod revival came a new generation of musicians and writers that would be pivotal influences throughout the era, largely un-matched by any generation since.

Above: Weller, Rawlings and Crowley on TV

The new Mod vision of the late 70's was initially explosive, pro-active, much more street-level than its predecessors and a refreshing alternative cultural follow-up to punk. At the time, it was without a doubt almost as relevant as punk before it in that it was initially self-contained and inspired by youth's energetic enthusiasm and optimistic attitude. For many it was their true musical calling card, a stamp of teenage identity and personal belief. Unfortunately, for reasons, which may vary for most of those involved, it was potentially doomed almost right from the start. Perhaps in balance, overall it lacked the soul and the deeper individual focus that the original period Mods were so imbued, whilst the over-exposure and journalistic cynicism already mentioned added further fuel to the fire of uncertainty. Frustratingly, the splintered factions of '79 Mods saw their scene lose its original impetus and progressive drive within a matter of mere months. Yet ultimately and most profoundly, the revival's stylistic influence, alongside its musical and cultural platform, was to inform and inspire many for decades to come - spawning legions of dedicated Mod believers and artistes that continue to add their creative Modernist sensibilities to popular culture and the Mod underground to this very day. This is the Modern World after all!

'MODS' A PERSONAL THING' BY TERRY RAWLINGS

Left: Terry Rawlings and friends and above centre

Contrary to popular myth Paul Weller was not the sole Mod-obsessive of the pre-punk mid-70's: True, Weller was a beacon of Mod style out in his Woking base, standing out amongst the period's plethora of denim and long hair... insular in his discoveries of all things Mod and like Terry Rawlings rapidly digesting and assimilating the whole phenomenon of sixties Mod. Both were short of like-minded partners in mohair, and neither were the last exclusive bastion of Mod! Whilst various scooter clubs across the country continued to 'keep the faith' and Mods' cousins on the Northern Soul scene lived a life of speed, back-flips and talc dusted dance floors - hair fit to match the times and strides outdoing past, present and future: a fast, highly-energised lifestyle with plenty of parallels to the earlier Mods... these young fans of the Small Faces, The Who and Soul lived out their personal reproduction of the life of a Mod. Quite possibly amongst a small number of Mod-leaning teenagers nationwide - few of whom knew of the other's existence - the paths of these two Mods of the 70's would come to join. Whilst one was to strike out and conquer the modern world with his Rickenbacker, youthful arrogance and goldmine of talent and embark on a career that many would come to envy, respect and applaud, eventually representing the soundtrack and voice for many of the punk and new Mod generation. The other was also destined to play an influential and important part in Mod's growth and longevity. In print, Rawlings paints a rich canvass illustrating Mod's 'great British phenomenon' and ongoing relevance... Though, Mod for Terry Rawlings is very much a personal thing!

Terry Rawlings - "I was working in the post room of Decca Records on Great Marlborough Street in the west end of London. It was a job recently vacated by my new best mate Gary Crowley, who had swanned off to the giddy heights of glamour working as the receptionist at the New Musical Express, up the road in Carnaby Street. A job incidentally made vacant by another old local mate of mine Danny Baker. I'd just been freshly rescued from the tediousness of work at a pure silk blouse warehouse in the garment district of London, in nearby Great Titchfield Street. My job there was to pack the blouses in boxes and load (load sounds like they were heavy, which obviously they weren't) them into a van for delivery. Dull, right? Well, yes and no!

I lived with my parents, who were of the sort that set down very basic yet rigidly enforced rules. The first being 'If you don't bring any money into the house for your keep then you can move out!' And boy, did they mean it. My Mum had me enrolled with a temp employment agency within days of my official school expulsion letter landing on our front door mat. Not that this had been my first and only soul destroying early work experience. Ooooh no! Before the relatively carefree days of stuffing women's clothing into my parka pockets, I'd been forced to toil away in many an unskilled, luckless, stink-pit in order to keep a roof over my head. However, I made sure my one stay at Watney's Brewery was worth my while. In order to make the best of a bad job, every morning I'd help myself to as many bottles of light ale as I could carry; plucked as I walked from the hundreds of beer crates stacked in the brewery yard and snuffled into my parka. Then I would walk, Great Escape-style though the yard with my pockets bulging, into the kitchen. Now I grant you, swigging bottles of warm light ale in a steaming hot kitchen in the middle of summer may not sound very refreshing, but let me tell you: when you're scrubbing out the remnants of two hundred industrial trays of sausage and mash, several light ales will help take the edge off.

Well, it made it tolerable at best; until one morning, when on my way to the kitchens the rattling of bottles in my parka gave me away to some jobs-worth and I was sent packing. Not that I gave a shit, for I knew my mother would have me back in that St. Paul's recruitment office first thing in the morning. And, sure enough that's where I was the following day - face to face with the pissed off filing cabinet operator who'd obviously been informed about my Watney's dismissal. The pair of them were discussing getting me a job with the local council, who were recruiting night road sweepers for the City of London. Now, for some thankful reason or another it turned out I wasn't eligible and so to cut a long story short I ended up boxing blouses!

So, back to my lunchtime trip to the Dog and Trumpet pub, and a chance meeting that would change the course of my life. I was walking past Liberty's department store on Great Marlborough Street heading towards Carnaby Street when I spotted a skinny ginger fella wrapped in an identical parka heading straight towards me. It was a mutual sighting and one that stopped us both dead in our tracks as Mod met Mod. I remember being struck about how well turned out he was, bronze tonic suit, checked button-down and (a pet hate of mine) well-polished Dr Marten shoes with white socks. Sounds ridiculous now I know, but back then, there just weren't that many Mods around - so few in fact that if you ever saw a fellow Mod you felt an instant camaraderie. This particular Mod was Gary Crowley, who (it just so happened) worked at the Great Marlborough Street offices of the once mighty DECCA record label, a few doors along from the back-stage of the London Palladium.

It being a lunchtime, Gary and me went for a couple of quick beers at the pub where, during the conversation, he mentioned he was leaving his job as post boy at Decca that Friday and that they needed a replacement. It was suggested I went for the vacancy, and that he'd put in a good word for me, which when all things were considered, was a magnanimous gesture seeing as we had only known each other for approximately three quarters of an hour and four beers. It was agreed we'd meet the next day, (Thursday) and he assured me he would have laid the ground work. Sure enough, as good as his word, we met back at the pub the following lunchtime and - yes indeed - an interview had been arranged for the next day!

Now I use the word interview in the lightest possible terms! What happened was I went with Gary on the Friday afternoon (dressed in cream Sta-Prest, navy blue Fred Perry, Hush Puppies and parka) and met with Decca's Marlborough Street boss a Ms. Sarah Bugle, who took one look at me stood next to an almost identically clad Gary and simply swapped like for like! I started on the Monday.

By the late seventies Decca's glory days as a major record company were history; it was way past its prime and a mere imitation of its once great and glorious self. However, the label's rich history still held me in awe. Yes, we all know they turned down the Beatles, but they made good with the Rolling Stones didn't they? Which reminds me - while we're on the subject of the label's cock-up with the Fabs - let me straighten out one of the music world's greatest injustices and misconceptions.

It has always been universally accepted that Decca A&R, Dick Rowe, was the poor unenlightened sap that turned down John, Paul, George and Pete/Ringo, with that now immortalised phrase 'Guitar Bands are on their way out'. Well, it wasn't dear 'ole Dick at all! It was, in fact, a company decision that actually went very much against what Rowe thought. Rowe simply became the scapegoat - the patsy as it were - and he spent the rest of his life telling the truth to everyone and anyone who would listen. This didn't do him a blind bit of good though; after all, who in the full glare of Beatle-mania was going to stand up and say 'by the way, Dick is telling the truth and it was me who fucked up!' Despite his signing of acts such as Small Faces, Moody Blues, Ten Years After, David Bowie and countless other legends, Dick Rowe is still only remembered as the man who turned down The Beatles.

Anyway, I digress! Life at Decca was a breeze; order stock up from the warehouse, which was next to the impressive Decca House on the Albert Embankment and (using a franking machine) select the right postage and come five o' clock, take the sacks round to the big post office on Broadwick Street. Apart from fetching the odd sandwich or cup of tea and occasionally manning the reception whilst the impossibly cute receptionist went for lunch - that was it! That was all that was required of me. I, of course, managed to sod up even those basic and simple tasks.

I was no better on my reception watch as no sooner would I take a call and patch it through to whoever's extension was required I'd have instantly forgotten who was calling. A typical call would go something like this: 'Hello - Decca Records'; 'Hi, can I speak to Sarah Bugle?' 'Yes, who's calling?' I'd get the name and switch the switches. 'Sarah, a call for you'; 'Who is it?' 'Errrrrrr... hang on!' It drove them all mad.

I did eventually get my act together and things ticked along nicely. I also had one of the greatest record collections building up at home, thanks to helping myself to whatever I fancied from the label's massive back-catalogue and simply posting it to myself. I had the entire Rolling Stones collection, singles, EPs and albums within my first month. Small Faces, then The Animals. Nashville Teens, Billy Fury, Marianne Faithfull, Brian Poole and the Tremeloes, John Mayall's Bluesbreakers and obscure stuff like The Poets, The Eyes of Blue and The Quik from Decca's off shoot label Deram. (Incidentally, my entire LP collection - bar a couple of dozen - would be stolen years later from a storage garage).

Life was good. Gary was still very much in my life and we'd meet up quite regularly for lunchtime beers in the Dog and Trumpet, where we were sometimes joined by another Mod called Don who worked in Lewis Leathers, the famous motorbike shop on Great Portland Street. It was through this connection Don managed to get a good deal on a really decent Lambretta LI which (I thought) he fucked up by having it entirely re-sprayed matt Black. He was also able to get his hands on a whole load of accessories, which was impressive because scooter parts were bloody hard to come by back then.

My life away from Decca was also becoming increasingly Mod. I'd managed to convince a couple of old school friends to take up the look, including the fella I'd convinced needed all those Monkees albums years back, but they were only semi-convinced and always looked half-arsed. We had taken to meeting regularly at the famous boxing gym/pub The Thomas a Beckett on the Old Kent Road every Tuesday night to watch a local Blues band called Stan's Blues Band. The group was headed up by a lead singer/guitarist called Dennis Greaves, and a harp player called Mark Feltham who between them shared such an incredible knowledge of the Blues and R n B, it belied their young age and seemed impossible. The fact no one in the band went by the name of Stan mattered not one jot! They totally blew us away, and once we'd witnessed the spectacle of Dennis playing a fifty foot guitar lead that enabled him to walk out of the pub and play from the traffic Island in the middle of the Old Kent Road, we adopted them as our own (he once got on a bus still playing.)

The Chords (left) and 9 Below Zero

Terry (at rear) Top of the Pops, March 79 for The Jam's 'Strange Town' performance

It was during one of our Tuesday nights out at The Beckett that I met Billy Hassett, a young Mod trying to hustle a gig for his Deptford-based band The Detours; an old school group he'd put together with his bass-playing cousin Martin Mason and two school mates; guitarist Chris Pope and drummer Paul Halpin. Billy had heard we had a good little live scene going at the pub and came in to check it out. He had the parka (complete with little yellow Esso petrol mascot key-ring and US military insignia), white Sta-Prest and button-down shirt. Well, suffice to say, nods were nodded, hands were shaken and bottles of light ales were exchanged. So began a lifelong friendship that continues today.

Billy's group were booked in for a couple of weeks' time - no questions asked and no need for a demo. The guv'nor of The Beckett liked our crowd even though he knew that everyone of us was underage, but so long as we kept a low profile and our noses clean, he in return turned a blind eye. I'm also sure the steady rounds of beer we bought helped.

Terry (centre) outside the Thomas a' Beckett pub

Billy invited me to a rehearsal his band was holding the following week at a studio space on Tower Bridge Road. This had been set up in order to rehearse for a forthcoming gig they had at The Deptford Arms and to also audition a new drummer. This resulted in the hiring of Buddy Ascott and a name change to The Chords which roughly coincided with Stan's Blue's Band morphing into 9 Below Zero. The Chords weren't called a 'Mod band', because that term hadn't been coined yet. This was 1978 and there weren't enough Mods around to be called anything like a scene, let alone a movement. Yes, we had our little pub crowd, but that was made up of a variety of individuals and very few Mods. The Chords had Billy who was a Mod, and Buddy who was more of a Who fan than a Mod. He'd joined the band because of their Who influences, and had slept on Brighton beach the day after Keith Moon died. He'd also got into the look the same way I had; via the 'Quadrophenia' photo booklet. Martin looked the part but he never declared one way or another, and Chris was more of a punk than anything else. We weren't aware that there was a similar crowd to ours meeting up regularly over in East London, to watch a local band who had recently changed their name from Jack Plug and the Sockets to The Purple Hearts.

9 Below Zero and The Chords played a few gigs together most famously at the Albany Empire in Deptford before their career paths sent them off along different roads; each establishing themselves in their own unique fashion, and both gaining a loyal following that slowly stretched beyond the South London pub circuit. This was all happening in tandem with the greater rise to

fame of The Jam who, as we now know, would go on to inspire (along with a certain film) 'the Mod revival' a year later in 1979. However in early '78 Mod was still a segregated affair, with little pockets of Mods in the South East and the West of London.

The Chords shifted up a gear with their now legendary residency at the Wellington Pub in Waterloo in '78 and also caused a stir when we all crashed the opening night of the stage musical 'Tommy' which had just opened in Shaftsbury Avenue. Now, here's another strange tale; this particular version of Pete Townshend's rock opera seems to have been successfully erased from people's memory. None more so than Pete Townshend's himself who, whilst raking in millions in the early '90s, billed that era's production of the show thus: 'For the first time on stage - 'Tommy''.

The Jam, early 1977 as seen in a fan club photo giveaway and Terry Rawlings and Mod pal, Gary Crowley

Anyway, we all tipped up at the Shaftsbury Theatre - a flash mob of green parkas and Desert Boots. The door security guys upon seeing us must have assumed we were part of the opening night because they stood aside as we all piled in. I remember spotting Townshend straight away standing in the foyer swaying and swigging from a bottle of vodka; he took one look at us and, instead of calling security, beckoned us over. That was when we heard about the film he was about to make based on the 'Quadrophenia' album and offered us all extras work. Then, one of our number somehow picked an argument with chat show host Russell Harty, and that was when most of us were shown the door. I actually slipped up the stairs and watched the entire first act before being finally ejected. That led to the Chords either auditioning in person to be the band in the nightclub scene of the film, or they recorded a demo! Whichever it was, they were rejected in favour of that group that did appear in the film and who were never seen or heard of again. We all blamed Russell Harty. I think the Chords not getting that film role was a blessing! Certainly if the group that landed the part are anything to go by career-wise. Besides, the Chords were about to land a far bigger break than a bit-part in a movie.

By this time, I had become friends with Paul Weller and I nagged him into coming down to watch The Chords one Saturday night at The Wellington - never thinking for a minute he ever would. However, long story short, turn up he did. He and his then girlfriend Gill strolled in to the pub just as the group took to the beer crate and plywood stage. The up-shot was Paul liked what he saw and generously gifted them the support slot to The Jam at the trio's forthcoming sell-out gig at The Rainbow, Finsbury Park. The rest, as they say, is history."

Terry Rawlings obsessive fascination with the 60's and Mod in particular has inspired his more than considerable output as a writer. Following his seminal 1982 Small Faces book 'All Our Yesterdays', published by Paul Weller's Riot Stories, Rawlings went on to pen further critically acclaimed Mod chronicles and most recently his version of events surrounding the death of Brian Jones, which is regularly updated and reprinted and has been the basis of a film screenplay 'Stoned'.

Like Terry Rawlings, the majority of the Mod-influenced bands that were slowly seeping through, had a distinct history of punk influence and involvement.

Robert John Manton (Purple Hearts) - "1977 and we got into the punk thing: we formed a punk group called The Sockets with Nicky Lake on drums and got our first gig supporting The Buzzcocks at North East London Polytechnic in Barking. We could barely play more than two chords but managed to get through it somehow aided by a few bottles of cider. We had a joke Punk Rock Opera called 'Reg', a sort of punk 'Tommy' but much shorter."

Simon Stebbing (Purple Hearts) - "It was Bob who first heard about The Jam. It was the spring of '77, me, Bob and Jeff were classmates, in our last year at school, music obsessed, and looking for a riot of our own.

After years of the musical tyranny of disco, and the stranglehold on the charts by bland family fodder such as Brotherhood of Man and Smokie, electric guitar based youth music was back on the agenda. The former flag bearers of British youth, our idols, The Who, were now considered too old, and were being supplanted by a new wave of hungry, socially aware bands. For us, stuck in the 'burbs of Romford, wishing it was the 60's, the burgeoning punk rock scene was definitely a step in the right direction, but not everyone wants to dress in bin bags or look like a junkie, the Punk revolution in style rapidly reduced to a clichéd development of 70's Keith Richards outsider heroin chic. and when you're 16, looks are important. From that first review, I think we knew The Jam would be *our* band; they had yet to release a record, so now we just *had* to see them.

Our chance came when they played at a West London college at the foot of a bill featuring Meal Ticket, a pub rock country band, and topped by Reg Presley and his legendary Troggs still churning out 'Wild thing' etc. Me and Bob took the bus up to London, and somehow managed to get into the students only gig. When The Jam took to the stage, with their matching suits and Rickenbacker's, me and Bob were instantly blown away - Bob describes it like a sledgehammer blow of adrenaline - he reckons the first number was 'I've Changed My Address', I do remember hearing 'In the City' and 'Route 66', but there was no doubt - this was the new idea, we had never witnessed such a furious blast of energy, this was a real band, as real as it gets - *our* band. Clearly visible from a side - stage window stood a mirror-bedecked scooter - Weller's. Little did we know that in the next few years our lives would cross over and be intertwined with these new heroes in waiting."

ED SILVESTER
'TRYING TO FORGET YOUR GENERATION'

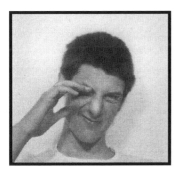  

Despite elements of Mod v Punk rivalry towards the end of the 70's, few can deny the importance of punk as an important musical and cultural force. Significantly, many '79 period Mods had sampled punk as one of the ingredients of their first musical apprenticeships.

By early 1978, the strong presence of Mods at Jam gigs was becoming yet more noticeable – almost pre-empting the soon to explode revival. When The Jam released their career defining 'All Mod Cons' album later that year, the scene was set in motion for a new generation of Mods. In contrast to their 60's Mod era ancestors, here was a new breed that shared different attitudes and conditions, often exhibiting a more distinctly aggressive stance - partly due to the social climate of the decade and the spectre of punk's recent influence. Ed Silvester is a perfect example of a punk youth who made the transition to Mod at the time.

Ed Silvester (West Essex Mod) - "I was born and bred an Essex lad, hailing from the last stop on the eastern end of the London underground's Central line - in the once sleepy market town of Epping. In the early 1970's I'd entered teenage life as the ubiquitous long haired smoothie, flared pants and DM boots – as seen on most football terraces on a Saturday afternoon, well, Leyton Orient in my case. Musically, I was a big fan of David Bowie and T-Rex - rushing to the local record store, to buy all their new releases.

At the back end of 1976, and by chance, (on the John Peel show, I think) I heard a record on the radio that changed life, New Rose by the Damned - so much power and energy, it near blew me away. This triggered an interest in the burgeoning punk rock scene, which was also starting to be covered in the music press as well, 'Sounds' being my rag of choice. At the time, Prog rock was popular with my fellow students, but this music left me cold – to me, it was just boring rubbish. I was studying in the sixth form at my local Comprehensive school at the time, but needed cash for clothes, records and to travel to gigs in the big smoke. So I lost interest in studying and decided to get any job, to fund my expanding social life. My long 'Geronimo' style centre parting locks were soon shorn off, and overnight I became the archetypical punk, with skinny jeans and a ripped and torn old white school shirt - the bondage trousers and Sta-Prest would come much later. I was more of a so called 'plastic punk' at the time, as I'd managed to obtain work as a messenger in the City of London – and my brother got a similar job in a shipping company in Holborn - although the 70's were painted as a grey and grim decade; jobs were far more plentiful for teenagers. A short trip to the local employment exchange, turn up for an interview; sign your name, quick chat, you'll do, you're in, job done! Mind you, I did wear an Oxford weave Ben Sherman shirt and 1950's style peg leg trousers to work - rounded off with some brogue like shoes – skinny tie was optional.

Seeing my idols on the few musical TV shows of the day, like The Old Grey Whistle Test and Top of The Pops, certainly whet my appetite, and I needed to see my heroes live. The excitement of putting cloths on that were intended to shock was very liberating at the time. The first punk gigs that I can clearly recall going to were, The Jam, Buzzcocks and Generation X in 1977 and early 1978 - mostly at the Marquee club in Wardour Street. I seem to remember also seeing The Clash at the Music Machine (Camden Town), where the group came on about 11 o'clock - which was a bloody ridiculous time to start. I annoyingly had to leave before the band had finished, otherwise I wouldn't have got home that night - so missed half the set, and I didn't want to lose my job. Generation X would sport Pop-Art t-shirts and jeans, and what caught my eye, was the soon to be adopted target t-shirt; which was the punk look that I stuck with. I always thought that the Generation X single, 'Your Generation' had similarities with 'My Generation' by the Who, and feel that was the real war cry for the, Blank Generation.

February 1978 was a seminal moment, as I was part of a gang of Epping punks who travelled West up the Central line, to see The Jam, at the Marquee club as part of their 'London Blitz', to promote the release of the 'News of the World' single. They were supported by the Scottish band, The Jolt. I suppose, at the time, we thought that The Jolt were heavily influenced by The Jam, working within a punk framework - in their snappy suits and power pop beat.

That evening The Jam wore their trademark black suit jackets, white shirts and thin black tie, but in a change to their usual attire; white Sta-Prest trousers - along with their usual black and white Jam shoes. Our little gang from Epping copied the skinny black tie and white shirt combination; our old 3 button school jackets became useful again! Most of us had also adopted Weller's spiky crew cut. Although, we still considered ourselves punk, it was a neater image, and unknowingly a look adopted by some of the later mod revivalists. The moment the band jumped on to the stage, and crashed into their opening number, the crowd started to furiously pogo. Even though it was freezing cold outside, we were all soon dripping with sweat; with shirts and ties all over the place - the kids wanted some action, and who could f-ing blame them now. We felt that we really were 'In the City'! The Jam were my favourite punk band (closely followed by the Clash, Buzzcocks and Generation X), and the transition to Mod was slow and subtle.

Paul Weller had never hidden his Mod influences, but had initially wrapped his angry teenage sound up as punk. The emergence of punk had given the Jam their big break, and a convenient platform. Weller wasn't going to disrespect the punk explosion that had made so many of the old dinosaur rock bands obsolete overnight. A short lived power pop revival happened that year and

260

that had also influenced us, with bands like the Pleasers having minor hits, one of which was an old Who number, 'The Kids are Alright'. We would read that Paul Weller loved sixties bands (especially the Beatles), and early Jam performances always included a few 60's covers – and novelty numbers like the Batman theme. We now wanted to hunt down the original versions, which naturally sparked an interest in 60's beat bands. We were discovering the bands influences, with The Who, The Kinks and the Small Faces being at the forefront.

Inspired by the 'News of the World' picture sleeve, my brother John, Alan Smith and myself travelled to Carnaby Street, as we wanted to check out the three button leather jackets at the Carnaby Cavern. We tried a few on, and told the shop assistant we'd buy them, and also have the jackets made to measure, which cost a bomb in those days – being a Mod was starting to be bloody expensive.

Paul Weller was clearly a Mod, but we still saw these bands as part of the post-punk and new wave scene. My brother John and myself both loved Bowie's Pinups LP, and the 'orrible Who album 'Quadrophenia', so we'd happily identified ourselves with this genre and style of music. We'd also taken the plunge and hunted down an old copy of the Who's compilation, 'Meaty, Beaty, Big and Bouncy', which had their 60's hits on it. I don't think that the punk elite or anyone in the music press expected the Mod revival to take off – with the exception of maybe, Garry Bushell – who I'd occasionally see at gigs.

As teenagers, we loved our music, and the gang would happily make the trip from Epping, to a little independent record store in Walthamstow, in East London; Small Wonder Records, a place where we were able to get all of the new punk and new wave releases, and the odd bootleg as well – a veritable goldmine. The guy who ran the place always wore a tea cosy on his head (the sometimes abusive, Pete Stennett), I guess he had been a hippie in a past life, but I always laughed when he told someone to 'fuck off'. But the driving force was the music, led by The Jam, and maybe, The Who as well. We wanted more than jeans and a target t-shirt, and craved additions to our wardrobe.

By 1979, the Epping gang (made up of a hard core group, Alan Smith, John Silvester, Dave Stokes, Michael Spencer, Kevin Russell and Mark Bradford) started to regularly travel by bus to Romford, to check out the Saturday market stalls for old 60's clobber, or make a pilgrimage to a cracking little shop called Mintz & Davis, (which was located just opposite the old Ind Coope brewery).

Photos: clockwise Alan Smith and John Silvester, Michael Spencer and Ed Silvester, Mark Bradford and Ed at the Marquee and Ed wearing target T-shirt

Mintz & Davis had started to sell retro and old 60's clothing on the back of the burgeoning power pop/Mod revival. This is where we all bought out first US Army parkas, now known by everyone as M51 parkas, although at the time we didn't bother with this type of description. Not surprisingly, demand soon picked up and they started to sell some off the peg three button tonic suits and Ben Sherman shirts as well. We'd occasionally see Jeff Shadbolt – of Purple Hearts fame - leaning against the counter, chatting to customers, a local Mod hero. I always felt that most of the burgeoning Mod-inspired bands at that time would have been labelled punk bands two years earlier - a more power pop/new wave sound.

Even by 1979, longish hair and flared trousers was still a common sight on the high street, which was the look for most of the male population, a hangover from the late 60's and early 70's hippy, rock style. The new wave Mod look, of parkas, target t-shirts, Fred Perry polo shirts and Desert Boots, had slowly started to seep into our little group of Epping punks and skinheads, as a result of The Jam, and reading the occasional review in the music press – especially 'Sounds' that often featured some of the new wave of Mod bands; and of course, the ever present influence of Paul Weller. Difficult to imagine now – with the plethora of modern clothing stores - but old 60's clobber could still easily be picked up from the odd market stall, charity shop and savvy clothing shop.

Weller was such an iconic presence at that time, and the release of the 'All Mod Cons' album of 1978 had really sealed this for us, this was the moment that we started to become totally absorbed by the Mod image. By March 1979, most of us had a parka and pair of Desert Boots, all you had to do was mix it with an old skinhead Ben Sherman button down shirt, and, hey presto, you were a Mod!

Prior to the release of 'Quadrophenia' the Who released a film retrospective of the band, named after one of their earlier songs, 'The Kids Are Alright', which came out in June 1979. I always felt that this film helped to raise the profile of The Who's Mod heritage, and also add fuel to the Mod revival. This certainly increased our enthusiasm before the release of the big one – 'Quadrophenia'! As part of the Mod revival, we were very keen to see our idols on screen, and to check out the clothes and to see old footage of the band playing live.

The film was first shown locally in South Woodford, a few stops up the Central line for us – so excitement was mounting. Even though it was a warm day, a few of the guys wanted to proudly wear their parkas, to announce that a new tribe was in town. On arrival at the cinema, we spotted a group of other parka-clad geezers. We wondered where these guys were from. Not knowing many other local Mods, we sauntered over and had a chat with these like-minded individuals. Their top fella turned out to be none other than Eddie Piller, of future Acid Jazz fame. Telephone numbers were exchanged, and after that, we all started to knock around together - we'd just doubled the amount of Essex Mods that we knew."

Simon Stebbing (Purple Hearts) - "We saw The Jam as much as possible, bunking off school in our O' level exam year, later that year they started releasing records and, along with many other new wave bands, began making their mark on the nation's consciousness. There was no real indication that The Jam's singles would soon be hitting number one in the charts in the first week of their release, but they soon began to gather a following of like-minded youth, who perhaps dressed a little smarter than their punk peers. By 1978 me, Jeff and Bob, along with new drummer Gary Sparks, had dropped all our jokey spoof punk songs and gone Mod too. Over the next year, we began to get more gigs in London and Southend under our new name the Purple Hearts.

There was a whole Romford contingent of proto-Mods, punks, and a few tame skinheads going to see The Jam and other new wave bands like Generation X and Buzzcocks along with other 60's-influenced groups like the Pleasers, and The Inmates. One time, the three of us (me Bob and Jeff) helped carry The Jam's gear into the Nashville, a West London pub on the rock circuit; this is where we first saw another Mod - Tony Lordan, soon to become designer of the Purple Hearts logo and later a member of Department S. I learned recently that Tony had thought we were going to fight him, because we kept looking over - in reality, we were surprised, and pleased to see that others were adopting The Jam's 60's dress sense and were just thinking of saying 'hello!' - pleased also because it might mean that there could be a possible audience for the newly named Purple Hearts brand of 60's flavoured teenage angst. Tony and Jeff soon became firm friends and he started designing flyers for our gigs."

Peter Maisey (North Herts Mod) - "When punk hit, it reflected the atmosphere to me that nothing was ever going to get better - it was all bleak and then we found a 'Ready Steady Go!' night at the Blitz and an alternative. Times might be hard and life shit but there was a future in the Mod way of life. In 79 Mod was a chance to replace the desperation of punk with hope and cool."

Ray Margetson - "The turning point for me was at the tail end of 1978 listening to the 'All Mod Cons' LP and being fascinated by the retro pics on the inside sleeve. It was also around this time when I used to go to a house in Hackney known as the '100 punks'. There was a guy who lived there called John, tall Mediterranean appearance with a leather jacket, who used to get punks from all over London come to his place for parties and hanging out listening to records. One of the guys who came along 'Surrey Docks' John, so called after the place where he lived, starting dressing differently in a parka and hush puppies, early 1979, and said you have to come over to South London to see this great new band called The Chords. We started dressing in that vein and getting into the Who, Small Faces, Kinks, Georgie Fame as well as Motown, Soul, Ska, (which was a natural progression for me as I already had some of these 60's dance sounds on vinyl from about three years earlier. I'd left school in 1978 and worked in a bank, so now had more money to buy clothes and records than ever before."

Simon Franklin (Luton Mod) - "By 1979 punk had lost its impetuous, it had virtually become mainstream. Inevitably when a subculture dies the youth looks back to see what it can revive or resurrect. At this time teenagers too young for the 60's but old enough to see their older brothers and sisters as Mods looked backwards to this sharp suited movement almost as a reaction to the scruffy DIY look of the punks! But they retained the angst against society and in this the reborn Mods were far more aggressive in their look and listening tastes."

By early spring '79, it was clear that the mood of youth was shifting away from the influence of punk towards the sharper street fashion of Mod - reflecting exactly how the disaffected post-punk generation wished to appear visually despite the imminent arrival of Thatcherism.

ROBERT LEE - MOD MAYDAY

Robert Lee's arrival with Mod was essentially - like many others of his age - a logical progression - a twist of fate that complimented his early love of the Small Faces and a chance photo session that would lead Robert to a date with Mod history as one of its most recognisable images of the era.

Robert Lee - "My interest in Mod began with music as a school kid in the early seventies through listening to Rod Stewart and the Faces and reading stories of Rod the Mod and of course The Small Faces all though I didn't actually listen to any Small Faces until they re-released 'Lazy Sunday' and 'Itchycoo Park' around 76. Those two singles prompted me to buy a Decca compilation of their A and B sides and from that moment I was hooked on anything Mod from the fashion to scooters and the beach fights but mostly the music because that was relatively easy and cheap to obtain.

By 1977 I had started work and had more money to pursue my interest in music and as well as the sixties records I was collecting. I also started following the new wave scene attending gigs in London most weeks. One band in particular that had a strong following from my town was Sham 69 (one of our crowd was a roadie for them and got us backstage access etc.) resulting in us becoming skinheads, or, in my case, Suedehead. Gigs sometimes led to trouble of some kind and attracted the attention of the police resulting in someone being arrested; thankfully, never I and I wanted it to stay that way, avoiding the right wing element that was creeping into the scene especially.

The Reading festival in 1978 featured our good mates Sham 69 on the Friday afternoon and the headline band that night was none other than The Jam. I had seen numerous new wave bands in the previous year but not The Jam. I owned their 'In the City' album and, although I thought their music was good, I hadn't made the connection with Mod, wrongly assuming them to be just another new wave band. That night changed my whole outlook, as they were the best live act I had seen to date and the penny then dropped with the Mod thing, Weller smashing his guitar like Townsend and covering the Vandellas' hit 'Heatwave'. The Sixties influence was plain to see; I came away a Jam fan and now had a new musical influence to align with.

The transformation from Suedehead to Mod wasn't that hard to achieve as I was already wearing tonic suits and tassel loafers; I just needed to tweak the look slightly and add a tie. By autumn, I had saved enough money to have my first (light grey) mohair suit made at a local tailor. I went on to have a further two suits made over the next few months; I liked his suits that much. And so by the winter of 78 I had completed the look - there was just one more thing to add, a scooter.

Photos from Robert's personal collection: above photo taken late 1978

I wasn't actively looking for a scooter, it was more a case of wishful thinking, but I knew that to complete the look and to be considered a Mod it was essential. Also I had started a new job that involved shift work so my own transport would certainly help with the commute. By chance just before Christmas I was passing a motor bike shop and a scooter for sale caught my eye in the window display. It didn't look that special and had after market indicators, large screen and a rear storage box but it was a scooter. After a bit of negotiating with the shopkeeper the scooter, a white Vespa 150 super, was mine and I picked it up the following Saturday and within a week I had removed the naff accessories to make room for my own additions.

The chrome accessories were added bit by bit on a weekly basis as my money allowed and I would ride for hours on end at every opportunity. I had stopped going to gigs, every spare penny was being spent on the scooter, and besides, apart from The Jam, there wasn't any bands I wanted to see that badly. Around Easter of 79, I was told about a film company needing scooter riding extras at Brighton for a film that was being made. To this day, I don't know if that was a fact or not because days before I intended to ride down, the Vespa and I parted company resulting in a fair amount of damage to the both of us. Thankfully, most of the damage to the scooter was only cosmetic so I made the decision to repaint the whole scooter black as a contrast to the chrome. My first Bank Holiday as a Mod was spent shaking rattle cans of spray paint in the back garden in an attempt to make the scooter look well again instead of riding to Brighton and having fun.

Around the same time, a good friend from the skinhead crowd who was still doing the gigs told me about the Mod Monday event at the Bridge House, East London featuring a Mod band called Secret Affair, and so the following Monday I got myself suited and booted and rode the twenty miles to Canning town. That first night I was expecting to find wall to wall Mod's with dressed-up scooters lined up outside; the reality was I was the only one wearing a suit let alone riding a scooter. There was, however, a lot of parka's being worn so I had at last found like-minded people.

The Bridge House became the centre of all things Mod over the next few months, mainly because there wasn't any other venues putting on Mod bands. Secret affair were the main band but gradually other bands began to appear and within a short time it seemed to be a new one every week. By then the crowds were getting bigger by the week and scooters were starting to appear. By the end of April there were about a dozen scooters turning up every week.

That May Day Bank Holiday, the Bridge House hosted an all-day event featuring most of the bands that had played the Mod Monday's before. The gig was recorded for the famous album 'Mod's Mayday79'. As we had already seen the bands at least once before, those of us with scooters agreed to ride down to Brighton for the day with the intention of returning to the Bridge House for the evening. We eventually got back to London around 10 o'clock to be greeted by what can only be described as a carnival atmosphere with the pub full to bursting point inside and as many people outside. Because we couldn't get in, we spent the rest of the evening hanging around outside exchanging stories with each other about the day's events whilst still being able to hear the music being played.

The following Monday evening, as I pulled up outside the pub, Terry Murphy the landlord and a photographer approached me and asked if they could take a couple of photos of me and the scooter to help promote the forthcoming album release. I agreed, not realising at the time that one of those photos would end up being used for the sleeve. By the time the album was released the Monday nights had grown in popularity so much that if you didn't get there early there was a very good chance you wouldn't get in at all: thankfully that wasn't a problem for me as Terry always allowed me in and even very kindly let me park the scooter behind locked gates beside the pub and away from the younger Mod's that always seemed to be hanging around outside.

The Bridge House was by then not only the focal point for live Mod bands it had also become the meeting place for scooter riding Mods. From there we very often went into the heart of London for a cruise around or attend other gigs at the Wellington, Dingwalls or the Marquee to name a few. From having no gig's at all we now had so many to choose from that it was difficult to keep up with them. In the space of four or five months, Mod had gone from nowhere to being everywhere; even in my home town Mod's and the occasional scooter were beginning to appear. I continued to attend the Bridge House every Monday for the rest of 79 with the exception of Bank Holidays when we would ride to the coast. The August Bank Holiday at Southend was a particularly memorable day, partly due to the number of scooters that made the journey, but also because the 'March of the Mod's' tour played at Canvey island that evening, Secret Affair, Back to Zero, Squire and the Purple Hearts all on the same bill, which truly capped a brilliant day.

By 1980 there was no need to travel to London to see bands as often as the previous year; it was possible to catch a lot of the bands playing gigs nearer to home and the local scene had grown to an extent that there were parties and dances most weeks. I still dropped in on the Bridge House occasionally to keep in touch with the crowd but by that Spring that had stopped. By the summer, I had sold the Vespa and switched to a Lambretta due to the tuning possibilities and the fact that the Vespa was attracting a lot of unwanted attention in the form of damage or parts being stolen. I was still a Mod but with a standard looking tuned scooter rather than the lights and mirrors that slowed the Vespa down, all though I have to confess that reliability was an issue.

The scooter side of things was at that time more important to me than the clothes and music. I relied on the scooter for transport to and from work and I was to become a father in the spring of 81 so money was soon to be a major problem. I did still attend a few gigs in 1981 such as the all day events at the Ilford Palais but the emphasis was more on the scooter runs, in particular the Bank Holidays. I also attended my first rally that summer at the Three counties park at Great Malvern, which was an eye opener if only for the lack of Mod's and trouble. In complete contrast to the Three counties rally the final Bank Holiday run of the year was to Brighton and there was certainly, no shortage of Mod's or trouble. About thirty of us travelled down from Essex complete with back up van and arrived early afternoon on the Sunday. After parking up on Marina drive, we went in search of refreshments only to find hostility instead, and so within one hour of arriving we were involved in a fight that pretty much set the tone for the weekend. After several more skirmishes and even more drinks, the pubs started kicking us out so we headed back to the scooters to find that the police had cordoned off Marina drive to contain hundreds of Mods. Luckily, we were parked at the right side of the slip road that led away from the trouble.

We headed east on the coast road and found a car park a few miles out of Brighton and set up camp for the night with the intention of returning the following day. The next morning, totally oblivious to how bad the previous night's events had been, we tried entering Brighton only to be met by a police road block and being escorted out of town and threatened with arrest if we returned. We later found out just how bad things had been with the miniature train station being burnt down and scores arrested but never found out the cause of the riot that had we parked a further thirty feet along Marina drive we would of been surely involved in. That Bank Holiday was to be my last run all though I wasn't aware of it at the time."

The Bridge House in Canning town, London was the leading pub rock venue of the 70's and also the first to be graced with its own record label. Landlord Terence Murphy was a keen and extremely active supporter of live music, not only of the emerging Mod influenced bands, but all musical genres. Many adopted The Bridge House as their second home with popular residencies from the likes of Steve Marriot (under the moniker of Blind Drunk) and Charlie Watts Rocket 88 (often alongside fellow Stones Jagger and Richards.) But, in 1979, it was the Mods who came to epitomise the venue for many. The famous Mods Mayday album was recorded there in one day, featuring tracks from Small World, Beggar, Squire, The Mods and rising scene leaders Secret Affair. The Robert Lee adorned front cover has become one of the iconic images of the late 70's Mod period.

The classic scooter rallies and weekenders were also boosted by the excitement of the times. Rotherham born Steve 'Zal' Downing had arrived at his Mod destination in 1978 through, first the Northern Soul scene, followed by punk and its associated Jam Mod element. Steve recounts a humorous 'Quadrophenia' out-take styled account of one of the many weekend rallies he attended.

Steve 'Zal' Downing (Rotherham Mod) - "Blackpool, Easter 1979. Me and my mate Parky's Lambrettas' just wouldn't do the distance so we went by train taking just our holdhalls and a change of clothes, opting to sleep rough in order to save our cash for the weekend. We found shelter just up from the central Pier and decided to make that our home for the night. Next to the shelter, the deck chairs were covered with a canvas sheet so we used that for security for our belongings. Parky had a sleeping bag and slept at the side of the sea while I only had my parka to keep me warm so slept on the Prom side.

After a couple of hours, I felt something on my foot. I awoke to find out that some Mod-hating robbers had stolen my loafers off my feet and swiped our holdalls as well. It then became like a scene from The Benny Hill show as we spotted them taking off with our gear and we chased after them across the beach. After realising that there were too many of them we turned back round and they then chased after us. Fight them on the beaches was simply not an option. We scarpered and lost them.

Later on around mid-day the rest of our scooter mates arrived and they looked after us and despite the robbing, we had a laugh and a great time. Our train tickets were gone so we ended up borrowing spare crash helmets off the local Blackpool folk and set off back home on the back of our mate's scooters."

THE CLASS OF 79 ▶

By the spring of 1979, the expanse of Mod styled bands had accelerated to the extent that the music weeklies were accommodating front cover and extensive inside features on the burgeoning scene. NME's well-presented April 14th issue featured a classic 64-period scooter pack of Mods and insights to both the original scene and the new bands active at that time, namely The Chords, Purple Hearts and The Fixations. These musicians largely considered themselves to be Mods as opposed to many of the 60's acts who merely performed to Mods. Bands were being signed up, fanzines set-up and the centre of the Mod live scene was The Bridge House in London. The Who's Double album soundtrack to their Rock-u-mentary 'The Kids are Alright' was being snapped up by young aspiring Mods as they excitedly awaited the release of 'Quadrophenia'. This was the first time since the punk explosion of a few years previously that a positive maelstrom of activity and involvement of youth had created such tidal waves across the country. The future of Mod's profile and ongoing influence seemed unstoppable; how could it fail?

Although bands such as The Chords included renditions of Soul covers (Sam and Dave's 'Hold on I'm Coming' graced their first album), the nucleus of this new Mod explosion were far more influenced by The Who, The Creation and a soundtrack of mid-60's beat. This was undoubtedly third generation Mod for the punk generation - ultimately much less soulful than say The Alan Bown Set or The Action of the 60's era.

In conjunction with the arrival of the new Mod bands, however, came a new appreciation of classic Soul by elements of their fans. To accommodate, some may say exploit, Atlantic records re-released choice selections of 60's originals across a series of E.P's and by late '79, the organ and unique guitar sound of Booker T and the MG's 'Green Onion's' had crossed over into the domain of fledgling teenage Mods the country all over.

It had begun with a small collective of 60's-influenced bands. With the exception of a few such as the R&B inspired Merton Parkas, the majority of them had been galvanised by punk - serving their initiation as garage bands who ventured little further than their local youth clubs, pubs and - if lucky enough, as in the case of The Sockets (now re-christened The Purple Hearts) and The Chords - a support slot with name punk and new wave acts such as Buzzcocks and Undertones respectively. By mid-79 this small and isolated band of young Mod upstarts were joined by scores of similar 60's-enthused bands. A new Mod movement was in the making.

THE LAMBRETTAS

The Lambrettas' (from Lewes East Sussex) original line-up consisted of Jez Bird (singer/guitarist), Doug Sanders (guitarist/vocalist), Mark Ellis (bassist) and Paul Wincer (drummer). Arriving on the scene prior to the media overkill, the band subsequently had their biggest hit with their cover of original Mod hit, The Coasters' 'Poison Ivy'.

Doug Sandom (Guitar/Vocals) - "When we first started, the Mod revival hadn't hit the High Street, so there wasn't much available in the clothing range - during our first year when we started to gig we used to go all over the country in a tatty old transit - we fitted in the band, crew, equipment, PA and even the audience! (joke!!) Each time we passed a charity shop, the van would screech to a halt and it was 'all for one - all for one!!' As we shared driving, the driver would lose precious time fighting for the best clothes!! In hindsight - great fun and we sometimes got some really good stuff. The early days were a really good time and what we lacked in experience, we made up for in enthusiasm.

The Mods around Brighton and Hastings all knew each other cos there were not many of us around. It dawned on us that things were becoming more popular when we did our first gig on Hastings Pier on 9th June 1979 - an all-day event which consisted of: The Purple Hearts, The Fixations, The Teenbeats, The Scooters, and (us) The Lambrettas. The town was full of Mods - where did they all come from? Within a short time, we were signed by Rocket Records and the recording career started.

For me, one of the landmark events was our first gig at the Marquee in London on 22nd September 1979. An hour before we went on stage, it was half full and we were quietly pleased with ourselves... 15 minutes to go, we looked through the stage curtain and the Club was full, someone went to look at the door and there was a queue half way up Wardour Street ... This was only a few months after Hastings, and not only were there loads of mods - they'd come to see us!! A really good night - a stage invasion, and one of my most memorable gigs to date..."

SECRET AFFAIR and their DAYS OF CHANGE

Perhaps the most vocal and assuredly confident of the new Mod acts were Secret Affair - led by Ian Page. Spawned from new wavers New Hearts (who released two singles and supported The Jam on their late '77 'Modern World' tour), Secret Affair offered a soulful take (brass section included) on the pedigree of 70's Mod. Building up a loyal following of 'Glory Boys', also the title of their debut album, they soon came to be viewed as the leaders of the new Mod movement with their punk-baiting anthem 'Time For Action'.

Ian Page (vocals) - "The Marquee club is perhaps the venue for which I have the fondest memories - with its perfect sized stage, decent equipment and staffed by people who were really into music, it was my favourite venue to both visit and play. First starting in 1958, I believe - it moved to its Wardour Street location in 1964.

Alongside The Bridge House, The Marquee was pivotal in helping promote the fledgling live scene of the new Mods. Prior to the 'March of the Mods' tour of that summer, the vibrant London scene thrived at the few Mod friendly venues at hand.

Ian Page for many the spokesman for the Mod movement of '79 - clearly recalls, the importance and influence of The Marquee.

Just a casual look at its gig history shows how important it was to the development of Jazz, R&B and rock. Always, it had a willingness to embrace all the latest developments of the current music scene, showcasing all kinds of music from all kinds of musicians. And the famous late-night marquee bar - post shows, was a vital place to meet and mix with other people on the music scene. I must confess I spent a lot of time there, it's even mentioned in our song, 'Days of Change' from the Glory Boys album.

The symbolic importance of the venue can't be underestimated. When Secret Affair at last secured a prized residency there, I knew we were poised on the threshold of finally establishing a foothold on the music scene. I remember turning up for the final week of the residency one bright sunny evening, From the ticket office.... all the way back to the Ship pub, there was a long line of people patiently queuing for our show. A number of people I knew who worked in the industry came up to beg for spots on the guest list for fear of not being able to get in. We were about to sell out the Marquee and I knew then, that Secret Affair had finally come of age."

Dave Cairns (guitarist/songwriter) - "The Sunday night Marquee residency was a make or break for new acts back in the 70s and the aim was to sell out the last gig over four Sunday nights by building your fan base, which Secret Affair achieved back in '79 not least by bringing our East London following up to the Soho venue.

It was also a great place to meet up with other bands and steal the odd player which is exactly what we did after we saw drummer Seb Shelton playing with 'The Young Bucks' there and he joined Secret Affair a week later.

Above: Dave Cairns. Across: New Hearts - Secret Affair's previous new wave incarnation

But my history with The Marquee goes back to playing there with our previous band New Hearts and going there to see bands when I was fourteen years old where I used to see all kinds of prog and heavy rock bands at the time but it was impossible to get a ticket for special gigs by big acts David Bowie and The Rolling Stones. I did manage however to get a ticket to see one of only two shows by Bowie as Ziggy Stardust at the Rainbow Theatre, Finsbury Park, in 1972.

Seven years later I found myself walking out onto that very same stage for Secret Affair's sound check and I'd just been given one of the first wireless radio mike systems for my guitar. It worked via UHF or VHF radio waves transmitting audio signals to a receiver unit placed high up in the theatre and meant you could move freely around the stage without getting tangled up in guitar leads, but being brought up on a diet of Pete Townshend, Steve Marriott and Jimi Hendrix I couldn't resist taking it a little further and during the guitar solo in 'New Dance' I suddenly appeared in the circle playing almost exactly where I sat watching Bowie which was a pretty surreal moment for me and the audience too.

I never would have dreamt that I could be playing a sellout show with my own band at the Rainbow but it wouldn't have been possible had we not worked our way up from the Marquee Club."

MILLIONS LIKE US – THE PURPLE HEARTS

Punk may have been over for The Sockets, but as The Purple Hearts, its influence continued within their sonic assault of Who-styled Mod Rock with a lyrical impetus that reflected the 'Frustrations' and teenage angst of their following of the time.

Robert John Manton (vocals) - "By early 1978 we were all a bit fed up with punk and thought about changing to a 60's style Mod band as we had retained our interest in that right through the punk thing. There may well also have been the consideration that The Jam had done very well being a 60's style band and also the power pop thing was happening as well. So in the spring of 78 we debuted as The Purple Hearts at the Albemarle youth club in Harold Hill. We were mainly doing 60's covers but did have the first Purple Hearts original 'What Am I Gonna Do?'

The band's name was taken from the sleeve notes from The Small Faces singles compilation 'Rock Roots'. We gradually got a set of songs together including 'Jimmy', 'Frustration' (which I wrote in ten minutes in my lunch hour at work), 'I've Been Away' and 'I Can't Stay here' (which was my take on 'Pushin' too Hard' by The Seeds. The rest of the set leaned quite heavily on the Rolling Stones - we would cover songs like 'The Last Time' but also their own covers – 'If You Need Me', 'Everybody Needs Somebody to Love' and 'Money' and so on.

We used to rehearse in Jeff`s parents garage so the point to make here is we were like a American 60's garage band but, instead of being separated from our influences by 3000 miles of ocean, we were separated by about 12 years of time.

The gigs in '78 were in small pubs in East London and Southend and on the remains of the pub rock circuit like The Hope and Anchor - Islington and The Nashville Rooms - West Kensington. At this time, we had all of our own gear including an old 1950's Marshall PA and some pretty cheap mic's. We used to like to end songs in a howl of feedback like The Who or the middle section of 'Watcha Gonna Do about It' by The Small Faces (which we also covered). Simon played a Les Paul copy and Jeff had an Ibanez semi-acoustic bass, which was great for feedback. For most of 78, we were unaware of anyone else doing the same sort of thing but towards the end of the year, we did notice the beginnings of what would become the Mod revival.

At first there was probably about 300 kids in London and the suburbs who all seemed to know each other and from this group came The Chords (Deptford), The Hidden Charms (Enfield) and Back To Zero (also Enfield). The Clothes were from charity shops and homemade or improvised.

We were lucky to have a shop in Romford called Mintz and Davis which had rode the wave of the Skinhead revival of 1978 - making Sta-Prest and loads of button downs, Harrington's etc... They also got hold of a lot of round toe Brogues from Poland, a pair of which I kept going into the mid 80's, as I liked them so much.

PURPLE HEARTS

I think the original kids in London/Essex on the scene were mainly ex-punks but there were a few people who had just been into the 60's and Mod fashions and had been independent of any mass youth movement. There was a very good article at the time in a fashion magazine Harpers and Queen, I think? Inside there were a couple of brothers aged 19/20 who had been working their way through sixties fashions. At this point they had the whole 'swinging London'/'smashing time' look with Nehru jackets and rectangular shades.

By Feb/March '79, it was clear that there was a scene going on. We were interviewed for Sounds by Gary Bushell at The Bridge House in Canning Town. Then there was the London Weekend Show with The Chords and the guys from the Maximum Speed fanzine. Around this time, at a gig in North London, we were approached by a guy called Terry Ork the founder of Ork Records in New York and once the manager of US new-wavers Television. He said we reminded him of Television and would we like to do a one off single. We didn't follow that up which I think is a shame in a way as it might have got us a foothold in America.

It was a busy year and there was now some record company interest. We did a demo for Jimmy Pursey's JP productions label including a proper stab at 'Millions Like Us', which was a new song at the time. It's a finished product but I had Laryngitis so not a useable vocal track. It's similar to the John Peel session version with the 12-string coda over the fade, probably lost now but I'd love to hear it again. In the end we signed for Chris Parry's Fiction label, it was the only deal in town by then and wasn't a bad deal. We also signed to Brian Morrison's Andson Music which also had Secret Affair, Back To Zero and The Jam. I found out many years later that Morrison had been instrumental in supporting The Pretty Things in recording 'SF Sorrow'.

The Clothes - well we started off trying to look as much like The High Numbers as possible! Look at the Polydor pics taken at the then derelict docklands. After that I can't remember, I think we got a bit scruffy? I had a nice two-tone blue mohair suit from a charity shop and a blue Paisley shirt and kipper tie combo at one time, lots of loafers and Desert Boots/Fred Perry's.

So what was our attitude to all this? Well I think with the arrogance of youth we pretty much took it all as our natural right but if you think about it clearly, it was a classic case of right place right time. Most bands in those days didn't get signed and didn't even get recorded. The album was recorded in Dec '79 and Jan '80 in two weeks. Chris Parry wanted to carry on doing singles and in hindsight, he was probably right. We did try and make the album different from the other bands on the scene, I like the 12 string on Side One and especially like the melodic use of feedback on 'Nothings Left'. The front cover was a nod to Andy Warhol's screen printing technique. We liked the idea of Pop Art - without knowing too much about it. A lot of our early handbills had pop-art themes and a friend of ours Tony Lourdan did a fantastic Batman poster for a gig at the Moonlight Club West Hampstead.

I did expect us to have top 20/40 hits and to have some sort of career probably only lasting a couple of years. Anyway we had a fantastic time, one gig at the Electric Ballroom was especially good as we had a dry ice machine: later on in 80/81 we did use pyrotechnics - smoke bombs etc..'Millions Like Us' got to number 57 in the charts and the follow up got to 92 - or did it? I say that at gigs but I think it's a number I pulled out of the air so if anyone knows I'd love to hear its true position?"

Simon Stebbing (guitar) - "We'd get more and more Mods turning up at our gigs, and pretty soon we were being invited to play at Mod events, these were often independently promoted affairs, below the radar of the mainstream music industry, and had a cliquey, underground vibe to them. The Purple Hearts were usually near or at the top of the bill, so we were obviously doing something right. But with the imminent release of 'Quadrophenia' (the film) and the massive investment by the Who's promotional machine (Mod clothing etc.) the stage was set for a full on Mod revival. The record companies were soon sniffing around, and the Purple Hearts were being courted by a few labels. We chose to record with Fiction Records, a subsidiary of Polydor records, which was run by Chris Parry who produced the first Jam records. Chris produced our album 'Beat that' and three singles released on Fiction records.

With the release of the film, 'Quadrophenia' Mod went mainstream, and for a few months in 1979, there were Mods to be seen on every High Street. A few bands released chart records, a lot more released non-chart records, until the next fad came along. The 70's were like that, a new craze every six months.

Later on when The Jam were one of the nation's top bands, and after the Purple Hearts had our brief brush with success, Paul Weller invited us to his Pimlico flat for an afternoon of disc spinning, and guitar strumming (I still have the tape) and invited us to his record label Polydor's studio (the same place that Jimmy Pursey from Sham 69 had recorded our first demos) to produce a couple of songs for his Respond label.

One of my proudest memories of the time was of me and Paul sharing a studio mic for backing vocals on 'Plane crash'. We also supported The Jam at secret gigs in their hometown of Woking, and a several dates on their penultimate British tour including the biggest audience (5000) that I have ever played in front of at the Brighton Conference Centre. I had often wondered at the time, when we crossed paths with The Jam, whether they recognised us as those spotty oiks hanging around at their earliest London gigs, occasionally helping them with their gear!"

THE CHORDS – MAYBE TOMORROW

Combining the influence of The Who at their peak with the energy and immediacy of punk, The Chords quickly found a place high up the ladders of the new Mod hierarchy.

Brett 'Buddy' Ascott (drums) - "Personally I was always more of a Who fan than anything else, be it a Mod, a punk or even a fan of music generally. The Who were the be-all and end-all for me – I started drumming because when I heard or saw Keith Moon play it just spoke to my inner soul – as a typically troubled teenager he embodied all that was creative and energetic, and paradoxically also destructive and rebellious. And as a band didn't they just look brilliant? Just like a gang. 'Quadrophenia', especially, was at the heart of everything I thought and did for years - and when the Mod revival came along, I couldn't believe it wasn't just me anymore! Blimey - kindred spirits!

The Chords had formed a year or so before I came along to audition, wearing a parka and a target t-shirt! They were started by cousins Martin and Billy, and they later recruited Chris [Pope] on lead guitar. I had been in a punk band called, variously, the Meat, NADA and The Bombshells, but it was basically always the same band, formed around some tough working class lads from SE London. We played the Roxy, the Vortex, upstairs at The Rainbow and all over London. The big turning point for me was when we became stranded in Paris in the summer of 1978. I ended up falling in love with a Swiss model called Evelyn, experimenting with amphetamines, shoplifting in order to feed myself, and then getting CS-gassed onstage at a free gig in front of 15,000 rockers! Dull it wasn't... I began to see that life on the road was the one for me. But joining The Chords was when it all came together musically, stylistically, completely – I'd found the band of my dreams. The set-up was so evocative of the early Who I thought I was in heaven! From a first rehearsal to playing the Rainbow took two months – ridiculous progress!

My second-eldest brother, Ryder, had been an original Mod in the Sixties, and he gave me some records to feed my new-found Mod-addiction – Fontella Bass, Dobie Gray, Jimmy Smith. Not very rock'n'roll – for that I invested in The Kinks, Small Faces, of course the 'Oo and various others. There were suddenly gigs on nearly every night in London in 1979, and clubs too, like The Oak in Tooley Street and Vespa's at Charing Cross. Not being a dancer I didn't visit these places as much as the live gigs – I'd be out 3-4 times a week no question. God knows how I found the money – but after we'd played The Marquee we could always get in there for free to see other bands. The revival had started off so fragmented - a few like-minded souls in SE London and also east London, but then LWT did a show on Mod (this was the same show where I'd first seen the

275

Sex Pistols and vowed to join a punk band, back in '76) and Sounds and the NME picked up on it in the spring of '79. Suddenly there were Mods everywhere, and Mod bands sprouting up all over – perhaps the media-driven frenzy was always destined to self-destruct, such was the rush to find the next-big-thing.

Although The Chords were fashioned most wholeheartedly on The Who, comparisons with The Jam appeared almost immediately – we played Rickenbackers and did Who covers – the people criticising us didn't seem to realise how big a debt The Jam owed to The Who. Although I love Rick Buckler as a bloke I never took any guidance or inspiration from his drumming – my mentor was Moon, so I'd get quite irate when comparisons were made. Billy sang with a London accent – but of course he WAS really from an estate in SE London, not Woking! He was the real deal, but he really suffered with the Weller comparisons, as did Popey of course. I think it had an adverse effect on his writing, after the Chords album was out of the way. Pope was a Dylan/Springsteen devotee, so again the accusations of being Jam copyists really dug under his skin – journalists can be a lazy bunch of twats."

Chris Pope (guitar/vocals) - "It's March 1979. I'm manic and manically driving through the back streets of Catford heading down towards Deptford. It's raining, it's a school night and I haven't even started that history essay on 'The rise and fall of Whoever' and it's got to be handed in first thing in the morning! .. AAH!... Fuck that! why? Cos it's our first gig with a new line up at the Kings Head.

I'm fully expecting three men and a dog not to turn up. But, low and behold! Its 'Jam' packed with local hipsters all suited and booted - a fair few barflies and more than a handful of Mods. How can this be? I remember very little about the gig. We had four original songs and a bunch of covers. It must have been good, we get a five star review in Sounds the week after. Here we go! I'm 17 !

Next stop. The Wellington, Waterloo. Somehow, we've managed to blag a Saturday night gig there with a promise of a crate of ale as payment. The ale never materialised but the gig did. The place subsequently turned into a veritable home for all and sundry of the Mod fraternity... gawd bless em! There's two - maybe three hundred - of 'em packed in for our inaugural turn there, including Paul Weller, who tells me that we were great. I disagree - not for the last time with the man! Oh! and London Weekend Television turned up and filmed it. This is a piece of cake this is!

We find ourselves signed to Jimmy Pursey's own record label with just those 4 toons of our own. Jimmy has big plans and big ideas, but it all ends within the month in deepest, darkest Surrey (well Guilford!). After a full scale riot, lighting rigs smashed to smithereens, PA speakers crashing into the audience - throw in a few Sex Pistols on stage with Jimmy Pursey wielding a mic stand like a machete. Well ... you get the picture.

So where now? Label-less and pot less two months into this CRAZY Thang. John Peel to the rescue. The session that saved our bacon (those 4 original songs again!). A bunch of record companies start sniffing around us at last. YES! Er..No ... Somehow by default, Polydor signed us (always read the small print, boys n girls!). Can't be too sure on this one, but no-one there really wanted us there – 'The snotty-nosed little brothers of bigger fish!' ... I heard it said, but I find it hard to believe. STILL we can MAKE F****** MUSIC at last YAH! Now it's Gone!"

BRIAN KOTZ – EVERYTHING IS BACK TO ZERO

The explosion of Mod bands in 1979 almost matched the punk onslaught of two years previously. As with punk, there were the first division leaders and the struggling lower ranks. So while bands such as Secret Affair and The Chords graced Top of the Pops, scores of bands such as Squire, Beggar, Wipeout, The Tones, Fixations and The Zeros would remain in the hearts of the truly dedicated gig-going Mods - their eventual vinyl collectability decades away. Back to Zero, formed in early 1979, found themselves part of the inner core of the Mod pack during that summer playing on the now legendary 'March of the Mods' UK tour and releasing their debut single 'Your Side of Heaven' that very same year. Vocalist Brian Kotz recalls his initial Mod calling and memories of the band.

BACK TO ZERO

BACK TO ZERO

Brian Kotz (vocals) - "I grew up in the Southgate/East Barnet area of North London. We'd moved from Stamford Hill when I was a baby. My brother, Alan, is 13 years older than me and was one of the younger Modernists in 'The Hill', living the life, going to all the clubs (Flamingo, Studio 51 etc.). He moved out when I was 9, leaving me with his record collection, which was full of rhythm and blues and Soul gems, such as 'Soulful Dress' by Sugar Pie De Santo, 'You're My Remedy' by The Marvelettes, etc. As I became older, my fascination grew with hearing about Mods in the 60's, reading what was available - for instance, in 1975 when the BBC series 'The Story of Pop' and its accompanying part-work featured Mods. Whilst I was the archetypal 70's pop kid, (winning teenage music quizzes on TV and radio to prove it)! I'd started collecting 60's records after finding a box of singles at my school's Summer fair in 1974, buying 38 for 3p each. This led to many years of visiting jumble sales and charity shops, building the backbone of my collection.

I was initially underwhelmed by punk when it came along in '77, until a school friend, Paul Williams, who was into it early and had leant me a record or two, told me that there was a band who punks liked, but they dressed in suits and sounded like The Who. I said to him that this had to be what I was waiting for. When I first heard 'In The City' being played on Radio Luxembourg two months later, it was a life-changer. In early '78, I read about The Jam's 'superfans' in Record Mirror, who referred to themselves as 'The Southend Mods' (including Chip Hamer, who eventually became a friend). That was my green light to do it too. In October '78, I met the Mods from Enfield at a gig The Crooks were playing at The Pegasus, Stoke Newington – the first like-minded people I'd me, and from whom the group that became Back To Zero would spring, with myself as vocalist.

We made our debut in March '79 at Southgate Technical College. Sam, the guitarist and songwriter, had brought his sister's boyfriend, Clive in to be involved; he started managing us with two of his friends. They started 'Maximum Speed' fanzine, and staged four gigs in April and May '79 that helped to bring bands and other Mods together. The Purple Hearts had played in Enfield in December '78, and The Chords started their brilliant Wellington residency in March '79. We'd all originally formed unbeknownst to each other, and now we knew we weren't alone.

The early clothes worn were more of a statement than an informed sartorial choice, it has to be said – hence the whole 'parkas in boiling hot clubs' stigma. As a general fan of 60's style, I wanted to follow my own taste, so I started scouring shops like Robot in Newburgh Street, especially for loud original shirts, paisleys in particular. At around the same time, I found two beautiful regency-style jackets at the Help the Aged shop in Southgate. You can see me wearing one of them (an original Lord John of Carnaby Street) in the official Back to Zero group photos, shot in September 1979. I remember taking it out of the bag at photo session. I announced 'this is my swinging 60's jacket'. Sam took the piss and said 'no, it's your swinging soul boy jacket'! He didn't get it at all!

The band developing a following became personally important to me, as what happened in '79 transformed my social life from a played-out local peer group to meeting people from all over the place - ironically, many of whom I had more in common with than the rest of BTZ. The 'March of the Mods' tour in August with Secret Affair and the Purple Hearts was the most intense 3 weeks of an intense year. Some of my favourite meetings with people occurred, as well as visiting towns and cities for the first time, but also some of the worst experiences of the year too. I witnessed some horrendous violence and aggression, and other unspeakable incidents. It wasn't what I was in the band for, and it wasn't what I got into the Mod thing for. I grew up fast that Summer!

The '79 bands had their champions in the music papers, and the writer who deserves to be mentioned above all is the late Phillip Hall of Record Mirror. He was enthusiastic and encouraging of all of us. He was only a year or two older. Others may be better known, but Phillip was my favourite by miles.

I was told that I was out of the band on New Year's Day 1980 which draws a convenient line on the BTZ experience. From there, Mod-wise, I followed my musical tastes. My short-lived band in 1980, Bees By Post, were doing covers by garage-punk bands from the Nuggets compilation among other things. In 1981, at a Jam gig in Amsterdam, I met Michel Terstegen and his friend from the Utrecht Mod scene. Michel was a fellow record collector, who went on own his own shop. I paid regular visits to Utrecht in the 80's, and had some of the best times of my life in the company of my friends there; they were into the music and style they happened to like, with none of the schisms that had occurred on the scene at home."

Perhaps it was inevitable that the purity and exclusive sense of belonging began to evaporate and lose its potency as soon as the media grasped the growing popularity of the '79 Mod phenomenon.

Terry Rawlings - "Mod slowly built up momentum as more bands began to spring up to join the Chords and the Purple Hearts. Bands like The Merton Parkas, Long Tall Shorty (then called the Indicators), Back to Zero and later, Secret Affair. The gigs were packed out with more and more new faces showing up week in week out. It was a fantastic and cultish little scene and it wasn't long before it caught the media's attention. The Chords and the Hearts were featured on a London Weekend Television show hosted by Janet Street Porter, and the music weeklies began reviewing the gigs; not in any positive way, mind you! The likes of the New Musical Express and Melody Maker never had a good word to say about any of the bands and forth-righteously wrote the whole Mod movement off as backward- looking revivalism. They would be savage in their dismissive and spiteful put-downs, whilst singing the praises of Fleetwood Mac and ABBA. Not that we cared one bit - we were too busy getting pissed and pilled in our own private world. Then the bubble burst! Or - to be more precise - it slowly deflated when 'Quadrophenia' the movie was released and within a few short months the Mod scene as we knew it was no more. What had once been a fairly underground movement was (quick as a flash) replaced by a cheap, mass-marketed high street monster image. The little hippie shops in the indoor market in Carnaby Street transformed themselves overnight - from Afghan coat-sellers to nylon parka-pushers. Where there had once been coke bottle ornaments with fake polystyrene foam, there were now big felt sew-on patches with the word 'Mod' printed either on a target or a Union Jack background. In place of the rows of cheesecloth and denim were cheap button-down shirts and skinny black ties, also sporting the word 'Mod'. And worst of all, Mods appeared from every side-street like a plague of horror film zombies.

The Jam was having their stage-wear made at a little theatrical outfitters in Newburgh Street (just off of Carnaby Street) and this was all of a sudden the Mecca of new Mod. They began offering off-the-peg Jam suits! These were offset by Shelly's Shoes, selling the newly-advertised Jam shoes which, when combined with a skinny tie and brand new nylon parka, kitted out the new want-to-be Mod in a single afternoon of retail retard therapy. Well, if the likes of the NME and Sounds hated the Mod (now officially tagged 'Mod Revival') scene in its infancy they now fucking detested it in its full flight. Anything that was even remotely associated with Mod was ridiculed and put down without pity, which was remarkable since we were now in the grips of a Ska and Rock-a-Billy revival. Both of these scenes were surely just as revivalist as Mod weren't they? Yes, of course they were but only Mod was singled out for persecution! Harsh and unfair you'd think, but when bands with names like the Lambrettas, the Scooters, the Vespa's and wait for it... the MODS began stinking it up, you sort of understood their point. Subtlety had left the building! And I, for one, could kind of understand why.

The phrase 'Plastic Mod' was often heard when describing a figure of fun who, during the week, dressed totally opposite to what we considered ... well, Mod. Come the weekend, they would ditch their conventional clobber and appear at places like the Wellington in Mod fancy-dress. The original crowd began slowly but surely dropping out of sight; the venues stopped allowing Mods in, due to a raised level of violence that saw the new breed fighting on all fronts with everyone from skin-heads, Rock-a-Billy's and a new nemesis called 'The Casuals'. I also stopped attending gigs and began spending nights down the local pub 'The Mayflower' in Rotherhithe, and Mod for me became a personal thing all over again."

DOWN AT THE MARQUEE
MOD ON THE FRONTLINE

Ed Silvester - "Although we had started to meet the odd pocket of parka clad geezers, there weren't actually that many Mods around at that time. We'd excitedly travelled to see the Teenbeats play at the Triad Centre in Bishops Stortford, in May 1979, and as that was local, a few of us had squeezed into my brother John's MkI Ford Escort, and made the short journey to see them. They were one of the first Mod revival bands that we saw, and can vividly remember their charismatic lead singer 'Huggy'.

A couple of weeks later The Sta-Prest played in our home town, Epping, at a local youth centre in St John's road. Although, the Mod bands were playing small venues, at a local level, we did feel that Mod was now beginning to gather a head of steam."

Above: Huggy of The Teenbeats

Ed Silvester - "We now began to feel like we were part of something exciting and little pockets of Mods, were now meeting up. We spent a lot of time that summer and autumn at the Marquee Club, seeing bands like the Chords, Secret Affair and the Teenbeats. Having a messenger job, I had a few extra quid in my pocket, the next stage was to become mobile, and buy a scooter."

Above: Little Roosters and Ed's Marquee card
Left: Vic Vespa of The Killermeters

Above: classic 1979 revival photo comprising of Ed and an iconic array of Mod posters

Ed Silvester - "By the beginning of 1979 the Marquee was becoming a second home to our little group of Epping Mods, as we'd already seen numerous punk bands play there over the preceding years - including The Jam, of course. The Marquee would become our Mod Mecca. For us, it was an easy and convenient journey by tube on the Central Line to Tottenham Court Road station; and from there it was only a 10 minute walk to Wardour Street. The excitement would build after we all met at Epping station, and we'd then hurriedly jump on the next London bound tube train. As we approached the City other Mods would join us, with large groups joining us at Loughton and Woodford stations. The DJ always played old sixties music a bit of Who, Small Faces and Motown, guess it was the resident DJ Jerry Lloyd spun those old classics."

From the left - friends of Ed's – including Eddie Piller (between heads), Dennis Smith of Secret Affair at the Marquee, Dolly Mixture's Debsey Wykes, Ken Copsey of The Teenbeats

Ed Silvester - "The Marquee club was actually quite a small dark club and could probably only accommodate a few hundred people, no wonder there was always a smell of sweat and beer hanging in the air. But the crowd were always within touching distance of the band, a punk ethic maybe, but the bands felt at one with the crowd, no stadium rock attitudes here. This made for some fantastic evenings and wonderful memories."

The Marquee, once the home of British R&B and The Who, was now a second home for the 70's Mods in and around London.

Despite much of the '79 period Mod's dress sense being maligned (mainly by journalists and often original Mods) the quest to achieve an authentic style was still a driving force. Although this was a totally different generation, with contrasting aspirations and backgrounds to their predecessors - many of the late 70's Mods were just as committed in their quest to ensure that, in their minds, they did look as authentic as original first generation Mods.

Ray 'Patriotic' Margetson - "For clothes we checked out second hand clothes shops in Tottenham – 'second time around', and local Jewish menswear shops in Stoke Newington, who blew the dust off the packaging of their shirts that they had still kept in stock since the 60's! We bought tonic suits, button down shirts and cuff-links to go with these old shirts on a mother of pearl style. I remember going to a Who concert at the Rainbow in Finsbury park (North London) in May 1979 and came across a guy called Goffa selling 'Maximum Speed' fanzine. He looked as though he was pilled up off his head (but I later found out that was just his gregarious persona!). I realised the guys who produced the fanzine only lived a short distance from myself, so I just turned up at their flat in Stamford Hill, introduced myself and said I was interested in what they were doing and what gigs did they go to? Before I knew it, I was helping with their fanzine and going to a lot of their bands gigs - Back to Zero - and then playing records before and after the band's sets at a few of their gigs.

Most gigs we went to by public transport, buses and tube, and it was only at the latter part of 1979 that I finally got a scooter. All of my money was spent on clothes, records and getting into gigs. We tried not to pay on the tubes as most of us just jumped the barriers - it gave you more to spend on clothes! Even in 1979 we were trying to look different in a small part of the style we dressed – unusual cuff-links, different patterns on jackets and sweaters, different colouring in the tonic mohair suits.

The early gigs I went to were at Edmonton, The Wellington in Waterloo, Pegasus in Stoke Newington, Hop Poles in Enfield, The Bridge House in Canning Town and The Marquee in the West End. By the end of 1979 I jacked in this business studies course I was paid to go on by my employers – a Merchant bank in the City – as I didn't do the sessions as was always out gigging and clubbing."

One thing is for certain, the energy, passion and enthusiasm for the Mod lifestyle, was just as pronounced.

By the summer of '79, the high-tide of Mod's resurgence had been reached - the future unknown?

CHAPTER 9

TIME FOR ACTION!

By late summer 1979, with the imminent screening of 'Quadrophenia' and a handful of key releases from the scene's prime contenders (The Chords, Secret Affair) and the success of 'Gangsters' by The Specials, along with a growing media profile, the new Mod explosion was pushing confidently into full gear. Little did the proponents and followers realise that the rallying call for a 'Time for Action' would soon be replaced by a mood of despondency and artistic frustration.

ALAN MAY'S TIME FOR ACTION!

The Mod revival - as it was conveniently termed by the music weeklies - was a distinct introduction to music and cultural pastures anew for a great number of young contenders. Many converts had been caught up in the maelstrom of first and second wave punk as it was drawing its last breath. They were drawn to the abrasive energy and idealism of punk yet were now shedding its fashion for a sharp wardrobe of sixties-influenced clothes. Revivalists... some may have accused? With such examples as Alan May and the legions of like-minded young Mods, taking inspiration from a Paul Weller quote, they could easily claim 'what do we know about revivals, we're Only 14!'?'

Alan May (St Ives, Cambridge Mod) - "The year 1979 was a very interesting time which would change my life forever. Firstly, there was a film to be released called 'Quadrophenia' and on Top of the Pops a new band were playing called Secret Affair. After watching Ian Page singing 'Time for Action' in his smart suit this had made my mind up. The punk thing was over for me and a new era had begun.

What was it all about this thing called Mod? Time for a chat with my brother-in-law Richard - based in London - who was a Mod in the sixties'. 'It'll be all about the way that you dress, the club's they went to, the music and the way they got around town cheaply on smart Italian scooters,' I'd been given a history lesson on a genre which I'd never heard of! And at 14, I thought I knew it all.

As I dug deeper into the scene I was discovering things which were not only new to me but also certain ideals started to make sense – like The Jam for instance, why did they wear suits and sing sixties Motown covers when the punks were wearing bondage and leather! Got it, they resemble the people in the books I was reading, youths smarting 3-button suits, looking sharper than Sweeney Todd's razor.... even as teenagers for fucks sake. Thank you Richard Barnes and the photographs in your book Mods! This alone should have set me up but with Dickie's input and his record collection, I was set up to discover a way of life, which is embroiled into me to this day 35 years later!

What was first then for a teenager without ten bob to rub together? It had to be the charity and second-hand shops for a decent 1960's suit. To my amazement, the racks were full of them to and I settled for a nice brown two-piece for all of three quid with 15 inch bottoms on the leg, and slanting pockets for the jacket; blade sharp lapels, three buttons up the middle and 6 inch rear vents - beautiful. I'd wear this suit to death along with a nice pink buttoned-down shirt - Ben Sherman of course - bought from Dave Pinks in Cambridge and topped off with a smart thin tie I lifted from my stepfather's wardrobe. As for the shoes I'd built up a collection from Black winkle pickers, Shelly's skunks or Jam shoes as they became known and of course Clarks 2 hole Desert Boots – any combination looked cool with the suit.

Other attire I sported was my first M51 fishtail Parka coat, which was from the Army and Navy store for just a fiver. I bought another to be different with a German ducktail number – which I chose not to wear much as certain faces would take the piss, but hey, it looked the business. I emblazoned the parka with patches of my favourite bands Secret Affair, The Chords, The Jam and The Purple Hearts along with button badges naming The Who, The Kinks, and The Yardbirds etc... One feature I always liked on my parka was a Blues and Royals cord placed around the epaulette and under the arm – I thought I was the business, well I was wasn't I?

I had started to build up some decent clobber as a year had passed and was wearing a grey red/blue striped boating blazer with Fred Perry's or cycling shirts: Levi 501 's were a hit but had to be bleached for the look.

With the fashion sorted and I'm now on minimum wage I had started to grow my collection of 45 inch singles and LP's, all the sixties stuff like early Rolling Stones, The Creation, The Action etc. and Motown faves like Little Stevie Wonder, Martha Reeves and the Vandellas sat nicely on my bedroom floor alongside the recent revival stuff from Squire, The Chords, Nine Below Zero, Purple Hearts, The Jam and of course the 'Mods Mayday' album which included such great bands as Beggar, Small Hours and The Mods from North London.

At 16, I needed transport and set about owning a Vespa 50 Special, which I bought on HP for five pound and 60 pence a week. It was light Blue and I purchased a chrome rack and crash bars for the front, a fly screen, wheel disk covers, six stemmed mirrors and some additional lights, which didn't work, and an ironing board backrest for the look. To my horror, 29mph wasn't good for fucks sake and I couldn't wait to get a bigger engine machine, you could almost run faster.

Owning a scooter not only gave me freedom but also enabled me to get a job 10 miles from home earning more money which was a bonus and my mates were getting scoots too. Soon there was a gang of us making a racket every Saturday riding around town playing the tunes on a cassette player strapped to the back rest and beeping air horns, oh the fuel we wasted going around in circles all afternoon. I remember buying a scooter for my mate in 1980 for £15 from a fellas' back garden, which I'd spotted as I walked by – we even called the police to ask permission to ride home if we could get it going to a reply of no problem! It was a slim style Lambretta TV175 in navy blue and was ridden by our mate Pinchard who was five or six years older than us and a face for sure."

SHEFFIELD MODS OF 1979

Not surprisingly, and reflecting the 60's Mod period, the fascination and euphoria of the youth cult spread far and beyond its London roots. As early as 1977, Mods appeared at Jam gigs in the north and by the following year, some pockets were established even before much of London had unified into a cohesive scene. Many of these northern Mods gestated from the still active scooter clubs across towns such as Barnsley and Huddersfield. Sheffield, the home of the famous Mojo club of the 60's, had held its own throughout the 70's with a heavy Northern Soul following and by 1979, whilst Huddersfield had ex-punks The Killermeters, Sheffield had its own Mod band, The Negatives, and an enthusiastic Mod scene of its own.

Pete Skidmore (Sheffield Mod) - "I can remember the August Bank Holiday of 1979. I was just about to return to school on what would be my last year before I was flung out into the great wide world. My mate John and myself sat at the side of the A61 Chesterfield road dual carriageway between Batemoor and Low Edges just idling the afternoon away when in the distance we could hear a funny sound getting louder and nearer. About a minute later around 20 scooters came past with the air filled with (beautiful) two stroke exhaust fumes and a mixture of 1 and 2 people on them, it was a mix of Lambrettas and Vespa's in various colours and with varying amounts of mirrors, lights, foxtails, whippy aerials, tents, bags etc., and all riders and passengers were wearing parkas. It was a truly awesome sight, and even now I get goose bumps when I see a few scooters together even more so when they are lammys! Over that afternoon, we must have seen good eight or nine varying groups of Mods speed past on which we presumed was their way home. As a 15 year viewing such a sight as this, you can't wait to be part of something like it, along with my obsession with The Jam and punk and Mod came my wanting of a scooter, which at the time was beyond my reach. Looking back now there was thousands of us school kids like that."

The self-expressed statements of these punk-generation born Mods absorbed many influences, the DIY approach of punk, creating the look, utilising punk's penchant for pin-on badges, avidly studying Mod fanzines, following 'sounds from the street' of young bands and the love of punk's 'black sheep trio of the new wave' - The Jam, even down to their pilfered footwear.

Phillip Wright (Sheffield Mod) - "True story this... One day we had seen pictures of the Jam in these sort of stripy shoes and I was wondering where you got them from, when my mate Neil Kitson (A massive Jam fan and now a famous photographer) said *'they are like bowling shoes, like when you wear when you play 10 pin bowling'* so I thought, *'cool!'* The next Saturday lunchtime I went up to Firth Park bowling alley in a pair of crappy old shoes, paid my money to play, swapped my shoes for the bowling shoes and just walked back out. I met my mates on Fargate in the afternoon and they were stunned. We were all wearing cycling shirts at the time - that was another part of the fashion. Most of the Mod wannabees just wore the parkas and stuff; we just tried to be cool and wore authentic Mod gear and anything that Paul Weller wore."

THE JAM, MODERNISM AND ME!
BY FRASER SMITH

Sheffield Mod Fraser Smith had also been inspired by the energy and self-expression of the punk explosion, in particular The Jam. From the ashes of the punk fall-out, Fraser was swept up by the sixties Mod-influenced Paul Weller and like many of his age, consequently discovered the world of Mod!

Fraser Smith's early post-punk Mod incarnation, Blackpool 1978

Fraser Smith (Sheffield Mod) - "As 1977 drew to a close, my world was about to open up somewhat. I was in the last year of what, to be fair had been a rather lack lustre education... And, the current economic climate was to say the very least quite bleak. I had been turned down by the Headmaster in my attempt to skank another two 'do nothing years' as he felt I would have 'too much freedom' in the 6th form, to be fair he had a point looking back - reality was starting to nibble, and it was time to start thinking about a real job. There was no such thing as ID in 1977, and by now, I was a regular on the Sheffield alternative night scene... Crazy Daisy – via the Golden Ball, Dove and Rainbow, and Blue Bell. Amongst others of course, for instance The Cannon, Hen & Chickens, but those places, to me where all about how 'hard' you were, and tended to attract young people out for a fight... Now that was certainly NOT my idea of a good night out. I had gone through a pretty intense, if short-lived punk period... The Sex Pistols, The Damned, Slaughter and the Dogs and so on... and to be completely honest the more acceptable the face of punk became, the less interested I was. I saw, and still see, punk more as a movement, a place in time. The music that mattered was based around not just the fun times, but also the austerity, and the shambles of a state the country was in. The youth saying ENOUGH, now, that was what I really buzzed off back then.

One Thursday evening in 1977 I had sat down with my mother as per usual to watch Top of the Pops; sneering at the usual dross – Boney M and Showaddywaddy blah blah - when out of nowhere came a 3 piece that to me (at the time) appeared to be a cross between 60's Pop/Rock and punk. Whether they were or not is academic, what mattered most was.... (to fill the void in my mind)... this is what I wanted to be into! The song was 'All Around the World' – The band, three lads from down south were called The Jam. I knew then, life, and music for me, was all starting to make sense.

I will never forget my mother saying 'Blimey, they make a lot of noise to say there are only three of them'. Noise? Had she forgot that I had been lead vocalist in the now defunct 'Fraser Boys'. The musician in the family was ME, well, kind of. From that day onwards, I continued to try and compile as much information as I could about The Jam, something I don't suppose I ever really gave up on.

In July of 1978, I started my first job: I managed somehow to get an apprenticeship in the printing trade as a compositor. On my first day I rolled up, all bright eyed and bushy tailed, and sporting more than one Jam badge, and the first person I bumped into was a lad around 24. His name was Gary Street, and he was COOL! He noticed my badges, and as it transpired, he had been an original Mod Well, his stories about bands like The Who, The Kinks, Dr Feelgood, Family, and many more intrigued and caught my imagination and instilled excitement. He actually gave me his badges that he had had back in the 60's, and actively encouraged me to get into Modernism. I mean come on.... At that time at least, Weller's favourite song was Waterloo Sunset by The Kinks so all must be good!

Back on the street, before long, I was something of a 'Face' or at least I thought so. Maybe it was the fact I had by far the best badges in Sheffield - Good old Gaza! We (myself and like-minded friends) soon realised that the clothes we needed, if we really wanted to carry off the look, were either going to have to come from London, or, we needed to find a reconditioned suit joint and one that was close by so that we could visit as often as possible. A lad who I was on day release with, not only had a scooter, but he also had inside information for the best place around to buy reconditioned proper Mod suits from the 60's; L & M Supplies in Barnsley. Well, it was an absolute treasure trove. So suited and booted our journey continued, having our pictures taken at the Amsterdam Bar in Huddersfield by giddy girls, oh how we posed: I just wish I had copies of the pictures. Being chased down West Street by Teddy Boys, who frankly were at an age where they should have had better things to do. And of course gigging.

The first time I saw the Jam live was at Sheffield Polytechnic in November 1978 on their 'Apocalypse tour' promoting their brand-new album 'All Mod Cons'. They were supported by (Punk poet with a guitar) Patrik Fitzgerald and The Dickies, who to be fair were fun, but silly: I mean we were the Mods after all and we took clothes and music seriously now!

That night, we were in the Students Union Bar, trying our utmost to look cool, and get pissed on 'Harp' Lager. The audience at the Poly gig was, to be fair much more leaning towards punk. But, it was clear from the lyrics, and the genuine aggression Paul, and Bruce showed that night that the Jam were not just a band to be labelled.

The next time I saw the Jam was at the Students Union at Sheffield University when they played two nights, Friday and Saturday. Both gigs were sell-outs, and fortunately for us we had tickets for the Saturday. Once again they were electrifying, I don't remember sweating so much, suit, tie, and fish tail parka is certainly NOT the best way to dress for a Jam gig. At this time the audience was much more Mod-influenced, in fact, we wore eyeliner (a la Jimmy in Quadrophenia, I imagine I must have looked like Bette Davis in the killing of Sister George by the end of that one!

Towards the end of 79 anyone who was anyone, in fact anyone who was NOT anyone had jumped on the bandwagon. I still struggle to this day to understand how people who bought the generic cover versions of Mod classics by bands such as The Lambretta's and Merton Parka's etc. could completely appreciate or understand the ethos of The Jam. Of course, It could always be me that didn't get it, but, I honestly don't think so."

Heather Quinn (Sheffield Mod) - "Without consciously setting out to become a Mod, I had started to dress like the bands I was listening to. At first I was quite masculine in my tastes - short hair with a Steve Marriott centre parting; button-down collar shirts - possibly Paisley, or spots (I used to buy these by mail order from Melandi's of Carnaby Street. I bought a fishtail parka with the regulation fur on the hood and a cringingly embarrassing Small Faces logo painted on the back. I had a green and navy boating blazer, which I bought from a 'Mod' stall in Leeds market. My shoes were usually from Rebina's, which had a shop just off High Street, Sheffield and a stall in Sheffield's Castle Market. I managed to get hold of a pair of black and white Jam shoes, which were made for girls. I was so proud of them and wore them until they fell to pieces."

It should also be noted, that for the '79-era Mods, the only real reference points available to them, older siblings aside, were the music weekly's coverage of the new scene alongside nostalgic overviews of the 60's along with the 1973 'Quadrophenia' LP photo album insert. Also, most importantly, Richard Barnes' highly informative book - Mods. The rest was mostly pure improvisation and instinctive invention.

Chesterfield and Nottingham were also home to burgeoning Mod scenes during this period. A short train ride from nearby Sheffield, aspiring young Mods would spend their time fluctuating between all three towns and cities.

Andy Bull (Chesterfield Mod) - "I never even knew what a Mod was, until the summer of 1979. We (me and my brother Jud) were on holiday in Skegness with my sister Karen and her fella Malc. The place was swarming with all these lads and lasses in Parkas, slim trousers (not flares like my other older brothers had seemed to be wearing forever), button down shirts and thin ties... Malc suddenly announced (to quote the sew on patch)... 'the Mods are back'... and then went on to explain about what it was like in Sheffield, his home town in the 60's, with our Karen pointing out one of my other sister Janis was a Mod too in that era and our house always had scooters parked outside. I was absolutely smitten and when I returned to school (my first year at William Rhodes secondary) - armed with my Jam, Beat, Madness and Specials records - I was a Mod!"

Andy Bull (holding camera) with his fellow Mod brother, Jud

Dave Bamford - "One Saturday afternoon around 1979, I was in the Broad Marsh shopping centre, Nottingham city centre with my mate when suddenly this massive gang of youths appeared through the crowds of shoppers, they were all dressed in green parkas, suits, boating blazers, pork pie hats and wrap around shades....What was this ? Who were they? I had to find out more. All I knew was that they looked good and I had to be a part of it!"

Fraser Smith - "From the outside L & M Supplies on Sheffield Road, just outside Barnsley Town Centre, looked like any other ex-army shop, but once inside, you felt as though you were 'Mr Benn'. The back of the shop was a room absolutely crammed with 60's suits, all reconditioned to their former glory. Mick Harrison, Stuart Heenan, Pluck, myself, and a few other 'invite only' Mods would make the Saturday morning pilgrimage on the 265 bus to see what gems we could treat ourselves to, and each suit was one price £5!! Four button jackets, (almost) drainpipe trousers finished off with Hush Puppies was the look we went for. And although the song may say 'Zoot suit, with side vents 5 inches long' we would not be seen DEAD with side vents in our jackets. I really don't know why, it was just one of those things for us at the time. Some of the lads would adorn their lapels with badges, the better the badge the better the Mod. But personally I used to carefully select just one in particular each time we went out. And pin it to my tie, as a sort of 'tie pin' if you will. I thought I was unique, but of course, I don't suppose I was. I always have, and still do think a badge says a lot about the wearer and I never understood the ethos behind wearing 90 badges with 50 different band names on. Lots of people would ask us where we got our suits from, and by mid-79 'cool' shops like 'Jonathan Silver' had started to sell phony Mod suits for around £60. But that completely defeated the object of being an individual, we stuck with dear old L&M, it made much more sense!"

ANDI BARNES AND THE EARLY DAYS OF THE BIRMINGHAM MOD REVIVAL!

Reflecting much of her generation, Andi Barnes' Mod association arrived with punk. Here she details her high tide of Mod, her love of classic 60's Soul and her disaffection with the eventual elitism that came as part and parcel of the new scene.

Andi Barnes - "Birmingham 1978. The music scene focused on Barbarella's. I had started 6th form college and all of a sudden a new world opened up for me. After five years at an all girl's grammar school, male company and punk music were a long awaited release. Blondie, The Clash, Magazine, the Adverts... the list of bands and a good night's entertainment was endless. I was alive and in the middle of an era that everyone knew was special. But with that came the negatives. Drugs, gobbing, violence and a spiraling negativity began to pervade the scene.

The beautiful people began to drift across the road to the Rum Runner. I dabbled in the early scene but was drawn to an emerging night on a Thursday at Samantha's. It incorporated the poseurs (who later became the New Romantics) and Mods. Both interested in fashion and appearance and a love of music and a good night out.

Although I adored the emerging electronic scene, for me, the fun of the Mods and the happy music was a draw. There was no fighting and heavy drinking. It was clean living and I preferred it. The crowd grew very quickly. By word of mouth and Saturday meet ups in town, within 6 months, the Mod scene was flourishing. The Top Rank in Dale End was a huge club and a natural progression for the dedicated followers of fashion. With a dance floor big enough to cater for the experimental dance moves of the ace faces, the Mods had a new home.

Some of the original 60's Mods came to visit. They would sit back telling stories of the old times. Visits to the Twisted Wheel in Manchester, scooter rides to the coast on Bank Holidays. None of this reminiscing was lost on the most eager of the Mods who hung on their every word and lived to emulate the faded days of the originals. I became totally wrapped up in the music. Despite the Jam, Secret Affair and other supposedly 'Mod' bands, the scene became increasingly purist. Ska was quickly sidelined as another avenue all together. Music snobbery took over and Reddington's Rare Records and record fairs were the places to be on Saturday mornings digging out the latest finds. Donny Elbert's 'Little Piece of Leather', 'Night Train' James Brown and anything [else] on the Sue label.

Clothes were to be had a plenty in the rag market when 60's cast offs were still freely available and cheap. I had an agreed routine with my mother that anything I bought would be left in the freezer room between the garage and the kitchen where she would inspect my second hand finds before they were allowed into the house... just in case they needed fumigating. Suede coats, ski pants, shirts and flats quickly replaced miniskirts and stilettos as the clothes to be seen in. The boys were able to buy fishtail parkas from the Army & Navy stores and a shop in Oasis Market in Birmingham did a flourishing trade in striped blazers.

My boyfriend at that time had a brother who lived in Brighton. So for us, every bank holiday became a pilgrimage. Before the M40, it was a five hour drive via every village between Birmingham and the south coast. Brighton at that time was very stuck in the 70's. It hadn't changed at all since the last decade and would become a Mecca for Mods again after the release of 'Quadrophenia'. We were there on the first Bank Holiday weekend that the fighting started up. There were very few rockers left to fight with and it was more like a scene from the Keystone Cops with hoards of Mods being chased up and down the sea front by truncheon wielding policemen. It was a non-event but still made the news and the horrified of Tunbridge Wells wrote of their disgust in the newspapers the following day."

Andi Barnes' love of Soul came with a particular love for the classic Sue label issues of the 60's.

Perhaps, the renewed fascination with Mod was compromised by its popularity. Back in April of '79', the outlook for the relatively small gathering of Mods, quickly assimilating new members and greater media profile by the week, had been positively refreshing. Yet by late '79' cynicism, division and violence had set in. Some, in hindsight, suggest that it would have been a more relevant addition to the ongoing cult of Mod had it been named something progressively new - the term 'Glory Boys' was advanced by some.

Glory Boys (so termed in homage to Secret Affair's debut LP) were actually active on the scene at the time; a collective of Secret Affair followers (their title often tattooed on their inside lips) they gained a reputation of solidarity and uncompromising loyalty for the band. One thing is certain, by late 1979, Mods, along with 2-tone and a new film named after a 1973 Who album, were featured in most young people's conversation or personal involvement.

'QUADROPHENIA' A 'MOD' WAY OF LIFE

Inspired by the lyrical theme and central character of the Pete Townshend penned 1973 double Who album of the same name, 'Quadrophenia' was directed by Franc Roddam and shot in 1978, placed in the time frame of 1964 and the Mod v Rocker seaside riots of that year, in particular Brighton. The original album itself had already garnered the interest of the previous decade's Mod era on release, whilst recent post-punk Mod-leaning teenagers had discovered Mod's past and influence since 1973 from the inner sleeve booklet of the LP. Although cited by many as the greatest youth film of all time and others as an inaccurate portrayal of the less stylised elements of Mod's past... even so the film (released September 1979) signposted both the high-tide of the Mod revival and the beginning of the end. Originally reputed that ex-Sex Pistol John Lydon would star as the main character, though others were also auditioned, the film featured a young and hungry ensemble of actors born of a new class of acting (both Gary Shail and Mark Wingett arrived for auditions as their punk selves ready to morph into their Mod roles). 'Quadrophenia' has now become a worldwide phenomenon and for many signifies the greatest and most significant inspiration for the dawning of Mod's 1970's re-birth and continuing influence.

David Birchall (60's period Mod) - "'Quadrophenia' is unquestionably the best movie of the era. I still remember walking down theatre row in Vancouver (never having heard of this movie) looking at the still photos that were posted outside all the movie theatres. Suddenly I was looking at scenes that I recalled as if they were yesterday. It was as if I recognised the people and the scenes. It was 'Quadrophenia' and nobody in Vancouver knew what the hell it was about. Another movie that captures the end of the sixties very well is 'Withnail and I'. That is how I remember it - long overcoats, always pissing with rain. He seems to be a bit more educated than anybody I knew then of course."

Robert John Manton (The Purple Hearts) - "The release of The Who's 'Quadrophenia' Film was a sort of dividing line for the original Mod revival as it took the scene nationwide and took [away] the 'exclusive club' feel of the early days."

Ed Silvester - "Just after the film was released we spotted an advertisement in the music press, saying that a lot of the clothes from the film were going to be sold off in a shop just off Petticoat Lane, called the Last Resort. This clothing boutique had previously been a hangout for skinheads, and the odd punk, but was now frequented by a few Mods looking for mementos. Initially I found the place very intimidating, but the owners would put punters at ease, and shout

out to any Mods walking by, that they had some clothes from the film 'Quadrophenia' for sale. As you entered and just next to a large statue of Marilyn Monroe, there was a huge box full of all the clothes that had been used in the film. My friend Dave Stokes was able to buy a lovely grey and green Ivy League jacket that was worn by an extra in the film - Dave wore that jacket religiously for months - nothing would fit me though. In the end, and along with my friend Alan Smith, we decided to buy some lovely Sta-Prest trousers instead.

I've lost count of the times that I've watched 'Quadrophenia' since it was released, but there is always something new to discover, however small. I don't think the film has really dated ,although at the time we were incredibly anal about the many mistakes in the film, especially the parts where you could see NF written on walls, and the long hair on some of the northern scooter boys at Brighton. But, we still love the film and can still recite lines verbatim. This was certainly the youth cult film for our generation."

Fraser Smith - "The first time I saw Quadrophenia was at the ABC on Snig Hill in Sheffield.... The Mod 'revival' was starting to gather pace by now. But in keeping up, the need for the cool cat clothing far exceeded its availability. To see the film I wore a sky blue 'bullshit' sweatshirt (you had to be there, they were cool) and a pair of rust-coloured 'Bowie' Trousers, from Harrington's in the Castle Market... not exactly 'The Ace Face'. Anyway, having seen the movie, and the imminent release of the Jam's new fourth album ('Setting Sons'), we needed to find a place to meet our fashion needs. This is where the wonderful L & M Supplies on Sheffield Road, just outside Barnsley Town Centre came into its own once again."

Heather Quinn - "I do admit, that perhaps watching Quadrophenia, donning a parka and a pair of Jam shoes does not necessarily qualify someone to be a Mod, but it was certainly a good place to start. However, I wonder how many wannabe Mods back then realised that Quadrophenia originally started life as a '70s rock album by the 'orrible Who."

Ginger Kevin Lawton (far right) and Barnsley Vikings Scooter club member Steve Orridge (far left) on the 'Quadrophenia' set. The club were prominent extras on the set.

GARY SHAIL 'SPIDER'

Gary Shail - "In the last Ten years Quadrophenia has been continuously voted as being one of the top ten British films of all time. But on the films general release back in 1979 the reviews certainly wouldn't have supported that fact. In fact it very nearly never got shown at all as certain factions wanted Quad banned due to its excessive use of bad language and scenes of violence, all of which seem remarkably tame by today's standards.

Quadrophenia was my first adult acting job and I can honestly say that in 35yrs I have never experienced another job quite like it. Even before filming commenced we were put to work, although it certainly didn't feel like work at all! Franc Roddam (Director) wanted absolute authenticity and that included the interactive relationships between main characters. We were actively encouraged to 'hang out' as a gang and get to know each other as well as possible. We had scooter riding lessons, dance lessons, which were hysterical, and parties where we were given handfuls of blues so the producers could see how we interacted whilst completely off out tits!!! It worked. By the time we headed off to Brighton to film the riot scenes, we were all firm friends. In fact Mark Wingate (Dave) moved in with me at my mum and dads for the duration of the filming. It was an exciting time!"

Ed Silvester - "'Quadrophenia' had been hyped, on giant posters, the music press and at the cinema. So, we all felt that the film had taken ages to be released. But, after seeing the film it did feel like a watershed moment and the key point when the Mod revival had started to become very popular. Especially, as a few of us went to see the film again in Oxford Street, and when leaving the cinema we were jumped by a gang of skinheads – Mods were already becoming an easy target – and groups of Mods shouting; we are, we are, we are the Mods, didn't help. A few of the gang had jumped over a counter and hidden in a nearby McDonalds, until it calmed down. The rest of us luckily escaped into the tube network."

QUADROPHENIA ON SET ⏸➡

Although 'Quadrophenia' came to commercially represent and inspire Mod's public face for years to come, in 1979 it would be the emergence of a new hybrid of punk-energised dance music - primarily Ska - that would come to captivate and excite many young Mod fans. Also attracting an audience of often right wing new breed skinheads, the record label and genre 2-tone - itself a multi-racial ideal - would eventually enter the record collections of youths of all tribes.

2-tone

2-tone released its debut platter in the summer of 1979 with 'Gangsters' by The Specials - a crafty and refreshing re-working of Prince Buster's Blue Beat classic 'Al Capone'. Following packed-out dates across the country with fellow 2-tone artists Madness (who consequently moved to Stiff Records after their debut 'The Prince') and the Selecter, the scene was set for a whole new youth-led contemporary scene. 2-tone - despite its troublesome reputation and occasional accompanying gig violence - brought young Mods, punks, skinheads and rude boys together beneath the umbrella of cultural and musical unity and the love of Ska!

Robert John Manton (The Purple Hearts) - "Then the 2-tone thing happened (which I loved) and that was the end of The Hearts - as a commercial proposition at least. The Two Tone explosion gave the kids a much more danceable/easier to understand 'off the shelf' culture and it played much better with the generally 'left/liberal' political culture of the music press of the time."

Simon Franklin - "Against the Thatcherism backdrop of the late 70's, early 80's the 2-tone movement emerged from a Mod revival movement not capable of carrying a political message. Most of us had never had any activist inklings at all, but with its derivative 60's Ska sound and 'enjoy yourself it's later than you think' message this music galvanised its followers – anti-racist and anti-Tory, dressing sharp with meaning. 2-tone subconsciously embedded it's message into us, whilst looking good, having fun and most important dancing! The perfect music for the time, and it hadn't fallen too far from the Modernist tree!"

Ed Silvester - "Initially, and certainly not during 1979, we didn't differentiate between the 2-tone groups and the new Mod revival bands – as they were all part of the same melting pot of what we considered as Mod – you'd see as many kids in parkas as skinheads at the early gigs – to us both genres had origins in the 1960's. We'd happily go and see both the Specials, and bands like the Lambrettas at the same time. Madness and the Selecter were even on the same bill as Secret Affair and the Purple Hearts at the Lyceum Ballroom in August 1979, which was one of the venues used on the 'March of the Mods' tour. So the 2-tone bands were happy to play alongside Mod bands at that time. An uneasy alliance between skinheads and Mods, didn't last that long though."

2-tone sped like an out of control locomotive, moonstomping its infectious dance fusion of punk energised Ska and rocksteady beat throughout the youth club discos of the land. Its impact on a young generation of working class youth should never be underestimated.

Charles Murphy (Glasgow Mod) - "By 1979 I had been a Mod for a year or so, I was 15 years old and was totally knee deep in music - anything to do with the 60's, that was me; I was absolutely spoiled for choice. People forget just how much music was blasting out of the radio, and of course religiously, watching TOTP. In '79, the first band for me to define 2-tone, was the benchmark 45 by The Specials 'Gangsters'. A flurry of 2-tone 45rpms followed and ruled the airwaves. I bought every record I could get my hands on, Madness, The Selecter, The Beat, and the totally funtastic Bad Manners, like a kid in sweet shop heaven. I never saw the 2-tone bands as Skinhead bands, or even Ska bands, just brilliant infectious music, PARTY MUSIC!

I remember at my Secondary school dance, I had my first 2 tone suit on red and purple - bought out of 'Gilt Edge' clothes shop' in the Saturday market here in Glasgow, by my big brother Mick who was working in the 'demolition game', and for the princely sum of £19.99. I bought (five pairs for a pound) white Terry Towelling socks down the famous Glasgow Barras market with some of my hard earned pocket money and a pair of black Loafers from City gents clothes shop (a mecca for Mods) and a ''Boston Pin Collar' shirt for £4.99 from 'Dees' of Trongate. I also bought a one-inch wide purple knitted wool tie to go with the suit, for £1.99. I had saved all of my pocket money and I knew exactly the way I wanted to look; the only difference was my hair, which was collar length. I wasn't into short hair, it was more of a "Beatles' style. I wanted to look my best but just be me, and was so nervous about going to the dance in case someone had the exact same suit on as me! Typical Mod.

The other 'problem', for me was getting to the school dance, was gangs. I was in the 'Den Toi' and my school, Lochend, was in "Drummy' - the gang we fought. Only us from Easterhouse know just how violent it was in those days. Still to this day I don't know how I managed to get there and home without being stabbed and seriously done in. I had to go a long way round dodging and looking over my shoulder, hoping no one recognised me as you really couldn't exactly miss me, and EVERYONE knew my face, and not for the right reasons. I still remember going into the School, and looking over and seeing in the middle of the football pitches people flying into each other with every kind of blade, hatchet, swords and bricks being thrown at each other: this was 'normal', this was how I was growing up right in the middle of it all. The music and the clothes, hoping to get a scooter when I left school, kept me sane, it was my escape.

I could hear Ottowans 'D.I.S.C.O' Blasting down the corridors as we made our way down to the school dinner hall where the dance was held. I walked in and looked around, being 15 and every girl looked like sex on legs, and I had to think 'bromide' and find somewhere to sit. The dance floor was just full of everyone I knew from school, and loads of guys dressed in black pork pie hats with the black and white checked bands round the hats, with matching black leather gloves, white button downs and black inch wide ties, and wearing shades - they looked so cool. I had been in for about twenty minutes, loads of Disco music was getting played and the teachers mixing with the pupils 'rowing' on the floor to the Gap Band's 'Oops Upside Your Head', then in a split second the next thing I heard was the opening 'scratching crackles' of 'Gangsters' By The Specials'. The floor was full of these Mods with Harrington's and Docs stomping about: an explosion of 'dressed to the 9's' Mods in suits and shades. I will never forget the rush I felt watching them dance. Such a buzz!"

Ed Silvester - "By 1980 sporadic outbreaks of violence occurred between Mods and skinheads. Skinheads would descend on Carnaby Street, and minor scuffles between Mods and skinheads were not that unusual – It really had become a dangerous place for Mods to meet and hang out. To this day, I have friends that have always preferred 2-tone and Ska styles of music, whilst others have pushed the boundaries, and embraced all aspects of Mod since the revival days. I have noticed that both Mods and 2-tone followers have never lost their love for scooters."

Ed Horwood (Somerset Mod) - "In 1980 as a white 13 year old growing up in a rural village 25 miles from the nearest big city (Bristol), what I knew about work, politics, race relations, sex, music, clothes etc. can be written on the back of a postage stamp. At this formative time, I was in danger of accepting all the stereotypes of the status quo. And then thankfully, I start to take notice of this thing called 2-Tone. It's the simple yet infectious beat that first hits me – it's unlike anything I've heard in my young life up until then and damn it, I can't keep my feet still when it comes over the airwaves. As part of a small but growing group of others turned onto this new sound, I start buying and borrowing the records. Then the lyrics introduce me to a gritty, often seedy urban landscape where prejudice, oppression and frustration are commonplace for all, regardless of skin colour. Yet despite this, a steely pride and determination to rise above the crap, to unite, to dress sharp, to dance, to live every day and celebrate life comes through. Two Tone was my introduction to all the values I was later to embrace within the Mod lifestyle and which to a large extent continue to inform my life to the present day."

STRAIGHT MUSIC PRESENTS

THE SPECIALS

MADNESS

DEXY'S MIDNIGHT RUNNERS

THE SELECTOR

ELECTRIC BALLROOM
184 CAMDEN HIGH ST. NW1 (NEAREST TUBE CAMDEN TOWN)

SATURDAY 21st JULY at 7·30

TICKETS £2·00 (INC. VAT) ADVANCE ELECTRIC BALLROOM BOX OFFICE. TEL: 485 9006
LONDON THEATRE BOOKINGS, SHAFTESBURY AVE., TEL: 439 3371; PREMIER BOX OFFICE, TEL: 240 2245,
OR ROCK ON RECORDS, 3 KENTISH TOWN RD., NW1, TEL: 485 5088

Soul ensemble, Dexy's Midnight Runners briefly aligned themselves with the 2-tone scene before taking their Soul revues to their own venues as leader, Kevin Rowland, was searching, not only for the 'Young Soul Rebels' but his very own intensely burning vision of Soul.

Simon Franklin - "Dexy's Midnight Runners were a Mod band, and I'd argue and debate this fact with anybody who likes to. They were more of a Mod band than any of the revival bands, more Mod than even The Jam! Now I'm being very careful with my words 'Mod band' not a band made up of Mods. In the purist sense the music of their first and ultimately definitive album, 'Searching for the Young Soul Rebels', is more derivative of the music Mods listened to and danced to than any of the new wave tinged Mod revival bands. Even their name was taken from a Mod drug of choice, but think of that too, the Midnight Runners bit, always moving, late into the night, like the Mods did trying to extract something meaningful out of every minute!

Dexy's were perfect for their time, their videos were stark, monochrome and very simple. They reflected the time period, mirrored the mood. You have to remember the Mod revival was not at a time of swinging Britain, Brit Pop may have been, but times were hard. It really was Mod (clean) living under difficult circumstances! The Soul music they copied was from an industrial Detroit and America, adding colour to people's drab lives - listen to early Dexy's and you can't fail to be transported.

At the time of the revival I'd been given a huge stack of Stax, Chess, Motown and Atlantic Soul 7" singles by my Uncle to listen to and dissect with a discerning ear and I couldn't understand how this was the music of the Mods when bands like The Chords, The Jam, The Purple Hearts et el were considered to be Mod bands? I then delved deeper, and came up with names like Geno Washington (via the Dexy's single 'Geno'), Jimmy James and Zoot Money. Their music was difficult to come by, but it was sweaty, stomping, soaring Soul music not unlike what the Midnight Runners played. It was passionate, meaningful and heartfelt like Kevin Rowland preached and sung. If you think Stax Soul revue or Otis Redding you'd be close to the feel and sound, banging and loud, all encompassing and involving.

Then there was the dress, straight out of the Brando film 'On the Waterfront', New York City dock worker - smart but practical, ready for the dance and fight. Donkey jacket, dark worker chino's or Sta-Prest, striped or plain t shirts, black Benny hats and monkey boots or DM shoes, hair cut short and tight. For a while me and my mates copied this attire, we really did, we adopted a gang mentality, a closed ranked thinking. It wasn't exactly 60's Mod but it did lend itself to a progression albeit ten years too late. From this some of them became scooterists, adopting the look further with bomber jackets, combat trousers etc.

I have no doubts that Kevin Rowland was and is a Modernist. He has that attention to detail that ultimately crippled him through mental illness. He was a purist and genius like Weller not falling far from the tree, occasional returning to take another bite of the fruit. Mod music, music liked listened to and danced to by an audience of Mods."

THE INFLUENTIAL FACTOR
BY GRAHAM LENTZ

Like others of Mod's diverse and eclectic cast, Graham Lentz has a wide influence and involvement in large periods of Mods ever-evolving history. Graham's journey evokes some familiar epiphanies and memories - many of which could well mirror the experiences of much of his generation.

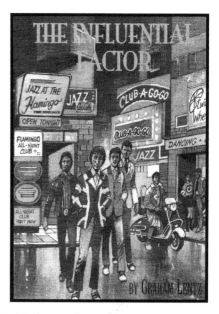

Graham Lentz (Author, Broadcaster, Reviewer and Mod Philanthropist) - "I suppose, if anyone was destined to be a Mod, I would possibly fit that category. My late father, Brian was an early Modernist of the 1950s: a fact that would impact on me years later.

My earliest memory of music is hearing 'Baby Love' by The Supremes and (I don't know how) but I must have seen them on 'Ready Steady Go!' as that footage is all too familiar. I didn't care for Diana Ross, I was drawn to another. Mary Wilson attracted my attention and is still one of the most beautiful women I've ever seen. That was the starting point of my life-long passion for Black music.

Music (and possibly Mod) has been the only 'constant' in my life even from that early age. Everyone listened to the radio all the time and music was culturally important. Growing up in Battersea, South London, I do have vague recollections of scooters and Mods. The film 'Up the Junction' was shot in my 'manor'.

By the late Sixties, I was very aware of skinheads and their style, although I was never allowed to adopt it. My mother made a few small concessions. A Ben Sherman for a 10 year-old was a big deal, as was my first 'Harrington'. By the age of 14 I went to Rutlish High School in Wimbledon where my fellow students included one Mick Talbot and his brother Danny. Danny and I were in the same year, Mick was a few years older, but I recall us taking music lessons there.

Fate decided I could not stay in London. My family moved to East Grinstead in Sussex where things didn't exactly go to plan. As 1976 became 1977, music became my refuge in my isolation as I struggled to make friends. I felt lost and in need of something. That something duly arrived one Saturday morning. I had a routine by then. I spent most of the morning listening to Peter Young and his chart show on Capital Radio. I would make a note of singles I liked and wanted to buy. He played a new single by a band called The Jam. It was 'In the City'. By the time it had finished, I was already out the door on my way to H.R.Cloakes Record Shop. The staff were like family to me as I was in there all the time. They had a copy of the single in a picture sleeve. They played both sides in the shop for me. I was blown away. I placed a permanent order with them to set aside anything they had relating to The Jam. LPs, singles, posters, and display material, anything Jam/Paul Weller-related. That order only came to an end in 1983 when the shop closed for the last time.

I was also an avid reader of the music press and it wasn't long before I started to see pictures of Jam fans as well as more prominent photos of the band themselves. The style, the image, it resonated with me so deeply, I knew this was how I wanted to look, it was ME!

Being a provincial in early 1978 wasn't much fun. The last train from London to East Grinstead was something like half-past ten at night, so going to gigs was not even a remote possibility. I did used to go to London a lot on Saturday afternoons, mainly to Carnaby Street where I would occasionally see other like-minded kids. By late 1978 I had a parka, three suits, Desert Boots, 'Jam' shoes and tasseled loafers. Obviously my appearance was noticed by my parents and one day while listening to The Jam in my room, my dad came in and asked me what I was listening to? I told him I was a Mod, to which he replied, 'Well that's not Mod music. I'll get you some proper Mod music.' He returned with two EPs and an album. They were all by the Gerry Mulligan Quartet with Mulligan, Chet Baker, Chico Hamilton and Carson Smith. For some reason, the first time I listened to those slices of pure Modern Jazz, I got it. I understood what it was about. It just said 'Cool', but a different kind of cool to The Jam who were also cool. The visual style was not a million miles away. You could see the similarities between the two. Then, by 1979, a band called The Merton Parkas had a single out called 'You Need Wheels' and there on the cover were my old school associates, Mick and Danny Talbot, so I followed their career closely.

Graham's Mod inspirations, Eddie Piller (left on group pic) and Ray 'Patriotic' Margetson

As the revival got into full flow, I became obsessed and consumed everything I could. The Richard Barnes' book 'Mods' vindicated my Dad's assertion about early Modernists. The 'Mods Mayday' LP was another important addition as it highlighted the new crop of bands. Decca's 'London Boys' EP, the reissued and repackaged Tamla Motown LPs, Randy Cousin's Mod 100 list and James Hamilton's helpful pointers in Record Mirror all contributed to expanding my understanding of Mod music beyond The Who, Small Faces, Kinks and The Jam. London Weekend Television's special programme, hosted by Janet Street Porter, which looked at the new Mod of '79 was another key moment for me. It had its faults and looking at it now, you can see how the producers and JSP had an agenda, but there on the screen were kids my age using the punk-ethos of DIY and producing 'Maximum Speed' fanzine. Little did I know that the very people who were my source of information in '79, Goffa Gladding, Eddie Piller (Extraordinary Sensations), Ray Margetston (Patriotic) etc. would eventually become friends, as have many of the members of the bands from that time.

By mid-1979 I had acquired a Lambretta 150 LI and had met about 7 or 8 kids who were Mods in East Grinstead and we would meet at The Glandfield pub as it was then. When 'Quadrophenia' came out, the whole Mod thing went into orbit. The late seventies was a very dangerous and violent time. I could wax lyrical about the gigs, the fights and our exploits, but there are many of us 'Revival' Mods who have countless stories like that. Suffice to say our little band of Mods eventually became The Defiance Scooter Club and its still going today."

DUBLIN'S MOD SUMMER - BY MORGAN NOLAN

The embracing of a new Mod scene of the late 1970's was not exclusive to the mainland of Great Britain. Evolving with many similarities to the recent revival over the Irish Sea, including the youthful zest to want to belong to a scene of their own, the Irish Mod scene - boosted with a visit by The Jam the previous year - would spawn a whole new generation of lifetime Mod enthusiasts. Teenager, Morgan Nolan personifies this new young generation of Mods.

Morgan Nolan - "I came from Donnycarney on Dublin City's Northside. I can remember getting into the Mod thing around the summer of 1979. This wasn't a conscious decision to be a Mod as I hadn't a clue as to what that term actually meant, little did I know then that this decision would to a large extent shape how my life has developed and lead to the type of person I am today.

Anyway back to the summer of 1979, I had just finished Primary school and would be entering Secondary School in September. There was definitely something in the water that summer; the charts were starting to reverberate with the sounds of The Jam, The Specials and Madness. I recall hearing Down in the Tube Station on the Dave Fanning show and been blown away, I had to find out about this band.

This naturally led to my first purchase, 'All Mod Cons', which introduced me to Sta-Prest, Button down shirts and Monkey Boots and of course a neat haircut. Without knowing it I was becoming a Mod.

With hindsight it is easy to understand why this image would appeal to a working class kid surrounded by the bland and grime of the rocker scene that was big in my part of the city. My mates were all into Led Zeppelin, AC/DC, Black Sabbath, etc. that they picked up from their older brothers, well that wasn't going to be my path. As the oldest in my family I had no role model to influence me so the future was mine to discover and 'All Mod Cons' was a great reference point for anybody willing to explore. The artwork of the album introduced me to scooters, Ska, Tamla Motown, Targets and Union Jacks, what was this all about. The answers I found in Richard Barnes book Mods, the closest thing I have to a Bible. Now I had a reference with the past that set the template for my dress sense, musical taste and if it isn't too clichéd to say attitude to life. Yes 1979 was a seminal year for me as I had begun to discover and explore the [whole] Mod thing."

Missing the initial months of underground Mod activity but observing from a distance with interest and attraction during the summer of 1979"s flowering of scooters, parkas and Mod gatherings, aspiring Sheffield teenagers such as Heather Quinn and Lee Radforth, along with Barnsley Mod, Stewart Hardman, absorbed the whole Mod phenomenon. They were soon backtracking to the very core of Mod's earliest beginnings, whilst assimilating in true Mod style, the ideology of moving forward with the latest sounds being created and grouped together under the broad umbrella of Mod music. In truth these young hipsters could well represent a whole new generation of post revival Mods who dismissed the notion that this was merely the latest fashion, but more a genuine lasting recognition of a music, style and sense of cool that would become a way of life in every way, shape and form.

HEATHER QUINN – THE MAGIC OF MOD AND THE SMALL FACES

"When I first started collecting records, back in the late '70s/early '80s, I wasn't very knowledgeable at all. I tended to choose those with the coolest picture sleeves and I basically took it from there. At the start of my quest to discover everything Mod, be it style or music, I found that album covers were a great source of '60s imagery and that's partly how I fell in love so much with the Small Faces. Not only did I like the way they sounded, but oh boy I adored the way they looked. Take their first Decca album released in 1966, the cover epitomizes Mod perfection. I would spend hours studying every inch of that album cover, back and front, as if there was a hidden message or secret clue to the Mod universe hidden somewhere.

There was a guy behind the counter (of Violet May's Sheffield record shop) and I asked him if he had any Small Faces records. I seem to remember him getting down a long, heavy wooden box full of 45s. He pulled out one of the singles and it was an original Small Faces' 'Hey Girl' on Decca. It cost £1.35. 'Hey Girl' isn't necessarily one of the Small Faces best songs; it's typically commercial for the times. I thought it was good, but it was Marriott's vocals, which caught my attention. I played the 'B' side instrumental, 'Almost Grown' - now I *really* liked this. I had to hear more. I took a trip to Bradley's Records and bought a Small Faces Greatest Hits LP. There was a branch of Bradley's on Fargate, and also one on Chapel Walk. I later bought a copy of the Who's 'Meaty Beaty Big and Bouncy', together with a Kinks Greatest Hits LP. I loved (and still do) all three bands, but Steve Marriott will always be my personal favourite.

I just couldn't buy records fast enough. Every penny I saved went on music - records, posters, magazines. I discovered Record Collector magazine and from that discovered record fairs. I was fuelling my addiction by reading up on anything and everything about records - labels; 45s, EPs, LPs; foreign pressings... and the *pièce de résistance*, I discovered Small Faces French EPs, which came complete with picture sleeves and were a particular delicacy. Just like the band themselves, they are diminutive and perfectly formed. The first French EP I bought was 'All or Nothing' and it cost £12, which was an arm and a leg in those days. The picture-sleeve was superb; the Small Faces looked immaculate. The EP was especially expensive considering I had managed to get hold of a copy of an original Small Faces Decca LP for a fiver! It's difficult to choose a favourite track from that album, but I think it would possibly be 'You Need Loving'. Marriott's vocals on the LP are just so raw and brilliant.

As the obsession for records continued, so did the clothes. My style of dress became more extreme. I dressed less like a guy. As I started to find a style of my own I grew my hair and had it styled in a typical, Sassoon inverted bob, with two V shapes cut into the neckline at the back. In those days, charity shops and jumble sales were brilliant for finding original label clothes. In one charity shop in town, I found a virtually unworn black and white, op-art Mac. I went on to collect anything and everything relating to Sixties' cool and in a pre-internet world, it took a lot of time and effort to track down illusive items."

Heather's commendable passion for 60's vinyl is a prime example of the revival era Mod's yearning to trace the back catalogues of their favourite Mod artists. In those days - years before the quick fix of the internet - it was still relatively easy to pick up piles of lost treasures of the 60's in charity shops, markets and the good old fashioned second hand record shop.

Right: The Chords. Mod, like its predecessor, punk, soon made its way to pop poster appeal

The traditional family holiday at the seaside frequently inspired numerous Mod epiphanies.

Stewart Hardman (Barnsley Mod) - "I had been into the music firstly during the summer of 1979 hearing the likes of The Jam and Secret Affair, The Lambrettas, Madness, The Specials, the Selector etc. on the radio. Eventually 1979 gave way to 1980, and the weather started to get warmer. During a family holiday to Great Yarmouth in the April, I got my first really sighting of Mods on a rally at the coast. During that week long holiday, I would walk the family dog before breakfast, and pass the scooters that were parked up on the green near us, some of the Mods camping nearby. So I used to be able to stare at the lights and mirrors on the scooters as I went by. During either the Saturday or Sunday, they all drove up the sea front in ranks of two and trees, the road was clogged up with the sights and smells of two strokes, crowds lined the road on either side staring at the sight they were witnessing, at some point a load of skinheads ran out and at them a big scuffle kicked off, police sirens rang out, cars were trying to get out of the way. All during the weekend where ever you looked there were Mods on scooters, or Mods walking around in fishtail parkas and suits, it was some sight.

All too quickly though, the weekend was over and they all made their way home, leaving again down the sea front in formations, leaving the blue vapour trails of 2 stroke everywhere, I was totally hooked. We saw them again later on in the summer, this time at a rally in Blackpool during August, but the seafront there is a lot longer so the effect was not as impressive as it had been at Yarmouth, but still something worth seeing which I still treasure and think about at times. The scooters all parked up outside the Pleasure Beach amusements, in the parking bays down the whole length of the place. I can still remember to this day, walking down the side streets and seeing various names The Jam, Secret Affair, The Chords, Purple Hearts, The Lambrettas, The Who, or targets, or Keyhole emblems of Secret Affair, on the backs of the various parkas..."

Lee Radforth (Sheffield Mod) - "Mod first touched me via the '79 revival and like most people of my age the soundtrack to my six week holidays, before going up to comprehensive school in the September of '79, was The Jam, Secret Affair, The Chords and the two-tone bands The Specials, Madness et al. My summer holiday was a week in Skegness, which fortuitously coincided with the August Bank Holiday. Sat in a traffic jam a never ending procession of parka wearing Mods streamed past on their scooters, I was transfixed; my life would never be the same again. The September day I walked into Aston High school for the first time the whole playground was a sea of Sta-Prest trousers, Harrington jackets (both courtesy of Harrington's in Castle Market) and Fred Perry's, I felt part of something."

As previously touched upon, what exactly differentiated the revival period Mods from their original heritage?

Peter Jachimiak (South Wales Mod) - "One word sums up the difference between the Revival period and Mod of the mid-60s: 'Anger'. The originals came about during a time of economic boom. The Revivalists existed in a post-Punk era of social deprivation. And the resultant frustration of all that comes out in the thrash'n'crash music of The Purple Hearts and The Circles ('Frustration', 'Angry Voices', and so on). 'Quadrophenia' certainly also captures that anger felt in the very late 70s.

Another major difference was the Parka. Back in the 60s, its sole purpose was to keep the scooter rider clean and warm. Yes, it was 'American' and not leather (that is, not 'British' and not something a Rocker would wear), but that's it, pure and simple. Come '79, however, and it became the symbol of Mod. Covered in button badges and sew-on patches, it was the instantly recognisable signifier of street-corner gang Mod."

Ashley Walker (Birmingham Mod) - "It was the perfect blend of punk's teenage angst and elements of 60's Mod. The Pistols had gone, The Clash had sold out many moons ago, new wave was ok but with hardly any real voice behind it."

Ian Snowball (Maidstone, Kent Mod) - "During the Mod revival period, we considered ourselves just as Mod as the 60's Mods. Only we were running away from skinheads and punks instead of rockers."

Ray 'Patriotic' Margetson - "Yes, we were heavily influenced by The Jam, went to their gigs and then these new bands that started to pop up in London. We were looking in a new direction and this was what was needed in a natural way. The more I delved into the 60's style and sounds the more absorbed I was, yet at the same time it was very contemporary because we were going to gigs to see bands who were roughly the same age as ourselves, bands that I really liked – The Chords because of the energy they put across, Secret Affair for their brass Soulfulness at times, Small hours with their Hammond organ sound etc.."

The logos of Mod bands old and new were common-place on parkas and the popular pin-on badges of 1979. The addictive nature of Mod cast a spell upon large proportions of the youth of the period. In reflection of punk, two years previously, Mods' direct appeal was just as all-consuming. But would the revival's influence and relevance be strong enough to sustain it into the 1980's?

CHAPTER 10

BACK TO ZERO

Left: Peter Sceats, autumn 1980. Centre: Key 79 era Mod Eddie Piller (wearing beret) and friends (including Ed Silvester, also right) walking down Oxford St, summer of 1980

By the spring of 1980, the recent Mod explosion, unlike its closely related 2-tone cousin which was spiralling in popularity, had in many ways reached its musical peak: certainly the craze for all things Mod and 60's influenced had passed its apogee of fashion status, although its influence had been profoundly felt and was integrated in the mainstream. Now, Post-'Quadrophenia', Mod was yet again a household name as a generation of teenagers in a search for self-identity saw in Mod clothing and music an ideal form of post-punk self-expression.

The music press, most of which never truly embraced or understood the resurgence anyway (the greatest and most enthusiastic supporter being Garry Bushell of 'Sounds'), began to stick the critical daggers into a splintering Mod movement. Even one of Mod's most respected icons Paul Weller declared much of the new Mod scene as uninteresting just as quickly as he had dismissed his 'Spokesman for a Generation' music press awarded moniker. The truly dedicated of stylist Mods remained committed to the diminishing scene, often being out-numbered by a mass sea of green parkas, many of whom didn't know their Soul from the sole of their Hush Puppies. But, fashion followers aside, this new flock of Mod-loving kids, now on their way to learning the codes and eclectic appeal of the ever-changing Mod religion were to flourish within the evolving scene; learning and digesting everything Mod-related- ultimately symbolising the 1980's new breed of Mod!

Despite the authentic Mod ethics of certain elements of the scene, a sense of déjà vu may well have been felt by those of an observant nature as the profit once again drove a mixed-bag of business-minded fashion moguls and establishments to exploit the original 60's Mod look. Even before the close of the previous decade, the back pages of the music weeklies had been selling suits 'as worn by The Jam', ex-army issue parkas (and from who's army it could be often debated?), target t-shirts, Jam shoes and occasionally genuine Mod gear. The race for commercial overkill had once more begun and Mods had once again lost firm control of what was essentially their very own youth-led movement. Yet, this was one mere facet of Mod's struggle to meet the new decade head-on.

The 1979 coastal Mod exploits also continued into the new decade as teenagers acquired their first scooters and excitely set out to their very first Mod rallies. Scarborough, Great Yarmouth, Clacton, Brighton and other towns all saw fresh invasions of Mods during 1980 and by the following year tabloid-induced seaside troubles and near-riots were once again making headline news. As Mods were herded into cages (Scarborough 1981) gaining the usual sensationalist headlines and Mod fought Mod in one of the unlikeliest of venues - the Lake District, many would not have given the cult much more than another six months of survival.

On the surface of it, the public face of Mod almost passed with those final journalistic coffin nails driven firmly in, burying the shallow representations purporting to be Mods. The truly devoted Mod once again disappeared back into his underground roots of clubs, scooter rallies and numerous upstairs pubs and club meetings. Other changes occurred when by 1982; some Mods had evolved into scooter boys, swapping suits, Italian knit wear and Brogues for combat trousers, denim and Dr Marten boots. As the decade wore on, if the media interest in Mod was anything to go by, Mods had become almost non-existent. Yet scratch beneath the surface and a whole plethora of various Mod-related cults and scenes could be found. Mod, in the true nature of its origins, had survived and rode the storm of populist fashion and expectations. In many diverse ways, the 1980's would prove to be as creative, idealistic and individual for the true Mods as the 1960's themselves.

During the closing months of the 70's and into the 80's, that diversity sadly saw, in addition to tribal indifference, violence break out between the various related Mod factions and their rivals. City centres, concerts, youth club and suburban streets alike often shared common occurrences of tribal hostility and random violence as skinheads and rude boys fought rockabillies, punk rockers and Mods. Unlike their 60's ancestors, this time round, however, Mods indulged in much less inter-Mod rivalry; the aggression being saved for the other suitable targets at hand.

Mods on the tube, Ed Silvester, Eddie Piller and friends in 1979

Above: Punk and Mod animosity, 1980

Above: Artane Mods 1980

Punk and Mod tensions were not exclusive to mainland UK. Dublin - certainly no stranger to the violence of the times in other forms - was also afflicted with typical examples of youths' intolerance to their opposite faction's fashion statements and stance.

Morgan Nolan - "So 1979 became 1980 as time dictates and Too Much Too Young was dominating the radio and my mind. To me the Mod and Ska thing were all the same but looking back it was funny how quickly they became too distinct things, particularly when the latter was tagged Rudeboy music.

At first this was like friendly family rivalry amongst same age cousins but in later years this turned nastier when the Rudeboys were overrun with plebs in Harrington jackets with Specials or Madness transfers on the back, these were really just yobs looking for a tribe to belong to. You can't think about this period without commenting on the Tribe mentality that existed at the time, Mods, Rudeboys, Skins, Punks, Teds, Rockers and whatever else you are having existed side by side and in a lot of cases in open hostility to each other.

At the centre of this universe was Dublin's Dandelion Market. This market was a mix of the semi-legal and the totally illegal were you could but anything from records, clothes, cannabis to novelty tricks. It was here that many bands got their first public notice including some outfit called U2. The market was set in a derelict site at the top of Grafton Street, Dublin's primary retail street. When approaching the market the first thing you encountered was ADVANCE records shop surrounded by a gang of Mohawks. You had to run the gauntlet with these phlegm challenged beauties if you wanted to enter and sieve through the vinyl inside, always a tough decision on a Saturday or Sunday afternoon. Traditionally the market was the reserve of punks and Hippies in search of weed and they gave each other a respectful distance but as the stall holders were catching on the emerging Mod and Ska thing they began to sell Parkas, Harrington, skinny ties, loafers etc. and this started to attract a trickle of interested young enthusiasts.

The trickle became a flood very quickly and this led to an inevitable confrontation with the punks who felt their space was being invaded. In 1980 it would be fair to say that your average Mod was a good three to four years younger than your average punk, and this naturally gave the physical advantage to the followers of Sid, but that is only an advantage so long as the numerical difference is reasonable. That summer the number of Mods and rude boys was so great that the inevitable happened. It is a mystery to me how these things happen and with little or no organisation a group of about 50 Mods/skinheads somehow decided that it was time for the punks to find a new home. I am going to stop here and leave the rest to your imagination for I swore I would not let this article fall into the usual cliché when referring to the 1980's and let it be dominated by accounts of random and mindless violence. Enough said.

Most people remember the 1980s as been very tribal, Mods, Punks, Teds, Skinheads, Boot boys, Hippies, Rockers, rude boys, Soul boys, New romantics all existed side by side and in parallel worlds of their own self-importance. Dublin's Mod scene was based around 'the Monument' on O'Connell Street, the main thoroughfare of the Capital. The Monument was in fact a statue (and it's very important pedestal at which one could sit and chat) of William Smith O'Brien, a Young

Irelander (Nationalist) and member of Parliament of the 19th century, in the centre median of O'Connell Street. I don't know how this came to be the main hangout for Mods in the City but its central location meant that it was the place to be seen. This fitted the Mod culture right to the T and every Saturday and Sunday male and female Mods would meet to discuss the latest styles, music, comings and goings of the local scene, etc. No matter what time of the day you were sure to catch somebody hanging about there, weather permitting of course, and this has ensured that the place has fond memories for most of us who ever spent time there. Friendships were formed that would last a lifetime.

Another very important social institution was Bubbles Night Club. Based in Adair Lane just south of the river Liffey in a Basement that you entered via a small lane. This was the music heart of our scene. When you entered the club via the stairwell it had a real 6Ts feel due to the low ceiling and velvet seating covers. The club originally ran on a Wednesday night (later adding Sunday night) for Mods going through many name changes throughout the week to cater for other musical tastes. As I explained in the early 1980s my mates and I were still school going, as were most of the Mods going to Bubbles. The venue didn't have an alcohol license and the owners probably reckoned it wasn't worth their while to risk selling alcohol to a bunch of kids; why would they when the soft drinks option was just as profitable. The music played was your standard Soul, R&B, 60's power pop and Garage, Revival and Ska tunes. To us it was a magical world of our own invention, something that set us apart from the mainstream and other tribes.

When a band came across from the UK it tended to be a big event, however, I reckon that the 'The Troubles' kept a lot of bands from venturing across. The Jam played in 1978 and as this was too early for most of us to attend it was mainly a punk/new wave event. However, I recently met the drummer from the their support band on the Irish tour (The Vipers). He recalls Paul as being difficult and withdrawn (not much change there) and Bruce and Rick as been very friendly, however he reserved his highest praise for John Weller who organised a lift for the support band and gave them plenty of advice. Over the years we had visits from Nine Below Zero, Squire, Purple Hearts, Makin' Time, The Kinks, various Soul Artists and a fair collection off of the 2-tone label."

Whilst in the Mainland, the usual suspects were still supplying the Mod soundtrack, the Mod spin-off genre - Northern Soul, began to make an impression on some elements of the Mod scene.

Ray (Inset) and outside the Mildmay Tavern 1980 with his girlfriend of the time, Donna

Ray 'Patriotic' Margetson - "I was attributed to being the first London Mod to play Northern Soul records in London clubs, so I've been told, and was influenced by the 6T's club I used to go to at the STARLIGHT club in West Hampstead (North West London). This was well before the 6T's club got going on Friday nights at the 100 club. I made contact with Ady Croasdell and bought records from him back at his flat, a short walk from the 100 club in London's West End. Ady and the Starlight club were a big influence on the Soul music I played wherever I went."

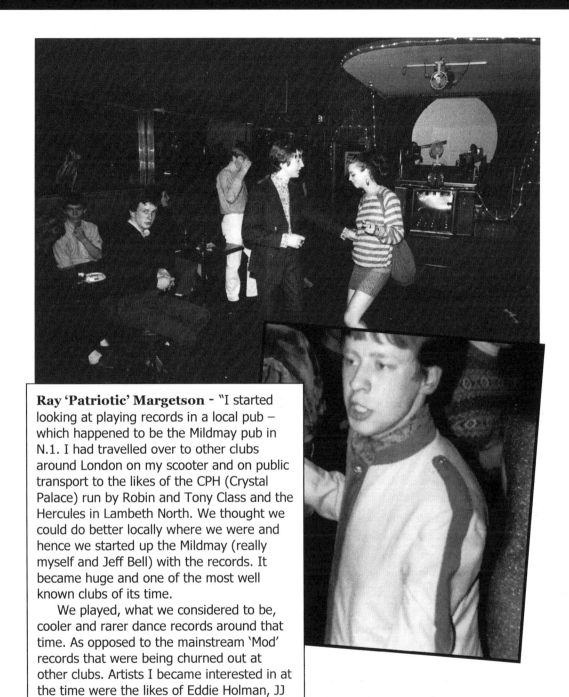

Ray 'Patriotic' Margetson - "I started looking at playing records in a local pub – which happened to be the Mildmay pub in N.1. I had travelled over to other clubs around London on my scooter and on public transport to the likes of the CPH (Crystal Palace) run by Robin and Tony Class and the Hercules in Lambeth North. We thought we could do better locally where we were and hence we started up the Mildmay (really myself and Jeff Bell) with the records. It became huge and one of the most well known clubs of its time.

We played, what we considered to be, cooler and rarer dance records around that time. As opposed to the mainstream 'Mod' records that were being churned out at other clubs. Artists I became interested in at the time were the likes of Eddie Holman, JJ Barnes, Darrell Banks, ZZ Hill, alongside Ska, R&B and Jazz tracks. I sourced out singles on the Sue and Chess records labels and 'discovered' great sounds by the likes of Jimmy McGriff and Phil Upchurch Combo."

**Above – Mildmay Tavern, 1980
Ray on the dance floor in 1979**

Sean Hampsey had followed the track of Northern Soul from its earliest incarnation. A regular on the scene, travelling the breadth of the country to all of the contrasting clubs of the '70's, Sean also held the connection to Mod and its emphasis on 'Modern' close to his heart.

Faces on the Northern Soul scene (including Sean's friends left to right: Simone – Alison – Jacko – Dave - Sue - Jimmy. Front: Yammy from Rotherham.) preparing for a night at Rotherham's Clifton Hall, Feb 81.

Sean Hampsey - "By 1980, it seemed that the Northern Soul scene was all but dead and buried, leaving a small hard-core of dedicated, long standing Soul boys and girls who were all of the same mind; we needed a new home and, despite the oncoming years, we weren't going to be calling it a day just yet.

Thankfully, and rather unexpectedly, this period of declining numbers at many of the well-established venues coincided with the late 70's Mod Revival, seeing many hundreds join the ranks and swelling the numbers. As the Wigan Casino came to its ultimate finale, (it had several 'last nights' and reprieves) my own town, Rotherham, was there to pick up the baton. The Clifton Hall was a large Victorian building on the edge of town. Opposite a car park and easily accessed by public transport, the building was the East Pennine bastion of the all-nighter tradition, from 1979 until 1983. I saw it as a 'one room paradise' as all kinds of Soul music was embraced. Initially I attended as a willing, paying, punter so receiving the call to join the DJ roster was a very proud moment for me. Having worked for years in the region, at the Charade, Tiffany's and Windmill clubs; here I had the chance to play to a huge room with a crowd that had come from all over the UK. The music policy was totally across the board, unfettered by politics or rigidity. The promoters gave free reign to the DJ's, to entertain and to keep the floor busy, so on the national stage and in an all-nighter environment I was able to get behind the records I'd been hammering on my local 'stomping ground' for many years, such as Brothers Guiding Light 'Getting Together', Bobby

Patterson 'I'm In Love With You' and Darrell Banks 'I'm The One Who Loves You'. Remarkably, these were very well received alongside the 80's 'new releases' and dozens of impossible 'grails' from the 60's.

A new generation had found Soul music and the old guard were understandably grateful. Without the Mod revival, the Northern Soul scene would have struggled to wash its own face, economically. The rise of the scooter clubs and events exposed new Mods to fresh 'nighter' music and staple Clifton classics, such as Prince Phillip Mitchell's 'I'm So Happy', Charles Johnson 'Never Had A Love So Good' and my Lincoln market discovery Ronnie Dyson's 'Lady In Red', were soon to become the new Mod anthems of the day.

**Wigan Casino dancers
above Sean Hampsey**

Cleethorpes Winter Gardens, a legendary east coast venue, was brought out of mothballs and became a magnet for the young soul vanguard. Back then I'd run a coach, from Sheffield, Pond Street Bus Station, picking up in Rotherham and Doncaster, more than 60 teenagers at a time, with a passion for the music every bit as strong as my own. Although 60's sounds were still being 'discovered' there are no doubts these young newcomers were much more ready to embrace and follow the new soul music of the time. They had a taste for it, related more to it... and it meant more to them. A further split was inevitable, thus the 'Modern Scene' was a breakaway dedicated exclusively to new music and its 'Modernist' followers went with it, never to return!

To intensify the separation, the '60's Mafia' set out to reverse the trend by kicking against the new establishment and playing unknown and underplayed 45's (sixties-newies!). This was seen as an antidote to the ever-shifting trend towards the 80's. Despite the further fragmentation, this dedication to unearth the obscure was no bad thing. Many fabulous Soul records were uncovered that might never have been heard and it would have been a crying shame had the likes of Sam Fletcher 'I'd Think It Over' Bobby Kline 'Say Something Nice' and Sam Dees "Lonely For You Baby" not been given that vital lease of life.

Simultaneously, young Mod's were rediscovering 60's RnB and the earlier sounds of Soul. Records from the legendary Scene Club and Flamingo started to come onto the playlist entwined with the new discoveries. 45's that 10 years earlier would have been considered 'too early' such as Benny Spellman's "Fortune Teller" were massive Northern spins. London's own 100 Club, the world's longest running Northern Soul All-nighter, owes more than a handshake to the latter day Mods. Both scenes and cultures penetrated the other and in so doing ensured survival for a further 30 years."

Yet, as Northern Soul became a relevant part of the equation for some, popular fashion outside the scene was also making an impact on the new bands.

Chris Pope (The Chords) - "Within a blink of an eye its 1980 and a new decade. Oh, Yes! Oh No! Here comes Maggie, strikes, the dole queue and the New Romantics. Still we got Rockabilly, rude boys, the Arse-end-of-Punk and the Modernists. 'Maybe Tomorrow' breaks the Top 40. It's Top of the Pops. 'So Far Away' hits no 30. Tours and Tours, we were on a roll! Too much of this, too little of that - suddenly its too many near misses. 'Something's Missing', and it's true and its summertime and 'The British Way of Life' ... the BIG one, the Ace in the pack? It stalls and splutters, Eek and Ouch, confidence shattered. Now the cracks are starting to show just twelve months in, how can this be... band on the verge!

Ah yes, the band. Billy the Ace-Face singer. He scared the shit out of me at the time. We never knew which Billy was going to turn up? Volatile and spiky and truly magnificent on stage. Martin, somewhat erudite, and just a little aloof, in all the perfect bass player. Buddy, the joker and all over the drum Kit - the man I roomed with on tour. We shared a lot - trashing rooms, TV sets, pot plants, furniture, beds ... you name it, all out of hotel windows. Setting off fire alarms, drinking all night. Being banned from every Trust (trash) House Forte in The UK, RESULT! And a REAL passion for the TOONS!"

Meanwhile, scooters, long associated with the image of the Mod in the 60's, unsurprisingly had begun to interest the late 70's crowd. By 1980, and as the decade progressed, this enthusiasm drove the formation of numerous new scooter clubs which subsequently absorbed the spin-off mixed bag of Mod with a growing presence of Northern Soul and for some scooter boys - punk.

Left: Ed and John Silvester in 1980
Below: members of Ed's contingent

Ed Silvester - "In early 1980, with my brother, and with our readies in our pockets, we made our way to Masons of Wanstead. We knew which scooters we wanted, and there and then purchased a couple of Vespa's, one white, one blue (many more scoots were to follow). Next, we would have to learn how to drive them! A daunting task, as teaching one's self how to drive one, was comical in those days. No proper lessons, just get on the damn thing and slam it into first gear, then drive bloody slowly, and pray you didn't fall off. How the hell we managed it I don't know, but we must have done as we were driving properly after a couple of weeks. I drove my new white Vespa 100 to my friend Alan Smith's house, in Epping, as he was keen to have a go. Little did I know that he hadn't actually ridden a motorized vehicle before, why did I let him ride it? - what a fool!

After waiting an hour for him to return, I started to understandably become worried. Then I noticed Alan nervously walking back up the road towards me. I knew something must have gone wrong, and he apologetically told me he'd stacked my scooter into a lamppost. Hadn't had it five minutes and it would need to go back to the garage for repairs. Luckily, all that needed to be done was some repairs to the cover over the front wheel. We're still good friends, so I must have forgiven him.

We expanded our reach, and now started to drive to see Mod bands at places all over the London area. This was also the first time that we drove to the coast as part of the annual scooter runs, to Brighton, Margate Clacton and Hastings. We steered well clear of the northern runs, mostly down to cost, as it would cost us too much to have a broken down scooter towed back home."

Pete Skidmore (Sheffield Mod) - "The area of Woodseats (Sheffield) had a lot of Mod and scooter boys and girls, with the Mods with scooters tending to be late teens to early twenties. From around 1979 to about 1982 there was always scooters parked up outside the 'Big Tree' and 'The Woodseats Hotel' on nearly any given night.

Along with most youth movements, there was always a trip to the coast. The Mod revival made this possible with transport easily available. Of what I can remember, there was loads of scooters about that had been found in garages, sheds, cellars etc. and, unlike owning a car, you could basically just walk into a dealer and buy a scooter and ride it away, even if you had never rode one. The trips I've had out over the years to places like Skegness, Ingoldmells, Bridlington, Scarborough, Blackpool, Southend, Torquay and loads more coastal resorts - all something that is our way of getting away from the dreaded 9-5!"

Paul Boddy (Devon Mod) - "I was (aged 15) with my parents in Torquay, with no real direction in my life, and whilst walking along the seafront, we heard this loud rumble behind us. So we all looked round and all I could see was a sight that changed my life from that moment on... a huge convoy of Lambrettas and Vespa's covered with lights and mirrors. As the sun shone down on the chrome I could now see all the riders had open-face helmets with either mirror or black shades on: nearly everyone was wearing parkas. They looked so cool.

As they parked up their scooters in a massive line along the seafront all the holiday makers and locals stood aside. I asked my mother 'who are they?' and she replied 'MODS'. 'What's a Mod' I enquired, and she looked at me saying 'trouble makers, just ignore them'. And with that I wanted to know more and more about these Mods; so when my parents were on the beach I wondered off along the seafront to have a look at the scooters. As I walked down the line of gleaming machines I noticed some Mods looking in their mirrors doing their hair, and adjusting their ties and collars: they looked so cool. I also noticed the girls (of course)... most were wearing black and white outfits with white lipstick along with dark eye liner, I was in love. Anyway after about an hour of posing, and checking each other's scooters out they kick started their machines and in a foggy haze of two stroke they pulled off one by one with one scooter blocking the road so all the other scooters could pull off together. Again I thought this was amazingly cool.

So once I got back to my home town I had decided I wanted to be a Mod. But where do you find a Mod? I asked a few people in Town and they told me that loads of Mods meet up at a certain café in Exeter. I had no idea about Mod dress sense, though I did buy a millets parka and a pair of Levis with a tatty pair of trainers.

I headed off to Exeter to this café and walking past a few times I could see loads of Mods inside in parkas. I was far too scared to go in, but after about half an hour of walking up and down outside this cafe I met a Mod outside and we did the Mod nod. 'Alright mate.' he said and I replied

'Err yeah.' he asked if I was a Mod and I answered 'I want to be.' He took one look at me in my millets Parka and tatty trainers and my hair all over the place... and said 'Well if you wanna be a Mod you gotta sort yourself out.... come inside.' So I did.

Everyone was eyeing me up. He introduced me to his friends who gave me the once over. one of them said 'For fucks sake mate what the hell are you wearing??' I could feel myself getting red with embarrassment until one said 'Don't worry we'll sort you out, sit yourself down and have a cuppa.' There must have been 30 to 40 Mods in there. Brilliant.... and from there on in I was given the basics of being a Mod: what to wear, what clubs to go to, what rallies to go to, where to meet at weekends and which girls were single and which ones to leave well alone."

Paul 'Smiler' Anderson (Reading Mod) - "Mod after the revival was a totally different animal from that of the 1960's. In the 60's the kids had a blank canvas and all ideas were truly original. Fashions could be in one week and out the next. By the time the 1980's had started the Mod scene was already being influenced by the past. An obvious influence on the culture was the Richard Barnes Mods!' book published in 1979. Kids would read up on original Mod fashions and incorporate them into the then standard Mod look."

Alan May - "When we got a little braver we would do some national rallies like Great Yarmouth, Scarborough and Southend but going on these, as fun as they were, always ended with an argument at home as the media always reported trouble with the skins or casuals – I never got into trouble but in 1981 at the Scarborough National I had my head set stolen from my Vespa PX150, along with two scooters owned by my mates... not funny at the time trying to source a cheap replacement with cables etc. to get home and your mates on the train pissed off!

From 79 to 1982 I had seen a number of bands play live: the fondest memories are on two occasions – firstly in November 1979, our youth club had booked The Teenbeats and we had sold out with over 350 Mods waiting in awe! Come 10 o'clock we had a call from the band from a phone box near Essex saying they were snowed-in and didn't think they'd make the gig... well all hell broke loose and the Youth Club manager was shitting himself until at 11-15pm they turned up to play a 45 minute set, which subsequently followed with a mass row with the local rockers who'd heard about the gig and were waiting outside with sticks, bricks and poles, albeit at midnight and in front of the police station which I recall was shut from 9pm!!

The rockers, grebs, or grebo's as we called them were always older and looked as scary as fuck to a teenager but then again we could re-live our own 'Quadrophenia' style beach battles in our own town. On another occasion the Radio Caroline road show came to town along with the local greb's (numbers being boosted by the Hells Angels from the Northampton area, who believe me were not to be messed with, but then that left their bikes to be sabotaged when they were in the gig, by who? god only knows!

Another gig I loved was at Ipswich Corn Exchange in 1981 to see The Chords. Myself and (my mate) Mick White went on the train, made our way to the pub next to the venue and low and behold The Chords were at the bar- I was in heaven! The gig was awesome and Buddy and Chris Pope invited us back stage to give us some memorabilia and sign our tickets, which I still have. All was good until we realised we'd missed our train home and slept in our parkas freezing our tits off on Ipswich station, cold, damp and miserable...with 3 fags and a tin of cider between us!

One thing I hated were the wannabies who wore parkas with Specials and Madness on the back - my favourite parka of the day was owned by Paddy from Huntingdon with 'Away from the Numbers' on the back and 'That's where I wanna be ...'

The saddest thing for me about the revival period was that Ska rode the back of it and had more success and with the music press slagging off the mod revival in the NME, Sounds etc. it never stood a chance and soon dwindled out to a much smaller movement and went underground until another wave in the mid to late eighties."

The allure of Mod did not end with the music-press damnation of the revival and subsequent loss of favour for the associated bands in 1979. Its wide-reaching influence spread into the provinces and suburbs. From the Isle of Wight to the streets of Glasgow, Barnsley and Nottingham and every city and town in-between, Mod left its presence and often life-defining impact on those affected by its undying influence.

Jeff Platts (Barnsley Mod) - "The Mod revival was well underway, 'Quadrophenia' was responsible for many a playground scuffle, 'We're Barnsley we're barmy we're off our fuckin heads!' and other staple footy chants of the day had been replaced by 'We are the Mods, we are the Mods!' etc. etc.' ex-army parka from Wakefield Army Stores in town. Mod drew me in. The ex-army issue parka from Wakefield's store in town, the hair, the shoes the pink Ben Sherman shirt ('It's a pastel shade sir honest, it says in the school rules 'Blue, grey, white, or pastel shades!'). I had the snappiest boating blazer in town, and if that came with a sewn in bird on the arm then all well and good! They were shallow times, in many ways, but Mod was about the fire, the soul, the unity and loyalty. A loyalty that still resonates with me to this very day 30 years on. The Mod image has long gone, but the fire still burns hot enough to scorch the odd seaside dance floor throughout the summer months."

Mark Thomson (Falkirk/Scotland Mod) - "It was all Jerry Dammers fault really. I was twelve when I watched an edition of BBC2's 'Rock Goes To College' featuring on this occasion, 2-tone's finest band The Specials. As they kicked off into 'Do the Dog' I could see, on a raised stage just over Terry Hall's shoulder, this madman with cropped hair playing a keyboard whilst running on the spot, with no front teeth, sunglasses on and a tight fitting suit. Full of energy. But it was his feet I was drawn to. Trousers about three inches too short, pristine white socks and a pair of tasselled loafers pounding the stage floor as he battered the keyboard into submission during that opening song. I can clearly remember thinking ' What the FUCK is THIS? 'and instantly liking everything about it.

This was late 1980, and the kids on our estate were a mish-mash of fashions and tribes. The common uniform amongst the hipper young bucks being black Harrington jackets and Dr Marten boots with the all-important yellow laces: Adidas t-shirts and Samba trainers in the summer, donkey jackets in the winter. Music wise, I had been buying the likes of Dexy's, The Jam and Blondie but 2-tone and the Mod thing hadn't really registered on my radar. Once I'd seen that Specials concert on our old Rediffusion telly though, my entire outlook, and indeed my wardrobe, was to change forever. I threw myself into the whole rude boy look, with Sta-Prest, Fred Perry's in various colours (the black with yellow tips and the West Ham maroon being early fave colourways) and the wonderful tasselled loafers, teamed with those cheapo market stall white towelling socks (three pairs for a pound) Magic!

The next pivotal moment in my young life was us getting our first video recorder. One of those big top-loading VHS numbers. A Ferguson Videostar I think it was. Anyway, on my first trip to the newly opened Video shop with my Dad, I was looking through the ones on display and there it was. 'Quadrophenia.' I badgered my old man to rent it out (along with the Wanderers) and when him and my mum popped out to the pub that Friday evening I sat alone and watched it. Then watched it all over again. Much the same as when I'd first saw that Specials gig I couldn't take my eyes off it. The parkas, the scooters, the hair, the music, the fighting. I thought it was the best thing I'd ever seen and I wanted in.

As luck would have it, it was my birthday shortly afterwards and I was intent on getting a parka. My Mum and I went to the local Army and Navy stores but all they had were those nasty German ones without the crucial, and ultimately deal breaking feature, the fishtail. I had to endure a two-pronged attack from both the salesman and my Mum that "it was a lovely parka, and just the same as that Quadrangle film you watched' but I stayed resolute. It was a fishtail or nothing.

My Mum, bless her, pushed me onto a train and we bombed through to Glasgow, finding a shop I'd heard of, 'Flip', very quickly and going in. And there they were. A long row of US Army fishtail parkas. A sea of army green just sitting there, calling out to me.

Now, I had on black Sta-Prest a white Fred Perry under a black Fred Perry cardigan, and my tasselled loafers on my feet. Standing in front of the mirror I slipped on a carefully selected, one size too big, fishtail parka and looked at the Mod looking back. Some things in this old life just make your heart soar and this was one of them. I looked every inch the Mod I wanted to be. I literally couldn't take my eyes off the image staring back at me. I kept it on, and as my Mum paid for it I clocked a display of sunglasses and managed to wheedle an extra gift for myself of those black wraparound spex out of my now exasperated parent.

The walk back to the train station was peppered with near misses; lampposts and parking meters were swerved as I checked my reflection out in the shop windows as we walked. I noticed something else, it was only faint, but it was a glimmer of what was to come later on, as I became a fully-fledged Mod. It was the hint of malevolence in the eyes of other youths. That look that's laced with a bit of dislike and the threat of menace. I didn't give a fuck though to be honest, and was over the moon with my new parka.

Pretty soon, there was a group of us, all about 14-15, on the estate and we were all following the Mod path. The Jam were our faves, but we'd listen to other stuff like The Chords, Secret Affair and The Who. Our parkas were adorned with target and Union Jack badges and our regular forays into the town centre were met with scuffles with the local skins, bikers and various other dafties who wanted a go. Nothing major but you had to watch your back. We were a tight little bunch, but that distinctly Mod thing of one-upmanship saw us competing to have the best clothes, the best haircuts and the best record collection. Actually, it was around this time I bought the Richard Barnes Mods! book and set about trying to get all the soul singles pictured within its pages. (it took me years but I finally did it). Those black and white pictures of 60s Mods had a profound effect on me and, as I was getting older, my Mod style tastes were evolving."

Andrew Harris (Nottingham Mod) - "The year 1979 had seen me swept into the second wave of Mod as a very young lad; being too young for 'Quad' and knowing little of the original Mods. My pals and I viewed it all as something very new without knowing or attempting to reproduce any bygone era. Due to the Two Tone explosion and the Mod Revival (being in my opinion interdependent on each other), I believe it caused the second generation of Mod to swell for more than perhaps it would have done if stood alone. Music being but one aspect of Mod, I personally found the Two Tone phenomenon and its fairly infectious mix of punk and Ska far more appealing to the ears than the actual Mod bands of the time.

In 1980, on one non-uniform day, we marched the school field in parkas, slim ties and loafers. We were chanting 'Geno' to be met by the sixth form rockers in a punch-up. This ended with me and another guy being forced to stand outside the staff room by the deputy headmaster for instigating and participating in a mini riot. After that, everyone seemed to morph into 'Rudeboys' and the then 'New Romantics'; these people being the average sheep-like followers of fashion who liked to be in vogue."

Ed Horwood is another Mod representative of a generation of 1980's youth who had been too young for punk and the early days of the Mod Revival explosion. Instead, he found almost instant empathy and identity with both classic period Jam and the 1980's fertile ground of 2-tone. Craving something far more potent and inspirational than the average run-of-the-mill chart sounds, Ed was poised on his musical starting block during the first year of the new decade.

Ed Horwood - "As far as my recollections of the 'youthscape' of the late 1970's and 1980's Britain go, I recall there being three main options laid out before me and my peers with regards to what would now be termed the 'lifestyle' choices teenagers had. Whichever option you chose would go onto determine the clothes you wore, the music you listened to and the crowd you hung with. Perhaps more importantly, for many of us, and as hindsight has proven, it would also determine the future course of our lives.

Option one, and by far the easiest for many teenagers, was to become what was loosely termed, a 'Trendy'. This was someone who, as the term implied, followed the high street fashions of the time and liked whatever music was in the top twenty. Were it not for the fact that these kid's tastes seemingly changed with every cycle of the moon, they might have been praised for merely being broad-minded. However, seeing them flit from trend to trend and become passionate about the latest big name band or the latest youth movement only to drop them like a stone when Smash Hits, Record Mirror or the NME decided that something or someone new was to be championed, soon dispelled any myths that these individuals were at all genuinely passionate about their tastes. Option 2 was to become a dedicated member of any of the many youth cults adding colour and excitement to what was in many respects as we entered the 80s, a dismal decade for many young people who were increasingly to experience the inequality, injustice and destruction wrought by Thatcherism. Option 3 was, in many respects, just a continuation of where most of us had been pre-teenage years and before the onset of puberty – a state of unquestioning normality. Normal kids or 'Nothings' were it seemed, either totally dismissive of youth culture, preferring instead to become conformist, upright, respectable young adults as soon as they could; or else, perhaps through their own timidity or the attitudes and controls put in place by their parents, they were unable to take the step to become a 'something' by becoming, for example, a Teddy Boy, a Skinhead, a Punk, a New Romantic or a Mod.

In the summer of 1980, I became a teenager. And almost overnight, I transformed from being a 'normal' football obsessed, comic collecting run of the mill kid into a fledgling adherent to youth culture. The separation of my parents a few years previously, the winter of discontent, the ever increasing threat of nuclear annihilation as the cold war continued to heat up, these things and the hormones racing through my body suddenly made me challenge my cosy childhood view of the world - and then, there was the 2-tone movement and the Mod revival bands.

Up until I hit thirteen, I had merely 'heard' music. This came to me via the radio or my Mother's record collection (The Beatles, rock 'n' roll, Johnny Cash, Lonnie Donnegan). In addition, like most of my generation, I had a collection of C90s stuffed with a variety of tracks crudely taped from the chart show on a Sunday evening on my portable cassette player. For some reason I can't fully recall, I found myself drawn to the likes of The Jam, the Specials, Secret Affair, Selecter, etc. In these groups and their contemporaries that together made up the closely linked 2-tone and Mod Revival movements, I found a sound and style that resonated with me and which made me actually stop hearing and to start 'listening' to music. Looking back, it was perhaps no surprise that I latched on to the '2-tone and Mod' thing. Punk came too early for me – after all, I was only ten when 'God Save the Queen' caused ripples in polite society. And, whilst much of punk's anger and attitude seemed to live on within the ranks of the Mod and 2-tone bands, these groups were to my young ears, far more melodic. Importantly, they dressed a hell of a lot better too. The latter point I used to full advantage with my Mother who still bought my clothes at that point. At my suggestion, she had no qualms kitting her oldest lad out in smart Sta-Prest, Ben Sherman's, Harrington jackets, an army trench coat and Hush Puppies and she even bought me a pair of black DM boots for school (after all, even the local police wore black DMs back then).

Later that summer I started in my first part-time job working weekends and Bank Holidays in a shop. This source of income was to provide me with the means of buying the all-important records and occasional extra clothes items, and, influenced by the older lads in my area zipping about on scooters, I soon started to save up money towards getting a scooter on my 16th birthday."

Morgan Nolan - "On the clothes front in the early years it was a real hunt for the good gear. Naturally vintage shops or to give them their contemporary title 2nd hand shops/Dead man shops were hit and miss for buys and it was a case of blind luck. The aforementioned Dandelion Market could be relied on for some of the staples of the Mod uniform. As the years went by dedicated shops such as Lord John's Parnell Street (Sta-Prest, Button down Shirts, Harrington and Monkey Jackets, etc.), Simon Harts (Shoes) and Murphy's (for off the peg suits and jackets). Custom made tailoring was a luxury and some great tailors operated on Gardiner Street and Caple Street. For something different a trip to London was always worth it, with Carnaby Street being considered good for quick grabs in Shelly's, Melanddi's, Merc, Pop and Brook Brothers."

Typical Mellandi and Cavern shop adverts of the 80's

So much occurred between the revival's high tide of '79 and '80. Lessons could have been learnt from punk's recent compromises and demise as a musical force, coming almost within shouting distance of the early Mod restoration period. Although Secret Affair added a soulful influence and Dexy's, The Step and Q-Tips drew obvious inspiration from the genre, perhaps, the distinct lack of Soul's influence was one downfall, as bands mostly drew influence from the energy of punk and classic 60's Mod Rock for inspiration? Regardless of this, it has to be recognised that fashion and youth culture are often fickle - not all involved take such a committed stance as the devoted inner core.

Chris Pope (The Chords) - "And so it implodes around mid to late October 1980: In Leamington Spa of all places. Not very rock n roll! The fact is (as the facts are), Billy left and we stayed. A new singer, Kip [joined] and a new direction [attempted]. One More Minute, not quite sure why? No one really came along for the ride with us this time. We didn't hang around. It was over by late September 81 - in less than two and a half years! PHEW and BLIMUS! Could have ... Should have, would have ... Yeah, you've heard it all before, countless of times. We Got LUCKY... and then very unlucky. No Big deal. For just a brief moment back then, having the best job in the world, what an amazing place to be for a teenager? Recording seven singles, one album, a handful of amazing tours and some brilliant memories. I wouldn't have missed it for the world!"

The lifespan of bands such as The Chords may have been short, but for some of the band's fans, the impact would be significant and have a lasting influence.

David 'Dizzy' Holmes (centre in photo) has spent a considerable period of time devoted to music: his early days were, like many, spent following the bands and sounds of the late-70's Punk Rock scene. His Mod initiation occurred while attending a performance by one of the most tuneful bands that the new wave had to offer... and in near perfect symbiosis the support was a punk-inspired Mod act!

Dizzy Holmes (West Sussex Mod) - "I was first touched by the hand of Mod when I was a budding Punk Rocker at a tender age of 17. I went up to the Guildford Civic Hall to see one of my favourite bands The Undertones. While we were outside queuing to get in, about fifty scooters turned up and rode into the car park. They were all shiny without stretched mirrors! They looked so cool and mesmerized me... Now thirty years on I can still vividly remember that night. I thought to myself, wow who were this lot. I had never heard of Mod until that night.

Anyway, while we were in the venue a support band came on stage that mirrored what I had seen outside. The band was called The Chords! They were brilliant and I was hooked! So we went home after the gig and became Mods overnight.

**Dizzy (above) and
with friends at Scarborough**

I sold my Wolseley Hornet car (Complete with The Clash printed on a green visor on the front windscreen) and set about buying my first scooter. A week passed and I was now a proud owner of a Lambretta TV200 for a measly price of £35.00. I set about stripping it down, re-sprayed it and re-built it. I rummaged through my dad's wardrobe, found a old suit and a pair of his old Hush puppies. I looked the dog bollox, so I thought!!!!

1981 was fast approaching and it was announced that at Easter was a mass Mod meeting at Scarborough (so we thought). So we put out the word that we would attend amongst all the local clubs! Well we set off on the Thursday morning to get to Scarborough for the Friday night. This wasn't to be as we had over 30 old scooters in our convoy. Literally every mile we had a breakdown. Then we would fix that and set off again followed by another breakdown. Finally we reached the seaside town of Scarborough on the Sunday lunchtime.

We were tired, hungry and exhausted... But we were there! The weather was bad, cold and it even started snowing! Not to be deterred, we all got cleaned up and donned on our best clobber to head into town! God we were in for a shock! We expected to see hundreds of similar dressed Mods. What we saw was hundreds of flared trouser tank topped scooter-riding yobs! We couldn't believe what we saw!

Anyway, we started to mingle and the beers started to flow. What I remember was that there was a pure hatred for us southerners. We didn't understand why at the time and several skirmishes broke out! It wasn't until afterwards we learnt that Mod never really died out up north and they resented all the southerners getting all the lime light since the release of 'Quadrophenia'. Flairs and Tank tops was the fashion up north through the Northern Soul clubs like the Wigan Casino and Twisted Wheel.

Anyway, we made our epic journey home with much to think about ... Then literally overnight we progressed to becoming Scooter boys! I returned my dad's suit and hush puppies back in the wardrobe and bought myself a flight jacket and a pair of camouflage army trousers. I still loved listening to Mod music but becoming a scooter boy was more appealing."

JAMMING

Nowadays, Tony Fletcher is a well-known author with such critically applauded titles as The Who drummer's biography 'Moon' and his own biographical foray into his formative punk/Mod days, 'Boy About Town'. Struck by the early sound of both The Jam and punk, Fletcher undertook the creation of his very own version of one of punk's greatest creative ideas - the fanzine.

Jamming was born at the height of punk in 1977 (initially for a school-printed run), but by 1978 Tony had struck up a healthy friendship with Paul Weller, after conducting exclusive Jam interviews, resulting in Weller's support and signing of his band 'Apocalypse'. The fanzine quickly came to embrace and cover the blooming Mod scene, interviewing the bands and reviewing the sounds with a true fan's critique and insider knowledge. Jamming was one of the most accomplished fanzines of the post-punk and Mod revival era eventually expanding into a glossy magazine format.

Elsewhere other street-wise Mods felt the compulsion to indulge in the creation of a fanzine. The enthusiasm and zerox-styled passion of the times echoed punk's 'Do it Yourself' idealism.

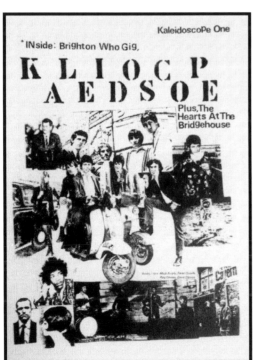

Ed Silvester - "In the summer of 1981, and inspired by fellow East London and Essex contemporaries, Ray Margetson (Patriotic), Eddie Piller (Extraordinary Sensations), my brother and I one drunken night decided to put together a Modzine, which we decided to name Kaleidoscope. The theme would be the emerging mini psychedelic revival of that year. We'd recently seen the Who in Brighton, (which included a few back stage passes – kindly donated by Jackie Curbishley) and we covered that gig as well. In addition, a few other bits and pieces were added, including a piece about the Regal, a place that sold psychedelic inspired clothing. The fanzine took us the best part of 3 weeks to put together, and was much harder to complete that we had first expected, and extremely time consuming. Luckily, I had a good friend (Dave Stokes) who worked at a printing firm in the city at the time. He arranged for the printing, and a mate's rate was agreed, basically a token fee was paid, and a few extra beers were paid for on the next scooter run.

My brother arranged for the articles to be typed up at his workplace - no computers in those days. By today's standards, some parts were not very PC, but we only ever wanted to cover our costs and spread the word of our Mod/psychedelic influences at the clubs we frequented. I seem to remember, we sold out on the first night at a Mod club being held at the Phoenix pub, located near Cavendish Square, just off Oxford Street – a few of us had taken them up there, packed in our scooter racks. We never did produce any further additions - as we just didn't want our social life interrupted."

Along with Ed Silvester's evocatively (psychedelic) entitled 'Kaleidoscope', Mod maestro, Eddie Piller's 'Extraordinary Sensations' and others - 'Direction Reaction Creation', 'Maximum Speed, 'Roadrunner,' Sheffield's reputable A5 sized 'Beyond All Limits' and a whole new influx of Mod zines (some still soldering on from '79), a new fanzine appeared in 1983. Named in tribute to the Jam song 'In the Crowd 'the fanzine surpassed the usual enthusiastic but limited run of a handful of issues and continued to inform and unite Mods with the latest news and happenings right into the start of the next decade.

IN THE CROWD - THE MOD FANZINE
BY DEREK 'DEL BOY' SHEPHERD

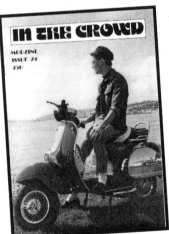

Whilst sampling the thrill of Mod as the revival was in full swing, Derek Shepherd used his outsider location to his advantage. His immediate passion for the Mod scene in mainland UK inspired Derek and girlfriend Jackie to aim to chronicle the movers and shakers of the revival with his own fanzine - one that benefited greatly from Derek's separation from the popular shifts in fashion of the time.

Derek 'Del Boy' Shepherd (Guernsey Mod) - "I was born and bred in Guernsey in the Channel Islands getting into Mod in the early summer of 1980 right at the tail end of the Mod revival. I was looking for a new direction in life at the time and, didn't have many friends; I was a bit of a Billy no mates really!

Then I went down to this disco club called 'Huggy's pit' and saw these smart looking people having a great time dancing to 2-tone and The Jam and just thought I want some of that so just joined in! I knew one of the guys called 'Sharp Mart' who played for my five a side footie team and he got involved with the small group of Mods which also included Mark Le Gallez who went on to form Mod band The Risk.

Anyway I decided Mod was for me, even those at the start I didn't have much of a clue what Mod was all about, but went out and brought the whole back catalogue of revival Mod records The Jam, Secret Affair, The Lambrettas etc. and have never looked back!

I used to get Extraordinary Sensations from Eddie Piller and loved the way it made me feel part of the bigger Mod scene even though I was a long way from the centre of the action in London, so when I saw the Modzine feature on the very first Tube show on Channel 4 I said to my girlfriend at the time Jackie let's do a Modzine to promote the scene. It was a bit of a leap for me as I was to be honest rubbish at school especially English, but lucky enough Jackie was still at school and was much more academic then me and also had use of the School photocopier so in 1983 'In the Crowd' was born.

We sent about 30 copies of the first issue off to the old Rockefeller centre in Carnaby Street and were amazed that we sold them all, so had to send more, we even got a few letters from Mods saying how refreshing ITC was compared to some other zines. We later moved to the Carnaby Cavern and then The Merc, which was managed by Jimmy (ex-Rockefeller). Carnaby Street was our biggest outlet, but we also sold a lot of copies in Birmingham, Belfast, and Dublin and in west coast USA through Bart Mendoza of Manual scan plus Mod societies selling them all over the UK and in Spain and even Japan! We had approx. 300 subscribers to 'In the Crowd' from all over the world, which pushed up sells to around 2500 per issue at its peak, especially with the flexi record issues.

We interviewed most of the main 80s Mod bands Makin Time, Small World, The Risk, The Prisoners, Direct hits ... 79 Mod heroes like Jez Bird of the Lambrettas, Buddy Ascott of The Chords. Most of interviews from the first issues of ITC were postal ones, because living in

Guernsey we could not get over to the mainland UK as much as we liked to do them our self's. Later on we built up a good group of friends on the mainland who were happy do interviews and articles for us. 'In the Crowd' was very much a collaboration and not just all about me and Jackie which I think is one of the reasons it was so popular.

We once got a phone call from a reporter from The Sun newspaper, someone had sent our zine in as they were doing a fanzine feature, and we were later one of only five fanzines reviewed in the feature. Unfortunately we also had a number of fall outs including a nasty letter from Long tall shorty after we slated them in a gig review, funny enough a few issues later we got nice letter from him after one of our reviewers gave them a good review, but that was ITC for you wasn't just our opinions expressed. We also get a very interesting letters from one or two Mods who did not like the fact we covered a lots overseas Mod scenes and bands, we soon put that one to bed!

Making loads of friends all over the world helping promote the Mod scene and keeping people inform on the latest scene news and bands etc. because the main stream media didn't want to know us, and of course not to mention all the free records and tapes! We always tried to make 'In the Crowd' better with each issue, with content or better layouts, making it glossy also, doing colour front covers made it more like a magazine, and I we think took it to a new level. I think the fact that we seemed to speak the language of the ordinary Mod in the street and didn't preach to them or tell them what they should wear or listen to was a positive for us.

We had loads of zines sent us to review, I Still have box loads of them and there was some really good ones like Chris Hunts 'Shadows and reflections' which was one of the best written Modzines of the time. We also liked GO GO, US zine Waaam! and 'Extraordinary Sensations' of course, most zines only lasted a few issues so for us to do 30 issues is quite good going and living in Guernsey helped a lot as we had less distractions.

I think fanzines helped keep the Mod scene going and informed when no one else was interested in Mod, it really was us against the world in the 80's and I don't think there wouldn't be a scene today without all the zines, newsletters and Mod societies' of the 80's. I'm very proud of 'In the Crowd' and the 30 issues we did, I don't think any other modzine did that many and that we played our part in keeping Mod alive during the 80s. A lot of people have told me since how much they looked forward to getting the latest copy of ITC because it kept them inform and involved in the scene which is what we set out to do!"

007 MEET AGENT PATRIOTIC!

Ray singing with 007 live at Liverpool Eric's 1981

007 at Sebright Arms, Hackney circa '81

Ray 'Patriotic' Margetson - "We even had Mods come over from Holland and Belgium on a Sunday morning after I had made contacts from Jam and Chords gigs in Paris, other parts of Northern France and Amsterdam, and via my fanzine I started up in 1980 called 'Patriotic'. The first one sold in one morning whilst waiting with 400 other scooters prior to a run down to Brighton!"

Attending a Jam gig with Andy 'Catford' (to the left, and Ray in the middle wearing the suit) in Amsterdam 1980

Ray 'Patriotic' Margetson - "007 were an East London band made up of five members, including brothers Gary and Russell Wood, with a decent following. They played support to the Jam at Wembley on one occasion and were around at the same time as North London band The Variations with some nice friendly rivalry!"

DOWN IN THE GROOVY CELLAR – PSYCHEDELIA 1981

Perhaps it was inevitable that an interest in pyschedelia – an immediate follow-on from the original Mod era - would gain interest with some elements of this latest Mod generation. The short-lived 1981 Psychedelic scene, which had its beginnings in a new clothes shop called The Regal, spawned its own clubs and bands (Mood Six and the High Tide etc.) and a well-received compilation LP 'A Splash of Colour', yet by the following year it was just about all over.

Ed Silvester - "By 1981, we'd started to notice a few hipsters at clubs wearing more flamboyant clothing, reflecting a more mid 60's psychedelic look, which began to interest us. This included paisley shirts and Edwardian style double-breasted jackets. This new more 'Freakbeat' look, we discovered, could be bought from a clothing emporium called the Regal - founded by Andy Yiannakou in 1980. The shop, which was originally located in South Kensington market (then just off Carnaby Street), had started to attract a Mod and a hippie chick crowd - for the ladies there was a shop called Sweet Charity. The clothes were outlandish and added excitement and colour to the streets, very different to the normal white Ben Sherman shirts and Levi Jeans, which we would normally wear, certainly a more mid 60's US garage band look. Now, Mod was always about looking smart and being different, and this was a big leap for a lot of the guys at the time, as some thought that the look was not strictly mod, and accusations of being a bit of a Dandy were being bandied about - even accusations of being a New Romantic!. But, the Epping Mods didn't really care and embraced the look.

We heard on the grapevine (and on flyers given away at the Regal) that a fantastic club had recently opened up, located just off Regent Street in London's West end, that now catered for this new scene; the aptly named, Groovy Cellar. We'd all drive up on our scooters and park outside.

Exclusive passes in our hands, we'd peel off our parkas to reveal a kaleidoscope of colours underneath. We would all eagerly jump down the stairs, to reveal a subterranean nightclub with psychedelic lights pulsating and loud psyche sounds pumping out of the speakers. I'm pretty sure that many a pill was being popped, but as we drove there most weeks, we stuck to a mostly alcoholic intake, in small quantities I might add - it was all about the clothes and music for us.

Virtually all of the music played at the club was originally from the mid to late 60's, although I did occasionally hear contemporary tunes like 'Treason' and 'Reason' by the Teardrop Explodes. This led to an interest in 60's US garage bands, and the discovery of a fantastic compilation, LP – Nugget's 'original artefacts from the first psychedelic era, 1965-1968', being its full title. Also, an interesting compilation album was released that year that featured most of the movers and shakers of the psychedelic revival - a Splash of Colour. Seemingly, the only collective piece of music new psychedelia produced that summer. The club became a magnet for members of aspiring psyche bands to frequent, and it wasn't unusual to spot someone from one of these groups. Mood Six seemed central to the scene, as they dressed the part and had a couple of catchy tunes, although they did become ever more flamboyant over time. Along with a guy they called the Doctor; the group put together a crazy film, to highlight the music and clothes of the moment - The Groovy Movie. They also filmed extensively at the Groovy Cellar and also a Thames boat trip, where the band played live and which we all briefly featured in.

Another cracking night that they organized was the Horror Happening at the London Dungeon, where Mood Six were the main act. We couldn't resist having a few photos taken with the exhibits, gruesome stuff really. Everyone seemed to be there that night, and this was probably the apogee of the scene. We all loved the Onlookers, and found out that a coach was booked to take paying guests from Carnaby Street to a venue in Croydon. A gang of us rode up to Carnaby Street on our scooters, where we found a safe place to park, and just managed to catch the coach. – it was great gig with a friendly crowd. But, I always remember the journey home though, as the one thing you didn't want to do was get stuck in heavy traffic in the West End - as there always seemed to be boneheads lurking about on every street corner. On this occasion, my brother had trouble changing gear on his Lambretta and had to stop, some of the fellas stopped to help him out. Understandably, we felt uncomfortable doing this, because at that time, an air of menace was always around you in certain parts of the Big Smoke, as tribes competed and continuously fought each other. Out of nowhere a drunken skinhead saw his opportunity, and ambled over to give us a mouthful of abuse, which was initially ignored. Just as a ruck was about to break out, half a dozen bikers pulled up, the Skinhead then made a hasty retreat. We thought, here we go we're in trouble now, but, luckily they only wanted to help out, and came over and tried to fix my brothers scooter. One of the bikers even managed to ram it into 2nd gear, and John was able to slowly drive home. Not all bikers were out to pick a fight with Mods."

Ray 'Patriotic' Margetson - "The Groovy Cellar in Piccadilly ... many a Paisley shirt was to be seen in there and mine I had made to measure, from original 60's cloth, at Regal in South Kensington."

1981 Psychedelia revival memorabilia and photos from Ed Silvester's collection including psyche act Mood Six (top of page)

'New Psychedelia' Dandy's outside the Regal clothes emporium in 1981
(photos courtesy of Anne-Marie-Newland)

New psychedelia gained the interest of certain elements of Mods, as well as enjoying a brief renaissance and 'flavour of the month' status with the music press, primarily The Face - which had hit the shelves as a monthly the previous year launched by ex-60's Mod Nick Logan. Whilst The Face utilised the title of Mod's highest accolade - the '79 bands, some of which also had a go at the psyche vibe, were seeing bleaker times.

Brett 'Buddy' Ascott - "Unfortunately it's true that some of the new 'Mod' bands springing up were bandwagon-jumpers of the worst kind (The Crooks anyone?) and that reflected badly on the good bands – amongst who I include the Purple Hearts of course, and Speedball. Secret Affair and the Merton Parkas were much slicker and possibly more contrived than The Chords, but at least they were there at the beginning and saw it happen from the very first stirrings of the revival. I could understand why they were popular, even if they didn't fill me with awe. I'm trying to be diplomatic here - I'm mates with so many from those bands now, all rivalries long forgotten! And Micky Talbot is one of the best musicians I've ever had the privilege to work with – he's a class act alright!

The biggest mistake we made was not signing to managers we could trust – in the end, when Billy fell out of love with the band and couldn't express his feelings, there was nobody to help us patch things up – I thought his leaving might be the beginning of Part Two, and really it was the beginning of the end. Billy had been a brilliant singer and front man – there's an edge of vulnerability and aggression to his voice that has never been replaced by whoever sings those Chords' songs. He made them his own. We struggled on for another year, with the very-lovely Kip, putting out two great singles that sold zilch, and by November '81 it was all over. We split up on a Friday and I was back at work on Monday!"

The Chords were not the only casualties. By 1982 the first wave of the Mod revival bands were mostly long gone or ignored by all but their shrinking loyal fan base. Obviously, the high tide of the Mod revival had passed, its legacy seemingly consigned to history. In later years, many of the involved band's back catalogues - including undiscovered songs - were revisited and re-appraised, belatedly enjoyed by Mods of all generations. However, during the early 80's, not all Mod-inspired youths necessarily looked to the recent revival for inspiration.

Sandra Hutchinson (Glasgow Mod) - "My Dad was a Teddy boy in the 50's and was also in the Merchant Navy, visiting America and Jamaica along the way. He managed to get his hands on vinyl that had not been imported to the UK so I grew up with his record collection. I fell in love with his R&B records and that's where it started for me."

SCOOTER RUNS AND NORTHERN SOUL

Far from the purple haze of new psychedelia, the influence of Northern Soul, along with changes in clothes, hair styles and scooters, coincided with the increasing popularity of scooter rallies.

Ed Silvester - "By the end of 1981, scooter runs to Clacton or Scarborough had started to take on a more 'Northern' look Scooter runs to South Eastern resorts were beginning to be full of scruffy Northern scooter boys – with their cut down scoots and Rockabilly music (well that's the impression we got anyway). At that time, we were all dead keen on Northern Soul music and the sound had really only become popular in the South East in the early 1980's - Jazz funk and soul were much more popular, complete with resplendent wedge haircuts and Pringle jumpers. Mind you, we were also happy to don our Adidas trainers, Lacoste polo shirts and Lois chords, when we went to footie - the Casual look couldn't be ignored. Suddenly, DJ's at Mod clubs dotted around the metropolis had started to play more Northern Soul. These theme nights had by then really started to take off - our favourite venue being the Mildmay Tavern in Islington, which also had a Sunday afternoon session as well, which catered for the younger Mod fraternity. The look was scruffy; the usual apparel being army greens accompanied by a Lonsdale/Keep the Faith style t-shirts. Northern Soul had been popular with a few revival mods since 1979, but it hadn't become really widespread until around 1981/2, after the pervasive influence of Northern scooter clubs invading the southern scooter rallies, and where DJs had started to play more Northern Soul based sets. Up to then we'd been happy to listen to Motown and revival bands, but this sound certainly piqued our interest. A friend of ours (Terry Stokes) was a big influence and had started selling R&B/Northern Soul records from his house in South Woodford - and was always available to recommend a track or two. He later expanded and opened a short-lived shop just off Carnaby Street; I've still got stacks of old Northern Soul singles bought from Terry stored in the loft. I'll have to dig them out, and give them a spin one day."

greater, or so he claimed. I admit I knew nothing about what to do if it went wrong-I was young and naïve and was more concerned with the look of the thing than what was the engine capacity! I can't say I even remember much detail about my first coastal journey other than freezing my arse off and worrying about my hair when I took off my crash helmet (bouffant and beehives were never a good combo for the crash helmet issue.) No one warned me how bloody cold it was going to be on such a long journey regardless of the weather-and my teeth were literally chattering at one stage. I was grateful for the old army coat (oversized or not)

Once we arrived though it was like a scene from 'Quadrophenia' as scooter after scooter cruised by with admiring glances. In my head The Who were playing 'My Generation' and 'Dr Jimmy' and I couldn't stop smiling. It felt like I was living 'the teenage Mod dream' and as a female of the species I was a rare breed by this time. In fact Mod girls were virtually extinct let alone on the back of a scooter by 1982: the Mod scene was in decline giving way to the New Romantic scene where the blokes had more lipstick on than the girls.

As for me I was happier with looking at the odd Mod god in black eyeliner a la Jimmy in Quadrophenia, the futuristic element passed me by and I tried hard not to acknowledge it even when Soft Cell released their excellent version of 'Tainted Love'. I was the only Mod girl in the entire school, and one of only three Mod blokes since there was a hard core Skinhead group in my area, plus a lot of Mods defected to Suedeheads and 2-tone before finally becoming 'casuals'.

For that reason scooter rallies became more and more important at this stage and were not just about the scooters of course, it was (and still is) very much a way of life. We lived and breathed it and like Jimmy we couldn't understand why anyone would want to leave it and we wanted to stay close to others that felt the same. Our evenings at scooter rallies were spent at pubs or make shift dance venues drinking cheap watery ber and smoking too many cigarettes. As a girl, for me being a Mod was not just about the music, which I loved, but also about the look, the clothes, the hair and being totally colour coordinated from shoes to bags to earrings. Unlike the bitchiness of school girls, Mod girls would want to know how you did you hair, where you got the shoes and bag, and complement you on getting it right. We admired the attention to detail and adored each other's loyalty to the scene.

The music of course was important but it was also the dancing that made these events come alive. If you couldn't dance how could you ever be a 'Face'? Stuff like that was important to me. I learned my steps from watching others and reading vintage books and magazines from the 60s archives. Many of us merged what we knew with the now hugely popular Northern Soul dance scene. Back then we also had the stamina to keep on dancing despite the hazards of beer splashed or talcum powdered floors and thick cigarette smoke that engulfed the room. On one rally we had an old barn that was used for the dancing-as the night drew on the dust from the floor rose and mingled with the smoke so that we could barely see the other side of the room-I emerged at 5am covered in dust and my nose clogged with black soot! In fact one rally I slept in an old barn and was terrified to hear rats crawling about in the middle of the night-luckily a few mods had torches and kept them at bay; certainly it was not a luxury experience.

One rally in the Isle Of Wight I recall was a particularly uncomfortable one for me. At the end of the night my then boyfriend was so drunk he forgot what B&B we had booked and we decamped to a deserted garage with other hapless Mods too drunk to care. While my fellow girlfriends sensibly shared the last few rooms that were available; I had to share one single sleeping bag with said boyfriend on a very cold floor. I was not impressed. The following morning bleary eyed I walked to the shops to buy him more cigarettes and watched while other mod zombies aimlessly walked about with grey dazed expressions, and black eyeliner and mascara smudged on their eyes and cheeks (and that was just the blokes!) It was bloody freezing that morning and all I wanted to do was go home at that point.

Later in the day though, having partially forgiven him, we sought comfort in one of the pubs, which had a mix of Mods, skins, and scooterists we knew. The Landlord was upset that someone had nicked some of his old pictures off the wall 'Those pictures have been up there for 50 bloody years', he bemoaned to which someone at the back shouted 'Well it's about time you bought some bloody new ones then!'"

As the decade progressed, original recordings of classic 60's groups, along with the complimentary Soul selections, were becoming less prominent, resulting in further shifts of musical preferences and the continuing taste for Northern Soul.

Morgan Nolan and scootering friends, Tramore scooter rally, July 1983

Morgan Nolan - "I think it would be fair to say that the type of Soul music played in the early years were mainly Motown and Stax in the early days of the club from Soul standards from Wilson Picket, The Supremes, The Marvelletes, Jackie Wilson The Four Tops, etc.; however this began to change in early 1983. If my memory on this is correct a couple of lads had come back from some event in the UK with a bag full of 7 inch vinyl of what I now know to be Northern Soul. The new style of dancing that they brought in (Northern) caused the first kind of divisions in the scene.

Gradually the Northern thing pushed the type of music I preferred out to the edges. I am what I would describe as a big fan of Power chords/Power Pop type bands. Into this genre I lump my favourites from the 60's such as The Small Faces, The Who, Fleur De Lys. The Creation, Yardbirds, and from later Dr Feelgood, The Jam, The Chords, Purple Hearts, Lambrettas, etc. The Northern craze became the dominant part of the scene in 1984 and increasingly people took to wearing combat trousers and sports T shirts. I remember at that stage feeling disconnected from what was happening in the Club and would say from late 1984 I became a very infrequent visitor and eventually stopped going in early 1985. The Club would continue in this venue for another few years up until 1987 when it moved.

Other musical outlets were based around clubs we would run ourselves. The earliest I remember were the R&B Clubs run first in various hotels and then settling into a residency in The

Ivy Rooms for a year or so. I used to DJ some of the early events and this came about because somebody told the guy organising it that I had some good records. As the organiser never checked the veracity of this statement nor ask me could I operate a set of decks, I made my debut to a packed club of unforgiving stylists. Was I nervous, was I fuck, I can remember getting the speed wrong on a few occasions and leaving dead air on one night for about 30 seconds but surprisingly I got asked back for several gigs. There were other clubs over the years such as the Pow club, Sleepless Nights, Emerald Soul Society etc. and others I can't remember the name of now."

Whilst the introduction of Northern Soul into the Mod clubs was not welcomed by everyone (it had been present in many 79-period Mod's playlists from the outset), the climate was now set for more cosmopolitan soundtracks across the scene at large.

Throughout the decade, live acts were welcomed at Mod rallies. Bands such as Direct Hits, Makin' Time, The Moment, The Threads, The Cynics, Small Hours and The Rage (touted as a sort of Mod supergroup featuring ex-Purple Hearts Jeff Shadbolt, Derwent of Long Tall Shorty and Brett 'Buddy' Ascot of The Chords on drums) and others performed sets to crowds of Mods often more receptive to Mod Rock bands own interpretations of Soul, R&B and beat than Mods in the 60's had been. In Dublin, it was much the same.

Morgan Nolan - "Live music was an integral part of the scene both from local bands and visiting UK bands. The most significant and influential Dublin band were the Blades, whom we consider our answer to The Jam. To this day I still rate them as a class act and a re-union gig in December 2013 reconfirmed for me that these boys really were an excellent band. The next most influential band were the Zen Alligators with drummer Eamonn Carr making a direct 60's connection through his involvement in such Beat groups as Tara Telephone and the legendary Horselips. There were a lot of unsigned bands such as Side 1, The Cherry Brogues, and Instant Party who were great live acts blending original works with favourite covers."

Paul 'Smiler' Anderson - "During 1981 there was definitely a more psychedelic look infiltrating the scene but the big change came a year later. By 1982, kids attending scooter rallies were influenced by what they saw over the weekend. At Morecambe and Isle of Wight in 1982 there was a huge surge towards a more scruffier looking image of army green fatigues, trainers, Doctor Martin boots and T shirts; the Scooter Boy look. This casual dressing down look had a huge impact on the Mod scene, and soon the more casual look became a more easy to manage and common look across future events and rallies. This was also aided by the fact that the many of the bands that had built up the scene, including Secret Affair and The Purple Hearts, split that year."

Not all gatherings of the conflicting youth styles of Mod were always as ambivalent as some. Even into the mid-80's and beyond, the clichéd rivalry between opposing youth cults still existed. Whilst the days of pitch battles between youths on the Kings Road in the 70's and the beach skirmishes of the previous decade were largely diminished and forgotten, displays of violence and intimidation from one youth cult to another still existed from time to time.

Ed Silvester - "Being from the London suburbs we'd always gravitated towards more original Mod events, like those put on by Tony Class. We'd been going to his functions since 1980, firstly at The Walmer Castle, in Peckham. One of the most infamous of Tony Class's scooter rally events was at Brighton in 1981 - at the Royal Artillery Hall. The event started quietly enough, but after a couple of hours all hell broke loose, geezers jumping off balconies – the national press were there that night - and a massive bottle fight erupted between rival Mod gangs. There was glass everywhere, it was like a fight in an old Wild West bar. Luckily, we escaped before the old bill arrived – which wrecked a really good night. Things were getting really nasty, and not what Mod was all about."

CULTURE CLASH - scooterists strike out at a lone motorcyclist

Graham Lentz - "The violence was one aspect I hated. It was the worst thing about being a Mod for me back then. You could never relax while you were out. It was the one thing that made me question if it was worth the bother, especially as I've never been a 'natural' in that respect. I could defend myself if I had to, but that was always a last resort for me."

Ed Horwood - "Much has been written over the years about the 'hatred' between Mods and 'rockers' or 'bikers' as they were then in the 80s, and as the decade rolled on, I was to have a few run ins with bikers myself. At a local level however, I never recall there being any real trouble between the two 'tribes'. Maybe living in a Somerset village (Cheddar) where everyone grew up with each other or their siblings had something to do with that. There were certainly enough members of both groups around to start and keep alive a hatred had there been a desire to do so, but any rivalry between the factions seemed limited to jocular banter and the odd impromptu 'burn up' between newly tuned scooters and old British iron that had by that time seen far better days. That's not to say that the two groups generally mixed openly however."

Meanwhile a younger set of Mods, inspired by their exposure to 'Quadrophenia', which was still playing in cinemas across the country, were ready to set out on their own 80's Mod journey.

Pete Wilky - "I saw 'Quadrophenia' whilst playing truant in 1980 (aged 13) and was a Mod the day after Mod was and is an identity as personal as my personality and a style as sharp as a stanley-knife!"

Andy Bull (Chesterfield Mod) - "The real birth of the Mod rallies for me was Scarborough. Myself, Jud and Tony Smith (the Suedehead Times) headed for the train station only to find it jammed with what seemed to be every Mod from the local area and as the train stopped at Sheffield and other stations the train looked like one of the old 'football specials'... but for Mods.
        The venue at Scarborough (with the Lemon Tree nightclub below) was fantastic as was the turnout. In fact, everything from the new music sounds I was hearing and the clothes just blew me away. We even had a small skirmish with some Geordie football lads and won (for a change). It was everything I'd ever wanted out of the Mod scene and more."

CHAPTER 11

AN EVER CHANGING DECADE

Mod was always concerned with change and moving forward, ever evolving and absorbing new and fresh styles from various forms of culture. As the 80's progressed - and the hip music press concerned themselves elsewhere - the post-revival generation (at least those that remained devoted to all things Mod) ventured even further underground. As a result, various interpretations of Mod regularly appeared across the country. From the capital to the suburbs, few could deny that the 80's were an ever-changing decade to be a Mod!

Brett 'Buddy' Ascott (The Chords) - "The media quickly moved on to Ska, then the Rockabilly revival, and it all came together in '82 in the New Romantic movement – that well and truly killed the name Mod."

Clearly, for those who felt a part of the revival period musician's take on Mod, there was only one remaining band left around to carry the torch.

Ed Horwood - "In 1982, aged 15, me and a schoolmate went to see The Jam on their Solid Bond Tour at the large Shepton Mallet (near Glastonbury) Showground venue. I had never seen so many Mods and scooters in one place before. The venue was a sea of parkas, and before the group came on, I had eyes on me like saucers trying to note every little detail - what people were wearing, what scooter club or band patches they had on their parkas, etc. As for The Jam themselves, well, at the risk of sounding pretentious, if you attended a Jam gig, no description is necessary, if you didn't, then perhaps none will possibly convey the connection and sheer electricity that existed in that building between the band and it's adoring and loyal followers. The Jam were the first band I ever saw live and every band out of the hundreds I've seen in the thirty plus years since has been judged against them – some have come close admittedly, but in my mind, none has ever rivalled them."

Mark Thomson - "The parka got dumped for a 'Mod Mac' (bottle green like Spider's one in Quad) and I was being heavily influenced by Paul Weller's look. In fact, to be honest, I became a 'Weller Clone'. I always had his hairstyle, culminating in the Marriott look, and I used to dress in the gear he wore too. Lonsdale sweatshirts, boxing boots, chisel toe bowling shoes and Levi's denim jackets with the Sheriff's badge and even at one point, a referee's whistle round my neck! And then The Jam went and split up!"

BEAT SURRENDER –THE JAM SPLIT!

Paul Weller Main photo (by Derek D'Souza). Top with Derek 'Del Boy' Shepherd.

The Jam's split signalled the end of an era for many of the punk and Mod revival generation: a period of their lives, of pure teenage excitement and euphoria, idealism - 'Direction, Reaction, Creation' - as the band's early punk years manifesto proclaimed, now contained within a time capsule of belief, gigs, records and empathy for a band that sound tracked their youth. For some, the decision by Weller to remove the band from out of their lives was a step too far. Yet, others managed to digest, take stock and risk a chance on looking to the future and the next project to be fired from the cannon of Paul Weller's soulful repertoire.

Ed Silvester - "When they announced that they were splitting up in 1982, it did feel like the curtain was slowly coming down on something special, and that it was time to move on."

Steve Parlett (Rotherham Mod) - "Having been a huge Jam fan, with Weller being my style icon, the announcement of the Jam's split was devastating."

Ed Horwood - "Like many of my generation, the headlines in the music press that The Jam were to split came as a huge shock to me. The announcement seemed to come out of the blue and appeared to make no sense at all, as the group were at the top of their game. The sense of dismay was compounded because this was not just a pop group coming to an end. If you were a Jam fan you understood that The Jam were always about more than just brilliant music, they were an institution and it's fair to say, in many respects 'mentors' to many second generation Mods. Certainly I (and I wasn't alone) scrutinised (and then tried to imitate) everything they wore; studied the lyrics of every song and the text of every interview, and religiously tracked down and listened to the musical influences that inspired Weller, Foxton and Buckler. To my mind, The Jam, more than any other group of the revival era were the link between the original Mod movement and those of us trying to recreate and redefine Mod in the late 70s/early 80s. The Jam certainly played a part in helping me make sense of the world and assisted me in forming a political viewpoint that I still hold in my late 40s."

Fraser Smith - "When Paul Weller decided to call time on The Jam for me; personally, he went from hero to villain in seconds. I believed at the time Weller's words that he would only split The Jam when he thought they had run the course. It is my opinion having heard the first Style Council single that the direction was the same, which commuted into my teenage brain as a personal insult. It took me until the release of 'Wildwood to learn how to completely forgive him. Childish and arrogant as that was I don't regret the decision. As for the the Style Council I have never acknowledged their existence. With hindsight, of course, it's possible I missed out. But life is a drink and you get drunk when you're young."

Paul 'Smiler'Anderson - "The year ended with the most influential group, The Jam, announcing the decision to disband too. Thousands of fans who had been heavily influenced by the lead singer, Paul Weller, seemed to drop out almost overnight. As 1983 dawned, there didn't seem a great future for the scene as more and more revival bands called it a day and music press hacks avoided commenting in the scene as if were the plague. I don't really have many memories of this year only that more and more Mods were attracted to the 'dark side' of the scooterboy world."

Following the premature demise of The Jam, one of the few remaining 'class of 77' bands to have stuck to their original ideals and intentions, how would Jam fans react towards Weller's next venture when it arrived?

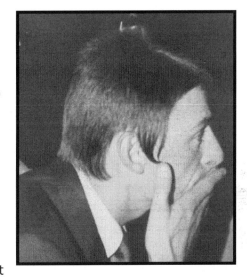

Mark Thomson - "We couldn't believe it and its fair to say our little mob were in a state of shock and mourning. Slowly though, bits and bobs about Weller's new band started to filter through. A new project called The Style Council with 'some bloke out of the Merton Parkas who'd played piano on 'Setting Sons' was being bandied about and we were all desperate for news. No internet or social media back then so info was sought through the music papers and word of mouth.

Soon enough, rumour became reality with the brilliant Speak like a Child video and we were all bang into it. For my part, I took a picture of Paul's new haircut to the hairdressers and came out with a spot on copy of his new French crop. I loved The Jam, but I had been too young when they started, so had played catch-up with their earlier LPs. With the Style Council, I was in at the start and I 'got' what they were all about right away. Different from The Jam with a more soulful edge that was going to take us on a rollercoaster ride before they split six years later. Those early days though, and I would say the first five or six singles, plus of course 'Cafe Bleu', I look back on with nothing but fondness. That (long hot) summer of 1983 we all hung about with pastel coloured jumpers slung over our shoulders and Wayfarer sunglasses on, white jeans, no socks and loafers. Still Mod, but very different to the parka-wearing 'Quadrophenia' boys we'd been before."

Graham Lentz - "By 1982, the whole thing had lost its focal point with The Jam splitting. I followed the Style Council because, again, I got it. I understood what Paul Weller was doing and I loved much of the early output from that band, but by 1984 I had lost interest in music."

Ed Horwood - "In the weeks and months that followed the news of the split I recall reading a series of interviews with Weller where he outlined his reasons for ending The Jam and his aspirations for the future. Unlike most of my peers, I remember being quite excited at the prospect of The Style Council when it was first muted. In many ways I had grown with The Jam and Weller's more overt nod to Soul music with the addition of Hammond Organ and Brass on tracks like 'Town called Malice' and 'Precious' had further encouraged me to dig deeper into Tamla Motown and sixties Soul. My feelings of loss for The Jam were therefore soon tempered by the promise of what Weller could achieve if freed from the restraints of what was essentially a power-pop trio. The Style Council's fusion of Soul, Jazz, funk, good clothes and socialist politics was soon to prove irresistible to me and I rapidly became as big a fan of Weller's new venture as I'd been of The Jam."

TRACEY WILMOT

Riding pillion to her much-cherished scooter rallies, Tracy Wilmot must have turned many a young Mod's head. Defying tribal differences, Tracy's experiences finely illustrate the early 80's scene - a transitional period of Post-revival enthusiasm preceding the division and splintering allegiances of the decade's later years.

Tracey Wilmot - "Back in 1982 a young Mod girl stood back and admired her first scooter-a black Vespa 90 with customized Union Jack side panels. Bleached blonde and bouffant - wearing a little too much black eyeliner and an oversized parka resplendent with badges and tippexed band names Secret Affair, The Chords, The Who, she looks fragile but somehow manages to grab the handlebars and pulls back the stand without falling over. She sits on the polished leather seat in her black ski pants and dolly shoes steadying her balance, as she is ready to take her first ride out. Mum and dad watch from the window-agitated. 'Be careful-don't go too mad!' shouts mum from the window. She looks back and smiles 'yes mum' she groans.

Yeah that was me back then, it's true to say I felt completely terrified and yet totally exhilarated that finally, I owned my very own scooter-now all I had to do was learn how to ride the bloody thing. Back in those days all you needed was a provisional license and not much else-scary to think of that now. Several moments stick in mind in the learning process, in fact I didn't even understand how the gears changed to begin with believing that as long as I stayed in second gear I would go slower-and almost managed to burn the engine out on my first trip out. Another time waiting at the lights the engine stalled and a gang of skinheads jeered at me out of the window of their car. I managed to get the engine started in the nick of time and made my escape.

Once while riding pillion on my boyfriend's Lambretta I forgot he had taken one of the back foot rests off-he reminded me repeatedly to put my right foot forward and after a few beers I managed to forget as we journeyed along-some moments later when we arrived at our destination my shoe was literally on fire the sole totally melted on the exhaust, much to everyone's amusement.

Two months later there I was, riding to the Isle of Wight scooter rally-the only girl in my group of eight other scooterist Mod types of the lesser known Carpenders Park Mods known as The Way Out Scooter Club we were later joined by some of the Hemel Mods on my first long trip to the coast. Although I had been on rallies before I had always been on the back of someone else's scooter so this time it felt strange that finally I had to worry about my own scoot and whether I would get there without it conking out (a common occurrence) My boyfriend made a good job of renovating the engine - and in fact although it was registered as a 90, the engine capacity was

A SOLID BOND OF MODERNISM

BY SIMON FRANKLIN

Simon Franklin - "My journey into Mod began and ended with the Mod revival of '79. When this faded my aspiration to be attached to this subculture declined but my desire to learn more increased. I still dressed with leanings towards Mod but I become more interested and immersed in its history, the music, counter culture and what it really stood for not the media or commerce's need to exploit the younger generation. Paul Weller's journey after The Jam was similar, and it was the style council – its look and music which became my guide above and beyond Modernism.

By the time of the demise of The Jam and the end of the Mod revival movement in 1982, Paul Weller had become disillusioned and had sought to dig deeper into Modernism, its roots and its values. Fast forward over 30 years and Eddie Piller, founder of Acid Jazz, had said 'that Mod was a broad church', Weller's next move after The Jam was to confirm and challenge this but he also alienated a section of his audience who were not prepared to join him for this journey.

Weller had long been a disciple of the Mod movement but with the Style Council, he sought to take it back to its earliest Modernist roots. He had long used Colin MacInnes's book 'Absolute Beginners' as a reference point, this document was the best description of the late 50's London Modernist landscape that existed. It described vividly the conception and birth of the youth subculture, which would later become the more popular and media friendly Mod movement of the mid-60's. Weller started to dress in the Ivy League look of crisp clean chinos, Bass Weejun loafers, red or no socks, Brooks Brothers button-down collar shirts with a bright v necked jumper draped over his shoulders. This differed starkly from the Desert Boot, parka-clad, Fred Perry wearing Mod revivalists. It looked more elitist, a more purist reflection. The Mod revivalist had always been hampered by what was available, which for them, at the time, was searching out second hand shops, buying dead stock of Ben Sherman's or Fred Perry shirts or cheap inferior copies. The original Modernist wore the best that was available, to make them stand out, with the Style Council Weller was reflecting this, but only a few got it.

Next were the sounds. The sharp angular angst of The Jam was gone and in came the more harmonic and rhythmic complexity of Modern Jazz, music of choice for the Modernist. Even fewer got this, especially given the political background of the time but Weller's lyrical prose was overtly political, just not obvious. You just had to think about it.

The Style Council's first album 'Cafe Bleu' replicated all these Modernist influences, the sharp dress, the more European influenced cafe culture (Internationalists) and the Jazz sounds. The sleeve was simple, mimicking the Blue Note albums of the 50's and early 60's. Weller continued in this vain for his next album 'Our Favourite Shop', the sleeve of which was cluttered with influences and pointers. Next, however, he went for a more urban and contemporary Soul Jazz influence (The Cost of Loving), then a blend of R&B, classical and Jazz (Confessions of a Pop Group).

During the later period (1987-1988), Weller had started to explore the trendier club music of garage and Deep House music. It was here that he had thought he had found the missing link between the youth subculture of the present day and that of the 60's. The vinyl-obsessed clubber seeking out the latest imported sounds mirrored that of the Mod finding rare Motown Soul grooves from American sailors. Whilst on a visit to the King's Road Weller watched a queue for the latest

Kicker footwear and mused over its resemblance of a mid-60's Carnaby Street scene finding the latest and most up-to-date fashions.

However, where he [Weller] took his view of Modernism next completely distanced himself from his audience. He recorded an album of Deep House music and called it 'Modernism: a New Decade', it was a leap of faith too far for his record company who dropped the band. It also resulted in the band's last concert at the Royal Albert Hall ending with torn tickets and programmes being thrown on the stage, Weller was no revivalist and he was not about to perform a concert of Jam or Style Council classics. The band disbanded, its followers disappeared and diluted and Modernism stuttered and receded, only to reappear under the guise and as a major influence for Brit Pop. Weller retreated, his next move invigorated by time out and fatherhood was a heavier R&B Soul, late 60's early 70's pastoral sound influenced by bands such as Traffic and artists such as Curtis Mayfield. He regained some of his lost audience, gained new influences and advanced forward on his journey.

For me, Weller's Style Council adventure deepened my journey into Mod. The avenues and boulevards it opened were tangible, my musical tastes widened greatly, my wardrobe got more colourful and diverse. Weller was seeing the whole horizon from the point of hindsight; he was able to combine all the subcultures influences, looks and musical tastes. This is something the Mods of today are able to do probably more resourcefully given our internet age and e-commerce ability – knowledge, clothes and sounds readily available, all the time, any time (anyway, anyhow, anywhere). For me the Style Council are that vital missing link between the Modernists of the late 50's, the Mods of the mid-60's, the Mod revivalists of '79 and today's scene – the broad church. For some it was Weller's less favourable period but this is because he split the revivalist subculture leaders and spokesmen 'The Jam' up. To me The Style Council was as creative as it could have been and definitely definitively shaped what came next."

FROM LE' PARIS WITH STEVE PARLETT
A MOD STYLIST MEMOIR

The legend of The Jam was to continue indefinitely, many fans never truly forgiving Weller's brave and controversial decision to split the band, and the issue generates division to this day. However, for some ardent Jam fans, a future still lay ahead still following the ex-leader of The Jam and a new vision of Mod and further possibilities. Formed almost in parallel with the demise of his previous band, Weller's new musical venture, The Style Council swapped Rickenbacker guitars and anthemic three-minute classic 'Jam sound' singles for the Hammond organ of ex-Merton Parka, Mick Talbot and a variety of eclectic musical influences along with a distinctly European cosmopolitan keen eye on fashion and influences. Northern Mod, Steve Parlett is suitably adept at describing this transitional and relevant Mod period when the religion of Mod returned to rediscover some of its roots and diversity.

Steve Parlett - "My Mod life began around the age of 11 in '79 when a friend in Junior School introduced to the early 2-tone singles. The Jam and Secret Affair. I kicked off with the little mode/rude boy uniform of Fred Perry shirts, tonic and coloured Sta-Prest, white socks, loafers and Harrington's. It was a sharp, bold and cool look that me and many other boys my age fell in love with. For many others it was a fashion thing and they soon moved on to Baggy pegs and buckled boots with strange Flock of Seagulls haircuts, but I was mesmerised and it has formed the basis of my whole ethos of dressing and music ever since.

Paul Weller himself was a true style icon to me, clearly influenced by the 60s Mods such as the Small Faces and the Who, and in fact many of my looks are influenced by him. The Style Council in particular was a kaleidoscope of sounds and looks that I draw on to this day.

The old 'Fire and Skill' had morphed into a more Soulful sound with the addition of the horn section and a Tamla beat, so I hoped amongst hope that the next venture would go in right direction. Hearing that Merton Mick had been brought to the party was another good sign but I was still had trepidations before I first heard 'Speak like a Child'. I was so relieved, he looked the part, the sound was great, and he seemed finally to be at ease and having more fun!

The next few years were a whirl of new sounds and experimentation, some joyfully successful, others testing the patience of a saint ('Strength of Your Nature' took some getting used to I can tell you). For me it was taking the modernist ethic forward, something those of my brethren thought was sacrilege (anything after 67 never happened etc.). Having read Absolute Beginners many years before, the whole late 50s pre-Mod world coupled with the European style influences (beautiful shoes, knitwear and tailoring) were Mod yet bang up to date in the 80s not buried in the 60s. Seeing him experiment with overcoats, scarves, cardigans was another step away from the 'three button, 5 inch vents suit' look we had all stuck so religiously to. I do confess I lost interest at the Cost of a Loving album, which felt a bit tired and formulaic, but the 'Confessions' album reignited our love of the Style Council, and so while we (me and Lee Radforth – Rad) were discovering lots of great new soul and Jazz bands like Tommy Chase, James Taylor Quartet in and around Manchester (where I was at University) we held firm to our TSC roots.

The idea of a trip to Paris to recreate the sleeve artwork for the A Paris EP no doubt formed over several beers in either Sheffield or Manchester. I had been at university in Salford for around a year, and while I was not in tons of debt like some of my friends, I did not have lots of money to splash around. I was making the most of the last few suits I had had tailored before I went to University and relying on a beautiful bespoke navy blazer, because that could form the basis of many a TSC inspired look. Lee meanwhile was doing really well in Sales at BT, so was a bit more flush.

We decided to make the trip, but to do it as cheaply as possible – which meant a coach and ferry trip. We booked some pretty cheap accommodation (a bit isolated and run-down) but we were in heaven. Clearly we were aiming for the area around the Eiffel Tower to try to imitate the loafer and tower shots, but we also decided to place ourselves at various landmarks around the

City, sometimes only a small part in a wider landscape shot. The Eiffel tower shots are brilliant, and I have to take my hat off to Lee for capturing my loafers with the Tower in the background perfectly. I also love the one he took of me sitting on the steps. We visited the Tower, Montmartre, Les Jardins de Luxembourg, L'Eglise de Sainte Eustache and many others – I particularly remembering us being outside Notre Dame church, eating French cheese and baguette with a rough bottle of red wine on a bench, and being joined by a proper Frenchman, in full raincoat/beret combo, who had come to feed the birds – he was only missing the string of garlic around his neck!

The young Soul stylists, Steve Parlett and Lee Radforth

Taking regular breaks in rue-side cafes and bars, we fell in love with the place. I am ashamed to this day to say that while I can read and speak French (A level grade A no less), I was too shy to do so, whereas Lee was more than happy to bowl straight in with his rudimentary command of the language, but it has to be said the locals loved him for it.

It was a coming of age for us I think, moving from teenagers to adults (I was about to hit 20) and one I remember very fondly.

Whilst Weller's Style Council meetings and well-crafted interpretation of Modernism would ultimately lose much of its initial appeal and optimistic creativity, it would not be the final chapter for Weller and much of his fan base's Mod journeys. Elements of Style Council fans continued to push forward in their musical tastes, the Jazz/Soul sounds of Working Week being popular for some; ultimately many would cross musical paths again with Weller a decade later. Others of Mod persuasion shifted into scooterist camps of relative, but not inclusive, Mod styles.

Morgan Nolan - "When The Jam split it was a seismic event for me and looking back as it was then I started to drift away from the mainstream Mod scene. My friends and I frequented Mod events in the City less and less. We were not as interested in the Soul obsessions of some of our peers and started to broaden our musical interests. The Style Council were central to this as was Weller's endorsement of bands that were not identifiably Mod but who could really put out decent records, such as the Housemartins, The Blow Monkeys, The Colourfield, etc. These musical tastes and the influence that these bands had on our style would carry me through the remainder of the decade. However even Weller wasn't doing it for me by 1988 and whilst I was lukewarm on the 'Cost of Loving' album I couldn't get into 'Confessions of a Pop Group'. Musically things didn't pick up until Weller returned as a solo artist in the early 1990s."

Mark Thomson - "Musically we were heavily into Northern Soul by this point, and we were snapping up 7 inch singles of this genre by the dozen. I remember tunes on the 'Inferno' and 'Kent' labels being big faves back then. I also diversified further with bands like the Redskins and Everything but the Girl as the 80s rolled on.

As our sixteenth birthdays came around, we started getting scooters, mostly Vespa's, and usually chromed up. I had a little dark blue Vespa PK50 before getting a PX125 later on. This opened up a completely new scene as scooter rallies were attended and new people were met. Some of our boys got into the Scooter Boy style with army trousers and green flight jackets covered in rally patches being the order of the day."

Much like the original Mods of the 60's and the 70's, the 80's Mod was committed to the cult of the scooter. Often garnering expert knowledge - especially within the ranks of the many scooter clubs of the period - original model Lambrettas' and Vespa's' were highly sought after, despite the costs of individual parts and the hours required to fix the ongoing technical problems that appeared with this preferred method of Mod transport. In the spirit of the scene's flair for improvising and catering to one's requirements, Mods and the emerging scooter boys took it upon themselves to organize scooter spares parts meetings to help solve this demand.

Ed Horwood - "Looking back, it's perhaps no surprise that a lot of scooter-riding lads and lasses from the more outlying areas of the UK were to ditch the Mod thing over the coming years for the far more 'practical' scooterist lifestyle, whilst most of the big cities managed to maintain a diminishing yet stylish and increasingly more authentically 60's influenced Mod scene."

In little over two years, certainly by 1982 and into the following year, the Mod scene had splintered into various - often rival - factions: the most notable offshoot of Mod was the shift from the classic smart Mod style to the much more casual and less-clothes conscious scooterist scene's dressed down focus.

Ed Silvester - "By 1983 Mods had evolved and split into many different branches, hipsters, scooter boys and casuals. Most Mod bands had been forgotten by the music press, and Mod had gone back to being an underground street culture. As the original revival Mods got older, they didn't want to ditch their scooters, so every year would still make the effort to attend the odd scooter rally. A love of the music and the camaraderie had not disappeared. No longer did we bother to ride to a resort wearing a tonic suit, but now we would don more practical army greens and Dr Marten boots. This was due partly to a need for better protection, but mostly to ape the Northern scooter boy look.

A journey to the Isle of Wight would take hours, and the English weather always seemed to be inclement. I can remember one scooter run to the Isle of Wight when one morning I'd opened the zip on our tent, to reveal two inches of water outside – being totally inebriated, I hadn't heard the thunderstorm during the night, it had become messy and dirty, and far removed from our original Mod revival roots. For a while, we would avidly collect the scooter rally patches that were very popular, and the excitement when sewing them onto our bomber or combat jackets. By the end of 1984, almost all of the original Mod revival bands had long since broken up, and we'd become more interested in listening to Northern Soul, with slower more R&B style records becoming popular. Although, a few Mod inspired bands had sprung up, for example The Prisoners and Makin' Time. Both bands should have been huge, but had missed the boat by a couple of years, which was a shame, as they were very good – they were short lived, but their influence still resonates to this day. Although our musical tastes had changed by the later part of the 1980's, we had still kept and rode our scooters, occasionally going on the odd scooter run."

Morgan Nolan - "Scooter runs would inevitably include the obligatory Bank Holiday trip to a sea side town. Our favourite site was Tramore in the sunny South East county of Waterford. The British tabloid press reportage of the violence in English coastal towns sent our own press into a frenzy about the June and August Bank Holiday trips of 1983. The press coverage before the runs practically called for martial law to be introduced and when the weekends passed of relatively peacefully the media could hardly contain its disappointment. During the weekends the frenzy that the media generated could be felt in the air and it was obvious that a lot of holidaymakers had stayed away due to the fear of violence. But apart from a few isolated incidents it was relatively quiet and looking back I am quite proud of this. I do remember one incident were a white Hiace van came cruising onto the part of the beach where a group of us had decided to kip and was sent quickly on its way under a hail of missiles. I have spent many years wondering were the occupants of that van a gang out looking for trouble or some unfortunate lovers looking for some privacy."

 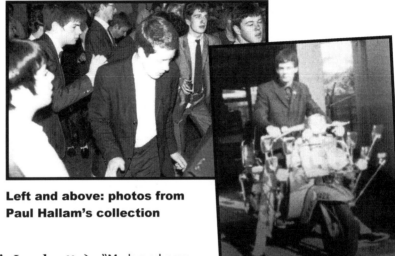

Left and above: photos from Paul Hallam's collection

Ed Horwood (right on his Lambretta) - "My brand new red Vespa 50 Special was delivered on the evening of my 16th birthday in May 1983. I remember the sense of excitement building for months, weeks, days then hours beforehand. For some reason I also remember the Troggs performing and being interviewed on the TV just prior to the local Vespa dealer's pickup arriving with my first set of powered wheels. The Vespa had been ordered up a month beforehand, my savings paying the deposit, insurance, road tax and also providing a Stadium open face lid and gloves. My mum, bless her, had signed the H.P. papers on condition that I paid her back weekly from my wages and that I agreed to complete some training. At that point, the only extras on the scooter were an indicator kit and two handlebar mounted mirrors.

Living in a small Somerset village may sound idyllic to adult ears. To a 16-year-old Mod with his own wheels though, the action was most definitely to be found further afield, especially ten miles away at the seaside town of Weston Super Mare with its long association with scooters and Mods stretching back to the 50s and 60s. Weston boasted a Vespa dealer, several shops selling 'Mod' clobber (including several old gents outfitters with some original 1960s stock left in their store rooms) and plenty of charity shops where Brutus, Jaytex, Ben Sherman's shirts, tootal scarves, suede cardies, etc. could thankfully still be picked up really cheaply. There were also a handful of record shops including the long since demolished Arcade Records ('the' place to go for the latest soul re-issues), a regular Soul/Mod night (in the skittle alley at The Long John Silver Pub at Sand Bay), several Mod/scooterist friendly cafes (most prominent in my mind being the exotically named Monte Carlo and Casablanca) and a large Mod/scooterist fraternity.

The town had two large scooter clubs and it was the newer of these (the Roundel Runners) that I joined, along with most of the lads from my village after being invited to one of their meetings by one of the local 'faces'. The Roundels got their name because initially meetings were held in the social club on the RAF Locking base where the club's 'number one' was posted. The 'Mod' association to the roundel emblem was secondary, not least because by that time, most of its members were starting to move away from the Mod thing and had become 'scooter boys/girls'. However, I recall the scooterist style then as still being quite cool and sharp. The psychobilly trend was still a year or so away from being 'mainstream' at that point. West country scooterists back then were mostly clothed in Ben Sherman's, denim jackets, well-fitting olive green combats, Levis, boxing boots, DMs, parkas and sheepskins – a very skinhead based look, but all items also worn by many Mods of the time as daywear. In many cases, the differences between whether someone considered themselves a Mod or a scooterboy/girl boiled down to whether they preferred chrome accessories on their scooter or instead went for a snazzy paint job and tuned engine; whether they wore 'denim and olive greens or a suit and tie on a Saturday night.

Unless I could bag a lift in a car from one of the older or wealthier lads or lasses, then like many country-based Mods of the time, I had to travel a good few miles on a scooter to access the main centres of 'the scene'. Bus services were crap even back then, and, thanks to Dr Beeching, little was left of any rail services outside of the cities and bigger towns. Most of us dreamed of owning a car one day (as well as a scooter of course), but for most of us, cars were still an impossible dream, with even the driving lessons and insurance etc. being way beyond what we could afford, let alone the cost of the vehicle itself. As a result, in all but the best summer weather many scooter-riding West Country Mods, myself included, would be clad in cheap waterproofs and what could be termed 'scooterboy/girl gear' as a real practicality to protect our smarter gear underneath. Once at our destination, these outer layers would be shed, revealing the smarter clothes underneath and hair would be combed and tidied, etc. I often envied my city/big town-based counterparts in this respect; after all, if it rained in Bristol, London, Birmingham etc., you could always get a train or bus, leave the scooter at home and arrive immaculate.

In the autumn of 1983, I started a four-year apprenticeship as a plumber and gas fitter, working with my Father. No clean, well paid office job for me. Instead, it was a five and a half day week - Monday – Thursday 'on the tools', day release at Tech College on the Friday and then work again Saturday morning. A big bonus of entering the building trade in the early 80s was that a large percentage of the brickies, sparks, chippies, etc. that I worked alongside had been Mods, skins, suedes, etc. within relatively recent memory and what's more, they were only too happy to reminisce in great detail concerning their clothes, music, scooters etc. to a fresh faced and enthusiastic young 'un like me.

Not long after I started work I even got my first suit – a black wool number with white pin stripe. It started as a 'two button hand me down' that my old man had got married in in the early 60s, and which had hardly been worn since. At the cost of £40 saved up from several weeks' wages, the original tailor who had made the suit worked wonders, transforming it into a three button; tailored article that looked like it could have been made for me personally. It may have been second hand, but it looked the biz and totally outshone the cheap Carnaby Street mail order efforts worn by a lot of my mates.

I was only destined to spend a year with the 'Roundels'. By my 17th birthday in mid-84, the club had pinned its colours very much to the scooterboy/girl wall, along with every other scooter club in the South West. At no point was I made to feel unwelcome at the club, I just found myself increasingly at odds with what the mainstream scooter scene was now becoming as I in turn, become more of a confirmed Mod. And, I wasn't alone. Before too long, I had joined with other Mods in the area and, following what seemed to be a national trend (if the editorials in the newly formed Phoenix List Mod newsletter were to be believed) had helped create a local 'Mod society'. Before I left the club however, I had experienced much of the excitement of what I then perceived to be the 'Mod lifestyle'. I had attended my first scooter rally (Weston Super Mare '83) where I had been amongst the biggest amount of scooters and their riders that I'd ever seen in my young life; I had witnessed a large gang of scooterists and Mods take retribution on a car and its owner who had hospitalised two of our members by deliberately running them and their scooters off the road; I had been kicked off my scooter by a gang of bikers at the Torquay National Scooter Rally in early '84; I'd found myself surrounded by right wing skins with broken bottles intent on blood after they had gate-crashed a Mod house party and for reasons I still can't explain, had been able to talk my way out of it without sustaining so much as a scratch, I'd made some great mates and was going steady with a smart and very pretty Mod girl. As my 17th birthday dawned, I felt that I had now served my 'apprenticeship' as a Mod and I had a feeling that the best was yet to come.

Ed (in Trenchcoat) with West Country Mod friends, November 1984 at a London National Mod meeting

My 17th birthday was immaculate. It was a glorious summer day of the kind that is seemingly very rare these days. I was up very early that morning. I had not been able to sleep much the night before. I was going to spend the day in Bristol with my girlfriend ice skating and shopping. I had my suit, a nice button down shirt pressed ready, shoes shined, and a reasonable amount of money saved up in readiness for the HMV store in the city centre. However, exciting as the prospect of spending time with my girl was, it really couldn't compare to the excitement of riding the recently acquired replacement for my Vespa 50.

A week previously, I had acquired a three-year-old Vespa P150X via a loan from my old man. As I pushed it out of the garage and then surveyed this big Vespa sat on the drive of our modest semi that morning, the scooter's standard bright red paint contrasted by a metallic silver horn cast and side panels and with its 150cc engine up jetted and fitted with a Fresco exhaust, I couldn't stop smiling from ear to ear. I already had the measure of just how fast it could go, having ridden it back home ten miles the night I'd bought it. Now, with a couple of hours to spare before me and my girl met to catch the Bristol bus, I excitedly started the PX up, eased it off the stand, selected first, released the clutch and rode off to complete a fast blast of a good few miles, my mind full of all the places my first 'proper' scooter was now going to take me.

The second half of 1984 was a real buzz. During that year, I did so much, including several National Scooter and 'Phoenix Society' Mod rallies, the National Mod Meeting in London and a large number of smaller Mod dos. A couple of events stick out vividly in my mind; Bournemouth Mod rally – which I went to as a passenger in a mate's down at heal Austin Maxi, using the car to kip in on the official rally campsite (all the seats folded flat on a Maxi making them really practical to sleep in).

That weekend we seemed fated to come into contact with boneheads as the rally campsite got bombarded with bricks and bottles by a large group of them who'd arrived in the town especially to cause trouble with us. Thankfully, nothing seemed to come of this and they were soon chased off by a far larger number of angry Mods. The highlight of that weekend had to be the Alljacks, a blistering R&B and Soul act that we're by then making a name for themselves on the scene and

who were included on the '5-4-3-2-1 Go!' Countdown Records compilation a year later.

The August Bank Holiday Scooter Rally to the Isle of Wight. A small group of us had ridden down to Bournemouth on the Friday for a pre-arranged meet up with a club called the Wessex Stylists (with whom one of our number had made some contacts with) at the pub where they held their meetings. We'd then kipped at various people's houses and had set off early Saturday morning as a big group for the ferry port. Once there, we were treated to a stern talk by a couple of plain-clothes coppers before we embarked. We were told to 'chuck all of our weapons and drugs over the side of the ferry if we knew what was good for us' as there would be a 'big police reception committee waiting' on the island. I remember there being puzzled looks and muffled laughter all around at this and more than one person suggested that they'd got us confused with the Hell's Angels.

As the ferry approached it's docking point on the island, the air was split by the sound, exhaust smoke and smell of multiple two strokes being impatiently revved by their owners. As the ramp went down, and the ship disgorged us, it's buzzing contents, I mentally prepared myself to meet the promised masses of police readying themselves that very moment to check our documentation, frisk us and to generally make our stay uncomfortable. As it transpired, the 'reception committee' was two motorcycle cops who, after bringing the column of scooters to a halt, informed everyone that we were now going to be led in convoy with them leading, to the official rally campsite. Clearly, it had not entered the minds of these officers that people might also be staying at B&Bs and other campsites all over the island...

That weekend Edwin Starr was headlining on the rally site stage. As we sat around on the site awaiting Edwin's performance, one of my mates turned around to see Edwin approaching us. He was then asked by Edwin if he'd give him a lift to the stage on his Vespa, which naturally, he duly did and subsequently never let us forget! Of course, whilst we were immersed in our youthful pleasures that weekend, elsewhere in the country, the Tories ideological war on the working class and its biggest and most well organised union, the NUM was in full flow. It was sobering, yet reassuring therefore, to find a stall on the rally site populated by the Labour Party Young Socialists who were collecting for the miners. I (like many others I witnessed), donated as much as I could comfortably spare. Perhaps my strongest memory of that weekend though, is of our group riding along a coast road without crash helmets in a light mist to catch the early morning ferry back to the mainland.

Musically, 1984 was a really exciting time for me. Influenced in no small way by the direction Paul Weller was steering the Style Council, guided by the music features of the hipper 'Modzines' and caught in the slipstream produced by the increasing number of people making a determined effort to re-discover and document the 'roots' of the original Mod scene, I found myself listening to an incredibly broad span of music. Alongside the sounds of the first wave revival bands, and the many new 'Mod' bands starting to emerge at that time, I was digging even deeper into the British Beat and US Garage bands of the 60s, ever more obscure Soul, R&B and Ska and discovering the joys of Modern Jazz from both the 60s and via contemporary UK acts. I was lucky that several mates had become serious vinyl addicts and DJs. They would gladly make me up regular C90 tapes of their latest finds. Other friends with London connections would get tapes in the post of some of the 'Mod' radio shows that existed at the time on the small independent stations there and run me off copies."

Tricia Hickling (Nottingham Mod) - "Whilst friends at school were busy reading the 2nd Diary of Adrian Mole, I was busy reading the play - A Taste Of Honey and the book - A Clockwork Orange. Already researching back to 60s and 70s publications and media - pretty hardcore for a 13-year-old girl. This combined with listening to my parents records, such as the Stones and the Kinks only meant one thing really - I was bound to be a Mod girl. Not a Modette as many were referred to; I hated the term as much as those associated with it! I hung around with the Nottingham Mods and being too young to attend rallies or other events, I hooked up with a group of younger ones in which we all enjoyed buying records and clothes plus talking music and film. Some of us have continued to do this to the present day and along the way I have produced and sold a popular fanzine/modzine, put on our own nights plus supported those of others."

For Nottinghamshire Mod, Andrew Harris, Mod had become a near-solitary lifestyle, until 1984.

Andrew Harris - "I was left alone, as the only Mod at school. I then started backtracking and delved far deeper into the 1960s. I went on to join a work preparation course in 1984 at a College in Nottingham and almost instantly became part of a Mod/scooter gang. They were Just friends really, having lots of laughs and involved in many incidents, which are beyond the scope of this brief overview. This also linked in with an existing and far bigger Mod scene in Nottingham, of which by 1987 (bar a handful of us who still exist today) had left the Mod scene to become somewhat ordinary."

Despite the relatively underground profile of Mod during the mid-80's, the scene was still accessible. Paul Boddy from Devon experienced his rally initiation in 1986, the first of countless others to come over the years.

(Photo) Paul Boddy and friends Dean Orton and Tappy off to The Lowestoft Bank Holiday Mod rally 1988 from Devon

Paul Boddy - "Brighton 1986 was my first Mod rally aged sweet 16. About 15 of us from Exeter and Crediton went down on the train and another load went on scooters. Most of us didn't have enough money for a B&B so we slept in a disabled toilet with the hand dryer stuck on to keep us warm (not very Mod). I loved every minute of the rally, so many scooters all Modded up and they looked so cool. So a scooter covered in lights and mirrors was the next thing I wanted, even if it was only a 50cc! I heard there was loads of fighting with skinheads and casuals but we stayed away from all that, the do's were packed and I met the drummer from Making' Time ... brilliant. I made so many friends who I still know today. There was also some fighting between Mods and other Mods in the do, which I didn't understand? I was really proud to be a young 16-year Mod back then and I was loving every minute of it."

Dave Bamford - "I adopted the Mod way of life and by 1985 I was attending the Phoenix Mod Rallies with the rest of the Nottingham crowd. The rallies were great in that they brought together hundreds of like-minded kids together for various weekends of music, dancing, mod bands and drinking. Some of the best rallies were Scarborough, Blackpool, Shanklin and Lowestoft. Live bands such as The Rage, Makin Time, The Moment and The Threads and discos and all-nighters with over a thousand smartly dressed Mods dancing till the early hours to the sounds of 'Wade in the Water' - Little Sonny, 'Bert's Apple Crumble' - The Quik, 'So far away' - Hank Jacobs and 'The Snake' by Maximillion to name a few."

Ed Horwood - "In 1985, I acquired my first Lambretta - a silver 1981 registered Spanish built Serveta LI 150 Special. The scooter had been bought new by one of the older Mods I had looked up to whilst still at school. As far as I was concerned, this scooter was the dogs! Its original owner had spent a fortune fitting front and rear crash bars, an ironing board backrest, front carrier and rear carrier and combined spare wheel holder. The scooter was still in excellent condition with only 6,000 on the clock - I just had to have it and my Vespa and some cash was duly traded against it. There was one fly in the ointment however. Knowing that I was still a provisional licence holder, the dealer had insisted on fitting a 125cc conversion kit to make the sale of the scooter completely legal. This meant a top wack of around 50mph, much slower than my Vespa, but I was prepared to compromise on speed in return for riding (as I saw it then) a real head turning Mod scooter.

Within a few months, I had bought up some of the many second hand mirrors, chrome stems and spotlights lying redundant in the garages of the local scooter lads and bolted them on. At its peak, the Serveta had eight spotlights and twelve mirrors fitted. However, none of my mirrors and stems protruded more than a foot from each side of the machine, which at the time was the maximum legally acceptable protrusion (or so the coppers used to tell us).

1985 was also the year that I started going to the Gloucester Mod Alldayers. These were accessed by train from Weston Super Mare - Gloucester being around 50 miles away from me. They were held at a black working man's club - the Jamaica Club in one of the more down at heel areas of the city. Back then, the idea that a group of smartly dressed lads and lasses would want to be taken to this venue would always confuse the taxi drivers at Gloucester station. I vividly recall on one occasion, a taxi driver only agreeing to take a group of us there on the proviso that he dropped us off a few hundred yards away from the venue as he was convinced there would be trouble. Nothing however could be further from the truth, as sharp young white kids danced away to their black musical heroes, sometimes, and especially when Ska was being played, we were joined by some of the older Jamaican fellas in the member's bar who'd break off their game of dominos to come show us how it was done. It was at these all-dayers that I became familiar with some of the top 'original' Mod sounds – tracks such as Billy Stewart's 'Secret Love', 'The Snake' by Maximillian, 'House of Bamboo' – Earl Grant, 'Bert's Apple Crumble' - The Quik, 'Blue Moon' – Bobby Bland and 'Smokey Joe's La La' by Rene Googie were all favourites with the well-dressed crowd there, along with the many Latin soul tracks that were all the rage on the scene that year."

The years 83 - 88 were awash with the funk and Soul that had partially grown from the soundtrack of Mod's original musical diet. Not all 80's Mods remained devoted to the post-revival sounds (or the classics of the 60's either!); many Modernist-enthused Soulsters keenly embraced the contemporary offerings of The James Taylor Quartet, Working Week, Blue-Ox Babes and selections of underground funk and Soul releases, incorporating continental fashion styles along the way. Not that greatly removed from this Mod aesthetic were the Casuals!

IT'S A CASUAL WORLD BY STUART DEABILL

Casuals had been around since the previous decade: The very first UK-spawned youth cult that was born with no musical scene to inspire it. True, they shared a love of music that many contemporary Mods would also appreciate, namely modern Soul, Funk and the new European Mod style of Weller's Style Council. But this cult came together on the football terraces, quickly spreading across the country on team's away days. It's fashion did not begin with some collective of musicians own preference of clothes, far from it. Yet, despite the separate ideologies and often violent opposition towards Mods and the other youth scenes of the time, the very ethos of the Casual shared its basic fundamental obsessional love of clothes with the Mod.

Stuart Deabill - "Casual – a look, a phrase, a different meaning to the individual, a code to forwardly project as setting yourself apart? Sound familiar?

Northolt Station Photo Booth Summer 83 and 'Sounds' music weekly front cover of Casuals The Accent

The link with Mod is not enough for me though. There's more to Casual than just a clothes link to a certain outlook. I certainly thought that back in 82 when I bought my first Pringle Jumper and Sergio Tacchini Track Suit and looked as far removed from a Mod Revival bod as I did a spaceman. The dress code of a golf course or tennis court had transcended to the look of urgent, street wise kids of London/Liverpool/Portsmouth etc. at different times of the late 70's / early 80's. The seats and terraces of decaying football grounds was the catwalk, not music based venues, as most other genre's cults seemed to be.

We wore it bold, we swaggered with a mix of youth arrogance and knowing that when you bowled across the country into alien towns that you had something that others envied or plainly just didn't get. Supporting Chelsea in the early 80's the supporters had an immense siege mentality as the team were so fucking poor on the pitch, but the exact opposite on the terraces. Not that I was really one for fighting but was none the less caught up in the mood of the heavy times.

As I left school in summer 1982 and started the dreaded Youth Opportunity Scheme in the September of that year and pulling the odd stroke, the dough I was suddenly receiving enabled me to start updating the wardrobe twice a month. Suddenly the names of Fila, Lois and Diadora pushed aside the MA1 Jacket, Levi Red Tags and Hush Puppies. The pride of wearing Lyle and Scott and Adidas Hawaii became unbelievably important. I was obsessed with my hair being the right length so I could do the flick as I walked down my road to impress on the locals that this is now! Northolt Golf Club was robbed weekly to feed the local's obsession as was the Sports shops of Greenford, Ealing and most famously Lilywhites in Piccadilly Circus. On a Saturday there would be teams of kids all waiting their chance to score some quality sportswear.

My clothing icons stopped being the likes of Terry Hall and Paul Weller but Bjorn Borg and John McEnroe, the racquet champions of the day. (Not Connors though, never rated the Cerruti gear he used to play in) My pals though were fully-fledged Soul boys, which to me was more the direct link to Casual. The other cities have all got their own take which but down south the roots of what became Casual was born out of West Indian Sticksmen - the Gabbici Cardigan, The Farah strides , the slip on croc Bally or Gucci shoes which spread to the white boys busting moves in the funk and Soul clubs of the capital .

Mods to Casuals, Alan Smith and John Silvester, 1984 and (below), Ed and John Silvester

The music of the time for me, it was still mainly The Jam until the end, but also Haircut 100 took pride of place next to UB40 next to I Level next to New Order next to Wham next to Jo Boxers next to David Joseph next to Everything But The Girl ... Then the beauty of The Style Council - Weller's direct about turn from the restrictions of the [Jam] Army to the civilian life of European panache! The first three singles - All diverse, all with contrary B-sides, all beautifully constructed and on to the first tour - Council Meetings. The old guard of Jam fans not feeling the change, the mood almost sombre sitting in the pubs around Tottenham Court Road before the first of two nights at The Dominion Theatre. Whilst I grabbed a cheeky half buzzing for the nights, proceedings I felt the full look of disgust dressed in a Fila Match day and frayed Light Blue Lois Jeans. As one particularly gruff large remedial muttered and pointed south towards Trafalgar Square - 'Wimbledon's that way you cunt'.

But to call the TSC a casual band would be a bit much but they did have all the elements that most of us on the outer reaches of West London dug, with its Jazz/Soul/Bossa Nova/Pop Technicolor. So to the question, was Casual a direct link from Modernism? Of course, there's elements of that, but I think it's just another youth cult that makes British street culture so unique and special. The working class quest to stand apart from the humdrum, the authoritarians, the daily grind and to do the exact opposite of what you was expected to be."

STEWART HARDMAN'S PHOENIX RALLY INITIATION

Stewart leading mid-80's Mods, North Bay Scarborough

CLASS presents
on the
SCARBOROUGH MOD RALLY '85
A SIXTIES EVENING FEATURING
YEH YEH & THE WAY
+ 60's DISCO featuring Tony Class, Shirley & Dom
at
THE SALISBURY HOTEL BALLROOM
Huntriss Row
on Saturday, 15th June, 1985
6 p.m. till 2 a.m.
Smart Dress Absolutely Essential
ADMISSION BY THIS TICKET ONLY

Stewart Hardman - "By 1986 a new Mod revival was just starting to take shape in the UK and I was on my way to my first 'Official' rally. The destination was the Phoenix rally (the then organisers), to Scarborough, alas not via scooter or car but by train. After a train change at York, the last leg of the journey, was met by a train about two thirds full of Mods travelling to the rally. The carriages were a sea of green parkas, it really was kind of mind blowing and added that extra nerve tingle of excitement heading for that unknown as yet proper rally feel. After eventually finding a bed and breakfast that was willing to take a group of five blokes (we were all from the same village and had travelled up together), it was off to the dinnertime do. Seeing sharp dressed Mods all over the place that day on the way to, and inside the venue was fantastic, the locals and the holidaymakers not really knowing what to do or think, mainly staring at us all the time.

I can now remember all the scooter cruises down the seafront, the sun glinting off all the chrome of the lights and mirrors, the whippy aerials. Also trying to get to the various seaside resorts before everyone else, so you could checkout the charity shops or the records shops before all the others, to be the one to find that mega rare record for next to nothing, or some fantastic 1960's shirt or top, maybe still in its original wrapping, so you could maybe wear it for that weekend, or to finish off an outfit that you have planned. A button-down high collared shirt to go with that new suit, or a pair of cufflinks, anything like that.

Spending a few hours on a Sunday morning maybe before or after breakfast making sure the scooters were all nice and clean ready for the scooter cruise later that day, the buzz riding down the main road and seeing people stop and stare as you all drove past, I realised that 'this is the life, this is our life'."

SMILER'S 80'S MOD RALLIES

Isle of Wight 1988

Paul 'Smiler'Anderson oozes Mod. He lives and breathes the whole ideal of being a Mod. First succumbing to the enigma of Mod in 1979, whilst also keeping a keen ear to the top drawers of punk, Paul immersed himself in the lifestyle of Mod, taking in the clubs, gigs and perhaps most avidly the classic Mod rally. Ironically, by the mid-80's, the sight of Casuals, as was so with many Mods of the period, did not represent anything Mod-friendly. The shadows of previous times' youth cult rivalry unfortunately still prevailed.

Paul 'Smiler' Anderson - "As I managed to raise myself on my arms from the cold tarmac I was aware of the blue Ford Capri wheel spinning away. I staggered to my feet to survey the scene – my scooter in a tangled heap and chrome debris scattered around. Only hours earlier I'd spent the afternoon cleaning and polishing the very same machine, preparing it for the following day's journey. I'd not reckoned on meeting the dreaded enemy of Casuals just a few hundred yards from my journey end. Welcome to tribal Britain 1984!

The day after this incident, I rode my dented chariot (with matching dented pride) to my mate's house for him to look at. Sadly my mate Martin shook his head and informed me that my forks were bent and the scooter was unsafe to ride. Deep down I'd known all along but the thought of attending the first ever National Mod meeting as a pillion truly gutted me. My 1966 Vespa Sprint would have to wait until another day for its moment of glory.

1984 had been a great year for the Mod scene up until that moment. It seemed as if a mini revival was taking place, which I welcomed with open arms. Many of the people I'd started out with had deserted Mod sensibility for combat trousers, stupid haircuts and cut-down scooters. I'd remained loyal to the cause, in fact I felt more drawn into Mod than ever before. I'd started to frequent London clubs instead of just pissing it up around Reading and attending local Northern Soul nights that I just couldn't seem to relate to. Bands were still very prominent such as The Scene, Long Tall Shorty, Small World, The Moment, Mark Le Gallez and The Risk, Fast Eddie and The Truth.

Fanzines spread the word, and kept you informed of what was going on in other parts of the country. Blimey, Sounds magazine even did a feature on Mod '84 in an edition at the end of July. The biggest change though that took place during that year was that the scooter rallies were divided since the first time since the revival.

There was definitely a feeling of difference between many Scooter boys and Mods although of course there were people who were scooterists who didn't feel aligned to either party. The Phoenix Society were a London based organisation that included Mark Johnson, Tony Class and Eddie Piller who set out to promote Mod orientated events throughout the country. Helped by the production of The Phoenix List, which was a free newsletter informing people of their events and other Mod related dos, they decided to hold Mod only runs. Coinciding with the 20th anniversary of the 1964 riots, the rallies were advertised as 'Southern Mod Scooter Runs' and held at the same coastal towns that the riots had taken place in.

Over the weekend of the 21ST to the 23rd of April whilst the National Scooter Run was to Morecambe, at least 2,000 Mods from all over descended on the town of Clacton. A week before the rally a journalist had visited Sneakers Mod club in Shepherd's Bush to gain an insight into what Mod culture was about and prepare a feature on the Clacton rally. The weather over that weekend proved to be lovely, with entertainment being provided by Fast Eddie and the All – Jacks for the live bands and Tony Class, Paul Hallam and others as DJ's. As usual, the rally was marred by violence, not from the Boneheads or punks of old but from the new Mod enemy of Casuals who sported modern day designer clothing and sportswear. When the article on the rally finally came out in June's edition of 'The Face' magazine it portrayed the Mod scene as something of a joke with very scathing remarks directed towards certain individuals.

The other Mod rallies for that season were: 28-29 April – Margate 23-24 June – Brighton 14-15 July – Bournemouth 18-19 August – Hastings. On the August Bank Holiday, the Phoenix Society had been involved with a rally to the Isle of Wight but it was not a Mod only rally, as it had to share the island with the Scooter mania Run and The Rallyist Scooter Run. Apart from all parties attempting to organise a combined rally of 10,000 people, they also had to take on the island's council who had tried to seek an injunction to stop the event. The scooter rally did go ahead but not without the Phoenix's solicitor's bill spiralling. Sadly, the weekend only proved that there was now lots of animosity aimed at Mods from the scooterists who made it clear that they were no longer welcome. To be honest I only attended Brighton rally that year as I'd started collecting rare records, attending London clubs regularly and getting lots of my clothes made. Brighton had been awful with constant rain, hassle from the police and a poxy disco in a tent. Still on a positive note, the music being unearthed to play in clubs such as The Phoenix in Cavendish Square London and Sneakers was getting better all the time. Each week that passed a newly discovered tune was being played , and it was thanks to DJ's like Del and Chad from Southend, Tony Reynolds from Birmingham, Toski, Paul Hallam and Richard Early from London that it happened. In September, there was a fantastic alldayer at the Ilford Palais in Essex featuring the Purple Hearts, The Scene, Makin' Time and Dee Walker. It was a great follow up to the one that had been held in July featuring The Truth and Small World. The Truth were also down to play at Fort Newhaven alongside Fast Eddie and The Co-Stars. Luckily I avoided that and heard stories of how awful it had been with plenty of violence from the Scooter Boy crowd. The division between Mods and Scooter Boys had grown wider than ever by now and I was looking forward to the first National Mod Meeting being held in London to see what was going to be done about it.

November the 3rd arrived. It was the day I had waiting so anxiously for. I'd spent most of the morning with my friends trying to fix my badly damaged Vespa but had to face up to riding pillion on the back of my mate Martin's Lambretta. I lent Martin my parka as I no longer wore it and had taken to wearing a wartime GI trench coat. We finally set off, two PX Vespa's and a Lambretta. There were five of us; Martin Ivey, Richard Molyneux, Chris Strong, Darren Brown and myself. By the time we'd finally got into the centre of London we were too late to take part in the Buckingham Palace run so we made our way to the Boston Arms in Tufnell Park.

The doors of the Boston Arms opened around 5pm and the place filled up very quickly. The Boston Arms seemed huge, and as we stood on the dance floor, we looked towards the stage, behind which was hung a huge map of the Britain. There were probably around 400 in attendance, not all Mods it has to be said, but all anticipating the chance this year to actually vote on where the rallies were to be held. Eddie Piller took to the stage first and read out a message especially written for the occasion by Ronnie Lane of The Small Faces. Sadly, at the time Ronnie was going downhill fast with his MS and could therefore not be present. Lane's speech spoke of how he'd got into Mod and how it was all about being smart and cool. This received a few heckles from some of the scooter boys present but Eddie gave as good as he got and we got to hear the rest of the speech. Mark Johnson of The Phoenix list was up on stage next, boos rang out as he tried to introduce the next guest 'Irish' Jack Lyons. Jack was an original 60's Mod who had known Pete Townshend in the 60's and is rumoured to be one of the inspirations for the Jimmy Cooper character in Quadrophenia. His speech talked of the state of Mod in '84 and also highlighted the problems of having '*fucking Mohicans riding around on stripped down Vespa's'*. The speech drew giant applause and a standing ovation... well at least from the Mods present.

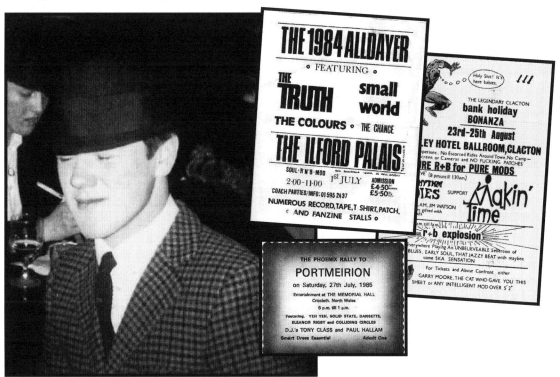

Mark Johnson then talked of 1984 being the year of the Mod and how successful the Mod only rallies had been. Tony Class took over as we got to vote on where the 1985 rallies were to be held. Lots of arguments ensued, and people debated on the pros and cons of certain locations. Big Bob Morris from Forest Gate got on stage and demanded a run to Southend '*to slap the boneheads!*' Roars of approval rang around the room, and as much as Tony Class tried to dismiss the idea the rally was voted in. The rest of the Mod meeting is a bit of a blur but I can remember the R&B band Fast Eddie playing and Paul Hallam and Tony Class DJ'ing. Two songs I remember dancing to that night were 'C'mon and Swim' by Bobby Freeman and 'Nobody But Me' by the Human Beinz which were both massive tunes at the time. So there it was, 1985's Phoenix Mod rallies had been decided.

The main difference to 1984's 'Southern' Mod rallies were that this time it had been divided into two Northern runs (opposite coasts), one to Wales, one in the west and four in the south. That evening both myself and Richard Molyneux made a promise to each other that we'd attend every Mod rally of 1985...a promise we kept.

1985 started quite gloomily with the news of Fast Eddie splitting up. I had found myself recently having been drawn more and more to records anyway but had to admit that losing bands on our scene was becoming more common and I felt a bit sad about it all. On the plus side, my weekends spent in London were fantastic. I'd take the half hour journey to Paddington by train and spend the afternoon in Carnaby Street visiting upstairs at the Flea market to buy fanzines, tapes etc. doing my best to avoid the boneheads who hung around on the stairs.

I'd stroll past The Cavern and Melanndi's, which were two clothing shops aimed at mass produced Mod clothing. Onwards to a small door with various little name plates and buzzers, press the button, announce your identity then up the stairs to Charlie Antoniou's – the Mod tailor of the 80's.

After Charlie's I'd go around to 7 Archer Street in Soho. Once again, up the stairs of some crumbling building and into a tiny room where you would find elderly Katy Steven, the best Mod shirt maker around. The trouble was though that the staircase was to the right of a 'live bed show', so as you exited the premises with your new shirt in a bag, everybody in the café across the road would see you emerging from a sex show with a brown paper bag! Saturday night I would pick up Dickie on my Vespa then ride back up to London to attend The Phoenix in Cavendish Square, which to me was one of the best Mod clubs of that period. Sunday's were spent chilling out before Dickie and myself found ourselves zooming back up to London on my scooter to The Bush Hotel in Shepherds Bush for the Sneakers Mod Club night where Paul Hallam and Richard Early reigned supreme behind the decks.

On Monday March 18th The Sun newspaper carried a small article entitled 'Scruff Toughs' that told of a youth cult war building up between Mods and 'Scooter Scruffs'. A supposed '*leading London Mod'* is quoted as saying 'All the trouble comes from them but Mods will fight back if attacked. Rockers are no longer our main enemies, it's the Scruffs and things are definitely going to get worse in the summer'. Tensions were already strained between both parties but that article practically lit the blue touch paper.

Soon enough April was upon us and the first Mod rally of the year was here. The Easter bank holiday event was from $5^{th} - 8^{th}$ of April and Clacton was the destination. The weather was still pretty chilly as we set off for 3 night's entertainment at The Westcliff Hotel and didn't really brighten up over the whole weekend. Dickie once again a passenger on my scooter as his was off the road as we headed for glorious Essex. There was a camp site for those wishing to rough it at the Warwick Castle car park but thankfully we booked into a B&B just up the road from The Westcliff. The Friday nights entertainment consisted of bands The 5.30, The Theme and The Direct Hits plus DJ sets from a selection of DJ's that included Tony Class and his brother Robin, Paul Hallam, Richard Early and Dom Bassett. I can't remember much about The Theme but I remember thinking that The 5.30 were awful, which is funny because several years later they progressed and became one of my favourite band's. The Direct Hits were really good and as I'd bought their album 'Blow Up' a year earlier, I really enjoyed their set. It was the DJ's that I'd really gone for though, and dancing all night to some great R&B and Soul supplied by Dom, Paul and Richard.

The Saturday daytime was spent hanging around Georgina's café, which boasted an original 60's glass jukebox and proved a popular meeting place. As for the remainder of the weekend, I remember little. I could tell you that the bands The Ugly Ones, Solid State, The Gents and The Moment played but I wouldn't be able to tell you what their sets had been like. I could tell you that in general I loved The Moment but despised The Gents, but that would be about it. One thing that does stick in my mind is that during the Sunday afternoon, a black convertible Golf pulled up outside The Westcliff and tear- gassed the venue, punch-ups ensued and I think somebody was stabbed. This was all apparently the work of the Hornchurch Casuals but proving again that Mods had many enemies during this period.

Lytham St-Annes was the next destination on the list. For those unacquainted with the geographical position of the place it is roughly five and a half miles from Blackpool. The dates of the rally were the weekend of $20^{th} - 21^{st}$ of April so with it not being a Bank Holiday we decided on good old National Express coaches to get us there. When we arrived, it was pouring with rain and things looked rather bleak. We walked down towards St Anne's Pier on the seafront, as we did so a few Vespa PX's passed us, so at least there were some Mods present.

On arrival at the pier we could only see about 25 scooters with little gangs of Moddy boys and scooter boys wandering around. Their average age must have been around fourteen. It was around this time I thought that things couldn't get any worse but then I bumped into Mark Johnson. I enquired where everybody was but he told me that everybody was getting changed for the evening's events. He also informed me that the venue had changed to one in Blackpool and they were going to organise vans from his hotel so we had to be there at 7.00PM. It was already 6.30PM and we still had nowhere to stay.

We walked around the town but it was not easy as the holiday season had not yet started so most of the B&B's were shut. We finally convinced a landlady of some holiday flats that we were executive businessmen on a business trip around Northern coastal resorts (thank god for mohair suits and full-length brollies!). We eventually found the transport to take us to the do and sat amongst people in Millets parkas and 'Mod Squad' badges. If that wasn't bad enough, things got a whole lot worse when we saw the venue: an under 18's trendy disco called 'Zowies' that didn't have a bar! There were a few smart Mods from Liverpool and Manchester present but the majority were just locals. It's funny but I do remember Richard 'Shirley' Early was there, who at the time was my favourite DJ but I really can't remember him DJ'ing, although he must have. Most of the music played that evening were '79 revival tunes. Then a local band called 'Yeh-Yeh' hit the stage and from what I heard of their first offering, 'no no' I thought! We headed outside to a local pub for some much needed alcohol. When we came back there was some clueless local DJ playing the likes of Gerry and The Pacemakers. The following day (Sunday) most of the Mods had gone home

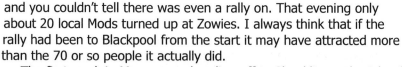

THE RHYTHM AND SOUL SET.
MEMBERSHIP CARD

rhythm, soul, jazz, beat, ska & fun!

NAME. *Paul Anderson*

SMART MOD DRESS ONLY!

and you couldn't tell there was even a rally on. That evening only about 20 local Mods turned up at Zowies. I always think that if the rally had been to Blackpool from the start it may have attracted more than the 70 or so people it actually did.

The first week in May saw us heading off to Shanklin on the Isle of Wight. This was the first year that the Mods had broken away from the scooterists on the traditional August Bank Holiday run. We left Reading around lunchtime on the Friday, and the journey down to Portsmouth was in beautiful sunshine. On arrival at the ferry port there was a policeman and policewoman pulling over scooters searching baggage for weapons and drugs. The policeman asked to see in my side panel toolbox then proceeded to rummage through my tools before pulling out a screwdriver. '*What's this for then mate?*' he demanded as if he'd just found a flick knife or iron bar. '*Er.....screwing officer!*' came my reply as the policewoman burst out laughing. Her partner looked slightly embarrassed as he ushered us on to the ferry. On arrival in Shanklin I remember a scooterboy enquiring as to the whereabouts of the campsite. Dickie replied '*I think it's in Clacton mate!*' (referring to Clacton National rally on the same weekend) The do's were all held on Shanklin Pier and the discos which Dom Bassett, Paul Hallam and Shirley played sets at. I may be wrong but I think Tony and Robin Class were both supposed to DJ but their mother had sadly passed away around this period, and cannot remember if they DJ'd for sure. I do remember that on the Sunday night Doncaster band The Gents played. To me, a truly awful band, decked out in cheap boating blazers and wraparound shades, that Mark Johnson had started managing. The other memory of this rally was large crowds of people doing 'Jimmy' leaps off the balcony...until somebody jumped but wasn't caught and hit the dance floor with a sickening thud. Luckily, he got up and walked away and the rest of the weekend passed without incident.

As May continued it was fantastic to see a group from Los Angeles called 'The Untouchables' sporting a very Mod image climb the UK charts with a tune called 'Free Yourself'. The Daily Mirror printed a small piece that hinted at a Mod revival for the summer. I could never envisage it myself especially after attending Great Yarmouth National rally held at the end of May. We had decided to attend this rally as Tony Class was holding an alternative Mod event at The Brunswick featuring Dom, Hallam and Shirley on the decks. We got the coach up to this as my scooter was off the road for some reason. Within about two minutes of being in town, lots of scooter boys were jeering Dickie at me because of our Mod attire '*Can I have your autograph Paul (Weller)*' '*We are the Mods*' etc. It was bloody obvious we were as welcome on their rallies as they were on ours. Walking along the seafront in our suits we were then accosted by five or six blokes dressed in camouflage '*Oi lads... Brighton's that way!*' '*Yeah*' I replied '*Vietnam's that way!*' pointing in the opposite direction. That evening Tony Class held competitions that involved scooter boys stripping, inserting sticks of rock up their arses and eating doughnuts off of each other's dicks. As we had no B&B, we slept in Paul Hallam's car that night and I really couldn't wait to get back home.

In June, The Style Council released the album 'Our Favourite Shop' full of reminders of 'Thatcher's Britain' and the miners' strike which had recently ended. It was conclusive proof to me that Weller had lost none of his edge and I loved that album. At the time, they were one of the few contemporary bands I bought records by. Live acts I would watch this year would include lots of gigs by The Prisoners, as well as gigs The Tommy Chase Quartet, The Moment, The Rage, The Scene, The Untouchables, Fast Eddie, and The Style Council amongst others. The most popular band that year though as far as most Mods were concerned were Wolverhampton's Makin' Time, a real rhythm and soul band with the gorgeous Fay Hallam on vocals and keyboards.

By and large, the people I was hanging around with in the London Clubs were fed up of The Phoenix membership cards and Boy Scout type attitudes. So another split in the scene was about to take place as the first 'pirate rally' had been booked in Hayling Island to substitute the Scarborough rally by Paul Hallam and some of the East London Mods. Both myself and Richard felt torn as we had promised ourselves to make all the rallies that year. A flip of the coin sealed our fate and destiny had favoured Scarborough. Coach tickets purchased, and so June 15th saw us dancing around at The Salisbury Hotel on the Saturday evening to some great tunes courtesy of Dom Bassett and Shirley who had also thankfully sacrificed the Hip Hayling Island run.

**Scarborough '85' DJ
Dom Bassett**

Two bands played that night, the first were called The Way, a young four-piece outfit, who were really very good although their own material sounded much better than the obvious covers they had chosen such as 'Batman', 'Pretty Green', 'Move On Up' etc. The other band were 'Yeh-Yeh' who I'd seen a bit of at Lytham St-Anne's and was so unimpressed I didn't bother watching this time either. Tony Class ended the evening playing his Mod classics set much to the delight of many of the locals. It had been a long trip just for an evening but we felt it had been worthwhile.

The last weekend of June, the scooter was fixed and it was to the nearby seaside town of Leysdown in Kent. I remember little about this rally other than that it was pretty shite. The trip down there on the scooter was awful because even though the sun was shining I had bloody terrible hayfever so Dickie had to take over the riding. Once there the actual turnout for a rally was poor, around 200 people all told, but the noticeable thing was that the majority were scooter boys and not Mods. At least quite a lot of the Mods present we knew from the London crowd. I have no recollection of any bands but remember the venue was sweltering. I do remember dancing to Jimmy McCracklin 'The Walk' for some reason but in truth it was a lousy rally.

July was an important month for me because fed up with only Northern soul do's being the local entertainment in Reading both Richard and myself held held our own event. Advertised as 'a night of 60's R&B and 60's soul' with the addition of 'requests for Northern Soul will be laughed at', the night was actually a success and started off my long and illustrious career as a DJ. An added bonus around this period was that Channel 4 was showing edited re-runs of the 60's programme 'Ready Steady Go!' so the weekend really did start there...and end with Sneakers on a Sunday night.

Looking at the map to see just how far away Portmeirion in Wales was from Reading didn't make for good viewing. Dickie then cheered me up by telling me not to worry as he had a scooter to take and wouldn't be riding pillion for such a long journey. Sadly, my elation soon came crashing back to earth when he told me the scooter was a Vespa 90. Even though the rally was stated as being to Portmeirion, the actual events would be held four miles west at the Memorial Hall in Criccieth. I remember the sun was shining for most of the journey, and after what seemed a lifetime on the scoots, we finally reached the Welsh border. I remember cheerily taking a photo of Dickie proudly stood by his Vespa 90 with the 'Welcome to Wales' sign behind him. Thank fuck that's over we both thought...well until we got around another bend and spotted just how far we still had to ride to get to Portmeirion. Christ, because it's in North Wales it was practically the same distance we had travelled! Riding through the Welsh valleys was a great experience that I'll never forget, dodging sheep, seeing it raining at the top of a hill and then entering the warm summer rain. By the time, we reached Criccieth it was too late to look around 'The Village' at Portmeirion where the TV series 'The Prisoner' was filmed. We found some digs at a lovely little B&B cottage, yes we really would travel that far without pre-booking accommodation first! There is certainly no doubt that Wales is great for scooter riding and the scenery was breath-taking. I remember we bumped into some of the Birmingham Mods that we knew, amongst which was Tony Byrne and his fantastic 1965 Modded up Lambretta.

We spent the day riding around, visiting a few pubs then it was back to the B&B to get ready for the evening do. The actual do was a major disappointment that I seem to have erased from my memory because I feel it abused my love of Mod. There were various bands playing live that night including Yeh Yeh and Eleanor Rigby that certainly didn't float my particular boat. I don't think we actually saw anyone play live because after about an hour at the do we decided to leave and spent the remainder in a pub along with a few other disappointed souls. The next morning at the B&B breakfast table, we struggled with the breakfast after heavily indulging in too much hooligan juice the night before. The landlady's little dog was yapping away under our table as our host told us of her love for the little terror. We packed our bags and set about loading up the scooters in the process leaving the front door and gate open. To our horror, we suddenly say '*mummy's little darling*' bounding out of the house and charging down the street yapping away to its hearts content. Dickie looked at me with that 'oh shit!' feeling then we shouted 'goodbye' to the landlady, started up the scooters and set off on our mammoth journey. I remember we passed the liberated pooch still eager on its great escape about a mile up the road! We finally reached home much later that evening.

My dad asked me if the long journey had been worthwhile. '*No, the do was rubbish so we went to the pub instead*' came my reply. I still remember seeing the look on my dad's face! He could not comprehend why anybody would travel well over 300 hundred miles in less than 48 hours on a scooter for such meagre rewards. Of course, what he failed to understand is that I was living '*the life*'. A great 'live now' type of life that came with being a dedicated young Mod.

August Bank Holiday had always meant a trip to the Isle of Wight but now the rallies were divided. Whilst the scootering fraternity were planning their assault on the island, the nation's Mods were looking at just how far is Newquay in Cornwall to travel to by scooter. From where I lived it was once again a journey of bloody epic proportions! I hadn't managed to book the Friday off work as Dickie had so it meant a very early start on the Saturday. Naturally preparing for such a rally would mean the Friday night being well used; making final adjustments to the long route or maybe a little last minute maintenance on our trusty steeds, instead of which we spent it on the piss in the pubs of Reading! The following morning at about 4.30 am, it was freezing cold and the rain tipping it down. Thankfully, it was just getting light as Dickie got a rear tyre puncture about two miles from Stonehenge. In truth, we were both bloody useless as neither of us had fitted a spare wheel or had any type of breakdown cover. My toolbox was pathetic to say the least, but I rummaged around and found a tube of 'Tyre Weld'. The wheel sorted we set off again, only for the tyre to go down about five miles up the road. It was decided the best thing was to ditch the scooter in some dense undergrowth by a slip road, and for Dickie to climb on the back with me. A few miles up the road, I ran out of petrol, so we now had to push the scooter for what seemed miles.

Refuelled we set off towards Exeter which we finally reached and stopped for a rest and a spot of dinner. After more trouble with the scooter, which was remedied after changing the spark plug, we cruised along, and finally found ourselves riding along a very bleak Bodmin Moor. We both agreed that this would be an awful place to break down. Needless to say, we got a puncture about four miles outside Bodmin (around twenty miles from Newquay). 'Fucking Hell why do we do this to ourselves?' I was thinking. I actually managed to flag down a car, and they gave me a lift to a garage to get some more 'Tyre Weld'. We waved the woman cheerily goodbye, set off and got as far as Bodmin roundabout before the tyre went deflated. Totally disgusted we dumped the scoot in somebody's garden, agreeing to pick it up next day. It was now 4.00pm and we hitched a lift to Bodmin.

At Bodmin, we found a bus to take us to St. Austell, and from there at great expense got a train to Newquay after changing at Parr. How long winded is this? We finally got to Newquay train station at 8pm. It was great to see loads of Mods about, but as usual, we hadn't booked a B&B! Thankfully, ten minutes later we had somewhere and hurriedly got changed for the evening do but there wasn't one. Saturday evening and The Phoenix Society in their wisdom hadn't booked a venue! We spent most of the night in the Cavalier pub chatting to the likes of Dom Bassett and Kurt Fricker. After the pub, there was the usual talk of a beach party, which as usual never materialised. Heading back to the B&B we couldn't help but notice the large amounts of Casuals and help thinking that maybe holding a rally in such a popular holiday resort over a Bank Holiday wasn't such a good idea after all.

The following morning the kind people who ran the B&B took Dickie and me over to our stranded scooter and brought it back on a trailer. I'd managed to convince some girl the previous evening into lending me her spare wheel so soon everything was fine and dandy. Around midday, we met up with everyone and spent the lunchtime drinking in some obscure pub. This was of course before all day opening so by 3pm we all had nothing to do until the evening do which was being held at a venue called Disco 5000.

Richard 'Shirley' Early made the Sunday night for us by playing a fantastic R&B set although it didn't seem to impress one young couple who were shagging in one of the corners of the giant room! At the end of the evening, the mythical beach party was again touted so everybody headed there. The trouble was though that to get to the beach you had to walk through the town centre. It was here that loads of fights kicked off as loads of holidaying 'Kevin and Trevor's' decided that Mods seemed like fair game. Several of our mates got arrested and dragged off to the local cells. We seemed to manage to avoid most of the trouble only for a gang to chase us yards from our digs. Dickie managed to get away alas I was finally caught, but did what I do best when outnumbered and simply blagged my way out of it!

The journey back was pretty uneventful, and as Dickie waited for his overjoyed dad to pick him up at the site of his stranded scooter. I rode back the last few miles alone smiling to myself. Although we'd had an unbelievable amount of aggro with the scooters, and a severe lack of actual Mod do's, the weekend had been great and more memorable than usual."

PAUL 'SMILER' ANDERSON – FACE OF THE 80'S MOD RALLY

HAYLING ISLAND 1985 – WHEN IT ALL CAME TOGETHER FOR PAUL HALLAM

Paul Hallam was one of the leading most respected Mod DJ's of the 80's, his love of R&B, rare Soul and Mod Jazz a great attribute to his popular sets. Yet - unlike many of his generation - his love of Mod did not arrive with the usual 79 period revival bands.

"As I have mentioned in more articles/books than I care to remember over the years, my introduction to Mod did not come via Punk/Jam/Secret Affair/Chords etc. but from my love of nostalgia as an 8-9 year old.

I remember sitting alone in the 'breakfast room' - we were a bit posh and called it that rather than a dining room of my parents' house in 1974 playing 7 inch records on an old Dansette of my sisters.

She was - and still is - 12 years older than me, and had been in the nice side of the 60s. Her idol was Cliff and the inside lid of the record player still had a photo of him cut out from some pop mag from a decade before.

Paul Hallam (Right) with Mark Edwards

But unlike my peers, I wasn't playing the latest from T-Rex, Slade, or even little Jimmy Osmond. I was playing a stack of singles that my mum/sister had acquired - then discarded - from a previous decade. Tommy Steele was (and still is) my hero. Add to that some Adam Faith singles, Max Bygraves and a George Formby album. I was officially the most Uncool kid in my school. Even the ones with national health glasses held together with plasters made me look nerdy if they wore flares and liked Mud.

I left music briefly in the mid-70s to pursue my passion for football. First Liverpool FC then Millwall. I dreamed of becoming the new Barry Kitchener. There was of course one problem. I wasn't actually very good at kicking a ball. Then in 1977, I discovered the Beatles. Actually, I didn't discover them. I immersed myself in them. I became obsessed. Everything else went out the window. I listened too and bought everything I ever could on the band. Even the Ringo 1970s solo Albums. I know. I apologise for this.

Then at some point in 1978 on a shopping trip to Kingston (Surrey not Jamaica) I bought a book called BEAT MUSIC by Derek Johnson. It was published in 1969 and it went through year by year the history of pop music from pre 1954 to 1968-69. It had a photo section with pictures of people I had at the time never heard of; Jefferson Airplane, Cream. As well as artists, I still don't know anything about - Caesar, Young Flowers, Iron Butterfly (I must check these out). It was a serious book that was not a lot of fun for a 12 year old to read in bed tucked up in his nylon pj's and hot water bottle. However, night after night, I would read it. And one quote stuck in my mind.

It talked of mid-1966 to mid-1967 and said it was the 'year it all came together'. It described Monterey festival as the event of events. The most important weekend in a year of teenage dreams. A brave statement for a book published a couple of years after. But I liked and remembered that statement.

The years past. I discovered Mod. I discovered RnB. I learnt of rare soul and cool Jazz. I bought Mose Allison and Snooks Eaglin records and burnt Dave Clark Five and Applejacks records. In addition, by mid-1984 I had made a bit of a name for myself on the Mod Scene as a DJ (OK I was at the top of my game and the best in the world at what I did I'm allowed to gloat (MOD-ESTY ALERT!). The autumn and winter of 84-85 was amazing. 'Sneakers' became the Scene Club of two decades earlier. Teenagers from Cardiff/Swindon/Belfast/Norfolk amongst other places were travelling up to a back room of a pub off Goldhawk Road to look good and dance to rare R&B until the ungodly hour of 10.30pm on a Sunday. All was good. Going in 1985 things just got better and better. And then...

We - the young soul rebels - decided we should put on a weekend away to the coast in the spirit of our mentors from 20 years earlier. I am not sure how but I was teamed up with Gary Moore (yes he the renowned inventor who now tours the globe shaking politicians hands while discussing his invention of the less water toilet). We had the whole of the British Isles to choose from. But where to start?

As I child me and my family had never gone abroad on holidays. The rest of my school were venturing off to Spain - Torremolinos usually or if they were REALLY rich Marbella. They came back with bits of wood that tasted of liquorice and stories of water sold in bottles. Some of it was fizzy. But me and my family choose the home comforts. Caravans (which made my Romany born mum feel at home) or camping. And one of our favourite destinations was Hayling Island. A jewel in the Solent. Off the coast of Portsmouth with a view across to the mythical land of the Isle of Wight. As a child, it was an amazing place.

Myself and Gary drove down one Saturday afternoon. We stopped on the sea front. Played some games in an arcade. Ate scampi and chips and then... we saw The Solent Club. A 1970s stand-alone building just off the seafront with a car park and room for 300 people to dance. It was tatty run down and perfect.

We nervously knocked on the door - I would have been 19 and Gary 20 - and a large man with a HUGE beer belly and braces on his trousers greeted us. This was Pete Sheppard. Former London boy made good who had invested his savings in this hidden gem. We negotiated a deal that was so in his favour it was shocking. He took the bar. We paid the DJ's the bouncers and everything. Then we split the door 50-50%. We didn't care we just wanted to do this 'pirate rally'. We shook hands - OK he squashed mine. And off we went. We were in business.

The next few weeks were full of excitement on the London scene. Gary and his cohort Jim Watson published leaflets announcing it was a 'Fuck the Phoenix rally' - the Phoenix was a London organisation that I was a member of and they were none too pleased with this headline. But the momentum grew. Whispers in the Shadows. Tickets were selling faster than we could print them.

The week before I remember going to a club in Southend and taking speed - which wasn't something I did so much in those days. South London Mod Tony Schockman was also partaking in amphetamines and was talking 500 words to the minute about the next week's event. 'It's gonna be wall to wall mohair at Hayling Island. Fucking wall to wall mohair', he repeated over and over and over and over again.

I got on my soapbox and told anybody who cared to listen that 'this was the start. Going forward we will have not just Mod musicians and DJ's. We will have Mod poets. Mod journalists. Mod in the Media and Mod Politicians.' I had an audience. This is gonna be it. This is WHEN IT ALL COMES TOGETHER.

featuring:- 'ANOTHER'
Sensational Seaside Special, at Hayling Island on 28th June

The 3rd **R+B** Party, is here!
Saturday night, at the Solent Club

D.j's **Paul Hallam, Garry Moore**
PLUS SUPRISE BASTARD! (definately NOT Shirley)

ADVANCE TICKET'S ONLY: £3·00 each

TICKETS AVAILABLE FROM THE ABOVE D.J's AND AT MOST SMART LONDON CLUBS

There will be no tickets on the day (so buy early you tight bastards)

Strictly SMART MODS only no scruffy scum

Four days before the event I returned home from work to find my mum concerned. 'You've had a call from Hampshire Police. Can you call them back?' I did and got a very worried chief of police. He had heard of our planned weekend and was pretty pissed off about it. The Phoenix would inform seaside town's months before of the events and often a senior police officer would judge the best scooter competition. But this was unannounced and maverick. We were turning up and doing what we wanted to do.

And party we did. I remember nothing of the night. 300 of the coolest people in England at the time turned up and danced until 2am. I think every single person there had a new suit/skirt/shirt or pair of shoes hand made for it.

A Policeman turned up early evening - for some reason he had a bicycle wheel in his hand and a walkie-talkie that just wouldn't work. 'Ello Ello' he said. 'Can you please make sure there is no trouble tonight. There are hundreds of you and only 3 of us on duty so do us a favour and keep it nice.' And keep it nice we did.

The night ended and I went back to my £10 B&B with rock solid mattress and flowered curtains. High on life and High on cheap speed I shed a small tear. This was the Pinnacle for me. The height of the mid-80s Mod scene. The weekend 'It All Came Together' and I didn't think it could ever be this good again."

For the majority, the mid-80's Mod soundtrack consisted of a mix of Soul, obscure R&B and blue-eyed Soul, yet what must not be underplayed was the importance and fondness some held for the contemporary bands of the day. Alongside the commercial cross-over success of under-rated artists such as Big Sound Authority (who blended a mix of brassy Soul and watered down Weller/Costello styled social comment), The Truth and LA Ska act The Untouchables - who enjoyed a chart hit with their 1985 single 'Free Yourself' - bands such as The Scene, The Threads, The Moment and who could forget Makin' Time's dance-friendly take on 60's beat fronted by the femme fatale of the Mod scene, Fay Hallam? However, top of the class in drawing the Mod crowd in were The Prisoners!

THE PRISONERS BY DAVID ABRAHAMS-EDLEY

Mod's of all period share an obsessive nature that often crosses over into the love of specific bands where the attention to detail remains just as important.

David Abrahams-Edley (Middlesbrough Mod) - "It wouldn't be much of a task if I had to name five bands that changed my life. The Small Faces of course and The Jam. The Chords and The Pretty Things and then there is the Prisoners. Whilst I love the Small Faces and the Pretty Things, which led me away from the Northern Soul I never, felt that comfortable with and into Beat and Psych, where I did. I got into the Mod thing in the first place because of The Jam and The Chords. If I had to distil and pinpoint, though, it would be the Prisoners that led me down the social and musical route that developed my musical styles, that in turn introduced me to new music and leading me to form friendships with kindred spirits that I still have, that in turn led me down the route that took me into the Mod lifestyle I chose, that in turn led me to be an avid vinyl junkie and that in turn led me to DJ, scooter collector and musician. True The Prisoners would be the last to nail their colours to that mast and it hardly helped their cause. But if it were not for the Prisoners I probably would have never gone to clubs and seen new bands, I would have never met other Mods and became part of a scene that was industriously rebuilding itself underground away from the carcinogenic music press that never got it anyway. I would almost certainly not have been instigated into the scene and would have never attended rallies and all-dayers and I certainly wouldn't have gigged, toured both in the UK and Europe or made records. I would have probably happily settled down into the nine to five life with a wife and 2.2 kids, a golden retriever and two weeks in the Costa del Shite that has always eluded me.

Memories of my miss-spent youth and I am grateful for every second and to which I thank the Prisoners. And I am certain I am far from alone in this, there must be hundreds out there that would share this view. I am equally certain that this revelation and the implications of it would horrify the band who I'm guessing just wanted to go out and play. But credit where credit is due and there it is.

The first time I heard of the Prisoners was in 1984. I was living in Kent recording a demo in a studio on the Sturry Road in Canterbury. The track was called 'Cardboard City' and to be honest sounded like a poor cross between 'Standards' by The Jam and 'In my Street' by The Chords. The studio owner came in whilst I was mixing it and remarked that he had recently recorded two bands who had a similar style to what we were (but clearly much better – he never said that but he clearly meant it). The bands were from just down the road in the Medway Towns – one was called the Milkshakes and the other was the Prisoners. In 1984 for a young Mod, the contemporary music scene was at best barren. Since the Jam split up in 1982 with the refreshing exception of the

Mandy (wearing helmet) and scootering friend and with Simone at Gorleston Rally 1989

Everybody dreaded Monday morning. Not only did you have to face work the next day, but it was a long journey home that you now had to cope with, made worse by the fact that you'd had hardly any sleep for the past three days, you ached from all the dancing and generally felt like shit and on a bit of a comedown with the prospect of going back to reality, and 9 times out of 10 it was raining!

The last thing to do before leaving though was to get a local paper to see if there was an article and pictures from the Rally, more times than not there was, I wish I'd kept these! I'd amuse myself and keep myself awake on the way home by reliving in my head the many events of the weekend only to be kept sane by the fact that at the very next Bank Holiday we'd all be doing it all over again! Happy days!"

Morgan Nolan - "One of the oddest fashion trends of the mid-80s was an attempt to give Mod icons an 'Irish twist', such as the target and Jam shoes. The image of Green White and Orange targets and Jam shoes still fills me with horror and as a proud Paddy I have to admit that Red White and Blue is far better. We also had our own media outlets through the numerous and various Modzines that could be purchased at any of the Mod events or from scooter outlets. I produced two different Modzines over 1983/4 Steppin' Out and Time for Truth. There were so many zines that it seemed every neighborhood had its own."

Perhaps this following reasoning goes in some way to best explain the 1980's Mod manifesto?

Andrew Harris - "I never changed my style, and Mod was never about dressing up like your favourite Mod pop band. Mod was always an attitude, a mannerism albeit it having some rules to the look that few know - old or young. The 80's Sawdust Caesar was different to the originals who stomped the dance floor to 'Let's Go' - The Routers; they had opportunities to either backtrack or move forward, or even better - do both!"

MODS OF THE 80'S

DEREK 'DEL BOY' SHEPHERD AND JACKIE OF 'IN THE CROWD' FANZINE

Various photos of the 80's Mod scene, including a pre-Charlatans Martin Blunt (middle photo left) from Paul Hallam's extensive collection (with the exception of photo directly above)

Vicky Walsh Knightley – Third from the left – and friends

Above: Mod duo at a Gorlston Rally, 1987

Left: 80's Face Gary Evans, Brighton 1986

SHEFFIELD'S 80'S MOJO REUNION

Left to Right: Mark Christian (aka Wingnut), CB, Dave Walton, Debbie, Lisa Abbott and Bell

Lee Radforth - "I'd heard so much about The Mojo from family friend Dave Drabble who virtually lived there in its heyday, and to say I was excited about The Leadmill hosting the first reunion since its demise would be an understatement. I guess I was expecting all the original Mods, who would only be in their late 30's early 40's to still be looking sharp, and the night to recapture the excitement and vibrancy of the original club.

To be honest it was a bit of a disappointment for me. While the crowd generally seemed to have a good time, it was more of an old friends catching up and chatting about their youth than the dynamic night a young Mod obsessed with the scene was hoping for. Looking back, I guess I was naive expecting anything more. The people attending had mostly had kids and settled down, and Mod had been a brief but bright burning flame of their youth that was now only flickering in the background. Thirty years on though, kids grown up, a lot of those exact same people are back renewing their love of the music, clothes, and scooters with renewed vigour."

By the end of a decade that had seen Mod triumph, fade and then return to its underground roots, the writing on the wall seemed to be once again appearing. This may seem to be an obvious prognosis for ardent 80's Mods - yet beneath that sense of finality lay the seeds of a future much healthier and forward-focussed than most of the post-revival period had enjoyed.

Graham Lentz - "The 80's was a time when culturally and particularly in music, the artists collectively lost their creative minds and I could find nothing that spoke to me. It was a desolate, vacuous period, dominated by electronically produced drivel and the whole 'greed is good', Thacherite mantra. I was so 'out of touch' even the whole Acid/Rave culture passed me by. I may not have dressed like a Mod during this period, but it was always in me. It never left. It was bands like the Stone Roses who began my reawakening."

Brett 'Buddy' Ascott (The Chords) - "I don't think the bands who carried Mod on and into the 80's get enough credit - The Chords et al had been riding the crest of a wave in '79, but these poor sods were putting up with no interest from the media, or major labels. Bands like Makin' Time, The Moment (with whom I'm lucky enough to be filling in for now!), The Risk etc. etc. - they really LOVED that scene, even though the rest of the world had moved on to Hip Hop, Duran Duran and Jive Bunny!. And Tony Class - Gawd bless him - he continued carrying the flame for all things Mod, he never wavered. He should take a lot of credit."

Andy Bull (Chesterfield Mod) - "Right up until around 1989 I thought it would never end, but little things like Cleopatra's nightclub in Lowestoft (the main venue) closing down, having to use the smaller room in the Winter gardens at Blackpool and a half empty Ocean Rooms at Gorleston on Sea. In the time between 85 and 89, I had heavily into the Mod scene, done a fanzine, organised events, but by 1991, it was all but over. Mates had got into the rave culture/Madchester scene. I became single, strangely enough finding myself in Skegness with a bunch of non-Mod mates answering questions about Ska, Soul & reggae to win beers for us all on a weekend piss up."

Lee Radforth - "Following on from The Attic came a more Jazz based night upstairs at Charlie Parkers on Cambridge Street and then Vout Oroonie at The Leadmill with a pre-famous (and blood brother) Richard Hawley on 'co-tune spinning' duties. We brought Jimmy McGriff and Big John Patton to Sheffield to name but two and played a wicked blend of dance floor Jazz, Hammond grooves, and boogaloo to a hip Acid Jazz (my latest incarnation of Mod) crowd that voted it in the top ten best clubs ever at The Leadmill. We even got an NME review that sadly I've lost."

Ed Silvester - "Initially I had liked Paul Weller's new band the Style Council, and their blue-eyed Soul and funky sound. But by 1985, I was listening to more Northern Soul and Jazz funk, and had got slowly bored and disinterested with the Style Council. As the 80's began to wane, we listened to bands on the Acid Jazz label and House music - with its parallels with the summer of love, of 1967. Everybody seemed to have embraced the Rave culture, popping pills and peace and love was all around. The fighting between different youth cultures did seem to evaporate, and a baggier look evolved. House music had arrived, and bands like the Happy Mondays, Inspiral Carpets and the Charlatans with their fusion of dance and rock music were starting to interest me.

By the late 1980's, Eddie Piller has started to DJ at a small club - on a Friday night - at the T&C 2, (the Town and Country club, near Highbury and Islington tube station) and this became our venue of choice every Friday night. The music was much more eclectic, Acid Jazz bands, a bit of Rare Groove, Jazz Funk, and 70's and 80's Soul. Sadly, this venue closed in the early 1990's."

Ed Horwood - "Post-1985, I continued on as a Mod until 1987, which was also the year I finished my apprenticeship and became a tradesman. In the spring of 1986 I passed my motorcycle test and later that year, traded the trusty Serveta for a new P200E. Although I attended a multitude of Mod rallies and events in 1986, my initial flush of enthusiasm for the Mod lifestyle was starting to wane. By that time, most of the lads and lasses I had known from my earliest Mod days had either gone over to the scooterist lifestyle or else had got married and settled down. The Mod scene was riven by countless divisions and agendas and frankly, it was all starting to become a little stale for me."

CHAPTER 12

INTO THE FUTURE

The Post-Acid House Rave scene seemed to swallow up music, fashion and club culture as the new decade arrived. The excess of flared jeans as 'Baggy' was born could not have been much further removed from the trim and sharp creases of the Mod's classic style. Superficially, at least, it appeared that Mod was now well and truly a cult consigned to the past once more. But, despite the garishly attired fashions, hedonism and near-hippie kudos of the new Ravers and their declaration of a brand new summer of love, beneath this acid-drenched Ecstasy flavoured circus of warehouse parties and illegal raves in farmer's fields, there was an undercurrent of Mod's legacy and (most importantly) it's very future bubbling away - if one only took the time to look.

Aside from the deliberate Mod leanings of Andy Weatherhall's 'Boys Own' collective, darlings of the Baggy scene, the Stone Roses also shared confirmed Mod pedigree within their ranks. Following their punk beginnings, both Manni and Ian Brown spent their time scootering across the north for Northern Soul and Mod all-nighters. Primal Scream's Bobby Gillespie not only sported a newly-shorn 1966 style Mod cut and target sweater to suit during the World Cup summer of 1990, he matched his choice of visual with a keen eye on Mods' 'primal' drive for creative progression across a refreshing hybrid of styles and musical ventures that promised to project any forward-thinking Mod of the new decade firmly into the future!

Elsewhere, post-Style Council demise and free agent Paul Weller took a career-rejuvenating glance back soon resulting in the moniker of 'Modfather'. Baggy exponents Inspiral Carpets converted many a Mod with their Farfisa organ-flavoured sixties-styled garage/pop and The Charlatans - who included ex Makin Time bassist, Martin Blunt in their ranks - celebrated late sixties Nuggets style pop and psyche and 80's Mod faves The Prisoners set their sights upon new funkier pastures. A new dawn of Mod-influenced music seemed to be just around the corner. Conclusively, Mod (Brit Pop era misfires Menswear aside) was not redundant by a long shot, merely doing what it does best in times of need - utilising its great capability as a subculture that was able to consistently evolve!

As for the Mods themselves? Scooter rallies were still religiously attended whilst music policies expanded, though not always to every Mod's taste. Northern Soul was still going strong after a much-needed boost from the previous decade's Mod revival itself... and authentic Mod R&B nights were still being organised, though not as regularly as later in the decade. Sadly Mod fanzine 'In the Crowd' called it a day after a successful 30-issue run. Alternatively, new mediums for Mod news and reviews were just around the corner.

Mods at a Bridlington weekender 1991

If there was one significant Mod-related genre that did evolve around this time it was the advent of Acid Jazz. Taking its cue from the recent Acid House explosion, Acid Jazz was in effect a product of the previous decade, but would come to signify the early to mid-90's alternative club culture that Mod elements would embrace.

Mark Thomson - "As I got older, the Northern Soul scene got me into Chicago House, which led me to Funk and rare groove, culminating in the Acid Jazz thing and the Madchester stuff. Trips to Northern Soul all-nighters and Southport Soul Weekenders. It was all linked really and a natural Mod progression."

In a similar replication of Mod's submission to LSD in the 60's, the new drug of choice of the 90's was Ecstasy. Yet, whilst some welcomed this relatively cheap (to begin with at least) drug, the most common Mod drug of choice remained speed, in spite of its notorious comedown effects.

Ultimately, unlike the originals, Mods by and large came to choose that sociably acceptable drug of choice of the Joe Normals, alcohol, as another of their recreational relaxants. Significantly, as the decade progressed and especially with the advent of Brit Pop, clubs that catered for Mods emerged in most towns and cities.

A new generation of bands arrived too, Psychotic Reaction, The Aardvarks and cult Mods The Clique impressed the majority of Mods with their Hammond-fuelled sounds. Inspired by the optimism of the times and encouraged by New Untouchables founder Rob Bailey, originals such as The Action re-formed and delighted fans at packed low-key gigs and a memorable outing at the popular Isle of Wight annual weekender.

Enamel Verguren (pictured above) - "The 1990s started where the 1980s had finished, basically; the Stylists had taken over the inner core of the Mod scene, and they were far more arrogant than their predecessors, to the point of being absolutely not communicative – I can say that because I was still a novice back then … it was a bit like the difference between upper-class and bourgeoisie, although we were all issued from the working class ('P'tit Blond' for example, from Paris, was a top Face at weekends but working in the kitchen of a restaurant the rest of the week)."

Class? Obviously a highly emotive subject in such times, had, along with elements of purism, seemingly re-entered the Mod scene. However, this was not an issue of outside social or political agendas, more a degree of inner group politics and a pecking order perhaps echoing the Tickets and Faces structure of their sixties relatives? Even so, one thing was for certain, once tasted, the recipe of Mod was rarely placed back on to the shelf.

In many ways, elements of the Mods of the 80's and, certainly the 90's, considered themselves to be an improvement upon the original 60's Mods. Without taking away any of the great respect that they had for the originals - using their pioneering blueprint of taste and influences - the contemporary Mod felt a compulsion to build upon those very foundations and increase their stature and influences to a greater level. In essence, the evolving Mod took the finest of all previous generations of Mod and aspired to top them all - surely the untainted true spirit of the original Modernists' aspirations? Yet, as Enamel has just explained, the negative aspect was also prevalent.

There had been a noticeable splintering within the late 80's Mod scene, as many of the revivalist Mods continued digging into more Northern Soul pastures and others delved even deeper into the traditional Mod sounds of R&B, along with a greater appreciation of British R&B groups and Mod Jazz. Each division appropriately adopted their own appointed clubs (Drummonds in Euston London had DJ Rob Messer spinning healthy doses of 'Northern' and filling the dance floor, whilst Paul 'Smiler' Anderson's The King's Tavern in Reading successfully held a strictly original Mod policy). Consequently, the musical template for the Mods of the early 90's was much more diverse and eclectic than ever before. However, while some accepted and endorsed the new sounds arriving from Manchester, ex-Mods such as the Stone Roses and The Charlatans and the 60's garage pop sounds of Inspiral Carpets, purists simply rejected their invidious presence on the dance floors of Mod clubs.

Highly respected Mod about town and member of the CCI Mod rally's committee, Paul 'Smiler' Anderson, not a fan of what could be seen as a compromise of Mod's long standing soundtrack, also held his own against the onset of Northern Soul. At one rally in Gorleston, where he was DJ'ing, he shouted out to the crowd "Sod this Northern Soul; get some R&B down your throats!" For all of the musical democracy that was shared across the Mod scene, the division was just as prominent. In contrast, Scooter clubs for instance, rarely had any musical objections and had been absorbing sounds that had taken a distinct departure from recognisably Mod sounds since the early to mid-80's.

Paul 'Smiler'Anderson - "The year 1989 ended with December's issue of iD magazine running a feature on 'Acid Jazz Mods' featuring a photo including well known Mods Jon Cooke, Paul Newman, Dom Bassett and Toby Fosh which was
more or less just an article saying that Mods were attending Gilles Peterson clubs. Nonetheless, it caused a few waves amongst the Mod scene and would have bigger impact the following year and the dawning of the new decade would change the Mod scene beyond recognition.

From the first week in January '90 a new Saturday afternoon club opened at the Dublin Castle in Camden featuring Thierry from Belgium, Noj, Jez Strickland and myself on decks with the cream of the current bands playing live such as The Clique, Aardvarks, The Immediates and others. Saturday Nights had me, Tony Class, Rob Bailey, Ian Jackson and 'Check It Out' John on the decks as well as bands playing at Drummonds in Kings Cross. Whilst I also ran a club at the Saint John Tavern in Archway on a Tuesday. 1990 will though in my mind stay in my mind for many reasons. Firstly a trip over to Blankenberge R&B weekend in Belgium in March ended in the most bloody and mental punch up with a load of boneheads. Secondly there was lots of chatter in the clubs about the Madchester scene and the whole baggy culture. Talk of bands such as The Farm, Charlatans, Happy Mondays and Stone Roses. The Charlatans had released 'The Only One I Know' as a single in May and as it featured Hammond organ and an obvious sixties feel it started to get a few plays in clubs. At the time I was quite a purist I must admit, and although I didn't particularly dislike the song I didn't feel it should be welcomed into club playlists. A small divide had already begun.

I also found myself getting drawn back to Jazz clubs and a couple of visits to Dingwalls in London on a Sunday afternoon to hear what Gilles Peterson and Patrick Forge were playing; a mixture of 60's organ, Jazz hip hop and Brazilian tunes amongst others. The music split continued, and spilled over onto the rallies. At Bridlington rally, that year there really was a strange atmosphere The Charlatans was played, as did Dee-Lite's 'Groove Is in the Heart'. I felt compromised, as I was not only a committee member but also a regular rally DJ by then. I spoke to my friends Putney Sean and Phil Otto about maybe starting our own little 'weekends away'. Later that year I handed in my resignation as a DJ/committee member to Tony Class.

Sometime, around late August '90, we had a meeting in the Pontefract Castle pub in West London. Present were Andy Hynd, Jamie Rave, Dom Bassett, Dom Strickland, Dave Edwards, Phil Otto, Putney Sean and myself to decide on the future of the rallies and clubs etc. Various names were thrown about as a name for the organisation until I came up with The Untouchables. It was decided that all profits from the clubs we ran would go on to fund the following years rallies. The first club we put on was at the Mildmay Tavern in Highbury. The opening night was on November 11th. Around the same month iD magazine did another feature on Acid Jazz styled Mods and I still felt drawn to this more casual style of Italian knitwear and Duffer St George clobber. As the year was coming to an end, the attendance at the Mildmay nights wasn't particularly great and I found myself sneaking off up the road to the Prohibition Jazz nights.

1991, started with the first Untouchables rally at the Queens Hotel in Brighton on the New Year's Eve. I was already feeling a bit of a fraud as I had less and less interest in the actual Mod scene and more and more on the Jazz scene. In the January edition there was a huge article about clubbers looking like Mods and once again featuring many of the scene's old regulars. In truth, it was just a bit of an in-joke but once again caused trouble on the Mod scene. I started putting on my Kings Tavern nights on fortnightly as I was finding it hard to get back to do them after attending the Sunday afternoon session at Dingwalls. I eventually closed it down as a Mod club and reopened it a few weeks later as a Jazz club that embraced the new Acid Jazz sounds. I sold off all my tailor made gear and handmade suits and was usually found in Duffer St George, Paul Smith and either Adidas Gazelles or Patrick Cox loafers. I was off watching bands like The Manic Street Preachers (early punk type gigs) or The 5.30. I stopped going to Mod clubs but did fulfil my

DJ spots for all The Untouchables rallies that year. On January 18th 1992 I announce my retirement from The Mod scene as a DJ."

Paul did not retire from DJ'ing, however: he devoted his DJ skills to Jazz events and later on ran a Mod/Funk/Indie based club 'Get Carter' and continued to DJ at various clubs, though, in his own words "I have never fully immersed myself back in 'the scene' as much since I walked away from it really around 1991."

Paul Hallam - "Once a Mod, always a Mod. If you were into it that much, your heart will always be in it."

In 1991, a memorable TV appearance from Paul Weller on the Jonathan Ross show would include an oft-quoted statement from the soon-to-be termed Modfather, himself on the cusp of a brand new artistic high and subsequent reappraisal of his talents and career:

Paul Weller - "I am a Mod, I'll always be a Mod, you can bury me a Mod."

Paul Weller Golddiggers, Chippenham 1990   Photos: copyright of Jody Maguire

Paul 'Smiler' Anderson - "All of a sudden, it helped me a lot to know that a person that first got me into being a Mod, was now involved with the Acid Jazz scene. It made me feel like it had gone full circle, I really got into Paul Weller because of this Punk/Mod guy that he was first, and then there he reappeared, he had evolved with his new material, and he was looking fantastically Mod, more than he had been for a long time.

He brought out 'Into Tomorrow', which to me, if there was any life-changing anthem, would be it. On the same 4-track EP you had 'Here is a New Thing', in which some of the lines, meant personally, for having been so heavily involved in the Mod scene (with the Untouchables) exactly how I felt at the time: 'Gotta let go of the past...' It all said it to me; that's the right thing to do, that's the way things were going."

392

Paul Weller - in adhering to Mod's forward-thinking ethics - was a keen participant in the underground Acid Jazz scene. His earlier proclamation of House Music being the new Mod may well have been slightly wide of the mark for some - though, not as wide as might be assumed and understandably may well have helped to nurture his vision of another new musical style for Mods steering them towards Acid Jazz's progressive soundtrack.

The brainchild of Eddie Piller and Giles Patterson, the Acid Jazz label and its soundtrack of alternative club sounds - incorporating elements of Funk, Jazz, Latin, Soul, Hip Hop, disco, Reggae and even poetry - grew in popularity, establishing club nights at London clubs such as Dingwalls in Camden and The Wag in Soho, bringing back Mod's Jazz heritage full circle in a return to its place of birth.

Yet, this refreshing new emphasis on the club aspect of Mod culture was not one based upon the discovery of previously unheard sounds exclusively promoted by the DJ, it was primarily a live scene featuring acts such as Galliano, The Last Poets, A Man Called Adam (who had achieved popularity within the earlier dance scene of the Rave period), Chris Bangs, The Night Trains, Snowboy and The Latin section, James Taylor Quartet and The Young Disciples amongst others.

The first compilation album was released in 1988, 'Totally Wired' – an ongoing collective of volumes with a mix of obscure 70's funk, Hammond grooves and horns-heavy club sounds. The label and style evolved further with Small Faces influenced Mother Earth, initially a studio based act, who included Weller as a guest on their sublime rendition of the Small Faces 'Almost Grown 'and also, not forgetting, Corduroy - perhaps the act most favoured by contemporary Mods?

Acid Jazz was positively creative and pro-active and for a while challenged the whole concept of club sounds along with the musical map of Modernism. Whilst its allegiances were fundamentally of a Mod persuasion, the inner core of the label and style would come to inform, inspire and influence the future of club culture on a wider scale.

Acid Jazz, was, yet again, a London-spawned musical development. However, as is consistent throughout Mod's history, its influence spread out of the capital, in turn instigating spin-off Acid Jazz scenes in various parts of the country - Sheffield is one such notable example.

ACID JAZZ IN SHEFFIELD BY LEE RADFORTH

Melody Maker Jul14 1990

BRAND NEW HEAVIES

VOUT: OROONIE, SHEFFIELD

THE club itself, situated in The Leadmill, is a strictly cool affair with a totally laidback vibe. Latin Jazz tunes mix with JB-style funk as the mood swings from mellow to wildly vibrant. The impeccably be-suited hipsters sit at tables around the floor. And there's beards; good beards, mind, like goatees and stuff.

Into this ambience step Brand New Heavies. And there's a lot of them, about eight, I think. The guitarist looks like all the faces and fashions of the late Sixties period Stones rolled into one body, with Brian Jones as the .... genes.

Cool. Way back in '88 this music would've been called Acid Jazz; but now, it's a loose funk-bassed groove with tinkling piano and cymbal t-sssing snappy drums. The rhythms are sinuous and snakey with wicka-wicka guitar slicing through and a brass section that two-steps from side-to-side as curves and waves of brass tumble out. Bass player is cool as DJ's Angel Pie and God Came For Breakfast are first to fast shuffle onto the floor, and they are the catalyst.

The man in shorts and sax controls the groove — stopping, starting, changing rhythms, and reshaping from bare beat to full-blown vibrancy. And, as the groove shifts, so different patterns and combinations of brass, keyboard, guitar and bass rise up in a seemingly seamless shape-changing flux. Subtle shades of percussion scrape and shuffle and donk in between the groove spaces. It all makes you feel dead

Lee with fellow South Yorkshire Mod, Steve Parlett during their Acid Jazz phase

Unsurprisingly Sheffield Mod Lee Radforth - a man, in the true ethos of Mod, constantly searching for new sounds and styles - came to identify with Acid Jazz. His already existing taste for Blue Note and the Jazz equation of the Mod playlist put Lee in good stead for this new venture. Not one for the political side of Mod or its recently developing division of styles and associated scenes, here was a young man from the steel city willing to put his Mod persona right into the core of the free-form dance floor of Acid Jazz.

Lee Radforth - "Acid Jazz... well I suppose it was mainly a London thing, and revolved round a certain Mr Eddie Piller and Gilles Peterson but it sent ripples and added some much needed vibrancy through the movement as far as I was concerned. The Mod scene in the mid 80's had always had its fair share of dance floor Jazz played tipping a nod to the scene's origins, which oddly a lot of the people I know that got into Mod in the 60's really don't get on with, seeing Mod as a purely soul thing music wise.

I think a certain amount of people that got into Mod through the revival and saw it evolve had become disillusioned by the late 80's with in fighting and politics, and I think we were always looking to keep the scene fresh and moving forward while obviously keeping one foot in the origins of the scene, and I guess that's where Acid Jazz hit a nerve for me.

The LP 'Acid Jazz and other Illicit Grooves' released on Urban in 1988 was the first time I saw the term, although the memory is a little hazy. Featuring the likes of James Taylor (ex of The Prisoners), Steve White (The Style Council), Simon Booth (Working Week), Jacko Peake (The Paul

Weller Movement), Alec Dankworth (son of John Dankworth) amongst others. It moulded Jazz/Latin/house and seemed a fairly natural progression or slight diversion of Mod as far as I was concerned. I-D magazine also ran an article 'Acid Jazz Mods' at the time.

I was by this time mainly listening to Blue Note/Prestige style soulful dance floor Jazz and Latin fuelled by the wonderful Baz fe Jazz compilations that got you searching out records by the likes of Eddie Jefferson, Ivan 'Boogaloo Joe' Jones, Lou Donaldson and James Moody. As luck would have it, I also became acquainted with Sheffield musician Richard Hawley who shared my love of funky Jazz. Sat playing records in his would you believe 'Hawley Street' flat he suggested we should start

a club night. The next week after a meeting with the then Leadmill head honcho Graham Wrench Vout Oroonie was born. The premise was simple enough, to try to create a night where hipsters could groove to Jazz/Latin/and Hammond instrumentals and when available we could book suitable live bands to complement the night. There was nothing else in Sheffield remotely like it. Vout Oroonie quickly garnered a cult reputation that saw the likes of Acid Jazz heroes The Brand New Heavies and Mod legends Jimmy McGriff and Big John Patton gracing the stage, while people tore up the dance floor to Jimmy Smiths 'Stay Loose', Oscar Brown Jnrs Mr Kicks, and Detroit City Limits 98 Cents Plus Tax alongside Lou Donaldson, Art Blakey and newcomers Galliano, The Jazz Renegades, The Young Disciples, Corduroy, and The James Taylor Quartet.

The Brand New Heavies gig was reviewed in Melody Maker with a brief outline of the vibe of the club itself, which helped spread the word, as did the club flyers, which were designed by Sheffield's Designers Republic and quickly became a collector's item in their own right.

As mentioned before Acid Jazz was predominantly a London scene so trips to the Wagg Club, Dingwalls Jazz Alldayers in Camden, Blow Up and upstairs at Ronnie Scott's in Soho, along with The Blue Note were made which also combined record buying and clothes shopping.

As for the clothes for me the casual Acid Jazz look revolved round Levi and Wrangler cords, Gabicci 'Yardie' style tops, that Mod stalwart, John Smedley jumper, and vintage 60's knitwear. Along with newer brands like Duffer of St George. Some would argue the scene was nothing to do with Mod and in some respects, I guess they would be right. But it was an underground scene with its own look, music, record labels (Acid Jazz now joined by Talking Loud) releasing a slew of material by new groups with a loose affiliation bonded by a love of Jazz, Latin, 60's Hammond instrumentals, Soul, Funk and house.

In essence, as far as I am concerned Acid Jazz was just a moniker under which a melting pot of musical styles and fashions loosely came together to dance and have a good time. At Vout Oroonie, as at Dingwalls the more Mod end of the crowd preferred the Hammond instrumentals, Boogaloo, and the Soulful Jazz, while the out and out Jazzers in their Zoot Suits and spats preferred hard bop. In my mind Vout Oroonie was as near to a modern day Flamingo Club as I could get, and it doesn't get much more Mod than that in my book."

WELLER IT'S A NEW THING!

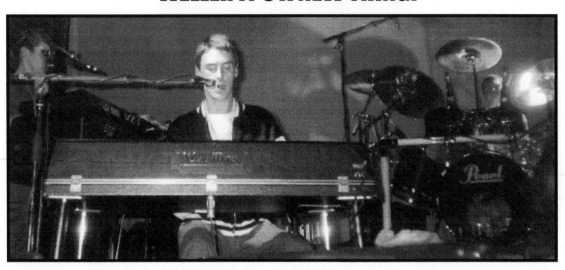

It seemed almost a lifetime since Weller's closing chapter with the Style Council - a cosmopolitan collective - the projectionists of wide-ranging musical genres, celebrating the early Modernist sounds of Jazz and injecting into it a mix of Soul, Funk, Latin, 60's Pop and various other experimental rhythms - perhaps Modernism as a musical soundtrack personified. Yet, in essence, Weller had merely taken a well-earned but unplanned breather due to the impact of record label dismissal and the critical outpouring of disenchanted fans, which surely reduced his confidence and prestige. However, following a series of outings as The Paul Weller Movement in 1990 and a distinct return to his roots, Weller was assuredly back on track, ready to start again and push the boundaries of Modernism in all directions - with nods to the past, sideways glances to recent styles and influences and (most importantly) a creative full-speed trajectory into tomorrow!

Simon Franklin - "After the demise of the Style Council Paul Weller retreated to a self-imposed exile a la John Lennon. Mod did the same, waiting for its third coming (which for all sense and purpose never happened).

When Weller emerged in May 1991 with his own self-financed single 'Into Tomorrow' on his own label 'Freedom High', he had truly gone back to his English (maximum) R&B roots. It was , also, around this time that Clarks reintroduced it's [famous] Desert Boots on the High Street, available (at first) exclusively in their shop in Regents Street - and definitely not at the price or colour variation of today's version. Ben Sherman and Fred Perry suddenly become more widely available in a better quality and closer to the original pattern than the cheaper '79 variety had been. As for Weller, he was about to unleash his own soundtrack - to this subtle revival - of a more purist shade of Modernism.

Ironically, Weller couldn't even get a UK label to release his self-titled resurrection album, it was left to a Japanese label to unleash it on the world, and it was only available on an expensive import. I made several pilgrimages to London before I laid my hands on a copy from the Virgin megastore in Oxford Street. Compared to the sharp angular sounds of The Jam and the Soulful struts of the Council, this was very lo-fi, the music and sound more complex, noticeably softer and more like a day in the country than one in the city or a La Paris. Less 'sup up yer beer', less cappuccino more herbal tea - looser and free from restraints or rules.

In Weller's own words, he was revisiting his roots (via frequent journeys back to Woking), adding further influences and heading forward. This definitely wasn't history textbook Mod i.e. parka, Levi's, Desert Boots, button-down shirt etc.. These were less orthodox Mod influences, taking as the starting point the late-60's bands and pastoral style of Traffic, psychedelic period Beatles, 'Ogden's' era Small Faces and 'Village Green Preservation Society' period Kinks.

On the cover, Weller was wearing a ruffle shirt, his hair a longer Marriott style and his trousers pinstriped and flared. It was almost full circle from the 60's, yet adding contemporary influences in the mix; it was derivative. It also meant that you could dress like this and not everyone would get it, it wasn't that obvious, well it was but only to yourself and your contemporaries. Acid Jazz broke into the mainstream and, with it, a more Soulful Jazz looking Mod, this naturally also went into the mix. So you had maximum R&B, late 60's 'Heavy Soul', free-form rock and all of its varied influences and looks.

Photos: copyright of Jody Maguire

Now I'm not sure that Weller's resurgence, which started with his solo debut release, heralded a Mod revival of sorts, but it certainly brought the subculture back into the sub-consciousness of the nation, where it's remained bubbling under as a stable subculture ever since. You can see it everywhere, it's clearly available to all. Only now, it's moving on, at its own steam. Weller, without knowing it, through his musical influences, introduced the theory 'what is Mod music and the answer 'it's music Mods listen to'. Ultimately, that can be anything, and with reason so can the dress code of Mods. Weller and his disciple cohorts prove it's not cool to look like some kind of fancy dress Carnaby Street styled Mod, take that as your influence if you must, but put a spin on it! Weller again challenged his audience, taking them on a musical and visual journey, touching the surface and making you do the homework to further enhance this life experience.

The early 90's were the start of Weller's revival (or rather return) and himself taking his place at the higher echelon of great British stylists and songwriters. He was our generation's Neil Young, Van Morrison and, if you like, Lennon and McCartney in one. Who else is still influencing what we listen to - from Krautrock through to Northern Soul and back and beyond whilst influencing how we dress and look? Morrissey? Costello? [the late great] Joe Strummer? They stood still - was Mod(ernism) supposed to do that? By its very inference and definition - no!

Through Weller you can trace second generation Mod revivalists (The Jam), the more considered Modernists (the Style Council) through to Mod today and it's integration and place as an important influential subculture. Weller's look, vision and sound takes you on the whole journey, the complete picture. From 'In the City' (the bastard sons' of Marriott, Townshend and Davis) to 'Cafe Bleu (Miles, Coltrane and Blue Note) to the solo years of Paul Weller, continuing onwards and upwards... and into the future!"

By 1993's 'Wild Wood', his follow-up to the reawakening of talent and influences that had been his 1992 self-titled début solo outing, Weller was experiencing in full flow a new critically applauded honeymoon of his art. Weller's stature and Mod pedigree as a solo artist grew significantly as old fans returned to the fold and ex-Mods and Brit Pop lovers embraced his fusion of classic 60's rock, Soul and R&B and a recent penchant for the folk/rock of Neil Young and Nick Drake amongst others. In truth, Weller had already rediscovered his muse well before any stirrings of Mod-ingested Brit Pop arrived.

Weller's reappraisal from the music press and fans alike, seemed to symbolise a period in which the former angry young man of The Jam and cosmopolitan Mod of the Style Council could simply do no wrong. Weller, too, embraced Brit Pop, proclaiming his favourite acts from The Charlatans to Primal Scream in 'Select' - the very magazine that had set the scene for Brit Pop with their 1993 front cover of Suede's Brett Anderson and a Union Jack headlined with 'Yanks Go Home' - in reference to the US Grunge acts that they were rallying against. Meanwhile Mod's evolving legacy was in full swing in a growing array of clubs across the country.

Tricia Hickling (Nottinghamshire Mod girl) - "One of my first favourite vinyl LPs purchased and that of a new band at the time was the The Money Spyder by The James Taylor Quartet. Any Mod inspired by a Hammond organ from the likes of The Small Faces, Driscoll and Auger, Graham Bond, etc. could not resist the charms of The James Taylor Quartet. Spy-themed links to the 60's and thumping instrumentals was bound to keep the 'Mod vein' throbbing. This paved the way to Acid Jazz with bands like Corduroy (previously Boys Wonder) and Mother Earth exploding with a refreshing organ sound. Various bands and nights out between 1987 and 1993 included a medley of Acid Jazz, organ grooves plus 60s/70s Soul and funk. In Nottingham, we attended late night bars or clubs (avoiding raves and house party types like the plague!) and always found some blasting organ and dance floor grooves to keep us happy!"

Tricia pictured in 1988

Enamel Verguren - "Then came the Acid Jazz explosion; The Prisoners had split up since '85, but JTQ was holding the flag and we truly believed, for a short period, that this new wave of music could hold the fight against the obnoxious invasion of Techno/House that was everywhere – of course we were wrong, due to the numbers of punters involved."

One particular club also flew the flag as an alternative to the post-rave period of splintered dance scenes - one that came to personify the period in creating a unique and very 60's influenced version of club culture. Not everyone's cup of English tea, 'Blow Up', however could not be ignored with its recognition of a wide selection of sounds for the dance floor of the 90's!

"It was a regeneration of Mod ... an agenda, new music, new style, to make a raid on the mainstream rather than being in the side-lines." - **Paul Tunkin 'Blow Up' founding DJ**

'Blow Up' club, originally located in the upstairs function room of a Camden pub, The Laurel Tree, opened in October 1993 by Paul Tunkin - quickly establishing a vibrant and energetic antidote to the prevalent Grunge and bland indie scenes of the time. In parallel with the emerging Brit Pop, the club signalled a continuation of a swinging London style for the 90's and beyond, incorporating the sounds of Easy Listening, French Pop, TV themes, Jazz, Brit R&B, Soul, psychedelia and much more with weekly guest DJ's adding to the eclectic catalogue of sounds. Andy Lewis from Watford was one such DJ.

Andy Lewis - "Right from the first night in October 1993 at down-at-hell Camden boozer The Laurel Tree, I knew that Blow Up would be a lot of fun. Between us, Paul Tunkin and I had a stack of great records and a desire to put a bit of style back into a world that was submerged by grunge or bludgeoned by repetitive beats.

To begin with, we were preaching to the converted. I'd managed to bring along a lot of the people who also went to Wendy May's Locomotion on the Friday night. We were joined by Paul Tunkin's art-school and indie scene friends. Bored with queuing in the autumn drizzle, the crowds waiting to get into the Jazz Cafe and grunge night Silver at The Underworld came to check us out instead. Discovering plenty of common ground, they mingled, danced, exchanged glances and phone numbers. Above all, they loved the music. Word began to spread.

Mod purists hated us. We weren't a Scene Club re-enactment society. We were playing bona fide soul or beat rarities next to Stereolab or whatever. Furthermore, we had records that they'd never heard of, and we were attracting crowds to our night that they could only dream about. But it wasn't a competition. It was a reminder that it wasn't supposed to be set in stone. It was supposed to be all about fun, dancing, dressing up, losing a few inhibitions, being young- or at any rate youthful-minded. They hated us, but they still came. Week after week.

Whether they liked it or not, the Mod purists were having a catalysing effect on the crowd. You could track the transformation in some of the clientele. The first time through the doors, they'd be grunging it in a plaid shirt with long hair. The following week they'd have had a haircut and got hold of a Fred Perry and DM's. After a month or so, some would be sporting slim-cut 60's suits, others no less sharp in their chosen look, possessed of a swagger and a sense of style.

We went on tour with Blur, and discovered that all across the country people were excited by our choice of music. The music press was full of it. Back in Camden, the queues got longer, the nights got wilder. The Laurel Tree was like a Tardis in reverse. It looked much bigger on the outside, where the queue now stretched round the block. Inside, a sweating crush of souls jostled rather than danced most of the time, up the stairs, at the bars, even on the snooker table downstairs. Condensed sweat fell like rain, and steam billowed out of the upstairs windows.

Eventually the West End beckoned. Blow Up transferred to The Wag, where it succeeded in pulling in the punters in big numbers until the day the venue closed its doors. By then it wasn't the only game in town. A rejuvenated Mod scene was welcoming those who'd decided they wanted to dig deeper into the lifestyle. British pop was fast becoming a global brand. Dance music had adopted, adapted and evolved the sounds and the beats Blow Up had helped popularize. Twenty years on, and the noise we made in that Camden pub is still being heard."

Graham Lentz - "In 1990/91 Paul Weller released his first solo LP and I became aware of this label called Acid Jazz who were doing some amazing and interesting things with new bands. Eventually I discovered Blur, then Oasis and the whole Brit Pop era. I was working in London again by this time and I noticed the influence of Mod returning, but it had changed into a more informal look. Three-buttoned suits were making a comeback, as was the parka (in an updated form). New twist-and-go scooters appeared.

I started to investigate more and realized there was something real happening and Mod was making itself known again. I found out about clubs like Blow Up, Mousetrap, Lordy Lord, Heavenly Blocked in the West Country, The Hideaway in Manchester and Brighton Beach which toured Universities in the north. These were hugely important clubs in the mid to late 90s."

By 1993, the continuing interest in the great British sounds of the 60's inspired further attention to the back catalogues of institutions such as The Kinks and Small Faces. The Kinks, in particular and their blend of pastoral musical images and the music hall lyricism of a England now lost was a profound influence on Blur, that ex-Baggy act of a mere three years previously.

Blur's 'Modern Life is Rubbish' was a crucial signpost in helping pave the way for Brit Pop's classic 60's Mod digestion. The band dismissed the then prevalent Grunge scene, instead calling for a return to the classic British pop of the 60's and a stripped down casual Mod look to match. By the following year, Blur had almost parodied this with 'Parklife', which featured 'Quadrophenia' star Phil Daniels on its title track. 1994 also saw a clutch of Mod acts, Manteray, Thurman (who perfectly celebrated The Kinks with their single 'English Tea'), along with Blow-Up regulars The Weekenders and others. That November, struggling music weekly Melody Maker decided that this increase in Mod profile warranted a front page and a further eight page inside feature.

That same year a bunch of 'foul mouthed yobs' yet again set the course of music onto an unexpected direction with a debut single and album that, for a generation, defined and sound tracked their hedonistic youth. The band, Oasis, though never quite bonafide Mods and without a doubt never accepted as a Mod band, managed to utilise the style and sounds of Mod within their influences. Their success spiralled to unexpected heights and came to define the post-Brit Pop era.

However, not all members of the Mod fraternity of recent years agreed with the relevance of Brit Pop within Mod's legacy.

Brett 'Buddy' Ascott (ex-The Chords) "I'm not sure that Brit Pop really had much to do with Mod as such, despite Liam's parkas! I thought Supergrass were the best band to come out of all that, and the drummer was great too!"

Without a doubt, Brit Pop, for all of its shortcomings, did help to salvage the profile and future of Mod. The genre may not have presented anything exclusively new to the table - with its condensed musical interpretation of Mod's past mixed with other influences such as punk. However, it helped inspire a whole new generation of music fans to discover the likes of The Action, The Creation and the song writing talent of Ray Davies etc. Consequently, many other acts left undiscovered since the 60's were given rediscovered.

Though the mid-90's may have belonged to Oasis and Blur in sales and media profiles (the summer 95 singles war between the two bands which achieved national headlines, as the world of pop awaited the victor, was the high-tide of Brit Pop), the era was also one of appreciation of less mainstream acts. A band such as the Prisoners, who had served their Mod apprenticeship tenfold, should have rightfully prospered greatly considering the musical climate of the times. But such bands were destined for something far more long lasting and untainted by the trappings of fame. The Prisoners must surely be one of the greatest cult bands of all-time, never losing the respect and admiration of their core fan base.

David Abrahams-Edley - "In 1996 I was DJ'ing at 'Brighton Beach' and writing 'Call it Something Nice', I was getting a lot of freebies of Brit Pop stuff to play and review. There was a company called Beatwax that sent me about half a dozen CDs a fortnight and out of the blue I received a copy of 'Shine on Me' by the Prisoners! It brought it all back. I bought a vinyl copy in Fopp Records, Devonshire Street, in Sheffield. This time I managed to get to see them four times: at the Leadmill in Sheffield and Subterranea and the Forum in London (where me and Scott Copeland DJ'd) to packed and sweaty crowds and Sankeys Soap on Manchester - to an almost empty room. This contradiction seemed to be a metaphor for the Prisoners. Of course I have a flowered view of this but I never understood why they never got a fraction of the credit they deserved and why so many others did so much better on the back of them. It is a tragedy of Faustian proportions."

Tricia Hickling - "The Acid Jazz scene with 'indie kids' belonging to The Stone Roses and the Inspiral Carpets were the beginnings of a whole new music chapter yet to follow. Whilst we were at clubs, such as The Dubble Bubble dancing to Acid Jazz and classics, such as 'You Really Got Me', new bands Oasis and Blur were already starting to grace the DJ's decks. Brit Pop was born and for us Mods it really was exciting. The bands exploding on the Brit Pop scene were back to basics - guitar bands and 'real' instruments taking influences from original 60s Mod bands through to punk/new wave, '79 revival to Acid Jazz and indie styles; there was something for any Mod still standing. We went to a Brit Pop night at The Zone in Nottingham every Saturday night and wore our 60s inspired clothing, mixed it up with some 70's [styles] and would not be laughed at.

My favourite band of the time was Supergrass, but I couldn't grow my sideburns to Gaz's extent! Mod nights were using the Brit Pop theme to get back on track with 'Brighton Beach' nights around the country and live gigs were enormous; made better as we could wear trainers and not ruin our best shoes. Myself and a handful of the original 80s mods loved the Brit Pop scene that encompassed Mod and kept the whole thing alive and youthful; if not slightly rebellious!"

Ed Silvester - "I think the rise of Brit-Pop in the early 1990's re-invigorated and saved Mod and added extra impetuous to the scene, which rekindled my interest in mod culture again. Although, none of the Brit Pop bands was strictly Mod, Oasis did have the swagger and confidence of a Mod band, they showed that they were influenced by the Mod revival, in terms of music and fashion. My interest in Mod had begun to wane by then, but was piqued again, and as a result of the popularity of Brit-Pop – with bands like Ocean Colour Scene and The Clique, I've never really lost touch since the mid 1990's."

Enamel Verguren - "Then came Brit Pop, which was far too commercial for me; that's when we realised that the media were using our culture, to their own advantage. Eventually, the majority turned to the Swinging London vibe by the mid-'90s, seeing it as the ultimate look and the accomplishment of the '60s Mods; but a lot of people, though, didn't see it that way (too much of a hippie influence obviously) and moved onto the Northern Soul scene."

Andrew Harris - "The Brit Pop era simply gave us more nights out; the clubs offered a mix of indie/Brit Pop and also sixties classics. One week we would be watching The Psychotic Reaction or The Flaming Stars and then the following week we would be at a Bluetones or even a Super Furry Animals gig. I recall being in Brighton at a Mod/freakbeat night in 1997. It was only half-full, but there were some great tunes being spun. A few days later at a different venue, we were able to attend a very full Brit Pop /Indie night which also played sixties tunes; it was a good mix overall. There were numerous opportunities in the evening for mod types. We made the most of this period, as we had grown so tired of empty rooms and Northern Soul music. Brit Pop brought with it a refreshing scene, which hit the country in a way that was reminiscent of the Two Tone era.

I believe that having your own taste in music and not conforming to what is deemed as Mod music by Mod historians is important. In 1984, I recall enjoying the bands, The Prisoners and The Milkshakes on The Tube. This was my first connection to my long-term passion for garage music, apart from the obvious of course; Them, Kingsmen, Kinks, Stones, Yardbirds, etc. - this introduced me to the 'Medway' sound. Several years later, I found myself collecting the 'Pebbles' compilations and various sixties garage tunes of all types. This also introduced me deeper into Surf Rock, by which I don't mean folk songs about surfin', but instrumental guitar played loud through fender amps; Wipeout and Pipeline had already been played at Mod nights in the 80s.

Garage and surf rock (in my opinion) go together like fish and chips; I was listening to surf and guitar instrumentals by the likes of Link Wray. In 1994, Tarantino's Pulp Fiction sealed the deal for me. No longer did I have images in my head of spotty kids dancing around campfires on the beach; it was now 'gangster'music! Of course, The Chantays had previously been effective during the action scenes in gang film, The Wanderers back in 1979."

The interest for all things Mod that re-emerged along with Brit Pop helped greatly to inspire new clubs with a distinct focus on 60's period Mod, mingled with the best of the day's sounds. The genre also invigorated club culture and its soundtrack along the way. A discerning Modernist of the period would have possibly indulged in the trip-hop ambience of Portishead just as avidly as the Charlatans? Classic examples of the integration of Mod's back catalogue with Brit Pop and the more Mod-flavoured indie hits of the day were the monthly Brighton Beach club nights in Sheffield and Leeds, in which the sounds of The Kinks and Booker T and the MG's shared a playlist with Pulp and The Jam. In a smaller adjacent room, the more obscure sounds of Freakbeat, R&B, Soul and Hammond-fuelled Soul/Jazz were enjoyed by a hardcore of more demanding purist Mods that desired something much closer to their roots and heritage.

Mods now enjoyed a broad canvas of styles and while some adhered faithfully to the obscure sounds of 60's Mod, the opportunity to also sample contrasting music styles was hard to resist – be it the revived Jazz of the Nick Rossi Set, the retro funk of Brothers Seven, the power chords of The Rifles, garage punk, post-Brit Pop, Acid Jazz and in more recent days the talents of The Moons, Andy Lewis and the new breed of R&B groups - to name a few available musical options. It could be fairly argued that this cosmopolitan soundtrack supplied part of Mod's legacy for the 90's and into the following two decades.

TAKE ME TO THE HIDEAWAY BY MIKE WARBURTON

The love of original Black American R&B has come full circle in recent years, with a healthy portion of the contemporary Mod scene casting aside much of the more obvious and often clichéd musical connections to Mod and instead opting for a return to the roots of their forerunners. Along with a respect and taste for the Modern Jazz sounds of the original Modernists, the more discerning Mod of today nurtures an ever-expanding sense of musical eclecticism - and none more profound than in the re-discovery of the sounds of Black America from the late 50's and early 60's, much of which had spent the last few decades largely under-appreciated or undiscovered. A need for like-minded clubs to enjoy and share the love of these dance floor-demanding sounds has spawned The Hideaway club, which paved the way for other like-minded clubs to follow.

Mike Warburton - "I got into the Mod Scene, like most people in the late 70's (late 78 to be precise). After a few years listening to the dreaded revival and frequenting the likes of Wigan Casino, a combination of the Richard Barnes book 'Mods' and visiting a club night called 'Jump and Grunt' at Rafters in Manchester promoted by original Twisted Wheel DJ and Manchester legend Roger Eagle, pointed me in the right direction. Original Mod tunes from the likes of Dobie Gray, Arthur Alexander, and Bo Diddley, were being spun, and the clientele were smarter than anything I had encountered, with an original Mod look starting to emerge. No more Weller and Wigan for me, it was a life changing experience like no other.

Over the next five years, I attended all of the top Mod clubs in the UK such as the legendary 'Sneakers' (London), 'Outrigger' (Birmingham), and 'The Polish Club' (Coventry). The best night of the lot had to be 'The Dolphin' (Liverpool), which spun quality upfront sounds from the likes of June Bateman, Ernestine Anderson, and my all-time hero Arthur Alexander when certain other clubs were succumbing to the dubious delights of 'Bert's Apple Crumble'. Additionally it was a club with 'Mods in it' instead of that most clichéd of clichés a 'Mod Club'

With the downturn of the Mod scene in the late 1980's I started attending the quality end of the Northern All-nighter scene such as the 100 Club (London) and the Wilton Ballroom (Yorkshire). Elements of the Northern scene had embraced the R&B/early 6T's sound in a big way. With my now extensive knowledge of the subject, I started recommending and selling tunes to DJS' and collectors alike. Soon enough I started DJ'ing, initially for Dave Callister at a new club in Liverpool called Move and Groove. Over the next few years I graced the turntables at a number of leading Mod/R&B Clubs such as the Mousetrap (London), Compared to What (London), and Heavenly Blocked (Weston Super mare). The highlight of this era was being asked to DJ with Roger Eagle, on his last ever DJ appearance at The Mitre in Manchester. To say I was blown away when he praised my selection of sounds such as 'My man called me' Big Mama Thornton (Peacock) and 'You're Funeral' and 'My Trial' Sonny Boy Williamson (Chess) was an understatement. It was on this night that myself and two other long standing Manchester Mods, Neil Henderson, and Paul Welsby decided to start a new club in Manchester that would follow in Roger's ground-breaking direction. That club would be called The Hideaway.

We were concerned that the majority of so-called Mod clubs of the time, were overloading on either Northern Soul or that freakybeat, and were neglecting the R&B and 6T'S Soul sounds, that were beloved of the original Mods.

Late February 1999, the Hideaway club opened its doors for the first time at The Mitre in Cathedral Gates, Manchester, and did so every month until March 2011. Named by me in a rare moment of inspiration when looking through my record box and stumbling across a certain Freddy king tune, Paul Welsby made the night even more distinctive by describing the music played as New Breed R&B. This moniker has certainly stuck with clubs to this day using it.

Mods at The Hideaway, 2001 (copyright Graham Lentz)

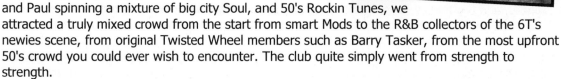

A typical Hideaway playlist from the early days would have featured among others the Latin Soul of the Caper Brothers, the Mod Jazz of Oscar Brown jnr, Ska from the likes of Laurel Aitken, and Prince Buster, and Northern R&B dancers from the likes of Patience Valentine and Arthur Alexander. Also through the varied collections of the three promoters/DJS with me concentrating on those big R&B newies with more than a smattering of Mod tunes, Neil playing the Soulful end of the R&B spectrum and introducing many quality new discoveries in the process, and Paul spinning a mixture of big city Soul, and 50's Rockin Tunes, we attracted a truly mixed crowd from the start from smart Mods to the R&B collectors of the 6T's newies scene, from original Twisted Wheel members such as Barry Tasker, from the most upfront 50's crowd you could ever wish to encounter. The club quite simply went from strength to strength.

We prided ourselves on booking the top DJ's from the Mod, Soul, and 50'S Scenes, names that have graced the Hideaway flyers over the years include the likes of Adey Croasdell, Roger Banks, Carl Willingham, Marc Forrest, Chris Dale, Alan Handscombe, and Frank (Hip Teens) Pop. 'The Hideaway' has brought such legendary DJ'S as Barry Tasker (Pendulum), Roger Fairhurst (Brazenoose St), and Paul Hallam and Richard Early (Sneakers) out of retirement. Additionally so many DJ's from both the Mod and Soul scenes have secured their first bookings at the Hideaway, names that spring to mind include Mike Hawkins, Bill Kealy, Nick Hudson, and the legendary 'Scouse Manc' John Kelly.

We also managed so many firsts such as membership cards, and a quarterly newsletter, keeping members informed of all future events and reviewing sounds worth looking for. The posters for the nights featuring Soul/R&B greats became very sought after. The membership grew to such an extent that after twelve months people were getting turned away, this resulted in a move to a venue, which will always be associated with the peak years of the Hideaway, The Waldorf in Gore Street, Manchester. So many memorable nights were had at this legendary venue, which reminded older members so much of the Brazenoose Street Twisted Wheel. Full Club and a full dance floor, to say The Hideaway was on the up was yet again an understatement.

July 2000 saw the introduction of the Mod Weekender (two days of sounds and styles) which has become the template for every other weekender in Europe. Kicking off with a write up in Record Collector (The R&B Scene), it has run continuously to this day. A combination of top DJ's and the occasional live act such as The Five Aces, Gene Drayton unit, and Soul legend Tommy Hunt has led to an event that is unequalled anywhere. Even the scooter riders are smartly dressed.

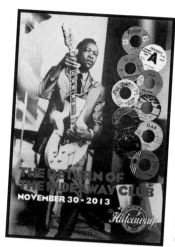

The success kept on coming, with the launch of a series of two 'New Breed R&B CD'S' on the legendary Kent label. The first was a Kent records compilation with the second one being the best of the R&B sounds from the legendary King label. Launched by Adey Croasdell at a packed Hideaway special and the next day on Richard Searling's Soul Sauce radio show, these CD's are talked about until this day.

Another stroke of inspiration saw the Hideaway bring back the original Twisted Wheel days of 63-65 with a Brazenoose St special that ran at Christmas for several years, and was warmly received by both original Twisted Wheel members and the new breed alike.

July 2008 saw a move from The Waldorf to the upmarket Deansgate Hotel Manchester, with even more success. 200+ attending the weekenders, a successful New Year's eve special, and yet more guest DJ's introduced such as Pete Griffin, Bill Kealy, and Davie Girvan. Of course not forgetting the legend that is Martin 'Sugar' Merchant, who introduced the whole re-wind concept from the reggae clubs to The Hideaway. And surprise surprise so many other clubs have followed us. Sugar's most memorable quote, was 'This goes out to the Hideaway massive'. If he was around in an earlier age, he would have given King Stitt a run for his money.

However a combination of the recession, and the dearest bar prices, led to a drop in the monthly attendances, although the bigger events such as the Mod Weekender and the anniversary led to the closure of the monthly Hideaway in March 2011. Tributes were overwhelming, after all The Hideaway had set the musical agenda for the previous 12 years, as well as introducing more than a sense of style to the Northern Soul obsessed North West. 'The Hideaway' had also made a big contribution to several weekend events, such as 'Prestatyn', 'Ace of Clubs' (various destinations in Europe), and 'Hipshaker' (Isle of Wight), and more recently the excellent Ham Yardies (Isle of Wight). Thanks to Guy Joseph for inviting me to DJ at one of the most popular events on the Mod calendar.

The Mod Weekenders have continued to his day, very successfully with a mix of UK and International DJ'S, the clientele getting smarter with each passing year. Paul Welsby however was changing direction, and was going increasingly towards that reggae train. He made the decision to no longer be involved early 2013, and has since launched his own skinhead reggae night.

Myself and Neil Henderson made the decision to continue with the Mod Weekender., at a venue that is increasingly becoming known thanks to the enthusiasm of the landlord Sean Brett as Manchester's s Soul Bar, the Nag's head at Jackson Row off Deansgate Manchester. In the meantime, several top Mod/R&B venues had successfully emerged such as The Ad Lib (Lincoln), and R&B 123 and Ham Yardies (London). Special mention goes out to another London venue which I had the pleasure to DJ at on several occasions, Hip City which successfully brought back the Mod sounds of the early 60's and quite rightly was regarded as the club for original Modernists. A visit to Sheffield's first rate King Bee club (thanks to Lee Radforth for promoting a first rate night which continues to set standards), convinced me with little persuasion from Neil it was the time to bring back the Hideaway on a four times a year basis. The Mod Weekender at the Nags Head was the start, first rate DJ sets from what was our best ever guest DJ line up (Bill Kealy, Chris Dale, and Alan Handscome, a smart and upfront crowd, made for a fantastic atmosphere that surpassed all of the previous events. After that, it was announced that starting November 2013 there would be along with the weekender 3 additional Hideaways, back in business with a new upfront audience. Along with king Bee the North West now has two of the top clubs in the UK."

THE NEW UNTOUCHABLES

Perhaps the most ambitious of Mod's movers and shakers of recent years is Rob Bailey, who, from a young age, decided that the world map of Mod's legacy should provide an inspiration and future.

Rob Bailey - "I was 12 years old and it was through the kids at our school and a couple of our teachers. One teacher Miss Potts was a Mod and rode a Vespa to School and was our home economics teacher (quite a few of us signed up for that class as she was a beauty) as well as some other sixth grade lads. One of our other teachers used to DJ and play stuff like 'Green Onions' at the Christmas disco (quite sure they don't play that anymore) along with The Jam and Specials and old Soul like Benny Spellman's 'Fortune Teller'. We also had some great local bands in the Medway area including the Prisoners and Milkshakes and later the James Taylor Quartet.

I started out playing records at our local 'Cool Running Scooter Club' nights when I was sixteen with fellow NU DJ Lee Miller. We had two old record players from home wired together through an amp into a pair of amateur speakers and that gave me the DJ bug. After that the group started our forays into the nearby London scene clubs like Sneakers and the Bizz and then very swiftly onto the Phoenix and CCI weekenders. Like many other it was Tony Class who got me started seriously first as the warm up DJ at sessions in the Bizz and then onto the weekenders in 1988. That same year I run my first club night in London together with two friends Tony Schockman and Check it Out John at the Crown and Sceptre in W1. In 1990/91 a group of friends from around the London area started The Untouchables. The New Untouchables were formed in September 1997 after personal differences in the group. The aim was simple and remains the same - to encourage young people into the scene and provide a platform for the converted with exciting events.

Our first event was an alldayer at the Dungeon venue under London Bridge in November 1997. It was a fantastic venue under the bridge comprising of several arches linked to one another with different sixties music and four live bands. This was quickly followed by a NYE event and a full set of rally dates in 1998 including Hastings, Scarborough, Brighton and Isle of Wight with the first ACTION show in thirty years. From a personal point of view getting all the original members of The Action back together to reform for a dozen shows was amazing and seeing the response the band received was heartwarming.

The first ever Sonics show outside the US was also a defining moment for the New Untouchables and the band. Other special original acts I had the honor to work with are Love with Brenda Holloway, The Velvelettes, Arthur Lee and Johnny Echols, PP Arnold, Yardbirds, Martha Reeves, The Pretty Things, Creation, Maxine Brown, Arthur Brown, Dean Parrish, The Flirtations, The Prisoners, Herbie Goins and the Nightimers, Brian Auger, Zoot Money, Rupert's People and The Remains. Great new acts worth a mention like Eli 'Paperboy' Reed, King Khan and The Shrines, The Strypes, Horrors, Nick Waterhouse have all been very successful and in some cases gone on to mainstream success.

We were sending our printed newsletters all over the World from the early Untouchables days and over the years, the list grew. Modstock in 1994 in Germany was the first big International event. In 1998 we started co-promoting events like Euro YeYe in Spain and Autumn Stone, Italy and by 1999 our first US event 66-99 in San Diego with Ugly Things magazine.

There had always been music and fashion fads within the scene ever since I can remember. I think the 80's and 90's scene took the same route that the original scene did after some years. Some Mods became skinheads and got into reggae, some became Soul boys and girls and some took LSD and got into Psychedelic styles.

Another important factor was the Brit Pop boom in the mid-90's which took its influence from the Kinks, Beatles and Pretty Things etc. These new kids found these sounds closer to the Brit Pop bands they followed. The love of the rare sixties black music would resonate with some of them later on.

I always thought that saying NU were Swirlies was just lazy and inaccurate when you consider that out of the six DJ's only Speed played solely Pop Art and Psychedelic sounds. Pid and I can play anything from the Mod and Sixties spectrum while all the other DJs play almost solely black authentic Mod sounds. Many of our events like mousetrap and crossfire for example had more than one room of music so there was an opportunity to play a broader range of sixties musical styles."

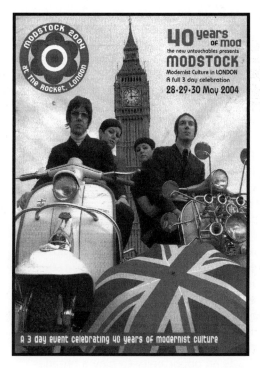

The success of the New Untouchables and Blow Up - with their focus on the appeal of not just the standard Mod recipes of Soul and R&B, but the Freakbeat and Psyche crossover sounds - coincided with London clubs such as The Purple Pussycat and Mousetrap. A resurgence of the lounge-styled TV incidental soundtracks of Tony Hatch and Tony Hawksworth was welcomed by some, though most purists cringed with disapproval with regards to the swinging London sounds of 1967-74 and its Regency period fashion influences. 'Swirlies' these long haired paisley shirt-wearing, Freakbeat obsessives, who mingled with Mods on the scene, were so christened (the connection to the Austin Powers film of the time is over-exaggerated), yet in retrospect, they were merely expressing a preference for a later period of Mod-influenced style of music and fashion.

Undoubtedly, the influence of Mod has spread globally, escalating considerably by the 90's and beyond. Europe, which has always had a profound influence on the culture, began to host Mod events, whilst the USA, Australia, New Zealand, Japan and Canada are also graced with prominent Mod-enthused scenes, the latter enjoying a thriving West Coast scene modelled upon the original UK Mods.

Penny Lane - "I live in Winnipeg, Manitoba, Canada - not really a beacon of Mod culture. I always loved 60's clothes, music, fashion. I was one of those people who was into the whole Mod thing before I knew what Mod was. I was graduating high school in 1997 and was becoming immersed in the whole Brit Pop movement that hit at the time. From Brit Pop, I discovered Mod and started to attend regular events and get more into it in the late 90's, early 2000s. We had a regular Saturday night here at a bar called 'Loaded Club' which was our weekly Mod night and it was fantastic - amazing dress, great music. I became very close friends with the DJ of the night, who hosted his own radio show on a campus and community radio station here in Winnipeg. At his urging, I applied for my own radio show, putting in a proposal to bring a Mod radio show to the air that would explore all aspects of the subculture. I started broadcasting my show, Punks in Parkas in May of 2005. I'm for a global scene, and I love seeing all the different variances of Mod around the world and how each generation reinterprets it for their own time and place. I know we can't all agree on everything and I love to see the difference of opinion in the scene!"

As Mod entered its official sixth decade at the start of the new millennium, its public profile was considerably high. The Who engaged upon their 'Maximum Hits' tour, Paul Weller's solo career was still riding the crest of a wave - sweeping up hordes of domesticated ex-Mods into the bag - Mod acts such as Ocean Colour Scene were selling out arena-sized venues, the vintage sounds of Soul, in particular those of a Northern Soul influence, were being channelled into the public's homes via TV commercials whilst scooters continued to be revered as the pinnacle of fashionable mobility. Mod had become the 'Great British Institution' it quite probably always promised to be? Yet, this commercialisation and acceptance of Mod's legacy and great influence compromised Mod's individualism. The influences, hair and styles may have changed over the years, but the Mods of the new millennium still yearned to be as exclusive - within a collective of similar aspiring souls - as their late 50's and early 60's predecessors.

Enamel Verguren - "The Mod scene had to evolve, as it always has, and it's all about feeling good with the look you display – some kept the cropped hair, some others preferred a more relaxed haircut ... it's silly to try to portrait the archetype of a Mod; it's what the media tried to do and it only led to the invention of the Plastic Mod - a parka, bowling shoes, Sta-Prest, etc..

After 2000, I must say that I got slightly fed up with it; I started seeing in the streets of London people who were buying into the look, but who had no idea whatsoever about the culture and the ideology behind it."

The north of England still yearned for more clubs in the vein of The Hideaway and its playlist.

THE AD-LIB BRINGS MOD BACK TO LINCOLN

Glen Field - "The Ad-Lib Club in Lincoln was born out of a need to re- introduce the early 50's/60's sounds that had helped to influence and shape the original Soul all-nighter scene of the mid-sixties. It was a conscious decision made by a group of lads in a local Lincoln pub 'The Jolly Brewer' who managed to put some rare/underplayed early Soul, R&B, Jamaican R&B and Ska, Doowop and Hammond grooves onto the pub's jukebox as a reminder of the social history behind the original Soul/Mod/R&B scene.

Photo: Michael Hill

The pub was a magnate for the Lincoln in-crowd from every musical genre, many playing in all sorts of bands. The jukebox tracks blew them away so the club was formed. The main thinking behind the club was entrenched in the old Soul club called The Duke in Lincoln from 1966. The 'Faces' from that era brought the rare underground music heard at Manchester's Twisted Wheel, Sheffield's King Mojo and Nottingham's The Dungeon and Beachcomber and London's Flamingo to the club. Tracks never heard played out anywhere else in the area. Fast forward and todays Ad-Lib Club gets its buzz from hearing rare, underplayed, newly discovered 50s and 60's tracks - taking the music back to its roots. That's why we call our club nights 'Back to the Roots' as it pays homage to those early black artists and to our own British R&B pioneers who helped bring to our attention to those great sounds. The club will keep growing and will keep bringing in the finest UK DJ's and collectors of the early scene with the aim of encouraging everyone into the CULT-STYLE-HISTORY that goes with a top R&B club."

Let it not be said that contemporary Mods depend purely on their established musical heritage. Throughout the 90's and beyond, Mod related acts such as Big Boss Man, The Nick Rossi Set Boogaloo Investigators, James Taylor Quartet, the Jazz of Tommy Chase, the updated 60's Garage Rock sound of Psychotic Reaction and the underground Funk soundtrack of Sugarman 3, amongst many others, have continued to whet the aural appetites of Mods young and old.

Whilst this recognisably eclectic love of the many styles of Mod-centric music continues - the shifts from orthodox Mod Rock, typically personified by Ocean Colour Scene and others, to much more cosmopolitan musical horizons is a constantly evolving aspect of today's Mod soundtrack. There is also a desire to revisit and re-inject that very same scene with the original sounds that inspired and gave Mods their birth, following their Modern Jazz conception in their formative years. Sheffield's Pow Wow club, graced with such class DJ's as Mik Parry, and, most recently, the birth of the King Bee club in early 2013 are prime examples of a 'back to the roots approach to the Mod soundtrack.

THE BIRTH OF KING BEE BY LEE RADFORTH

Taking heed of The Hideaway and Lincoln's Ad-Lib, Sheffield Mod Lee Radforth decided that it was now time to inject into his home town of Sheffield a much-needed club of its own. The King Bee - a worthy and welcome descendent of the earlier mentioned Pow Wow club was so born.

Lee Radforth - "I'd been thinking about putting another club night on in Sheffield for a while and standing in Lincolns brilliant Ad-Lib Club one Saturday night I casually muttered to Mick Marston that since The Pow Wow nights had stopped we were having to travel for a good night out. He just glanced at me said; well put a night on in Sheffield then. So that was the birth of The King Bee.

By the next Monday morning I'd emailed three of Sheffield's finest DJ/collectors, Gav Arno (of the aforementioned Pow Wow nights), Joe Dutton (Back Beat and Flipside) and Graham Wright (The Sheffield institution that was Moke) and asked if they would consider being the house DJs for a monthly night. The music policy was deliberately narrow, mainly mid 50's to mid-60's rhythm and blues, and the venue I had earmarked Shakespeare's Ale House, seemed perfect. A bit ramshackle but oozing character. The upstairs room had actually been used as a gym in the 50's and the walls had been covered in pictures of body builders which looked like something straight out of Vince's Mans shop in Soho in the early 60's, which I took as an omen!

Gav, Joe and Graham all immediately said yes and so as is the want these days a Facebook page was duly set up and to my amazement, we hit the 200 members mark in a matter of weeks, and the momentum just kept building. There seemed to be something in the air in the north of England, as no sooner as I had begun promoting The King Bee, Ed Horwood got in touch about a club night he was starting in Scarborough called 'Melting Pot', and Glenn Merrifield about a night he was starting in Hull called 'Mojo'. All three along with the already existing 'Ad Lib' and Dearne Valley 'Back to the Roots' shared a common theme of playing early club soul, and R'n'B with a

411

smattering of Ska, and dance floor Jazz and Latin. None of them is promoted as Mod clubs but all attract a healthy percentage of Mods.

Opening night in February 2013 with my old sparring partner (and now rather more famous musician) Richard Hawley being the first guest DJ saw that many people turn up we had to open the doors and spin the first record 30 minutes earlier than advertised as people were unable to get in the pub downstairs. In less than an hour, we were sold out with 120 people crammed onto the dance floor and the room literally dripping in sweat.

If I had envisaged one of my previous clubs, Vout Oroonie to be a modern day Flamingo, my vision for The King Bee was a modern day Scene Club. I had always seen the distinction between rhythm 'n' blues and a lot of what some call rock 'n' roll as somewhat arbitrary and always remember reading some of Guy Stevens set lists and seeing the likes of Carl Perkins being played. I also had a few friends on the Rocking scene, and many records being played on the Mod scene post The Hideaway Club were played at Rocking nights. So I was so pleased to see the room was a mix of Mods, Hep Cats, Northern Soulers and the downright curious. Karl Flavell from Nottingham posted on the Facebook page the next day it was the nearest he could imagine to what The Scene Club must have been like; I was rather pleased with that.

While writing this I happened to read an interview with Jeff Dexter (original Mod) talking about the dance halls being where Mods originally went prior to clubs like The Scene. Interestingly he commented that Mods would do a rather stiff Jive (did not want to crease your sleeve) with the dances evolving as the clubs became smaller and more cramped. He also mentions playing The Everly Brothers alongside Soul and R&B. I like to think he'd approve of both our music policy and the fact that he'd more than likely see Mods jiving again (as well as doing The Block) at The King Bee.

Twelve months on and the night sells out every month with people travelling from all over the country. It would be nothing of course without the DJ's who continue monthly find new records to keep the night fresh. The beauty of Mod for me is to consistently strive to find or hear new sounds and I think that's been one of the strengths of the night. The amount of people that at the end of the night come up to me and say they had never heard one of the records played before but had not stopped dancing is testament to Gav, Joe and Graham.

The King Bee couldn't have happened without Manchester's Hideaway, a true legend of a club that single handed brought rhythm 'n' blues back to the forefront of the Mod scene and invented the genre New Breed R&B. One of its founders the legend that is Mike Warburton regularly makes the journey over the Pennines for 'The King Bee' and now 'The Hideaway' is back putting on regular nights Sheffield and Manchester once again have two clubs echoing 'The Mojo' and The Wheel two of the most important clubs of the 60's outside London."

The Melting Pot club in Scarborough has adopted the eclecticism of the dedicated Mod's open-minded acceptance of various musical styles, but also openly welcoming other like-minded cults, past and present, to share the joy of quality sounds.

Ed Horwood - "Established in Scarborough in January 2013 by myself and Doug Lewis, 'Melting Pot' seeks to showcase the underplayed or obscure sounds from a variety of retro-based scenes all under one roof. Our playlist takes in Jump Blues, Doo-Wop, Rock 'n' Roll, Rockabilly, Popcorn, R'n'B, Soul, Surf, Exotica, Ska and early Reggae. As the name implies, Melting Pot welcomes everyone regardless of age, fashion, musical knowledge etc. All we ask is that people arrive with an open mind and the intent to have fun. As a fundamental principle, every penny taken on the door goes to charity."

Ed Horwood – 'Melting Pot' co-founder

The zest for Mod's return to its R&B roots, as exemplified by clubs such as 'The King Bee' and 'The Hideaway', Hull's Mojo r&b Club and Scarborough's 'Melting Pot' continues to influence and attract crowds of like-minded souls the length of the country.

Likewise, the scooter scene thrives, enjoying an eclectic mix of many of the genres embraced by Mods throughout the decades. A plethora of scooter clubs and organisations across the country celebrate their individual interpretations of Modernism in the 21st century.

Right: Aimee Hall, New Originals Scooter Club member, 2010

An equally potent return to the primal beginnings of Black American music is also prevalent within new clutches of young bands eager to infuse their music and song writing with the timeless appeal of rhythm and blues.

THE NEW BREED!

Mixing their sound with classic influences of Mod Rock and punk, The Spitfires from Watford, who have released three critically acclaimed singles, refuse to toe the party line of Mod's profile.

Billy Sullivan (The Spitfires) - "I'm not into nostalgia trips and pantomimes of the beach fights. Mod for me is a mind-set, state of thinking - not a genre, a look, and a mode of transport or a symbol. There can't be an anniversary because it exists in all subcultures - the attention to detail. It's just the anniversary of kicking seven shades of shit out of each other. I don't get this attitude towards it, like we get called a new Mod band - what's a Mod band? Geezers in parkas playing guitars? There's something gripping young people at the moment, more and more kids are waking up. That excites me more than anything."

The fast-moving, yet stale and shallow, digestion of music in a modern age of MP3 and downloads has been rejected by an ever-increasing number of music fans, with a healthy return to Vinyl. Though never truly dying out, the single and long playing record have returned with a cultish popularity while the live music scene has never been healthier. Mods too have, yet again, evolved. Continuing a Modernist approach, the studious Mod of today may share an often obsessive love of R&B, Soul and 60's garage punk and beat (not forgetting the appeal of Modern Jazz) with an open-minded approach to the developing contemporary sounds of the day. Bands such as 3-piece Mods with punk attitude The Spitfires are often equally embraced as keenly as King Mojo, DC Fontana, Button Up, The Indigos, The High Hazels, The Sherlock's, Soul ensemble The Stone Foundation and the energetic Brit-R&B of the 45's and The Strypes amongst others.

The appreciation and love of the rhythm and blues embraced by the original Mods of the 60's and consequent generations since, has now come full-circle. Young artists such as Nick Waterhouse, who references early R&B along with Jazz and authentic blues as great influences and the talents of Hannah Williams and the Taste Makers have proven to be popular with contemporary Mods. The Strypes, however, appear to have divided opinions. 1979 era Mod Heather Quinn - always attentive for new Mod sounds - has keenly taken to these new hip young gunslingers of the music scene.

Heather Quinn - "There are a whole host of promising young bands emerging out there and one very young band in particular, The Strypes, has caught the attention of numerous famous musos such as Paul Weller, Noel Gallagher and Roger Daltrey.

The Strypes are a four-piece from Ireland and are barely out of school, yet they play gritty, harmonica filled rhythm and blues and draw their inspiration from the likes of Bo Diddley, T-Bone Walker and Howlin' Wolf – legends who were born generations before these teenagers and indeed their parents. Then there is the equally young and talented local boy John Lennon McCullough, whose name just says it all and his style is reminiscent of early Bob Dylan or Nick Drake.

Mod clubs and scooter runs still continue to thrive as new generations of young, dedicated Mods continue to appear and join forces with the more mature of us to keep the scene alive... a scene which is arguably just as strong now as it was half a century ago."

Lee Radforth - "There is still a lot of interest in Mod be it from the likes of Miles Kane or The Strypes. Standing in a sold out Strypes gig in Camden watching young people singing every word of Bo Diddleys 'I Can Tell' and Jessie Hills 'Ooh Poo Pah Doo' filled me with optimism that the music I feel so passionately about will never die.

The dearth of tailors apart [tailoring legend Colin Starsmore's imminent retirement], Gillian Long 'Cock o' the walk' being one of very few newcomers to the trade, there has probably never been a better time to be a Mod clothes wise. Some heritage British brands bring out some lovely pieces and there are a number of Shops and manufacturers specialising in Mod-related apparel. Claudio's 'DNA Groove' being one of my personal favourites. Living in Sheffield the John Smedley factory is only an hour's drive away and they still produce some of the best fine gauge knitwear in the world. And of course Andy Bull, Mod and friend since the early 80's runs the factory shop."

Today's Mod scene is not one totally comprised of ageing originals and revivalists alongside those that wish they had been born years earlier. The legacy of Mod has imbued many with a genuine and eternal passion for the Mod style and various related aspects of its culture and this is celebrated globally. Aside from the cash-in Union Jack, target and plastic imitations of Mod, a cast of true connoisseurs grow older gracefully, constantly adapting to modern living in (often) difficult and age-defying circumstances. Their love of the Mod ideal is shared worldwide with like-minded souls; it is truly in their blood. They are Modernists, living the eloquence, style and commitment to detail that all before them have aspired to - it never subsides and remains significant. All of this resonates with the new young breed of Mods. Individual and in contrast to each other's visions, yet - in unison - looking ahead into the future of Mod!

Ben Stone (Present day Mod) - "I'm 30, from Sheffield and I've been involved in the Mod scene for around eight or nine years. I was brought up listening to Soul and rhythm and blues, and the music of the 50's and 60's had always been somewhat of an obsession of mine, but back then I just wasn't aware that a thriving contemporary Mod scene existed. I'd experienced a few of the mawkish, insipid Northern Soul nights which crop up in town hall function rooms and hotel ballrooms but they held no thrall for me, they felt soulless, lacking real passion and wrapped up in sentimentality.

Then a friend introduced me to Sheffield's now lamented 'Pow Wow club' and my mind was blown; these people weren't sentimental weekend Soulies, their lives were defined by the music they loved. They spoke, danced and dressed with an obvious obsessive zeal that I could easily identify with. Soon I discovered similar nights all over the country; dark sweaty basement clubs full of sharply dressed people dancing all night to the sounds of obscure rhythm and blues on crackly black vinyl. I was instantly hooked.

I predominately listen to and collect R&B and early Soul, but I'm partial to a wide range of music which falls under the broad umbrella of 'Mod'. I adore late 50s Jazz, Boogaloo, 60s beat and garage, through to a few more Psychedelic sounds. It's often all too easy to get bogged down in your own particular niche, and whilst there's some music related to the Mod scene which just doesn't float my boat, I try to keep a relatively open mind. I will admit, however, that I'm a complete Luddite when it comes contemporary music. I'm led to believe that there's a whole range of 21st century acts pumping out an authentic Mod sound, but I'm still uncovering unbelievable tunes from the original era and there's simply not enough time to add in anything new.

Clothes-wise, I try to adopt a very early-to-mid 60s style, the aim is to look like I could pass for an extra in the back of an old French new wave film. I'm an absolute sucker for a slim-fitting, three or four buttoned suit and so a good tailor is an absolute must. It's becoming increasingly hard to source original vintage clothes in wearable condition, but there are still gems to be found for those willing to put in the time either online or trawling the backstreet shops, and a piece of unworn original knitwear is always a beautiful thing. When it comes to clothes, it's ultimately an overt attention to detail, which unites all Mods. The classic Mod look isn't an especially outrageous style, it's even somewhat reserved, but there's a certain undeniable confidence, which comes from dressing 'well', especially in an age where casualness and informality is the norm.

As for Mod's future relevance, as far as I can see, Mod's future seems secure. Club nights, festivals and weekenders up and down the country are filled with a new generation of Mods rubbing shoulders with the old guard, and sadly, I can really no longer consider myself to be one of the younger members of the scene. In the modern world, it's easy for people to sample the music and styles of virtually any subculture, which takes their fancy, and it seems a healthy number are rejecting contemporary pop culture and embracing the Mod style. I think this also explains the relevance of Mod today; it's simply a celebration of glorious, timeless music and classic style. There's no real ethos or political slant, there are no barriers to joining the Mod scene other than a drive to seek it out.

There will always be in-fighting, bickering and banter between the various factions within the scene, endless cries of how 'Mod has lost its way...', and the persistent irritation that the public perception of Mod is so firmly rooted in targets, union jacks and fishtail parkas; but it's the changing trends within the scene which keep it alive. For example, the New Breed R&B sound which was so prevalent when I first became involved in the scene has somewhat dwindled in popularity with some younger DJs, many of whom who prefer a slightly more funk-edged Soul style, but this or yet another niche genre that will be rediscovered and championed by a future influx of young Mods wanting to stamp their mark. I'm sure they too will scoff at the new bloods when their sound is no longer in vogue, but this is exactly how Mod manages to remain fresh and vital, while still remaining firmly tied to its roots. Moving forward while standing still."

Kevin and his Modfather.
Above: Kevin's band The Hamfat Four

Kevin Smith (Present day Mod from Glasgow) - "I have always had a desire to be the centre of attention. As a child, I would turn the coffee table upside down, stand in the middle of it, a guitar in hand and mimic whoever was my dad's record player. This sort of behaviour in my family was encouraged. My dad would often take to me his band rehearsals, usually in a really run-down manky studio, that stank of fags, beer and dampness. But it was watching my dad and his band, and hearing live music played really loud that inspired me the most.

There was always music on around the house, both old and new. At that point, the sound that grabbed me the most was Paul Weller. I began obsessively taping everything I could, I memorised performance dates and all the other band members names and details. There was something so exciting about the performances, the image, the style and the presence. It was around age 12 or 13 that I wanted to ditch the tracksuits and start looking smart.

Around that time my Dad brought me back 3 films from the library; 'Easy Rider', 'Blue Velvet' and 'Quadrophenia'. These three films inspired me in different ways; it nurtured my passion for film, introduced me to new music and inspired me to explore more things that were not in the mainstream.

I started tracing Weller's influences back, listening to Blues tapes that were around the house. I remember my dad buying me three CDs Albert King, Freddie King and BB King and it was at this point I discovered the music that was to remain my passion in life.

At 14, I knew a chap who was 18 who sold me his driver's licence. This was my ticket to explore a world of music, unrestricted by my age. We looked nothing alike but I memorised every detail on that drivers licence, even his star sign. It became a foolproof method of getting into clubs and pubs unbeknown to my parents.

With my Saturday job, I saved up and bought a double-breasted, blue pinstriped, Hardy Amies suit, second hand from Mr Bens in Glasgow's Trongate. My Mum helped to match me a nice tie and shirt. My Mum always made sure that from a young age that our clothes were coordinated and matched appropriately. She told me what colours would go with what and what patterns would clash. This suit became my going out uniform. Any clothes I wore, I made sure matched and looked good together. I would look in the sleeves of the Paul Weller albums and copy the clothes that were in there.

The only people I knew at that stage of my life who went to pubs were punks. No one around my age that I knew was interested in Modernism. A middle ground for me and the punks I hung around with was a garage and psyche night called Eyes Wide Open. It was there that I learned there was a real mod club called Friday Street. I attended my first Friday Street aged 14 in the Cuba Notre in Glasgow, in a suit that was slightly too big. I couldn't believe there were other people who liked the same type of music as me. From there I went to Divine in Glasgow's Art School union where I first saw *The Boogaloo Investigators*. To this day, I haven't heard a sound like it live. This was the most authentic sounding RnB band around. Everything down to the real Hammond and Leslie speaker, the old Selmer PA, and even the unusual way that they chose to mic up the drum kit. They only used one mic, and it was just behind the drummer! I was playing gigs locally at this point with a Brit Pop sounding band, and the sound was always terrible at gigs and I didn't know why. I didn't really question why every engineer at every venue would put a mic right in front of everything. The resulting sound was the wall of incoherent muddy-ness. I knew at this point that I had to be in an RnB band and I had to achieve this sound.

I had bought *the Boogaloo's* album Dynamighty on Vinyl, which gave me an excuse to buy a record deck for my first flat at 16 years of age in Govan. I studied sound engineering and worked as free-lance sound engineer wherever I could. I played in bands, I worked in call centres, I worked as a handyman and I busked in the town on Friday evenings just to make enough money to make it out to a mod club. I got myself into thousands of pounds debt, buying records, music equipment, clothes and going out four or five times a week, and then pissing the rest away on rent.

Life hasn't changed much since then, I still pursue that pure sound that I first heard in the Art School, I now play in an RnB band with the drummer of The Boogaloo Investigators and we are called The Hamfat Four. I have started DJ'ing and organise mod and RnB events most months.

At 25, I have had 11 inspiring years on the Mod scene and it is still fresh, I still hear new music weekly. It is more than just the parkas and the scooters. It's about meeting passionate people, who share an obsession no matter their age or sex. It's about good taste; it's about not being part of the mainstream guff and standing apart from the mundane. For me it's taking pride in everything I do, from how I colour code my sock drawer to how I organise my records, It's my ethos as individual and collectively its respected and understood."

Kristopher Dunn (Present day Mod from Sheffield) - "It's hard to say how and when Mod took over my life. I was born in '84 so grew up during Brit Pop and just about caught the tail end of [the later spin-offs of] Acid House (to which the connection to Northern Soul now seems so obvious). Weller, Mani and Johnny Marr are obvious influences, although at the time I didn't consciously associate myself with Mod. I didn't really think of myself as a Mod until my 20s, which I suppose is unusual.

My dad is a big Blues fan and I grew up around John Lee Hooker and Lightnin' Hopkins so I've always had an interest in black music in general. Exploring the influences of the likes of Weller was a natural continuation of this interest. The House music that we danced to in clubs soon lead me to Soul. I also lived in Brixton for a few years and got turned on to Reggae. I suppose a range of influences converged to bring me to Mod, and it's partly the breadth of styles that fall under the Mod umbrella that is so appealing; there's always more to discover.

Why I find Mod so captivating is easier for me to answer. At the core of its appeal is the fact that Mod allows you to differentiate yourself - to stand out from the crowd - whilst also feeling that you belong to something. Mod is about self-expression, within certain boundaries, which I love. The attention to detail also plays to my slightly obsessive nature; I'll spend as long deciding which socks to wear as I will on choosing my jacket.

Breaking down Mod into its constituent parts - particularly separating the music from the style in general - is hard, but for me the clothes probably come first. I'm often frustrated by my lack of creativity - I can't write music, draw or play an instrument - and I think the way I dress helps satisfy the urge to be creative and express myself.

As a Modernist, I try not to be too nostalgic for a time I've never know. It should always be about now, albeit with a healthy reverence for the past. I imagine the experience of being a Mod in my generation differs fundamentally from others because of the ease of access to things like music and clothes. Being able to listen to John Coltrane's back catalogue on YouTube is great, but I think some of the joy of discovery must have been lost. Youth culture in general is far more disparate than in the past and for better or worse, I'm not sure there is the same sense of tribalism as before."

SCARLETT BAYLIS – YOUNG LADY OF MOD

Meticulous, sharp, cool and photogenic; with a love of timeless rhythm and blues mixed with the Mod soundtrack of today, Scarlett Baylis perfectly represents the future of Mod - a love of Mod's past, injected with her own individual twist to the Modernist style.

Scarlett Baylis (Present day Mod) - "I'm Scarlett, a 15 year old Mod (2014) from Canterbury, Kent. The culture first came about by the influences of my parents as I've always been brought up around the music. I finally watched the film 'Quadrophenia' a few years back, went away, and educated myself into the scene. I was and still am completely blown away with how important individual details were and took it upon myself to look as cool and as sharp as the originals did.

I enjoy sounds from previous decades, not always just the sixties. Rhythm and blues is my favourite and I'm yet to discover so many more wonderful foot stomping tunes. I do favour music from the past however recently the 21st century has brought some amazing young sixties influenced up and coming bands into the scene that I've had the opportunity of seeing live. It's hopeful to see such talent from teenagers who really know what they are doing as well as playing. The original material however has aged with elegance and means so much more to me to know that it was made over half a century ago and I have the pleasure of listening to it now.

Since a meeting with Stacie Stewart and an appearance in Afro-mic productions' 'For the love of Mod' documentary, I have built up a great circle of wonderful likeminded people with a variety of ages who have the same thirst for it as I do and show great respect for me as I do for them. Despite them all being scattered across the country, our similar interests seem to make us feel like we've known each other for years and we belong. It's fantastic to know so many people from a range of places who you can get together with at events across the country. Surprisingly the Southeast lacks subculture meaning I'm one of very few and have to travel to meet these people. Having never met the majority of them, I have become friends with quite a few big faces within the scene who I look up to immensely.

Personally I'm not influenced by specific individuals, I find my styles through the pictures of past mods who really knew how to style. I buy my clothes from everywhere and anywhere, as I don't believe it matters where they originate from as long as they're dapper and look the part. Being the age I am, I don't have a lot to be spending on tailor made outfits, so I try my best while working with what I've got. I like to combine both of the past Mod periods, as I respect them all for how they got it so right and smart. I'm recently beginning to incorporate my own twist on bought items only to then alter them to suit me. Despite not all of my clothes being bespoke pieces and usually high street fashions, the way I pair them makes them different to everyone else's. I'd like to think I've developed a style, which accommodates me best, and one that makes people respect me for how I've interpreted the scene at such a young age.

Mod haven: Scarlett surrounded by images and varied sounds of Mod's past and future

Mod is a culture that will never date. We don't look back in embarrassment unlike previous fads and fashions. We just like dressing smart and taking pride in our appearance. The majority of the younger generation involved in the scene have captured the essence of the culture incredibly well, and I have no doubt that it'll be carried on through further decades, each one adding a new story to be told. It's all been said before, and I believe as long as everyone enjoys it to the utmost that they can, then it'll continue to thrive everywhere."

Nathan Prescott (Present day Mod from Middlesbrough) - "All my family were Mods in the house and there was always Northern Soul or Paul Weller playing. I started getting interested in the Mod scene when I was eleven years old after watching 'Quadrophenia' and reading books about the 60s and the early Mods. I just loved the whole thing about the Mods, the clothes, the scooters the music and the haircuts. Bands like The Who, The Jam, Small Faces and Northern Soul will always be a big part of my life. I met some amazing people on the scooter rallies and also the Northern Soul and Mod scene, and to this day, they are still my great friends who are family to me for me. The Mod scene will never die, there always be that little flame keeping it alive and I will never stop being a Mod - it's in my blood. Mod for me it's not just a phase it really is a way of life."

Nathan Prescott (right) and his family of Mod

The Mod's love of scooters continues its tradition with clubs such as the one run by Modernist Bradley Hall of Stamford Hill. The club, based at Starting Gate pub, Alexandra Palace, North London, played a key role in organizing the Mod exhibition at Hackney Museum, which celebrated the fiftieth anniversary of the ground breaking Mod article 'Faces without Shadows.' The New Originals opened the event with a fanfare of roaring two strokes during their drive by on 7th November 2012. And so the journey continues.

Below: Bradley Hall's New Originals Scooter Club outside Hackney Town Hall at the opening of the Mark Feld Mod Exhibition, November 2012

Copyright of Stephen Hughes

So, the phenomenon of Mod has reached its appointment with the modern age. From its original inception in the late 50's and the decades beyond, though interpretations and influences may have changed and been recycled over the years, the crucial common ethics of Mod remain just as healthy and valid as ever. Mod was (and still is) about moving forward, adapting to one's possibilities and surroundings; taking the utmost care to stay clean, true to personal belief and promotion of detail, surely a Mod's eternal manifesto is to live a focused life to a soundtrack as sharp as their clothes, and to always make sure that they are looking good!

Those individualists so termed Sawdust Caesars by the realms of the establishment decades ago, along with the Mod-influenced generations since - how do they feel about its influence and lasting legacy now?

IT'S A MOD LIFE

Rob Nicholls - "Mod gave me freedom in style and expression. I found it liberating and as a result I have never been fearful of being unique—standing out as an original or speaking out on matters I believe in, in hippie terms, of 'doing my own thing.' I got a degree in Art and my love of Black music took me to Africa, the Caribbean, and also to Washington DC where I obtained a doctorate in African Studies. I am currently a professor of Social Science at the University of the Virgin Islands."

Roger Ames - "What are my thoughts about embracing Modernism and how it affects my life fifty years on? Well, we were 'the transient mobile disposable generation' (title of my thesis at Hornsey art school) and the idea of Modernism was to keep moving on in all areas. Originally, to make a statement, to be a Face, you had to be innovative and this has led me through many changes of direction in design and manufacturing (I worked in publishing as art director and magazine publisher, and then moved onto the design and manufacture of lighting systems), always trying new concepts and creations and Mod has been a guiding force in my life."

Steve Austin ('Sawdust Caesars' cover star) - "One of my old friends lived just off Hedge Lane, we had a lot of parties in his house, and we saw the Motown revue at Finsbury Park Astoria in 1964. We had wonderful teenage years.

For a brief four to five year period in the early 60's Britain influenced the whole world. We led the world in Fashion, music, and lastly, how to be cool. The driving force behind this revolution was summed up in one word - Modernists. These three influences have been with me all my life. I have never lost interest in clothes, music is still very important to me, and am I still cool, probably not."

Gary Maxton - "I would never be so boring as to say to kids today 'It was so much better in my day', but one thing is for sure but one thing is for sure they will never see the biggest acts in venues holding 200 like we used to."

John Leo Waters - "Mod was a coming of age, a voice for teenagers where none existed before, an ethos, a beginning - it was (and is) everything."

Ted Reynell - "You never forget being a 'Mod'. It's a way of life and an attitude of mine. I am still as much a 'Mod' today as I was then. I like to keep myself smart with a bit of style. When we walked down the street we were proud to be 'Mods'. We were dead smart and thought we were 'the best of British'."

Ella Donnor - "I enjoyed my life as a Mod as it made me fashion conscious, street wise and gave me a fantastic social life with great friends, something I will cherish always."

Adrian Stern (left) - "Mod, whatever it was, couldn't have shaped my life as it was we who were shaping it by what we did, how we behaved, the music we listened to and most importantly the clothes we wore. There was never any kind of 'Mod philosophy' since we were mostly just kids having fun and although not rebellious exactly we were at the very least dressing in a very different way to what had come before. So Mod as a life shaper - No, no influence then or since. I still dress as I did at 18 - though the clothing is hard to find and doesn't always fit. But I still wear loafers, straight 501's, Baracuta jackets (despite the current poor quality), and Lacoste shirts etc., etc. Lack of hair means I can't have a parting but otherwise it's about what it was."

Roy Allen (right) - "When I became a Mod it changed my life. I began looking for great clothes and music and smartened up all together. It gave me pride in my appearance and in being an individual. Later in life it gave me the confidence, as the song goes, 'I did it My Way!' Stay Kool',"

Lloyd Johnson - "It [Mod] was a teenage youth culture, a teenage lifestyle that we aspired to. When I think of the Mod era, the period from 59-62 was the most important. That was before it went national with the '64 coverage and all that."

David Birchall - "The Mod scene was of the time and the generation (I hope I don't offend anybody with that opinion). Nobody had any money - my father used to borrow my bicycle to go to the pub since he couldn't afford a car. We all lived in Council houses - I didn't know anybody who owned their own house. None of us passed the eleven plus. There is a reason for that - we were not expected to! The eleven plus was written initially as a class-based method of keeping us in our place. It was changed around 1960 to become an IQ based exam but prior to that, it was not. If you look at the photos, of Mods of the sixties, you notice one thing - they are all skinny! We couldn't afford to eat well - there were no 'fast food' places. We were lucky to get peas with our fish fingers!"

Dave Fawcett - "Back in Mod Manchester ('65 to '68) we were able to go our own way with our own style and rules, looking good and sharp and living the lifestyle we wanted."

Kath Chambers - "I got back into the Soul/60's R&B scene through social networking – and got to know some of the DJs in Manchester and did some gigs. I also met some fellow Soulies and have met up with them to go to some Soul nights, including going back to the Twisted Wheel over 40 years later.

What stays with you over the years? The music; that feeling when a record starts and you have to dance; the sound that takes you back to a dusty dance floor in 1968. A certain sense of what looks stylish – even if you're not quite the same shape these days. Most of all, the friends; the ones you have kept in touch with over the years; the ones you have found again and the new ones the music has brought."

Alfredo Marcantonio (left) - "It was the cult that changed our culture. Before it, everything and everyone in Britain was grey. We created the first street fashion by blending the colourfulness of the Continent with the cool of the States. And now, more than 50 years later, most of us are still doing just that."

Right: John Hellier with Ray Davies of The Kinks

John Hellier - "Looking back on my own involvement in 50 years of Mod fills me with nothing but pleasure. I still dig exactly the same things clothes-wise and music-wise as I did back then. The Small Faces were the benchmark for my wardrobe and I guess they still are. If I'm considered old fashioned because I wear proper shoes instead of trainers and my trousers don't drag along the floor I couldn't give a toss! The old adage 'Mod is for life, not just for Christmas' was surely written with me in mind."

Tony Foley - "As regards the influence and relevance of Mod, it's an all-encompassing life style. You only have to look around you for that."

Keith How - "Being Mod set you apart. It gave me style, purpose and identity in a grey world. Music, art and fashion... it keeps you alive."

Steve Bush - "I spent more time getting my hair 'just right' than my girlfriend did!"

Irish Jack Lyons - "I was nobody until I became a Mod. It seemed so anti-establishment, so rebellious. I used to live for every minute of it."

425

Glenn Field (above left) - "Mod to me is a mind-set that you will always have. Attention to detail. Care in appearance, independence and individuality - away from the mainstream, be it music or clothes. It is CULT, it is STYLE. It is a sense of belonging to a scene ... It is as strong today for me as it was when I was a teenager. These values have always held me in good stead and I am proud to say they have been adopted by the next generation of my family."

Maurice Moore (above centre) - "Lots of the people around in the 60s still see each other and share the same interests. Recently I went to a 60s Soul and Motown Disco, where 500, mostly from the 60s, danced to their favourite music all night long. I now write music with my wife, and we play in a band, MozMicDawn, which plays many of the songs I played all those years ago in the Salty Dogs, as well as our own original music. We also make videos, take many photographs and I create podcasts of the Soul music I grew up dancing to. The Mod movement gave us direction, style, friendships and helped to launch a certain creativity and artistry; we never 'grew up' and still retain that exuberance. Mod gave me an optimism and energy which shaped my life; the identity and style stayed with me and ensured I still have that youthful outlook."

Don Hughes (above right) - "When I look back to those halcyon days of the early 60s I smile fondly, for I hold cherished memories of the Mod era, many of which I shared with you all in my book, 'Friday On My Mind'. Mod was apolitical, and still is, but out of my passion for the movement spurned an inner consciousness. To 'judge people by the content of their character not the colour of their skin' as Martin Luther King famously said. Mod, together with the thoughts of King, showed me a way forward in life. And at 65, I have no regrets over the decisions I made for my beautiful rainbow family is a testament to my Mod roots. It all goes back there."

Paul Clay - "We do have to be careful that we don't look back with rose tinted glasses, but in all honesty I would give my right arm to be back the 60's."

David Middleton - "Being a Mod was great. I was just one of lots of Mods at that time and it really did mean something back then. It was all new to us and at the time no one liked us and we didn't care: it took first generation Mods less than five years to get a bad name and fifty years to be goody goodies."

Reggie Webster - "I don't ever recall becoming a Mod. I think I was just the type of kid that was always going to be one. We were far from stupid but were street smart, outgoing and working class. Our Dads' had been to war and (rather than moving along with the tide) had a similar dislike of the officer class and people [often] deemed their betters: those men are in every generation.

It wasn't new, just more blatant. But I will say a scooter was the most obvious. It didn't mean anyone with a scooter was a Mod, because there were plenty of kids around riding them. But they weren't a part of the crews that appeared locally. There was no motive to it all; it wasn't a movement and [importantly] not anyone could join. It was laddish and aggressive at times, but the crew were your family in a way. It wasn't elitist, it was separatist, we were selfish, arrogant and cocky - local celebrities in a strange kind of way."

Dennis Munday - "My stint as a Mod lasted about four years, though it seemed longer and it shaped me into the person I am now. Many of my contemporises wallow in this era, something that I don't. Yeah, I still listen to a lot of the music from my callow youth, but I also listen to music from the subsequent decades."

Steve Bush (left on photo) - "It's a shame that the Skinhead movement became so associated with violence, and we were never really able to shake off the stigma of the so-called 'Bovver Boys'. There were stories of football hooliganism, gang vandalism, and even a degree of racism all connected with the skinhead movement. The Press likened it to Teds 'ripping up cinema seats while watching The Blackboard Jungle in the mid fifties', and the confrontations on the beaches of Brighton and Margate between Mods and Rockers in 1964, but having been at the very heart of it I can only say that we were there purely for the clothes and the music, and that it was great fun while it lasted. Would I do it again? You bet I would..."

Sean Hampsey - "In the early 80's came the first of many trips to the USA, looking to discover new sounds. The size and quality of the record collection was always the key and I was asked to work at most of the big all-nighters of the time. Cleethorpes, Bradford, Rotherham, Warrington were my weekend stints and even to this day, I get out on a regular basis on the line up for the Prestatyn, Cleethorpes, Whitby, Great Yarmouth, Rimini and other major Soul Weekenders and events. When I am in the mood (and have the energy) I still work the occasional all-nighter, such as Oxford Street's famous 100 Club and others across the north and Midlands. Rugby, Stoke and Sheffield, while squeezing in the odd transatlantic trip, purely to track down the music. The temptation to get behind the decks or get stuck into a store full of records is always too strong.

Being Mod and into Soul were essentially intertwined for me. There have been many Brit artists associated with Mod culture, and I like to think I'm a fan of all good music, but I was always far more attracted to the sound of Black America than any other genre. As a brass musician, it just seemed a natural progression, being ignited by those Stax Horns, into a lover and collector of Soul music. It has been a remarkable journey that actually went full circle for me when some 40 years after hearing that first tune I got to spend an entire day in the company of Wayne Jackson himself. The coolest guy on the planet. He showed me around the Stax studios in Memphis, where the likes of Otis Redding, Carla Thomas and Sam and Dave recorded those incredible records and where this love affair with all things soulful was born. I've been privileged and very fortunate and wouldn't have had it any other way."

Gary Shail - "Although we [the 'Quadrophenia' cast] all stayed in touch and remained friends, it was not until the early 90s that we were all back together again. I had given up acting to pursue a career in advertising music production and was working in a recording studio in London's Soho when I received a phone call from a company who had bought the rights to release Quad on DVD. They had planned a massive launch party in Brighton to promote the event and had even hired a special 'Quad Train' leaving at 5.15 (Geddit!) to ferry us all back to the scene of the crime. I said I would definitely attend as long as I could take whoever I liked. They agreed to my demands, so I took everybody from the studio who had had no idea that I had appeared in the movie and treated the whole affair like a 'works? 'outing.' I even took Goldie the jungle R&B star who was recording in the studios downstairs. I even managed due to my advertising contacts to secure a sponsorship with Jack Daniels who promised me free booze for a year if I wore one of their jackets whenever I was interviewed by one of the many TV crews that were covering the event. That train certainly rocked that night! Almost 20 years on and 'Quadrophenia' now seems to be more popular than ever. I am constantly asked from fans across the world what it is like to be in a cult movie, and I always tell them the same thing. I remember my mum waking me up one morning in 1978 and saying...'FOR FUCK SAKE GET UP AND MAKE A CULT MOVIE WILL YA!"

Terry Rawlings (right) - "I've always said the same thing when asked what influence MOD has had on my life! Apart from there being a Mod or Mod-related music theme to most of my books, the essential and important thing is how Mod set the standard as to what I would never wear rather than what I would. It's like having a sixth sense where by you instinctively know what's right and what's not""

Brett 'Buddy' Ascot (The Chords) - "Of all the 'tribes', or youth cults, it appears that 'Mod' has withstood the ravages of time better than most. It has retained its air of style hitched to a love of certain music, clothes, and a defined lifestyle. I think hundreds, possibly thousands of people stopped going out while their kids were growing up, but now that '79-'81 lot are up for a party again! It blows my mind sometimes! And some of the music still stands up!"

Robert John Manton (Purple Hearts) - "I think it was not just about 'Mod' but also an idea that 70's teenagers had of the mythical 'Swinging Sixties' - a time that seemed like some sort of golden age for youth compared to the rather grey and repressiveenvironment of the mid-70's."

Brian Kotz - "What happened to me in 1979 laid the foundations for the rest of my life in so many ways, as I know it did for many more. My involvement in the '79 Mod scene in London as an 18-year-old 60's fan (who could sing a bit) was inevitable and absolutely right. When people slag off what is known as the 'Mod revival', they are slagging people's lives off, and myself and others have every right to take it personally. It is a vital part of the overall story and structure of Modernism. I could bang on about the reasons for ages. I insisted on the Back to Zero 2003 reunion album being called 'It's All Relative' for that reason. Having said that, I don't need to live in the shadow of '79, and I don't need to constantly re-live being 18 at the age of 53.

So does Mod still influence me now? Last year, for the first time, I went to more exhibitions than gigs - shows of work by pop artists such as Peter Blake and Pauline Boty (travelling to Wolverhampton for that one) and photographers such as Gered Mankowitz, my interest 110%

traceable to my interest in Mod and digging deeper into the culture when I was younger. I'm still just as big a fan of the music, and I'm still discovering new things all the time. So is it still a part of me? I'd say that's a big yes! A couple of weeks ago, I was trying to explain to a colleague that when my barber retired, I had to go online to research the most suitable hairdresser in London to replace him. When she remarked that it was a bit obsessive of me, my immediate response, without even having to think about it, was 'I'm an old Mod'."

Alan May (right) - "What does being a Mod mean to me now? Well it's the combination of still enjoying Music, fashion to a point and the scooter. I agree that as a teenager it purely started as a fashion and evolved as I got older into something a little deeper. It's about a sense of well-being and pride.

As you get older, you need to balance things in your life like your family and business. It doesn't mean you can't have both, but being a Mod isn't a label at nearly 50, it's more of a statement (and as the genre is becoming popular again 'everybody seems to be Mod these days') but you have to have lived through the tough times, divorces, the job loses, the large waist bands etc. to appreciate what it is and was all about. I still can't nail it down though, as I guess it's an inner self-ideal. The truth is, if you consider yourself a time served Mod, then I'm sure you'll understand. For the new generation I say 'good luck', keep it going, but do your own thing and don't be tempted to follow the media or the masses."

Robert Lee - "My priorities changed with the birth of my son and four wheels became more important than two; unfortunately I couldn't afford to run a scooter and car. However I did keep the scooter and still own it to this day and have no intention of ever letting it go as it symbolizes the three happiest years of my life."

Fraser Smith - "My interest in seeing The Jam live never waned, and I saw all there future gigs in Sheffield, as John Weller famously ALWAYS said, 'Please welcome the best rock 'n' roll band in the world....THE JAAAAAM! They were, and for my money, they always will be. Gail and I went down to London to see their last ever hometown gig, at Wembley Arena. Great gig, very emotional. I remember Bruce asking for the house lights to be turned on during the encore, and he was sobbing his heart out. That moment will remain with me forever, so will the things I experienced, and of course, the friends I made, being a Jam fan was my best decision ever. And to quote the great man himself - 'I was born a Mod; they will bury me a Mod'"

Derek 'Delboy' Shepherd - "Mod is very much part of me. I still love the clothes and the music, I can't imagine what I would be like if I'd not found Mod back in the 80s."

Tracey Wilmot (with Dave Cairns and Ian Page of Secret Affair) - "Towards the end of the Mod Revival the antagonism between the many youth cults was waning- Mods started dancing to Ska and Skins danced to Northern Soul and everything was blurred and less defined. Maybe everyone was growing up and realizing that actually it was pretty pointless fighting or just that we all knew the scene was dying and we just wanted to enjoy the last moments of misspent Youth in peace.

Fast forward to today, here I am again at scooter rallies but this time with the Mod icons of the day, Secret Affair. I see the Mod scene evolving and growing again, young faces stare up at the band on stage resplendent in boating blazers and Fred Perry's. Some come to the gigs and rallies with whole families and kids decked out with their own tribute to the scene. It seems the scooter rally and the mod scene never really died but is still very much intertwined with Ska, skins and reggae and is now reawakening, reviving and reminding us of good times and good friends we met along the way-while the new Mod waits in the wings for the next encore."

Dizzy Holmes - "30 odd years on, I run Detour Records that specialises in Mod Music and run a mail order business that caters for the Scooter scene."

Ed Horwood (left) - "By mid-1987 I had pretty much gone over to the scooterist side of things and had started to dress tidy scooterboy and focus on National Rallies. However, the advent of the 'Acid-Jazz' and 'Neo-Mod' scene of the late 80's and early 90's also saw me return to a certain extent, to the Mod fold. The spirit and fresh approach of the 'Neo-Mod' scene really appealed to me with its mix of traditional 60's Mod, funky 70's retro and contemporary influences. Catching the likes of Galliano, JTQ, Corduroy or Mother Earth live, getting the bus to London to buy Duffer of St George or Chipie gear and attending Acid Jazz nights repackaged the whole buzz of my early mod days in a fresh new style. Since the mid-nineties, I've re-visited the Mod scene on a number of occasions, along with other styles, but now, aged 46, the time for pigeon-holing myself to one particular lifestyle is well and truly over - I'm content to just be me, a conglomerate of all the musical, cultural and stylistic influences that have touched me over the years. However, scratch the surface and many of the attitudes and passions that informed that wide-eyed young Mod are still very much there."

Graham Lentz - " By 1995, I had already decided that I would use my journalism training to write a book about Mod. Up to that point, Richard Barnes's 'Mods' had been the only reference material, so I set to work doing the research, then tracking down people I wanted to talk to and the project took on a life of its own.

Let's not forget, the internet was in its infancy, there was no social media. The only Mod website I was aware of was David Walker's 'modculture.com'. If anything, I was ten years too early with 'The Influential Factor'. People from bands like Secret Affair, Chords, Purple Hearts, Merton Parkas etc.; they didn't want to talk about the 'Revival' period at all, well, at least not to me they didn't. But, thanks to people like Paul Welsby, Dizzy Holmes and Rob Bailey, I had interviews with Chris Farlowe and Long John Baldry. Anthony Meynell (Squire) and Brian Kotz (Back To Zero) to name a few.

Graham Lentz with Mick Talbot

I was the first (in 2002, and possibly still) the only writer to highlight international mod with people from Japan, Sweden, Italy, Germany, USA, Australia, Spain and France. I couldn't get a publisher interested, so I self-published with no marketing budget at all, but with support from Scootering Magazine and others, I sold the entire 2,000 print run and broke even. With the rapid advances on the internet, and the phenomena of social media, I have been able to reconnect with old friends in the international mod community and make new friends as well.

In 2008, Paolo Hewitt called me to ask if I would mind having the first chapter of 'The Influential Factor' included in his new edition of 'The Sharper Word – A Mod Anthology'. Of course, having my work alongside people like Nik Cohen, Tony Parsons and Dick Hebdige was a huge honour. Then in 2010, a day spent as an extra during the filming of 'Outside Bet' written by Mark Baxter and Paolo Hewitt is another massive moment in my Mod life. That was when I met members of Stone Foundation, Darron Connett (Last Of The Troubadours) and many others who have been firm friends ever since.

In July 2012, New Untouchables founder Rob Bailey offered me the job of Reviews Editor for his Nutsmag online publication. It soon became obvious to me that there were a lot of really good Mod-influenced bands who deserved some help and support, so I made it my mission to do whatever I could for them. That has led me to sitting in with The Spitfires while recording their single 'Spark To Start b/w Sirens' at Paul Weller's Blackbarn studios. Seeing Stone Foundation supporting The Specials on a UK tour, and now I am a permanent co-host on 'We Are The Mods' podcast with Warren Peace and DJ Penny Lane as well as presenting 'Nutscast' with Rob Bailey which is devoted to new bands and new music. I go to as many gigs and events as I possibly can, and I lend my support to any band, promoter or clothing/shoe company who is doing something to keep it all alive. Primarily though, the New Untouchables come first. Without them, none of this would have happened for me in the last couple of years.

So here I am, 36 years after I first became a Mod, and I'm probably more Modernist and more committed than ever. I'm not in the same league as people like Weller, Ady Croasdell, Russ Winstanley, Rob Bailey, Eddie Piller, Dizzy Holmes or The Hideaway lads - Paul Welsby, Neil Henderson and Mike Warburton. I've never put on a gig, set up a record label or organized an event. But I will always salute those who have over the years. Without them, it would have died out completely and most of them are still doing it; still promoting the 'broad church that is Mod culture'. Who knows, maybe this is my time to join those illustrious names?"

Paul Boddy (left) - "All these years down the line I am still clubbing, doing the rallies here and abroad.... trying my best to be different whilst having the same idea as everybody else. I realize now that being a Mod then has made me the person I am now. It's all about the detail; going that extra mile, getting your first suit made, looking the dogs bollocks. And to be told you're a 'face' in the crowd is one of the best feelings you can have. Then you can look back and remember the times when you used to wear a millets parka, have scruffy hair, wear tatty trainers and no idea what decent music was... and now smile."

Dave Bamford - "I made many lifelong friends during this time, many of whom are still on the Mod scene. Me? Well by the end of 1988, I had got the urge to move on and dropped out of the scene never to return. Many of the old seaside haunts have long since gone, Kelly`s, Lowestoft pier, The Salisbury Hotel in Scarborough and Shanklin pier on The Isle of Wight, but the memories of that special time remain. The good times, the bad times, the highs, the lows... A way of life, yes it was!"

Mark Thomson - "Mod for me was all about style. About attitude. About the music, the clothes and the footwear. About your mates, your code and your scooter. About rare Soul records and life changing bands like the Jam. About the gigs and the soul nights. About being clued-up and knowing the score. To sum up my life following the Mod path, I have always said this, if you were ever a Mod, and I mean a proper one, it never leaves you. That attitude to life is always with you. It's all about the details.

If I wear a suit its three buttons with just the top button done up. A handkerchief in the top pocket. Tie clip and cufflinks. Button down shirts. Bass Weejun loafers. Good knitwear. A paisley pattern scarf. Fred Perry. Rare Adidas trainers. Harrington's and Barbour jackets. Stylish sunglasses. John Smedley. Levi's jeans. Clarks Originals. Aquascutum.

It was about bowling around in your parka, being young, impulsive and sussed and knowing, just knowing, you were in the coolest club you could possibly be in. I didn't want to be the same as everybody else. That's why I was a Mod, see?"

Steve Parlett - "My kids think I look ridiculous in some of the photos (Paris trip), but they are of a time, about something that really mattered to us, and I'm so pleased we did it."

Heather Quinn (right) - "Recently I rushed into the newsagents to buy the latest issue of Mojo magazine, simply because the Small Faces were the main feature. On the cover, there was a superb photo and a multitude more within, all of which I'd seen many times before. At my age, it seems rather childish to be so excited. Some would say I should have grown out of it by now, but inside I feel no different to when I first discovered what Mod was - and that was around 35 years ago."

Andy Bull (Chesterfield Mod) - "I've tried the new Mod rallies they are too Austin Powers for me. I've also done many nationals, but still feel an outsider. The Mod rallies of the 1980's, for me, will never be equalled! They were literally the time of my life!"

Lee Radforth (right) - "Over 50 years since Mod went nationwide, and thirty-five years since I became aware of and obsessed with the movement. It's still something of a curate's egg and means so many different things to so many people. Most aspects of British youth culture since its birth have been touched and shaped by it and you cannot walk down a high street without seeing someone wearing the ubiquitous Parka. Or notice Mod imagery or music advertising something. Most cities have a 'Mod for It' type night playing The Who, Small Faces, Tamla, Stax, Oasis et al and for some people that is all there is to Mod. But there will always be those that want to dig deeper and keep moving forward.

It has to be said that the majority of people I see at club nights got into Mod in the late 70's and early 80's, or before and the Brit Pop era didn't see people getting into the scene like the '79 revival did. Young people don't appear as interested in youth cults either and with the onset of digital media don't see music quite as compartmentalised as I think people in the past did.

So let's bring things up to date... Well I'm still buying my suits from my friend Colin Starsmore (sadly about to retire that will leave a huge hole in my life), I buy more records than ever courtesy of eBay (and where possible actual record shops), I still ride a 1960's Lambretta and my car of course is a Mini (until the lottery win and an E Type sits in the garage). And the weekends? Well the north of England is enjoying something of a renaissance as far as club nights are concerned, all playing mid 50's to mid-60's R&B, Club Soul, dance floor Jazz, Ska and Boogaloo. The Ad Lib in Lincoln, The Melting Pot in Scarborough, The Mojo in Hull, and well my very own 'The King Bee Club' based in Shakespeare's on Gibralter St. in Sheffield. It started, if the truth were told, due to the legendary 'Pow Wow' nights in Sheffield folding, and wanting somewhere to go in Sheffield rather than travelling elsewhere every weekend. I envisaged myself and a few friends sitting round taking it in turns to play a few tunes once a month but I appear to have unwittingly created a monster. The first night (February 2012) sold the 120 capacity out in 30 minutes and thanks mainly to the three awesome resident (all Sheffield)

DJ/collectors Gav Arno, Joe Dutton and Graham Wright we have quickly built a reputation as one of the best clubs in the country with people travelling from all over Britain every month.

I still love live music, which is what originally got me into the Mod scene in the first place and play a Rickenbacker (not that well). I'm currently rehearsing (with some King Bee regulars) and trying to get a band together, have just been offered the chance of playing keyboards in my long standing friend Chris Blackburn's legendary garage band The Mourning After (which bearing in mind I've just started learning seems a tall order....but), and still DJ regularly with Hawley. I also recently got to meet Weller. Spent two hours in his dressing room pre gig, walked on stage with the band at Sheffield Arena, and watched the gig lent on Weller's guitar amp. If you would have told me aged eleven that would happen I would have thought you were mad.

Mod has (and still does) shape my life. It sets you apart and gives you a unique viewpoint on life be it clothes, music, literature, art, design, and most importantly, it has helped me meet and befriend the most wonderful people who share my passion. Here's to the next 35 Mod filled years."

Ed Silvester - "The recent popularity of numerous Mod Facebook sites has spread the Mod gospel to another generation, with old and recent bands tapping into a new younger audience. Mod culture will always wax and wane, but ageing Mods are spoilt for choice nowadays, as there seems to be a Soul/Mod/Brit Pop event every weekend.

Ed Silvester (2nd Left) and friends 2014

Mod inspired culture, continues to define the way that I dress, the music that I listen to, and the books and magazines that I read. Although, I have had many different looks and musical interests since the 1980's ended, I have always been a Mod at heart and have maintained an interest in the whole spectrum of Modernism. It doesn't matter what style one has adopted in the past, it's where you end up that matters. I believe through thick and thin, that I've always kept the faith. What a journey, from punk to paisley... it's all about style, music and art."

Enamel Verguren - "I come from the old school whose motto has always been: Mod for life. But is it really good to be a purist? I must say that I missed a lot of things by being impervious when I was younger - I didn't follow what happened in the 1990s because I was stuck in the 1960s, and I had to re-discover that decade much later.

I used to ask this question to people I interviewed when I was preparing my second book: What's the most important thing for you between your scooter, your clothes or your music? And I came to this conclusion: it must be the music. Scooters and clothes, everybody can buy into it nowadays, as I said earlier. But the music you listen to, and that you love, defines who you really are. And that's how it all started, with the Jazz and RnB of the late '50s."

Simon Stebbing (Purple Hearts) - "For most it was a passing fad, for many others, Mod has been an enduring way of life. The Purple Hearts recording career on a major label lasted roughly a year, but many of the original fans from '79 still came to see the band on our reformation in 2009."

Rob Bailey - "Each new generation will add something to the rich tapestry of Mod and our aim [New Untouchables] is always the same, to attract new interest to the scene and provide a platform for the converted with fun, ambitious and exciting events for many years to come and help keep this wonderful lifestyle and culture alive in the 21st century."

Andi Barnes - "Like all good things, they come to an end. For me, the day I heard Japan for the first time and cast an eye over Sylvian, I was lost to the world of the frilly blouse and make up for men. I left behind the Mod scene but still retained a lifelong love for Motown and Soul. The poetry of Ray Davies and the sheer brilliance of the Small Faces have stayed with me and my love of music was deeply enriched by those early days of the Mod revival."

Morgan Nolan (left) - "I am still as into this thing as I was in the early 80s. I don't really think about it anymore as it is just who and what I am. I have my wardrobe and my music and that is how it is. I could never imagine dressing in anything that was not sharp or stylish and my music taste covers the full range of this Broad Church of music from early R&B, Modern Jazz, Original and 2-Tone Ska, Soul in all its variations, Garage and Psych and still my favourite, the Power Chord/Power Pop bands of the 60s, The Revival and right up to the present. As each decade goes by I wonder how long I will stick with it, now as I approach 50 I try to think will I still feel comfortable in the type of clothes I have been wearing since I was 13. Hand on heart I think the answer is yes.

It is a funny thing that today in Dublin there are more Mod clubs running than there were in the height of the 80s. Obviously when a lot of us turned 40 something kicked in and the events that had struggled through the 90s with two men and a dog present were packing people into bigger and bigger venues. This thing still has life in it and perhaps we will still be gathering in a further decade."

Julian Leusby - "Mod was my youth, my religion and my life, the best days of my life with great music, great friends, great clothes; no other youth movement comes even close."

Andrew Harris - "I would say that it (Mod) has been a part of me since 1979, from Mod to skin/Suede to finally resulting to smoothie; a term I shall use for the purpose of this book and also for a similar purpose as in 1971."

Paul 'Smiler' Anderson (left) - "Mod, apart from my family and friends, is the most important thing in my life. It has been with me for the majority of my time on earth and will go to the grave with me. It pumps through my veins, fills my mind and still manages to excite me beyond belief. I cannot even imagine how dull life would be without it."

Sandra Hutchinson - "Mod gave me an education in style. An appreciation of the best music and a scene to express how much I fuckin' rock!! "

THE STYLE OF SANDRA HUTCHINSON

From the age of 14 in 1981, Sandra Hutchinson has pursued and enjoyed with great passion the Mod aesthetic of clothes, music and style. Detail, attitude and a supreme sense of cool add to her exceptional personification of the Mod image.

Sandra Hutchinson - "Personally, I had/have no interest in the Mod revival, it never really spoke to me. My interest music wise has always been Blues, Jazz, Gospel, Doo Wop, R&B and Soul! I still take my inspiration from the very early Mod girls, my dress is and always has been androgyny."

Sandra Hutchinson successfully blends the many relative styles and influences of Mod throughout the decades within her ever-evolving image; from the smart skinhead girl look to early Mod and hints of '66 transitional period. She integrates the whole essence of the female Mod style - with respectful nods to its heritage and a positive forward emphasis on projecting the class of Modernist visuals for the future with confidence and charisma.

Sandra's musical soundtrack consists predominantly of original Blues, rhythm and blues, Jazz and early Soul: this passion for the traditional template for Mods takes us almost back to the very beginning of Mod's illustrious and often controversial, yet invigorating journey. A timeless soundtrack that transports today's aspiring Modernists back to a world where the musical and fashion choices of the individual was influencing contemporary culture. The journey has come full circle: the Modernist subculture thrives and exists in the 21st century with a profound lasting influence.

A LASTING INFLUENCE

The phrase 'Sawdust Caesar' appears to have been drawn from a reference to Italian dictator Benito Mussolini - who was originally viewed as the new Caesar by many Italians up to and including the early period of WW2 - but after Italy's capitulation he was regarded as a 'Sawdust Caesar' - emperor of merely the chipboard maps that had been used to plan troop movements and failed campaigns. Further searches for its origins reveal that the term was used in reference to Mussolini even earlier within a 1935 published George Seldes book entitled 'Sawdust Caesar: the Untold History of Mussolini and Fascism.' Whether Magistrate Dr. George Simpson was knowledgeable of these facts and references is open to conjecture? What is certain, however, is that Modernism - often derided for its sense of contradiction - has outlived all British youth cultures of the last 50 years. The 'Sawdust Caesars' - not exactly the teenage hoodlums that Magistrate Dr. George Simpson lazily pigeon holed in 1964 have since proven their worth and longevity without question. These cosmopolitan hipsters - who have consistently overcome all cultural obstacles sent their way - these chameleon-like purveyors of diversity and originality - most likely deserve, instead, the accolade of 'eternal connoisseurs of taste'?

   Of course, it's all subject to opinion and how the concept of Modernism is perceived. Is it, for instance, an anachronism, maybe an ironic contradiction in that, what was once considered new and modern during its infancy is now the new retro - a continuing tradition and an identifiable style with immediate roots to the 1960's? Considering its legacy, Mod subculture is a bonafide British institution, but also a Global commodity. It is no longer perceived as a subversive threat to society or a sign of rebellious youth and is consequently welcomed at the very same Great British seaside resorts that the Sawdust Caesars famously ran amok through in 1964. It can also be found across all aspects of popular culture and mediums of entertainment. From Bradley Wiggins to Miles Kane, Martin Freeman and mass-produced roundel-adorned seaside mugs, it is all around us. 'We are all Modernists now' it has been suggested, and in some ways that is quite true, in that we all absorb and partake, taste and experience a portion of what Modernism has injected into the modern age - be it fashion, music, architecture, furniture, cinema, TV, media and art or the recognizable symbol of Mod, the scooter. Yet this is only a broad consideration!

The true central ethos of Mod is within the individual. It is not an 'off the peg' style that can be universally purchased at leisure: as one voice within this book states 'Not everyone could be a Mod!' And... as another one declared 'If you need to ask what Mod is, you clearly are not one.' That's it, clearly in a nutshell, it is indefinable, subject to the individual's perception of what it is and means to themselves. Yet, significantly, despite Pete Meaden's claim that 'Anyone can become a Mod' it is not always easily attainable by everyone. Subjectively, the down to basics code of Mod disallows those of questionable taste and of dubious commitment - the recent years label of 'Comedy Mods' and even 'Fantasy Mods' being two such disapprovals, whilst division still continues between the purist original themed crowd and the post-79 Mods. Clearly, its one-upmanship and sense of what is cool or not clearly indicates that only a certain type of individual can truly tune into and project the requirements of Modernism. The eternal narcissistic purveyor of the essential codes of supremacy - these Sawdust Caesars simply wished to be the very best and to emerge out of their surroundings to create much more desirable circumstances for themselves whilst looking better than everyone else - even their fellow Mods... Especially their fellow Mod!

   In context, no one particular individual has the definitive grasp of Modernism, except within their personal choices and sense of self-identity, belief, confidence and the admiration and respect of others. It is fundamentally a personal ideal exclusive to each person - it's not something that can be craftily absorbed without considerable personal input and most importantly it is consistently a stylistic extension of the individual.

The faces of Modernism 2014: Niamh, Katie and Scarlett Baylis
(On an Art Gallery Clothing Shoot - Photography by www.clivetagg.com)
and Nathan Prescott

Ironically - and Mod is quite obviously not the only perpetrator of this - Mods - the cool, clean and clear symbol of youth culture, now has no best before date or age limit to it. Mods of the present day do not merely confine their forays into its style and culture to their days of youth and teenage autonomy, they continue onwards with their journeys - defying the onsets of age, approval and changing contemporary fashions. From the immaculate style of Rolling Stone Charlie Watts to the confidence and sense of modernity of Paul Weller (an artist consistently welcoming the 'new') and the young guns' impeccable perceptions of Mod via the likes of Billy Sullivan and Nick Waterhouse, the whole spectrum of Mod surrenders to no definable expectations of finality. To be expected, there is occasionally a small but considerable price to pay for this. Successfully and respectfully projected by some in their 50's and 60's and beyond with grace and consideration, the Mod style can just as easily be slaughtered by an 18 year old in a poor-fitting Ben Sherman and a High Street parka. In short, if you don't put in the time and effort, you won't pass the test of Modernist cool.

The subject of Mod is also highly emotive and evokes conflicting versions and opinions - from the street-wise working class 'punch-up ready scooter boy of spartan-stripped-down basics (who we should not readily dismiss as the hoodlum of the story: they often being of high intelligence, knowledge and wit) to the pristine embellishment of Modernist ambiguity so persistently portrayed by the inner elite of Mod. From 60's original to northern pill-popping Mojo Club youth and punk in a parka and two-tone suit revivalist to Acid Jazz enthusiast - few opinions and ideas of what makes a Mod are similar and all are just as equally relevant as the other. Furthermore, although the relevance and importance of being at the cusp of the movement is a considerable attribute and a supportive means to being a much more than average authority on the history and culture of the subject, the means test of Mod credence is not conclusive to age, location, class nor circumstance.

No matter what a Mod's beginnings or social prestige, the onus is on the present and the future, it's not where you are from it's where you are at and going to!

Personal tastes in clothes and music - and other mediums - are not the sole requirements of Mod subculture. It is not what the clothes are, more a case of how they are worn, it has been said. A Mod will often, consistently, be confident in style and self-projection, sure in their decided tastes and will, most likely, continue their obsessive attention to detail and image in how they stand, speak, walk, wear a watch, smoke a cigarette and assert themselves and much more besides. The present day Mod may well interact with other cults and in turn possibly borrow aspects of their once adversary - the rocker. He/she will absorb and integrate the desired influences of the present and mingle the results within the melting pot of their past influences and styles. Contrary to some popular perceptions, some elements of nostalgic themed events and associations aside, the Mod is every inch the forward thinking Modernist and personification of the present as he was in 1959 when the first small gatherings of like-minded connoisseurs of taste and style first appeared and took it upon themselves to indulge in what would become the most important style culture ever experienced. Misunderstood by plenty, hijacked and abused by some, yet equally life-defining and hugely important for others. Just as controversial and divisional in the modern world that we now live in as it was at any time within its illustrious past, Mod is here to stay!

Perhaps the final words should belong to two of the originals within this story?

John Leo Waters - "I cannot speak for others but the 'Mod' influence on my life has never really left me. They say you are always eighteen in your mind and that may have something to do with it!

I still love the same music now that I loved then (although my tastes have broadened somewhat). Soul music has had a huge influence on my life and although I am far too old to 'boogie' I still can be spotted on occasions at venues such as the Jazz Cafe whenever a relevant artist is visiting town although these days the first thing I look for when I enter a club is a seat!

Two of my favourite spots are Soho and Brighton - Why? I don't really know - just something about the vibe. Maybe the spirit of the sixties is still embedded in the fabric of the walls!

I am not stupid enough to dress as I did when I was seventeen. There is nothing as sad as an old guy trying to look young! I have not yet resorted to a ponytail and a Harley Davidson! However, I still take care in my appearance and have a penchant for Desert Boots, loafers, button down shirts and my two top jacket buttons done up! I still feel the adrenalin pump through my veins whenever I see a group of present day Mods (and a tinge of jealousy perhaps!). It must be something in the genes - Once a Mod........."

Gill Evans - "I've often tried to explain how I feel about my style - that it's something I visualise in my head and I put it all together: then it is exactly how I envisaged. Del did the same as well. How can you explain it - it is just right and it is an extension of your inner self. The whole concept of being a Mod was to be an individual with an eye for detail. It was perfect."

ESSENTIAL MODERNISM CONTINUES THROUGH THE DECADES

Photo by Paul Hallam

Acknowledgements

A HUGE THANKS TO ROB NICHOLLS – WITHOUT WHOM THIS PROJECT WOULD QUITE PROBABLY HAVE NEVER HAPPENED AND WHO HAS BEEN AN INVALUABLE PARTICIPANT AND SOURCE OF INSPIRATION!

ALSO SPECIAL THANKS AND APPRECIATION TO THE MIGHTY SIX - JOHN LEO WATERS, GILL EVANS, GLENN FIELD, LEE RADFORTH, JOHN HELLIER AND ED SILVESTER

THANKS TO SUE MCALPINE EXHIBITIONS/COLLECTIONS MANAGEMENT, HACKNEY MUSEUM FOR THE KIND USE OF WORDS AND PHOTOS FOR THE STAMFORD HILL MODS AND MARK FELD SECTIONS

THANKS AND APPRECIATION TO THE PROOF READERS – ROGER AMES AND ROB NICHOLLS EXTRA PROOFING FROM VANESSA MATHISON AND SEAN HAMPSEY. COVER DESIGN BY DAVE SPENCER. INDEX CREATED BY ROB NICHOLLS AND PROOFED BY VANESSA MATHISON

And the following people who contributed and helped immensely with this project - Irish Jack Lyons, Lloyd Johnson, David Middleton, Andy Lewis, Derek D' Souza (The Jam and Spitfires images), Terry Rawlings, Mickey Tenner, Stephen Hughes (New Originals scooter club photo), Glenn Field and Eric South (for numerous Lincoln scene photos and page 13 Teds photo), Nigel Brandt Bellamy, Tony Foley, Kate Harrison, Sally Stevens, Ed Horwood, Tracey Wilmot, Paul 'Smiler'Anderson, Graham Lentz, Alan May, Ray Margetson, Robert Lee, Eddie Piller, Carl Myers, Louise Mckenning, Anne-Marie-Newland, Michael Hill (Ad-Lib photo), Mark Charlton, Andrew Harris, Chris Pope, Brett 'Buddy' Ascot, Charles Murphy, Ben Stone, Kristopher Dunn, Mike Warburton, Tiggs Keywood-Wainwright (Dungeon days photo), Bill 'Wiggy' Hildred, Robert John Manton, John Reed, Arthur Cliffe, Roy Allen, Jeremy Norman, Steve Austin, Alfredo Marcantonio, Paul Clay, James Bowden, Maurice Moore, Adrian Stern, Ian Kleinberg, Pete Sugar, Miki Simmonds, Benny Hall, Kenny Silver, Don McCullin, Wayne Kirven, Frank Cooper, Rick Brocklume, Reggie Webster, Gordon Rath, Brian Kotz, Jody Maguire (Paul Weller images), Geoff Green, David Birchall, Sandy Sergeant, Derek Glover, Carol Mcfee, Pat Beckett, Jackie Bain, John McNally, Gary Maxton, Kenney Jones, Keith How, Dave Fawcett, Ella Donnor, Mick and Carol Gregory, Dave Manvell, Rob Taylor, John Wood, Ted Reynell, Jim Ferguson, Sean Hampsey, Steve Bush, Rob Bailey, Simon Franklin, John Silvester, Alan Smith, Enamel Verguren, Michael Spencer, Mark Bradford, Doug Sandom, Dave Cairns, Ian Page, Pete Eason, Pete Skidmore, Phillip Wright, Fraser Smith, Heather Smith, Andy Bull, Andi Barnes, Gary Shail, Ginger Kevin Lawton, Steve Orridge, Rob Wasteney, Stuart Deabill, Steve 'Zal' Downing, Morgan Nolan, Stewart Hardman, Scarlett Baylis, Nathan Prescott, Paul Boddy, Jeff Platts, Dave Bamford, David 'Dizzy' Holmes, Mark Thomson, Derek 'Del Boy' Shepherd, Steve Parlett, Kevin Smith, Paul Hallam, David Abrahams-Edley, Mandy O' Connor, Bell, Vicky Walsh Knightley, Gary Evans, Penny Lane, James Farrow, Billy Sullivan, Neil Sheasby, John Lennon McCullough, Steuart Kingsley-Inness, Pete Wilky, Tricia Hickling, Sandra Hutchinson, Berit Boettcher (Enamel Verguren photo), Amanda Sanders, Ann Axeberg, Derek Pearson (Northern Soul photo), Johnny Powell, Giovanni Napolitano, Jenny Spires (Cambridge Mods photos), Peter Jachimiak, Ian Snowball, Ashley Walker, Simone Wilson (Style Council photos), Sid Poulton, On an Art Gallery Clothing Shoot - Photography by www.clivetagg.com, Ann and Eddy Barry (Dungeon club photos), Sally Stevens photos by Ian Spratt, Stewart Poustie, Frank Cornelli, Gerry Lambe, Steve Longworth (Northern Soul 80's photo), Lynn Corbett, Graham Cooper, Hard Mods photo thanks to Charles Murphy, Elaine Andrew now Smith, Dennis Munday, Lester Owers,Kristan James Melik, Kevin Wells (Strypes photo), Neil Anderson, David Growns, Clive Garnett.

Finally a massive thanks to my fiancée Vanessa for the support and patience

Readers of this book may Enjoy 'KEEP LOOKIN' – 80 MORE MOD, SOUL AND FREAKBEAT NUGGETS'

on RPM records

Contributor Rob Nicholls has also been involved in the production of CD sets that commemorate the Mod era. They are:

Boogie Chillen: Early Mods First Choice Vinyl. A three CD compilation of 75 R&B tracks. London: Future Noise Music, FVTD156. (2013)

Trojan Presents Mod Ska: Forty Original Ska Anthems from 1962-67, London; Two CD compilation (2012)

Other books by Tony Beesley

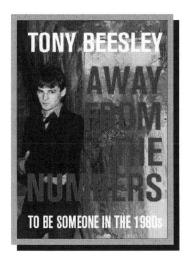

FURTHER RECOMMENDED READING

'Friday on My Mind' and 'Pushin' and Shovin' - Don Hughes
Mods: the New Religion - Paul 'Smiler' Anderson
Mod: A Very British Phenomenon - Terry Rawlings
The Influential Factor - Graham Lentz

RECOMMENDED MEDIA

The official website

www.tonybeesleymodworld.co.uk

Alan Mays 'Glory Boys' radio show Sundays 7pm – 9pm at

www.6towns.co.uk
www.mixcloud.com/gloryboy

www.themodgeneration.co.uk

www.modculture.co.uk

Roger Smith's excellent site on the Club a 'GoGo' at www.readysteadygone.co.uk/club-agogo-newcastle

R.I.P

Ian McLagan
Del Evans
Randy Cozens
Roger Mason
Tony Class
Heather-Jane Soper
Pip Carter
Rob Hughes
Dave Fawcett
Ted Reynell
Joe Dutton
Bert Ansell
Ashley Walker

DISCLAIMER

INDEX